Lecture Notes in Computer Science 8244

Commenced Publication in 1973
Founding and Former Series Editors:
Gerhard Goos, Juris Hartmanis, and Jan van Leeuwen

Valeria Bertacco   Axel Legay (Eds.)

Hardware and Software: Verification and Testing

9th International
Haifa Verification Conference, HVC 2013
Haifa, Israel, November 5-7, 2013
Proceedings

 Springer

Volume Editors

Valeria Bertacco
University of Michigan
Department of Electrical Engineering and Computer Science
BBB4645, 2260 Hayward Avenue
Ann Arbor, MI 48109-2121, USA
E-mail: valeria@umich.edu

Axel Legay
Inria Rennes, Campus de Beaulieu
263, Avenue du Général Leclerc
35042 Rennes, France
E-mail: axel.legay@inria.fr

ISSN 0302-9743   e-ISSN 1611-3349
ISBN 978-3-319-03076-0   e-ISBN 978-3-319-03077-7
DOI 10.1007/978-3-319-03077-7
Springer Cham Heidelberg New York Dordrecht London

CR Subject Classification (1998): D.2.4-5, D.3.1, F.3.1-2, D.2.11, I.2.2-3

LNCS Sublibrary: SL 2 – Programming and Software Engineering

Typesetting: Camera-ready by author, data conversion by Scientific Publishing Services, Chennai, India

Printed on acid-free paper

Springer is part of Springer Science+Business Media (www.springer.com)

Preface

This volume contains the proceedings of the 9th Haifa Verification Conference (HVC 2013). The conference was hosted by IBM Research - Haifa and took place during November 5–7, 2013. It was the ninth event in this series of annual conferences dedicated to advancing the state of the art and state of the practice in verification and testing. The conference provided a forum for researchers and practitioners from academia and industry to share their work, exchange ideas, and discuss the future directions of testing and verification for hardware, software, and complex hybrid systems. This year HVC introduced a special track on software testing. This track, which was chaired by Amiram Yehudai and Itai Segall, expands the scope of HVC and attracted 11 submissions from a broader community.

Overall, HVC 2013 attracted 49 submissions in response to the call for papers. Each submission was assigned to at least three members of the Program Committee and in many cases additional reviews were solicited from outside experts. The Program Committee conferred about the submissions, judging them on their perceived importance, originality, clarity, and appropriateness for the expected audience. The Program Committee selected 23 papers for presentation, including five from the software testing track, resulting in an acceptance rate of 47%.

Complementing the contributed papers, the conference featured five invited keynote talks: "EDA in the Cloud" by Leon Stok, "Challenges in Enabling the Next Generation Mobile Experience: Are You Ready?" by Scott Runner, "Recent Advances in Model Checking" by Robert Brayton, "Synthesis of Concurrent Programs Using Genetic Programming" by Doron Peled, and "Opportunities and Challenges for High Performance Microprocessor Designs and Design Automation" by Ruchir Puri.

The conference itself started with a tutorial day including tutorials on: "Hardware Functional Verification - Present and Future" by Yuval Caspi; "SystemVerilog Assertions for Formal Verification" by Dmitry Korchemny; "Verification and Performance Analysis of Interconnects Within the SoCs" by Mirit Fromovich; "SAT, CSP, and Proofs" by Ofer Strichman; and "The System Simulation as a Tool for Development and Validation of Complex Systems" by Racheli Kenigsbuch.

We would like to extend our appreciation and sincere thanks to Sivan Rabinovich for serving as General Chair and handling the conference details so successfully. Our thanks also go to Arkadiy Morgenshtein for arranging the tutorials day. Finally, we would like to thank our arrangements support team: Eti Jahr for managing the technical aspects of the conference, Ettie Gilead and Chani Sacharen for handling communication, Yair Harry for web design, and Tammy Dekel for graphic design. HVC 2013 received sponsorships from IBM,

Cadence, Mellanox, Jasper, Quallcom, and Mentor Graphics. Submissions and evaluations of papers, as well as the preparation of this proceedings volume, were handled by the EasyChair conference management system.

September 2013   Valeria Bertacco
                                                        Axel Legay

Organization

Program Committee

Valeria Bertacco	University of Michigan, USA
Armin Biere	FMV
Roderick Bloem	Graz University of Technology, Austria
Hana Chockler	King's College London, UK
Myra Cohen	University of Nebraska, USA
Alexandre David	Aalborg University, Denmark
Giuseppe Di Guglielmo	Columbia University, USA
Harry Foster	Mentor Graphics
Alex Goryachev	IBM Israel
Ian Harris	University of California, Irvine, USA
Michael Hsiao	Virginia Tech, USA
Alan Hu	University of British Columbia, Canada
Axel Legay	Inria, France
Jeff Lei	The University of Texas at Arlington, USA
João Lourenço	Universidade Nova de Lisboa, Portugal
Rupak Majumdar	Max Planck Institute, Germany
Oded Maler	Verimag, Grenoble, France
Leonardo Mariani	University of Milan, Italy
Amir Nahir	IBM, Israel
Preeti Panda	IIT Delhi, India
Hiren Patel	University of Waterloo, Canada
Itai Segall	IBM, Israel
Martina Seidl	FMV, Linz, Austria
Mark Trakhtenbrot	Holon Institute of Technology, Israel
Shobha Vasudevan	University of Illinois at Urbana-Champaign, USA
Sergiy Vilkomir	East Carolina University, USA
Ilya Wagner	Intel
Li-C. Wang	University of California, Santa Barbara, USA
Elaine Weyuker	DIMACS, Rutgers University, USA
Amiram Yehudai	Tel Aviv University, Israel

Additional Reviewers

Amin, Mohamed
André, Étienne
Chen, Wen
Dimitrova, Rayna
Khalimov, Ayrat
Kloos, Johannes
Könighofer, Bettina
Lanik, Jan
Liffiton, Mark
Meller, Yael
Mens, Irini
Mishra, Prabhat

Ferrere, Thomas
Gladisch, Christoph
Heule, Marijn
Kaushik, Anirudh
Poetzl, Daniel
Prähofer, Herbert
Sharma, Namita
Shomrat, Mati
Strichman, Ofer
Tyszberowicz, Shmuel
Vale, Tiago

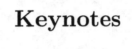

Keynotes

EDA in the Cloud

Leon Stok

Electronic Design Automation Technologies, IBM

Abstract. A large number of compute intensive applications are moving to the cloud at a fast pace. EDA, has been on the forefront of computing for the last 25 years and should certainly be one of them. How come this has not happened yet at a noticeable scale? In surveying the attendees to the 50th Design Automation Conference cloud and IT was certainly at the forefront of their thoughts for the future of EDA. This talk will describe why EDA has not taken off in the cloud, but why it is inevitable to happen and what needs to be done to bring real value to the design and verification teams.

Opportunities and Challenges for High Performance Microprocessor Designs and Design Automation

Ruchir Puri

IBM Research

Abstract. With end of an era of classical technology scaling and exponential frequency increases, high end microprocessor designs and design automation methodologies are at an inflection point. With power and current demands reaching breaking points, and significant challenges in application software stack, we are also reaching diminishing returns from simply adding more cores. In design methodologies for high end microprocessors, although chip physical design efficiency has seen tremendous improvements, strong indications are emerging for maturing of those gains as well. In order to continue the cost-performance scaling in systems in light of these maturing trends, we must innovate up the design stack, moving focus from technology and physical design implementation to new IP and methodologies at logic, architecture, and at the boundary of hardware and software, solving key bottlenecks through application acceleration. This new era of innovation, which moves the focus up the design stack presents new challenges and opportunities to the design and design automation communities. This talk will motivate these trends and focus on challenges for high performance microprocessor design, verification, and design automation in the years to come.

Recent Advances in Model Checking

Robert K. Brayton

Uniersity of California, Berkeley

Abstract. Model checking, either for property checking or equivalence checking, continues to advance towards shorter runtimes and the ability to handle larger problem instances. These advances have been due to:

1. improved underlying engines such as SAT solvers, BMC, and semi-formal simulation,
2. new methods such as property directed reachability - IC3/PDR,
3. improved data structures for representing logic,
4. improved synthesis methods, such as signal correspondence, retiming, reparametrization, use of isomorphism
5. improved abstraction methods, such as localization and speculation,
6. use of parallelism and general availability of multi-core servers.

This progress is partially documented by the annual hardware model checking competitions and the growing set of competition categories, such as the liveness checking and multi-output categories. These competitions have also encouraged contributions of challenging industrial examples, all of which has greatly stimulated research and development in the model checking area.

This talk will discuss the various advances of the past few years and give examples of the progress made.

Synthesis of Concurrent Programs Using Genetic Programming

Doron Peled

Bar Ilan University

Abstract. We present a method to automatically generate concurrent code using genetic programming, based on automatic verification. As the problem of constructing concurrent code is in general undecidable, the user needs the intervene by tuning various parameters and supplying specification and hints that would steer the search for correct code in the right direction. We demonstrate how various hard-to-program protocols are generated using our method and our developed tool. We show how a commonly used protocol for coordinating concurrent interactions was found to be incorrect using our tool, and was then subsequently fixed.

Challenges in Enabling the Next Generation Mobile Experience: Are You Ready?

Scott Runner

Qualcomm

Abstract. In the next decade, consumers are going to be treated to an array of new use case experiences in mobility that one can only dream of today. The HW and SW IP and systems integration that will enable these experiences are prodigious. The design and verification challenges which must be surmounted to enable such high levels of integration and functionality are daunting. And doing so in the timeframes required to satisfy the appetites of smartphone and tablet customers, while delivering to cost, power, performance and quality targets demands novel approaches. We will explore these challenges in the design of the most popular devices in the wireless world.

Challenges in Enabling the Next Generation
Mobile Experience: Are You Ready?

Scott Bright

Introduction

Table of Contents

Session 4: Supporting Dynamic Verification

Session 5: Specification and Coverage

Keynote Presentation

Session 6: Abstraction

Session 7: Model Representation

Backbones for Equality

Michael Codish[1], Yoav Fekete[1], and Amit Metodi[2,*]

[1] Department of Computer Science, Ben-Gurion University, Israel
{mcodish,fekete}@cs.bgu.ac.il
[2] Cadence Israel Development Center, Israel
ametodi@cadence.com

Abstract. This paper generalizes the notion of the backbone of a CNF formula to capture also equations between literals. Each such equation applies to remove a variable from the original formula thus simplifying the formula without changing its satisfiability, or the number of its satisfying assignments. We prove that for a formula with n variables, the generalized backbone is computed with at most $n+1$ satisfiable calls and exactly one unsatisfiable call to the SAT solver. We illustrate the integration of generalized backbone computation to facilitate the encoding of finite domain constraints to SAT. In this context generalized backbones are computed for small groups of constraints and then propagated to simplify the entire constraint model. A preliminary experimental evaluation is provided.

1 Introduction

The backbone of a search problem is a fundamental notion identified to explain why certain problem instances are hard. The term originates in computational physics [8,17,16]. It identifies decisions which are fixed in all solutions, and so need to be made correctly. Typically, a decision is the value of a variable, and if that value is fixed in all solutions then the variable is called a backbone variable. If a problem has a backbone variable, an algorithm will not find a solution to the problem until the backbone variable is set to its correct value. Therefore, the larger a backbone, the more tightly constrained the problem becomes. As a result, it is more likely for an algorithm to set a backbone variable to a wrong value, which may consequently require a large amount of computation to recover from such a mistake [20].

For SAT, the backbone of a satisfiable propositional formula φ is the set of variables which take the same truth value in all satisfying assignments of φ. In this case, the backbone can also be seen as the set of literals which are true in all satisfying assignments of φ. Computing the backbone of a propositional formula is intractable in general [7]. Janota proves that deciding if a literal is in the backbone of a formula is co-NP [6] and Kilby et al. show that even approximating the backbone is intractable [7].

---

* This research was carried out while the third author was a graduate student at Ben-Gurion University.

V. Bertacco and A. Legay (Eds.): HVC 2013, LNCS 8244, pp. 1–14, 2013.
© Springer International Publishing Switzerland 2013

Backbones appear in a number of practical applications of SAT. If a backbone is known, then we can simplify a formula without changing its satisfiability, or the number of satisfying assignments. Assigning values to backbone variables reduces the size of the search space while maintaining the meaning of the original formula. On the other hand, computing the backbone of a SAT problem is typically at least as hard as solving the SAT problem itself. Investing the cost of computing a backbone (or part of it) can pay off when the application must solve the same formula many times. Typical examples are model enumeration, minimal model computation, prime implicant computation, and also in applications which involve optimization (see for example, [12]). Another useful application, examplified in [10], is when SAT solving is incremental, and a backbone can be computed for a small portion of the CNF but used to simplify the whole CNF.

Backbones are often computed by iterating with a SAT solver. For a satisfiable propositional formula φ and literal x, if $\varphi \wedge \neg x$ is not satisfiable, then x is in the backbone. For a formula with n variables and a backbone consisting of b literals, a naive approach requires $2n$ calls to the SAT solver from which b are unsatisfiable and typically more expensive. In [12], the authors survey several less naive options and introduce an improved algorithm. For a formula with n variables and a backbone with b literals their algorithm requires at most $n - b$ satisfiable calls and exactly one unsatisfiable call to the SAT solver.

This paper generalizes the notion of the backbone of a CNF formula φ to capture all equations of the form $x = \ell$ implied by φ where x is a variable, and ℓ is either a truth value or a literal. In this case we say that x is a generalized backbone variable. The (usual) backbone of φ is the subset of these equations where ℓ is a truth value. The motivation for generalized backbones is exactly the same as for backbones: each implied equation represents a decision which is fixed in all solutions, and if we know that $x = \ell$ is implied by the formula then all occurrences of x can be replaced by ℓ thus fixing the decision and simplifying the formula without changing its satisfiability, or the number of its satisfying assignments.

We prove that generalized backbones (with equalities) are not much more expensive to compute than usual backbones. We show that for a formula with n variables the generalized backbone is computed with at most $n+1$ satisfiable calls and exactly one unsatisfiable call to the SAT solver. We also illustrate through preliminary experimentation that computing generalized backbones does pay off in practice.

In previous work described in [14,13,15], we take a structured approach to solve finite domain constraint problems through an encoding to SAT. With this approach we partition a CNF encoding into smaller chunks of clauses, determined by the structure of the constraint model, and we reason, one chunk at a time, to identify (generalized) backbone variables. Clearly, any (generalized) backbone variable (or an implied equation) of a single chunk is also a (generalized) backbone variable (or an implied equation) of the entire CNF. Moreover, a backbone variable identified in one chunk may apply to simplify other chunks. In [14], we termed the process of identifying such equations, and propagating them to other chunks, equi-propagation. We introduced a tool called BEE (Ben-Gurion Equi-propagation Encoder) which applies to encode finite domain constraint models to CNF. During the encoding process, BEE performs optimizations based on equi-propagation and partial evaluation to improve the quality of the target CNF. However, equi-propagation in BEE is based on ad-hoc rules and thus incomplete.

In this paper we describe the extension of BEE to consider complete equi-propagation (CEP) which is about inferring generalized backbones for chunks of the CNF encoding and propagating them to simplify the entire CNF. In this setting, chunks of CNF designated for complete equi-propagation are specified by the user in terms of sets of constraints. For each such specified set, an algorithm for generalized backbone computation is applied to its CNF encoding. For typical constraint satisfaction problems, removing some of the constraints renders a CNF which is much easier to solve. Hence, here too, the cost of computing the (generalized) backbone of an individual chunk can pay off when applied in the global context to solve the whole CNF.

2   Related Work

Simplifying CNF formula prior to the application of SAT solving is of the utmost importance and there are a wide range of preprocessing techniques that can be applied to achieve this goal. See for example the works of [9], [2], [4], and [11], and the references therein their work. Detecting unit clauses and implications (and thus also equalities) between literals is a central theme in CNF preprocessing. The preprocessor described in [5] focuses on detecting precisely the same kind of equations we consider for generalized backbones: unit clauses and equalities between literals.

There are also approaches [9] that detect and use Boolean equalities during run-time, from within the SAT solver. Perhaps the most famous example is the SAT solver of Stålmark [19] which has extensive support for reasoning about equivalences and where formulae are represented in a form containing only conjunctions, equalities and negations [18].

The approach taken in this paper is different from these works. The above mentioned works apply various techniques (resolution based and others) to track down implications. They are not complete techniques. Ours is a preprocessing technique with a focus on the computation of complete equi-propagation implemented using a backbone algorithm (with equalities). A key factor is that by considering only a small fragment of a CNF at one time enables to apply stronger, and even complete, reasoning to detect generalized backbones in that fragment. Once detected, these apply to simplify the entire CNF and facilitate further reasoning on other fragments.

When compiling finite domain constraints to CNF using the BEE compiler, the structure of the constraints can be applied to induce a partition of the target CNF to such fragments.

3   Backbones and Equalities

In this section we first describe an algorithm for computing backbones and then detail its application to compute generalized backbones (with equality). Our approach is essentially the same as Algorithm 4 presented in [12].

To compute the backbone of a given formula φ, which we assume is satisfiable, we proceed as follows: the algorithm maintains a table indicating for each variable x in φ for which values of x, φ can be satisfied: *true*, *false*, or both. The algorithm is initialized by calling the SAT solver with $\varphi_1 = \varphi$ and initializing the table with the information relevant to each variable: if the solution for φ_1 assigns a value to x then that value is tabled for x. If it assigns no value to x then both values are tabled for x.

The algorithm iterates incrementally. For each step $i > 1$ we add a single clause C_i (detailed below) and re-invoke the same solver instance, maintaining the learned data of the solver. This process terminates with a single unsatisfiable invocation. In words: the clause C_i can be seen as asking the solver if it is possible to flip the value for any of the variables for which we have so far seen only a single value. More formally, at each step of the algorithm, C_i is defined as follows: for each variable x, if the table indicates a single value v for x then C_i includes $\neg v$. Otherwise, if the table indicates two values for x then there is no corresponding literal in C_i. The SAT solver is then called with $\varphi_i = \varphi_{i-1} \wedge C_i$. If this call is satisfiable then the table is updated to record new values for variables (there must be at least one new value in the table) and we iterate. Otherwise, the algorithm terminates and the variables remaining with single entries in the table are the backbone of φ.

In [12] the authors prove[1] that for a formula with n variables and a backbone with b literals the above algorithm requires at most $n - b$ satisfiable calls and exactly one unsatisfiable call to the SAT solver. The following example demonstrates the application of the backbone algorithm.

	x_1	x_2	x_3	x_4	x_5	φ_i
$i=1$	1	1	0	0	1	φ
$i=2$	1	0	0	1	0	$\varphi_1 \wedge \neg\theta_1$
$i=3$			*unsat*			$\varphi_2 \wedge (\neg x_1 \vee x_3)$

Fig. 1. Demo of backbone algorithm (Example 1)

Example 1. Assume given an unspecified formula, φ, with 5 variables. Figure 1 illustrates the iterations (three in this example) of the backbone algorithm: one per line. The columns in the table detail the iteration number i (left), the the formula φ_i provided to the SAT solver (right), and the model θ_i obtained (middle). The example illustrates that $\varphi_1 = \varphi$ has a model θ_1 depicted in the first

---

[1] See Proposition 6 in http://sat.inesc-id.pt/~mikolas/bb-aicom-preprint.pdf

line of the table, and that requesting a second (different) model, by invoking the SAT solver with the formula $\varphi_2 = \varphi_1 \wedge \neg\theta_1$, results in the model θ_2. Notice that the variable x_1 takes the same value, *true*, in both models, and that the variable x_3 takes the same value, *false*. In the third iteration, the call $\varphi_3 = \varphi_2 \wedge (\neg x_1 \vee x_3)$ requests a model which is different from the first two and which flips the value of (at least) one of the two variables x_1 (to false) or x_3 (to true). Given that this call is not satisfiable, we conclude that x_1 and x_3 comprise the backbone variables of φ.

Now consider the case where in addition to the backbone we wish to derive also equations between literals which hold in all models of φ. The generalized backbones algorithm applied in BEE is basically the same algorithm as that proposed for computing backbones. Given formula φ, generalized backbones are computed by extending φ to φ' as prescribed by Equation (1). This is straightforward. Enumerating the variables of φ as $\{x_1, \ldots, x_n\}$. One simply defines

$$\varphi' = \varphi \wedge \{ e_{ij} \leftrightarrow (x_i \leftrightarrow x_j) \mid 0 \leq i < j \leq n \} \tag{1}$$

introducing $\theta(n^2)$ fresh variables e_{ij}. If the literal e_{ij} is in the backbone of φ' then $x_i = x_j$ is implied by φ, and if the literal $\neg e_{ij}$ is in the backbone of φ' then $x_i = \neg x_j$ is implied by φ. As an optimization, it is possible to focus in the first two iterations only on the variables of φ. However, there is one major obstacle. The application of backbones with equalities for φ with n variables involves computing the backbone for φ' which has $\theta(n^2)$ variables. Consequently, it is reasonable to assume that the number of calls to the SAT solver may be quadratic. Below we prove that this is not the case, but first we present the following example.

	x_1	x_2	x_3	x_4	x_5	e_{12}	e_{13}	e_{14}	e_{15}	e_{23}	e_{24}	e_{25}	e_{34}	e_{35}	e_{45}	φ_i
$i{=}1$	1	1	0	0	1	1	0	0	1	0	0	1	1	0	0	φ'
$i{=}2$	1	0	0	1	0	0	0	1	0	1	0	1	0	1	0	$\varphi_1 \wedge \neg\theta_1$
$i{=}3$	1	0	0	0	1	0	0	0	1	1	1	0	1	0	0	$\varphi_2 \wedge \left(\begin{array}{l} \neg x_1 \vee x_3 \vee e_{13} \vee \\ \neg e_{24} \vee \neg e_{25} \vee e_{45} \end{array} \right)$
$i{=}4$			unsat													$\varphi_3 \wedge (\neg x_1 \vee x_3 \vee e_{13} \vee e_{45})$

(Column header θ_i spans the x and e columns.)

Fig. 2. Demo of the generalized backbones algorithm (Example 2)

Example 2. Consider the same formula φ as in Example 1. Figure 2 illustrates the iterations, one per line, (four in this example) of the backbone algorithm but extended to operate on φ' as specified in Equation (1). The first two lines of the table in Figure 2 detail θ_1 and θ_2 which are almost the same as the two models of φ_1 and φ_2 from Figure 1, except that here we present also the values of the fresh variables e_{ij} indicating the values of the equations between literals. The two variables x_1 and x_3 (and hence also e_{13}) take identical values in both models, just as in Figure 1. This time, in the third iteration we ask to either flip the value for one of $\{x_1, x_3\}$ or for one of $\{e_{13}, e_{24}, e_{25}, e_{45}\}$ and there is such a model θ_3 which flips the values of e_{24} and e_{25}. In the first three models the variables x_1, x_3, e_{13}, and e_{45} take single values. Hence in the fourth iteration the call to the SAT solver asks to flip one of them. Figure 2 indicates that this is not possible and hence these four variables are in the generalized backbone.

We proceed to prove that iterated SAT solving for generalized backbones using φ' involves at most $n+1$ satisfiable SAT tests, and exactly one unsatisfiable test, in spite of the fact that φ' involves a quadratic number of fresh variables.

Theorem 1. *Let φ be a CNF, X a set of n variables, and $\Theta = \{\theta_1, \ldots, \theta_m\}$ the sequence of assignments encountered by the generalized backbones algorithm for φ and X. Then, $m \leq n+1$.*

Before presenting a proof of Theorem 1 we introduce some terminology. Assume a set of Boolean variables X and a sequence $\Theta = \{\theta_1, \ldots, \theta_m\}$ of models. Denote $\hat{X} = X \cup \{1\}$ and let $x, y \in \hat{X}$. If $\theta(x) = \theta(y)$ for all $\theta \in \Theta$ or if $\theta(x) \neq \theta(y)$ for all $\theta \in \Theta$, then we say that Θ *determines* the equation $x = y$. Otherwise, we say that Θ *disqualifies* $x = y$, intuitively meaning that Θ disqualifies $x = y$ from being determined. More formally, Θ *determines* $x = y$ if and only if $\Theta \models (x = y)$ or $\Theta \models (x = \neg y)$, and otherwise Θ *disqualifies* $x = y$.

The generalized backbones algorithm for a formula φ and set of n variables X applies so that each iteration results in a satisfying assignment for φ which disqualifies at least one additional equation between elements of $\hat{X}$. Although there are a quadratic number of equations to be considered, we prove that the CEP algorithm terminates after at most $n+1$ iterations.

Proof. (of Theorem 1) For each value $i \leq m$, $\Theta_i = \{\theta_1, \ldots, \theta_i\}$ induces a partitioning, Π_i of $\hat{X}$ to disjoint and non-empty sets, defined such that for each $x, y \in \hat{X}$, x and y are in the same partition $P \in \Pi_i$ if and only if Θ_i determines the equation $x = y$. So, if $x, y \in P \in \Pi_i$ then the equation $x = y$ takes the same value in all assignments of Θ_i. The partitioning is well defined because if in all assignments of Θ_i both $x = y$ takes the same value and $y = z$ takes the same value, then clearly also $x = z$ takes the same value, implying that x, y, z are in the same partition of Π_i. Finally, note that each iteration $1 < i \leq m$ of the generalized backbones algorithm disqualifies at least one equation $x = y$ that was determined by Θ_{i-1}. This implies that at least one partition of Π_{i-1} is split into two smaller (non-empty) partitions of Π_i. As there are a total of $n+1$ elements in $\hat{X}$, there can be at most $n+1$ iterations to the algorithm.

Example 3. Consider the same formula φ as in Examples 1 and 2. Figure 3 illustrates the run of the algorithm in terms of the partitionings Π_i from the proof of Theorem 1 (in the right column of the table). There are four iterations, just as in Figure 2, and $\varphi_1, \ldots, \varphi_4$ and $\theta_1, \ldots, \theta_4$ are the same as in Figure 2, except that we do not make explicit all of the information in the table of Figure 3. To

	$\overbrace{x_1 \; x_2 \; x_3 \; x_4 \; x_5}^{\theta_i}$	Π_i
$i=1$	1 1 1 0 0 1	$\{\, x_1, x_2, x_3, x_4, x_5, 1 \,\}$
$i=2$	1 0 0 1 0	$\{\, x_1, x_3, 1 \,\}, \{\, x_2, x_4, x_5 \,\}$
$i=3$	1 0 0 0 1	$\{\, x_1, x_3, 1 \,\}, \{\, x_2 \,\}, \{\, x_4, x_5 \,\}$
$i=4$	*unsat*	

Fig. 3. Demo of the generalized backbone algorithm performing a linear number of calls as in the proof of Theorem 1 (Example 3)

better understand the meaning of the partition observe for instance the second iteration where Π_2 indicates that the set $\Theta_2 = \{\theta_1, \theta_2\}$: (a) determines the equations between $\{x_1, x_3, 1\}$ (for both assignments, $x_1 = 1$ is *true*, $x_3 = 1$ is *false*, and $x_1 = x_3$ is false), and (b) determines the equations between $\{x_2, x_4, x_5\}$ (for both assignments, $x_2 = x_4$, $x_4 = x_5$, and $x_5 = x_2$ are *false*).

4   Complete Equi-propagation in BEE

BEE is a compiler which facilitates solving finite domain constraints by encoding them to CNF and applying an underlying SAT solver. In BEE constraints are modeled as Boolean functions which propagate information about equalities between Boolean literals. This information is then applied to simplify the CNF encoding of the constraints. This process is termed *equi-propagation*. A key factor is that considering only a small fragment of a constraint model at one time enables to apply stronger, and as we argue in this paper, even complete reasoning to detect equivalent literals in that fragment. Once detected, equivalences propagate to simplify the entire constraint model and facilitate further reasoning on other fragments. BEE is described in several recent papers: [14], [13] and [15].

In BEE, each constraint is associated with a collection of simplification rules. The simplification of one constraint, may result in that we derive an equality of the form $x = \ell$, where x is a Boolean variable and ℓ a Boolean literal or constant, which is implied by one or more of the given constraints. The compiler then propagates this equality to other constraints, which may in turn trigger simplification rules for additional constraints. BEE iterates until no further rules apply.

Figure 4 illustrates a constraint model in BEE for the Kakuro instance depicted as Figure 5(a). In a Kakuro instance each block of consecutive horizontal or vertical white cells must be filled with distinct non-zero digits (integer values between 1 and 9) which sum to a given clue. For example, in the bottom row of Figure 5(a) the four cells must sum to 14 and a possible solution is to assign them the distinct values 5,1,6,2. The constraints in the left column of Figure 4 declare the finite domain variables of the instance. Each cell is associated with a finite domain variable taking values between 1 and 9. Each block of integer variables (horizontal and vertical) in the instance is associated with a `int_array_plus` constraint (middle column) and an `allDiff` constraint (right column).

The simplification rules defined in BEE consider each individual constraint to determine (generalized) backbone variables in its underlying bit-level representation. These rules are "ad-hoc" in that they do not derive all of the equalities implied by a constraint. Moreover if an equation is implied by a set of constraints but not by an individual constraint, then BEE may not detect that equation. Figure 5(b) illustrates the effect of applying BEE to the constraint model of Figure 4 and demonstrates that 7 of the 14 integer variables in the instance are determined at compile time.

In this paper we propose to enhance BEE to allow the user to specify sets of constraints to which a generalized backbone algorithm is to be applied. We call this process complete equi-propagation (CEP). Figure 5(c) illustrates the effect of the enhanced BEE where each pair of constraints about a given block: one int_array_plus and one allDiff are grouped for CEP. Here we see that all 14 integer variables in the instance are determined at compile time.

new_int($I_1, 1, 9$)	int_array_plus($[I_1, I_2], 6$)	allDiff($[I_1, I_2]$)
new_int($I_2, 1, 9$)	int_array_plus($[I_3, I_4, I_5, I_6], 17$)	allDiff($[I_3, I_4, I_5, I_6]$)
new_int($I_3, 1, 9$)	int_array_plus($[I_7, I_8], 3$)	allDiff($[I_7, I_8]$)
new_int($I_4, 1, 9$)	int_array_plus($[I_9, I_{10}], 4$)	allDiff($[I_9, I_{10}]$)
new_int($I_5, 1, 9$)	int_array_plus($[I_{11}, I_{12}, I_{13}, I_{14}], 14$)	allDiff($[I_{11}, I_{12}, I_{13}, I_{14}]$)
new_int($I_6, 1, 9$)	int_array_plus($[I_3, I_7], 11$)	allDiff($[I_3, I_7]$)
new_int($I_7, 1, 9$)	int_array_plus($[I_4, I_8, I_{11}], 8$)	allDiff($[I_4, I_8, I_{11}]$)
new_int($I_8, 1, 9$)	int_array_plus($[I_1, I_5], 3$)	allDiff($[I_1, I_5]$)
new_int($I_9, 1, 9$)	int_array_plus($[I_2, I_6, I_9, I_{13}], 18$)	allDiff($[I_2, I_6, I_9, I_{13}]$)
new_int($I_{10}, 1, 9$)	int_array_plus($[I_{10}, I_{14}], 3$)	allDiff($[I_{10}, I_{14}]$)
new_int($I_{11}, 1, 9$)		
new_int($I_{12}, 1, 9$)		
new_int($I_{13}, 1, 9$)		
new_int($I_{14}, 1, 9$)		

Fig. 4. Constraints for the Kakuro instance of Figure 5(a)

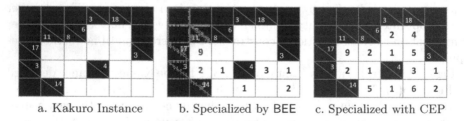

a. Kakuro Instance   b. Specialized by BEE   c. Specialized with CEP

Fig. 5. Applying complete equi-propagation to a Kakuro Instance

The compilation of a constraint model to a CNF using BEE goes through three phases. In the first phase, bit blasting, integer variables (and constants) are represented as bit vectors. Now all constraints are about Boolean variables. The second phase, the main loop of the compiler, is about constraint simplification. Three types of actions are applied: ad-hoc equi-propagation, partial evaluation, and decomposition of constraints. Simplification is applied repeatedly until no rule is applicable. In the third, and final phase, simplified constraints are encoded to CNF.

In order to enhance BEE with CEP we introduce syntax for users to specify constraints or groups of constraints designated for CEP. We introduce a new phase to the compilation process which is applied after the first phase (bit blasting) and before the second phase. In the new phase, we first apply two types of actions, ad-hoc equi-propagation and partial evaluation, repeatedly until no rule is applicable. Then we apply generalized backbone computation on the CNF of the user defined groups of constraints. If new equalities are derived from applying the CEP algorithm on one of the user defined groups, then these are propagated to all relevant constraints and the simplification process is repeated until no more equalities are derived.

At the syntactic level, we have added two constructs to BEE: cep(C) specifies that the CEP algorithm is applied to the CNF of constraint C instead of the ad-hoc rules in BEE; and cep_group(G) specifies that CEP is applied to the conjunction of CNF's corresponding to the constraints in a group G. For instance, the user might specify cep_group([int_array_plus([I_1, I_2], 6), allDiff([I_1, I_2])]) for pairs of constraints in the Kakuro example.

5 Preliminary Experimental Evaluation

We demonstrate the potential of CEP with 2 experiments. Our goal is to illustrate the impact of CEP on the BEE constraint compiler. We demonstrate that, in some cases, enhancing the compilation of constraints to consider CEP (using a SAT solver) at compile time leads to much better results than those obtained when using BEE's polynomial time compilation based on ad-hoc equi-propagation rules. To this end we view CEP as yet one more compilation tool that the user can choose to apply.

5.1 The First Experiment

We illustrate the impact of CEP with an application of extremal graph theory where the goal is to find the largest number of edges in a simple graph with n nodes such that any cycle (length) is larger than 4. The graph is represented as a Boolean adjacency matrix A and there are three types of constraints:

1. Constraints about cycles in the graph: $\forall_{i,j,k}.\ A[i,j] + A[j,k] + A[k,i] < 3$, and $\forall_{i,j,k,l}.\ A[i,j] + A[j,k] + A[k,l] + A[l,i] < 4$;
2. Constraints about symmetries: in addition to the obvious $\forall_{1 \leq i < j \leq n}.\ (A[i,j] \equiv A[j,i]$ and $A[i,i] \equiv false)$, we constrain the rows of the adjacency matrix to be sorted lexicographically (justified in [1]); and
3. Constraints that impose lower and upper bounds on the degrees of the graph nodes as described in [3].

Further details on this benchmark can be found in [1].

Table 1 illustrates results, running BEE with and without CEP. Here, we focus on finding a graph with the prescribed number of graph nodes with the known maximal number of edges (all instances are satisfiable). In our encoding, if CEP is applied, then there is a single CEP group consisting of all of the constraints related to symmetry breaking and node degrees (items 2 and 3 detailed above). All of the other constraints related to graph cycles (item 1 detailed above) remain ungrouped. The table details for each instance:

- in the first two columns: the number of nodes and edges;
- in the next two columns: the size of the single CEP group which is input to the CEP algorithm (number of clauses and variables, after ad-hoc simplification by BEE);
- in the next two sets of 4 columns: for each CEP choice: the BEE compilation time, the (total) number of clauses and variables in the target CNF encoding, and the subsequent sat solving time.

The table indicates that CEP increases the compilation time (within reason), reduces the CNF size (considerably), and (for the most part) improves SAT solving time.[2] The CEP groups in this example involve, in average, about half the number of variables and one third the number of clauses when compared to the encoding without CEP, with up to 10,000 variables and 50,000 clauses. We note, that as explained above, BEE iterates over CEP groups, propagating equations learned from one group to simplify other groups which as a result may yield further CEP information. The group sizes presented in Table 1 indicate the initial group sizes. During iteration the size of the groups decreases.

5.2   The Second Experiment

We consider the 12 instances from the **armies** benchmark from category DEC-SMALLINT-LIN of the PB'12 competition.[3] Each instance consists of a set of cardinality and pseudo Boolean constraints.

For this experiment we consider a grouping of the constraints into two (overlapping) groups. These are obtained by considering a connectivity graph where the nodes are constraint variables. There is a weighted edge (u, v) with weight $dep(u, v)$ between variables u and v if their degree of dependency $dep(u, v) > 0$ which is defined as follows:

Given a set of constraints Cs. Let V be the set of (Boolean and integer) variables occurring in Cs. For a variable $v \in V$, let $C(v)$ denote the set of constraints that involve v. For a pair of variables $u, v \in V$, $dep(u, v) = |C(u) \cap C(v)|$ is a simple measure on the potential dependency between u and v.

We also define $level(v) = max \{ dep(u, v) \mid u \in V \}$, a measure on the dependencies of variable v: a variable v has a high dependency level if there is another

---

[2] Experiments are performed on a single core of an Intel(R) Core(TM) i5-2400 3.10GHz CPU with 4GB memory under Linux (Ubuntu lucid, kernel 2.6.32-24-generic).

[3] See http://www.cril.univ-artois.fr/PB12/

Table 1. Search for graphs with no cycles of size 4 or less (comp. & solve times in sec.)

		group size		with CEP				without CEP			
nodes	edges	clauses	vars	comp.	clauses	vars	solve	comp.	clauses	vars	solve
15	26	8157	1761	0.24	13421	2154	0.07	0.10	23424	3321	0.08
16	28	10449	2200	0.26	18339	2851	0.19	0.12	30136	4328	0.34
17	31	11996	2558	0.39	21495	3233	0.07	0.16	37074	5125	0.12
18	34	14235	3030	0.49	26765	3928	0.12	0.21	45498	6070	0.13
19	38	16272	3433	0.46	30626	4380	0.11	0.22	54918	7024	0.15
20	41	21307	4354	0.55	43336	6005	5.93	0.25	68225	8507	12.70
21	44	24715	5037	0.77	52187	7039	1.46	0.31	81388	9835	69.46
22	47	28296	5762	0.88	61611	8118	71.73	0.35	96214	11276	45.43
23	50	32213	6556	1.10	73147	9352	35.35	0.38	113180	13101	27.54
24	54	35280	7278	2.02	81634	10169	96.11	0.50	130954	14712	282.99
25	57	40942	8344	1.40	99027	12109	438.91	0.53	152805	16706	79.11
26	61	44817	9208	4.58	110240	13143	217.72	0.73	175359	18615	815.55
27	65	50078	10282	2.16	127230	14856	35.36	0.75	201228	20791	114.55

variable u such that u and v occur together in a large number of constraints. For a grouping, we first take all of the constraints which contain a variable of maximal level. Denote $max = max \{ level(v) \mid v \in V \}$ and define

$$G_1 = \{ c \mid v \in V, \ level(v) = max, \ c \in C(v) \}$$
$$G_2 = Cs \setminus G_1$$

In the context of our experiments G_1 was small in comparison to G_2, and we extended it by defining

$$G_1' = \{ c \mid v \in V, \ level(v) \geq k, \ c \in C(v) \}$$

for a suitable value $k < max$ such that the size of G_1' and G_2 are more or less equal. Note that we did not redefine G_2 so the two groups overlap. We found this redundancy useful.

Table 2 illustrates the encoding sizes for the instances of the `armies` benchmark. In the first 2 columns we indicate the instance name and the number of original instance variables (ι-vars). Next we illustrate the encoding sizes for three configurations: using BEE (with ad-hoc equi-propagation), using BEE with a backbone algorithm, and using BEE with a CEP algorithm. For backbones and CEP we group constraints into two groups (G_1' and G_2 described above), more or less equal in size. For encoding sizes we indicate the number of CNF variables and clauses as well as the percent of the original instance variables eliminated during the compilation process ($\Delta\iota$). So in average, BEE with CEP eliminates 6.3% of the original instance variables, while BEE with backbones eliminates 3.7% and BEE alone (with its ad-hoc techniques) eliminates 2.0%. These reductions, although small, may be significant as we are eliminating variables on the input to the SAT solver.

Table 2. The Army benchmarks — Encoding sizes

instance		BEE (regular)			BEE (backbones)			BEE (CEP)		
name	ι-vars	vars	clauses	$\Delta\iota$	vars	clauses	$\Delta\iota$	vars	clauses	$\Delta\iota$
$8 \times 9ls$	220	2136	8072	0.0	2136	8072	0.0	2096	7932	3.6
$8 \times 9bt$	220	2893	11567	5.0	2488	9962	10.5	2438	9784	15.0
$9 \times 12ls$	266	2778	11077	0.0	2778	11077	0.0	2738	10937	3.0
$9 \times 12bt$	266	3522	14441	4.5	3204	13101	7.1	3172	12994	10.2
$10 \times 14ls$	316	4008	14450	0.0	4008	14450	0.0	3978	14345	1.9
$11 \times 17ls$	370	4914	18447	0.0	4914	18447	0.0	4874	18307	2.2
$10 \times 14bt$	316	6433	25553	4.1	5711	22969	8.5	5657	22771	11.7
$11 \times 17bt$	370	7446	29425	3.8	6914	27290	5.9	6882	27183	8.1
$13 \times 24ls$	490	7240	28645	0.0	7240	28645	0.0	7210	28541	1.2
$13 \times 24bt$	490	15298	60988	3.3	13858	55675	5.1	13826	55568	6.7
$12 \times 21bt$	428	14094	55614	3.5	12515	49725	7.2	12457	49507	9.6
$12 \times 21ls$	428	5912	23144	0.0	5912	23144	0.0	5872	23004	1.9
Average		6390	25119	2.0	5973	23546	3.7	5933	23406	6.3

Table 3. The Army benchmarks — solving times (seconds) with 1800 sec. timeout

instance	BEE (regular)			BEE(Backbones)			BEE (CEP)		
name	comp.	solve	total	comp.	solve	total	comp.	solve	total
$8 \times 9ls$	0.0	0.6	0.6	0.4	0.1	0.5	0.7	0.5	1.2
$8 \times 9bt$	0.1	1.0	1.1	0.7	0.6	1.3	1.3	0.7	2.0
$9 \times 12ls$	0.1	5.9	6.0	0.5	3.0	3.5	1.0	1.1	2.1
$9 \times 12bt$	0.1	3.4	3.5	1.0	7.5	8.5	1.4	1.7	3.1
$10 \times 14ls$	0.1	17.0	17.1	0.7	1.0	1.7	1.5	8.2	9.7
$11 \times 17ls$	0.1	4.5	4.6	0.9	65.4	66.3	1.8	8.1	9.9
$10 \times 14bt$	0.1	45.2	45.3	1.9	100.4	102.3	4.1	6.9	11.0
$11 \times 17bt$	0.2	267.8	268.0	2.5	344.0	346.5	4.0	26.9	30.9
$13 \times 24ls$	0.1	833.8	833.9	2.2	880.8	883.0	3.5	652.2	655.7
$13 \times 24bt$	0.3	1072.7	1073.0	8.9	∞	∞	14.9	768.7	783.6
$12 \times 21bt$	0.3	∞	∞	7.0	∞	∞	18.9	∞	∞
$12 \times 21ls$	0.1	∞	∞	1.7	∞	∞	3.1	∞	∞

Table 3 details the solving times for the three encodings of the army benchmarks: using BEE (with ad-hoc equi-propagation), using BEE enhanced with backbones, and using BEE enhanced with generalized backbones (CEP). For each encoding and instance we indicate the compile time, the SAT solving time, and the total solving time (sum of the previous two).

First, we comment on compile times. Compile times increase for backbones and even more for generalized backbones. But this increase comes with a discount in solving time. Consider the instance $13 \times 24bt$. Compilation time for CEP goes up from 0.3 sec. to 14.9 sec, but total solving time goes down from 1073 sec. to 784 sec.

These instances are hard, although they are relatively small. The largest instance, $13 \times 24bt$, has only 490 (Boolean) variables and involves 1085 constraints.

Only four out of the 42 solvers tested on these instances in the PB'12 competition manage to solve instance $13 \times 24bt$ within the 1800 second timeout (the same timeout is used in our experiments). From these four solvers, the two SAT-based solvers require more or less 1600 seconds (on the competition machines) whereas our solution for this instance is under 800 seconds.

6 Conclusion

This paper generalizes the notion of a CNF backbone to capture also equalities between literals. We prove that computing generalized backbones, just as usual backbones, involves only a linear number of calls to a SAT solver. We describe the integration of backbones with equality to enhance the BEE constraint-to-CNF compiler and demonstrate the utility of our approach through a preliminary experimentation.

Acknowledgments: We thank Peter Stuckey for helpful discussions and comments.

References

1. Codish, M., Miller, A., Prosser, P., Stuckey, P.J.: Breaking symmetries in graph representation. In: Rossi, F. (ed.) IJCAI. IJCAI/AAAI (2013)
2. Eén, N., Biere, A.: Effective preprocessing in SAT through variable and clause elimination. In: Bacchus, F., Walsh, T. (eds.) SAT 2005. LNCS, vol. 3569, pp. 61–75. Springer, Heidelberg (2005)
3. Garnick, D.K., Kwong, Y.H.H., Lazebnik, F.: Extremal graphs without three-cycles or four-cycles. Journal of Graph Theory 17(5), 633–645 (1993)
4. Heule, M.J.H., Järvisalo, M., Biere, A.: Efficient CNF simplification based on binary implication graphs. In: Sakallah, K.A., Simon, L. (eds.) SAT 2011. LNCS, vol. 6695, pp. 201–215. Springer, Heidelberg (2011)
5. Heule, M., van Maaren, H.: Aligning CNF- and equivalence-reasoning. In: Hoos, H.H., Mitchell, D.G. (eds.) SAT 2004. LNCS, vol. 3542, pp. 145–156. Springer, Heidelberg (2005)
6. Janota, M.: SAT Solving in Interactive Configuration. PhD thesis, University College Dublin (November 2010)
7. Kilby, P., Slaney, J.K., Thiébaux, S., Walsh, T.: Backbones and backdoors in satisfiability. In: Veloso, M.M., Kambhampati, S. (eds.) AAAI, pp. 1368–1373. AAAI Press / The MIT Press (2005)
8. Kirkpatrick, S., Toulouse, G.: Configuration space analysis of traveling salesman problems. J. Phys. (France) 46, 1277–1292 (1985)
9. Li, C.-M.: Equivalent literal propagation in the DLL procedure. Discrete Applied Mathematics 130(2), 251–276 (2003)
10. Manolios, P., Papavasileiou, V.: Pseudo-boolean solving by incremental translation to SAT. In: Bjesse, P., Slobodová, A. (eds.) FMCAD, pp. 41–45. FMCAD Inc. (2011)
11. Manthey, N.: Coprocessor 2.0 - a flexible CNF simplifier - (tool presentation). In: Cimatti, A., Sebastiani, R. (eds.) SAT 2012. LNCS, vol. 7317, pp. 436–441. Springer, Heidelberg (2012)

12. Marques-Silva, J., Janota, M., Lynce, I.: On computing backbones of propositional theories. In: Coelho, H., Studer, R., Wooldridge, M. (eds.) ECAI. Frontiers in Artificial Intelligence and Applications, vol. 215, pp. 15–20. IOS Press (2010), Extended version: http://sat.inesc-id.pt/~mikolas/bb-aicom-preprint.pdf
13. Metodi, A., Codish, M.: Compiling finite domain constraints to SAT with BEE. TPLP 12(4-5), 465–483 (2012)
14. Metodi, A., Codish, M., Lagoon, V., Stuckey, P.J.: Boolean equi-propagation for optimized SAT encoding. In: Lee, J. (ed.) CP 2011. LNCS, vol. 6876, pp. 621–636. Springer, Heidelberg (2011)
15. Metodi, A., Codish, M., Stuckey, P.J.: Boolean equi-propagation for concise and efficient SAT encodings of combinatorial problems. J. Artif. Intell. Res. (JAIR) 46, 303–341 (2013)
16. Monasson, R., Zecchina, R., Kirkpatrick, S., Selman, B., Troyansky, L.: Determining computational complexity for characteristic phase transitions. Nature 400, 133–137 (1998)
17. Schneider, J.J.: Searching for backbones – an efficient parallel algorithm for the traveling salesman problem. Comput. Phys. Commun. (1996)
18. Sheeran, M., Stålmarck, G.: A tutorial on stålmarck's proof procedure for propositional logic. Formal Methods in System Design 16(1), 23–58 (2000)
19. Stålmark, G.: A system for determining propositional logic theorem by applying values and rules to triplets that are generated from a formula. US Patent 5,276,897; Canadian Patent 2,018,828; European Patent 0403 545; Swedish Patent 467 076 (1994)
20. Zhang, W.: Phase transitions and backbones of the asymmetric traveling salesman problem. J. Artif. Intell. Res. (JAIR) 21, 471–497 (2004)

PASS: String Solving with Parameterized Array and Interval Automaton

Guodong Li and Indradeep Ghosh

Fujitsu Labs of America, CA
{gli,ighosh}@fla.fujitsu.com

Abstract. The problem of solving string constraints together with numeric constraints has received increasing interest recently. Existing methods use either bit-vectors or automata (or their combination) to model strings, and reduce string constraints to bit-vector constraints or automaton operations, which are then solved in the respective domain. Unfortunately, they often fail to achieve a good balance between efficiency, accuracy, and comprehensiveness. In this paper we illustrate a new technique that uses parameterized arrays as the main data structure to model strings, and converts string constraints into quantified expressions that are solved through quantifier elimination. We present an efficient and sound quantifier elimination algorithm. In addition, we use an automaton model to handle regular expressions and reason about string values faster. Our method does not need to enumerate string lengths (as bit-vector based methods do), or concrete string values (as automaton based methods do). Hence, it can achieve much better accuracy and efficiency. In particular, it can identify unsatisfiable cases quickly. Our solver (named PASS) supports most of the popular string operations, including string comparisons, string-numeric conversions, and regular expressions. Experimental results demonstrate the advantages of our method.

1 Introduction

A string solver is used to determine the satisfiability of a set of constraints involving string operations. These constraint can be mixed with numeric constraints, in which case we call them *hybrid* constraints. This paper is about how to solve hybrid constraints efficiently using SMT solving and automaton approximation.

Hybrid constraints may be produced by a static analyzer or a symbolic executor. For example, a symbolic executor for web applications may produce thousands of path conditions containing non-trivial hybrid constraints. Solving these constraints efficiently is the key for the tool to be scalable and practical. A typical web application takes string inputs on web pages and performs a lot of string operations such as `concatenation`, `substring`, `>`, and `matches`. There are also three more typical requirements: (1) strings are converted into numeric values for back-end computations; (2) string values are constrained through regular expressions; and (3) unsatisfiable hybrid constraints should be identified quickly. This poses unique challenges to many symbolic execution tools [5,12,13,17] which usually handle only numeric constraints well.

V. Bertacco and A. Legay (Eds.): HVC 2013, LNCS 8244, pp. 15–31, 2013.
© Springer International Publishing Switzerland 2013

While there are some external string solvers [2,20,8,18,15,9] available, none of them meets our need to obtain a good balance between efficiency, accuracy, and comprehensiveness. Roughly, existing solvers can be divided into two categories: (1) bit-vector (BV) based methods, which model a string with a fixed-length bit-vector; and (2) automaton based methods, which model a string with an automaton. A BV method needs to compute the lengths of all strings before constructing bit-vectors, hence it may enumerate all possible length values in order to prove or disprove a set of constraints. Such enumeration often leads to exponential numbers of fruitless trials. In contrast, an automaton method models a string with an automaton capturing all possible values of this string. String automata can be refined according to the relation of the strings. Essentially, an automaton is an *over-approximation* of string values, and the refinement is often insufficient, requiring the enumeration of concrete string values and/or string sequences to find out a valid solution. The methods combining these two models inherit many of the disadvantages while circumvent some.

In this paper we propose a new way to model strings so as to avoid brute-force enumeration of string lengths or values. We model a string with a parameterized array (*parray* for short) such that (1) the array maps indices to character values, (2) both the indices and the characters can be symbolic, and (3) the string length is pure symbolic. With this model, string constraints are converted into quantified constraints (*e.g.* $\exists$ and $\forall$ expressions) which are then handled through our quantifier elimination scheme. Our conversion scheme follows a declarative and non-recursive style. The produced quantified constraints are often beyond the capacity of modern SMT solvers such as Yices [19] and CVC [1]. To handle them, we propose an efficient quantifier elimination algorithm. This conversion scheme is our first contribution. It precisely models string operations and string-numeric conversions. The quantifier eliminator is our second contribution.

Our third contribution is to use interval automata to build an extra model for strings, and reason about string values via automata. We use automata to not only handle regular expressions (RegExps), but also enhance the solving of non-RegExp cases. We demonstrate how to refine the automata through deductive reasoning and fixed-point calculation.

Our fourth contribution is to combine the parray and automaton model to determine satisfiability efficiently. For example, when the automaton domain finds unsat, the solver can safely claim unsat. While the automaton model is mandatory in modeling RegExps, we can use the automata to refine the parray model for locating a solution fast.

We perform preliminary experiments to compare different methods, and show that our method outperforms existing ones in general.

As far as we know, our P-Array based String Solver (PASS) is the first to explicitly use parameterized arrays to model strings and apply quantifier elimination to solve string constraints. It is also the first to combine interval automaton and parray for fast string solving. As for comprehensiveness, it handles virtually all Java string operations, regular expressions, and string-numeric conversions.

```
String s1, s2; int i; // symbolic      String s; // symbolic input
if (s1.beginsWith("a1")) {             if (s[0] == '-') {
  if (s2.contains("12")) {               if (s.match(".\d+,\d{3}"))
    if ((s1 + s2).endsWith("cd"))          ...;  // path 1
      ...;  // path 1                     else {
    else ...;  // path 2                    int i = s.lastIndexOf(',');
  }                                         if (i == -1) ...; // path 2
  else if (s2.toLower() > s1)              else {
  { ...; return; } // path 3                String s1 = s.substring(i+1);
  int j = parseInt(s2.substring(i,i+2));   int x = parseInt(s1);
  if (j == 12) ...; // path 4              if (x > 100 + i)
  else (toString(i) == s2)                  ...; // path 3
    ...; // path 5                         else if (s1 < "1000")
  else ...; // path 6                        ...; // path 4
}                                           else ...; // path 5
else ...; // path 7                     }}}
        (a)                             else ...; // path 6
                                                (b)
```

Fig. 1. Two example programs producing hybrid constraints

2 Motivating Examples and Background

Figure 1 shows two Java examples. The first one contains string operations substring, beginsWith, $>$, etc.. Inputs $s1$ and $s2$ are symbolic strings, and i is a symbolic integer. Consider the path conditions (PC) of Path 1 and Path 4. A possible solution for PC1 is $s1 = $ "a1" $\wedge\ s2 = $ "12cd". PC4 is unsatisfiable since constraint $\neg s2$.contains("12") contradicts with the "toInt..." constraint. Here numeric and strings may be converted back and forth.

PC1 :   s1.beginsWith("a1") $\wedge$ s2.contains("12") $\wedge$ (s1+s2).endsWith("cd")
PC4 :   s1.beginsWith("a1") $\wedge\ \neg$s2.contains("12") $\wedge$ s2.toLower() $\leq s1$
          $\wedge$ toInt(s2.substring($i, i + 2$)) $= 12$

The second example checks whether the symbolic input s starts with '-'. If yes, it checks whether s is of a popular format depicted by a RegExp (*e.g.* starting with any character, followed by at least one digit, and a comma, and then 3 digits). Then it checks whether ',' appears in s. If yes then the substring after character ',' is taken and converted into an integer x, which is later compared with $100 + i$. This is a typical computation in web applications, *e.g.*, first, performing format checking, then, converting strings to numeric, and finally, branching over the numeric. For example, a valid test case for path 3 is "-,103".

The satisfiability of string+numeric constraints is an undecidable problem in general (see [2] for some discussions). Hence practical solutions are important to tackle string-intensive programs. Existing string solvers cannot fulfill our needs. For example, Microsoft's solver [2] encodes string operations with bit-vector but does not support regular expressions. Hampi [8] and Kaluza [15] also use bit-vector encoding and provide limited support for hybrid constraints and regular expressions. The Rex tool [18] uses automaton and an SMT solver, and represents automaton transitions using logical predicates. Stranger [20] uses an automaton-based method to model string constraints and length bounds for abstract interpretation. A lazy solving technique [11] uses automaton with transitions annotated with integer ranges. A good comparison of the automaton-based approaches is given in [10]. Many of these solvers provide no support or only very limited support for hybrid constraints (*i.e.* combinations of numeric constraints, string constraints, and RegExp constraints). An interested reader may refer to [9] for more discussions. Moreover, even for the supported features, they often use iterations or brute-force enumerations, hence harming the performance. Now we briefly introduce the two main existing string models.

Bit-Vector Based Model [2,8,15]. A string of length n is modeled by a bit-vector of $8n$ (or $16n$ for Unicode) bits. Note that n has to be a concrete value before the bit-vector can be instantiated. Hence, a BV method first derives length constraints, then solves them to obtain a concrete assignment to the lengths, and then instantiates the bit-vectors and builds value constraints whose solving gives the final string values. For example, from constraints s1.beginsWith("ab") $\wedge$ s1.contains("12") we can derive $|s1| \geq 2$ (we use notation $||$ for the length), then obtain a concrete length value, *e.g.* $|s1| = 2$, then instantiate a $16b$ bit-vector v and build value constraints $extract(v, 0, 7) = $ 'a' $\wedge$ $extract(v, 8, 15) = $ 'b' $\wedge$ $extract(v, 0, 7) = $ '1' $\wedge$ $extract(v, 8, 15) = $ '2', which is found unsat by the SMT solver. Next, a new length constraint like $|s1| > 2$ is used to start a new iteration. After a few trials a valid solution $s1 = $ "ab12" is found with $|s1| = 4$. Clearly, separating the solving of length constraints and value constraints may result in wasted effort. This is also evidenced by the solving of PC1, where the minimum lengths for $s1$ and $s2$ is 2 and 4 respectively. Since the length constraints specify that $|s1| \geq 2 \wedge |s2| \geq 2 \wedge |s1| + |s2| \geq 2$. there are 2 wasted iterations before the right length values are reached.

The case of the unsatisfiable PC4 is worse. A BV method can infer $|s1| \geq i \wedge 2 \leq i + 2 \leq |s2|$, then build the value constraints after assigning concrete values to $|s1|$, $|s2|$ and i. After the value constraints are found unsatisfiable, new iterations are performed in an attempt to find a valid solution. Suppose the lengths and i are bounded to 100, then $O(100^3)$ iterations may be needed until time-out occurs. In contrast, our parray method requires no such fruitless iterations and is able to return sat or unsat quickly.

Automaton Based Model [16,21,18,20,11,9]. A string is modeled by an automaton which accepts all possible values of this string. There are two kinds of automata: (1) bit automaton, where each transition is labeled 0 or 1, and a string value is represented by the bits from the start state to an accept state; (2) interval automaton, where each transition represents a character whose value is within an interval (or range) $[lb, ub]$ for lower bound lb and upper bound ub. Since bit automata [21,20] assembles bit-vectors, here we investigate only interval automata. Note that a bit-automaton method may also require deriving and handling lengths constraints separately from value constraints [21].

Take PC1 for example. Initially, $s1$'s automaton accepts any string starting with "ab"; $s2$'s automaton accepts any string containing "12"; and the automaton concatenating $s1$ and $s2$, say $s3$, accepts any string ending with "cd". We can refine each automaton using the relation between the strings, $e.g.$ $s3$'s automaton should also contain "ab" and "12", and $s2$'s automaton should contain "cd". Then $s2$'s shortest solution is "12cd", which is valid.

Unfortunately, although automaton refinement can narrow down the possible values of the strings, it may fail to capture precisely the relation between strings. Consider the following path condition.

$$\text{PC3}: \quad s1 + s2 + s3 = \text{"aaaa"} \wedge s1 \geq s2 \geq s3$$

Obviously, after some (imperfect) refinement we can infer that $s1$'s value can be "", "a", ..., "aaaa". The next step is to assign concrete values to $s1$, $s2$ and $s3$. Suppose we starts with $s1 = $ "", then the second constraint enforces $s2 = s3 = $ "", which falsifies the first constraint. Similarly $s1 = $ "a" does not work. It may take multiple trials before we reach a valid solution like $s1 = $ "aa" and $s2 = s3 = $ "a". One main problem here is that an automaton represents a set of possible string values, but not the exact relation between strings, $e.g.$ only when $s1 = $ "" do we know that $s2 = s3 = $ "". While such a relation can be encoded in a production of two automata [21], the product-automaton may be too large. Searching strategies and heuristics [11] may help, but are too ad-hoc. We show in this paper a more general and comprehensive technique.

Moreover, the connection between strings modeled by automata and the numeric constraints may be weak. Consider the unsat PC4, where $s2$.substring($i, i + 2$) is converted to an integer for numeric computations. Since both $s2$ and i are symbolic, the values of this expression comprise an infinite set, and encoding them symbolically is not trivial (see Section 4 for more details). As a consequence, an automaton method may find it hard to disprove PC4. In our parray method, no automaton is required to handle PC4, and the unsat result can be obtained without enumerating string lengths or numeric values.

Nevertheless, the automaton model is extremely useful to handle RegExps. We propose a technique to convert automaton representation to parray representation parameterizedly after performing a sophisticated automaton refinement scheme. This scheme is crucial for both the accuracy and the performance.

This work is largely motivated when we built string solvers for Java and JavaScript Web applications. Our automaton-based solver in [9] suffers from above-mentioned issues, which are addressed by PASS.

Overview of Our Parray Based Model. A string is modeled by a parray of symbolic length. The main procedure to solve a set of hybrid constraints is:

1. All string constraints not involving regular expressions are converted into equivalent quantified parray constraints (Section 3).
2. If a string is constrained by a regular expression, build a string relation graph for all string variables in the constraints, perform refinement to infer more relations and possible values of the strings (Section 4).

3. For each string associated with a regular expression, build extra parray constraints from this string's automaton (Section 4). If no regular expression is involved in the original hybrid constraints, we can skip steps 2 and 3.
4. Perform quantifier elimination to remove quantifiers iteratively, solve the remaining numeric+array constraints (Section 3.1). This overcomes the limitations of modern SMT solvers like Yices [19].

3   Parameterized Array Based Model

A parameterized array (parray) maps symbolic indices (natural numbers) to symbolic characters. Unquantified parray constraints can be solved by an SMT solver supporting the array theory and the numeric theory. We convert string constraints into quantified parray constraints. Figure 2 shows some simple cases, where the conversions are mostly self-explanatory. Take lastIndexOf for example, integer i marks c's last position in the string. i is either -1 or $< |s|$. If $i = -1$, then $c \notin s$; otherwise, $s[i] = c$. Each character after index i does not equal to c, which is modeled by $\forall n.\, i < n < |s| \Rightarrow s[n] \neq c$.

All exists constraints can be eliminated by introducing fresh variables. Thus all remaining quantified constraints are of format $\forall n.\, n < l \Rightarrow P(n)$ where P is an unquantified constraint or a simple exists constraint. One main rule here is that we avoid using recursions in the conversion. For instance, we may introduce a helper function indexOf' to model indexOf: $s.\text{indexOf}'(i, c) = \texttt{ite}(s[i] = c, i, s.\text{indexOf}'(i + 1, c))$. However this recursive form may bring difficulties in quantifier elimination. Another example is $s > s_1$, whose recursive encoding is easy to specify but hard to solve. We describe below a novel way to encode it.

Figure 3 shows the conversions for some tricky cases, which represent our novel encoding. For $i = s.\text{indexOf}(s_1)$, if $i \neq -1$ then i is the first position in s such that s_1 appears, hence s_1 will not appear in any prior position m. The $i = -1$ case is the same as $\neg s.\text{contains}(s_1)$.

Consider $s_1 = s.\text{trim}()$, i.e. s_1 is obtained from s by removing all blank characters from the beginning and ending of s. As shown below, we introduce a natural number m to mark the first non-blank character in s. The conversion reads: all characters before m and after $m + |s_1|$ are blank, others are shared by s and s_1 in the same order, with the characters at two ends are not blank.

$s[0]$	...	$s[m-1]$	$s[m]$	...	$s[m+|s_1|-1]$	$s[m+|s_1|]$	...
' '	...	' '	$s_1[0]$	...	$s_1[|s_1|-1]$	' '	...

The conversion of $s > s_1$ is through introducing a natural number m to mark the first position where s and s_1 differs. As shown below, the characters from 0 to $m - 1$ are the same. Next, if s_1 is of length m and s's length is greater than s_1's, or $s[m] \neq s_1[m]$, then $s > s_1$. The case of $s \geq s_1$ is similar except that s can equal to s_1, e.g. $|s| = |s_1| = m$. The conversions of $s < s_1$ and $s \leq s_1$ are done through $s_1 < s$ and $s_1 \geq s$ respectively.

$s[0]$	$s[1]$	...	$s[m-1]$	$s[m]$
$s_1[0]$	$s_1[1]$	...	$s_1[|s_1|-1]$	

Case 1: $m = |s_1|$

$s[0]$	$s[1]$	...	$s[m-1]$	$s[m]$
$s_1[0]$	$s_1[1]$	...	$s_1[m-1]$	$s_1[m]$

Case 2: $|s_1| > m \wedge s[m] > s_1[m]$

String Constraint	P-Array Constraint
$s_1 = s_2$	$(\forall n.\, n < |s_1| \Rightarrow s_1[n] = s_2[n]) \wedge |s_1| = |s_2|$
$s_1 \neq s_2$	$(\exists n.\, n < |s_1| \wedge s_1[n] \neq s_2[n]) \vee |s_1| \neq |s_2|$
$s = s_1 + s_2$	$(\forall n.\, n < |s_1| \Rightarrow s_1[n] = s[n]) \wedge$ $(\forall n.\, n < |s_2| \Rightarrow s_2[n] = s[|s_1| + n]) \wedge |s| = |s_1| + |s_2|$
$s_1 = s.\mathrm{substring}(n_1, n_2)$	$(\forall n.\, n < |s_1| \Rightarrow s_1[n] = s[n_1 + n]) \wedge$ $n_1 < n_2 \leq |s| \wedge |s_1| - n_2 - n_1$
$i = s.\mathrm{lastIndexOf}(c)$	$(i = -1 \vee (0 \leq i < |s| \wedge s[i] = c)) \wedge$ $(\forall n.\, i < n < |s| \Rightarrow s[n] \neq c)$
$i = s.\mathrm{indexOf}(c)$	$(i = -1 \vee (0 \leq i < |s| \wedge s[i] = c)) \wedge (\forall n.\, n < i \Rightarrow s[n] \neq c)$
$s.\mathrm{beginsWith}(s_1)$	$(\forall n.\, n < |s_1| \Rightarrow s_1[n] = s[n]) \wedge |s| \geq |s_1|$
$\neg s.\mathrm{beginsWith}(s_1)$	$(\exists n.\, n < |s_1| \wedge s_1[n] \neq s[n]) \vee |s| < |s_1|$
$s.\mathrm{endsWith}(s_1)$	$(\forall n.\, n < |s_1| \Rightarrow s_1[n] = s[|s| - |s_1| + n]) \wedge |s| \geq |s_1|$
$s.\mathrm{contains}(s_1)$	$(\exists m.\, m \leq |s| - |s_1| \wedge (\forall n.\, n < |s_1| \Rightarrow s_1[n] = s[m + n])) \wedge$ $|s| \geq |s_1|$
$\neg s.\mathrm{contains}(s_1)$	$(\forall m.\, m \leq |s| - |s_1| \Rightarrow (\exists n.\, n < |s_1| \wedge s_1[n] \neq s[m + n])) \vee$ $|s| < |s_1|$
$s_1 = s.\mathrm{toUpperCase}()$	$(\forall n.\, n < |s| \Rightarrow s_1[n] = \mathtt{ite}(`a' \leq s[n] \leq `z', s[n] + `a' - `A', s[n]))$ $\wedge |s_1| = |s|$

Fig. 2. Conversion of simple cases (excerpt). Operator $|s|$ denotes string s's length. m and n are natural numbers; i is an integer; c is a character.

String Constraint	P-Array Constraint
$i = s.\mathrm{indexOf}(s_1)$ $i \neq -1$	$i \geq 0 \wedge i + |s_1| \leq |s| \wedge (\forall n.\, n < |s_1| \Rightarrow s_1[n] = s[i + n]) \wedge$ $(\forall n.\, n < i \Rightarrow (\exists m.\, m < |s_1| \Rightarrow s_1[n] \neq s[m + n]))$
$s_1 = s.\mathrm{trim}()$	$\exists m.\, m + |s_1| \leq |s| \wedge$ $(\forall n.\, (n < m \vee m + |s_1| \leq n \leq |s|) \Rightarrow s[n] = `\,') \wedge$   $(\forall n.\, n < |s_1| \Rightarrow s[m + n] = s_1[n]) \wedge$   $s[m] \neq `\,' \wedge s[m + |s_1| - 1] \neq `\,'$
$s > s_1$	$\exists m.\, m \leq |s_1| \wedge (\forall n.\, n < m \Rightarrow s_1[n] = s[n]) \wedge$ $|s| > m \wedge (|s_1| = m \vee |s_1| > m \wedge s[m] > s_1[m])$
$s \geq s_1$	$\exists m.\, m \leq |s_1| \wedge (\forall n.\, n < m \Rightarrow s_1[n] = s[n]) \wedge$ $(|s| = |s_1| = m \vee |s_1| = m \vee |s_1| > m \wedge s[m] > s_1[m])$
$i = \mathrm{parseInt}(s) \wedge$ $i \geq 0$	$(|s| = 1 \Rightarrow i = s[0] - `0') \wedge$   $(|s| = 2 \Rightarrow i = (s[0] - `0') \times 10 + s[1] - `0') \wedge \ldots \wedge$   $(|s| = 10 \Rightarrow$   $i = ((s[0] - `0') \times 10 + (s[1] - `0')) \times 10 \cdots + (s[9] - `0'))$

Fig. 3. Conversion of more tricky cases (excerpt)

The conversion of parseInt is one of the rare examples where the string length has to be bounded concretely. Since a 32-bit integer can have up to 10 digits, the conversion case splits over the possible length values to produce unquantified constraints. The conversion of parseFloat is similar. In Section 4 we show the automaton model can help infer possible lengths so as to simplify the encoding.

3.1 Solving P-Array Constraints with Quantifier Elimination

The generated forall constraints conform to a specific form: $\forall n. L(n) \Rightarrow P(s)$ or $\forall n. L(n) \Rightarrow \exists m. P(n)$, where P is a non-self-recursive predicate comparing two corresponding elements in two parrays, and L constrains n with respect to string lengths, *e.g.* $n < |s|$. In some cases, this simple format can be handled by a modern SMT solver like Yices [19]. But this is not the case in general. For instance, the most recent Yices version v1.0.36 cannot solve (in 10 minutes) the following simple forall constraints produced from string constraint $s + s = $ "aa", while it can solve $s_1 + s_2 = $ "aa" $\wedge |s_1| = |s_2| = 1$.

$$2 = |s| + |s| \wedge \_s_0[0] = \text{'a'} \wedge \_s_0[1] = \text{'a'} \wedge$$
$$(\forall n. n < |s| \Rightarrow \_s_0[n] = s[n]) \wedge (\forall n. n < |s| \Rightarrow \_s_0[|s| + n] = s[n]) .$$

Inspired by the work in [4], we propose an iterative quantifier elimination (QElim) [1] algorithm for the generated constraints. Note that [4] cannot handle most of our parray constraints, *e.g.* when an access's index is $m + n$ or $|s_1| + n$.

The basic idea is to calculate an *index set* and use its elements to instantiate forall constraints so as to eliminate the quantifiers. Given a set of constraints $\mathbb{C}$, parray s's index set (IS) includes all the indices of the accesses to s not bounded by a quantifier. By definition, $\{e \mid s[e] \in \mathbb{C} \wedge \text{qnt\_vars}(e) \neq \phi\} \subseteq \text{IS}(s)$, where qnt_vars gives the set of quantified variables. That is, for access $s[e]$, if e does not involve any quantifier, then $e \in \text{IS}(s)$. In addition, for each constraint of format $\forall n. n < k \Rightarrow P(s[n])$, the upper bound $k - 1$ is in $\text{IS}(k)$. This is for taking into the upper bound case into account.

Data: Quantified Constraints $\mathbb{C}_q$ + Unquantified Constraints $\mathbb{C}_{uq}$
Result: Unquantified Constraints $\mathbb{C}_{uq}$
forall s **do** $\text{IS}_{old}(s) = \{\}$; calculate $\text{IS}(s)$ **end**
while $\exists s. \text{IS}_{old}(s) \neq \text{IS}(s)$ **do**
$\quad$ **forall the** $e \in \text{IS}(s) \setminus \text{IS}_{old}(s)$ **do**
$\quad\quad$ **forall the** $(\forall n. L(n) \Rightarrow P(s[f(n)])) \in \mathbb{C}_q$ **do**
$\quad\quad\quad$ **if** $\text{sat}(\mathbb{C}_{uq} \wedge L(f^{-1}(e)))$
$\quad\quad\quad\quad$ add $L(f^{-1}(e)) \Rightarrow P(s[e])$ into $\mathbb{C}_{uq}$
$\quad\quad$ **end**
$\quad$ **end**
$\quad$ **forall** s **do** $\text{IS}_{old}(s) = \text{IS}(s)$; append new indices into $\text{IS}(s)$ **end**
end

Algorithm 1. Basic QElim algorithm for P-Array Constraints

After s's index set is calculated, we use each element e in it to instantiate constraint $\forall n. L(n) \Rightarrow P(s[f(n)])$ by replacing n with $f^{-1}(e)$, where f^{-1} is the inverse function of f. If P is an exists constraint, then its quantifier is removed by introducing a fresh variable. The intuition behind this is: if e matches $f(n)$, then we need to instantiate n with $f^{-1}(e)$, *i.e.* we should consider the special case

---
[1] Strictly speaking, our algorithm is not a conventional QElim which converts quantified constraints to equivalent unquantified ones. Here we reuse this term to indicate that our approach removes or instantiates quantifiers to find solutions.

$f^{-1}(e)$ for the forall constraint. Note that f is a linear function whose inverse is trivial to compute.

The next steps are described in Algorithm 1. For each new index e in $\mathrm{IS}(s)$ but not in $\mathrm{IS}_{old}(s)$, we use e to instantiate all forall constraints containing s. For such a constraint, if its assumption is satisfiable upon the current unquantified constraints $\mathbb{C}_{uq}$, then this constraint is added into $\mathbb{C}_{uq}$; otherwise it is ignored. The algorithm continues until no more new indices are found, in which case we remove all forall constraints, leaving a set of quantifier-free constraints.

Consider the above example, in the first round, $\_s_0$'s index set is $\{0, 1, |s| - 1\}$. After instantiating the two forall constraints with this set, we obtain six new constraints as following (note that $|s| - 1 < |s|$ is always true).

$$(0 < |s| \Rightarrow \_s_0[0] = s[0]) \wedge (1 < |s| \Rightarrow \_s_0[1] = s[1]) \wedge$$
$$(0 < |s| \Rightarrow \_s_0[|s|] = s[0]) \wedge (1 < |s| \Rightarrow \_s_0[|s| + 1] = s[1]) \wedge$$
$$(|s| - 1 < |s| \Rightarrow \_s_0[|s| - 1] = s[|s| - 1]) \wedge (|s| - 1 < |s| \Rightarrow \_s_0[|s| + |s| - 1] = s[|s| - 1])$$

Since constraint $2 = |s| + |s|$ conflicts with $1 < |s|$, we remove the two new constraints with assumption $1 < |s|$. In the next round, the remaining new constraints give us updated index sets $\mathrm{IS}(\_s_0) = \{0, 1, |s| - 1\} \cup \{|s|\}$ and $\mathrm{IS}(s) = \{0, |s| - 1\}$. The next index used for instantiation is $|s|$. Since $|s| < |s|$ is false, no new constraints will be added. Now there exists no new index, hence the algorithm terminates. The two forall constraints are removed, resulting in the following final constraints, whose valid solution is $s =$ "a" (and $\_s_0 =$ "aa").

$$2 = |s| + |s| \wedge \_s_0[0] = \text{`a'} \wedge \_s_0[1] = \text{`a'} \wedge$$
$$(0 < |s| \Rightarrow \_s_0[0] = s[0]) \wedge (0 < |s| \Rightarrow \_s_0[|s|] = s[0]) \wedge$$
$$(\_s_0[|s| - 1] = s[|s| - 1]) \wedge (\_s_0[|s| + |s| - 1] = s[|s| - 1])$$

The reduction of PC 1 results in the following constraints, which can produce a valid solution $n_1 = 0 \wedge |\_s_0| = 6 \wedge s_1 =$ "a1" $\wedge s_2 =$ "12cd".

$$|s_1| \geq 2 \wedge |s_2| \geq n_1 + 2 \wedge |\_s_0| = |s_1| + |s_2| \wedge$$
$$\_s_0[0] = s_1[0] = \text{`a'} \wedge \_s_0[1] = s_1[1] = \text{`1'} \wedge \_s_0[|\_s_0| - 2] = \text{`c'} \wedge \_s_0[|\_s_0| - 1] = \text{`d'} \wedge$$
$$\_s_0[|s_1| + n_1] = s_2[n_1] = \text{`1'} \wedge \_s_0[|s_1| + n_1 + 1] = s_2[n_1 + 1] = \text{`2'} \wedge$$
$$(\_s_0[|s_1| - 1] = s_1[|s_1| - 1]) \wedge (\_s_0[|s_1| + |s_2| - 1] = s_2[|s_2| - 1])$$

For a bounded string (i.e. whose length is bounded), its largest index set can contain all indices up to the bound. Hence the algorithm, similar to BV methods, always terminates (a careful reader can realize that our algorithm may terminate faster due to its symbolic index calculation). The obtained $\mathbb{C}_{uq}$ are equiv-satisfiable to the original (quantified + un-quantified) ones. More discussions on the soundness and termination of Algorithm 1 are given in the Appendix. Note that the soundness proof technique in [4] does not apply here since we (1) allow arithmetic operations in array accesses, (2) calculate index-set iteratively, and (3) permit array relations other than =.

Theorem. Algorithm 1 terminates on bounded strings, and generates un-quantified constraints equiv-satisfiable to the original (quantified + un-quantified) ones.

An Optimized Version: Iterative Quantifier Elimination and Solving.
Algorithm 1 may unnecessarily compute too many index sets and terminate
slowly. Hence in practice we use a slightly revised version shown in Algorithm 2
that can prove sat or unsat much faster. The revisions are on the main procedure
of each iteration: (1) we record the new un-quantified constraints in $\mathbb{C}_{cur}$ and use
it to compute the new index sets IS_{cur}, and then use IS_{cur} to instantiate forall
constraints; (2) after the instantiation, solve all un-quantified constraints using
an SMT solver, if unsat then the algorithm terminates and safely reports unsat;
(3) otherwise we check whether the current solution $solution(\mathbb{C}_{uq})$ satisfies the
original string constraints $\mathbb{S}$. If yes then the algorithm terminates with a true
valid solution; otherwise go to the next iteration. If the bound $limit$ is reached,
then return "unknown". Note that the algorithm does not need to iterate over
string lengths. In practice only a couple of iterations are needed in most cases.

The soundness of this algorithm is straight-forward, *e.g.* the sat case is war-
ranted by the check on $\mathbb{S}$. We give more details in the Appendix.

Theorem. Algorithm 2 terminates on bounded strings, and
reports sat (or unsat) when
the original constraints are indeed sat (or unsat).

Data: $\mathbb{C}_q + \mathbb{C}_{uq}$ + String Constraints $\mathbb{S}$
Result: sat, unsat, or unknown
$\mathrm{IS}_{cur} = \mathbb{C}_{uq}$;
for $i = 0$; $i < limit; i{+}{+}$ **do**
  calculate IS_{cur} w.r.t $\mathbb{C}_{cur}$;
  $\mathbb{C}_{cur} = \{\}$;
  forall the s **forall** $e \in \mathrm{IS}_{cur}(s)$ **do**
    forall $(\forall n.\, L(n) \Rightarrow P(s[f(n)])) \in \mathbb{C}_q$
      add $L(f^{-1}(e)) \Rightarrow P(s[e])$ into $\mathbb{C}_{cur}$
  end
  $\mathbb{C}_{uq} = \mathbb{C}_{uq} \cup \mathbb{C}_{cur}$;
  if unsat$(\mathbb{C}_{uq})$ **return** unsat ;
  if solution$(\mathbb{C}_{uq}) \Rightarrow$ sat$(\mathbb{S})$ **return** sat ;
end
return unknown ;

Algorithm 2. Iterative QElim

4   Enhancement with Automaton Based Model

We use an interval automaton to represent a string
such that all possible values of this string constitutes the language accepted
by this automaton. Our implementation is based on
the automaton package
`dk.brics.automaton` [6]. A
transition is labeled the lower
bound and upper bound of the associated character. For example, the automaton for the regular expression ".\d+,\d{3}" in the motivating example is shown
below.

The implementation of many operations is intuitive. For example, the
concatenation of s_1 and s_2 is implemented by adding ϵ transitions from all accepting states of s_1's automaton to all initial states of s_2's automaton, and then

removing ϵ to make the resulting automaton deterministic. Many operations such as `intersection` and `minus` are supported by the `dk.brics.automaton` package.

However, we have to model more string operations such as `trim`, `substring`, and `toUpperCase`. For example, `substring(2,4)` returns a substring from index 2 to index 4 (exclusive). To implement it, we first advance 2 transitions from the start state q_0, then mark the reached states as the new start state q_0', and then identify all states reachable from q_0' in 2 transitions as new accepting states. Finally, we intersect this automaton with the one accepting all words of length 2 to get the final automaton. Due to space constraint we will skip the details of implementing the new operations, which we extend from [16,9].

Automaton Refinement. Given a set of string constraints, we build a relation graph with the string automata as the nodes and string relations as the edges. Then we perform iterative refinement to (1) refine each automaton so as to narrow the possible values of the associated string, and (2) derive extra relations.

The first set of refinement rules, including the following, refine automaton values. For better readability, we reuse string names for the automata. Here notation s' denotes the new automaton for s. Operators $\cap$ and $\cdot$ denote intersection and concatenation respectively. Automaton s_{any} accepts all strings, and c_{any} accepts any character. We implement some helper operations: `mk_all_accept`(s) marks all the states in s as accepting states, and `mk_all_start`(s) marks them as start states. Operation `first`(s, s_2) returns the automaton that accepts any string whose concatenation with any string in s_2 is accepted by s. It is implemented over the production of s and s_2 with time complexity $O(n^2)$ for n nodes.

relation	$\implies$	refinement
$s = s_1$		$s' = s \cap s_1 \wedge s_1' = s_1 \cap s$
$s = s_1 + s_2$		$s' = s \cap (s_1 \cdot s_2) \wedge s_1' = \text{first}(s, s_2) \wedge s_2' = \text{second}(s, s_1)$
$s.\text{beginsWith}(s_1)$		$s' = s \cap (s_1 \cdot s_{any}) \wedge s_1' = s_1 \cap (\text{mk\_all\_accept}(s))$
$s.\text{endsWith}(s_1)$		$s' = s \cap (s_{any} \cdot s_1) \wedge s_1' = s_1 \cap (\text{mk\_all\_start}(s))$
$s.\text{contains}(s_1)$		$s' = s \cap (s_{any} \cdot s_1 \cdot s_{any}) \wedge$ $s_1' = s_1 \cap (\text{mk\_all\_accept}(\text{mk\_all\_start}(s)))$
$|s| = n$		$s' = s \cap (c_{any_0} \cdot \ldots \cdot c_{any_{n-1}})$

The refinements for `substring`, `lastIndexOf` and `indexOf` are similar to that for `contains`. Some rules are effective with assumptions, $e.g.$ length constraint $|s| = n$ or $|s| < n$ is performed only when n is constant. Similarly, we refine some $\neg$ cases only when one of the strings are known to be constant, $e.g.$ $\neg s.\text{contains}(\text{"abc"}) \implies s' = s - \{\text{"abc"}\}$. The refinement process is fixed-point calculation and will stop when no automaton can be refined further.

The second rule set is to refine the relations by inferring new facts from a pair of relations. In general, we may apply source-to-source transformations [14] to simplify the path conditions and then derive new facts. We present below an excerpt of these inference rules, which are repeatedly applied until no more new relation is inferred. They are particularly useful in finding some unsat cases early, *e.g.* $s_1 > s_2 \wedge s_2 \geq s_3 \wedge s_3 \geq s_1$ is unsat. We also define a consumption relation to simplify the relations, *e.g.* with $s.\text{beginsWith}(s_1)$ we can safely remove $s.\text{contains}(s_1)$.

relations	$\implies$	inferred relation
op $\in \{\geq,>\}$: $s_1 > s_2 \wedge s_2$ op s_3		$s_1 > s_3$
op $\in \{\leq,<,=\}$: $s_1 > s_2 \wedge s_1$ op s_2		false
$s.\text{beginsWith}(s_1)$		$s \geq s_1$
$\neg s.\text{contains}(s_1) \wedge s.\text{endsWith}(s_1)$		false

From Automaton to P-Array. For constraint $s.\texttt{matches}(re)$, s's automaton is refined by regular expression re. When we encode this automaton in the parray domain, the main challenge is on loops. For example, consider the following automaton corresponding to RegExp "$([l_0\text{-}u_0][l_1\text{-}u_1]\ldots[l_{n-1}\text{-}u_{n-1}])^*$", which accepts an infinite set of strings. Clearly, it is impossible to enumerate all the possibilities.

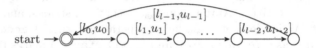

Here we propose a conversion which again uses **forall** constraints to encode the loop: we introduce a new number m to specify the limit of loop iterations. For each iteration, *e.g.* the nth one, we specify the value interval of each character, *e.g.* the kth character is within $[l_k, u_k]$. Here $n \times l + k$ gives the position of this character in s (l has to be a constant since we use the linear arithmetic of Yices).

$$\exists m. \forall n. \, n < m \Rightarrow \bigwedge_{k=0}^{l-1} (l_k \leq s[n \times l + k] \leq u_k)$$

This encoding method can be generalized to handle *well-formed* loops. A loop is well-formed if it contains no embedded loops and all its sub-sequences between a fork node and the next join are of the same length. A well formed loop is shown below on the left.

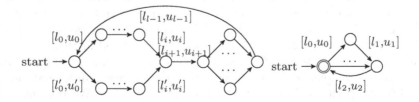

This loop can be encoded with the following parray constraint.

Table 1. Experimental results on toy examples. Here pc marks the path condition numbers. Time (T) is measured in seconds.

Program	set 1		set 2		set 3		set 4		set 5		total	
	pc	T.	pc	T.	pc	T.	pc	T.	pc	T.	#pc	T.
easychair	2,3,4	< 0.01s	5	0.03s	1,6,7	0.04s	8	0.06s	9	0.2s	9	0.4s
+our QElim	2,3,4	< 0.01s	1	0.07s	5,6	0.015s	7	0.02s	8,9	0.015s	9	0.2s
easychair*	1	0.04	2,5	0.003s	3,6,8	0.004s	4,7	0.005s	9	0.02s	9	0.1s
+our QElim	2,3,4	< 0.01s	1	0.05s	5,6	< 0.01s	7,8	0.01s	9	0.03s	9	0.12s
lastIndexOf	1	0.05s	2	0.01s	3,4	0.02s	5	0.1s	6	0.24s	6	0.5s
+our QElim	1,2	0.02s	3	0.015s	4	0.04s	5	0.11s	6	0.25	6	0.46s
+automaton	1	0.03s	2	0.2s	3	0.5s	4	0.35s	5,6	0.65s	6	2.34s
example (a)	1	1.02s	2	0.3s	3,7	0.01s	4	0.4s	5,6	0.8s,3.1s	7	7.3s
+our QElim	1	0.04s	2,3	< 0.01s	4,6	0.01s	5	0.1s	7	< 0.01s	7	0.16s
example (b)	1	0.23s	2	< 0.01s	3	0.02s	4,6	0.015s	5	0.15s	6	0.45s
+our QElim	1	0.23s	2	< 0.01s	3,4	0.015s	5	0.02s	6	0.01s	6	0.29s

$$\exists m. \forall n. n < m \Rightarrow$$
$$(\bigwedge_{k=0}^{i}(l_k \le s[n \times l + k] \le u_k) \vee \bigwedge_{k=0}^{i}(l'_k \le s[n \times l + k] \le u'_k)) \wedge$$
$$(l_{i+1} \le s[n \times l + i + 1] \le u_{i+1}) \wedge \ldots$$

The loop on the right is not well-formed: path 1 $[l_0, u_0] \to [l_1, u_1]$ and path 2 $[l_2, u_2]$ may alternate in the iterations, e.g. path 1 $\to$ path 1 $\to \ldots$ or path 2 $\to$ path 1 $\to \ldots$. For a non well-formed loop, we unroll the iterations to a pre-defined limit and disjoint the paths to produce parray constraints.

Our encoding of a well-formed automaton is complete and sound; but it is incomplete for non well-formed automata. Hence it is crucial to use refinements described in Section 4 to refine the automaton. In many cases non well-formed loops (e.g. embedded loops) are refined to well-formed ones. Even if a refined loop is not well-formed, it contains more information for better unrolled paths.

Note that we only convert an automata related to a RegExp All others need not to be converted since they have been modeled precisely in the parray domain. For example, in the motivating example (b), s but not s1 will be converted. In example (a), no automaton is needed to built at all (unless we want to use the automaton domain to help the solving)!

The facts obtained from automata can be fed to the parray domain, e.g. the minimal string lengths, the known values of the characters at some positions, etc.. This can sometimes help the parray encoding and solving.

5 Evaluation Results

Our solver is written in Java. We run it on benchmark programs on a laptop with a 2.40GHz Intel Core(TM)2 Duo processor and 4GB memory. We evaluate the parray solution and the one with parray+automaton.

We first test the main benchmark programs in [2], easychair and lastIndexOf, as well as the two motivating examples in Section 2. Table 1 shows the results on these toy programs. This includes the results for the comparison with Microsoft's BV-based solver. For `easychair`, with the parray encoding and Yices we can solve all 9 valid paths in 0.4 second ([2] takes about 1 second [2], but we do not include the exception paths that are trivial to compute). With our QElim method (Algorithm 2) the time is reduced to 0.2 second. Since a BV method needs only one iteration to handle these paths, we mutate them by introducing tricky unsat cases, which a BV method may need many iterations to disprove. Our pure parray method can prove sat or unsat for all of them in 0.1s without any iteration. With our QElim method it is 0.14 second. In the `lastIndexOf` example, string s is searched for different non-overlapping substrings with a common long prefix (*e.g.* > 30 chars). As shown in [2], a BV method may iterate on the lengths many times before finding out a solution. Our pure parray method needs no iteration and solves all the cases in 0.5 second, while the best method in [2] takes about 15 seconds (note that their input substrings may be different from ours). Interestingly, this example can be solved in the automaton domain too, *i.e.* after the automaton refinement, valid solutions can be found in the automata. This takes 2.34 second in total. Clearly, automaton building and refinement incur extra overheads. The pure automaton method handles other examples poorly, hence the results are not shown.

For these examples, our QElim is not mandatory. But applying it can improve the solving performance, *e.g.* reduce the time of Example (a) from 7.3 second to 0.16 second. In addition, since Yices returns a partial model which may be incorrect, we need to double check this model when Yices's search is used. In the appendix we show some results comparing Yices's algorithm with ours. It is apparent that our QElim is essential in solving parray constraints.

Method	set 1 (70)		set 2 (30)	
	#solved	T.	#solved	T.
Pure P-Array	53	17.6s	0	–
+ our QElim	55	4.1s	21	18.5s
Pure Automaton	34	72s	3	2.6s
P-Array+Autom.	68	20.4s	3	2.6s
+ our QElim	70	6.3s	26	28s

Fig. 4. Evaluating various methods on Benchmark set I. #solved gives the number the solved cases (sat or unsat).

Benchmark set I consists of 100 tricky path conditions collected from (1) real Web applications, and (2) manual stress tests. It excludes those easy to solve. These benchmarks are divided into two sets: set 1 that Yices can handle `forall` constraints well, and set 2 where our QElim algorithm is required. We evaluate the solutions with pure parray, with pure automaton, or with parray+automaton, with results shown in Figure 4. The results also show the advantages of our method over automaton-based ones such as [9].

For set 1, Yices performs well, solving 55 cases quickly, but 2 of them are incorrect partial models. The other 15 involve regular expressions and needs the support of the automaton model, which allows the parray model to solve all cases. However, using the pure automaton model only 34 cases can be solved since this model handles pure string constraints better than hybrid constraints.

---

[2] Time comparison is rough due to different evaluation environments.

Set 2 demonstrates the effectiveness of our QElim algorithm and automaton enhancement. Among these 30 cases, the "parray + automaton + QElim" method can solve 26, and the remaining 4 fails because the QElim algorithm hits the pre-defined limit (using a large limit can solve them). Missing any of these three components will lead to much inferior results, *e.g.* the pure parray method and pure automaton method can solve 0 and 3 respectively (time is counted for successful cases only). A closer look reveals that these two pure methods can prove unsat in short time, but are not good at finding solutions for sat cases. The combination of them does not help either since Yices seems to get stuck in handling the quantifiers.

Method Comparison. We compare PASS with two baseline implementations by us: an automaton-based method and a BV-like method . The former mimics the one in [9], with many details described in Section 4. The latter does not use bit-vectors directly. Instead *concrete* arrays are used to simulate bit-vectors with concrete lengths and indices. This can reuse our parray model and simplify the implementation: we first derive lengths constraints, then solve them to obtain length values, then instantiate the lengths in the forall constraints depicted in Tables 2 and 3, and then unroll all these constraints. Note that we do not directly compare PASS with existing tools since they assume different string operations and running settings, *e.g.* they accept much more restrictive syntax.

We run the three methods on several hundred non-trivial path conditions. Preliminary results indicate that PASS outperforms the simulated BV method in $\sim$ 80% cases, and can be up to 150 times faster for some sat cases. For the rare cases where PASS performs worse, it is up to 4 times slower than other methods. Compared with the automaton-based method, PASS usually gains performance improvement in a magnitude of 1 or 2 orders, although the automaton-based method can sometimes (1) solve RegExp intensive path conditions faster, and (2) prove unsat faster. However, this comparison might be neither accurate nor conclusive since we simulate other methods and optimize PASS more. We leave the experimental comparison with external tools such as [8] and [7,3] as future work.

6   Conclusions

We propose modeling strings with parameterized arrays, applying quantifier elimination to solve parray constraints, and using automata to model regular expressions and enhance the parray model. We show that all of these are essential to construct an efficient and comprehensive solver for numeric-string constraints with regular expressions.

The parray model needs much less enumeration of string lengths or values than existing methods since it encodes the string values and relations using quantified constraints of particular format. This format allows us to apply a simple algorithm to handle the quantifiers. Other enhancements are possible, *e.g.* more interactions between the parray and the automaton domains can further improve the performance.

References

1. Barrett, C., Conway, C.L., Deters, M., Hadarean, L., Jovanović, D., King, T., Reynolds, A., Tinelli, C.: CVC4. In: Gopalakrishnan, G., Qadeer, S. (eds.) CAV 2011. LNCS, vol. 6806, pp. 171–177. Springer, Heidelberg (2011)
2. Bjørner, N., Tillmann, N., Voronkov, A.: Path feasibility analysis for string-manipulating programs. In: Kowalewski, S., Philippou, A. (eds.) TACAS 2009. LNCS, vol. 5505, pp. 307–321. Springer, Heidelberg (2009)
3. Bjørner, N., Tillmann, N., Voronkov, A.: Path feasibility analysis for string-manipulating programs. In: Kowalewski, S., Philippou, A. (eds.) TACAS 2009. LNCS, vol. 5505, pp. 307–321. Springer, Heidelberg (2009)
4. Bradley, A.R., Manna, Z., Sipma, H.B.: What's decidable about arrays? In: Emerson, E.A., Namjoshi, K.S. (eds.) VMCAI 2006. LNCS, vol. 3855, pp. 427–442. Springer, Heidelberg (2006)
5. Cadar, C., Dunbar, D., Engler, D.R.: KLEE: Unassisted and automatic generation of high-coverage tests for complex systems programs. In: OSDI (2008)
6. Christensen, A.S., Møller, A., Schwartzbach, M.I.: Precise analysis of string expressions. In: Cousot, R. (ed.) SAS 2003. LNCS, vol. 2694, Springer, Heidelberg (2003)
7. de Moura, L., Bjørner, N.: Z3: An efficient SMT solver. In: Ramakrishnan, C.R., Rehof, J. (eds.) TACAS 2008. LNCS, vol. 4963, pp. 337–340. Springer, Heidelberg (2008)
8. Ganesh, V., Kieżun, A., Artzi, S., Guo, P.J., Hooimeijer, P., Ernst, M.: HAMPI: A string solver for testing, analysis and vulnerability detection. In: Gopalakrishnan, G., Qadeer, S. (eds.) CAV 2011. LNCS, vol. 6806, pp. 1–19. Springer, Heidelberg (2011)
9. Ghosh, I., Shafiei, N., Li, G., Chiang, W.-F.: JST: An automatic test generation tool for industrial java applications with strings. In: ICSE (2013)
10. Hooimeijer, P., Veanes, M.: An evaluation of automata algorithms for string analysis. In: Jhala, R., Schmidt, D. (eds.) VMCAI 2011. LNCS, vol. 6538, pp. 248–262. Springer, Heidelberg (2011)
11. Hooimeijer, P., Weimer, W.: Solving string constraints lazily. In: ASE (2010)
12. Li, G., Ghosh, I., Rajan, S.P.: KLOVER: A symbolic execution and automatic test generation tool for C++ programs. In: Gopalakrishnan, G., Qadeer, S. (eds.) CAV 2011. LNCS, vol. 6806, pp. 609–615. Springer, Heidelberg (2011)
13. Li, G., Li, P., Sawaga, G., Gopalakrishnan, G., Ghosh, I., Rajan, S.P.: GKLEE: Concolic verification and test generation for GPUs. In: PPoPP (2012)
14. Li, G., Slind, K.: Trusted source translation of a total function language. In: Ramakrishnan, C.R., Rehof, J. (eds.) TACAS 2008. LNCS, vol. 4963, pp. 471–485. Springer, Heidelberg (2008)
15. Saxena, P., Akhawe, D., Hanna, S., Mao, F., McCamant, S., Song, D.: A symbolic execution framework for JavaScript. In: S&P, Oakland (2010)
16. Shannon, D., Ghosh, I., Rajan, S., Khurshid, S.: Efficient symbolic execution of strings for validating web applications. In: 2nd International Workshop on Defects in Large Software Systems (2009)
17. Tillmann, N., de Halleux, J.: Pex–white box test generation for .NET. In: Beckert, B., Hähnle, R. (eds.) TAP 2008. LNCS, vol. 4966, pp. 134–153. Springer, Heidelberg (2008)

18. Veanes, M., de Halleux, P., Tillmann, N.: Rex: Symbolic regular expression explorer. In: ICST (2010)
19. Yices: An SMT solver, http://yices.csl.sri.com
20. Yu, F., Alkhalaf, M., Bultan, T.: STRANGER: An automata-based string analysis tool for PHP. In: Esparza, J., Majumdar, R. (eds.) TACAS 2010. LNCS, vol. 6015, pp. 154–157. Springer, Heidelberg (2010)
21. Yu, F., Bultan, T., Ibarra, O.H.: Symbolic string verification: Combining string analysis and size analysis. In: Kowalewski, S., Philippou, A. (eds.) TACAS 2009. LNCS, vol. 5505, pp. 322–336. Springer, Heidelberg (2009)

Increasing Confidence in Liveness Model Checking Results with Proofs

Tuomas Kuismin and Keijo Heljanko

Aalto University School of Science
Department of Computer Science and Engineering

Abstract. Model checking is an established technique to get confidence in the correctness of a system when testing is not sufficient. Validating safety-critical systems is one of the use cases for model checking. As model checkers themselves are quite complicated pieces of software, there is room for doubt about the correctness of the model checking result. The model checker might contain programming errors that influence the result of the analysis.

When a model checker finds a counter-example, it is straightforward to simulate the model and check that the counter-example is valid. Some model checking algorithms are also capable of providing proofs of validity. In this paper we describe a way to get proofs of correctness for liveness properties. This works by transforming the liveness property into a safety property using a reduction, and then getting a proof for that safety property. This changes the need to trust the model checker into the need to trust our reduction and a proof checker, which are much simpler programs than model checkers. Our method is intended to be usable in practice, and we provide experimental data to support this. We only handle properties that hold: counter-examples should be detected with other methods.

1 Introduction

Safety-critical automation systems, such as those deployed in e.g. nuclear facilities, need to be inspected for design errors. They tend to be complicated systems, because they often need to react to multiple measurements as well as inputs from the plant operators. It is therefore tedious and error-prone to analyse them manually. Model checking has proven to be a valuable tool in becoming more confident in the correctness of these designs. The use of model checking in the nuclear context is described in e.g. [17].

Unlike testing and simulation, model checking goes through every possible behaviour of the design, making sure that it conforms to its specifications. In theory, if the model checker reports no errors, then all possible behaviours of the design conform to their specifications. Because testing for all possible scenarios is impossible in practice, model checking a design can significantly increase confidence in it.

Since the model checker must verify that all behaviours of the design conform to specifications, and since the number of behaviours is exponentially large, a

V. Bertacco and A. Legay (Eds.): HVC 2013, LNCS 8244, pp. 32–43, 2013.
© Springer International Publishing Switzerland 2013

model checker must use advanced optimisations to keep computing time and memory usage within acceptable limits. Because of this, model checkers can be quite complicated pieces of software. Therefore, they inevitably contain programming errors, which could even affect the verification result. Especially when checking safety-critical designs, one would like to alleviate this concern. We propose a practical solution for getting independently verifiable proofs for liveness properties from the model checker.

1.1 System Models

In the context of this paper, models of systems are assumed to be finite logical circuits. The circuits may contain inputs from the environment and memory (latches). They operate synchronously, i.e. all latches get their new value simultaneously based on the inputs and on the previous values of latches. Cycles in the logical circuit are permitted only if they contain a latch. Inputs are considered to be non-deterministic, i.e. they can take any value at any time-point.

A state of the system is a mapping that gives a boolean value for each latch. In the initial state all latches have the value false. The *transition relation* determines the successors of a state, i.e. which states are possible after one time step.

Our tool works with the AIGER [1] format, which is used in the Hardware Model Checking Competition (HWMCC) [7]. It has good tool support because of the competition, and many benchmark sets are available from the AIGER and HWMCC web pages.

1.2 Liveness and Safety Properties

The formal properties in model checking can be divided into two main categories: safety properties and liveness properties. Intuitively, a safety property states that the system must not perform some bad action. A counter-example to such a property is a finite sequence of system states. It begins with the system in its initial state, and contains a sequence of states that corresponds to a bad action. To prove that a safety property holds, it is necessary to prove that a bad action can not be reached from the initial state.

Intuitively, a liveness property states that some event needs to take place. An example of this would be that all requests must be answered eventually. A counter-example to a liveness property is an infinite sequence of system states, where the system starts in its initial state, but fails to produce the required event. Verifying liveness properties is harder in general than verifying safety properties. To prove that a liveness property holds, it is necessary to prove that a *bad cycle* can not be reached from the initial state. A bad cycle is a sequence of states that the system can repeat indefinitely without producing the required event. Because systems can only have finitely many states, a bad cycle is needed to form a counter-example. In the context of this paper, liveness properties are represented as a set of *justice* signals that should not become true infinitely often. If all of the signals do become true infinitely often, i.e. in a cycle, a counter-example to the specification has been found.

A *liveness to safety reduction* is a way to transform a liveness checking problem into a safety checking problem. The first such reduction was introduced in [5]. Reducing liveness checking to safety checking entails changing the model to include some form of book-keeping. The burden of cycle detection is shifted from the model checker to the book-keeping part in the resulting model.

1.3   Symbolic Model Checking and SAT-Based Model Checking

Model checking a design is hindered by the *state explosion* problem: a system usually has exponentially many states with respect to its size. Representing each of them separately in memory is likely to exhaust the available memory. To deal with this problem, different *symbolic model checking* [10] techniques have been developed. They use a compact way to represent a set of states in memory.

In addition to the method in [10], another way to represent a set of states compactly is to use a propositional logic formula. A state belongs to the set iff the formula becomes true when assigning the values of the state variables (latches). Model checkers that use this technique usually make queries to propositional satisfiability (SAT) solvers, i.e. tools that decide whether a given propositional logic formula can be satisfied (made true). SAT-based model checking was first suggested in [6]. Our implementation works with SAT-based model checking, but the general idea does not depend on it.

1.4   Related Work

The IC3 [8] algorithm by Bradley, also known as property-directed reachability (PDR), is a complete[1], SAT-based algorithm for checking safety properties. One of its advantages is that it can provide a proof of correctness when the system meets the specification. The proof is an *inductive invariant*, i.e. a propositional formula that must hold in the initial state, and that will not be changed from true to false by the transition relation. If the model checker finds an inductive invariant that implies the specification, the system necessarily meets the specification.

Biere et al. introduced a liveness to safety reduction in [5]. That reduction changes the model to force a loop, and then checks whether a bad trace can be found. Compared to that, ours makes for a simpler implementation, which we consider to be important.

Claessen et al. describe an algorithm [11] for liveness checking that is based on bounding the number of times a justice signal becomes true. Gan et al. independently discovered this method in [15], where it is applied to model checking software designs. We also use this idea, but [11] implements it in their own specialised model checker, and they do not discuss proof generation. Moreover, their implementation uses pre-processing, which they state is important for performance. Using pre-processing adds more code to be trusted, which we try to

---

[1] In the sense that given sufficient time and memory, it will always terminate with the correct result.

avoid. Our implementation also differs from [11] in that they search for a bound by incrementing it by one, whereas we, like [15], double the bound at each step.

Others have also studied the issue of trusting the model checker when it claims correctness of a liveness property. Namjoshi takes a similar approach to ours in [18], in that the paper also describes a way to get proofs from the model checker. It does not make an implementation available, however, and makes no experimental evaluation. The proofs in that paper explicitly enumerate the states of the model, making them too big to verify in practice. Sprenger describes in [20] a model checker for μ-calculus that is proven to be correct. The model checker in that paper is verified using a theorem prover. Benchmarks or applicability to real world models is not discussed. Esparza et al. also describe a verified model checker in [13]. They first prove a simple model checking algorithm to be correct, and then make provably correct refinements to make it faster. Their implementation is not comparable to the state-of-the-art tools in efficiency, however. They describe it as a reference implementation against which optimised tools can be tested.

Compared to the model checkers above, our tool is designed to work with the same models that can be checked with the state-of-the-art tools. Our approach can work together with any PDR-based model checker that supports the AIGER-format, which includes many state-of-the-art model checkers thanks to the HWMCC. Moreover, improvements to those model checkers also benefit our tool.

2   Liveness to Safety Reduction

The key to getting better confidence in the result of the model checking algorithm is the liveness to safety reduction. Our reduction is as simple as possible, which makes it easy to understand and thoroughly test. This is crucial because the benefits of proof checking are lost if our implementation is suspected to be faulty. Because of the safety-critical context, we wish to get a high degree of certainty in the correctness of the model checking result. One key concern is the possibility of programming errors in model checkers. Requiring a proof from the model checker and validating it will increase confidence in the model checker, but it does not exclude the possibility of an error in our implementation. Therefore there is a great burden on our implementation to demonstrate reliability. We believe that a very simple algorithm is necessary for that.

Algorithm 1 shows the pseudo-code for our liveness to safety reduction. It expects as input a boolean circuit and a liveness property, expressed as a set of justice signals. The variable $count\_latches$ is an array of latches, and we use $count\_latches_i$ to denote the ith element of the array. The variable $wait\_latches$ is a mapping from bits in the $justice$-set to latches, and we use $wait\_latches_{bit}$ to denote the element that corresponds to bit, where $bit \in justice$. We use the latch itself, e.g. $count\_latches_i$, to denote the the value of the latch, and add $.input$ to it, e.g. $count\_latches_i.input$, to denote the wire that gives the next value of the latch.

The property is violated iff the circuit gives a true value for each of the justice signals infinitely often. In other words the property holds if there is a point in time after which at least one of the justice signals will stay false forever. Our algorithm assumes that the property is true, and tries to prove that. It should therefore be used when the system design is likely to be correct, and a proof of correctness is desired.

To deal with multiple justice signals, we first condense them into a single signal. Each signal in the original justice set will be assigned a latch that waits for it to become true. When all of these latches have been set to true, they will all be reset, and will start waiting again. The conjunction of all these latches will be true infinitely often iff all of the signals in the original justice set are true infinitely often. Lines 5–7 in the algorithm handle this part. An example of two latches waiting for two justice signals is shown in Figure 1.

Algorithm 1. Algorithm for getting a proof of a liveness property

---

1: **function** LIVE2SAFE-CHECK(circuit, justice)
2:      $count\_latches$ ▷ n-bit counter
3:      $wait\_latches$ ▷ each latch waits for a bit in the $justice$-set
4:      $increment \leftarrow \bigwedge_b wait\_latches_b$ ▷ when to increment the counter
5:      **for all** $bit \in justice$ **do**
6:          $wait\_latches_{bit}.input \leftarrow \neg increment \wedge (bit \vee wait\_latches_{bit})$
7:      **end for**
8:      **for** $n = 1 \to \infty$ **do**
9:          $carry \leftarrow increment$
10:          **for** $i = 0 \to n - 1$ **do**
11:              $count\_latches_i.input \leftarrow carry \oplus count\_latches_i$
12:              $carry \leftarrow carry \wedge count\_latches_i$
13:          **end for**
14:          $bad \leftarrow count\_latches_{n-1}$
15:          **if** MODEL-SAFE?(circuit $\cup$ count_latches $\cup$ wait_latches, bad) **then**
16:              **return** proof
17:          **end if**
18:      **end for**
19: **end function**

If the *increment*-signal will be true only finitely many times, the liveness property holds. To get proof of this, the algorithm uses a binary counter to keep track of the number of times it has become true. Lines 10–13 in the algorithm build the counter, line 14 defines the signal that denotes a bad state, and line 15 calls the safety property model checker. Figure 2 shows an example of a two-bit counter. If the counter never overflows, the *increment*-signal does not become true infinitely often, and the property must hold. On the other hand, if an overflow of the counter is detected, we assume that a larger counter is required, and restart the proof search with one more latch in the counter. The for-loop on line 8 of the algorithm implements this.

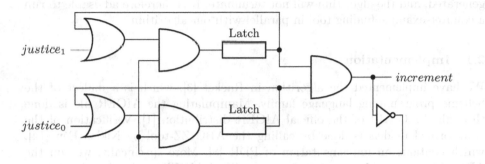

Fig. 1. Latches that wait for two justice bits to become true

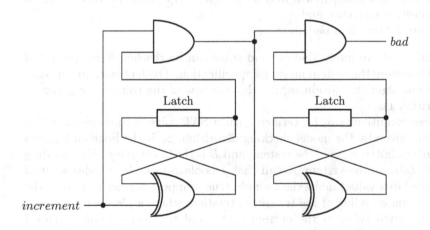

Fig. 2. Binary counter with two latches

If the circuit meets the specification, the algorithm will eventually generate a counter that is large enough to contain all the times the justice signals become true, after which the safety property checker will provide a proof of correctness. On the other hand, if the specification is not met, larger and larger counters are generated, and the algorithm will not terminate. It is therefore advisable to run a counter-example finding tool in parallel with our algorithm.

2.1   Implementation

We have implemented the algorithm in Racket [3], which is a dialect of the Scheme programming language family. Manipulating the AIGER file is done through the C API of the official AIGER distribution [1]. Verification of the transformed models is done by calling the ABC/ZZ-tool by Niklas Eén [14], which contains an implementation of PDR [8]. More specifically, we run the ABC/ZZ command `bip ,pdr2` on the modified AIGER model. Our implementation is available as a binary package and as source code at [16].

3   Verifying the Proof

If our algorithm is successful in finding a proof for a property, the next step is to verify it. The proof given by the model checker is an inductive invariant, i.e. it satisfies all of the following conditions:

- it is true in the initial state of the system,
- if it is true in a state, it will also be true in every successor (according to the transition relation), and
- it can not be true in a bad state.

The conditions above imply that no bad state can be reached from the initial state, and therefore the system meets its specification. The bad state in this case is the one our algorithm produces, i.e. the overflow of the counter we generate (see Algorithm 1).

The three conditions can be verified with a SAT solver[2]. Suppose that I is the invariant given by the model checking algorithm, S_0 is the boolean formula encoding of the initial state of the system, and B is the boolean formula encoding of the bad states of the system. Recall that a boolean formula encodes a set of states whose latch values make the formula true. Suppose further that R is the boolean formula encoding of the transition relation, where a plain variable (e.g. v) denotes a latch value in the current state, and the corresponding primed variable (e.g. v') denotes the latch value in a successor state. We generalise this notation to boolean formulae: adding a prime to a formula means adding a prime to every latch variable in it. We can now encode the conditions for the inductive invariant as boolean formulae, respectively:

---

[2] This is not limited to SAT-based techniques: any model checking method that can provide an inductive invariant as above could be used.

- $S_0 \Rightarrow I$
- $(I \wedge R) \Rightarrow I'$
- $I \Rightarrow \neg B$

The validity of the above formulae can be checked with the SAT solver by negating it. If the solver reports that the negation of the formula is unsatisfiable, the formula itself must hold.

To get further proof that no error has been made, even the SAT solver may be requested to give a proof of unsatisfiability. The SAT solver competition [4] features a track for solvers that provide such proofs. Many of the solvers are freely available for download, and many also provide their source code.

4   Experiments

We have evaluated the practicality of our tool by testing it on models with liveness properties available from the AIGER [1] and the HWMCC [7] web sites. We dropped out models for which a counter-example was found, as our tool would not terminate on those. We compared our implementation against three other model checkers: ABC/ZZ [14], which to the best of our knowledge uses [5] combined with PDR, IIMC [2], whose liveness algorithm is described in [9], and TIP [12], which to the best of our knowledge uses [11] combined with PDR. The latter two placed first and second in the liveness track of the HWMCC [7]. All the tests were run on a Linux machine with an Intel 2.83GHz processor and 8GiB memory. A time-out of 10 minutes was used.

The run-time of our algorithm includes the transformation of the model and all of the model checking work. Verifying the proof is not included. We anticipate that the proof verification time is small compared to the actual model checking.

The run-times are plotted against our algorithm in Figures 3, 4, and 5. Each figure plots the run-times of one algorithm against the run-times of another algorithm. A data point in the south-east half of the figure means our algorithm was faster, and a data point in the north-west half means our algorithm was slower. A data point on the inner border means a time-out occurred, and a data point on the outer border means that memory was exhausted.

Figure 3 shows the run-times of our algorithm compared against ABC/ZZ. We used a version that was retrieved from the code repository on June 24 2013. ABC/ZZ was run with the command `bip ,live -k=12s -eng=treb`, which also employs a liveness to safety reduction. There are quite many data points on both sides of the figure, meaning that neither algorithm is consistently better than the other.

Figure 4 shows the run-times of our algorithm compared against IIMC. We used version 1.2 of IIMC with the default options. The figure shows that our algorithm is faster in many cases, but also runs out of time in many cases where IIMC does not. Again, neither algorithm seems to be a clear winner.

Figure 5 shows the run-times of our algorithm compared against TIP. We used a version that was retrieved from the code repository on July 17 2013, with the default options. The figure shows that TIP is faster than our algorithm is the

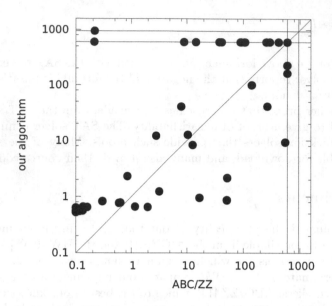

Fig. 3. Run-times (in seconds) of our algorithm and ABC/ZZ

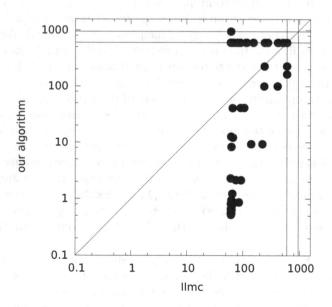

Fig. 4. Run-times (in seconds) of our algorithm and IIMC

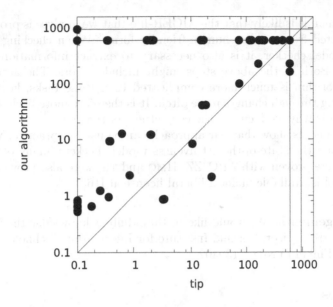

Fig. 5. Run-times (in seconds) of our algorithm and TIP

majority of cases, although our algorithm wins in a few cases, even proving two
where TIP ran out of time.

While it is clear that our algorithm does not beat the state of the art ones
in speed, it still manages to prove many of the benchmarks. We argue that the
simplicity combined with the proofs from PDR make it a practical way to become
more confident in the correctness of models with liveness properties.

5   Conclusion and Discussion

Our approach to getting more confidence in model checking results relies firstly
on a simple liveness to safety reduction, and secondly on getting an independently verifiable proof from the safety model checker. Our main contribution is
the use of the simple reduction algorithm in a way that gives good performance
and still results in proofs of correctness.

Model checkers are very complex pieces of software, and therefore are liable
to contain programming errors. It is conceivable that they might claim to have
proven a property that in reality does not hold. When applying model checking to safety-critical systems, it is desirable to alleviate this concern. We argue
that our approach increases confidence in the model checking result, because our
algorithm is very simple. It is therefore relatively simple to inspect our implementation and become convinced that it does not contain errors.

Our approach can not eliminate all concerns of whether the model checking
result actually applies to the real system. Even if the model corresponds to the

physical system, it is likely that the AIGER-file that we analyse is programmatically converted from a more human-friendly form.[3] When checking the proof from the model checker, it is also necessary to extract information from the AIGER-file. Both of the above steps might include errors. The actual model checking algorithm is much more complicated than these tasks, however, and typically going through changes more often. It is therefore more likely to contain errors, which is why we focus on the correctness of that part.

Our experiments show that our approach can be used in practice. While it is not faster than the state-of-the-art liveness model checkers, many of the properties that were proven with ABC/ZZ, IImc and TIP were also proven with our tool. The tool is available under a liberal license at [16].

Acknowledgements. We would like to thankfully acknowledge the funding of the SAFIR 2014 project, Helsinki Institute for Information Technology, and the Academy of Finland project 139402.

References

1. AIGER: A format, library and set of utilities for And-Inverter Graphs (AIGs), `http://fmv.jku.at/aiger/`
2. The IImc model checker, `http://ecee.colorado.edu/~bradleya/iimc/`
3. The Racket programming language, `http://racket-lang.org/`
4. Balint, A., Belov, A., Heule, M., Järvisalo, M.: The international SAT competition, `http://satcompetition.org/`
5. Biere, A., Artho, C., Schuppan, V.: Liveness checking as safety checking. Electr. Notes Theor. Comput. Sci. 66(2), 160–177 (2002)
6. Biere, A., Cimatti, A., Clarke, E., Zhu, Y.: Symbolic model checking without BDDs. In: Cleaveland, W.R. (ed.) TACAS 1999. LNCS, vol. 1579, pp. 193–207. Springer, Heidelberg (1999)
7. Biere, A., Heljanko, K., Seidl, M., Wieringa, S.: Hardware model checking competition 2012 (2012), `http://fmv.jku.at/hwmcc12/`
8. Bradley, A.R.: SAT-based model checking without unrolling. In: Jhala, R., Schmidt, D. (eds.) VMCAI 2011. LNCS, vol. 6538, pp. 70–87. Springer, Heidelberg (2011)
9. Bradley, A.R., Somenzi, F., Hassan, Z., Zhang, Y.: An incremental approach to model checking progress properties. In: Bjesse, P., Slobodová, A. (eds.) FMCAD, pp. 144–153. FMCAD Inc. (2011)
10. Burch, J.R., Clarke, E.M., McMillan, K.L., Dill, D.L., Hwang, L.J.: Symbolic model checking: 10^{20} states and beyond. Inf. Comput. 98(2), 142–170 (1992)
11. Claessen, K., Sörensson, N.: A liveness checking algorithm that counts. In: Cabodi, G., Singh, S. (eds.) FMCAD, pp. 52–59. IEEE (2012)
12. Eén, N., Sörensson, N.: Temporal induction by incremental SAT solving. Electr. Notes Theor. Comput. Sci. 89(4), 543–560 (2003)
13. Esparza, J., Lammich, P., Neumann, R., Nipkow, T., Schimpf, A., Smaus, J.-G.: A fully verified executable LTL model checker. In: Sharygina, N., Veith, H. (eds.) CAV 2013. LNCS, vol. 8044, pp. 463–478. Springer, Heidelberg (2013)

---

[3] For an example on work that encompasses higher level descriptions of systems, see [19], which discusses formalisation of a hardware description language.

14. Eén, N.: The ABC/ZZ verification and synthesis framework,
    https://bitbucket.org/niklaseen/abc-zz
15. Gan, X., Dubrovin, J., Heljanko, K.: A symbolic model checking approach to verifying satellite onboard software. Science of Computer Programming (2013),
    http://www.sciencedirect.com/science/article/pii/S0167642313000658
16. Kuismin, T.: Liveness to safety reduction, implementation,
    http://users.ics.aalto.fi/tlauniai/live2safe/
17. Lahtinen, J., Valkonen, J., Björkman, K., Frits, J., Niemelä, I., Heljanko, K.: Model checking of safety-critical software in the nuclear engineering domain. Rel. Eng. & Sys. Safety 105, 104–113 (2012)
18. Namjoshi, K.S.: Certifying model checkers. In: Berry, G., Comon, H., Finkel, A. (eds.) CAV 2001. LNCS, vol. 2102, pp. 2–13. Springer, Heidelberg (2001)
19. Ray, S., Hunt Jr., W.A.: Mechanized certification of secure hardware designs. In: Abadir, M.S., Wang, L.C., Bhadra, J. (eds.) MTV, pp. 25–32. IEEE Computer Society (2007)
20. Sprenger, C.: A verified model checker for the modal μ-calculus in Coq. In: Steffen, B. (ed.) TACAS 1998. LNCS, vol. 1384, pp. 167–183. Springer, Heidelberg (1998)

Speeding Up the Safety Verification of Programmable Logic Controller Code

Tim Lange[1], Martin R. Neuhäußer[2], and Thomas Noll[1]

[1] RWTH Aachen University, Germany
{tim.lange,noll}@cs.rwth-aachen.de
[2] Siemens AG, Germany
martin.neuhaeusser@siemens.com

Abstract. Programmable logic controllers (PLC) are widely used in industries ranging from assembly lines, power plants, chemical processes to mining and rail automation. Such systems usually exhibit high safety requirements, and downtimes due to software errors entail intolerably high economic costs. Hence, their control programs are particularly suited for applying formal methods; in particular, bounded model checking (BMC) techniques based on satisfiability modulo theories promise to be highly beneficial in this domain.

In this paper, we investigate adaptations and extensions of property dependent static analyses which operate on a novel form of intermediate code and which are tailored specifically to model checking PLC programs. In our experiments, our program transformations drastically reduce the size of formulae for BMC and speed up the verification times by orders of magnitude.

Keywords: Programmable logic controllers, Bounded model checking, SMT-based verification algorithms, Static analysis.

1 Introduction

Programmable logic controllers are embedded systems specifically designed to control automation processes. As such, they are at the heart of all major industries, controlling manufacturing, logistics, chemical, oil & gas, energy, and rail automation tasks.

A PLC and its control algorithm constitute a reactive system with a cyclic execution scheme: At the beginning of each cycle, the operating system reads inputs from sensor in the physical environment. The PLC program then operates on the inputs and its internal state to produce outputs that are sent to actuators upon termination of the PLC program. This scheme is repeated cyclically. As each cycle is highly time-critical, its execution is required to terminate within a pre-defined *cycle time*. Due to this strict bound on the execution time, PLC programs usually exhibit statically predetermined control flows. In particular, dynamic heap structures and loops whose number of iterations is determined dynamically are avoided, if possible.

V. Bertacco and A. Legay (Eds.): HVC 2013, LNCS 8244, pp. 44–60, 2013.

Many automation systems have high safety requirements. Errors in their control programs lead to intolerably high economic costs due to downtimes or the destruction of the automation system. Even worse, they may constitute threats to the life of workers and the environment. Hence, the correctness of such control programs is of utmost importance, making the use of formal methods advisable.

In this paper, we propose model checking (MC) of safety properties of the control program and focus on its logical correctness. In particular, we do not model time or the PLC's physical environment. As MC is mostly automatic, it can easily be used by non-experts, making it applicable in practice. Moreover, given the execution model and the simple control flow of PLC programs, bounded symbolic model checking (BMC) of safety properties — and especially simple assertions — promises to be highly beneficial. We focus on the verification of safety properties of the PLC program logic For example, an assertion could state that upon termination of the cycle, a flag must be set iff the speed of a drive is outside its admissible range.

For a correctness proof, all reachable states of the PLC program must be checked for violations of the assertion. In a classical setting, this can be accomplished by explicitly representing all reachable states of the system in terms of program locations and variable valuations. However, explicit state model checking generally suffers from the state space explosion problem, i.e. the exponential increase of the number of states depending on the input variables. One successful approach that mitigates this problem are symbolic representations of the state space as used in, e.g. BMC. Here, both the executions of the program (up to a pre-determined number of steps) and the safety property are encoded as propositional formulae which are input to a propositional satisfiability (SAT) solver that searches for program runs violating the property. BMC is generally incomplete due to the bound on the length of executions that are considered. However, this restriction fits very well with the cyclic execution scheme of PLC programs.

The contributions of this paper are twofold: Firstly, we further mitigate the state space explosion problem by adapting program transformations from optimizing compilers to minimize the size of the input program. In particular, we compile PLC programs written in the Instruction List (IL) language into a simple intermediate code which is subsequently minimized by constant folding, property dependent program slicing, and a new variant of forward expression propagation. Due to the redundant semantics of IL, the minimized intermediate code programs are much simpler and substantially easier to verify. Secondly, we define a formal semantics of our intermediate code by means of quantifier free first order formulae over the array and bit vector theories. To decide the satisfiability of such formulae, we use a satisfiability modulo theories (SMT) solver instead of a SAT solver. This allows us in particular to reason about simple dynamic addressing in the PLC programs — something that can hardly be done in the purely propositional fragment.

We evaluate our approach on several case studies, including safety-critical industrial PLC programs and hand-written artificial code. The empirical evaluation employing a prototypical tool implementation shows promising results.

The remainder of this paper is organized as follows. First, Sect. 2 compares our approach to existing work. Sect. 3 introduces the intermediate code on which our formal analyses build. Sect. 4 presents the model minimization techniques for mitigating the state-space explosion problem. Sect. 5 provides a formal semantics for the intermediate code and defines the structure of the BMC formulae. In Sect. 6, we evaluate the impact of our model minimizations on the verification times by means of a number of case studies. Finally, Sect. 7 concludes the paper.

2   Related Work

Several attempts to applying formal methods to PLCs have been made; a survey can be found in [1,2].

For verifying railway interlockings, [3] model checks ladder logic diagrams, applies simple program slicing to the Boolean formulae, and verifies invariants with HeerHugo [4]. Verification of correct signalling in railways based on SAT is described in [5]. Both approaches differ considerably from ours, as the verification does not incorporate control flow and focuses only on Boolean conditions.

Symbolic model checking of IL programs based on binary decision diagrams (BDDs) is proposed in [6], where the transition relation is directly derived from the input program without any optimizations. No benchmarks or remarks on the scalability of the approach are provided. The papers [7,8,9,10,11] address verification of instruction list programs based on propositional satisfiability. None of these approaches use static analyses for model minimization; [8] requires manual tuning to obtain manageable state spaces (even for an eight-bit input), and [7] does not allow for loops in the input program. An operational semantics of a subset of IL can be expressed in the higher order theorem prover Coq [12]; also here, no model minimization techniques have been applied.

This paper presents techniques that reduce the number of program locations that need to be considered in (bounded) model checking. A similar approach also involving SMT reasoning has been investigated in [13] where single transitions represent larger portions of the program under consideration.

3   Intermediate Code

Instruction List (IL) is the low-level language among the five programming languages defined for PLCs in the IEC 61131-3 standard [14]. It strongly resembles an assembly language of a complex instruction set computer (CISC). In particular, the semantics of an IL instruction generally depends strongly on the values of the processor flags and is best described by a sequence of simpler operations that affect a variety of registers and memory cells.

Whereas previous approaches to IL code verification derived models directly from the IL code [7,8,9,10], we first compile the input program into a simple intermediate code (IC), making all registers and side effects explicit. This has many advantages: Firstly, IL consists of approx. 170 instructions with intricate semantics and handling each of them explicitly in a verification tool is an extremely tedious task. Even worse, the complex instruction semantics effectively prevents any data flow analyses on IL code. Surprisingly, the IL semantics turns out to be highly redundant and inefficient. In fact, our experiments show that almost all register operations performed in the original IL code can be removed by static analysis of the intermediate code without altering the program semantics.

To enable strong model minimization, IC modifies at most one variable at a time and allows for arbitrarily nested arithmetic and Boolean expressions. IC consists of seven instructions: (1) a skip command that does not modify control flow or variables; (2) a stop command, indicating the end of a program execution path; (3) an unconditional jump to a program label; (4) a conditional jump to a program label equipped with a Boolean guard; (5) an assignment of an expression to a variable; (6) a call statement to invoke a procedure, and (7) a return statement to exit a procedure.

Definition 1 (Data types). Data types *of IC are defined by the following context free grammar:*

$$DataType := Ref(DataType) \mid Bool \mid Word \mid \ldots$$

Definition 2 (Domains). *The* domains *of the data types are as follows:*

$$D_{Word} := \{-2^{15}, 2^{15} - 1\}$$
$$D_{Bool} := \{true, false\}$$
$$D_{MemLoc} \subseteq \{(seg, offset, dt) \mid seg, offset \in \mathbb{N}, dt \in DataType\}$$
$$D_{Ref(dt)} := \{enc(seg, offset, dt) \mid (seg, offset, dt) \in D_{MemLoc}\}$$
$$D := \bigcup\{D_{dt} \mid dt \in DataType\}$$

where D_{MemLoc} is the set of typed memory locations, and $enc : D_{MemLoc} \rightarrow D_{Word}$ is an injective encoding function.

Definition 3 (Intermediate code). *The complete grammar of* intermediate code *is given by:*

$$
\begin{aligned}
Const &:= D_{Word} \\
Bool &:= true \mid false \\
MemLoc &:= (Const, Const, DataType) \\
Loc &:= MemLoc \mid deRef(Ref) \\
Ref &:= getRef(Loc) \mid Read(Loc) \\
Exp &:= Const \mid Bool \mid Ref \mid Exp + Exp \mid Exp \vee Exp \mid \ldots \\
Cmd &:= \mathsf{Skip} \mid \mathsf{Stop} \mid \mathsf{Jump}(Const) \mid \mathsf{CJump}(Exp, Const) \mid \\
&\quad \mathsf{Assign}(Loc, Exp) \mid \mathsf{Call}(Const, Exp^*) \mid \mathsf{Return} \\
Proc &:= \mathsf{Procedure}\ Const(DataType\ Const)^*\ \mathsf{is}\ Cmd^*
\end{aligned}
$$

An IC program $\mathcal{P}$ is defined as a tuple $\mathcal{P} = (P, i)$, where P is the set of procedures defined in $\mathcal{P}$, and i denotes the start *procedure.*

When compiling IL programs into IC, all internal flags and processor registers are represented by memory locations of the respective data types and the semantics of each IL instruction is formalized by an equivalent sequence of IC instructions.

4   Model Minimizations

The number of program locations, followed by the number of variables define the size of an IC program. Hence, we aim at program transformations that yield equivalent IC programs with fewer program locations and fewer variables. For the sake of verification, we relax the equivalence condition and only require each minimization step to yield an IC program that is equivalent w.r.t. the properties that need to be verified. As our experiments and the results in [13] show, minimizing the number of program locations and simplifying the control flow speeds up verification times tremendously. Hence, in our optimization, we trade more complex expressions in the IC code for smaller IC programs.

In Sect. 4.1 we present constant folding; Sect. 4.2 shortly describes a program slicing technique that removes irrelevant code, and Sect. 4.3 defines the forward expression substitution which enables us to reduce the number of program locations even further. Section 4.4 explains the fixed point iteration used to obtain the minimized IC program. All transformations are based on dataflow analyses [15]. A dataflow system is essentially given by a tuple $(L, F, (D, \sqsubseteq), \{\varphi_l \mid l \in L\})$ with

- a finite set of program labels L,
- a flow relation $F \subseteq L \times L$,
- a complete lattice $(D, \sqsubseteq)$, given by a domain D and an ordering relation $\sqsubseteq$ with least upper bound $\sqcup$ and least element $\bot$, and
- a collection of monotonic transfer functions $\{\varphi_l \mid l \in L\}$ of type $\varphi_l : D \to D$.

As is well known, computing the solution of a dataflow system amounts to solving the corresponding equation system over a collection of variables $\{AI_l \mid l \in L\}$ for obtaining the analysis information using fixpoint iteration.

4.1   Constant Folding

The first optimization to be applied is constant folding, in order to simplify expressions. It is based on a standard interval analysis [15], which additionally offers more opportunities for subsequent optimization steps, e.g., to statically evaluate inequations and to compute results of pointer arithmetic. To enable constant folding using the results of interval analysis, we use degraded intervals covering only a single value. This analysis is defined as follows.

Definition 4 (Domain of intervals). *The complete lattice $(Int, \sqsubseteq)$ is given by $Int := \{[x, y] \mid x \in \mathbb{Z} \cup \{-\infty\}, y \in \mathbb{Z} \cup \{+\infty\}, x \leq y\} \cup \{\bot\}$ with $\bot := \emptyset$. It is partially ordered by $\bot \sqsubseteq [x, y] \sqsubseteq \top$ (where $\top := [-\infty, +\infty]$) and $[x_1, y_1] \sqsubseteq [x_2, y_2]$ iff $x_2 \leq x_1$ and $y_1 \leq y_2$, entailing $[x_1, y_1] \sqcup [x_2, y_2] = [\min\{x_1, x_2\}, \max\{y_1, y_2\}]$.*

Note that this domain exhibits infinite ascending chains. In order to ensure the ascending chain condition (ACC) which guarantees termination of the fixed point iteration, widening is required. However, the standard widening operator $[x_1, y_1] \triangledown [x_2, y_2]$ (which sets the lower/upper bound x_1/y_1 of the first interval to

$-\infty/+\infty$ when it is underrun/exceeded by the next iteration x_2/y_2) often leads to imprecise results when joining the analysis information coming from different predecessor branches in the control flow graph (CFG). This problem is usually solved by narrowing. But in contrast to widening, narrowing does not necessarily terminate due to the presence of infinite descending chains [15].

To circumvent the overhead of obtaining imprecise results at first and trying to make them more precise afterwards, we introduce the lazy widening operator ∇_{Pre_l}. It is parametrized with a set of predecessors of label l in the CFG and allows each incoming edge to trigger one precise meet operation before applying widening. This way for loop-free code, we obtain the same precision as applying standard widening followed by standard narrowing without the additional overhead induced by narrowing. For code containing loops, we get the same results as applying standard widening.

Definition 5 (Lazy Widening). *Let $l \in L$, and let $Pre_l \subseteq \{l' \in L \mid (l', l) \in F\}$ be a subset of the predecessors of l. The lazy widening operator $\nabla_{Pre_l} : Int \times Int \to Int$ is applied when re-computing the analysis information at label l after an update at label l': $AI_l := AI_l \nabla_{Pre_l} \varphi_{l'}(AI_{l'})$ with*

$$[x_1, y_1] \nabla_{Pre_l} [x_2, y_2] := \begin{cases} [x_1, y_1] \sqcup [x_2, y_2] & \text{if } l' \in Pre_l \\ [x_1, y_1] \nabla [x_2, y_2] & \text{otherwise.} \end{cases}$$

Here, Pre_l is initialized with $\{l' \in L \mid (l', l) \in F\}$, and set to $Pre_l \setminus \{l'\}$ after each update.

4.2 Program Slicing

The next step in minimization is to remove all program instructions that do not have any effect on the validity of the properties under consideration. Technically, a standard needed variables analysis is applied, starting with the initial information of all variables occurring in the assertions at each label [15]. The desired result is the least set of needed variables, as we want to remove as many computations as possible, keeping only these which contribute to the values of needed variables. Based on this set, we check for every element of $\{l \in L \mid cmd_l = \mathsf{Assign}(x, exp)\}$ whether x is needed at the exit of l. If this is not the case, l can be removed from program p.

4.3 Forward Expression Propagation

In most cases, the IC program that results from constant propagation and slicing of irrelevant code fragments is already smaller than the original IL program. In addition, it employs a much simpler instruction set. Thus, a first improvement has already been achieved. However, due to the assembly-like structure of IL, all remaining assignments have small right-hand sides, such that complex expressions are still computed by a sequence comprising multiple IC instructions. But IC supports arbitrarily nested expressions. To further reduce the number of program locations, we combine multiple assignments into one by propagating expressions forward. Note that standard compiler optimization aims for the opposite: By introducing new assignments for expressions that are repeatedly evaluated ("available expressions"), one usually tries to reduce the overall number of evaluation steps at the expense of the number of program locations.

To propagate expressions forward from the point of their assignment, an available expression analysis (AvExp) is applied, which records the variable on the left hand side of the originating assignment [15]. Propagation is complicated by programs that exhibit a control flow as in Fig. 1. Here, we aim at propagating the expressions on the right-hand side of line 1 to the read access in line 2, as well as combining the expressions from lines 6, 9, and 14 with the assignments in lines 11 and 15. At line 2, however, expression "counter+1" is not available because of the assignment to variable counter in line 1. We refer to such critical assignments as recursive assignments.

```
1   counter=counter+1
2   CJump (counter>n) 16
3   CJump (state=1) 13
4   CJump (state=2) 8
5   {control speed}
6   overpow=overpow∨(speed>max)
7   Jump 11
8   {speed up}
9   overpow=overpow∨(speed>max)
10  CJump (speed=target) 15
11  warning=overpow∨emergency
12  Jump 16
13  {initialize motor}
14  overpow=false
15  warning=overpow
16  Stop
```

Fig. 1. Recursive propagation blocked

```
    counter=counter+1
    CJump (counter>n) 16
    CJump (state=1) 13
    CJump (state=2) 8
    {control speed}
    overpow=overpow∨(speed>max)
    Jump 11
    {speed up}
    overpow=overpow∨(speed>max)
    CJump (speed=target) 15
    warning=overpow∨emergency
    Jump 16
    {initialize motor}
    overpow=overpow∨(speed>max)
    warning=overpow
    Stop
```

Fig. 2. Recursive propagation safe

```
1   CJump (counter+1>n) 16
2   CJump (state=1) 13
3   CJump (state=2) 8
4   {control speed}
5   Jump 11
6   {speed up}
7   CJump (speed=target) 15
8   warning=overpow∨(speed>max)∨emergency
9   Jump 16
10  {initialize motor}
11  warning=overpow∨(speed>max)
12  Stop
```

Fig. 3. Result of propagation

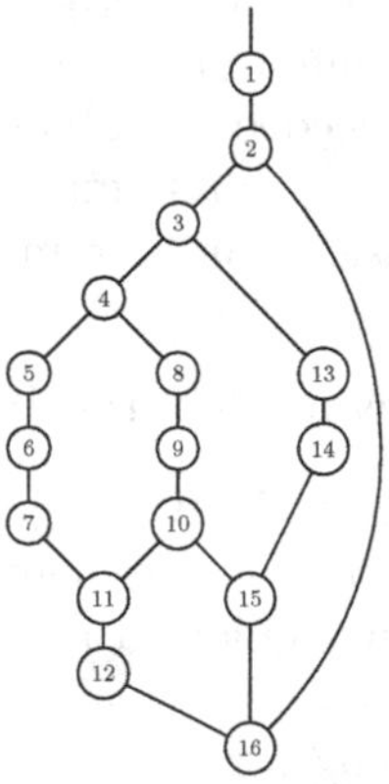

Fig. 4. CFG of Fig. 1 and Fig. 2

Definition 6 (Recursive assignments). *An assignment* Assign(x, exp) *is recursive if* $x \in V(exp)$, *where* $V(exp)$ *is the set of all variables occurring in* exp.

For forward expression propagation, we first need AvExp to handle recursive assignments. By slight abuse of notation, we sometimes refer to an expression as being *recursive* if it originates from a recursive assignment. In the standard approach, these expressions are excluded by the *gen* function [15], as they are not available in subsequent lines. Therefore, simply propagating them would not preserve the semantics of the code. In this case, termination of propagation is not guaranteed as propagating the assignment Assign(x, exp) to an expression exp' replaces the occurrence of x in exp' by exp and keeps x in exp', making the original assignment live. This results in a cycle, where in each iteration, exp is propagated. Thus, AvExp does not suffice for forward expression propagation.

The key to a semantics-preserving propagation of recursive assignments is the insight that replacing a variable with the assigned recursive expression is only allowed if the original assignment can be removed. To be able to remove a recursive assignment Assign(x, exp) while preserving the semantics, every read of x which can be reached from the assignment must be replaced by exp. For this purpose we need to extend AvExp by a label information to determine the origin of an expression. To maintain the original behaviour of AvExp, we define the partial order by applying the standard one of AvExp to the projection on variables and expressions.

Definition 7 (Extended available expressions analysis). *The* extended available expressions analysis *is given by*

- *the complete lattice* $(D, \sqsubseteq)$ *with* $D := 2^{L \times V \times Exp}$ *and* $A \sqsubseteq B$ *iff for each* $(l, v, e) \in B$ *there exists* $(l', v, e) \in A$ *(which yields* $A \sqcup B = \bigcup \{(l, v, e), (l', v, e) \mid (l, v, e) \in A, (l', v, e) \in B\}$ *and* $\bot = D$*) and*
- *the transfer functions* $\{\varphi_l \mid l \in L\}$ *given by*

$$\varphi_l(T) := (T \setminus kill_l) \cup gen_l \text{ with}$$

$$gen_l := \begin{cases} \{(l, x, exp)\} & \text{if } cmd_l = \text{Assign}(x, exp) \\ \emptyset & \text{otherwise} \end{cases}$$

$$kill_l := \begin{cases} \{(l', x', exp') \in D \mid & \text{if } cmd_l = \text{Assign}(x, exp) \\ \quad x \in Var(exp') \text{ or } x' = x\} \\ \emptyset & \text{otherwise} \end{cases}$$

The corresponding analysis information is denoted by $\{AE_l \in D \mid l \in L\}$.

For additional information about dependencies between reading and writing accesses to variables we employ a standard reaching definitions analysis [15]. Following the notion of reaching definitions, we call an assignment a *definition* or short *def* and a read of the assigned variable a *use*.

Definition 8 (Reaching definitions). *Let* $\{RD_l \mid l \in L\}$ *with* $RD_l \subseteq V \times (L \cup \{?\})$ *be the information obtained from* reaching definitions *analysis. Here*

$(x, ?) \in RD_l$ means that the input value of x possibly reaches l without being overwritten. For $x \in V$ and $l \in L$, we let $RD_l^x := RD_l \cap (\{x\} \times (L \cup \{?\}))$ be the reaching definitions of x in l.

Definition 9 (Filtered available expressions information). *Given* $\{AE_l \mid l \in L\}$, *we let* $AE_l^x := AE_l \cap L \times \{x\} \times Exp$.

Let us characterize the conditions for propagating an expression from an assignment to a use of the corresponding variable: At label $l \in L$, variable $x \in V$ can be replaced by expression $exp \in Exp$ if

- there exists $(l', x, exp) \in AE_l^x$ such that $x \notin V(exp)$ (non-recursive assignment) or
- there exists $(l', x, exp) \in AE_l^x$ such that $x \in V(exp)$ (recursive assignment) and for all $(l'', x, exp) \in AE_l^x$, the assignment $cmd_{l''} = \mathsf{Assign}(x, exp)$ can be removed.

The second condition holds if the assignment can be propagated to *every* use, i.e. if in every label $m \in L$ with $l'' \in RD_m^x$, x can be replaced by exp.

Note that this definition is recursive, meaning that it amounts to computing the greatest solution of the constraint system. The following paragraphs describe the implementation of the corresponding fixpoint algorithm. Its pseudo code is given in Fig. 5.

To keep track which labels can be removed and which cannot, we maintain two sets of labels: a set of *blocked* labels, which cannot be removed because at least one use cannot be replaced, and a set of *possibly safe* labels, which can be propagated into all uses that have been inspected so far. Thus, blocking a label, we add it to the blocked set and remove it from the possibly-safe set. Analogously, if we mark a label as safe we add it to the possibly-safe set.

First, we check for every element $l \in ExpL := \{l \mid \exists x, exp, l'' : cmd_l = \mathsf{Assign}(x, exp) \lor cmd_l = \mathsf{CJump}(exp, l'')\}$ and every variable $x' \in V(exp)$ whether l is not reached by any existing definition of x', i.e., whether $RD_l^{x'} = \{(x', ?)\}$. If this is the case, x' is not written on any path leading to l, i.e., x' is an input and we proceed with the next $l \in ExpL$. Otherwise we can distinguish three cases:

1. There exists no AvExp information for variable x', i.e., $AE_l^{x'} = \emptyset$. For all recursive assignments to x' at l' with use in l, i.e., $(x', l') \in RD_l^{x'}$ with $cmd_{l'}$ a recursive assignment, we mark l' as blocked. As the value assigned to x' at l' can reach l, but the assigned expression does not according to AvExp, it cannot be propagated. Therefore not all reads of x' can be replaced by the corresponding expression and the original assignment at label l' cannot be removed. This can trigger a "domino" effect of blocking recursive definitions through the corresponding def-use chains.
2. There exists exactly one entry in $AE_l^{x'}$, e.g., (l', x', exp'). If $cmd_{l'}$ is recursive and l' is not blocked, we mark l' as possibly safe.
3. There exists more than one entry in $AE_l^{x'}$. Then every entry must assign the same expression exp' to x' but from differing labels, in the following

Input: $RD_l^{x'}, AE_l^{x'}$
Output: safe, block

```
1   For l ∈ ExpL do
2     For x ∈ V(exp_l) do
3       If (RD_l^{x'} ≠ {(x',?)}) then
4         If (AE_l^{x'} = ∅) then
5           For (x',l') ∈ RD_l^{x'} do
6             block := block ∪ {l'};
7           EndFor
8         ElseIf (AE_l^{x'} = (l',x',exp') && exp'.isRecursive(x')) then
9           If (!isBlocked(l')) then
10            safe := safe ∪ {l'};
11          EndIf
12        Else
13          If (isBlocked(AE_l^{x'})) then
14            For (x',l') ∈ AE_l^{x'} do
15              block := block ∪ {l'};
16            EndFor
17          Else
18            For (x',l') ∈ AE_l^{x'} do
19              safe := safe ∪ {l'};
20            EndFor
21          EndIf
22        EndIf
23      EndIf
24    EndFor
25  EndFor
```

Fig. 5. Computing safe recursive expressions for propagation

referred to as L'. If the assignment $\mathsf{Assign}(x', exp')$ is recursive and there exists no $l' \in L'$ which is blocked, then we can mark all $l' \in L'$ as possibly safe, otherwise we block all $l' \in L'$.

When executing the above algorithm starting with the possibly-safe and blocked sets of the previous iteration until reaching a fixpoint, the result is the greatest set of safe recursive assignments. Iterating multiple times is necessary as the "domino" effect of blocking labels cannot be handled in a single iteration. For example, consider Fig. 1 where the occurrence of overpow in label 15 cannot be replaced due to conflicting AE and thus blocks the propagation of label 9. However, label 11 has marked label 6 and 9 as possibly safe before. Therefore in the next run, label 11 will see the blocking of label 9 and also block label 6.

When reaching a fixpoint, the resulting safe recursive assignments are not blocked by any other assignment and can therefore be propagated and removed without altering the semantics. Note that when replacing some variable in an expression at some label l" with a safe recursive expression, we have to block l" in order not to propagate wrong expressions.

4.4   Combining the Optimizations

In order to obtain the "best" program with regard to our optimizations that preserves the semantics of the original program with respect to the verification property, it is not sufficient to run the previously presented analyses and optimizations just once, as some optimization potential is only enabled by subsequent program transformations.

The obvious solution to obtain a minimal program is to execute the optimizations in an iteration until a fixpoint is reached. This procedure terminates as each optimization reduces the number of code lines. When we reach a fixpoint, i.e., the program does not change after optimizations, no optimization potential is identified and the result is the best program w.r.t. our optimizations.

While some of the analyses could benefit from using static single-assignment (SSA) form [16], e.g. constant folding or reaching definitions, for the common case of loop-free PLC code the time complexity of computing a fixpoint is linear in the size of the program, as is the conversion to SSA form. Thus the effect would be negligibly small in comparison to the verification time (see Table 2).

5   Bounded Model Checking

In principle, a PLC executes a main routine which computes a set of output signals based on dedicated input signals and internal state variables cyclically ad infinitum. Accordingly, the set of program variables V is partitioned into the sets V^{in}, V^{out}, and V^{mem} of *input, output,* and *persistent* variables, respectively. The state space is given by $\mathcal{S} = \{s : V \to \mathcal{D}\}$; adopting the notation from [17], we define $V' = \{v' \mid v \in V\}$ and $V_i = \{v_i \mid v \in V\}$ to refer to the next state and the i-th step variables, respectively.

We use $\mathsf{post}(s)$ to denote the successor states of state s and $\mathsf{FO}(V)$ to refer to the set of quantifier-free first order formulae over variables in V.

5.1   Bounded Model Checking

The transition relation ψ of a PLC program $\mathcal{P}$ is derived as a first order formula over free variables $V \cup V'$ such that two states s, s' satisfy ψ (denoted $(s, s') \models \psi$) iff $s' \in \mathsf{post}(s)$. Intuitively, ψ is satisfied by s and s' iff executing one step of $\mathcal{P}$ starting in state s may yield state s'. The control flow is modeled explicitly in ψ by a special variable $pc \in V^{mem}$, representing the *program counter.* Moreover, the initial states of $\mathcal{P}$ can be constrained via a state predicate I over V; in particular, $I = (pc = 0)$ specifies that any valid execution starts at the first instruction in $\mathcal{P}$. For simplicity, we assume that all call instructions in $\mathcal{P}$ have been inlined.

Table 1. First order semantics of inlined intermediate code instructions

$$[\![\mathsf{Jump}(j)]\!] = \big(pc' = j\big) \wedge \textit{trans}\,(\{pc\})$$

$$[\![\mathsf{CJump}(b,j)]\!] = \big([\![b]\!] \wedge \big(pc' = j\big) \vee \neg[\![b]\!] \wedge \big(pc' = pc + 1\big)\big) \wedge \textit{trans}(\{pc\})$$

$$[\![\mathsf{Assign}(x, exp)]\!] = \big(x' = [\![exp]\!]\big) \wedge \big(pc' = pc + 1\big) \wedge \textit{trans}\,(\{x, pc\})$$

$$[\![\mathsf{Skip}]\!] = \big(pc' = pc + 1\big) \wedge \textit{trans}\,(\{pc\})$$

$$[\![\mathsf{Stop}]\!] = \big(pc' = term\big) \wedge \textit{trans}\,(\{pc\})$$

$$\textit{trans} : 2^V \rightarrow \mathsf{FO}(V \cup V') : X \mapsto \bigwedge_{v \in V \setminus X} (v = v')\,.$$

For a PLC program of length n, we define the *transition formula* ψ over free variables in $V \cup V'$:

$$\psi = \psi_{term} \wedge \bigwedge_{0 \le l < n} (pc = l \rightarrow [\![instr_l]\!]) \qquad (1)$$

where $\psi_{term} = (pc = term) \rightarrow trans(\emptyset)$. As formally defined in Tab. 1, $trans(X)$ transfers the values of all variables apart from those in X to the next state.

Each subformula $[\![instr_l]\!]$ formalizes the semantics of the instruction at program label l by encoding the state transformation from variables in V to variables in V'. The subformula ψ_{term} corresponds to a self-loop once $\mathcal{P}$ has terminated. Table 1 defines the semantics of each intermediate code instruction, where $term$ is a special program label representing termination. The expression semantics is omitted for brevity.

We verify invariants $\varphi \in \mathsf{FO}(V)$ over the current state's variables.

Definition 10 (BMC formula, [17]). *Let $\mathcal{P}$ be a PLC program, $I \in \mathsf{FO}(V)$ an initial constraint, $k \in \mathbb{N}$ be a bound, and $\varphi \in \mathsf{FO}(V)$. The bounded model checking formula for $\mathcal{P}$, I, k, and φ is defined as*

$$\Psi_\varphi^k = I(s_0) \wedge \bigwedge_{0 \le i < k} \psi(s_i, s_{i+1}) \wedge \bigvee_{0 \le i \le k} \neg\varphi(s_i). \qquad (2)$$

Proposition 1. Ψ_φ^k *is unsatisfiable iff φ holds in $\mathcal{P}$ up to k steps.*

If Ψ_φ^k is satisfiable, P satisfies the negation of the property along one of its computation paths, starting in an initial state satisfying I, and after at most k steps. If $\eta \models \Psi_\varphi^k$, then η is a counterexample, i.e., a satisfying assignment which corresponds to a computation path in $\mathcal{P}$ violating φ.

5.2   Termination

Checking the satisfiability of the formulae $\Psi_{term}^0, \Psi_{term}^1, \ldots$, where

$$\Psi_{term}^k = I(s_0) \wedge \bigwedge_{0 \le i < k} \psi(s_i, s_{i+1}) \wedge (pc_k \ne term) \qquad (3)$$

yields a semi-decision procedure for termination of $\mathcal{P}$ under initial constraints I.

Proposition 2. *Execution of $\mathcal{P}$ terminates after at most k steps starting in states satisfying I if Ψ_{term}^k is unsatisfiable.*

Using assumption literals and an incremental SMT solver, termination can be detected during bounded model checking with low additional overhead. The execution model of a PLC requires any PLC program to terminate within a short cycle time (e.g. $0.1s$); complex control structures are generally avoided, which renders a semi-decision procedure for termination viable in practice.

5.3   Pruning Formulae

Most PLC programs have a very simple control flow due to their cyclic execution model, where inputs are read, processed, and outputs are generated. When deciding the satisfiability of Ψ_{term}^k and Ψ_φ^k, the SMT solver constructs the control and data flow of the PLC program. The complexity of this task can be reduced considerably by pruning the subformulae ψ in (2) and (3). We reduce the size of Ψ_φ^k and Ψ_{term}^k by precomputing the set of feasible program paths. Therefore, let

$$
succ(l) = \begin{cases} \{l'\} & \text{if } instr_l = \mathsf{Jump}(l') \\ \{l+1, l'\} & \text{if } instr_l = \mathsf{CJump}(exp, l') \\ \{term\} & \text{if } l = term \vee instr_l = \mathsf{Stop} \\ \{l+1\} & \text{otherwise.} \end{cases}
$$

be the set of successor labels for a given program label l. The sets $\Pi_i \subseteq L$ of program labels reachable in i steps are inductively defined by

$$
\Pi_0 = \{l \in L \mid \exists s \in \mathcal{S} : s \models I \wedge s(pc) = l\} \text{ and}
$$
$$
\Pi_{i+1} = \bigcup_{l \in \Pi_i} succ(l).
$$

The sets $\Pi_0, \ldots, \Pi_k$ allow us to prune infeasible computation paths from Ψ_φ^k.

Lemma 1 (Pruning formulae). *Let $\mathcal{P}, \varphi, k$, and the sets Π_i be as before, and define*

$$
\psi_{opt}^i = \bigwedge \{(pc = l \rightarrow [\![instr_l]\!]) \mid l \in \Pi_i, l \neq term\} \wedge \tag{4}
$$
$$
\bigwedge \{\psi_{term} \mid term \in \Pi_i\} \text{ and}
$$
$$
\Psi_{\varphi,opt}^k = I(s_0) \wedge \bigwedge_{0 \leq i < k} \psi_{opt}^i(s_i, s_{i+1}) \wedge \bigvee_{0 \leq i \leq k} \neg\varphi(s_i). \tag{5}
$$

Then $\Psi_\varphi^k \equiv \Psi_{\varphi,opt}^k$.

Note that analogously to Lemma 1, restricting to program labels in Π_i yields a formula $\Psi_{term,opt}^k$ which is equivalent to the termination check in (3).

5.4   Multiple Cycles

Conceptually, variables in V^{in} and V^{out} correspond to sensor and actuator signals. Hence, they can only be read or written to, respectively. On the other hand, elements from V^{mem} are variables that reside in the PLC's memory which keep their values from one cycle to the next.

Upon termination of $\mathcal{P}$, the values of the output variables $v \in V^{out}$ control actuators which affect the automation environment. Thereby, they indirectly determine the inputs for the next execution of $\mathcal{P}$. As the environment is not modeled anywhere in the input program, we consider the map from output variables of cycle k to the inputs of cycle $k+1$ as *underspecified*.

Replacing all occurrences of ψ_{term} by

$$\psi_{glue} = (pc = term) \rightarrow (pc' = 0) \wedge trans\left(V^{in} \cup \{pc\}\right)$$

in the transition formula ψ and ψ_{opt}^{i} from (1) resp. (4) formalizes a non-terminating loop where $\mathcal{P}$ is executed infinitely often; requiring $v' = v$ for all except the next cycle's input variables and the program counter transfers the internal state and the output values to the next cycle while leaving its input variables unconstrained. As free variables are existentially quantified in satisfiability checking, this corresponds to a non-deterministic abstraction from the effect of the environment on the next cycle's input variables.

Note that although our verification approach abstracts from concrete timing, considering multiple cycles allows to draw restricted conclusions of the system's temporal behaviour by taking the cycle time into account.

6   Evaluation

Correctness properties of two types of IL programs are formally verified using Z3 [18] to handle the BMC formulae. Firstly, we consider safety related control programs which monitor the speed and direction of a drive, check that its position is outside a pre-defined danger range and detect standstill, respectively; these programs contain no loops and have a simple control flow but exhibit large state spaces due to their unconstrained input variables. Secondly, we verify some non-trivial properties of a greatest common divisor and a Fibonacci number implementation.

Table 2 lists the verification times[1] for each input program along with the number of instructions and variables (in brackets) in its original version and intermediate representation, both before and after model minimization. Most IL instructions have a complex semantics which often affects many processor registers. Generally, each IL instruction is transformed into an equivalent sequence of IC instructions; moreover, all registers are treated as variables. Therefore, the number of instructions and variables increases drastically by the first transformation step. However, given the simple control flow and the highly redundant

---

[1] All times are averages measured on a Core i5 processor with sufficient memory to avoid swapping.

Table 2. Number of program locations and variables (in parentheses) in each transformation step, and the model minimization and verification times

PLC program	verification property	SMT	IL	IC	opt	time min	BMC
danger range monitoring	flags ok (pre-release)	SAT	247(26)	792(42)	5(10)	0.2s	<0.1s
	flags ok (release)	UNSAT	255(26)	821(42)			
speed control	control flags correct	UNSAT	116(17)	362(27)	3(10)	0.7s	0.9s
direction detection	flags ok (error)	SAT	88(11)	287(23)	3(7)	<0.1s	<0.1s
	flags ok (release)	UNSAT					
standstill detection	flags set correctly	UNSAT	112(15)	347(29)	3(9)	0.5s	0.6s
$gcd(a,b)$, $a,b \leq 10$	$gcd(a,b)$ divides a,b	UNSAT	21(5)	50(15)	10(4)	<0.1s	27.7s
$gcd(a,b)$, $a,b \leq 50$	$gcd(a,b)$ divides a,b	UNSAT					863.3s
Fibonacci	$\forall x{<}12.\ fib(x){<}100$	UNSAT	26(4)	57(14)	11(4)	<0.1s	7.7s
	$\forall x{<}13.\ fib(x){<}100$	SAT					8.6s

semantics of IL, the model minimization techniques from Sec. 4 reduce the size of the IC program drastically and restrict to the relevant variables. On the one hand, this is due to constant folding and program slicing; on the other hand, our intermediate code allows for complex Boolean and arithmetic expressions whereas IL is assembler-like. Using forward expression propagation extensively, we eliminate temporary variables and trade more complex expressions for reducing the number of program locations. In our experiments, almost all basic blocks of the resulting control flow automaton consist of a single IC instruction.

The effect on the verification times of a semantics preserving transformation into our intermediate code and strong model minimizations becomes obvious when comparing to an earlier implementation which directly translates the IL code into a BMC problem. It finds the error in the pre-release version of the danger range program after 57s; the correctness proof of the released version takes 364s.

The greatest common divisor and the Fibonacci examples are hard to verify due to their complex control flow and the properties that are verified. While being atypical for PLC programs, such algorithms provide an interesting benchmark. As can be seen from Table 2, model minimization is still effective; it reduces the number of program locations by half, removes temporary variables in the gcd example, and yields an equivalent program expressed in a semantically much simpler intermediate code. Proving and disproving simple properties such as $gcd(45, 27) = 9$ and $gcd(45, 27) \neq 9$ completes in 0.1s and 0.2s, resp. However, even though the more complex properties listed in Table 2 yield the same optimized IC program, their verification by the SMT solver takes exponentially longer. On the one hand, this is due to the larger bound required for completeness of BMC in these cases; on the other hand, in the gcd example, the runtime of the SMT solver grows rapidly for the same BMC formula if the restrictions on the input values are loosened only slightly.

7   Conclusions

We presented and evaluated an approach to optimize the verification of safety critical PLC code. By bringing advanced BMC techniques involving SMT-based reasoning to PLCs, we enable engineers to verify safety properties in a more complete way than testing allows, and to efficiently find counterexamples. By introducing a new intermediate code and by presenting successful adaptations and extensions of compiler optimization techniques to improve SMT solving, we highly improved usability of automatic verification using BMC techniques for PLC code. The evaluations show that for large industrial PLC programs, the verification time can easily be improved by three orders of magnitude.

In future work, we intend to investigate more advanced verification techniques, such as inductive reasoning [19,20,21] and interpolation techniques [22].

References

1. Frey, G., Litz, L.: Formal methods in PLC programming. In: Systems, Man, and Cybernetics, vol. 4, pp. 2431–2436. IEEE Computer Society (2000)
2. Younis, M.B., Frey, G.: Formalization of existing PLC programs: A survey. In: CESA, pp. 234–239 (2003)
3. Fokkink, W., Hollingshead, P.: Verification of interlockings: From control tables to ladder logic diagrams. In: FMICS, pp. 171–185 (1998)
4. Groote, J.F., Warners, J.P.: The propositional formula checker HeerHugo. Journal of Automated Reasoning 24(1-2), 101–125 (2000)
5. Kanso, K., Moller, F., Setzer, A.: Automated verification of signalling principles in railway interlocking systems. ENTCS 250(2), 19–31 (2009)
6. Canet, G., Couffin, S., Lesage, J.J., Petit, A., Schnoebelen, P.: Towards the automatic verification of PLC programs written in Instruction List. In: 2000 IEEE Int. Conf. on Systems, Man, and Cybernetics, pp. 2449–2454. IEEE (2000)
7. Meulen, M.: Verification of PLC source code using propositional logic. Master's thesis, Technical university of Eindhoven (2010)
8. Pavlovic, O., Pinger, R., Kollmann, M.: Automation of formal verification of PLC programs written in IL. In: Verification Workshop. CEUR Workshop Proceedings, vol. 259 (2007)
9. Loeis, K., Younis, M.B., Frey, G.: Application of symbolic and bounded model checking to the verification of logic control systems. In: ETFA, pp. 247–250 (2005)
10. Pavlovic, O., Ehrich, H.D.: Model checking PLC software written in function block diagram. In: ICST, pp. 439–448 (2010)
11. Sülflow, A., Drechsler, R.: Verification of PLC programs using formal proof techniques. In: FORMS/FORMAT, pp. 43–50 (2008)
12. Blech, J.O., Ould Biha, S.: Verification of PLC properties based on formal semantics in Coq. In: Barthe, G., Pardo, A., Schneider, G. (eds.) SEFM 2011. LNCS, vol. 7041, pp. 58–73. Springer, Heidelberg (2011)
13. Beyer, D., Cimatti, A., Griggio, A., Keremoglu, M.E., Sebastiani, R.: Software model checking via large-block encoding. In: FMCAD 2009, pp. 25–32. IEEE (2009)
14. John, K., Tiegelkamp, M.: IEC 61131-3: Programming Industrial Automation Systems. Springer (2010)

15. Nielson, F., Nielson, H.R., Hankin, C.: Principles of Program Analysis. Springer (1999)
16. Muchnick, S.S.: Advanced Compiler Design and Implementation. Morgan Kaufmann (1997)
17. Biere, A., Cimatti, A., Clarke, E., Zhu, Y.: Symbolic model checking without BDDs. In: Cleaveland, W.R. (ed.) TACAS 1999. LNCS, vol. 1579, pp. 193–207. Springer, Heidelberg (1999)
18. de Moura, L.M., Bjørner, N.: Z3: An efficient SMT solver. In: Ramakrishnan, C.R., Rehof, J. (eds.) TACAS 2008. LNCS, vol. 4963, pp. 337–340. Springer, Heidelberg (2008)
19. Bradley, A.R., Manna, Z.: Checking safety by inductive generalization of counterexamples to induction. In: FMCAD, pp. 173–180. IEEE (2007)
20. Bradley, A.R.: SAT-based model checking without unrolling. In: Jhala, R., Schmidt, D. (eds.) VMCAI 2011. LNCS, vol. 6538, pp. 70–87. Springer, Heidelberg (2011)
21. Cimatti, A., Griggio, A.: Software model checking via IC3. In: Madhusudan, P., Seshia, S.A. (eds.) CAV 2012. LNCS, vol. 7358, pp. 277–293. Springer, Heidelberg (2012)
22. McMillan, K.L.: Interpolation and SAT-based model checking. In: Hunt Jr., W.A., Somenzi, F. (eds.) CAV 2003. LNCS, vol. 2725, pp. 1–13. Springer, Heidelberg (2003)

Modeling Firmware as Service Functions and Its Application to Test Generation

Sunha Ahn and Sharad Malik

Princeton University, NJ, USA

Abstract. The term firmware refers to software that is tied to a specific hardware platform, e.g., low-level drivers that physically interface with the peripherals. More recently, this has grown to include software that manages critical hardware platform functions such as power management. This growing firmware needs to be shipped with the hardware and shares many of the same critical design concerns as the hardware. The two that we address in this paper are: co-design with the other system components, and validation of the firmware interactions with the connected hardware modules. To this end we introduce a specific *Service-Function* Transaction-Level Model (TLM) for modeling the firmware and interacting hardware components. A service function provides a service in response to a specific trigger, much like an interrupt-service routine responding to an interrupt. While TLM has been used in the past for HW-SW codesign, we show how the particular structure of the proposed service function based model is useful in the context of firmware design. Specifically, we show its application in automatic test generation. Recently concolic testing has emerged as an automated technique for test generation for single-threaded software. This technique cannot be used directly for firmware, which, by definition, runs in parallel with the interacting hardware modules. We show how the service function model proposed here can be used to analyze these interactions and how single-threaded concolic testing can still be used for an important class of these interaction patterns. The model and the test generation are illustrated through a non-trivial case study of the open-source Rockbox MP3 player.

1 Introduction

Firmware is the specialized class of software that directly accesses hardware. It can be in the form of software semi-permanently embedded in chips, drivers for specific physical components, or low-level OS code that directly interacts with hardware. In each case, the firmware is placed between the hardware and higher-level software (OS or applications) as in Fig. 1, thereby enabling them to communicate, via firmware, with each other. More recently, this category has grown to include software that manages critical hardware platform control functions such as power and even security management. These functions were previously implemented in dedicated hardware controllers, but their increasing complexity, coupled with the increasing availability of on-chip processing cores, has led to their migration to firmware [1]. This growing firmware needs to be shipped with the hardware and thus shares many of the same critical design concerns as the hardware. The two that we address in this paper are: co-design with other system components, and validation of the firmware interactions with the hardware.

V. Bertacco and A. Legay (Eds.): HVC 2013, LNCS 8244, pp. 61–77, 2013.

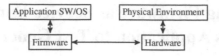

Fig. 1. Computer System Components

In a system-on-a-chip design the firmware needs to be developed at the same time as the hardware it interacts with. *Thus, at the least, a model is needed for the firmware-hardware interface that correctly captures the interactions.* The firmware also needs to be validated in the context of this interface model. Often the hardware model is missing, and only a natural-language specification is available in the early stages of design development. When available, the model is written in a hardware design language such as Verilog. However, the firmware itself is developed largely in a high-level language such as C/C++ with some assembly code to access specific registers/memory/pins that connect with the hardware. Validating a C/C++/Assembly program in the context of Verilog is challenging. One way this has been overcome in practice is by developing early design models for both the firmware and hardware in a common modeling language such as System-C that enables their co-simulation. These System-C level models are generally Transaction-Level Models (TLMs) [2,3,4], i.e., a functional model that captures the interaction between components without necessarily providing all the low-level details. Co-simulation of the firmware and hardware TLMs is then the workhorse for validating the firmware and hardware. *However, the main challenge associated with this methodology is that the System-C scheduler typically does not/cannot consider the prohibitively large number of possible interleavings between the concurrent hardware and firmware.* Thus, this simulation is incomplete with an unknown coverage of interleavings.

We address these challenges through the use of a specific TLM that captures some high-level information in the hardware and firmware transactions. Specifically, a firmware transaction is a service function in response to an input from the hardware or the higher-level application/OS software. Similarly a hardware transaction is a service function in response to an input from the physical environment or the firmware (Fig. 1). A service function provides a service in response to a specific trigger, much like an interrupt-service routine responding to an interrupt. *In structuring the transactions in the form of service functions, we can exploit specific interaction patterns between the transactions to address the validation challenges mentioned above.* These patterns can be used to automatically derive tests using concolic testing [5] based methods. Concolic (= *conc*rete + symb*olic*) testing has recently emerged as a promising technology for automatically developing test cases for unit testing of software. Concolic testing uses symbolic analysis of the software to generate concrete tests that test specific code paths. Current concolic testing techniques and test generation tools (e.g., KLEE [6], DART [7]), yet, are limited to single threaded code. However, a firmware thread runs concurrently with hardware and possibly other firmware threads, which would preclude the direct use of single-threaded concolic testing. We show how the interaction patterns enable single-threaded concolic testing to be used for multi-threaded testing for a large and important class of interaction patterns (the *stateless producer-consumer* case discussed in this paper). This paper makes the following contributions:

- It presents a novel service function based transaction-level model for the co-design of firmware and its interacting hardware components and shows how this model enables a useful characterization of their interactions. (§ 3.1-3.2 §)
- It shows how specific interaction patterns (the stateless producer-consumer case) enable the use of a single-threaded concolic testing framework to generate a complete test set for a firmware thread even when it is interacting with other concurrent firmware/hardware threads. (§ 4.1-4.2 §)
- It demonstrates the practical applicability of the proposed modeling methodology through its application to a non-trivial public domain Rockbox MP3 player system and the practical applicability of the proposed concolic test generation technique through the use of a public domain concolic test generator, KLEE [6], on the firmware threads in Rockbox [8]. (§ 3.3,4.3 §)

Overall this paper takes an important step towards bringing high-level functional modeling techniques to firmware/hardware modeling and exploiting the interaction patterns between the concurrent firmware and hardware threads for automatic test generation.

2 Rockbox Case Study

Our running example Rockbox [8] is composed of application code and firmware code including device driver threads which access the hardware device using assembly level driver APIs. These APIs are device-specific since Rockbox supports wide range of MP3 players. We use iAudio X5 device as an example in this work. The main Rockbox firmware is the device driver threads: the power thread for power management, the USB thread handling USB insertion/removal events, the backlight handling thread, the ATA disk management thread, etc. *Each thread executes its service function in response to an input from the hardware or application level software.* As an example of a service function, the power thread's job in each call is to (1) update the charger connection status, and (2) keep watching the battery level by reading the device (PCF50606 controller chip [9]) status. Hence, these service actions in each call depend on the inputs from the PCF50606 device. Similarly, *the hardware device provides service functions in response to the firmware.* For instance, one of the iAudio X5 chips [10], PCF50606, which manages the physical power supply provides a number of services. One example service of this chip is converting the analog battery level to digital and updating the value on the shared register in response to the physical voltage level change. Another service is to update the charger connection status. In the next section, we explain our novel service function based TLM with this example.

3 Transaction Level Model

3.1 Model Definition

Definition 1. *A High-Level State Machine (HLSM) [11] is defined as* $(S, I, O, V, s_0, v_0, \omega, \nu, \delta)$ *where S is a set of states, I is a set of inputs, O is a* *set of outputs, V is a set of storage values, $s_0 \in S$ is the initial state, $v_0 \in V$ is the initial storage value, $\omega : S \times I \times V \to O$ is the output function, $\nu : S \times I \times V \to S$ is the state transition function, and $\delta : S \times I \times V \to V$ is the storage update function.*

HLSM extends the Finite State Machine by treating the data state V as separate from the control state S. This allows the HLSM to describe algorithmic computation as a series of data updates (possibly conditional). In the following, $s \in S$ (possibly subscripted) represents a specific value of state. v represents *a variable* that can take values from V.

Definition 2 (Transaction). *A transaction T is an HLSM with a start state $s_s \in S$ with no incoming transition and an end state $s_e \in S$ with no outgoing transition.*

These characteristics are important to capture the service function nature of our transactions. A firmware service function starts in response to an external input from hardware or application/OS and ends at the completion of the service task. This is modeled by means of a single departure from the start state, and a terminating end state.

For a transaction, V represents both data values that are local to the transaction and data values that are shared with other transactions. Thus, $V = L \times G$ where L is the set of local storage values and G is the set of shared storage values. Equivalently, $v = (l, g)$ where v, l, g represent variables that take values from V, L, G respectively. Note that V may be composed of several different sets of storage values $V_1, V_2, \ldots, V_k, \ldots, V_p$, i.e., $V = V_1 \times V_2 \ldots \times V_k \ldots \times V_p$. Equivalently, $v = (v_1, v_2 \ldots, v_k \ldots, v_p)$, where v_k represents a (either local or shared) variable that takes a value from V_k. Different transactions communicate through these shared storages. A state s in a transaction reads variable v_k if some storage update in s depends on v_k, or some transition from s depends on v_k. s writes v_k if it modifies the value of v_k.

To illustrate this model through the Rockbox example, the service function of the power thread can be modeled as one transaction which starts by updating the charger connection status and ends by reading the battery level in order to receive the physical status.

Definition 3 (Transaction Execution Model). *A transaction instance t_i is an execution of a transaction T. When T executes, t_i starts from the start state s_s and continues execution till it reaches the end state s_e. t_i is followed by the next instance t_{i+1}.*

Depending on the values of i and v, a transaction instance may follow different paths through the transaction. Also, only one instance of a transaction can be active at a time while instances of different transactions can be executed concurrently.

Definition 4. *A Transaction Level Model (TLM) $\mathcal{T}$ is a set of concurrent transactions.*

A TLM can consist of both firmware and hardware transactions where each transaction is a specific service function. Their interactions are captured through the shared variable g. For instance, the two services of the PCF50606 chip can be modeled as two hardware transactions providing the physical battery level and the charger status to the power firmware transaction through the shared variables. These three transactions run concurrently. *This uniform modeling of the hardware and software as transactions provides a uniform analysis framework for studying their interaction patterns as well as a consistent modeling method for both firmware and hardware.*

The shared variables g provide the interactions between concurrent transactions. However, concurrency can result in many possible interleavings between the transactions that can impact the values of g and thus the paths taken in the transaction instances. Consider two concurrent transactions T_1 and T_2 where T_1 reads v, and T_2 writes v in every instance. Note that, in our TLM model, individual reads/writes to shared variables are atomic, but the entire transaction is not. In this example, t_1 (an instance of T_1) reads the value updated by the last instance of T_2 executed before t_1. This last instance of T_2 is determined by the relative speed of T_1's instances and T_2's instances and their interleaving. Thus, to get the complete set of possible behaviors of the transactions, all possible interleavings need to be considered.

3.2   Analyzing Data Dependencies between Transactions

We now show how specific interaction patterns between transactions can be exploited to reduce the number of interleavings. In Rockbox, we observed that there are a few interesting interaction patterns between transactions based on the data dependencies. We first define the notions of data dependence and data dependence graph and describe the specific interaction patterns of interest based on this. While these terms are well known in the compiler context it is useful to define them in the current TLM context.

Definition 5 (Data Dependence). *Variable v_l in state s_m in transaction T_n is data dependent on variable v_i in state s_j in T_k if s_j updates v_i, and this update determines the update of v_l in s_m.*

Definition 6 (Data Dependence Graph). *The data dependence graph D for a given TLM, $\mathcal{T}$, is a directed graph with vertices (v, s, T) where $v, s \in T$ and $T \in \mathcal{T}$ and v is updated in s in T. Edge $((v_i, s_j, T_k), (v_l, s_m, T_n)) \in D$ if and only if v_l in s_m in T_n is data dependent on v_i in s_j in T_k.*

In Fig. 2a, v_l in s_m is data dependent on v_i in s_j. Note that the above definition is not constructive, i.e. it does not provide an algorithm for determining data dependence. That is beyond the scope of this paper[1]. In the above, T_k and T_n may be the same transaction and v_l is updated by a transaction instance subsequent to when v_i is updated in a previous instance. This form of data dependence is referred to as a *cross-instance data dependence*. Different interaction patterns within and across transactions can now be defined in terms of data dependence and the data dependence graph.

Definition 7 (Transaction Independence). *Transaction T_n is independent of transaction T_k iff for each (v_i, s_j, T_k) there is no path to any (v_l, s_m, T_n) in D.*

Thus, for validating T_n, T_k is immaterial. This happens often in firmware transactions. Many firmware transactions are independent of the hardware transactions they interact with when they are only responsible for setting the state of the hardware transactions.

Definition 8 (Producer Transaction). *Let $U = (v, s_j, T)$ be the set of all vertices in D with a write to v in T. Further, for each $u \in U$, the only vertices in D with paths to u are in T. In this case T produces v.*

---

[1] Available in the compiler literature [12].

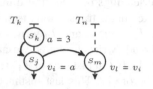
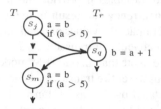

(a) Producer T_k and Consumer T_n (b) Stateful transactions T and T_r

Fig. 2. *(dashed arrow: a transaction instance, solid arrow: edge of the dependence graph)*

Intuitively, in this scenario T produces data that is independent of other transactions. Thus, we do not need to consider the interleaving of other transactions with T in computing this data. In Fig. 2a, the variable v_i is only written in s_j, and the only edge to s_j is from s_k, which is within T_k. Thus, T_k produces v_i.

Definition 9 (Producer Consumer Interaction). *Let $((v_i, s_j, T_k), (v_l, s_m, T_n))$ be an edge in D and let T_k produce v_i. In this case T_n is said to consume v_i.*

In Fig. 2a, T_k are the producer and T_n are the consumer of v_i. Note that a producer consumer interaction is defined specific to the value produced. Thus, it may be possible for T_1 to produce x and consume y and T_2 to produce y and consume x. Thus, neither of the threads in a producer consumer relationship may be independent of the other.

Definition 10 (Stateful Transactions). *A transaction, T is said to be stateful iff (1) there is a cross-instance edge $((v_i, s_j, T), (v_l, s_m, T)) \in D$ or (2) there is a path from (v_i, s_j, T) to (v_l, s_m, T) that goes through some vertex (v_p, s_q, T_r) and $T \neq T_r$.*

Intuitively the first case in this definition corresponds to v_l using a value written to v_i in a previous instance of T. In the second case, since v_p is from some other transaction, depending on the relative speeds of the execution of individual instances, v_l can use a value that is written to v_i in a previous instance of T. In Fig. 2b, both T and T_r are stateful. In a stateful transaction, an instance of the transaction depends on previous instances and provides values for future instances. Thus, multiple transaction instances need to be unrolled to cover all possible scenarios for this transaction. (Assuming the initial states of both a and b are zero, without unrolling T and T_r multiple times, the condition $(a > 5)$ will never be explored.)

A transaction is said to be *stateless* if it is not stateful. Intuitively, the values produced by a transaction instance of a stateless transaction do not depend on any previous instance of the transaction. Hence, in a stateless transaction, only one instance of the transaction is needed to cover all possible scenarios for that transaction. This is quite common with a service function based TLM. Each instance of a service function for the firmware is in response to some input from the application/OS software or from the hardware. Similarly, each instance of a service function for the hardware is in response to an input from the firmware or the physical environment. These responses are typically independent of previous invocations of this service function. In the next section, we examine the practical prevalence of the statelessness and the producer-consumer relationship.

3.3   Prevalence of the Interaction Patterns in Practice

We developed the Rockbox TLM model using the service function based TLMs proposed in this paper. It consists of a set of firmware transactions and *a set of hardware transactions that the firmware transactions depend on* in SystemC. For the firmware we used reverse engineering to model the TLM specification out of the C/assembly open-source firmware implementation. The hardware transactions were written by manual analysis of the relevant datasheets [13,9,10]. We modeled 6 firmware and 3 hardware transactions (Table 1a) and observed the model's interaction patterns. To show that these patterns are not only observed in the specific Rockbox case but are meaningful in general cases, we studied the interaction patterns of several Linux device drivers [14] and the corresponding x86 QEMU device emulator code [15] as well. Table 1c shows the different types of peripherals emulated in x86 QEMU and how many specific devices are emulated for each category. (Here, we selected some important representative categories from QEMU. The complete list is over 53 devices and more than 91961 lines of code, and thus a full analysis of QEMU interaction patterns is beyond the scope of this paper.) We chose one device per each category and analyzed its interaction patterns with the corresponding Linux device driver.

Independence: Often the transaction interaction is one-way, i.e. one is independent of the other when the two transactions are interacting. For example, in the backlight thread, the function setting the backlight brightness only writes to the hardware device but does not read from it. Thus the backlight thread is independent of the LCD device. 6 of 7 Rockbox transactions (third column of Table 1b) are independent of the interacting firmware transactions (first column). For QEMU, 7 of the 15 Linux transactions are independent of the QEMU transactions.

Producer-Consumer Relationship: The most common case in both Rockbox and Linux-QEMU is that a shared variable is shared only between one firmware and one hardware transaction, or one firmware and another firmware transaction, and this sharing has the producer-consumer interaction pattern. In these cases the shared variables are I/O pins or registers in a device that are shared with a dedicated device driver, or global variables across the firmware transactions. This pattern is easy to find in embedded systems since many I/O pins or registers are dedicated to a specific purpose and written by a master module. In fact, 6 of 7 pairs of interacting transactions in the Rockbox and 6 of 9 devices in Linux-QEMU are in the producer-consumer relationship.

Statelessness: As shown in Table 1b and 1c, stateless transactions occur frequently since a firmware transaction instance tends to be interested in only the current status of the device and hence processes a fresh set of device input values in each instance. For example, the power thread reads the current battery level, which is naturally stateless because the past battery level does not decide the current value. In Table 1a, 8 of 9 transactions are stateless, and 19 of 30 Linux or QEMU transactions are stateless.

Table 1. Interaction Patterns of Practical Examples

Transaction	Type	Main Functionality
Power	FW	Monitor charger connection and battery level
USB	FW	Monitoring USB status
Backlight	FW	Manage to turn on/off the LCD backlight
ATA	FW	Stop or restart the ATA bus depending on the USB status
Button	FW	Post the button value to other threads
Charger stat	HW	Provide the physical charger status [9]
Battery level	HW	Convert the analog battery level to digital [9]
USB detect	HW	Detect the physical USB presence [13]
ATA transfer	FW	Transfer data from/to the disk

(a) Rockbox transactions and their functionality (FW: Firmware, HW: Hardware)

Trans-action	Shared storage	Related Transaction	Relationship
Power	batvolts	Battery level	Both stateless & p-c
	GPI56	Charger status	Both stateless & p-c
	usb_state	USB	Both stateless & p-c
USB	id	USB detect	Both stateless & p-c
		Backlight	Both stateless & p-c
Backlight	remote_hold _button	Button	Stateless-stateful & p-c
ATA	sleeping	ATA transfer	Not p-c
	spinup	ATA transfer	Both stateless & p-c
Button	-	-	Stateful

(b) Relationship of the interacting Rockbox transactions (p-c means producer-consumer)

Category	# of devices supported	Representative device	Linux Transaction	Related QEMU Transaction	Relationship
Storage	5	ATAPI IDE	ide_transfer_pc(SF)	cmd_read(SL)	p-c
Graphics	2	Cirrus CLGD 54xx VGA	cirrusfb_bitBLT(SL)	cirrus_vga_iowrite(SF)	not p-c
Network	5	Ne2000 ethernet card	block_input(SL), block_output(SL)	ne2000_iowrite(SL),ne2000_ioread(SL)	p-c
Port	2	16550A UART	rx_chars(SL),tx_chars(SF)	serial_iowrite(SF), serial_ioread(SL)	not p-c
Bus	13	USB UHCI	uhci_readw (SL), uhci_writew(SL)	uhci_iowritew(SF),uhci_ioreadw(SL)	not p-c
Input	4	Microsoft serial mouse	sermouse_interrupt(SF)	msmouse_event(SL)	p-c
Sound	4	Intel 82801AA	codec_read(SL),codec_write(SL)	nabm_read(SL),nabm_write(SF)	p-c
Clock	2	i8253 PIT	i8253_read (SF)	pit_iowrite(SF),pit_ioread(SF)	p-c
Interrupt handler	3	i8259 interrupt handler	irq_pending(SL),mask_irq(SL), unmask_irq(SL)	pic_iowrite (SF),pic_ioread(SL)	p-c

(c) Linux-QEMU pair (p-c : producer-consumer, SL : stateless, SF : stateful)

4   Using Transaction Interaction Patterns in Firmware Testing

This section shows how the transaction interaction patterns presented in the previous section can be exploited to simplify test generation as well as increase test coverage. We show how the interaction patterns can be analyzed, and the results of the analysis can be encoded as constraints to be used during concolic test generation. This enables using a single threaded test generator such as KLEE to generate tests for a firmware transaction while accounting for other interleaving hardware and firmware transactions.

4.1   Automatic Test Generation Using KLEE

Concolic Testing: Concolic testing [5] combines symbolic execution [16] with concrete execution. It uses a constraint solver with the symbolic execution to cover all feasible paths related to the given symbolic variables. The user is responsible for identifying a set of variables as symbolic and instrumenting her test code. Then the concolic testing tool executes the code concretely except for branches controlled by the symbolic variables. For these branches, the tool explores both paths while attaching the corresponding constraints of the symbolic inputs for each path. At the end of each path, the tool asks its solver to generate the concrete values, or test cases, satisfying the constraints. In our work we chose to use KLEE [6] since it is open and well-maintained.

Code 1.1 is an instrumented test code for KLEE. KLEE executes the code as usual until it hits a symbolic value (line 4). Then, it forks execution and adds the constraint

```
1  void main(void){
2      unsigned int i, ret;
3      make_symbolic(&i);
4      if(i > 0) ret = i;
5      else      ret = 1/i;
6  }
```

Code 1.1: Instrumented code for KLEE

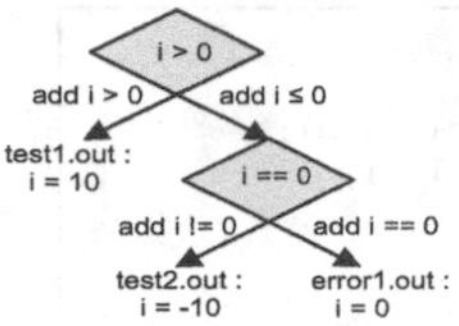

Fig. 3a. Generated test cases

$i > 0$ on the true path and $i \leq 0$ on the false path (Fig. 3a). The true path ends after line 4, and the solver picks a random value, say 10, for i among those values satisfying $i > 0$. On the false path with the path constraint $i \leq 0$, KLEE continues execution, eventually reaches line 5, and detects a dangerous operation, division by zero. Now, KLEE adds $i == 0$ as a constraint to the solver, and generates the error case. KLEE continues the other path, $i \leq 0 \wedge i \neq 0$, and generates the test case $i == -10$ at the end. As shown, KLEE explores all feasible paths for this case and generates the interesting test cases.

Concolic Testing and Concurrency: Concolic testing has been used largely for unit testing single-threaded code, not a multi-threaded program. [2] There have been approaches to extend concolic testing to multi-threaded programs [19,20]. These involve searching for all possible interleavings (or equivalently, schedules) of concurrent threads. However, due to the large number of possible interleavings, this tends not to scale. Partial Order Reduction (POR) [21] can help mitigate this. It generates only one representative interleaving among all interleavings which result in the same state. However, even with POR the number of interleavings can still be very large. In this work we show how the transaction interaction patterns can be used to address this issue.

4.2   Test Case Generation for Stateless Producer-Consumer Transactions

As seen in the previous section, stateless transactions and producer consumer interaction pattern are prevalent. Also, as discussed, if the firmware is the producer, the firmware thread is independent of the hardware thread. Hence, the most interesting case is when the firmware thread is the consumer. Here, what/when the hardware thread produces can impact the paths that the firmware thread takes, and thus impact the test cases of the firmware. We now show how the interactions of the hardware thread can be modeled through additional constraints provided to the constraint solver used for test case generation of the firmware thread. The overall procedure is as follows. The transactions to be tested are minimally instrumented manually for two purposes. The first is to identify certain variables as symbolic. These are the variables that need to be explored to cover various program paths in the firmware. This is standard in concolic testing. The second is to add constraints that capture the producer consumer interaction among the transactions. This is specific to our methodology. As we will show, these constraints completely eliminate the need to consider interleavings for this interaction pattern.

---

[2] The survey paper [17] on concolic testing tools indicates that only jCUTE [18] supports concurrent programs, but it is not open source.

```
1 | void T1(){
2 |   int rand, result;
3 |   klee_make_symbolic(&rand);
4 |   if(rand < 0){ x = 1; }
5 |   else
6 |   {   x = 2;
7 |       x = 3; }
8 |   result = y; // error if result is
                  0
9 | }
```

Code 1.2: Producer for x / consumer for y

```
1 | void T2(){
2 |   int r1, r2;
3 |   r1 = x;
4 |   r2 = x;
5 |   if(r1<0 || r2<0)
6 |       y = 0; //error
7 |   else
8 |       y = 7;
9 | }
```

Code 1.3: Consumer for x / producer for y

Example Transaction: We will illustrate the procedure using a simple example that captures the essence of the procedure. (This example focuses on two different producer consumer interactions, each with one shared variable, between two transactions. However, the procedure can extend to producers sharing multiple variables with multiple consumers.) In Code 1.2 and 1.3, $T1$ is a producer for x and a consumer for y at the same time. $T2$, on the other hand, consumes x and produces y. In the Code 1.2, the variable $rand$ is used to take either one of the paths in each execution. If $result$ is 0, it is considered to be an error. *While these transactions, as constructed, are not computationally very meaningful, their structure has been selected to illustrate the key points of the test generation procedure while keeping the transactions themselves small.* By manual analysis, we can easily conclude that in the concurrent execution of $T1$ and $T2$, each of $r1$ and $r2$ could independently store 1, 2, or 3. The order of write does not matter, i.e. $r1 = 3, r2 = 2$ is possible in an instance of $T2$, since a new instance of $T1$ keeps getting executed and $T2$ can read any of the value produced by the new instance. Note that $r1 = 0$ or $r1 = r2 = 0$ is also possible in case $T2$ executes first before $T1$ ever executes. Accordingly, we see that the condition in line 5 in Code 1.3 will never be true. This means $T1$ will not read 0 from y. It is important that the transaction instances do not have to be unrolled for testing since $T1$ and $T2$ are stateless. We now show how the results of this analysis can be captured through instrumenting the code in KLEE.

Instrumenting the Input Code: *The overall goal of instrumenting the producer is tracking the different values that could be produced by the producer for use by its consumer.* In the instrumented version, T1, the producer for x, takes an integer pointer $*wx$ as an argument in Code 1.4 (wx is short for $writex$). The value of x updated by $T1$ will be stored in wx later, so that the test generator code (Code 1.5) which calls $T1$ can access this value. In line 1, $w[NUM\_WRITE]$ saves all values of x written by $T1$ during the execution of an instance. $write\_len$ tracks the number of multiple writes on x during the instance, and it can be either 1 or 2 at the end of a path taken. Lines 12-14 let KLEE pick a constrained-random number between 0 to $write\_len - 1$, to pick one of the written values during the path. Thus, $w[c]$ can be either 1, 2, or 3. In other words, every time $T1$ is called, wx will record one of the three values. Note that, in general, the producer transaction may have many possible paths, and each of these paths may have many possible writes to the shared variable. With this instrumentation, for each path, we gather *only one of the written values during the path*. Similarly, $T2$ (Code 1.4), the producer of y, is instrumented in the same way in terms of y (line 23-24). We directly

```
1  void T1(int *wx, int *ry){
2    int w[NUM_WR],rand,c,temp,write_len=0;
3    klee_make_symbolic(&rand);
4    if(rand>0){
5      w[write_len] = 1;  write_len++;//write x
6    }else{
7      w[write_len] = 2; write_len++;//write x
8      w[write_len] = 3; write_len++;//write x
9    }
10   klee_make_symbolic(&temp);
11   *ry = temp;//read y
12   klee_make_symbolic(&c);
13   klee_assume(0≤c<write_len);
14   *wx = w[c];
15 }
16 void T2(int *rx1,int *rx2,int *wy){
17   int temp1, temp2;
18   klee_make_symbolic(&temp1);
19   *rx1 = temp1;//read x
20   klee_make_symbolic(&temp2);
21   *rx2 = temp2;//read x
22   if(temp1<0||temp2<0)*wy = 0;//write y(error)
23   else *wy = 7;//write y
24 }
```

```
1  int main(){
2    int st_x = 0; // initial state of x
3    int num_st;
4    int wx1,wx2,wx3,wy;//pointers for writes
5    int rx[2]; // pointers for read x
6    int ry1,ry2,ry3;//pointers for read y
7    int read_len = 2;
8    T1(&wx1, &ry1);
9    T1(&wx2, &ry2);
10   T1(&wx3, &ry3);
11   T2(&rx[0], &rx[1], &wy);
12   klee_make_symbolic(&num_st);
13   klee_assume(0 <= num_st <= read_len);
14   int i;
15   for(i=0; i<num_st; i++)
16     if(rx[i] != st_x) klee_silent_exit(0);
17   for(i=num_st; i<read_len; i++)
18     if(rx[i]!=wx1&&rx[i]!=wx2&&rx[i]!=wx3)
19       klee_silent_exit(0);
19   if(ry1!=wy) klee_silent_exit(0);
20   if(ry2!=wy) klee_silent_exit(0);
21   if(ry3!=wy) klee_silent_exit(0);
22 }
```

Code 1.4: Instrumented T1   Code 1.5: Test Generator Code

store the written value in wy rather than introducing $write\_len$ and c here because $T2$ only writes y once along any of the feasible paths. In the above instrumentation, $w[]$ stores all possible values written to the shared variable. As we saw in Code 1.2, this set of values, not the order in which they were written, is what matters in terms of interaction with the consumer. The consumer can read any one of these values with every read. Also, the size of $w[]$ is known statically in this case. If this is not the case, then $w[]$ can be dynamically allocated.

On the other hand, in the instrumented consumer Code 1.4, the consumer of x, T_2, takes integer pointers $rx1$ and $rx2$ as arguments for every read of x in the transaction (rx is short for $readx$). The pointers $rx1$ and $rx2$ are to store the values that the transaction reads in order to deliver them to the test generator code. Every time the transaction is supposed to read from x, the value is instead read from a symbolic variable, e.g., $temp1$ or $temp2$ (line 19,21). This forces the read value to explore all possible values as it is symbolic. Later, as shown in the next section, this symbolic value will be constrained to the possible written values gathered from the instrumented producer.

The Test Generator: In Code 1.5, the test generator code combines $T1$ and $T2$ into a single thread and adds some constraints that connect the values shared by the producer and consumer. This code first executes $T1$, the producer of x, as many times as the total number of writes to x in $T1$. This allows KLEE to assign independent values for each write. From each call of $T1$, it collects one of the write values from the producer in $wx1$, $wx2$, and $wx3$. Next, the consumer of x, $T2$, is called in line 11. Now, what we want is to make $T2$ read one of the collected values written by $T1$. In line 18, if $r[i]$, one of the read values, is not the same as one of the collected values of x, KLEE exits without generating any case for that path. This forces KLEE to select one of the collected values. Also, the case that $T1$ is not even executed before $T2$ executes, is covered with $T2$ reading from the initial state of x. KLEE picks the number of how many times the consumer reads from the start state, num_st, again randomly but constrained by the total number of reads (line 12, 13), and forces $rx[0]$ to $rx[num\_st-1]$ to read from the start state as in line 16. Similarly, matching values for y works in the same way except that we omitted the start state of y here for brevity. Note that there are multiple paths in the consumer of x, $T2$. As the values written by the producer $T1$ are stored in the symbolic variables $wx1$, $wx2$, and $wx3$, *KLEE will try and find all possible values that can be written to $wx1$, $wx2$, or $wx3$ in order to exercise all the paths in the consumer.* It may be possible that there is no value for $wx1$, $wx2$, nor $wx3$ that can exercise some path, in that case no test case will be generated for that path. In this example, since $T1$ only produces 1, 2, or 3, for x of which the initial value is 0, the true path in $T2$ can never be exercised. In contrast, if the consumer was unit tested alone, then this path would be exercised by assigning some value to x, even though that value could never be produced by the producer. This may result in some undesirable result, and thus be classified as a bug, but it would be a false positive as this path cannot be exercised in the full system context. This is the key value of this integrated testing procedure. *Note also that the service function aspect of the transactions was key to enable the characterization of the transaction interaction pattern as stateless producer consumer, which was critical to completely capture the space of shared values needed for the test case generation.*

General Algorithm: Code 1.6 is the general algorithm for generating test cases of stateless consumer transaction with multiple producer transactions. Here, T_1 is the target firmware transaction, and $T_2, \ldots, T_n$ are the producer transactions of T_1 where each transaction is instrumented as explained in the previous section. v_{ijk} represents the k-th variable among the shared variables produced by T_i and consumed by T_j. We use fresh variables for multiple readings on the same variable, i.e., rv_{ijk1} and rv_{ijk2} are multiple readings (r stands for read) on v_{ijk}. In contrast, we gather only one value of v_{ijk} written by T_i for multiple times during an instance, and save into wv_{ijk}. Note that we assume that static analysis of the data dependence graph is already able to determine the interaction patterns. For example, nw_{ijk}, the total number of writes on v_{ijk} in all paths of its producer T_i, or $read\_len_{ijk}$, how many times v_{ijk} is read during an instance of its consumer, are given. Lines 2-5 in the Code 1.6 runs all transactions including T_1 and its producers. Each runs as many times as the maximum number of writes on its shared variables. This forces generating of all possible write values since KLEE tries to assign different values as much as possible for the wv_{ijkx} of each instance (x represents each instance). Lines 7-8 decide among multiple reads from the same variable v_{ijk} during an instance, how many read from its initial states, not from its producer. Lines 9-11 force the variables to have the corresponding initial values as decided. Line 10 drives KLEE to generate results only satisfying desired conditions by killing the cases satisfying the negative conditions. The rest of the code matches values of all rv_{ijk} and wv_{jik}. A fresh variable rv_{ijklx} can read from any values of wv_{jikx} generated from all producer instances. *This algorithm forms the template which can be automatically instantiated with specific instances.* To automate the algorithm, tracking accesses to the shared variables in both producer and consumer code and instrumenting the code to store the set of values are needed. To sum up, the algorithm executes the producer transactions as many times as they can generate all possible values for the shared variables thus the target transaction can consume these values where each case corresponds to a feasible path. This algorithm guarantees the complete coverage of the consumer since it collects all values of shared variables written by the producers. Also, the testing result is sound since we constrain the consumer with only realizable

```
 1  testGenerator(T₁,...,Tₙ){
 2   for each Tᵢ where 1 ≤ i ≤ n{
 3    for(x=0; x < max(nwᵢⱼₖ∀j,k); x++)
 4     Tᵢ(...&wvᵢⱼₖₓ,...&rvⱼᵢₖₗₓ,...);//The index x represents the particular
         instance
 5   }
 6   for each rvᵢⱼₖ{
 7    klee_make_symbolic(&num_st_ijkx);
 8    klee_assume(0 ≤ num_st_ijkx ≤ read_lenᵢⱼₖₓ);
 9    for(l = 0;l < read_lenᵢⱼₖₓ;l++){
10     if(rvᵢⱼₖₗₓ ≠ INITᵢⱼₖ)klee_silent_exit(0);//INITᵢⱼₖ is the initial value of
         vᵢⱼₖ
11    }
12    for(l = num_st_ijkx; j < read_lenᵢⱼₖₓ;j + +){
13     if(rvᵢⱼₖₗₓ ≠ wvⱼᵢₖ_1 &&rvᵢⱼₖₗₓ ≠ wvⱼᵢₖ_2 && ... rvᵢⱼₖₗₓ ≠ wvⱼᵢₖ_max(nwⱼᵢₖ∀j,k))
          klee_silent_exit(0);
14    }
15   }
16  }
```

Code 1.6. Test Generator Algorithm

values from the producers. Lastly, in case only a subset of the interaction patterns among transactions are the stateless producer-consumer relationship, this algorithm can be used to partially test the system.

Limitations: This paper focuses on the stateless-producer-consumer pattern as this is the most common. The procedure presented here will need to be extended to other interaction patterns. We expect to add complexity as it will require exploring some transaction interleavings and unrollings. Further, determining the interaction patterns and the set of readers and writers in the interacting transactions required data dependence analysis. While this is a well studied area, practical data dependence is often not complete due to incomplete alias analysis. Another limitation lies on the manual instrumentation process. For our Rockbox study we were able to analyze data dependence manually. This needs to be replaced by coupling with an automated analysis in a compiler framework such as LLVM [22].

4.3 Experimental Results

We applied the proposed procedure to the set of the producer-consumer stateless transactions listed in Table 1b. For fair experiments, we only tried to extract a unit of work, or a transaction, from Rockbox but did not change its code and functionality. (In this work, the physical input values such as physical battery value are made symbolic. Also, since KLEE only allows C input, we made a C version of the Rockbox transactions.) For comparison, we performed unit testing using KLEE on the consumer transaction by itself first. For instance, unit testing of the Power transaction in Table 2 resulted in 800 test cases. For unit testing, initial values of the inputs and the shared/local storages were made as symbolic. Next, we performed the testing with the producer transactions. The Power transaction has three producer transactions; three shared storages constrained randomly in the unit testing are now to be constrained by the producers. We gradually introduced the producers one by one to see the effect of introducing these. For example,

Table 2. Test cases of Rockbox transactions

Consumer	LOC (Original/ Instrumented)	# of test cases of unit testing	Run time (sec)	# of symbolic variables	Producer	LOC (Original/ Instrumented)	# of test cases with the producers	Run time (sec)	# of symbolic variables
Power	973/991	800	302.56	8	Battery level	89/105	404	241.00	4
					Charger status	129/141	404	252.71	2
					USB	807/824	128	39.82	3
USB	807/821	18	1.86	6	USB detect	21/30	14	1.97	1
					Backlight	1003/1017			3
ATA	1538/1568	14	1.78	7	ATA transfer	226/243	19	2.36	3

we tested the power transaction only with the battery level transaction first while still making the shared variables with charger status and USB transaction symbolic. As a result, we got 404 cases. Next, we tested the power transaction (consumer) and the two producers, battery level and charger status, together and got the same 404 cases. Finally, we tested with all three of the producers and got 128 cases. By adding the producers, the test cases decrease since the producers restrict the possible values of shared storages more accurately than how the concolic testing tool constrained them during unit testing. For ATA, the number of test cases increased slightly when we tested with the producer transaction. This is because some of the values written by the producer are read multiple times along the same path in the consumer. With the producer, these values can be distinct. However, when unit-testing with KLEE alone, they will all be the same as KLEE does not consider the volatility of the shared variable. Thus, in this case, integrating the producer and the consumer during test generation provides for increased coverage.

5   Related Work

Firmware: Recently, many works have emphasized the importance of the high-level specification modeling of firmware and hardware for their concurrent development. Jerraya et al. [23] introduced high level programming model for HW/SW interface, and Heinen [24] et al. introduced formal specification of the HW/FW interface for consistency in system verification.

Transaction Level Models: There are a variety of notions of transactions used in hardware/software modeling. Among the earliest uses is in the context of databases where a transaction is an atomic execution of operations accessing a shared database [25]. In the hardware modeling context, Ghenassia [3] defined a transaction as data exchange between modules at the high level, replacing low-level signals or buses to raise the design abstraction level. Cornet [26] enriched [3] by adding a novel synchronization principle and a micro-architecture level TLM with timing. Many TLM models used SystemC OSCI [27], the SystemC library allowing standard TLM modeling. Perhaps closest in spirit to our TLM is the micro-architecture level TLM by Mahajan et al. [4] where a transaction is a unit of work performing data computation with clearly defined functionality. This shares the explicit start and end characteristics of our service function based TLM. However, their model is suitable for hardware rather than firmware/software as their detailed semantics match the underlying hardware components.

Testing Concurrent Programs: Testing concurrent programs is difficult due to the large space of interleavings. Previous works [28] [29] have used POR to cover complete interleavings of asynchronous SystemC models. SCOOT [28] used the commutativity of transitions between processors to reduce unnecessary interleaving in SystemC. Edelstein et al. [30] used a heuristic to increase the probability of observing race conditions by injecting seeded delays instead of exploring all interleaving. In contrast, our work directly uses the interaction patterns to add constraints to a single threaded concolic testing program to capture the effect of all interleavings. Also related is the work on formal verification of device drivers [31,32] but beyond the testing focus of this work.

Concolic Testing for Concurrent Programs: There has been some work in extending concolic testing to support concurrent programs. Sen et al. [20] combined POR with concolic testing to reduce all redundant paths which result in the same states. Rungta et al. [19] takes possible error states of the target concurrent system as an input, and uses guided symbolic execution to check reachability of the error states with continuous refinements. In contrast our work directly uses the interaction patterns to add constraints to a single threaded concolic testing program to capture the effect of all interleavings.

6   Conclusions and Future Work

Validating firmware poses several key challenges: (1) it is inherently hard to validate due to the higher complexity of software verification relative to hardware verification, (2) it inherently executes concurrently with hardware modules that it interacts with and this concurrency adds additional complexity to the validation task, and (3) the firmware and hardware have inherently different computation models, and thus their concurrent validation needs unified models for these heterogenous components. In this work we address these challenges by developing a novel TLM for modeling both the firmware and hardware components where the transactions correspond to service functions. We show how this notion of service functions naturally captures typical firmware-hardware interactions. Further, we show how this model allows for analyzing the interaction patterns between different transactions. Among the different interaction patterns, we observe that the stateless producer-consumer interaction pattern is most common. We then show how single threaded concolic testing generation tools such as KLEE can be used to generate tests for firmware with this interaction pattern. This test generation can potentially generate a complete test set with no false positives. We demonstrate the applicability of this modeling and testing methodology through a non-trivial practical case study of the Rockbox MP3 player. We model 3 hardware and 6 firmware transactions, characterize their interaction patterns, and generate complete test cases for the 6 pairs that have the stateless producer-consumer interaction pattern.

While the test generation part of this paper focused on the stateless producer-consumer case, it underlines a broader principle that can be brought to bear to simplify test generation for concurrent execution. The main idea exploited here is the higher level information captured by the service function transaction model which enabled static code analysis to determine the various interaction patterns. The next step in this research is to explore the cases that, unlike the clean stateless producer consumer case, require exploration of transaction unrolling and interleaving. We suspect that further analysis of the data-dependences for these cases can help bound the unrolling/interleavings needed.

References

1. Straunstrup, J., Andersen, H., Hulgaard, H., Lind-Nielsen, J., Behrmann, G., Kristoffersen, K., Skou, A., Leerberg, H., Theilgaard, N.: Practical verification of embedded software. Computer 33(5), 68–75 (2000)
2. Cai, L., Gajski, D.: Transaction level modeling: an overview. In: Proceedings of the Int. Conference on HW/SW Codesign and System Synthesis, pp. 19–24. ACM (2003)
3. Ghenassia, F.: Transaction-level modeling with SystemC: TLM concepts and applications for embedded systems (2005)
4. Mahajan, Y., Chan, C., Bayazit, A., Malik, S., Qin, W.: Verification driven formal architecture and microarchitecture modeling. In: IEEE/ACM MEMOCODE, pp. 123–132 (2007)
5. Majumdar, R., Sen, K.: Hybrid concolic testing. In: 29th International Conference on Software Engineering, ICSE 2007, pp. 416–426 (2007)
6. Cadar, C., Dunbar, D., Engler, D.: KLEE: Unassisted and automatic generation of high-coverage tests for complex systems programs. In: Proceedings of the 8th USENIX Conference on Operating Systems Design and Implementation, pp. 209–224 (2008)
7. Godefroid, P., Klarlund, N., Sen, K.: DART: directed automated random testing. ACM Sigplan Notices 40, 213–223 (2005)
8. Rockbox - Free Music Player Firmware, http://www.rockbox.org
9. http://www.rockbox.org/wiki/pub/Main/DataSheets/pcf50606.pdf
10. http://www.rockbox.org/wiki/IaudioX5HardwareComponent
11. Vahid, F., Wiley, J.: Digital design. Wiley (2006)
12. Kuck, D.L.: Structure of Computers and Computations. John Wiley & Sons, Inc. (1978)
13. http://www.rockbox.org/wiki/pub/Main/DataSheets/CY7C68310.pdf
14. Corbet, J., Rubini, A., Kroah-Hartman, G.: Linux device drivers. O'reilly (2009)
15. Bellard, F.: Qemu, a fast and portable dynamic translator. In: USENIX Annual Technical Conference, FREENIX Track, pp. 41–46 (2005)
16. King, J.: Symbolic execution and program testing. CACM 19(7), 385–394 (1976)
17. Qu, X., Robinson, B.: A case study of concolic testing tools and their limitations. In: International Symposium on ESEM, pp. 117–126. IEEE (2011)
18. Sen, K., Agha, G.: CUTE and jCUTE: Concolic unit testing and explicit path model-checking tools. In: Ball, T., Jones, R.B. (eds.) CAV 2006. LNCS, vol. 4144, pp. 419–423. Springer, Heidelberg (2006)
19. Rungta, N., Mercer, E.G., Visser, W.: Efficient testing of concurrent programs with abstraction-guided symbolic execution. In: Păsăreanu, C.S. (ed.) SPIN 2009. LNCS, vol. 5578, pp. 174–191. Springer, Heidelberg (2009)
20. Sen, K., Agha, G.: A race-detection and flipping algorithm for automated testing of multi-threaded programs. In: Bin, E., Ziv, A., Ur, S. (eds.) HVC 2006. LNCS, vol. 4383, pp. 166–182. Springer, Heidelberg (2007)
21. Godefroid, P., van Leeuwen, J., Hartmanis, J., Goos, G., Wolper, P.: Partial-order methods for the verification of concurrent systems: An approach to the state-explosion problem. LNCS, vol. 1032. Springer, Heidelberg (1996)
22. Lattner, C., Adve, V.: LLVM: a compilation framework for lifelong program analysis transformation. In: International Symposium on Code Generation and Optimization, pp. 75–86 (2004)

23. Jerraya, A.A., Bouchhima, A., Pétrot, F.: Programming models and hw-sw interfaces abstraction for multi-processor soc. In: Proceedings of DAC, pp. 280–285. ACM (2006)
24. Heinen, S., Joost, M.: Firmware development for evolving digital communication technologies. In: Hardware-dependent Software, pp. 151–171. Springer (2009)
25. Bernstein, P.A., Hadzilacos, V., Goodman, N.: Concurrency control and recovery in database systems, vol. 370. Addison-wesley New York (1987)
26. Cornet, J.: Separation of functional and non-functional aspects in transactional level models of systems-on-chip. Grenoble INP Group, PhD thesis (2008)
27. Rose, A., Swan, S., Pierce, J., Fernandez, J.M., et al.: Transaction level modeling in systemc. Open SystemC Initiative 1(1.297) (2005)
28. Blanc, N., Kroening, D.: Race analysis for SystemC using model checking. ACM Transactions on Design Automation of Electronic Systems (TODAES) 15(3), 21 (2010)
29. Helmstetter, C., Maraninchi, F., Maillet-Contoz, L.: Full simulation coverage for SystemC transaction-level models of systems-on-a-chip. Form. Methods in Systs. Des. 35(2) (2009)
30. Edelstein, O., Farchi, E., Nir, Y., Ratsaby, G., Ur, S.: Multithreaded java program test generation. IBM Systems Journal 41(1), 111–125 (2002)
31. Ball, T., Cook, B., Levin, V., Rajamani, S.K.: SLAM and static driver verifier: Technology transfer of formal methods inside microsoft. In: Boiten, E.A., Derrick, J., Smith, G.P. (eds.) IFM 2004. LNCS, vol. 2999, pp. 1–20. Springer, Heidelberg (2004)
32. Qadeer, S., Wu, D.: KISS: keep it simple and sequential. ACM SIGPLAN Notices 39 (2004)

Symbolic Model-Based Testing
for Industrial Automation Software

Sabrina von Styp[1] and Liyong Yu[2]

[1] Software Modeling and Verification
Department of Computer Science
[2] Chair of Process Control Engineering
RWTH Aachen University Germany

Abstract. In industrial automation software controls systems whose failure can be critical and expensive. Testing this software is very crucial but so far done manually, an expensive and not very thorough method. Model-based testing is an emerging concept in computer science for automatically testing a real implementation. It uses a formal specification describing the system behaviour. This specification is the blue print against which an implementation is tested. This paper presents how to use model-based testing in industrial automation. In detail it shows how the known concepts such as sequential function charts, used in industrial automation to describe a system, can be translated to a format that is required for model-based testing, including an automatic derivation of test-cases and its execution. A concrete case study illustrates the strength of this approach.

1 Introduction

Software testing is crucial especially for safety critical systems such as controllers in industrial automation. Unexpected execution results can be caused by semantical inconsistencies among requirements defined by function designers, comprehension on part of human programmers, and runtime characteristics of hardware. Considering the last aspect, automation functions are generally implemented on Programmable Logic Controllers (PLCs) or PLC-based Decentralised Control Systems (DCSs). PLC programs are characterised by their cyclic execution. Single PLC programs are cyclically executed without supporting multitasking, meaning that components of a program (e.g. steps and transitions of the same procedure) are not executed simultaneously, but sequentially. As a result, execution results can be influenced by scheduling of program parts, for instance function blocks within a function block network, actions of procedure step, steps and transitions of a procedure. Discussions with more details can be found in [3],[11] and [29]. PLCs and DCSs often control plants whose failure can be expensive and dangerous. Thorough testing therefore is crucial but also time consuming and expensive.

One attractive method to automate the test process, and therefore reduce time and cost, is *model-based testing* [6]. Model-based testing is a so-called black

V. Bertacco and A. Legay (Eds.): HVC 2013, LNCS 8244, pp. 78–94, 2013.

box testing technique, which automatically derives the test-cases from a formal specification describing the desired behaviour of the implementation under test (IUT). These test-cases are then executed against the real IUT by stimulating the IUT and observing its output. The underlying notion of correctness of an implementation, with respect to its specification, allows to show that testing can not yield false alarms.

One well-known theory for model-based testing is the *ioco framework* [26], where the specification is given as a labelled transition system (LTS) with input and output actions. The conformance relation, called *ioco*, describes that after a trace an implementation may only produce outputs or be silent if the same outputs or silence are also produced by its specification. Several tools exist for the derivation of *ioco* test-cases, e.g. JTorX [5], AGEDIS TOOLSET [10] and TGV [18]. The disadvantage of using an LTS as a specification is the state space explosion that occurs when using variables with larger domains, i.e. integers. To avoid this problem, the *sioco* framework [7,8], using symbolic transition systems (STS) as specification, has been developed. STSs allow a symbolic representation of data as well as a data dependent control flow, and therefore avoid the problem of infinite branching and infinite state space. The notion of symbolic testing has been implemented in the test tool JTorX [5].

There exists two approaches [16,17] to apply model-based testing in industrial automation engineering. Both approaches use the modelling language UML and only work for special application cases. Even though symbolic model-based testing has been successfully applied in many areas, to the best of our knowledge it never has been used in industrial automation engineering using sequential functional charts (SFCs), a well-known formalism which formally describes the steps a system can execute and under which circumstances it has to change into a different step. Bauer et al. [2] have successfully applied formal verification, precisely model-checking, in industrial automation. They used SFC as modelling language and provided a translation from SFCs to timed automata and used the tool UPPAAL [27] for model checking. Their approach can be used to verify the correctness of the provided formal specification, but does not verify if the real implementation is correct to its specification. For model-based testing only observable in- and outputs are of interest and therefore the approach of [2] is not suitable for model-based testing. There is also no notion of handling variables symbolically, leading to the state space explosion problem when handling variables domains such as reals or integers. To circumvent this problem Bornot et al. [4] used symbolic modelling verification [19] for applying model-checking on SFC. Their work also considers internal behaviour of the SFC and is therefore not suitable for model-based testing. Hence, we provide a new translation from SFCs to symbolic transition systems, where only observable behaviour is considered. In previous work [25], a translation of SFC to LTS has been introduced. This approach encounters a state space explosion when testing larger variable domains. To circumvent this state space explosion this paper provides a translation from SFC to STS and presents two case studies, showing how to do model-based testing with the *sioco* framework in industrial automation. The case studies demonstrate that real errors such as an imprecision in representing floats can be found by our approach. The first case study of this paper was inspired by previous work [25].

First, this paper gives an introduction on functional description methods in industrial automation. Then the underlying theory of the *sioco* framework is introduced. Section four presents the translation of *SFC* to *STS*. Section five describes the environment used for the case studies. Section six presents two case studies and demonstrates how to apply the introduced concept in practice. Finally, the paper is concluded in the last section.

2   Sequential Function Charts as Functional Description

The clear description of requested functions, especially the internal discrete logic (e.g. state machines and sequential procedures), is a logical prerequisite to the test of PLC-implementations. In todays industrial automation, there still exists no standardised description method. Discrete logics on PLCs can be described in various forms, for instance in Petri nets, UML/Statecharts or Procedure Function Charts (PFCs)[14]. Although existing methods with different expressive power can well represent functions in specific application domains, most of them do not consider execution semantics on PLCs. In order to ensure a consistent implementation, many automatic code generators have been presented in a series of research works. However, mapping rules that have been taken are usually developer-specific, and are often only suitable for hardware from certain vendors.

In the landscape of description methods for discrete logics, SFC is an approach that provides standardised graphical description and vendor-neutral implementation technique at the same time. *SFC* follows the specification language *GRAFCET* [12], which is based on Petri nets. *SFC* is proven to have the potential of being developed to a general description method [29][28].

Sequential functions of any complexity can be precisely described by simple graphical elements: steps and transitions between steps. All *SFC*s begin with an initial step (marked with a double boundary line), and they can either end with a final step or jump back to a previous step at the end of the chain. The former design is normally used to describe chemical production procedures, which only need to be worked through once. In turn, the latter one can describe a permanently active state machine. A discrete function described in SFC language can be directly implemented in a PLC. However, there are also systems that do not support graphical *SFC* programming, or whose implementation should not be programmed in *SFC*. For instance, the function block for a single motor controller discussed later in this paper is coded in most automation systems by using a textual programming language. Nevertheless in these cases, the internal execution progress and state machines of the encapsulated function block can also be intuitively and exactly described by using *SFC*. In this way, the programming engineer can exactly understand requirements given by the designer with the help of the *SFC* graphic; on the other hand, if an existing implementation needs to be optimised, its *SFC* description can help the engineer to understand the working principle and define solutions. In this paper, we show how *SFC* descriptions can also be used for automatic testing by automatically deriving and executing test-cases from them.

As a programming language, specifications of SFC in IEC 61131-3 [13] are not suitable to be directly applied as a description language. Improving SFC is part of a further research work [29], which intends to develop a general description method for discrete functions in a wide range of automation domains. For this paper, we consider a simplified SFC with the following features:

- Inspired by UML/Statechart, only three alternative action qualifiers for controlling action occurrences are applied: $P1$, N and $P0$. Their semantics correspond respectively to entry, do and exit.
- Actions of the same steps are executed sequentially from top to bottom (cf. the example SFC in Figure 9).
- Simultaneous sequences are not allowed. Only one step can be activated, and it represents the overall execution progress of the *SFC*.
- Only one alternative sequence can be chosen (compare Figure 9). In case of branching, transitions are evaluated from left to right.
- The SFC precedes its execution by the sequence in which the transition is evaluated as switchable at first.

3   Testing with Symbolic Transition Systems

Model-based testing is a well known technique for automatically generating test-cases and its execution. It is based on a conformance relation, e.g *ioco* [26] for labelled transition systems and *sioco* [7,8] for symbolic transition systems (*STS*), which formally defines when an implementation is correct with respect to a given specification. For the conformance relation it is assumed that the real *IUT* could theoretically be described by a transition system, see Figure 1.

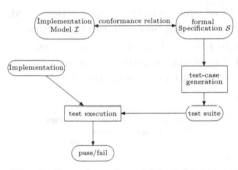

The conformance relation formally describes when an implementation is correct with respect to its specification. The ioco-relation basically requires that an implementation may only produce an output if the specification can produce the same output after executing the same trace. Based on this, the test-cases can automatically be generated from the specification and build a so-called test suite. These test-cases are used to test the

Fig. 1. Overview of model-based testing

real *IUT*. The verdict is either fail together with a trace leading to the error, or pass, provided the state space is finite. In case of an infinite state space, which mostly is the case, the implementation is tested until an error is found. Although this procedure is not complete, the advantage of model-based testing over manual testing is, that the implementation can be tested without any human interaction. After the execution of a certain amount of test-cases it could also be considered to test a copy of the implementation in the background while already using the implementation, to find additional errors.

Most controllers in industrial automation use variables of large, or even infinite domains such as integer or real numbers. In order to allow these variable domains and a data control flow without state space explosion, symbolic testing is indispensable. For symbolic model-based testing, symbolic transition systems (*STS*s) are used. *STS*s introduced by Frantzen et al. [7,8], are labelled transition systems extended with *in- and output gates* omitting interaction variables, *guards* over variables mostly written in first-order-logic (FO-logic) and *variable updates*, which manipulate the values of variables while performing transitions.

3.1 Symbolic Transition System

A symbolic transition system consists of locations including a initial location, interaction variables, location variables, in- and output gates containing interaction variables and an edge relation. Interaction variables are used in in- and output gates to transmit values. Location variables are internal variables and can be used to store the value of interaction variables, which can be edited from outside the system.

Definition 1 (Symbolic Transition System). *A symbolic transition system STS is a tuple $\mathcal{S} = (L, l_0, \mathcal{V}, \mathcal{I}, \mathcal{G}, \rightarrow)$, where*

- *L is a finite set of locations where $l_0 \in L$ is the initial location*
- *$\mathcal{V}$ is a finite set of location variables*
- *$\mathcal{I}$ is a finite set of interaction variables, where $\mathcal{I} \cup \mathcal{V} = Var$ and $\mathcal{I} \cap \mathcal{V} = \emptyset$*
- *$\mathcal{G} = \mathcal{G}_{out} \cup \mathcal{G}_{in}$ is a finite set of gates, where every gate has a tuple of interaction variables of certain length. $\mathcal{G}_{out}$ is the set of output and $\mathcal{G}_{in}$ the set of input gates, where $\mathcal{G}_{out} \cap \mathcal{G}_{in} = \emptyset$;*
- *$\rightarrow \subseteq L \times \mathcal{G} \times \mathfrak{F}(\mathcal{V}) \times \bigcup_{V \subseteq \mathcal{V}} \mathfrak{T}(Var)^V \times L$ is the edge relation.*

The notation $\mathfrak{F}(Var)$ denotes the set of FO-formulas over all interaction- and location variables. $\mathfrak{T}(Var)^V$ denotes the set of mappings of interaction variable to variables of Var. As usual we write $l \xrightarrow{g, \varphi, \rho} l'$ to denote an element of $(l, g, \varphi, \rho, l') \in \rightarrow$, where g is a gate with interaction variables, φ a guard over variables and ρ a mapping of interaction variables to location variables.

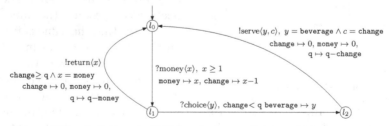

Fig. 2. A sample STS-beverage-vending-machine

Example 1. *Figure 2 shows an STS with the locations l_0, l_1, l_2 modelling a beverage vending machine. The machine expects money in bills (parameter x of input ?money), a choice for a beverage and returns change (parameter c of* *output* !serve*). If there is not enough change in the machine on a bill, the bill is returned (output* !return*). Otherwise, the user can choose a beverage for the cost of one unit, the change is returned and the beverage served (parameter y of output* !serve*). Parameters* x, y, c *are so-called* interaction variables. *Variables* q, change, beverage, money *are so-called* location variables. *Interaction variables represent the possible values that can be passed during input and output.*

The symbolic trace semantics is defined by Frantzen *et al.* [8] and expressed by transition relation $l \xrightarrow{\sigma,\varphi,\rho} l'$ where σ is a sequence of gates that are executed on the trace from l to l', φ is a conjunction of constraints over variables that need to be satisfied to reach location l', and ρ is a concatenation of variable mappings denoting the possible variable valuation after l' has been reached. Frantzen *et al.* [8] also define a conformance relation *sioco* describing when an implementation is correct to a specification. The conformance relation is based on *ioco*, introduced by Tretmans [26], and describes that an implementation can only produce an output, after executing a trace σ, if the specification can produce the same output after executing σ. Quiescence of the implementation is only allowed if the specification is also quiescent after executing the same trace. Going into further details would go beyond the scope of this paper and we refer to Frantzen *et al.* [8] for more details.

3.2 Testing with JTorX

The test-tool JTorX [5] is a platform-independent tool for model-based testing. It automatically derives test-cases from a given specification using the *sioco* relation. It therefore considers the traces in the specification and instantiates the input variables with concrete values regarding to the corresponding guard. Outputs are verified by checking if the output gate can also be mimicked by the specification and if the variable values satisfy the corresponding guard.

The specification of the program is provided to JTorX in XML format. In order to communicate with the *IUT*, JTorX supports standard input and output as well as the network protocol TCP/IP. JTorX requires these inputs and outputs to have the same format as the one given by the specification. Therefore, it is common to provide an adaptor that coordinates the different input and output formats. The test-case generation in JTorX happens on-the-fly, meaning that test-case generation and execution are done at the same time. Only the next steps that are needed are computed, and the information, which has already been traced, is stored in a log file and can be executed again if requested later. For modelling the *STS*, JTorX uses the *STSimulater*-framework [22].

4 Translation of *SFC* to *STS*

The previous section shows that for model-based testing with data the specification has to be a symbolic transition system. However, in industrial automation *SFC*s are used to formally describe the system behaviour. Therefore, this section addresses the translation of *SFC*s into *STS*s. Since model-based testing is a form of black-box testing, the translation only focuses on observable actions, such as inputs and outputs. In an *SFC*, variables are changed by the system when executing a step, while requirements for a transition are usually changed by some external components. As the transitions control which step is executed, and therefore how variables change, the variables enabling the transition are considered as input variables and the variables changed by the implementation, when executing a step, are considered as output variables. In theory it is possible that variables can be used for input and for output, as allowed in the following theory, but in practice it might be necessary to prohibit this.

4.1 Formal Description of *SFC*

In order to provide a translation from *SFC* to *STS* we first give a formal definition of *SFC*. As only observable actions are of interest, the definition is restricted to those. An *SFC* has a set of steps that can be executed and end with a set of observable variable configurations. The execution of an *SFC* is cyclic. This means every step and therefore all actions in one step are executed within one cycle. At the end of every cycle it is checked if one of the following transitions is enabled. Subsequently, the transition which is satisfied is taken and its successor step executed in the next cycle. In case more than one transition is enabled, the one with the highest order, the left most in a drawn graph, is taken.

Definition 2 (Sequential Function Charts). *A Sequential Function Chart (SFC) is a tuple $\mathcal{S} = (S, T, \mathcal{X}, \mathcal{Y}, \mathcal{R}, \rightarrow_{SFC})$ where:*
- *S is a finite set of steps containing actions, e.g., set variables, over output variables*
- *T is a finite set of transitions containing FO-formulas over input variables as guards*
- *$\mathcal{Y}$ is a finite set of output variables and $\mathcal{X}$ is a finite set of input variables*
- *$\mathcal{R} \subseteq T \times T$ is a total ordering on the set T.*
- *$\rightarrow \subseteq S \times T \times S$ an edge relation*

In a step s_k, variables $y_{k1}, \ldots, y_{kn}$ are set to certain values. Such a setting is of the form $y_{ij} := a \oplus b$, where $\oplus \in \{*, -, +, /\}$ and $a, b \in \mathcal{X} \cup \mathbb{R}$. The execution of a step s is repeated until a following transition t is enabled, written as $t \in en(s)$. A transition t_l has conditions $c_{l1}, \ldots, c_{lm}$ over input variables $x_{l1}, \ldots, x_{lp}$. They are concatenated by disjunctions or conjunctions, where c_{ij} is of the form $a \otimes b$ with $\otimes \in \{<, >, \leq, \geq, =\}$ and a, b being arithmetic expression over the set $\mathcal{X} \cup \mathbb{R}$. If more than one transition is enabled, transition t with the highest order wrt. $\prec$, written as $\forall_{t' \in T, t \neq t'} en(t') : t' \prec t \wedge en(t)$, is taken.

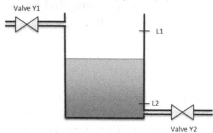

Valve Y1

L1

L2

Valve Y2

Fig. 3. Tank System

We write **trans**(s) to denote all transitions that can be enabled after step s. Let us consider a simple example. Figure 3 shows a tank system for some fluid. The input can be controlled by valve Y1 and the output by valve Y2. Is the fluid level above sensor L1, the value of L1 is true. The same holds for sensor L2 if the fluid level is below L2.

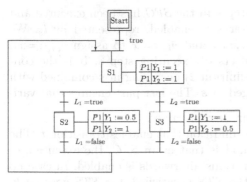

Fig. 4. SFC of tank system

Figure 4 shows the *SFC* of the controller for the tank system. The steps of this *SFC* are $S1, \ldots, S3$ and the transitions are the conditions between the steps, e.g. $L_1 =$ true. On the right side of every step the boxes describe the actions that are executed if the step is active, e.g. in step $S3$ the variables $Y_1 := 1$ and $Y_2 := 0.5$ are set. $P1$ in front of the actions stands for exactly one execution of the following action, see also Section 2. In the beginning both valves are 100% open. In case the fluid level is above $L1$ valve Y_1 is set to 50% and valve Y_2 to 100%. Is the fluid level to low and $L2$ is true, step $S3$ is executed.

4.2 From *SFC* to *STS*

The formal definition of an *SFC* now allows to define the translation to an *STS*. The idea is to consider the variables of a step as outputs and the ones at the transitions as input, as they allow to control the flow of the system. In an *SFC* every step is followed by at least one transition. This yields that in the *STS* every output is followed by one input, representing all possible inputs. Executing a step more than once can be accomplished if the input does not enable any guard of edges representing next steps. The only guard that then is enabled is the guard of the edge representing the previous output. Inputs have no guards, since the input values are usually changed by some external events and cannot be controlled. Every input action is followed by at least one output action. Every output action has a guard making sure the correct previous transition has been enabled before and the variable output is correct. An *STS* $\mathcal{T} = (L, l_0, \mathcal{V}, \mathcal{I}, \mathcal{G}, \to)$ obtained from an *SFC* $\mathcal{S} = (S, T, \mathcal{X}, \mathcal{Y}, \mathcal{R}, \to_{SFC})$ is defined as follows:

- $L = \{l_s | s \in S\} \cup \{\hat{l}_s | s \in S\}$ set of locations with initial location l_0, representing the edges between location and steps of the *SFC*
- $\mathcal{V}$ location variables
- $\mathcal{I} = \mathcal{X} \cup \mathcal{Y}$ interaction variables
- $\mathcal{G}$ set of in- and output gates containing interaction variables
- $\to$ a edge relation where every $s \xrightarrow{t}_{SFC} s'$ induces
  1. $l_s \xrightarrow{g, true, \rho} \hat{l}_s \xrightarrow{g', \varphi', \rho'} l_{s'}$ where
     - $g = ?in\langle \overline{x} \rangle$,
     - $\rho = (\overline{v}_{in} := \overline{x})$,
     - $g' = ?out\langle \overline{y} \rangle$,
     - $\varphi' = (\bigwedge_{t \in en(s), t \prec t'} \neg F(t')) \wedge F(t) \wedge F(s)$ and
     - $\rho' = (\overline{v}_{out} := \overline{y})$
  2. $\hat{l}_s \xrightarrow{g', \varphi'', \rho'} l_s$, where $\varphi'' = (\bigwedge_{t \in \mathbf{trans}(s)} \neg F(t)) \wedge F(s)$

The location l_s represents that the step s in the SFC has been executed and next it is checked which transition after s is enabled, represented by $\hat{l}_s$. We write $\overline{x}$ to denote the vector $\overline{x} = x_1, \ldots, x_n$ and $\overline{v}_{in} := \overline{x}$ to assign $v_{in_i} := x_i$. The FO-formula $F(s)$ describes the effects of executing step s. It is the conjunction of all variable settings (see Definition 2) occurring in s combined with $\bigwedge_{1 < i \leq n} y_i == v_{out_i}$ where y_i is not changed in s. The last part ensures that variables that are not changed, remain their current values.

The FO-formula $F(t)$ represents the condition that enables transition t. The second clause in the definition above models that in an SFC, the execution of a step is repeated until one of the transitions afterwards is enabled. In case no condition for the next output edge in the STS is satisfied, the STS goes back, with the same output as before, to location s.

Example 2.

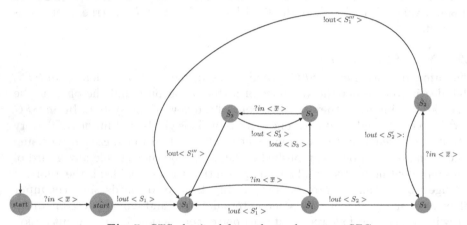

Fig. 5. STS obtained from the tank system SFC

$?in < \overline{x} >:\quad ?in< x_1, x_2 >, l_{x_1} = x_1, l_{x_2} = x_2$

$!out < S_1 >:\quad !out< y_1, y_2 >, y_1 == 1 \wedge y_2 == 1, l_{y_1} = y_1, l_{y_2} = y_2$

$!out < S_1' >:\quad !out< y_1, y_2 >, y_1 == 1 \wedge y_2 == 1 \wedge \neg l_{x_1} == 1 \wedge \neg l_{x_2} == 1,$
$\qquad\qquad\quad l_{y_1} = y_1, l_{y_2} = Y_2$

$!out < S_2 >:\quad !out< y_1, y_2 >, l_{x_1} == 1 \wedge y_1 == 0.5 \wedge y_2 == 1,$
$\qquad\qquad\quad l_{y_1} = y_1, l_{y_2} = y_2$

$!out < S_3 >:\quad !out< y_1, y_2 >, \neg l_{x_1} == 1 \wedge l_{x_2} == 1 \wedge Y_1 == 0 \wedge Y_2 == 1, l_{y_1} = y_1, l_{y_2} = y_2$

$!out < S_2' >:\quad !out< Y_1, Y_2 >, l_{x_1} == 1 \wedge Y_1 == 0.5 \wedge Y_2 == 1, l_{Y_1} = Y_1, l_{Y_2} = Y_2$

$!out < S_3' >:\quad !out< Y_1, Y_2 >, l_{x_2} == 1 \wedge Y_1 == 0 \wedge Y_2 == 1, l_{Y_1} = Y_1, l_{Y_2} = Y_2$

$!out < S_1'' >:\quad !out< Y_1, Y_2 >, l_{x_1} == 0 \wedge Y_1 == 1 \wedge Y_2 == 1, l_{Y_1} = Y_1, l_{Y_2} = Y_2$

$!out < S_1''' >:\quad !out< Y_1, Y_2 >, l_{x_2} == 0 \wedge Y_1 == 1 \wedge Y_2 == 1, l_{Y_1} = Y_1, l_{Y_2} = Y_2$

Figure 5 shows the STS obtained from the SFC in Figure 4. The edge from $start$ to $st\hat{a}rt$ is an input for enabling t_0, the first transition in the SFC. All input edges consist of a gate with the interaction variables x_1, x_2, standing for the level sensors. These variables are mapped to location variables l_{x_1} and l_{x_2}. All output edges have a gate with the variables y_1, y_2 for the valves, a guard and a mapping of interaction variables to location variables. The edge from $st\hat{a}rt$ to S_1 is the output, namely the observable result, of step S_1 in the SFC. S_1 to $\hat{S}_1$ is an input representing possible enabling of t_1 or t_2. If none of the guards, representing the transitions in the SFC, is enabled, output $!out < S_1' >$, leading back to location

S_1, has to be observed. This models the behaviour of the *SFC* repeating a step if no transition afterwards is enabled. If a transition t_1 or t_2 is enabled $!out < S_{2,3} >$, depending on the previously enabled transition, is executed. Is more than one transition enabled the one with the lower index is taken, as this is the transition order. After that output the system is in state S_2 or S_3 depending which $t_{1,2}$ has been enabled. Then a repetition of the execution of the state is possible if the transition afterwards is not enabled. This is modelled by the edge $!out < S_{2,3}' >$. Is the required edge constraint satisfied the output $!out < S_1'' >$ or $!out < S_1''' >$ can be observed. S_1'' and S_1''' both have a guard requiring the correct execution of step S_1 in the *SFC*, but their condition regarding the previously enabled edges differs as required by the *SFC*.

5   Case-Study Set-Up

The previous section described the usage of *SFC* as a formal description language and its translation to *STS*. This is presented in the upper part of Figure 6. The formal description, given as an *SFC*, describes the desired behaviour of the implementation. The implementation itself runs in an industrial operative environment (e.g. a runtime server on a PLC), and is cyclically executed with a predefinable and constant cycle time. Industrial communication protocols like OPC UA [15] and ACPLT/KS [1] allow standardised and system-neutral access (e.g. get and set of variables) to the current datas from external clients. The cyclic execution of the implementation can be controlled by a certain variable. It allows the general starting and stopping as well as exactly one cyclic execution. The feature of executing exactly one cycle is crucial for the test case execution.

The *STS* is obtained from the *SFC* before the testing process is started. It is then provided to JTorX [5], which uses it as a basis to generate test-cases. The adapter handles the communication between JTorX and the operative environment. It receives the input from JTorX, sets the corresponding variable values while the implementation is offline and executes the implementation exactly one cycle. When the implementation is offline again, the adapter gets the values of the variables and passes them on to JTorX, which interprets them as an output by the implementation.

5.1   Operative Environment

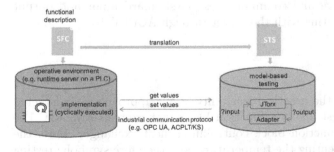

PLCs from different vendors often provide different software and hardware structure as well as execution behaviours. In order to develop a generic testing approach without dependence on specific

Fig. 6. Application Structure

execution platforms, we have applied a generic operative environment named ACPLT/OV [20]. ACPLT/OV is an open-source object management and run-time environment which permits the development of reference models and object-oriented applications that can be operated in real-time industrial automation. ACPLT/OV provides an object-oriented API for ANSI C, and allows a platform-independent evaluation of different models and execution behaviours. So far, an OV-server can be installed on industrial PCs supporting Linux and Windows and some micro controllers. An ACPLT/OV application is hosted on a server, which contains the executed program as well as object models. An OV-server can be directly applied as operative environment, but may also be set up on a conventional computer to act as an emulator of the industrial operative environment in prototyping tasks.

OV-servers offer an ACPLT/KS [1] interface for the information exchange with external servers and clients. ACPLT/KS is an open-source client/server communication protocol designed for decentralised control systems (DCS) and related applications. It uses object-oriented meta-modelling, where the predefined elements of the communication protocol (variables, domains, links, etc.) are generic, and can be used to manipulate virtually any concrete object model of a control system. ACPLT/KS clients have been developed in C++, Tcl/Tk, JavaScript and VB at present.

In our case study, every function that has to be implemented is programmed manually and encapsulated in a function block according to the IEC 61131-3 standard [13]. Internal logic of one function block is cyclically executed as far as the function block is activated (i.e. enabled). Information exchange with the environment is realised by input and output variables.

5.2   Client-Server Communication

The input and output vectors that are provided and observed – respectively – by JTorX, are given by the *SFC* specification. JTorX does not have a direct way of setting or getting variable values of the tested system, but the OV server provides the means to set and get these values exclusively through ACPLT/KS. Additionally, it has to be ensured that input variables are set at the right time on the server, and that JTorX always receives the current variable values, i.e. JTorX and the tested system have to be synchronised. This requires an adapter that sends and receives values in between JTorX and the server, and which also performs the required synchronisation by starting and stopping the IUT. The adapter is written in Java and communicates via standard input and output with JTorX, while interacting with the server through ACPLT/KS.

6   Case Studies

In order to demonstrate the practical feasibility of our approach we conducted two case studies. The first one is a function block that controls a motor. The second case study is a function block controlling a heat exchanger. Here, the variables are reals representing the temperature, and therefore symbolic testing is inevitable. For both case studies, the translation from PLCopen XML, an XML format for IEC 61131-3 languages [21] to .sax was done manually. A program for automatic translation is currently developed. For more detailed information about the case studies we refer to [23].

6.1 Case Study Motor

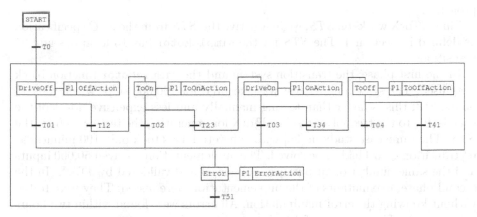

Fig. 7. SFC specification for the simpleMotor function block

For our case study, we chose a simple function block that controls an on/off motor with five steps. The function block has the following Boolean inputs: Con and Coff indicate that the motor should be switched on and off, respectively; CACK indicates that the user has acknowledged an error; and chkbOn indicates that the motor has confirmed that it has switched itself on, known as check back. In turn, the Boolean outputs are: ACT signals the motor to switch on (true) or off (false); DriveOn indicates that the motor is on; DriveOff indicates that the motor is off; and ERR indicates that an error has occurred.

The intended behaviour of the function block is described as follows. The motor is initially switched off, and the user may set Con to TRUE in order to start the motor. The function block then sets ACT to TRUE in order to switch the motor on, and waits for a confirmation signal with the value TRUE from the motor on chkbOn. If the confirmation signal arrives, the DriveOn indicator is set to TRUE and the function block stays in this state until the user sets Coff to TRUE in order to stop the motor. In this case, the function block sets ACT to FALSE in order to switch the motor off, and waits for a confirmation signal with the value FALSE from the motor on chkbOn. When this occurs, the function block returns to its initial state. In any case, an error state may be reached whenever an unexpected confirmation signal from the motor is received. In this case, the function block sets ERR to TRUE and stays in this state until the user acknowledges the error by setting CACK to TRUE, which clears the error indicator and returns to the function block's initial state.

The control logic for the simpleMotor function block has been specified by the SFC in Figure 7. Here, the steps DriveOff, ToOn, DriveOn, ToOff and Error represent the different states of the `simpleMotor` function block, and their corresponding actions set the function block outputs to the expected values. Furthermore, the transitions evaluate the conditions for a step change which depend on the function block inputs. Based on the *SFC* specification, the `simpleMotor` function block was implemented in C. In addition to this object class, five test classes were produced as exact copies of the original class, but with manually introduced errors, with the purpose of validating the model-based testing approach.

Since JTorX works on *STS*, we first derive the *STS* from the *SFC* specification as defined in Section 4. The *STS* for the `simpleMotor` has 13 locations and 21 transitions.

In the first phase, the transition system and the `simpleMotor` function block were used. The system under test was executed for 100,000 steps which took 13 hours. Still this is faster than testing manually and less expensive. Most of the time is due to the tree solver used in JTorX for generating the test-cases from the *STS*. The same case study in [25] with concrete labels took only 190 minutes as no transition guard had to be solved. The implementation received 50,000 inputs and the same number of outputs were observed and validated by JTorX. In the second phase, five mutants of the implementation were tested. They were tested without knowing the error manipulation. All errors were found within two hours using JTorX. There were no false alarms.

6.2 Case Study Heat Exchanger

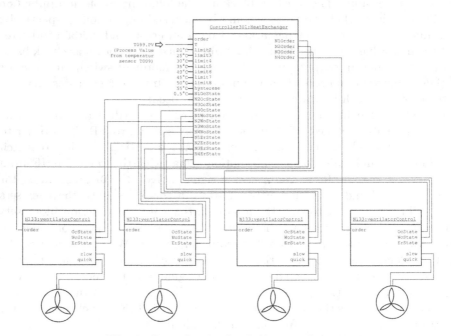

Fig. 8. Control units for the heat exchanger

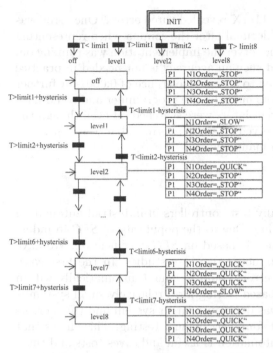

Figure 8 illustrates the structure of a water cooling system for a metallurgical furnace. The core of this cooling system is a heat exchanger composed of pipelines, four identical ventilators and one temperature sensor. Every ventilator can be operated in three modes: stop, slow and quick. By applying different combinations of ventilators, the water temperature can be kept in a certain range.

The control logic of the heat exchanger is described as an SFC, see Figure 9. Altogether 8 control levels (i.e. control states) are defined. According to the measured temperature, the control logic moves to the corresponding control level and operates the ventilators differently. The con-

Fig. 9. *SFC* specification of the function block class *HeatExchanger* (simplified)

trol program was programmed in ANSI C and executed on an industrial PC from a commercial vendor. It has about 1400 lines of code, excluding header classes and the server it is running on. During a typical production, temperature in the furnace is over $3000°C$, while temperature of the cooling water should be kept under $55°C$. Considering production safety, the heat exchanger should be operated in a reliable manner.

In the control program, 4 ventilator controllers and one group controller for the whole heat exchanger have been used. The group controller is implemented as a function block that realises the control logic in Figure 9. The main inputs and outputs of this block are declared as follows:

Name	data type	variable type	description
$N_x Order$	STRING	output	commando for ventilator N_x (x=1,2,3,4.)
$N_x OcSt$	UINT	input	occupancy state of N_x
			(10=free, 20=hand, 30=automatic)
$N_x WoOcSt$	UINT	input	working state of N_x
			(10=off, 20=starting up, 30=stationary, 40=stopping)
$N_x ErSt$	UINT	input	error state of N_x
			(20=undifined, 20=good, 30=alarm, 40=warning)

Test-Case Execution. The *STS* obtained from the *SFC* has 22 states and 63 transitions. The highest limit in the heat exchanger is $50°C$, after which all four ventilators have to run. To avoid that JTorX tests arbitrary high temperature values and to speed up the test process, the maximal temperature value was restricted to $100°C$ and was chosen randomly by JTorX.

Testing the heat exchanger with JTorX revealed three errors. One error was due to an imprecision in the fourth decimal after the comma when representing floats, e.g. 23.99998 was shown by the server the implementation was running on. This problem could not be fixed and such an accuracy is not needed in practice most times, so the model was changed to accept a tolerance of 0.0001 for further tests. The other two errors were errors made by the programmer and could have resulted in a system state were all ventilators were switched off even though the temperature exceeded $50°C$. All observed errors were errors that were not found when intensively testing the system manually.

7 Conclusion

This paper proposed to automatically test controllers in industrial automation by using symbolic model-based testing. Due to the popularity of *SFC* in industrial automation our testing approach is based on *SFC* specification. We have implemented our approach and conducted two case studies. In the first case-study, a controller for a motor, all errors could be found automatically within two hours. This shows that model-based testing for a relatively small system is profitable. The second case-study was done on a larger system and three errors where found. These errors were not found by manual testing. This shows that model-based testing in industrial automation is useful and saves costs and time. It is also more thorough than manual testing.

Future work will focus on incorporating real-time aspects in this setting using the theory in [24].

Acknowledgement. The authors wish to thank Prof. Dr. Ir. Joost-Pieter Katoen for comments on an earlier version of this paper.

References

1. Albrecht, H.: On Meta-Modeling for Communication in Operational Process Control Engineering VDI-Verlag (2003), VDI Fortschritt-Bericht, Series 8, No. 975, Düsseldorf, Germany, 3-18-397508-4, RWTH Aachen University
2. Bauer, N., Engell, S., Huuck, R., Lohmann, S., Lukoschus, B., Remelhe, M., Stursberg, O.: Verification of PLC Programs Given as Sequential Function Charts. In: Ehrig, H., Damm, W., Desel, J., Große-Rhode, M., Reif, W., Schnieder, E., Westkämper, E. (eds.) INT 2004. LNCS, vol. 3147, pp. 517–540. Springer, Heidelberg (2004)
3. Bauer, N., Huuck, R., Lukoschus, B., Engell, S.: A Unifying Semantics for Sequential Function Charts. In: Ehrig, H., Damm, W., Desel, J., Große-Rhode, M., Reif, W., Schnieder, E., Westkämper, E. (eds.) INT 2004. LNCS, vol. 3147, pp. 400–418. Springer, Heidelberg (2004)
4. Bornot, S., Huuck, R., Lukoschus, B., Lakhnech, Y.: Verification of Sequential Function Charts Using SMV. In: PDPTA 2000: International Conference on Parallel and Distributed Processing Techniques and Applications, Las Vegas, pp. 2987–2993 (2000)

5. Belinfante, A.: JTorX: A Tool for On-Line Model-Driven Test Derivation and Execution. In: Esparza, J., Majumdar, R. (eds.) TACAS 2010. LNCS, vol. 6015, pp. 266–270. Springer, Heidelberg (2010)
6. Broy, M., Jonsson, B., Katoen, J.-P., Leucker, M., Pretschner, A. (eds.): Model-Based Testing of Reactive Systems. LNCS, vol. 3472. Springer, Heidelberg (2005)
7. Frantzen, L., Tretmans, J., Willemse, T.A.C.: Test Generation Based on Symbolic Specifications. In: Grabowski, Nielsen (eds.) [19], pp. 1–15
8. Frantzen, L., Tretmans, J., Willemse, T.A.C.: A Symbolic Framework for Model-Based Testing. In: Havelund, K., Núñez, M., Roşu, G., Wolff, B. (eds.) FATES/RV 2006. LNCS, vol. 4262, pp. 40–54. Springer, Heidelberg (2006)
9. Grabowski, J., Nielsen, B. (eds.): FATES 2004. LNCS, vol. 3395. Springer, Heidelberg (2005)
10. Hartman, A., Nagin, K.: The AGEDIS Tools for Model Based Testing. SIGSOFT Softw. Eng. Notes 29(4), 129–132 (2004)
11. Hellgren, A., Fabian, M., Lennartson, B.: On the Execution of Sequential Function Charts. Control Engineering Practice 13, 1283–1293 (2004)
12. IEC International Electrotechnical Commission. IEC60848: GRAFCET Specification Language for Sequential Function Charts (2002)
13. IEC International Electrotechnical Commission. IEC 61131-03: Programmable Controllers - Part 3: Programming Languages, 2nd edn. (2003)
14. IEC International Electrotechnical Commission. IEC61512-2: Batch Control - Part 2: Data Structures and Guidelines for Language (2001)
15. ICE International Electrotechnical Commission. IEC62541-5: OPC Unified Architecture (2001)
16. Iyenghar, P., Pulvermueller, E., Westerkamp, C.: Towards Model-Based Test Automation for Embedded Systems using UML and UTP. In: ETFA 2011. IEEE (2011)
17. Kumar, B., Czybik, B., Jasperneite, J.: Model Based TTCN-3 Testing of Industrial Automation Systems - First results. In: ETFA 2011. IEEE (2011)
18. Jard, C., Jéron, T.: TGV: Theory, Principles and Algorithms: A Tool for the Automatic Synthesis of Conformance Test Cases for Non-Deterministic Reactive Systems. J. STTS 7(4), 297–315 (2005)
19. McMillan, K.L.: Symbolic Model Checking. Kluwer Academic Publishers (1993)
20. Meyer, D.: Objektverwaltungskonzept für die operative Prozessleittechnik. VDI-Verlag (2002), VDI Fortschritt-Bericht, Series 8, No. 940, Düsseldorf, Germany, 3-18-394008-6, RWTH Aachen University
21. PLCopen. Technical Committee 6 Technical Paper: XML Formats for IEC 61131-3. Version 2.01 - Official Release (2009)
22. STSimulator homepage, http://java.net/projects/stsimulator/
23. von Styp, S., Yu, L.: Two Case Studies for Applying Model Based Testing in Industrial Automation, AIB-2013-11, RWTH Aachen (2013)
24. von Styp, S., Bohnenkamp, H., Schmaltz, J.: A Conformance Testing Relation for Symbolic Timed Automata. In: Chatterjee, K., Henzinger, T.A. (eds.) FORMATS 2010. LNCS, vol. 6246, pp. 243–255. Springer, Heidelberg (2010)
25. von Styp, S., Yu, L., Quiros, G.: Automatic Test-Case Derivation and Execution in Industrial Control. In: iATPA 2011: First Workshop on Industrial Automation Tool Integration for Engineering Project Automation. CEUR-WS, pp. 7–12 (2011)

26. Tretmans, J.: Test Generation with Inputs, Outputs and Repetitive quiescence. Software - Concepts and Tools 17(3), 103–120 (1996)
27. UPPAAL homepage, http://www.uppaal.org
28. VDI/VDE Society for Measurement and Automatic Control. VDI/VDE 3681 Guideline: Classification and Evaluation of Description Methods in Automation and Control Technology (2005)
29. Yu, L., Quirós, G., Grüner, S., Epple, U.: SFC-Based Process Description for Complex Automation Functionalities. In: EKA 2012: Entwurf Komplexer Automatisierungssysteme, 12. Fachtagung, pp. 13–20. ifak, Magdeburg, Germany (2012)

Online Testing of LTL Properties for Java Code*

Paolo Arcaini[1], Angelo Gargantini[2], and Elvinia Riccobene[1]

[1] Dipartimento di Informatica, Università degli Studi di Milano, Italy
{paolo.arcaini,elvinia.riccobene}@unimi.it
[2] Dipartimento di Ingegneria, Università di Bergamo, Italy
angelo.gargantini@unibg.it

Abstract. LTL specifications are commonly used in runtime verification to describe the requirements about the system behavior. Efficient techniques derive, from LTL specifications, monitors that can check if system executions respect these properties. In this paper we present an *online* testing approach which is based on LTL properties of Java programs. We present an algorithm able to derive and execute test cases from monitors for LTL specifications. Our technique *actively* tests a Java class, avoids false failures, and it is able to check the correctness of the outputs also in the presence of nondeterminism. We devise several coverage criteria and strategies for visiting the monitors, providing different qualities in terms of test size, testing time, and fault detection capability.

1 Introduction

In the software system life cycle, program requirements are often given as properties using a declarative approach. In this paper we assume that these properties are formally specified in Linear Temporal Logic (LTL) [19], which often provides an intuitive and compact means to specify system requirements, especially in the presence of nondeterminism due, for instance, to underspecification. In this context, LTL declarative specifications can be easier to write than operational ones, such as finite state machines (FSM) and labeled transition systems (LTS).

The use of declarative specifications and nondeterminism poses several challenges to testing. For instance, it is well known that derivation of tests from nondeterministic models is computationally more difficult than from deterministic models, or even impossible [1]. In most cases, developers limit the use of LTL properties to runtime verification or *passive* testing, where a *monitor* observes the execution of the system to check that the behavior conforms to the specification. The use of LTL for runtime monitoring is well known, see for instance JavaMOP [5], LTL₃ [4], and LIME [13].

In this paper we focus on *active online* testing of Java programs starting from their LTL properties. In online (on-the-fly) testing, test generation and test execution are performed at the same time: a test is applied to the implementation under test (IUT) while it is generated. We propose to re-use the LTL properties

* This work is partially supported by GenData 2020, a MIUR PRIN 2010-11 project.

V. Bertacco and A. Legay (Eds.): HVC 2013, LNCS 8244, pp. 95–111, 2013.

of the program, not only for runtime verification but also for test generation and we are able to address the following issues.

Oracle problem: Our methodology is able to assess if the *outputs* produced during testing by the program under test, given in terms of return values of certain methods, are the expected ones.

Nondeterminism: Specification nondeterminism can be due to i) the restricted predictability of the systems, ii) underspecification because some implementation choices are left abstract, iii) abstractions used to reduce complexity or to remove aspects which can be (initially) ignored (e.g., time metrics aspects). Our methodology deals with both external and internal nondeterminism. *External* nondeterminism is limited to monitored (external) quantities (e.g., which method has been called or what values have been used as actual parameters); it is only due to the unknown usage of the code by a user. *Internal* nondeterminism refers to the fact that the same method call, executed in the same state, can produce different outputs at different times. In this case, techniques based on the "capture and replay" approach, like [20], or off-line testing approaches which produce test sequences together with oracles [10], generate tests which may fail because of the nondeterministic behavior of the implementation. Online testing approaches, like ours, which combine test generation and test execution, are more suitable [27].

No separate behavioral model: Our approach does not require the tester to write a separate operational model (e.g., a Kripke structure) besides the LTL properties which are directly linked to the code. This assumption is similar to the "Single Product Principle" of the design by contract [15].

Method call ordering: Our methodology deals with requirements about the order in which methods must be called. Sometimes a specific order among methods is required. For instance, the subject-view pattern is characterized by required calls from the subject to the view, and potential callbacks from the view to the subject, with a required order among the calls. In these cases, the traditional design-by-contract concepts of pre- and post-conditions [15], which refer to single methods, are not enough, while (P)LTL properties can describe correct sequences of method calls with ease. The problem of monitoring sequences of Java method calls is tackled also in [16]. Methodologies that ignore the requirement about methods' call order may generate many tests that fail only because they do not respect the ordering, and such false positives are a burden for testers which must manually discard tests that *falsely* fail [12].

Coverage: Our methodology is able to give feedback on how much properties are covered (as in LTL$_3$). This can be useful also in the case of passive testing, since it gives a measure of the adequacy of the testing activity.

Our *online* testing approach tackles all the issues mentioned above by introducing methodologies and techniques: *a)* to specify the behavior of Java programs by means of LTL properties, *b)* to translate all the LTL properties into one monitor (similar to a Büchi automata), *c)* to monitor if the program behaves correctly, and *d*) to generate online the test sequences by visiting the monitor with several policies.

Points *a-c* have been addressed in the past using several approaches. The original contribution of this paper consists in devising a technique for online test generation (point *d*), and an annotation-based technique for linking method calls and their return values (if any) to LTL properties (point *a*). A further contribution is the integration of these techniques into one single process.

Sect. 2 introduces the necessary background. The following sections present the proposed approach: Sect. 3 introduces some formal definitions, Sect. 4 presents a case study we use throughout the paper, Sect. 5 describes how a monitor is derived from an LTL specification, Sect. 6 introduces some coverage criteria for LTL monitors, and Sect. 7 describes how to perform the online testing. Sect. 8 presents the experiments we made to validate the approach. Sect. 9 relates our work with similar contributions, and Sect. 10 concludes the paper.

2 Background

For the sake of brevity, we assume that the reader is familiar with the use of *Linear Temporal Logic* (LTL) [19]. There is an extended literature on how an LTL specification can be converted to a Büchi automaton and this automaton to a monitor. Typically, a *monitor* is an automaton used to check system runs: in each state the monitor can show that (i) the corresponding LTL specification has been violated (a *bad prefix* is found [14]), (ii) *any* continuation of the run can not violate the specification (a *never violate* state is reached [6]), (iii) *there exist* continuations of the run that may or may not violate the specification.

In our approach we use *minimal deterministic monitors* as proposed by Tabakov and Vardi [22] and implemented in SPOT [7]. The monitors are obtained by determinizing and minimizing a Büchi automaton using several techniques like state minimization and alphabet minimization. The final monitor guarantees to reject minimal bad prefixes, i.e., to detect wrong behaviors as early as possible.

3 Formal Definitions

Given a Java class C, let M be the set of methods of C the user wants to monitor. For each method $m_i \in M$, let D_i be the set of all its possible return values (for void methods $D_i = \{void\}$). We consider only Boolean and enumerative types for the return value, but the approach can be extended to other types (see below). Moreover, we also assume that methods in M have no parameters.

We need to introduce suitable labels (*atomic propositions*) each univocally identifying a method call and its return value. To this purpose we define the finite set $MD = \bigcup_{i=1}^{n} \{m_i\} \times D_i$, and we introduce a set of atomic propositions $AP = \{ap_1, \ldots, ap_r\}$, $r = |MD|$, such that there exists a bijective function $id: MD \to AP$ identifying each monitored method and its return value by a unique atomic proposition. AP is built as follows: for void methods, the atomic proposition is the name of the method (i.e., $id(m_i, void) = m_i$); for non-void methods, an atomic proposition is built for each return value $d_i^j \in D_i$ and it is obtained by concatenating the name of the method with the return value (i.e., $id(m_i, d_i^j) = m_i d_i^j$).

Inverting the function id leads to the definition of the function $met\colon AP \to M$ and the function $eo\colon AP \to \bigcup_{i=1}^{n} D_i$ associating an atomic proposition with, respectively, the method and its return value representing the $e$xpected $o$utput.

Dealing with Large Domains. The suggested construction method for AP is not feasible when types of return values contain many values (e.g., integers) or are infinite (e.g., some reference types). In this case we should relax the condition that the function id is injective, so different return values can be represented by the same proposition, and/or assume that the function could be partial, so some return values are not considered – e.g., an atomic proposition $getValueGT0$ can be used to indicate that a method `getValue` returns a value greater than 0.

Trace Semantics. The semantics of the labels is the following: ap (with $m = met(ap)$ and $v = eo(ap)$) means that the method m has been called and returns the value v (if it is not void). On the contrary, the label $\neg ap$ means:

– for void methods: "the method m is not called";
– for non-void methods: "the method m either is not called or it is called but it returns a value different from v".

Since we assume that at every instant only one method is called, we have to add an *assumption* on traces. Usually [19], a trace is a word $\omega = \sigma(0)\sigma(1)\ldots$ over the alphabet 2^{AP} where a letter $\sigma(i)$ is a *set* of atomic propositions representing their truth evaluations (i.e., $\sigma(i) \in 2^{AP}$). However, since we assume that only one method is called in each time instant, we consider a trace valid only if one proposition in AP is true in every letter, so that a trace is a sequence of atomic propositions in AP.

A *test* is a finite sequence of methods calls and their expected values, so formally a test is a valid trace.

4   Running Case Study

As a running example we use the simple case study of a battery (class), whose schema is shown in Fig. 1: the method `init` initialises the battery; `charge` and `discharge` are called to charge/discharge the battery; `isC` checks if

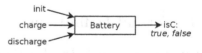

Fig. 1. Battery

the battery is charged or not. All methods are void, except `isC` that returns a boolean.

The set of monitored methods and the set of atomic propositions (computed as suggested in Sect. 3) are $M = \{\text{init}, \text{charge}, \text{discharge}, \text{isC}\}$ and $AP = \{init, charge, discharge, isCfalse, isCtrue\}$.

The requirements on the correct usage and behavior of the battery can be captured by LTL properties exploiting classical patterns as those in [8].

The following requirements regard the correct methods invocation:

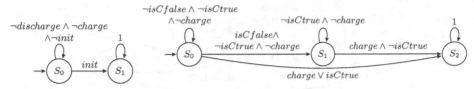

Fig. 2. Monitors for P_a (left) and for P_{d_init} (right)

$a)$ **charge** and **discharge** can not be executed before executing **init**;
$b)$ **init** must be called only once.
   They can be easily specified in LTL as follows.

$$P_a)\ (\neg\ discharge \wedge \neg\ charge)\ \mathbf{W}\ init \qquad \text{and} \qquad P_b)\ \mathbf{G}(init \rightarrow \mathbf{X}(\mathbf{G}(\neg\ init)))$$

The following requirements concern the correct battery behavior.

$c)$ After executing **discharge**, any invocation of **isC** can not return *true* until **charge** is called:

$$P_c)\ \mathbf{G}(discharge \rightarrow (\neg\ isCtrue\ \mathbf{W}\ charge))$$

$d)$ Anytime the battery is uncharged, it stays that way until it is charged.
   To model requirement (d), let us introduce the temporal formula f equal to $(\neg\ charge\ \mathbf{W}\ isCtrue) \rightarrow (\neg\ isCfalse\ \mathbf{W}\ isCtrue)$. f means that if no **charge** is issued before the battery is observed charged, it cannot happen that the battery is uncharged and charged again thereafter. This formula f must be true initially and always after the battery has been observed charged:

$$P_{d\_init})\ f \qquad\qquad \text{and} \qquad\qquad P_{d\_G})\ \mathbf{G}(isCtrue \rightarrow \mathbf{X}(f))$$

$e)$ The charging operation (after the execution of the **charge** method) is not instantaneous and, when the battery becomes charged, it can spontaneously loose the charge over time. So, repeatedly calling method **isC** after method **charge** can either return *true* or *false*, but it will eventually return *true*.

$$P_e)\ \mathbf{G}((charge \wedge \mathbf{X}(\mathbf{G}(isCfalse \vee isCtrue))) \rightarrow \mathbf{F}(isCtrue))$$

5   Monitor Construction

Given a Java class C, the user selects some methods $M = \{m_1, \ldots, m_n\}$ representing the behavior of C to be tested. Then, the set of atomic propositions $AP = \{ap_1, \ldots, ap_r\}$ is derived as described in Sect. 3. Using AP, the user can write several LTL properties of the expected behavior of the class methods and, if necessary, of the correct method invocation order.

   The first step of our approach consists in automatically deriving a monitor from every property by using the technique proposed in [7,22]. Two monitors for the battery properties are shown in Fig. 2.

   We then add to these monitors the trace assumption that at every step only one atomic proposition in AP is true, and then we use SPOT [7] to build the product monitor PM among all the single monitors. Although computing the

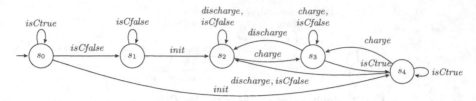

Fig. 3. Product monitor PM$_{batt}$ for the battery case study

product can be time-consuming, PM is built only once and it provides a useful global view of the system behavior. Every trace that is accepted by PM is also accepted by all the monitors and respects the trace semantics. In PM, every transition is labeled with a list of atomic propositions, each representing one possible action (method call and return value) causing the state transition.

Fig. 3 shows the product monitor derived from the monitors for the LTL battery specifications.

Note that obtaining the PM from LTL properties offers several advantages w.r.t. directly writing it as an automaton (e.g., FSM or LTS). First, the user can adopt a declarative notation like LTL. Writing the complete monitor from scratch may be more difficult than writing single LTL properties and then automatically deriving the PM. Moreover, the user can proceed incrementally adding new LTL properties and enriching the behavior, while being always sure that the PM still formalizes all the requirements given so far.

6   Coverage Criteria over the Monitor

In the literature, monitors have been used for runtime verification purposes: while the monitored program is running, the monitor checks that the program is used and behaves correctly. The monitor, at each step, observes the invoked method and the returned value, and changes its current state accordingly.

In this paper we extend the use of the monitor to testing. We devise the following coverage criteria over the product monitor for measuring the testing activity. These criteria work regardless the way the monitor is built.

- **State Coverage (SC)**: each state of the monitor must be visited.
- **Method Coverage (MC)**: for each state of the monitor, each *exiting method* must be visited. It means that, for each atomic proposition *ap* of each exiting transition, the corresponding method m_i (i.e., $met(ap) = m_i$) must be executed.
- **Transition Coverage (TC)**: each transition of the monitor must be taken. TC does not imply MC because a transition could be labeled by more than one atomic proposition (identifying different methods), and MC does not imply TC because the same method could appear on different transitions outgoing from the same state (but only one transition is taken).
- **Atomic Proposition Coverage (APC)**: each atomic proposition *ap* on each transition of the monitor must be covered. Covering *ap* requires to

execute the related method m_i (i.e., $met(ap) = m_i$) and that the returned value v is the expected one (i.e., $eo(ap) = v$). It implies both method and transition coverage.

- $n-$**Transition Coverage (TCn)**: every transition of the monitor must be covered at least n times.
- $n-$**Atomic Proposition Coverage (APCn)**: every atomic proposition on each transition of the monitor must be covered at least n times.

Given a monitor, a criterion identifies a set of *goals*. For instance, the state coverage identifies the set of states to be covered.

Criteria hierarchy A partial order exists among the coverage criteria, as shown in Fig. 4. p-atomic proposition coverage implies q-transition coverage when $p \geq q$.

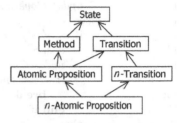

Coverage criteria for runtime monitoring The aim of runtime verification techniques is to observe a system while it runs and determine if it assures some properties expressed, for example,

Fig. 4. Criteria hierarchy

in LTL. Empirically, the more the system is executed and monitored, the higher is the confidence that the system is correct. But, how to measure such degree of confidence? To do this we can use the coverage criteria previously defined. The percentage of covered goals is as an indicator of how much the system has been monitored; the user could decide, when coverage reaches a threshold K, to stop monitoring, because (s)he is confident enough that the system is correct. Using Büchi automata or LTL properties for measuring the coverage has been already proposed in several works [24,23].

7 Online Testing of LTL Properties

We now describe the approach we propose for online testing Java code starting from its LTL properties. The coverage criteria defined in Sect. 6 are used to measure the testing activity and to address the generation of tests.

The overall process is depicted in Fig. 5. Given a Java class, the user selects the set of methods to be monitored, derives the atomic propositions, writes the LTL specifications and automatically obtains the product monitor from them.

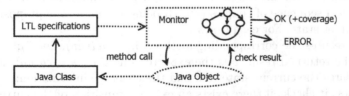

Fig. 5. Proposed approach – Online testing of LTL properties

Algorithm 1. Visiting algorithm of the monitor using the guided walk

---

Require: coverage criterion $CRIT$, class C
 1: **while** $existsNotCoveredGoal(CRIT)$ **do**   ▷ check if $CRIT$ is achieved
 2:     $currS \leftarrow initState$
 3:     $currObject \leftarrow$ **new** $C()$ ▷ create a new object of class C
 4:     **while** $existsReachableGoal(currS, CRIT)$ **do**
 5:         $path \leftarrow computePath(currS, CRIT)$ ▷ compute the path to the next goal
 6:         **for all** $(ap, s) \in path$ **do**
 7:             $v \leftarrow currObject.met(ap)$ ▷ execute the method associated with the ap
 8:             **if** $v = eo(ap)$ **then**   ▷ check if the result is the expected one
 9:                 $currS \leftarrow s$
10:                 $updateCoverage(CRIT, currS, ap)$
11:             **else**   ▷ check if the returned output is still correct
12:                 **if** $\exists (ap', s') \in out(currS)\colon met(ap) = met(ap') \wedge v = eo(ap')$ **then**
13:                     $currS \leftarrow s'$
14:                     $updateCoverage(CRIT, currS, ap')$
15:                     **if** $s \neq s'$ **then**   ▷ check if there is a deviation from the $path$
16:                         **break**
17:                     **end if**
18:                 **else**
19:                     $throwException$ ▷ the LTL specification has been violated
20:                 **end if**
21:             **end if**
22:         **end for**
23:     **end while**
24: **end while**

The test sequences are built by *visiting* the monitor with the aim of achieving the full coverage of a given criterion $CRIT$. We identify two kind of visits:

- **Random walk**: the criterion $CRIT$ is only used as stopping rule, but it is not considered to drive the monitor visit, since each step is randomly chosen.
- **Guided walk**: the criterion $CRIT$ is also considered when computing the paths to execute.

The visiting procedure in case of guided walk is shown in Alg. 1. Until all the goals of the selected criterion $CRIT$ are covered:

1. It starts the visit from the initial state of the monitor (the initial state is the current state $currS$), and creates the object $currObject$ of the Java class C;
2. Until no goals are reachable from the current state, it computes the shortest path to the nearest uncovered goal (line 5) using a standard greedy algorithm. A path is a sequence of couples (ap, s), being ap an atomic proposition and s the target state. For each (ap, s):
   (a) It executes the corresponding method (i.e., $met(ap)$, line 7);
   (b) If the returned result v is the expected one (i.e., $v = eo(ap)$, line 8), it updates the current state to s and the coverage information;
   (c) If not, it checks if there exists an exiting transition of the current state, labeled with an atomic proposition ap' that identifies the same method

and the returned result (i.e., $met(ap) = met(ap') \wedge v = eo(ap')$, line 12).
To check the existence of ap' we make use of the set $out(s)$ containing
all the couples (ap_i, s_i), where ap_i is an atomic proposition occurring
in a label of an exiting transition of s, and s_i the target state of the
transition.

    i. If a label ap' is detected, it takes the corresponding transition and it
updates the coverage info. Then, it checks if the expected path has
not been followed, i.e., if the reached state is different from the expected one. Note that ap' could indeed belong to the same transition
of ap. If the path is not followed, its execution is interrupted.

    ii. Otherwise, it throws an exception stating that the LTL specification
has been violated.

A single test is the sequence of the atomic propositions selected along the
paths built for the object $currObject$, i.e., a test is built during the iteration of
the inner loop of Alg. 1.

In case of random walk, $computePath$ (line 5) randomly chooses a transition
exiting from the current state and the check at line 15 is not executed since any
transition taken is acceptable.

Example 1. Let us consider the visit of the monitor in Fig. 3 following the state
coverage and using the guided walk. (1) In s_0 the path $[(init, s_4)]$ is produced
to cover s_4. Since the method is void, the method execution surely brings to
s_4. (2) From s_4, the path $[(isCfalse, s_2)]$ is produced to reach s_2. Consider the
method execution returns *true*, which is not the expected output, but it is correct.
So, the loop transition is taken and s_4 remains the current state. (3) From s_4, the
path $[(charge, s_3)]$ is produced to reach s_3. Since the method is void, s_3 is surely
reached. (4) In the same way, s_2 is reached from s_3 with the path $[(discharge, s_2)]$.
(5) Since there are no more uncovered states reachable from s_2 but there are still
uncovered states, the visit restarts from the initial state. (6) For covering s_1, the
path $[(isCfalse, s_1)]$ is produced. The method execution returns the expected
output, so reaching s_1. (7) Since there are no more uncovered states, the visits
terminates, achieving the full state coverage with the test suite $T=\{[init, isCfalse,$
$charge, discharge], [isCfalse]\}$.

Limiting the Unsuccessful Retries. Covering a test goal could be very difficult because the expected output of a given atomic proposition is seldom produced. Indeed, if a method is nondeterministic, one given value may be returned
with very low probability or, if the implementation is faulty, it may never be
returned. In order to avoid to continuously try to cover a *difficult* or *unreachable*
goal, in Alg. 1 we can impose a limit to the number of unsuccessful attempts. For
the guided walk, the limit is the maximum number of times k that the algorithm,
for each goal, can build a path for it; when the limit k is reached, the goal is
discarded. For the random walk, instead, the limit is given by the couple (m, t):

  − m is the maximum number of consecutive steps during which any goal is not
covered; when, during a test, m is reached, the test execution is terminated;

  − t is the maximum number of tests that can be executed.

Fault Detection Capability Our monitors guarantee to catch a wrong behavior (called *bad prefix* [14]), i.e., a violation of an LTL specification, as soon as it occurs. However, if no violation occurs, we cannot exclude the presence of faults since there exist properties for which a finite observation is not sufficient to draw an affirmative verdict. For instance, *non-monitorable* [4] properties can never be violated by a finite trace. Moreover, even for monitorable properties, it is always possible to build a program that behaves correctly until the monitoring is finished and it starts a wrong behavior only afterwards. However, for some properties, we can stop the testing activity at some point and exclude that continuing testing would find any fault. For instance, for the property P_a and its monitor given in Fig. 2, if the visit reaches state S_1, further testing would be useless. That state is also called *never violate* [6] and we can affirm that, if the monitor stops in a never violate state, no further activity from that state would find any fault. We suspect that unfortunately, states of this kind are quite rare (for instance, PM_{batt} does not have never violate states), especially for reactive systems, but we plan to perform further experiments in this direction.

8   Experiments

We have implemented a prototype based on the use of Java annotations for specifying the set of monitored methods M and the LTL properties. The tool exploits SPOT for monitor generation and composition. We have run all the experiments on a Linux machine, Intel(R) Core(TM) i7, 4 GB RAM. All the reported experiments data are the average of 2000 runs.

8.1   Coverage Criteria Evaluation

We here want to experiment the coverage criteria described in Sect. 6.

Criteria and Walk Comparison. We apply our approach using all the criteria over a correct implementation of the battery case study, always obtaining the full coverage of the goals. Table 1 reports, for each coverage criterion, the results of the experiment in terms of number of goals it requires to cover, time taken to cover all the goals, number of tests executed, and total number of methods executed. We experiment the two kind of visits that can be used in Alg. 1, i.e., *guided* (*G.* in the table) or *random* (*R.* in the table).

As expected, the time, the number of tests, and the number of methods grow with the number of goals to achieve (with both kind of visits).

Since we want to compare the two kind of visits, we also report the percentage change between the data in the two visits (being the guided visit the basis of the comparison). The random walk always obtains worse results for the three indicators. This means that computing the shortest path for achieving a given goal is more successful than visiting the monitor randomly. In the experiments regarding the fault detection we use the guided walk.

Table 1. Criteria comparison (achieved full coverage with minimum limit) – The acronyms of the criteria have been introduced in Sect. 6

Criterion	# goals	Time (ms)			# tests executed			# methods executed		
		G.	R.	± %	G.	R.	± %	G.	R.	± %
SC	5	0.007	0.013	86	1.87	2.02	8.2	6.3	15.4	143
MC	13	0.052	0.101	92	2.5	4.68	87	25.9	92.1	256
TC	13	0.058	0.094	61	3.48	6.05	74	26.9	76.2	183
APC	10	0.098	0.182	85	3.89	6.03	55	35.3	146.8	316
TC2	26	0.113	0.159	41	5.41	9.04	67	50.6	129.0	155
TC3	39	0.164	0.24	47	7.49	11.71	57	74.4	184.5	148
TC10	130	0.52	0.604	16	21.54	29.17	35	234.9	528.2	125
TC50	650	2.571	2.829	10	101.17	119	18	1155.3	2481.4	115
TC100	1300	5.138	5.692	11	201.02	227.36	13	2313.3	4892.1	112
APC2	32	0.193	0.373	93	5.93	9.21	55	69.8	263.2	277
APC3	48	0.28	0.532	90	7.88	11.83	50	104.8	395.0	277
APC10	160	0.926	1.664	80	21.59	29.45	36	348.9	1221.8	250
APC50	800	4.593	10.292	124	101.08	118.89	18	1746.6	6062.7	247
APC100	1600	9.11	19.221	111	201	226.96	13	3496	12021	244

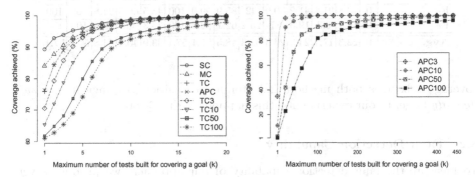

Fig. 6. Limit of unsuccessful retries – Guided walk

Limiting the Unsuccessful Retries. In the experiment above, we have not limited the number of attempts to achieve a goal: so, testing a correct implementation, we have always been able to obtain the full coverage. To investigate how limiting the number of attempts in achieving a goal influences the obtained coverage, we apply our approach to the correct implementation of the battery, using an increasing limit to the number of attempts. Fig. 6 shows the relation, for the different criteria, between the coverage and the limit of attempts using the guided walk. *Weak* criteria (e.g., state coverage) require a low limit to obtain the full coverage, since they are easy to achieve. *Strong* criteria (e.g., 100-atomic proposition coverage), instead, require a higher limit, since they are difficult to achieve and so several attempts must be made.

Subsumption Relation. Our experiments confirm the expected hierarchy among the coverage criteria (Fig. 4). Moreover, they reveal that, in practice, there exists a relation of subsumption between some criteria: n-transition

Table 2. Faulty implementations of the battery case study

Fault	Description
F_1	The battery is always discharged and so isC always returns *false*.
F_2	isC returns a random value, not related with the actual status of the battery.
F_3	Sometimes it is charged even if no charge method has been called.
F_4	Not charging battery: the charge method does nothing.
F_5	Not discharging battery: the discharge method does nothing.
F_6	The discharge method charges the battery (like charge method were called).
F_7	Before the init method execution, the battery is always charged.

Table 3. Fault detection capability (% of failing tests over 2000 test executions)

Fault	SC	MC	TC	APC	TC2	TC3	TC10	TC50	TC100	APC2	APC3	APC10	APC50	APC100
$F_1 - F_4 - F_7$	0	0	0	0	0	0	0	0	0	0	0	0	0	0
F_2	0	75.1	63	75.5	86.1	95	100	100	100	93.1	98.7	100	100	100
F_3	0	38.8	29.5	38	49.9	64.2	96.1	100	100	61.6	75.9	99.1	100	100
F_5	0	23.8	21.1	41.2	30.9	42	85.9	99.9	100	48.5	60.5	94.8	100	100
F_6	0	18.1	8.3	19.3	17	25.2	62.1	99.6	100	35.3	48	89.9	100	100
Avg.	0	22.3	17.4	24.9	26.3	32.3	48.5	57.1	57.1	33.9	40.4	54.8	57.1	57.1

coverage subsumes both method and atomic proposition coverage if n is *sufficiently* large. In our experiments, this happens with $n \geq 50$.

8.2　Fault Detection Capability

To measure the fault detection capability of our approach, we produce seven possible faulty implementations (described in Table 2) of the battery case study, and apply the approach to each faulty implementation with all the criteria.

Table 3 shows, for each faulty implementation, how the different criteria are able to detect the fault, and their average fault detection.

We found that three faults (F_1, F_4, and F_7) can not be detected: their resulting behavior is still acceptable by the given specification. These faults can not be detected by *finite* monitoring by any specification. In fault F_4, for example, the charge method never charges the battery, instead of charging it eventually in the future. The specification P_e describing the behavior of charge is non-monitorable and it can never be violated by a finite trace.

Note that, also when no fault is found, one can suspect that the implementation is faulty by observing the coverage obtained by the criteria. Indeed, if a coverage remains low, it may mean that some parts of the monitor can not be reached because the behavior of the faulty implementation does not exercise them. For the three faulty implementations we are not able to discover (F_1, F_4, and F_7), we achieved lower coverage than that obtained for the correct version; in particular, the stronger the criterion is, the lower the achieved coverage is.

Table 4. JTorX experiments

	Stopping criteria (# tests - # steps)									
	1-5	1-30	1-50	8-25	10-5	10-30	10-50	20-5	20-30	20-50
Fault Detection (%)	2.1	25	37.1	57.1	15.7	56.4	57.1	19.3	57.1	57.1
Testing Time (ms)	2017	7790	13541	53723	15620	82813	132957	29152	162276	272652

Among the faults that can be detected, some are easier to catch than others. In fault F_2, when the method isC is called, it returns a random value. This fault can be detected in all the states of the monitor in which method isC can be called and it is expected to return only a given value (states s_1 and s_2 where it can only return *false*). Such kind of faults are quite easily detected also by weak criteria as transition coverage (63 % in the table).

Some faults are more difficult to detect. In fault F_6, the method discharge behaves as the method charge. A necessary (but not sufficient) condition to detect such a fault is that the method discharge is called (from state s_3, s_4 or s_2), and then (from state s_2) the method isC is called: the fault is actually detected only if isC returns *true*. However, since the charging is not immediate, isC could return *false* without revealing the fault. Only strong criteria (n-transition and n-atomic proposition coverage with $n \geq 10$) have a good fault detection.

8.3 Comparison with LTS

We initially compared our approach with classical off-line test generation techniques. We chose two tools, namely EvoSuite [9] and Randoop [17], which generate test cases with oracles for Java classes. However, since both frameworks build test suites recording the current behavior, they produced many *falsely failing* tests (tests that may fail when replayed) because of the nondeterminism of the case study, leading to an unfair comparison. Therefore, we focus on techniques able to explicitly deal with nondeterministic systems. Among them, one of the most used is the Labelled Transition Systems (LTS) [26] (that are sometimes also called I/O automata).

In order to test a Java class, the user has to write an LTS specifying the program behavior and connect methods with LTS inputs and outputs. Inputs could be method calls while outputs the return values (if any). Tests check if the implementation satisfies a conformance relation (e.g., **ioco**) w.r.t. its LTS specification. In the LTS approach, a test case is a particular tree-like deterministic LTS with finite behavior leading to a verdict.

The LTS approach is suitable for online testing and for this reason we compare our approach with LTS and its supporting tool JTorX. We have run JTorX over the correct and faulty batteries implementations for 2000 runs. Since JTorX does not use coverage criteria for stopping testing, we have to fix the number of tests to execute and the length of such tests (couple of values (# tests, # steps)). Selected experiments data are reported in Table 4, including the experiment that obtained the best fault detection in the minimum time (in grey in the table).

Fault detection capability is the same as ours (see Table 3), while the testing time is several orders of magnitude greater than the time needed by our tests (see Table 1). Moreover, while we exploit coverage criteria also for testing guidance, JTorX randomly traverses the LTS representing the tests (also called *synthesis*), possibly leading to longer tests.

9   Related Work

Although monitoring of programs can be performed by means of behavioral specifications, like Abstract State Machines in [2], the use of temporal properties is more widespread. In order to link the Java program with the LTL specification, several approaches as J-LO [21], JavaMOP [5], and LIME [13] use Aspect Oriented Programming (AOP): the atomic propositions are *pointcuts* that can represent complex events related to method calls and fields accesses. In terms of JavaMOP, for example, the proposition *isCtrue* would be

event isCtrue **after**(Battery batt) returning(**boolean** b):
                call($*$ Battery.isC()) **&&** **target**(batt) **&&** **condition**(b) {}

Thanks to AOP, these approaches can monitor a wider set of events than ours since we target only method calls. However, it would be very difficult to generate tests from AOP pointcuts, although we plan to investigate this possibility.

The use of requirements given as LTL properties for test generation has been proposed by several approaches, especially in the model-based testing (MBT). In [24] the authors propose a property coverage metric which measures the quality of test sequences in terms of the coverage they provide over the LTL properties of the model; in [18] the notion of MCDC has been extended to temporal formulas. They both use a classical approach based on model checking for test generation. However, the tests they generate are abstract test sequences, i.e., sequences of values for atomic propositions, leaving unresolved the use of such tests to test implementations. Indeed, in case of nondeterminism, implementations can diverge from the test sequences generated in advance [10].

Another difference of our technique with classical MBT [24,18] is that we do not need the operational description of the system, since we directly derive the tests from LTL specifications. Moreover, they derive tests according to some criteria on the syntactical/semantic structure of the LTL specification, whereas our coverage criteria are defined over the monitor of the specification.

The idea of reusing runtime verification techniques for testing purposes has been proposed also in [3]. From a model of the input domain, a test generator produces, with the model checker *Java PathFinder*, input sequences for the application together with temporal properties that must be guaranteed during the execution. The runtime verification framework *Eagle* checks that the properties are satisfied during the execution of the application over the generated inputs.

An online testing approach has been also proposed in [27], where testing of reactive systems is seen as a game between the tester and the IUT. The conformance between a IUT and its operational specification is given in terms of *alternating simulation*.

In [25], in the context of hardware Assertion-Based Verification, the authors introduce a way to measure the coverage of properties and to generate test sequences from assertions.

10   Conclusion and Future Work

We presented an online testing approach in which system requirements are specified in LTL. We identified some coverage criteria for LTL monitors, i.e., automata used to check the conformance of system runs with their LTL formal specifications. The procedure we propose builds test sequences by visiting an LTL monitor with the aim of achieving the full coverage of a given criterion. The approach is *online* since tests are executed as they are built.

In the future we plan to devise other criteria addressing the interaction of methods calls; for example, we could introduce a criterion that requires that each couple of *consecutive* transitions are executed in sequence.

Our approach could have the disadvantage that, since non-monitorable behaviors are not considered in the monitor, we may not test some behaviors that, although they can not influence the evaluation of the specification, could however produce some faults (e.g., NullPointerException). As future work we plan to derive the test sequences using some criteria over the specification, and use the monitor only as oracle during testing.

Another future work is to ascertain which LTL property is violated when an error occurs. In order to do this, we should monitor the program execution using also each individual monitor of each LTL property. A weakness of our approach is that creation of LTL formal specifications may be difficult, also because little tool support exists. We plan to combine our approach with assisting LTL creation tools like Prospec [11], pattern based techniques [8], or tools for finding software properties automatically like Daikon. This will permit us to experiment our approach over real-world case studies.

In our approach, monitored methods can have parameters, which, however, are currently ignored. We plan to deal with them in the future.

References

1. Alur, R., Courcoubetis, C., Yannakakis, M.: Distinguishing tests for nondeterministic and probabilistic machines. In: Proc. of the 27th Annual ACM Symposium on Theory of Computing, STOC 1995, pp. 363–372. ACM, New York (1995)
2. Arcaini, P., Gargantini, A., Riccobene, E.: CoMA: Conformance Monitoring of Java Programs by Abstract State Machines. In: Khurshid, S., Sen, K. (eds.) RV 2011. LNCS, vol. 7186, pp. 223–238. Springer, Heidelberg (2012)
3. Artho, C., Barringer, H., Goldberg, A., Havelund, K., Khurshid, S., Lowry, M., Pasareanu, C., Roşu, G., Sen, K., Visser, W., Washington, R.: Combining test case generation and runtime verification. Theoretical Computer Science 336(2-3), 209–234 (2005)

4. Bauer, A., Leucker, M., Schallhart, C.: Runtime verification for LTL and TLTL. ACM Transactions on Software and Methodology (TOSEM) 20 (2011)
5. Chen, F., Roşu, G.: Java-MOP: A monitoring oriented programming environment for Java. In: Halbwachs, N., Zuck, L.D. (eds.) TACAS 2005. LNCS, vol. 3440, pp. 546–550. Springer, Heidelberg (2005)
6. d'Amorim, M., Roşu, G.: Efficient monitoring of ω-languages. In: Etessami, K., Rajamani, S.K. (eds.) CAV 2005. LNCS, vol. 3576, pp. 364–378. Springer, Heidelberg (2005)
7. Duret-Lutz, A., Poitrenaud, D.: SPOT: An extensible model checking library using transition-based generalized Büchi automata. In: MASCOTS 2004, pp. 76–83 (October 2004)
8. Dwyer, M., Avrunin, G., Corbett, J.: Patterns in property specifications for finite-state verification. In: Proc. of ICSE 1999, pp. 411–420 (May 1999)
9. Fraser, G., Arcuri, A.: Evosuite: Automatic test suite generation for object-oriented software. In: Proc. of ACM SIGSOFT ESEC/FSE, pp. 416–419 (2011)
10. Fraser, G., Wotawa, F.: Nondeterministic testing with linear model-checker counterexamples. In: Proc. of the 7th International Conference on Quality Software, QSIC 2007, pp. 107–116. IEEE Computer Society, Washington, DC (2007)
11. Gallegos, A., Ochoa, O., Gates, A., Roach, S., Salamah, S., Vela, C.: A property specification tool for generating formal specifications: Prospec 2.0. In: Proceedings of SEKE, Los Angeles, CA (2008)
12. Gross, F., Fraser, G., Zeller, A.: Search-based system testing: high coverage, no false alarms. In: Proceedings of the 2012 International Symposium on Software Testing and Analysis, ISSTA 2012, pp. 67–77. ACM, New York (2012)
13. Kähkönen, K., Lampinen, J., Heljanko, K., Niemelä, I.: The LIME interface specification language and runtime monitoring tool. In: Bensalem, S., Peled, D.A. (eds.) RV 2009. LNCS, vol. 5779, pp. 93–100. Springer, Heidelberg (2009)
14. Kupferman, O., Vardi, M.Y.: Model checking of safety properties. Formal Methods in System Design 19(3), 291–314 (2001)
15. Meyer, B.: Applying "Design by Contract". IEEE Computer 25(10), 40 (1992)
16. Nobakht, B., Bonsangue, M.M., de Boer, F.S., de Gouw, S.: Monitoring method call sequences using annotations. In: Barbosa, L.S., Lumpe, M. (eds.) FACS 2010. LNCS, vol. 6921, pp. 53–70. Springer, Heidelberg (2012)
17. Pacheco, C., Ernst, M.D.: Randoop: feedback-directed random testing for Java. In: OOPSLA 2007 Companion, pp. 815–816. ACM, New York (2007)
18. Pecheur, C., Raimondi, F., Brat, G.: A formal analysis of requirements-based testing. In: Proc. of ISSTA 2009, pp. 47–56. ACM, New York (2009)
19. Pnueli, A.: The temporal logic of programs. In: Proceedings of FOCS 1977, pp. 46–57. IEEE Computer Society, Washington, DC (1977)
20. Steven, J., Chandra, P., Fleck, B., Podgurski, A.: jRapture: A capture/replay tool for observation-based testing. In: Proceedings of ISSTA 2000, pp. 158–167. ACM, New York (2000)
21. Stolz, V., Bodden, E.: Temporal assertions using AspectJ. In: 5th Workshop on Runtime Verification. ENTCS, vol. 144, pp. 109–124. Elsevier (July 2005)
22. Tabakov, D., Vardi, M.Y.: Optimized temporal monitors for systemC. In: Barringer, H., et al. (eds.) RV 2010. LNCS, vol. 6418, pp. 436–451. Springer, Heidelberg (2010)

23. Tan, L.: State coverage metrics for specification-based testing with Büchi automata. In: Gogolla, M., Wolff, B. (eds.) TAP 2011. LNCS, vol. 6706, pp. 171–186. Springer, Heidelberg (2011)

24. Tan, L., Sokolsky, O., Lee, I.: Specification-based testing with linear temporal logic. In: Proc. of Information Reuse and Integration, pp. 493–498. IEEE (2004)

25. Tong, J., Boulé, M., Zilic, Z.: Defining and providing coverage for assertion-based dynamic verification. Journal of Electronic Testing 26(2), 211–225 (2010)

26. Tretmans, J.: Model based testing with labelled transition systems. In: Hierons, R.M., Bowen, J.P., Harman, M. (eds.) FORTEST. LNCS, vol. 4949, pp. 1–38. Springer, Heidelberg (2008)

27. Veanes, M., Campbell, C., Schulte, W., Tillmann, N.: Online testing with model programs. In: ESEC/SIGSOFT FSE, pp. 273–282. ACM (2005)

Modbat: A Model-Based API Tester
for Event-Driven Systems

Cyrille Valentin Artho[1], Armin Biere[2], Masami Hagiya[3], Eric Platon[4],
Martina Seidl[2], Yoshinori Tanabe[5], and Mitsuharu Yamamoto[6]

[1] Nat. Ins. of Advanced Industrial Science and Technology (AIST), Amagasaki, Japan
[2] Johannes Kepler University, Linz, Austria
[3] The University of Tokyo, Tokyo, Japan
[4] KVH, Inc., Tokyo, Japan
[5] National Institute of Informatics (NII), Tokyo, Japan
[6] Chiba University, Chiba, Japan

Abstract. Model-based testing derives test executions from an abstract
model that describes the system behavior. However, existing approaches
are not tailored to event-driven or input/output-driven systems. In particular, there is a need to support non-blocking I/O operations, or operations throwing exceptions when communication is disrupted.

Our new tool "Modbat" is specialized for testing systems where these
issues are common. Modbat uses extended finite-state machines to model
system behavior. Unlike most existing tools, Modbat offers a domain-
specific language that supports state machines and exceptions as first-
class constructs. Our model notation also handles non-determinism in
the system under test, and supports alternative continuations of test
cases depending on the outcome of non-deterministic operations.

These features allow us to model a number of interesting libraries
succinctly. Our experiments show the flexibility of Modbat and how language support for model features benefits their correct use.

Keywords: Software testing, model-based testing, test case derivation.

1 Introduction

Software testing executes parts of a system under test (SUT) [20]. A series of
inputs is fed to the SUT, which responds with a series of outputs. In *model-based
testing*, test cases are derived from an abstract model rather than implemented
directly as code. This approach has several advantages: A high-level model is
easier to develop and understand than program code; and partially specified
behaviors give rise to many possible combinations, from which many concrete
test cases can be derived.

Many existing test generation tools are designed to generate test *data* to
test a given function or method [9,17,21]. Our work covers test *actions* instead,
spanning sequences of multiple function calls.

Existing tools to generate test actions [9,15,16,21,28,29] define a programming
interface against which the model is coded; the programmer defines classes and

V. Bertacco and A. Legay (Eds.): HVC 2013, LNCS 8244, pp. 112–128, 2013.

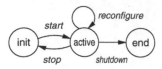

Fig. 1. A finite-state machine modeling component behavior

functions that implement the semantics of the model. It was shown that this introduces a layer of abstraction in the model that makes it difficult to clearly express the behavior of event-driven systems, which include databases, file systems, and cloud computing middleware [2]. Such systems also often depend on possibly unreliable hardware or communication links, which introduce possible delays and failures.

Our tool *Modbat* provides a domain-specific language to model test executions in such systems succinctly. In Modbat, system behavior is described using extended finite-state machines (see Figure 1). They provide a graphical, intuitive base of the model, which can be refined using a domain-specific language provided by Modbat. For example, the user can add additional preconditions about when given events are permissible. Results can be checked using assertions, or stored in model variables to be used in subsequent calls.

1.1 Usage of Modbat

Modbat strives to simplify test modeling by offering a flexible modeling platform. A tester uses Modbat as follows:

1. The tester defines a model as an extended finite-state machine. The model is compiled against a library provided by Modbat. For example, a transition from Figure 1 could be written as
   `"init" -> "active" := { c = new Component; c.start }`.
2. The tester runs Modbat against the compiled model. Modbat explores the possibilities defined by the model (the state space) using a random search, executing the SUT in tandem. After each completed test, the model and the SUT are reset to their initial state.
3. Modbat either executes a predefined number of tests, or it runs until a failure is found. A failure is detected when a test run violates a property. When a failure is found, Modbat writes an error trace to a file, giving the necessary information to analyze the error. For debugging, a failed test can be replayed.

1.2 Outline

This paper is organized as follows: Section 2 gives the necessary background and describes related work. Section 3 presents our modeling notation, and Section 4 describes our tool Modbat. Section 5 covers projects carried out with Modbat. Section 6 concludes and outlines future work.

2   Background

2.1   Terminology

A system under test (SUT) exposes its functionality to other software via an application programming interface (API). APIs may be organized in libraries.

Testing executes parts of the SUT [20]. A *test trace,* implemented as a *test case,* is a series of function calls (method invocations in object-oriented languages). A *test run* is the execution of a test case at run-time. The *test harness* serves to set up and manage test execution. A *test suite* is a set of test cases.

Our *test model* is based on extended finite state machines (EFSM) [8]. Formally, an EFSM is defined as a 7-tuple $M = (I, O, S, D, F, U, T)$ where

- S is a set of states, I is a set of input symbols, O is a set of output symbols;
- D is an n-dimensional vector space $D_1 \times \ldots \times D_n$;
- F is a set of *enabling functions* $f_i : D \to \{0, 1\}$,
- U is a set of *update functions* $u_i : D \to D$, and
- T is a transition relation $T : S \times F \times I \to S \times U \times O$ [8].

In an EFSM, D models the internal state of the model; the enabling functions describe when transitions are enabled; and update functions change the internal state of the model based on the outcome of a function call to the SUT.

In the formal definition, D is a vector space of fixed dimension. In our tool (see Section 3), we allow dynamic memory allocation, but for the purpose of describing the tool behavior, this difference is not important.

A test model usually has a large degree of uncertainty so that it can describe many possible test executions. *Test derivation* (test generation) describes the action of deriving individual concrete test cases from the abstract test model.

Techniques that rely solely on the specification of a system are called *black-box* techniques, while approaches that consider the implementation during analysis are known as *white-box* techniques. In our case, the specification is sufficient to write a test model; hence we consider our approach black-box.

2.2   Online vs. Offline Testing

Test derivation techniques can be divided into online testing and offline testing [28]. In online testing, the test generation (derivation) tool connects directly to the SUT. Each test is directly executed while it is generated (see Figure 2).

In offline test generation (see Figure 3), the test derivation tool does not execute the SUT directly. Instead, it generates an intermediate representation of test cases that is turned into executable tests later [28]. Existing literature also covers generation of manually deployable tests, which is elided in this paper [28].

Online testing is more efficient than offline testing, as no test code needs to be generated and compiled. A model can be set up to handle non-determinism in the SUT (also see Section 3), and may even dynamically fine-tune the test model based on earlier test executions.

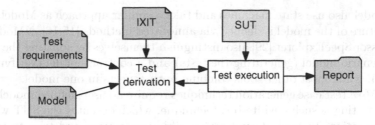

Fig. 2. Online testing. Test requirements include configuration options for the test tool, such as the number of tests to be generated; IXIT refers to *implementation extra information,* which is information needed to derive executable test cases [28]. Such information includes system configuration (such as library locations).

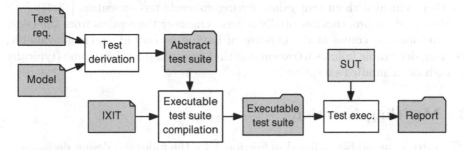

Fig. 3. Offline testing: Abstract tests are turned into executable tests later

Offline testing has the advantage that the test execution platform does not depend on the test derivation tool. The execution platform is therefore simpler and has a higher chance of not introducing unwanted behavior. Offline testing is also applicable when test cases have to be executed on a platform that is not supported by the test derivation tool. Modbat supports both online and offline testing, so it can handle a large set of use cases and platforms.

2.3   Related Work

Unit testing experienced a widespread rise in software development in the late 1990s [6,7,19]. In particular, JUnit is widely used for Java programs [19]. Modbat supports offline code generation for JUnit, allowing it to complement legacy test suites with automatically generated tests.

Many model-based testing tools allow a model to be defined against a programming interface (API). Such tools include QuickCheck [9] and ScalaCheck [21], which generate data based on predicate constraints; that data is then used to execute a given function in the SUT. One of the earliest practical model-based test tools that generates test sequences was ModelJUnit [28], which is also based on extended finite state machines. In ModelJUnit, a lot of the structure of the EFSM is implemented by the user (also see Section 3). A tool that motivated Modbat was actually implemented as a preprocessor to ModelJUnit [2]. Osmo and NModel also use state machines and take a similar approach as ModelJUnit; the structure of the model is defined via annotated methods [15,16]. NModel and its successor SpecExplorer [29] also distinguish themselves by splitting the model into a scenario model (generating the tests) and a contract model (verifying the outcome), while most other tools combine both aspects in one model.

Model-free test case generation techniques require no user-defined model. Randomized testing is such a white-box technique, which executes the SUT without any specification. Instead, it explores possible test actions and tries to execute as many aspects of the SUT as possible. Such testing may be primarily randomized [10,24] or more systematic and coverage-driven [11].

Concolic testing tools also optimize test coverage by keeping track of *(symbolic)* constraints that describe if a code branch can be taken; these constrains are then refined with current values during *concrete* test execution [13,27].

Model-free approaches essentially reverse engineer the models from the code. Full automation comes at the expense of having no output oracle is available, limiting detectable failures to executions that result in a fatal outcome (typically a crash or unhandled exception).

3   Modeling Notation

We address the problems listed in Section 1 by the following design decisions:

1. The underlying model is an extended finite state machine (EFSM), which is well understood by the formal methods community and developers alike. Transitions in the EFSM are directly linked to program code.
2. The model is not expressed as a program, but in a domain-specific language (DSL). Our DSL supports non-determinism both in the specification (to simulate faults or non-deterministic events) and in handling the resulting SUT behavior (to handle faults or exceptions). It is, to our knowledge, the only tool both supporting non-determinism and exceptions as primary constructs.

Figure 4 shows an example. Class `SimpleCounter` offers two methods that can increase its counter value (initially 0). The first method has the added property that a successful outcome depend on a flag (initially *true*). If the flag is set to *false* by calling `toggleSwitch`, then calling `inc` does not change the counter value. A corresponding test model calls the given methods in random order until value 2 is reached. In doing so, it does not take the side-effect of `toggleSwitch` into account. Modbat finds sequences of actions in the model that result in violating the assertion in the model, such as `toggleSwitch`, `inc`, `inc`, `assert`.

Note that a labeled state in an EFSM does not reflect the full model state; in our example, states correspond to the counter value but do not include the state of the switch in the counter (see Figure 5). This design is deliberate: The choice of a more abstract model state keeps the model size small. Model variables are used instead to define details matching the precise system state [28].

As a consequence of this design approach, different paths resulting in the same model state may correspond to different system states. In other words,

```
public class SimpleCounter {          class CounterModel extends Model {
  int count = 0;                        var counter = new SimpleCounter()
  boolean flag = true;                  // transitions
                                        def instance() = { new MBT (
  public void toggleSwitch() {            "zero" -> "zero" := {
    flag = !flag;                           counter.toggleSwitch
  }                                       },
  public void inc() {                     "zero" -> "one" := {
    if (flag) {                             counter.inc
      count += 1;                         },
    }                                     "one" -> "two" := {
  }                                         counter.inc
  public void inc2() {                    },
    count += 2;                           "zero" -> "two" := {
  }                                         counter.inc2
  public int value() {                    },
    return count;                         "two" -> "end" := {
  }                                         assert (counter.value == 2)
}                                       })}}
```

Fig. 4. Example system (left) and Modbat model (right)

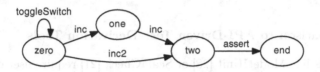

Fig. 5. Visualization of example model

model state $\langle s, D \rangle$ and SUT state do not necessarily match for two traces where $s = s'$ due to abstractions in the model. We are not aware of an established best practice for choosing the best level of abstraction, but it is well-known that choosing the right level of abstraction is a challenging task [18].

3.1   ESFM Notation

The notation of our model is motivated by previous work [2], which used a model that is based on graphs expressed in the notation used by Graphviz [12]. We decided to move to a new notation, because the Graphviz format is not extensible and not designed for model-based testing, but for visualization.

Our notation is designed as an embedded DSL [31] on top of the Scala programming language [22]. Transitions are declared with a concise syntax:

`"pre_state" -> "post_state" := { transition_action }`.[1]

Transition actions include calls to the SUT API, and assertions that check return values against given properties. Transition actions can be modified by adding declarations on exceptional or non-deterministic behavior.

---

[1] The first declared state automatically constitutes the initial state of the model.

Exceptions can be specified succinctly in Modbat. If an exception of a given type is always expected, `throws("ExceptionType" {, "ExcType"})` gives a list of possible exceptions, where one of them *must* occur during the transition. If an exception *may* occur, `catches` can be used, which specifies the target state for the model if the exception occurs:

```
"pre" -> "post" := { action } catches ("Exception" -> "errorState").
```

Related to the formal definition of ESFMs in Section 2, Modbat does not use explicit input and output symbols; input/output functions of Java's libraries are available instead. D is represented by model variables. F is implemented by Modbat itself as a check of the predecessor state, and whether declared preconditions evaluate to *true*. Update functions U are transition actions as shown above; and the transition relation T, implemented by Modbat, takes into account the given successor states, exceptions, and the semantics of `nextIf` as shown below.

Modbat also supports some shorthand definitions, for example to model a set of transitions with the same action and end state, and to model multiple transitions with the same predecessor and successor states but different actions. We believe that automatically combining user-defined annotations for preconditions and exceptions with transitions derived from the EFSM, is a key to making a test derivation tool both expressive and easy to use. Earlier work has shown that managing the model state as user-defined code is tedious and error-prone [2].

3.2   Comparison to API-Driven Test Derivation Tools

Existing tools like ModelJUnit [28] or ScalaCheck [21] require user-defined code to manage the model state. To show the benefit that Modbat provides, we compare the necessary code to manage the model state for normal transitions and transitions throwing exceptions. The overhead of user-defined code becomes particularly high when exceptions have to be managed. Figure 6 shows, for different tools, the code for managing the model state, and for ensuring that an exception *always* occurs (for example, when `action` is executed in the wrong system state). Code to manage optional exceptions is similar in ModelJUnit and ScalaCheck; it updates the next state instead of a boolean and contains no assertion.

Compared to other tools, Modbat's notation is more concise (see Table 1). When counting the additional code to handle certain features, we assume a non-trivial EFSM with non-empty preconditions and do not count the action function itself, or lines containing only curly braces. We also count a state transition in Modbat as two lines, as it is usually formatted as such (see Figure 4). We can see that our notation reduces the amount of model code by 75 % for each transition while also eliminating error-prone repetitive code that manages internal information.[2]

Preconditions (which may not contain side-effects) are supported by all tools in similar ways. In Modbat, preconditions are declared using `require`, using the same syntax as in normal Scala code.

---

[2] Defining additional helper functions in ScalaCheck could partially alleviate the overhead of exception checking, but not of state management.

Modbat	ModelJUnit	ScalaCheck

`"pre" -> "post" :=`
`{ action }`
	`boolean action0Guard() {`
	`  return state == 0; }`
	`@Action void action0() {`
	`  action();`
	`  state = 1; }`
		`case object Transition0`
		`extends Command {`
		`preConditions += (s==...)`
		`def run(s: State) = action`
		`def nextState(s:State)=...`

Modbat	ModelJUnit	ScalaCheck

`{ action }`
`throws("Exception")`
	`{ boolean ok = false;`
	`try {`
	`  action();`
	`} catch(Exception e){`
	`  ok = true; }`
	`assert (ok); }`
		`{ var ok = false`
		`try {`
		`  action`
		`} catch { case e:`
		`  Exception => ok=true }`
		`assert (ok) }`

Fig. 6. State transitions (top) and exception handling (bottom) in different tools

Table 1. Lines of additional code needed (per use) to handle certain model features

Feature	Modbat	ModelJUnit	ScalaCheck
State transition	1	4	4
Precondition	1	1	1
Expected exception	1	5	5
Optional exception	1	4	4

As can be seen, Modbat's embedded DSL supports model constructs efficiently while still leveraging the host language, Scala. Other related tools also use models defined in program code against a given API (see Section 2.3); the coding overhead compared to our DSL-based approach is similar to the cases shown in Table 1.

3.3 Advanced Modeling Features: Non-determinism and Annotations

We consider non-determinism a powerful modeling feature and therefore support multiple operators that deal with different types of non-determinism:

Choose returns a random number in a given range. It is intended to cover relatively simple use cases. We do not model complex data such as supported by generator functions in ScalaCheck [21], because the generators from ScalaCheck can be combined with Modbat as long as replay and offline testing (see below) are not used.

Maybe executes code probabilistically, with default probability of 0.5. This is useful when testing SUT functionality that is expected to fail sometimes (such as input/output). In a normal test setup, failure probability may be too low to be observed. With `maybe`, faults can be simulated (injected) on the model level.

NextIf models alternative outcomes on the SUT side. For instance, non-blocking input/output (I/O) operations return immediately but may be incomplete. Using `nextIf`, the model can account for both possible outcomes of such an operation.

When using non-blocking I/O, a failed or partial I/O operation usually has to be retried later. In Modbat, `nextIf` overrides the normal successor state if its predicate is *true*. The following code models a non-blocking accept call in `ServerSocketChannel`, which is part of package `java.nio` in the standard Java library [23]:

```
"accepting" -> "connected" := {
  connection = ch.accept()
} nextIf ({ () => connection == null} -> "accepting").³
```

The documentation of `accept` states that the non-blocking variant immediately returns a new connection handle if it is successful and `null` otherwise [23]. The normal successor state in the model (*connected*) covers the case where the operation is successful, but `nextIf` defines an alternative to remain in the current model state otherwise.

Using `nextIf` allows exhaustive testing of component-based systems which are often I/O-driven and have to be able to continue after communication problems. It is similar to next-state declarations in modeling languages such as Promela [14] used for the exhaustive verification of algorithms. As Modbat tests implementations, exhaustive verification cannot be attained directly. To observe all possible outcomes, either a large number of test runs is needed, or a platform that can simulate delays, such as Java PathFinder [30]; also see Section 5.

As our modeling language is embedded in Scala, all Scala language features are available. In particular, longer blocks of code can be written as separate functions. Functions may also be *annotated* so they have a special significance outside a test run: Functions annotated with `@init` and `@shutdown` are executed before the first and after the last test run, respectively. In our case studies, we used these annotations to run a server in the background while client tests were being executed, and to shut the server down cleanly at the end. While this task could also be handled externally (e. g., by shell scripts), having a built-in mechanism allows us to refer to model data. Similarly, annotations `@before` and `@after` execute a function before and after *each* test. Such functions set up and tear down auxiliary data structures without complicating the test model itself.

3.4 Other Features

Modbat records any decisions taken by its own random number generator (RNG), so tests can be replayed in full (with a given random seed) or partially (with a subset of the trace of random numbers generated). Unfortunately, replaying currently does not support third-party data generators such as ScalaCheck's.

---

³ The parentheses followed by the arrow, () =>, are a Scala syntax artifact to encapsulate the condition in an anonymous function, which is then passed to Modbat.

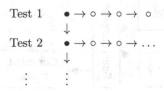

Fig. 7. Master (filled circle)/slave (unfilled circle) RNG usage in Modbat

Modbat uses random numbers in a tree-like fashion: Instead of one RNG, a *master RNG* and a *slave RNG* are maintained (see Figure 7). The master is advanced by one step at the end of each test run and only used to seed the slave RNG for a new test run. Because the RNG is restored to a new seed before a new test is started, changes in the number of (slave) RNG calls in previous test cases do not affect the new state at the beginning of a new test. This keeps test runs within a test suite consistent across minor modifications of the model (such as adding an extra choice that does not affect the outcome of most test runs). Precomputing master RNG states even allows parallelization of test executions.

Modbat supports multiple ESFMs, which are executed using an interleaving semantics. Modbat starts a given state machine first, which then uses the `launch` function of Modbat to launch a (parametrized) instance of another ESFM.

Modbat supports both online and offline testing, even when random numbers are used. For offline testing, the trace of random numbers is recorded for each transition, so test case minimization can be performed later [32].

Modbat also supports coverage measurement; currently, state and transition coverage are measured. Coverage can be visualized (along with the test model) using Graphviz [12].

4   Implementation Architecture

Modbat's test models are defined in an embedded DSL [31] on top of Scala [22]. Scala was chosen for its extensible syntax (allowing the definition of domain-specific languages on top of Scala) and its compatibility with Java. We use the Scala compiler to parse the test model and compile it against a model library that defines the syntax of our DSL and its operators (see Figure 8).

Modbat supports a variety of configuration options. Test requirements include the total number of tests and the option to abort after a failure. The length of test runs can also be limited by setting a probability to abort a test after each step. Implementation-specific information (IXIT in Figure 2) includes library locations, log file locations, and the option to set a random seed.

Modbat loads the compiled model and tests it against the SUT. Normally, Modbat runs in the normal Java Virtual Machine (JVM), and executes test cases online against the test specification. Failed tests are reported and can optionally

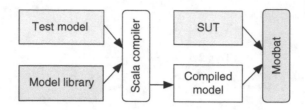

Fig. 8. Implementation architecture (online testing)

be written to a Java or Scala source file as unit tests. Modbat supports JUnit-style test code generation or a stand-alone format that uses its own test harness.

Offline test code is compiled against the test model for later execution. Both the compiled unit tests (defining the test traces) and the test model are used for offline testing, as the latter holds model variables and state transition functions.

5   Usage of Modbat in Software Development

To find defects in Modbat itself, Modbat is tested internally against a number of test models. Tests range from parsing command line arguments to online and offline test derivation. About 200 such tests are used as regression tests during development, to validate Modbat itself. Online test case generation is tested by running Modbat on the compiled test model, and observing the outcome (test coverage reported, number of failures found, contents of error traces). For offline testing, two more stages are added: First, the generated source code is compiled and compared against a previous run; then, the output of the executed offline tests is also verified.

5.1   Testing the SAT Solver Lingeling with Modbat

Our first project illustrates how Modbat is used to test SAT solvers, which are very complex and highly optimized programs. As SAT solvers often serve as reasoning backends in verification frameworks, their correctness is of particular importance. In general, efficiently implemented SAT solvers are too complex to be fully verified themselves, so testing approaches like model-based testing are required to ensure their robustness. Previous work [3] shows how model-based testing compares to standard testing techniques for the SAT solver Lingeling, which is the winner of several major tracks at the SAT solver competition 2013. Besides standard reasoning techniques found in almost all recent SAT solvers, Lingeling additionally implements several preprocessing rules which are very effective, but which also increase the complexity of the solver's code and API.

An earlier testing framework [3] realizes a model-based testing approach where the model is expressed in plain C code. The generation of the test cases based on this model was also manually implemented in C, requiring about 650 lines of code. We formulated the same model, consisting of 12 states with 18 transitions, in Modbat with only 300 lines of code for the same functionality. As Lingeling is written in C, we used the Java Native Access (JNA) framework to make Lingeling's API accessible in Modbat. We did not experience any restrictions concerning the expressiveness of neither Modbat nor Scala used for describing the generation of the input data. Because each test run consists of hundreds of transitions with almost equally many (uncovered) branches, 99.98 % of all generated paths by Modbat were unique after 100,000 tests.

We performed a similar experiment as described in earlier work [3], applying our tests to 373 different defective versions of Lingeling. The faults were randomly seeded into Lingeling's code by removing arbitrary lines or by introducing abort-statements. Each generated test case was then applied to each defective version, with a timeout of 100 seconds per test case (on a given instance of Lingeling). In our setup, 55 % of the defects were found with the model written in C [3] within that timeframe. With Modbat we found 60 % of the defects. When looking at the execution performance, we experienced that the hand-coded model in C is only twice as fast as the generic Modbat framework.

5.2   Java PathFinder

To evaluate Modbat to an input/output (I/O) driven system, we applied it to an implementation of `java.nio`, Java's network library for non-blocking, selector-based I/O. This library is used in Java PathFinder (JPF) [30], which is a software model checker for Java bytecode. In a concurrent SUT, JPF explores the outcomes of all possible thread interleavings by backtracking executions to a previously stored program state, and exploring the other remaining outcomes from that point. By itself, JPF cannot handle network I/O, because backtracking the SUT causes it to be out of sync with its environment [5].

In JPF, a *model library* can provide the missing functionality that JPF does not support. Other work describes the implementation of `java.nio` in JPF and its application to a web server in depth, along with a preliminary evaluation of an earlier model [4]. In this work, we describe our enhancements to the earlier model [4], the new defects that Modbat revealed, and its behavior in JPF in more depth.

JPF implements software model checking by running the SUT in its own virtual machine (VM) that is capable of backtracking the entire SUT state. JPF currently supports only the execution of entire programs; therefore, the test harness also needs to be executed inside JPF, even if it is entirely deterministic. In our case, Modbat is the test harness, and the `java.nio` library is the SUT.

5.3   Evaluation of Models for Non-blocking I/O

Non-blocking I/O is difficult to test: A non-blocking operation returns immediately, but the result may be incomplete. The correct use of non-blocking I/O therefore requires state and buffer management code to ensure completion of an operation. While more difficult to implement than blocking I/O, it often provides better performance and has become prevalent in modern servers [26].

Table 2. Experiments on testing the `java.nio` client API in JPF

# tests	Model coverage		JPF states		other JPF statistics		
	# states	# trans.	new	visited	ins. [1,000s]	mem. [MB]	time
100	5	13	1,070	5	11,667	616	0:15
200	6	15	2,142	3	23,316	1,173	0:31
300	6	19	6,256	24	68,312	2,913	1:51
400	6	20	16,302	61	177,605	4,802	6:03
500	6	20	26,054	121	283,699	6,127	10:20

Table 3. Experiments on testing the `java.nio` server API in JPF

# tests	Model coverage		JPF states		other JPF statistics		
	# states	# trans.	new	visited	ins. [1,000s]	mem. [MB]	time
100	7	17	676	0	7,185	294	0:16
200	7	17	4,798	223	52,128	551	1:10
400	7	17	6,917	230	74,823	1,131	1:46
800	7	17	11,973	273	128,910	2,607	3:37
1,200	7	17	14,760	282	158,872	4,396	5:33
1,600	7	17	20,194	338	217,039	5,996	9:57

We applied Modbat to three related models: one for the server API that focuses on accepting connections on an open port, and two for the client API that model connection usage and selectors, respectively. Out of these models, the server model is the smallest (having fewer states and less inherent non-determinism than the client models), and the client model that includes selector usage is the largest.

Modbat is first applied to our test model on the normal Java VM, taking the standard implementation of `java.nio` as a reference implementation. The model is written such that no (false) positives are reported in that case. Model execution in this case is very fast; for models without external communication, we measured 3,000 test per second on an 8-core Mac Pro workstation running Mac OS 10.7.

Execution in JPF is much slower than in the normal Java VM. The overall architecture remains the same, but Modbat and the SUT run inside JPF instead of the normal Java VM to analyze non-deterministic operations. While Modbat itself is deterministic, non-determinism in non-blocking I/O generates multiple possible successor states. When the outcome of a given test case is analyzed exhaustively (in JPF) rather than for only one execution (in the normal Java VM), coverage information maintained by Modbat diverges as well. This causes a state space explosion across multiple test executions (see Tables 2 and 3). In that table, the number of "visited" states in JPF indicates the effect of non-determinism on coverage information, and thus a super-linear increase in the state space.

Because of this growing memory usage by the state space generated JPF, generating a large number of test runs in a single execution is not possible. We

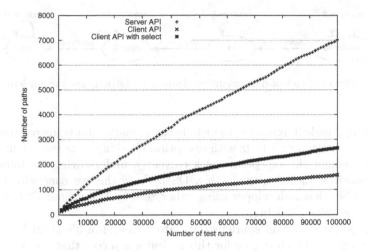

Fig. 9. Paths covered (out of infinitely many possible paths) during 100,000 test runs

solve the problem by splitting 100,000 tests into small test suites, and multiple executions of Modbat in JPF. Taking advantage of our random number generator (see Section 3), we use the successor of the master random seed of the last test run in the next execution of Modbat. Coverage information is aggregated by post-processing the log files.

Full state and transition coverage was reached quickly in all models, after fewer than 1,000 test runs.[4] As the models include loops, the number of possible paths is infinite. However, most tests reach an end state after ten or fewer transitions. Due to this, the probabilistic test exploration of Modbat ends up covering previously derived test traces (see Figure 9). After 1,000 tests, between 13.7 and 21.3 % of all generated traces are unique; after 10,000 tests, that number drops to 4.4–12.2 %; after 100,000 tests, to 1.6–7.0 %. We consider these diminishing returns not to be a huge problem: Similar case studies have shown that a large number of significant SUT behaviors is covered after 2,000–5,000 cases [3].

5.4 Defects Found

We found two previously unknown defects in our `java.nio` library for JPF:

1. The wrong exception was thrown when `finishConnect` was invoked after `close`. This scenario is easily overlooked as manually written tests and (even our own earlier models) tend to focus on key operations of the SUT and neglect operations that come after "difficult" ones [25]. The bug was found after introducing a short-hand in Modbat to model similar transitions more

---

[4] We found that for a large number of models, state and transition coverage was even easier to obtain. However, a model state may reflect many system states, depending on the level of abstraction. Therefore, we think that more complex coverage metrics [1] are needed; their usage is future work.

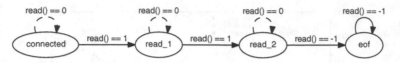

Fig. 10. Model of end-of-file semantics; dashed transitions are incomplete reads

succinctly, made it expedient to include the scenario that triggered the defect. Manually written unit tests with exception checking code (see Figure 6) did not implement the exception check correctly, underscoring the importance of supporting such features with a DSL. From this we conclude that it is conceivable that a developer using other test tools (without DSL support) may have missed this bug.

2. It was possible to read spurious data after an end-of-file (EOF) token had been received. The test case for this includes a server that sends two bytes and then closes its connection. The model has to verify correct reception of data in the presence of possibly incomplete reads. The defect in the library related to a mismatch between the EOF event and its internal state when non-blocking reads are used. The problem was found thanks to improved monitoring code in the model. In this case, the property to be monitored was expressed programmatically, and was initially too weak. In hindsight, using extra model states and Modbat's `nextIf` feature would have expressed the same property more succinctly and clearly (see Figure 10).

From these case studies, we conclude that Modbat is effective at modeling APIs of I/O-driven systems. The fact that it allows to express certain features directly was related to finding defects that were not detected by manually written tests (because of faulty checking code) and earlier models (because of a less expressive DSL available then). Still, we also concur that creating a succinct and correct model of system states and actions as a compact EFSM is a challenge. The choice of appropriate model states and variables at the right level of abstraction requires experience and precise reasoning about the system specification.

6   Conclusions and Future Work

Modbat is a model-based tester based on extended finite-state machines. It differs from existing test generation tools by providing a domain-specific language that assigns system actions to transitions between model states. Modbat directly supports exception handling and non-deterministic system actions such as non-blocking input/output.

Our experience with Modbat shows that its notation is very versatile and allows the developer to focus on the system semantics and properties. Using Modbat, we successfully found previously unknown defects in a complex system. This was made possible because Modbat allows one to easily express a variety of system actions, including non-deterministic operations. The fact that previous attempts missed these defects suggests that model expressiveness is an important factor for the effectiveness of model-based testing.

Our current approach to test case derivation uses only a random seed as persistent state. This allows for parallelization of the search, but limits the number of unique paths found for a given number of test cases. In future work, we would like to investigate coverage-driven approaches, in a way that still allows splitting large test suites into small parts. We also plan to integrate Modbat with other test data generation tools, and consider searching finite models exhaustively.

Acknowledgements. This work is supported by *kaken-hi* grant 23240003. We would like to thank Dimitra Giannakopoulou, Falk Howar, Richard Potter, Rudolf Ramler, and Franz Weitl for their suggestions and feedback during our discussions.

References

1. Ammann, P., Offutt, J.: Introduction to Software Testing, 1st edn. Cambridge University Press, New York (2008)
2. Artho, C.: Separation of transitions, actions, and exceptions in model-based testing. In: Moreno-Díaz, R., Pichler, F., Quesada-Arencibia, A. (eds.) EUROCAST 2009. LNCS, vol. 5717, pp. 279–286. Springer, Heidelberg (2009)
3. Artho, C., Biere, A., Seidl, M.: Model-based testing for verification back-ends. In: Veanes, M., Viganò, L. (eds.) TAP 2013. LNCS, vol. 7942, pp. 39–55. Springer, Heidelberg (2013)
4. Artho, C., Hagiya, M., Potter, R., Tanabe, Y., Weitl, F., Yamamoto, M.: Software model checking for distributed systems with selector-based, non-blocking communication. In: Proc. 28th Int. Conf. on Automated Software Engineering (ASE 2013), Palo Alto, USA. IEEE Computer Society (to be published, 2013)
5. Artho, C., Leungwattanakit, W., Hagiya, M., Tanabe, Y.: Efficient model checking of networked application. In: Paige, R.F., Meyer, B. (ed.) TOOLS EUROPE 2008. LNBIP, vol. 11, pp. 22–40. Springer, Heidelberg (1974)
6. Beck, K.: Extreme programming explained: embrace change. Addison-Wesley Longman Publishing Co., Inc. (2000)
7. Beck, K.: Test driven development: By example (2002)
8. Cheng, K., Krishnakumar, A.: Automatic functional test generation using the extended finite state machine model. In: Proc. 30th Int. Design Automation Conference, DAC 1993, pp. 86–91. ACM, New York (1993)
9. Claessen, K., Hughes, J.: QuickCheck: A lightweight tool for random testing of Haskell programs. SIGPLAN Not. 35(9), 268–279 (2000)
10. Forrester, J., Miller, B.: An empirical study of the robustness of Windows NT applications using random testing. In: 4th USENIX Windows System Symposium, Seattle, USA, pp. 59–68 (2000)
11. Fraser, G., Arcuri, A.: Whole test suite generation. IEEE Transactions on Software Engineering 39(2), 276–291 (2013)
12. Gansner, E., North, S.: An open graph visualization system and its applications to software engineering. Software—Practice and Experience 30(11), 1203–1233 (2000)
13. Godefroid, P., Klarlund, N., Sen, K.: Dart: directed automated random testing. SIGPLAN Not. 40(6), 213–223 (2005)

14. Holzmann, G.: The SPIN Model Checker. Addison-Wesley (2004)
15. Jacky, J., Veanes, M., Campbell, C., Schulte, W.: Model-Based Software Testing and Analysis with C#, 1st edn. Cambridge University Press (2007)
16. Kanstrén, T., Puolitaival, O.: Using built-in domain-specific modeling support to guide model-based test generation. In: Proc. 7th Workshop on Model-Based Testing (MBT 2012). EPTCS, vol. 80, pp. 58–72 (2012)
17. Kitamura, T., Do, N.T.B., Ohsaki, H., Fang, L., Yatabe, S.: Test-case design by feature trees. In: Margaria, T., Steffen, B. (eds.) ISoLA 2012, Part I. LNCS, vol. 7609, pp. 458–473. Springer, Heidelberg (2012)
18. Kramer, J.: Is abstraction the key to computing? Commun. ACM 50(4), 36–42 (2007)
19. Link, J., Fröhlich, P.: Unit Testing in Java: How Tests Drive the Code. Morgan Kaufmann Publishers, Inc. (2003)
20. Myers, G.: Art of Software Testing. John Wiley & Sons, Inc. (1979)
21. Nils, R.: ScalaCheck, A powerful tool for automatic unit testing (2013), https://github.com/rickynils/scalacheck
22. Odersky, M., Spoon, L., Venners, B.: Programming in Scala: A Comprehensive Step-by-step Guide, 2nd edn. Artima Inc., USA (2010)
23. Oracle. Java Platform Standard Edition 7 API Specification (2013), http://docs.oracle.com/javase/7/docs/api/
24. Pacheco, C., Ernst, M.: Randoop: feedback-directed random testing for Java. In: OOPSLA 2007 Companion, Montreal, Canada. ACM (2007)
25. Ramler, R., Winkler, D., Schmidt, M.: Random test case generation and manual unit testing: Substitute or complement in retrofitting tests for legacy code? In: 36th Conf. on Software Engineering and Advanced Applications, pp. 286–293. IEEE Computer Society (2012)
26. Reese, W.: Nginx: the high-performance web server and reverse proxy. Linux Journal 173 (2008)
27. Sen, K., Marinov, D., Agha, G.: CUTE: A concolic unit testing engine for C. SIGSOFT Softw. Eng. Notes 30(5), 263–272 (2005)
28. Utting, M., Legeard, B.: Practical Model-Based Testing: A Tools Approach. Morgan Kaufmann Publishers, Inc., San Francisco (2006)
29. Veanes, M., Campbell, C., Grieskamp, W., Schulte, W., Tillmann, N., Nachmanson, L.: Model-based testing of object-oriented reactive systems with Spec Explorer. In: Hierons, R.M., Bowen, J.P., Harman, M. (eds.) FORTEST. LNCS, vol. 4949, pp. 39–76. Springer, Heidelberg (2008)
30. Visser, W., Havelund, K., Brat, G., Park, S., Lerda, F.: Model checking programs. Automated Software Engineering Journal 10(2), 203–232 (2003)
31. Wampler, D., Payne, A.: Programming Scala. O'Reilly Series. O'Reilly Media (2009)
32. Zeller, A., Hildebrandt, R.: Simplifying and isolating failure-inducing input. Software Engineering 28(2), 183–200 (2002)

Predictive Taint Analysis for Extended Testing of Parallel Executions

Emmanuel Sifakis and Laurent Mounier

VERIMAG laboratory – University of Grenoble
2 Av. Vignate, 38610 Gieres, France
{esifakis,mounier}@imag.fr

Abstract. Dynamic information flow analysis is utterly useful in several contexts. Its adaptation to parallel executions of multi-threaded programs has to overcome the non-deterministic serialization of memory accesses. We propose an offline sliding window-based prediction algorithm for taint analysis. It infers explicit taint propagations that could have occurred under plausible serializations of an observed execution.

1 Introduction

Over the past ten years parallel platforms, especially multi-cores, have invaded every aspect of computing. Their capability to increase performance of concurrent applications did not come for free. The parallel execution model introduced by these platforms raises some new challenges to the (static and dynamic) analysis of (concurrent) programs executing on such platforms.

1.1 Executing Multi-threaded Applications in Parallel

Concurrency is often exposed to programmers through the notion of *threads*, which are schedulable streams of code. With the introduction of multi-cores, the execution model of multi-threaded programs switched from *sequential*, where the threads were serialized by the operating system, to *parallel*, where threads are executed simultaneously, and conflicting memory accesses are serialized by the execution platform. Fig. 1 illustrates an abstract view of a sequential and parallel execution of two threads. In the sequential case, on the left, the order in which instructions are executed is clear and it is guaranteed that thread B will assign variable y the value 0, since x=0 precedes. Dually, in the parallel case, on the right, threads A and B are executed simultaneously and it is *uncertain* if y is assigned value 1 or 0.

This uncertainty in the ordering of memory accesses is caused by the *execution platform*. More precisely, processing units of the architecture may issue simultaneously memory accesses which are eventually *serialized* on the physical memory. Also, for performance reasons, almost all architectures implement some type of *relaxed memory model*[1], where a thread A may observe a different ordering of memory accesses than that observed by a simultaneously executing thread B. All these elements introduce some non-determinism at the execution level of applications, which impacts the classical validation techniques.

---

[1] [1] provides a thorough presentation of relaxed memory models.

V. Bertacco and A. Legay (Eds.): HVC 2013, LNCS 8244, pp. 129–144, 2013.

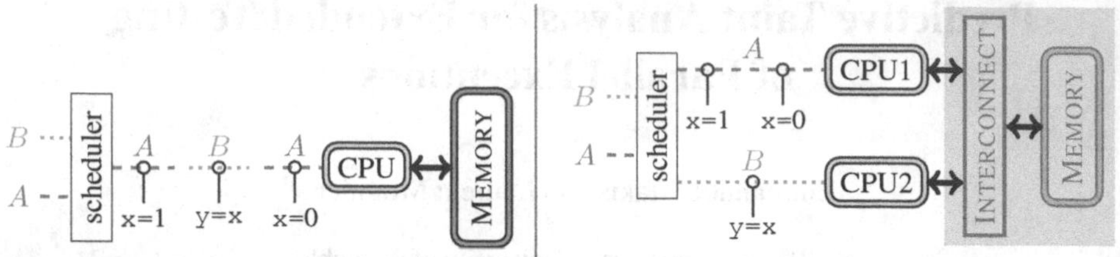

Multi-threaded execution on mono-processor   Multi-threaded execution on multi-processor

Fig. 1. Execution of multithreaded application

1.2   Concurrency Bug Analysis

The situation described on Fig. 1 is a typical example of a *race*, occurring when the outcome of a program depends on the order some shared resources (e.g., memory locations, files) were accessed. Races are a fundamental complication of concurrent programs. Their effect is also observable on sequential executions, when a schedule that triggers the race is executed. Because the scheduling of concurrent programs is (in general) non-deterministic, races are hard to detect and reproduce. Thus, to eliminate them synchronization mechanisms such as *mutexes* are used. The misuse of synchronization mechanisms may reduce performance, or introduce other concurrency bugs such as deadlocks and starvation. Therefore, (supposedly) benign races are often allowed in programs

As a result, identification of concurrency bugs has been widely studied in the literature. Many analyzes have been proposed to expose data races or synchronization issues such as deadlocks. Static approaches [2,3] provide global results, i.e. concerning all executions of a program, but they tend to produce many false positives due to necessary abstractions. On the other hand, dynamic analyses [4,5,6] are much more precise, since they are based on finite concrete executions, but their verdict holds only for the (very small) subset of observed executions, depending on the chosen program inputs.

In the case of parallel executions on a multicore architecture, this later point becomes even more critical. Indeed, the non-determinism introduced by the execution platform (in addition to the one produced by the interleaving between threads) further reduces the coverage level of a dynamic analysis (re-playing the application with the same input may lead to a different ordering access on shared resources, and drastically change the programs behavior). Moreover, observing a parallel execution is a very challenging task. This is usually achieved either by (arbitrarily) producing some particular serialization, or by using specialized hardware e.g, [7,8]. Note that the same problem occurs from a testing point of view: repeated executions of a same test case may produce different verdicts.

To overcome this limitation, a technique called *runtime prediction* has emerged over the past years. It consists in collecting sufficient information while observing a single execution to *infer* concurrency bugs that could occur in *other plausible* executions. This can be achieved using either algorithms operating on abstract program representations (as in [9,10]), or more sophisticated ones based on *symbolic* computations to better take into account data assignments (e.g., [11]). Our objective in this paper is to apply this technique on a specific information flow analysis.

1.3 Taint Analysis

Taint analysis is a very popular dynamic information flow analysis. It is widely used in several contexts such as vulnerability detection, information policy enforcement, testing and debugging. A significant effort has been put on optimizing taint analysis for sequential programs. However, adapting taint analyses to programs executing in parallel is utterly difficult due to non-deterministic memory accesses.

Taint analysis consists into marking/tainting data associated to a memory location/ variable and tracking them as they propagate inside a program. A taint analysis is characterized by (i) *taint sources*, which specify what data should be tracked; (ii) *taint propagation policy*, which specifies how taintness propagates between memory locations; and (iii) *taint sanitizers*, indicating when data can be considered as un-tainted. In the context of vulnerability detection, user input and network traffic are most commonly designated as taint sources. The propagation of taintness occurs either *explicitly* through direct copy of data, or *implicitly* through some covert channel (e.g., control flow). Un-tainting (i.e., sanitization) occurs when a static value (i.e., user independent) is assigned to a variable. Implicit flows are very tedious to track dynamically and are often dropped in the literature. Similarly, in our work we focus exclusively on *explicit* taint propagations.

Most existing dynamic taint analyses [12,13,14,15] are implemented using some *dynamic binary instrumentation* framework [16,17]. The instrumentation code aims to maintain a so-called *shadow memory*, i.e., a mapping between each memory location accessed and a "taint value" in $\{T$ (tainted), U (untainted)$\}$. Note that, to track taintness correctly, the instruction that taints or un-taints a memory location and the update of the shadow memory must be performed atomically.

1.4 Objectives and Contribution

The objective of this work is to propose a predictive dynamic taint analysis for parallel executions of multi-threaded applications. More precisely, it consists in extending the results obtained by observing *a single parallel execution* to the set of *all plausible serializations* that *could have occurred* at the memory level (and were not necessarily observed along this execution).

Our main contribution is therefore to provide a dynamic taint-analysis addressing the following issues: (i) it does not require a sequential execution of the application, i.e., the results are obtained without constraining its *parallel execution* on a multi-core platform; (ii) it takes into account the *non-determinism* introduced by the execution platform, i.e., the results obtained are valid for a larger set of plausible executions than the one being observed; this allows to increase the *confidence level* provided by a given test or dynamic analysis campaign; (iii) it preserves the semantics of critical sections implemented by means of synchronization primitives (like mutexes).

The rest of the paper is structured as follows. In section 2 we give a general overview of the analysis technique we propose. Taint analysis with respect to a sequentially consistent memory model is described in section 3, and it is then extended in section 4 to take into account synchronization primitives. In section 5 we show that our results also hold for a weaker and more commonly used memory model (TSO). Finally, section 6 makes a short comparison with related work and section 7 concludes and gives some perspectives.

2   An Offline Window-Based Analysis

In this section we present our offline sliding window-based analysis for taint prediction. Fig. 2 illustrates an overview of our approach which consists of two phases:

online phase: execute the target application, on a given set of inputs, without any scheduling restrictions. The execution produces a set of log files (one per thread);
offline phase: analyze the log files to predict taint propagations that could occur on plausible serializations of the observed execution.

The logged information consists of all program statements involving some memory access (to a shared or private location) in the form of use/def relations, as well as the locking/unlocking operations on mutexes. Each log entry is associated with a *timestamp*, allowing to identify offline the "simultaneous" memory accesses. The lower part of Fig. 2 presents the *offline processing* which consists into:

1. slicing the logs into *epochs* (dotted boxes)
2. predicting taint propagation inside a window ($\mathcal{W}$), consisting of two consecutive epochs, and
3. summarizing the execution down to the analyzed window ($ST_{\mathcal{W}}$).

We introduce hereafter some notations used in the remaining of the document as illustrated on Fig. 2. First, each log entry corresponds to a runtime observation of a use-def relation between memory locations initiated by a thread. We denote log entries as *events* e_k^A where A is the thread identifier and k is a thread specific counter used to infer the observed program order. We introduce the functions $Def(e), Used(e)$ which return the set of defined/written and used/read variables respectively, for an event e. The logs are sliced into *epochs* which we refer to as l_i. The currently analyzed window $\mathcal{W} = \{l_b, l_t\}$ consists of two specially labeled epochs, where l_b is the *body* and l_t the *tail* epoch respectively [2]. The preceding window is called $\mathcal{W}' = \{l_h, l_b\}$, where l_h stands for the *head* epoch.

2.1   Slicing the Log Files

As mentioned earlier, our goal is to infer plausible serializations from a parallel execution. Thus, we slice the logs into uncertainty epochs of *fixed time intervals* τ. The period τ is platform dependent, such that each epoch contains a set of events "potentially executed in parallel". Thus, each epoch not only contains events occurring strictly at the same timestamp, but a set of events occurring within a "small" temporal window corresponding to some possible execution overlaps. Note that if this period is too large

---

[2] Label names are inherited from [18].

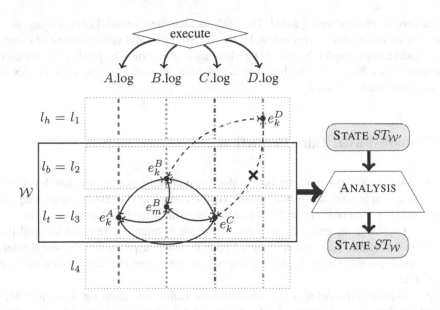

Fig. 2. Overview of our approach

it may also encompass event overlaps caused by the inter-thread scheduling. These interleaving also correspond to valid executions. The effect of the epoch size is illustrated through a handcrafted example in [19].

To simplify the presentation of our prediction analysis we assume first that the program order is not necessarily respected: events produced by a same thread can be interleaved. This (irrealistic) assumption will be dropped on section 3.2. Moreover, because the slicing of epochs is done arbitrarily i.e., there is no runtime synchronization to guarantee a happens before relation between events, we extend the interleaving assumption to events of two consecutive epochs.

Fig. 2 illustrates this point by depicting several events connected with a bidirectional edge denoting they can interleave (under the current assumption). The dashed edge connecting event e_k^B to e_k^D although valid, since these events belong to adjacent epochs, concerns the preceding window $\mathcal{W}' = \{l_h, l_b\}$. There is no possible interleaving between e_k^D and e_k^C (as shown by the crossed out edge connecting them) because they do not belong to adjacent epochs. Denoting event e_k^A occurring in epoch l as (l, A, k), we define a binary operator $\lhd_{cr}$ to express that an event (l, t, i) *may precede* an event (l', t', j) under the current assumption of *completely relaxed* (cr) interleaving of events, and a binary operator $\blacktriangleleft_{cr}$ which restricts $\lhd_{cr}$ to events belonging to the same thread.

- $(l, t, i) \lhd_{cr} (l', t', j) \equiv l' \geq l - 1)$
- $(l, t, i) \blacktriangleleft_{cr} (l', t', j) \equiv t = t' \land (l, t, i) \lhd_{cr} (l', t', j)$

2.2 Sliding Window Prediction

We apply our analysis using a sliding window consisting of two adjacent epochs. The window slides over epochs, thus all interleavings of an event with events in its preceding and succeeding epochs are explored. The analysis identifies potential taint propagations inside the currently analyzed window $\mathcal{W}$ by inferring all valid serializations of events with respect to the completely relaxed interleaving assumption. The predictions are then summarized in a *state ST*, which acts as the *shadow memory*. That is, all variables in ST are considered as tainted.

3   Window-Based Taint Prediction

Hereafter we present our taint prediction algorithm operating at the window level. We start with a simple case where we assume (i) the completely relaxed interleaving assumption (even events of a single thread can be arbitrarily interleaved) and (ii) untainting of variables is ignored, i.e., once a variable is tainted it remains so until the end of the execution. Next, we refine prediction by using sequentially consistent interleaving assumptions (program order is respected) and taking into account un-tainting of variables.

Fig. 3 illustrates the definition of window-based taint prediction for the completely relaxed interleaving assumption. As illustrated, taint predictions down to the preceding window are summarized in $ST_{\mathcal{W}'}$. The prediction algorithm must infer taint propagation for all valid serializations of events in the currently analyzed window. That is, for all predicted $x \in ST_{\mathcal{W}}$ there exists a *valid serialization* $\sigma_{\mathcal{W}}^i = (e_1, ..e_j, ..e_k, ..e_n)$ of all events in $\mathcal{W}$ such that $taint(\sigma_{\mathcal{W}}^i, last(\sigma_{\mathcal{W}}^i), x)$ holds, where $last(\sigma_{\mathcal{W}}^i)$ is the last event of $\sigma_{\mathcal{W}}^i$ and $taint$ is a predicate that indicates if variable x is tainted at event e_k after executing $\sigma_{\mathcal{W}}^i$. We consider here the usual taint propagation policy telling that a variable defined (i.e., assigned) at e_k is tainted as soon as one of the variables used to define it is tainted. The predicate $taint$ is then defined recursively as follows:

$$taint(\sigma_{\mathcal{W}}^i, e_k, x) \equiv \begin{cases} x = T \quad \vee \quad x \in ST_{\mathcal{W}'} \quad \vee \\ \exists j \leq k \text{ such that:} \quad \begin{aligned} &Def(e_j) = x \quad \wedge \\ &\exists y \in Used(e_j) . taint(\sigma_{\mathcal{W}}^i, e_j, y) \end{aligned} \end{cases}$$

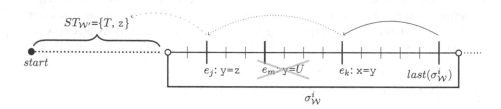

Fig. 3. Window-based taint prediction

3.1 Iterative Taint Prediction

A straightforward way to predict taint propagation for a window is to compute explicit taint propagation (Algorithm 1) for each of its valid serializations. Recall that state ST contains tainted variables. Thus, the condition on line 3 asserts there exists a tainted variable in the used set of the current event. Note that, in the case of un-tainting no action is taken, which conforms to our current assumption.

Algorithm 1.	Algorithm 2.
In: $\sigma^i_\mathcal{W}, ST_{\mathcal{W}'}$	**In:** $\sigma^i_\mathcal{W}, ST_{\mathcal{W}'}$
1: $ST^i_\mathcal{W} \leftarrow ST_{\mathcal{W}'}$	1: $ST_\mathcal{W} \leftarrow ST_{\mathcal{W}'}$
2: **for all** $e \in \sigma^i_\mathcal{W}$ **do**	2: **for all** $e \in \sigma^i_\mathcal{W}$ **do**
3: **if** $Used(e) \cap ST^i_\mathcal{W} \neq \emptyset$ **then**	3: $tv = TaintingVars(e)$;
4: $ST^i_\mathcal{W} \leftarrow ST^i_\mathcal{W} \cup Def(e)$	4: **if** $tv \neq \emptyset$ **then**
5: **end if**	5: $TH_\mathcal{W} \leftarrow TH_\mathcal{W} \cup \{(Def(e), (e, tv))\}$;
6: // ignore kills, do nothing	6: $ST_\mathcal{W} \leftarrow ST_\mathcal{W} \cup Def(e)$;
7: **end for**	7: **end if**
Out: $ST^i_\mathcal{W}$	8: // ignore kills, do nothing
	9: **end for**
	Out: $ST_\mathcal{W}$

The enumerative approach we just presented is illustrated in the left side of Fig. 4. It necessitates the processing of $|\mathcal{W}|!$ serializations, where $|\mathcal{W}|$ denotes the number of events in $\mathcal{W}$. This is not acceptable considering windows containing hundreds of events. However, we propose an alternative algorithm sketched on Fig. 4 (right). It consists in iterating Algorithm 1 on an arbitrary serialization of $\mathcal{W}$ until $ST_\mathcal{W}$ is stable (hence in at most $|\mathcal{W}|$ iterations).

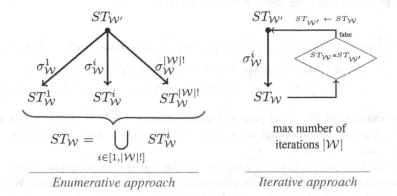

Enumerative approach   Iterative approach

Fig. 4. Enumerative prediction of taint propagation

We show hereafter how to extend this solution considering interleaving of events that respect *sequential consistency* and how to take into account un-tainting operations.

3.2 Iterative Taint Prediction under Sequential Consistency

According to *sequential consistency* program order should be respected. That is, events of a single thread cannot be interleaved. We define here the precedence operator for *sequential consistency* $\lessdot_{sc}$ which restricts the interleaving of events accordingly:

$$(l,t,i) \lessdot_{sc} (l',t',j) \Rightarrow (\, t = t' \,\wedge\, (l < l' \,\vee\, (l = l' \,\wedge\, i < j))\,) \,\vee\, (\, t \neq t' \,\wedge\, l' \geq l - 1\,)$$

Then, we say that a serialization $\sigma = (e_1, \ldots e_n)$ is sequentially consistent, and we note $is_{SC}(\sigma)$ if and only if for all $1 \leq i \leq j \leq n$ we have $e_i \lessdot_{sc} e_j$.

To ensure that all predicted taint propagations respect sequential consistency, we maintain a *taint history*. The taint history is associated to the currently analyzed window, and maps each memory location x to a set of pairs (e, V). The information captured in taint history makes taint propagation more explicit. Each pair (e, V) associated to x indicates that e taints x ($Def(e) = x$) through a (tainted) variable $y \in V$ where $V \subseteq Used(e)$. More formally, we define the *taint history* mapping function as follows:

$$
\begin{aligned}
TH_\mathcal{W}(x) = \{(e,V) \,|\; & e \in \mathcal{W} \,\wedge\, Def(e) = x \,\wedge\, \\
& V = \{y \,|\, y \in Used(e) \,\wedge\, \exists\, \sigma_\mathcal{W}^i \text{ s.t. } taint(\sigma_\mathcal{W}^i, e, y)\}\}
\end{aligned}
$$

Detailed information maintained in taint history allows us to compute *taint dependency paths* (TDP) for a given memory location. A *taint dependency path* $\mathcal{P} = (e_1, \ldots, e_n)$ specifies the execution ordering of a subset of events in the current window allowing to taint $Def(e_n)$. That is, taintness is propagated from the source event e_1 (tainted from $ST_{\mathcal{W}'}$) to the destination event e_n, through successive propagations from e_k to e_{k+1}. Here is the definition of such a path:

$$
\begin{aligned}
\mathcal{P} = \{(e_1, \ldots, e_n) \,|\; & \forall k \in [1, n] : e_k \in \mathcal{W} \,\wedge\, Used(e_1) \cap ST_{\mathcal{W}'} \neq \emptyset \,\wedge\, \\
& \forall k \in (1, n] : \exists\, (y, e_m, V) \text{ s.t. } y \in Used(e_k) \cap Def(e_{k-1}) \,\wedge\, \\
& (e_m, V) \in TH_\mathcal{W}(y) \,\wedge\, e_m = e_{k-1} \}
\end{aligned}
$$

In the example of Fig. 3 the path that taints variable x is $\mathcal{P} = (e_j, e_k)$. Assuming $e_k \lessdot_{sc} e_j$, this serialization is not valid under *sequential consistency* because it violates program order.

To update the *taint history* of a window and check that only *sequentially consistent* taint propagations are inferred, we need to modify the processing algorithm. We introduce Algorithm 2 which updates accordingly both the state of the current window but also the *taint history*. Note that, the check of whether the variable defined by an event gets tainted or not depends on the outcome of $TaintingVars$. This function returns the set of variables that propagate taintness to $Def(e)$.

Algorithm 3 sketches the implementation of $TaintingVars$. For each variable y used in event e it collects all taint dependency paths $\mathcal{P}$ that can be inferred in $TH_{\mathcal{W}}$ for y (line 3). Next, the function $isValid$ is applied to each path $\mathcal{P}$ to assert all propagation restrictions. At this stage, $isValid$ is equivalent to just calling $is_{SC}(\mathcal{P})$

Algorithm 3. $TaintingVars(e)$ return tainting variables

In: e

1: $tv \leftarrow \emptyset$
2: **for all** $y \in Used(e)$ **do**
3:     **for all** $\mathcal{P} \in TDP(TH_{\mathcal{W}}, y)$ **do**
4:         $\mathcal{P} \leftarrow e \,.\, \mathcal{P}$ // add event e as first event of $\mathcal{P}$
5:         **if** $isValid(\mathcal{P})$ **then**
6:             $tv \leftarrow y \cup tv$; break;
7:         **end if**
8:     **end for**
9: **end for**

Out: tv

3.3 Taking Un-tainting into Account

Un-tainting of variables affects taint prediction in two ways: (i) it prevents taint propagation by breaking a TDP and (ii) it removes (untainted) variables from $ST_{\mathcal{W}}$. These two points are handled separately.

To verify a path is not broken by an un-tainting we re-enforce $isValid$ by adding the predicate $noKill(\mathcal{P})$ which asserts events $\mathcal{P} \cup \{e_k \,|\, \exists e_m \in \mathcal{P} \text{ s.t. } e_k \blacktriangleleft_{sc} e_m\}$ can produce a sequentially consistent serialization $\sigma^{\mathcal{P}}$ such that (i) the ordering of events in $\mathcal{P}$ is respected and (ii) the variable that propagates taintness between two consecutive events of the path is not re-defined in-between.

A formal definition and representative examples of $noKill(\mathcal{P})$ are presented in section 4.2.1 of [20]. Hereafter, we present the principle of the checks through the examples of Fig. 5. In the upper part of Fig. 5(a) we illustrate the tainting path $\mathcal{P}$ using labeled edges, where the label corresponds to the variable that propagates taintness between events. In the lower part of the figure we juxtapose the tainting path $\mathcal{P}$ which is used as the back-bone of the serialization that $noKill(\mathcal{P})$ must infer. At the bottom, we denote as $\sigma^{\mathcal{P}} \setminus \mathcal{P}$ the events that must be positioned on $\mathcal{P}$ to produce $\sigma^{\mathcal{P}}$. The arrows illustrate where each event can be positioned while respecting sequential consistency. In this example the events can only be placed on a single position, thus we must check e_2^A and e_1^B do not define y and w respectively. In the example of Fig. 5(b) while the events breaking the path could be individually placed on $\mathcal{P}$ such that they do not break the path. These choices are not compatible as denoted by the crossing dashed arrows. Thus the path is inevitably broken.

Variables that end up un-tainted on all valid serializations of events in $\mathcal{W}$ should be removed from $ST_{\mathcal{W}}$. For instance, in the example of Fig. 5(b) while y is successfully

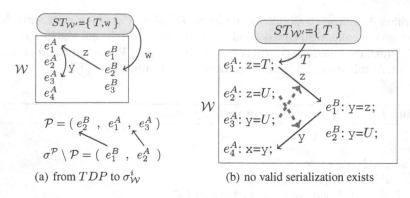

(a) from TDP to σ_W^i (b) no valid serialization exists

Fig. 5. Inferring a valid serialization for a path P

tainted at event e_1^B, it is subsequently un-tainted on all sequentially consistent serializations of W. Thus y should be excluded from the summarization of the window. Note that, due to the sliding of windows, variables un-tainted by events in the *tail* epoch of a window should be kept in ST_W. These un-tainting events have not yet been interleaved with events in the tail epoch of the next window, and thus un-tainting these variables could under-approximate taint propagation.

3.4 Precision of the Analysis

We presented so far an iterative algorithm that predicts explicit taint propagations within a window, while respecting sequentially consistent interleavings of events and the *un-tainting* of variables. There are two sources of over-approximation in our analysis. First, we might consider infeasible paths with respect to data valuations.

The second source of over-approximation is the sliding of windows which allows to propagate taintness through incompatible serializations. Fig. 6 illustrates such an example. In the first window $W' = \{l_h, l_b\}$ variable x is tainted through $P_1 = (e_1^A, e_3^A, e_1^C, e_1^B)$ traced with a solid line. The summary $ST_{W'}$ correctly contains x as there exists a serialization which taints it. Sliding to the next window, $W = \{l_b, l_t\}$, variable x can be used to propagate taintness. In this example, it taints variable y through $P_2 = (e_3^B, e_2^A, e_4^A)$, illustrated with a dashed line. Taint dependency path P_2, although valid in W, it is *not compatible* with the one that initially tainted x (which is the tainting source for variable y). Namely, the two TDPs cannot be merged and hence they do not provide a concrete serialization demonstrating how y gets tainted.

Merging TDPs computed in different windows is not always feasible. However, TDPs indicating why a variable is tainted within a window are not unique (although finding a single path is sufficient with respect to our taint propagation policy). For instance, with a closer look at Fig. 6 we can identify a second path $P_3 = (e_1^A, e_2^B)$ (illustrated with dash-dotted edges) for variable x which is compatible with P_2.

The incompatibility of TDPs over-approximates our predictions. To reduce the number of false positives we can classify the tainted variables into two categories *strong* and *weak*. *Strongly* tainted variables are those for which taintness propagation occurred

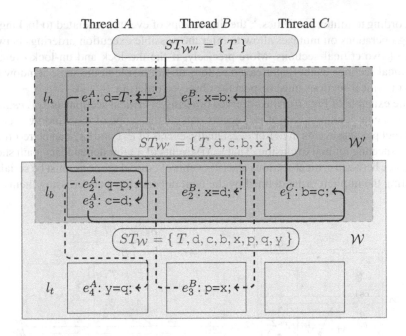

Fig. 6. Propagating taintness through incompatible TDPs

through mergeable tainting paths. Dually, *weakly* tainted variables are those for which non-mergeable tainting paths may exist. For the strongly tainted variables a witness execution can be constructed.

We provide hereafter two heuristics that can be used to identify *strongly* tainted variables without exhaustively exploring all paths:

1. If a tainting path $\mathcal{P}$ contains only events from the window's body and its tainting source variable is strongly tainted, then it defines a strongly tainted variable as well. Since $\mathcal{P}$ contains only instructions in body epoch it has no conflicts with paths in the succeeding window.
2. If a variable x is tainted in two consecutive epochs and (i) there is no kill of this variable in the common epoch and (ii) the variable that made it tainted in the first epoch is *strongly* tainted, then x is strongly tainted.

4 Respecting Synchronization Mechanisms

To control the execution of a multi-threaded application several synchronization mechanisms are provided. *Mutexes* are binary semaphores defining a *lock* and *un-lock* operation to respectively obtain and release exclusive access to a shared resource. *Mutexes* are widely used to implement *critical sections*, portions of code that must be executed atomically, by surrounding them with lock/un-lock operations on the appropriate mutex. Hereafter, we briefly explain how logged information on mutexes is used to refine taint propagations.

According to mutex semantics [3], the timestamps of events associated to locking/un-locking operations on mutexes allow to infer the possible execution orderings between events of two critical sections. More precisely, if the the lock and un-lock events of two critical sections cannot interleave i.e., they do not reside in the same window then events of critical sections must respect the observed ordering.

In the example of Fig. 7(a) the observed ordering of critical sections is $cs1, cs2, cs3$. Because the un-locking event of $cs3$ occurs outside the scope of the window events in $cs3$ cannot precede events in $cs1$ or $cs2$. Dually, events of $cs1$ and $cs2$ can be re-ordered while respecting mutual exclusion. That is, (i) events of a taint dependency path should not bounce between critical sections and (ii) events of critical sections must be serialized respecting the implicit order defined by the taint dependency path crossing them.

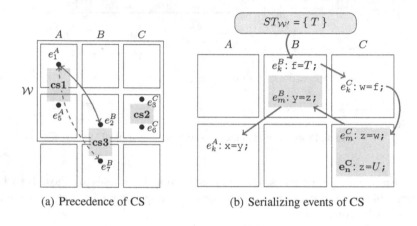

(a) Precedence of CS   (b) Serializing events of CS

Fig. 7. Respecting mutex synchronization

In the example of Fig. 7(b) the tainting path designated by the solid edges implies the critical section of thread C was executed prior to that of B. Thus, all events of critical section in C are executed before executing B. The corresponding possible serialization is therefore (e_k^B, e_k^C, e_m^C, e_n^C, e_m^B, e_k^A). Variables x and y cannot be tainted since event e_n^C always "breaks" the taint dependency path.

5 Taint Analysis and TSO Memory Model

All the results we presented so far are based on the assumption that program excution respects *sequential consistency*. However, for efficiency considerations, current multi-core architectures usually implement *weaker* memory models, potentially leading to a larger set of valid serializations of a parallel execution. We discuss in this section how our results are impacted when considering TSO ("total store ordering"), one of the most commonly used memory model[4].

---

[3] At any time at most one thread may hold a given mutex.

[4] e.g, on Intel x86 machines.

The main characteristic of *TSO* is that it allows the *write to read* relaxation: a read operation may complete prior to a preceding write operation to a different memory location. To formalize the precedence operator for *TSO* ($\blacktriangleleft_{tso}$) we need to reason at the level of individual *read/write* operations. Thus, we now consider events being either $\mathbf{R}(x, reg)$ (read variable x into register reg) or $\mathbf{W}(x, v)$ (write imediate value or register v to variable x). We introduce the functions $R(e)$ and $W(e)$ which return respectively the variable *read* or *written* by event e. The precedence operator $\blacktriangleleft_{tso}$ between events of the same thread (and the corresponding predicate is_{TSO} over serializations) is defined as follows:

$$\blacktriangleleft_{tso} \equiv \blacktriangleleft_{sc} \cup \{(e_m, e_k) \mid e_k \blacktriangleleft_{sc} e_m \wedge (\forall k \leq j < m.\ R(e_j) = \emptyset \wedge W(e_j) \neq R(e_m)\}$$

A natural question is now to check if considering TSO executions may impact taint propagation, and, if yes, how our algorithm could deal with this memory model. However, as expressed by Property 1, it happens that, under our taint propagation hypothesis, if a valid TSO serialization σ_W^i taints a variable x at event e_k, then there also exists a valid SC serialization σ_W^j tainting x at event e_k. Thus, considering sequential consistency is sufficient to predict taint propagation of parallel executions on TSO architectures.

Property 1. For a window W containing an event e_k, and for each variable x, we have:

$$(\exists \sigma_W^i.\ is_{TSO}(\sigma_W^i) \wedge taint(\sigma_W^i, e_k, x)) \Rightarrow (\exists \sigma_W^j.\ is_{SC}(\sigma_W^j) \wedge taint(\sigma_W^j, e_k, x))$$

Proof. (Sketch). First of all, if $is_{SC}(\sigma_W^i)$, then the property trivially holds. Otherwise, it is sufficient to show that introducing a valid TSO re-ordering (but not valid w.r.t. SC) in the events of a given thread does not change the taint value of the variables. Without loss of generality, lets assume that a thread T contains a sequence of events of the form $(\ldots, e_k, e_{k+1}, \ldots, e_{k+n}, e_k', \ldots)$ such that, for all $0 \leq i \leq n$: e_{k+i} is a write event; e_k' is a read event, $R(e_k') = x$, and $W(e_{k+i}) \neq R(e_k')$.
In a valid TSO serialization σ_W^i, event e_k' may *precede* events e_{k+i} ($e_k' \blacktriangleleft_{tso} e_{k+i}$), whereas it must *follow* them in any valid SC serialization ($\neg\ e_k' \blacktriangleleft_{sc} e_{k+i}$). But:

- variable x is not modified by events e_{k+i} ($W(e_{k+i}) \neq R(e_k')$);
- if variable x is modified by another thread T', i.e., there exists an event e_l such that $W(e_l) = x$ and e_l precedes e_k' in σ_W^i, then it is always possible to build another serialization σ_W^j such that $is_{SC}(\sigma_W^j)$ and e_l precedes e_k' in σ_W^j (since e_l and e_k' do not belong to the same thread).

Consequently the value read by e_k' on σ_W^i and σ_W^j corresponds. ∎

It is worth noting that Property 1 is no longer valid when a stronger taint propagation policy is considered. Lets assume for instance that a variable defined by a statement i becomes tainted if and only if *all* variables used to define it are tainted (e.g., if i is x=y+z then x is tainted iff both y and z are tainted). The example below shows that, under this assumption, considering TSO or SC memory models does not produce the same sets of tainted variables.

Example 1. Let us consider 3 threads A, B and C executing respectively :

A	B	C
x = U ;	y = U ;	z = a + b ;
a = y ;	b = x ;	

When individual read/write events are considered, the log file obtained is the following:

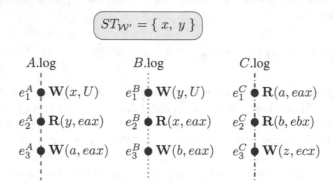

$$ST_{W'} = \{\ x,\ y\ \}$$

A.log	B.log	C.log
e_1^A • $\mathbf{W}(x, U)$	e_1^B • $\mathbf{W}(y, U)$	e_1^C • $\mathbf{R}(a, eax)$
e_2^A • $\mathbf{R}(y, eax)$	e_2^B • $\mathbf{R}(x, eax)$	e_2^C • $\mathbf{R}(b, ebx)$
e_3^A • $\mathbf{W}(a, eax)$	e_3^B • $\mathbf{W}(b, eax)$	e_3^C • $\mathbf{W}(z, ecx)$

Fig. 8. Log files produced from Example 1

According to TSO definition, event e_2^A (resp. e_2^B) and e_1^A (resp. e_1^B) can be swapped. Thus, the following serialization is valid under TSO: $(e_2^A, e_2^B, e_1^A, e_1^B, e_3^A, e_3^B, e_1^C, e_2^C, e_3^C)$. This serialization taints variable z. However, there exists no valid serialization under SC able to taint z with respect to this strong taint propagation hypothesis: a and b cannot be simultaneously tainted when event e_3^C is executed.

6 Related Work

Several dynamic taint analysis tools handle multi-threaded programs by serializing their execution. To the best of our knowledge the only works considering parallel executions of multi-threaded programs are [18], which inspired us, and [15]. In [18] they focus on implementing lifeguards for simpler data-flow problems such as undefined variables, reaching expressions etc. and provide technical details on how to implement taint analysis. The taint analysis they propose does not take into account any type of synchronization primitives and it is unclear whether they consider un-tainting of memory locations or not. Finally, their work is based on a specialized architecture which slices the execution into epochs at runtime. Their analysis uses a sliding window of three epochs which in our opinion makes the algorithms more complicated without any gain in precision.

In [15] they propose a two-phase taint analysis to reduce information recorded by re-players. Initially, they perform thread-local taint analysis at execution time. That is, each thread tracks taint propagation independently and logs the memory accesses uniquely to shared memory locations along with their thread-local taint status. Next in the off-line phase, they analyze the logs to predict taint propagations. Their prediction aims to identifying the effect of different schedules. Thus, they do not account for un-tainting of variables since any inter-thread interleaving could occur. However, they use happens before relations to refine their predictions. Finally, their logs are more concise than ours since they only log accesses to shared variables, but this implies they cannot precisely predict taint propagation offline.

7 Conclusion

In this work we addressed the problem of dynamic taint analysis for parallel executions of multi-threaded programs. We proposed a sliding-window based analysis which allows the prediction of taint propagations that could have occurred under plausible serializations of an observed execution. Prediction of taint propagation inside a window uses an iterative algorithm which avoids an explicit enumeration of all serializations. This algorithm holds when we assume a completely relaxed interleaving of instructions and a propagation of taintness through a single variable. We adapted this algorithm to sequentially consistent interleaving of instructions and proved that it is also capable of capturing taint propagations for TSO executions.

Our prediction algorithm has been implemented in a proof of concept tool chain. The tool chain consists of a front-end which instruments, statically, programs written in *C* that use the *Pthreads* library. The instrumenter is developed in *Java* on top of the CETUS [21] library. It adds the necessary logging instructions to capture the Use/Def relations required by the analysis, but also all mutex locking and un-locking events. The input accepted by the instrumenter is a sub-set of the *C* language. Note that the limitations are purely syntactical, yet they restrict the experimentations to hand-crafted examples. The back-end consists of a slicer (*Perl* script) which marks the epochs inside log files and the analyzer itself which parses the log files and performs the iterative analysis. We have three types of prediction implemented (i) completely relaxed interleaving assumption; (ii) sequentially consistent interleaving and (iii) sequentially consistent with synchronization restrictions. Apart the computation of taint propagation the analyzer also produces a visualization of taint propagations inside a window which facilitates back-tracking of taintness.

Initial experimentations on some hand-crafted examples allowed to infer correct taint propagations that were not observed at execution time. The execution time overhead for producing the logs is only 50% (which is quite reasonable regarding classical dynamic information-flow analysis). The performance of the offline phase is encouraging as well.

Several perspectives are envisioned for this work. At the theoretical level, it would be interesting to consider other propagation policies e.g., like the one mentioned in section 5. This would allow to adapt our algorithm to other information flow properties such as non-interference. At the practical level, the log files could be produced at the binary level which would increase analysis precision and allow arbitrary applications to be analyzed (even when the source code is not available). Moreover, we could introduce the classification of strongly and weakly tainted variables in our analysis, to reduce the number of false positives. Finally, the resulting tool could be integrated into some existing testing and vulnerability detection platform, making this plateform able to handle multi-threaded parallel executions.

References

1. Adve, S., Gharachorloo, K.: Shared memory consistency models: A tutorial. Computer 29(12) (December 1996)
2. Pratikakis, P., Foster, J., Hicks, M.: Locksmith: Practical static race detection for c. ACM Trans. Program. Lang. Syst. 33(1) (January 2011)
3. Engler, D., Ashcraft, K.: Racerx: effective, static detection of race conditions and deadlocks. In: SOSP 2003. ACM, NY (2003)
4. Yu, Y., Rodeheffer, T., Chen, W.: Racetrack: efficient detection of data race conditions via adaptive tracking. In: SOSP 2005. ACM, NY (2005)
5. Jannesari, A., Bao, K., Pankratius, V., Tichy, W.: Helgrind+: An efficient dynamic race detector. In: IPDPS 2009. IEEE Computer Society (2009)
6. Savage, S., Burrows, M., Nelson, G., Sobalvarro, P., Anderson, T.: Eraser: a dynamic data race detector for multithreaded programs. ACM Trans. Comput. Syst. 15(4) (1997)
7. Ozsoy, M., Ponomarev, D., Abu-Ghazaleh, N., Suri, T.: Sift: a low-overhead dynamic information flow tracking architecture for smt processors. In: Proceedings of the 8th ACM International Conference on Computing Frontiers, CF 2011, pp. 37:1–37:11. ACM, New York (2011)
8. Dalton, M., Kannan, H., Kozyrakis, C.: Raksha: a flexible information flow architecture for software security. In: Proceedings of the 34th Annual International Symposium on Computer Architecture. ISCA 2007, pp. 482–493. ACM, New York (2007)
9. Wang, L., Stoller, S.: Runtime analysis of atomicity for multithreaded programs. IEEE Trans. Softw. Eng. 32(2) (February 2006)
10. Sorrentino, F., Farzan, A., Madhusudan, P.: Penelope: weaving threads to expose atomicity violations. In: FSE 2010. ACM, NY (2010)
11. Wang, C., Ganai, M.: Predicting concurrency failures in the generalized execution traces of x86 executables. In: Khurshid, S., Sen, K. (eds.) RV 2011. LNCS, vol. 7186, pp. 4–18. Springer, Heidelberg (2012)
12. James, N., Dawn, X.: Dynamic taint analysis for automatic detection, analysis, and signature generation of exploits on commodity software. In: NDSS (2005)
13. Cheng, W., Zhao, Q., Yu, B., Hiroshige, S.: Tainttrace: Efficient flow tracing with dynamic binary rewriting. In: ISCC 2006. IEEE Computer Society (2006)
14. Zhu, D.Y., Jung, J., Song, D., Kohno, T., Wetherall, D.: Tainteraser: protecting sensitive data leaks using application-level taint tracking. SIGOPS Oper. Syst. Rev. 45(1) (February 2011)
15. Ganai, M., Lee, D., Gupta, A.: Dtam: Dynamic taint analysis of multi-threaded programs for relevancy. In: FSE 2012. ACM, New York (2012)
16. Bruening, D.L.: Efficient, transparent and comprehensive runtime code manipulation. Technical report (2004)
17. Luk, C., Cohn, R., Muth, R., Patil, H., Klauser, A., Lowney, G., Wallace, S., Reddi, V.J., Hazelwood, K.: Pin: building customized program analysis tools with dynamic instrumentation. In: PLDI 2005, NY, USA (2005)
18. Goodstein, M., Vlachos, E., Chen, S., Gibbons, P., Kozuch, M., Mowry, T.: Butterfly analysis: adapting dataflow analysis to dynamic parallel monitoring. In: ASPLOS 2010. ACM, New York (2010)
19. Sifakis, E.: Towards efficient and secure shared memory applications. PhD thesis, University of Grenoble (2013)
20. Sifakis, E., Mounier, L.: Offline taint prediction for multi-threaded applications. Technical Report TR-2012-08, Verimag Research Report (2012)
21. Dave, C., Bae, H., Min, S.J., Lee, S., Eigenmann, R., Midkiff, S.: Cetus: A source-to-source compiler infrastructure for multicores. Computer 42, 36–42 (2009)

Continuous Integration for Web-Based Software Infrastructures: Lessons Learned on the *webinos* Project

Tao Su[1], John Lyle[2], Andrea Atzeni[1], Shamal Faily[3], Habib Virji[4],
Christos Ntanos[5], and Christos Botsikas[5]

[1] Dip. di Automatica e Informatica, Politecnico di Torino, 10129 Torino, Italy
{tao.su,shocked}@polito.it
[2] Department of Computer Science, University of Oxford, UK
johnplyle@gmail.com
[3] School of Design, Engineering & Computing, Bournemouth University, UK
sfaily@bournemouth.ac.uk
[4] Samsung Electronics, UK
habib.virji@samsung.com
[5] National Technical University of Athens, Greece
{cntanos,cbot}@epu.ntua.gr

Abstract. Testing web-based software infrastructures is challenging. The need to interact with different services running on different devices, with different expectations for security and privacy contributes not only to the complexity of the infrastructure, but also to the approaches necessary to test it. Moreover, as large-scale systems, such infrastructures may be developed by distributed teams simultaneously making changes to APIs and critical components that implement them. In this paper, we describe our experiences testing one such infrastructure – the *webinos* software platform – and the lessons learned tackling the challenges faced. While ultimately these challenges were impossible to overcome, this paper explores the techniques that worked most effectively and makes recommendations for developers and teams in similar situations. In particular, our experiences with continuous integration and automated testing processes are described and analysed.

Keywords: continuous integration, automated testing, web-based software infrastructure, functional testing.

1 Introduction

As web-apps become more pervasive, the reliance on web-based software infrastructures, such as middleware products and libraries, is growing. However, because end-users do not interact directly with such infrastructures, then devising appropriate strategies for detecting and preventing hidden software defects is challenging.

Four complementary approaches are typically used to identify such defects. *Unit tests* target isolated modules, *integration tests* target the integration of

V. Bertacco and A. Legay (Eds.): HVC 2013, LNCS 8244, pp. 145–150, 2013.

components, *functionality tests* target source code functions, and *system tests* target high level functionality. Carrying out these tests sequentially can be time-consuming as developers need to wait for the results of these tests before they can continue working. Moreover, integration problems of the source code of different contributors commonly occur for a myriad of reasons. To address these problems, Fowler [1] introduced the idea of *continuous integration*. This entails continuously downloading, integrating, and testing the source code and project libraries contributed by each developer. Following this approach, software can be tested for defects that might not otherwise be noticed by an individual developer.

A continuous integration strategy is difficult to devise when testing distributed software infrastructures because it needs to simulate all required devices and services. In this paper, we describe our experiences developing and applying continuous integration to test the *webinos* platform. *webinos* provides an overlay network between an individual user's set of personal devices, including their PC, smartphone and TV, and then allows web applications to access services on these devices through a set of standard JavaScript APIs. The complex interactions between web-based devices through browsers make *webinos* particularly hard to effectively test from one side, and particularly interesting as a case study from the other.

2   Related Work

Most web-based application testing researches focus on client-server applications that implement a strictly serialised model of interactions, generating test cases based on user-session profiling [2][3], or on testing the correct functioning on the client side or the server side separately [4][5].

Currently, there are no similar methods to test web-based software infrastructures like *webinos*, which appears to be the first platform for sharing services from different types of devices through browsers. One approach for using continuous integration testing is described in [6]. The authors presented a neat plug-in for Selenium implemented on a continuous integration server; this hooks every AJAX call made by the tested web application to verify requested data before application processing. This helps narrow down the location of a fault irrespective of whether it is situated in server- or client-side code. However, compared with our approach, this work only narrows the error position, and it is already covered by available functionality tests.

3   *webinos* Architecture

webinos is a secure platform which can be accessed by multiple types of web-enabled devices. In its life cycle, more than 30 organizations, mostly based in Europe, contributed to its development. It introduces the *Personal Zone* concept, where all the devices (*Personal Zone Proxies*) belonging to the same zone support and expose standard JavaScript APIs for accessing services such as device features (cameras, geolocation, networking and etc).

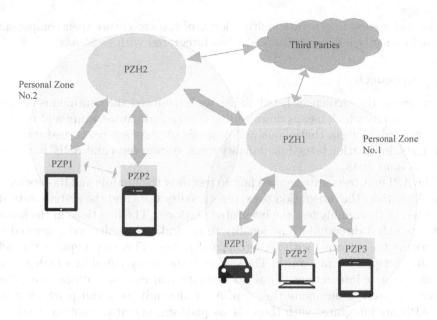

Fig. 1. *webinos* architecture

As shown in Figure 1, the *Personal Zone Hub* (PZH) is the focal point of the personal zone. The interactions might take place between PZHs and PZPs in the same zone or from different zones in different modes, when they try to share the resources or communicate with each others.

4   Testing *webinos*

As a web-based software infrastructure, *webinos* is designed to work on different browser-enabled systems and devices. This makes the testing extremely challenging. The interpretations of different browsers for the same JavaScript code are not identical, especially for browsers with different JavaScript engines. Implementing the same testing code on device with different architectures and computing power, is also challenging. For example, modules accessing OS specific functionality such as accessing path or network connectivity, provide different responses.

To simplify the development process, the platform was modularised; this meant that each API had its own git repository. This also made testing more complex. Since the APIs and core components are under continuously development by groups which apply rapid development methodology, it would be very easy for certain API to break other components and even the whole platform despite having passed its own unit test.

The testing infrastructure was created relatively late in the project. This meant that testing engineers were busy catching up with the developed components, and needed to generate multiple levels of tests to ensure their components worked correctly independently and when integrated with *webinos*.

4.1 Approach

To overcome the challenges listed above, we introduced the continuous integration technique, which means downloading source code, integrating and running various levels of tests continuously. Five levels of tests are performed, the API unit tests, integration tests, functionality tests, system tests and APIs' integrate-with-*webinos* tests.

The API unit tests are executed first to test only the module and its dependencies. After that, the integration tests, functionality tests and the system tests are executed to thoroughly test the integrated platform. The functions in the source code are called directly in functionality tests, and the results are generated by comparing the returned with the predefined values. This step requires the help of a JavaScript test framework. The system tests are executed in a higher level, mimicking user interactions. Thus, to simulate real case operations, a headless browser is used to automate this step. After the unit tests and platform tests, the APIs are integrated with the *webinos* platform one after another, testing if they can work correctly after integration.

Setting the order as mentioned is to make the discovery of errors easier: each unit test is delimited to a specific module, so the test failure means the problem is circumscribed to the module or its dependencies. The integration tests and functionality tests are executed before the system tests for similar reason, since they are more comprehensive and can provide more information on why the test fails.

To minimise the testing work, the tests are integrated with continuous integration servers. They are set to download the newest source code, execute the listed tests one after another in the defined order, and notify the testing engineers if error happens. For unit tests which only take a short time, the continuous integration server is set to perform the tests after the developer commits, while the other tests which take longer time are performed in the middle of the night.

4.2 Lessons Learned

The sub-sections below characterise three lessons learned in developing and applying our continuous integration system for *webinos*.

Continuous Integration Is Shaped by the Revision Control System Used. In *webinos* project, git is chosen to revision control source code. In the github model, developers build components within their own sandboxes and once the components are stable, they ask for pull request to the official repository running on github. Automated tests of pull requests minimises the time that maintainers spend reviewing submissions, but delays accepting pull requests cause merge conflicts, means that multiple incompatible pull requests occur. Therefore, open source development approaches using systems like github need very active maintainers and prioritise accepting contribution. For the maintainer who is also a developer, the rule of "you should not merge your own pull request" is effective to avoid errors brought by blind confidence, but causes the mentioned problem.

As an example, several thumb developers worked together and updated the *webinos-pzh* module, but according to the rule, they can not merge their pull request themselves. Therefore discussions were held on this pull request. However, at the same time the other pull requests were merged directly. After the discussion, the pending request was merged, caused a lot of failed tests, these developers had to rework the updates to incorporate with the new merged changes.

Maintaining the Test Infrastructure Is Harder Than Maintaining the System. For *webinos*, a comprehensive testing system may be more difficult to create than the infrastructure itself.

As an example, to test *webinos* on various OSes, we use three different continuous integration servers: one cloud-based infrastructure, one self-hosted infrastructure and one self-developed node.js module. The infrastructures focus on Linux platforms, which do not work very well on proprietary platforms. Therefore the node.js module is developed to cover this inadequacy. Beside that, the tests also break frequently because of rapid development of the components.

From the *webinos* experience, we believe the best option should start testing from low level to up level as state in section 4.1. The test cases for individual components can be generated by the developers, this way may fasten the testing procedure. Also in the most cohesive and loosely coupled components, fairly good unit tests would help to discover some problems which should be found in the integration tests. Integration and functional tests work better if it is possible to assign several developers who have detailed knowledge of the source code to write these test cases, as these tests are the most important part for testing a modularised system like *webinos*. Even if this would require a quite large amount of resources, bugs raised in the cooperation with other modules are exactly the kind of problem that an individual developer can not find out. Generating the system test cases is easier, the developers of these test cases only need to know how to operate with the *webinos* platform and use a headless browser to simulate the operations.

Thus, in our opinion, the best way to assign the resources and speed up the testing procedure is to assign developers the individual component test responsibility. Also system tests can be generated by single developers, while more care and resources are needed for integration and functional tests, requiring cooperation from different modules developers.

Developers Only Test for a Single Platform. Developing *webinos* for multiple platforms raised several issues that were hard to overcome. Ideally, the dependencies and modules should be tested on all the platforms before further implementation and development. For the reason that dependencies or modules may behave differently on each platform at runtime. Similarly, the binaries for native modules should be compiled separately on all platforms. In reality most developers worked only on a single platform at a time, and tend to only concern the tests passed on their own systems. This may led to subsequent bugs and incompatibilities piling up on other platforms.

For example, *webinos* widget packaging required the *zipfile* library; which was included and built on Linux developer's machines. Although fully functional at runtime on both Linux and Windows machines, the library failed to be built on Windows. Even though the testing system was totally functioning, this error remained undetected for several months until a Windows developer tried to compile it. This subsequently led to several days being spent re-adapting this library.

5   Conclusion and Future Work

Using continuous integration system to automate various levels tests increases development efficiency, it also increases our confidence about the quality of *webinos* platform. However, the testing system has its own limitations. At present, the system is unable to cover all of *webinos'* supported operating systems. Since *webinos* applies security as a pre-requisite, security tests are being introduced as an important part of our testing approach in the future.

Acknowledgements. The research described in this paper was funded by the EU FP7 *webinos* project (FP7-ICT-2009-05 Objective 1.2).

References

1. Fowle, M.: Continuous integration in martin fowler's blog (2000),
   http://martinfowler.com/articles/continuousIntegration.html
2. Sampath, S., Sprenkle, S., Gibson, E., Pollock, L., Greenwald, A.S.: Applying concept analysis to user-session-based testing of web applications. IEEE Transactions on Software Engineering 33(10), 643–658 (2007)
3. Elbaum, S., Rothermel, G., Karre, S., Fisher, M.: Leveraging user-session data to support web application testing. IEEE Transactions on Software Engineering 31(3), 187–202 (2005)
4. Di Lucca, G.: Testing web-based applications: the state of the art and future trends. In: 29th Annual International Computer Software and Applications Conference, COMPSAC 2005, vol. 2, pp. 65–69 (2005)
5. Marin, B., Vos, T., Giachetti, G., Baars, A., Tonella, P.: Towards testing future web applications. In: 2011 Fifth International Conference on Research Challenges in Information Science (RCIS), pp. 1–12 (2011)
6. Falah, B., Hasri, M., Schwaiger, S.: Continuous integration testing of web applications by sanitizing program input. Cyber Journals: Multidisciplinary Journals in Science and Technology 3(2) (2013)

SLAM: SLice And Merge -
Effective Test Generation for Large Systems

Tali Rabetti[1], Ronny Morad[1], Alex Goryachev[1], Wisam Kadry[1],
and Richard D. Peterson[2]

[1] IBM Research - Haifa, Israel
{talis,morad,gory,wisamk}@il.ibm.com
[2] IBM Systems & Technology Group, Austin, TX
petersn@us.ibm.com

Abstract. As hardware systems continue to grow exponentially, existing functional verification methods are lagging behind, consuming a growing amount of manual effort and simulation time. In response to this inefficiency gap, we developed *SLAM*, a novel method for test case generation for large systems. Our verification solution combines several scenarios to run in parallel, while preserving each one intact. This is done by automatically and randomly slicing the system model into subsystems termed *slices*, and assigning a different scenario to each slice. SLAM increases simulation efficiency by exercising the different system components simultaneously in varied scenarios. It reduces manual effort of test preparation by allowing reuse and mix of test scenarios. We show how to integrate SLAM into the verification cycle to save simulation time and increase coverage. We present real-life results from the use of our solution in the verification process of the latest IBM System p server.

Keywords: Functional verification, Test generation, Verification IP reuse.

1 Introduction

The ever-increasing demand for higher performance computer systems is driving digital designs to become increasingly complex. Advances in process technology are making it possible to squeeze more logic into a single chip, enabling the growth of the multi-core trend. This, in turn, is helping achieve better throughput with less power consumption. Today, it is common to find computer systems with hundreds of components, including processors, I/O bridges, and special purpose hardware units.

The functional verification of these larger systems is one of the most time- and resource-consuming aspects of a system's development cycle. The main portion of this effort is pre-silicon verification, which is performed before the chip is fabricated. Pre-silicon verification relies heavily on simulation-based techniques.

In pre-silicon verification, engineers seek good coverage of the design functionality. This can only be achieved by creating high-quality stimuli. Hence, test case development is a key activity for ensuring successful verification of the system.

V. Bertacco and A. Legay (Eds.): HVC 2013, LNCS 8244, pp. 151–165, 2013.
© Springer International Publishing Switzerland 2013

To increase productivity and reduce effort, many chip development companies use test generators that are based on test templates [2,9] as the main vehicle for creating test cases. A test template is a description of a verification scenario, written by the verification engineer in a high level language. The test generator uses these templates to create random test cases that match the high level scenario. Most test templates are developed to verify a specific functionality and therefore exercise only a subset of the full system.

When it comes to the system-level verification of large systems, verification needs to target the various interactions between the numerous components, and the stress on common resources (i.e., caches, buses) as a result of their simultaneous work.

Verification engineers can choose one of several practices to verify such large systems. One approach is to run individual test cases separately on a full system model, with each test case covering a different part of the system. This approach suffers from low utilization of system resources, since many of the components are idle during the execution of one test case. This approach is also limited when it comes to stressing the system.

Another option for verification engineers is to construct a smaller model that better fits a particular scenario. While this approach increases simulation utilization, it involves a large effort to build and maintain numerous models. Moreover, it cannot reach the level of stress on resources that is reached when all the components of the full system work together.

Verification engineers can also develop test cases that target the full system. However, in large systems with many components, it is difficult to come up with scenarios that truly exercise all the components in an interesting way. Therefore, this approach requires a lot of effort and tends to miss important corner cases.

In this paper, we introduce *SLAM*, a novel method for effective test generation for large systems. In this method, the system components are divided into groups, called *slices*. Each slice is assigned with a different test template. The test generator then generates a specific test case for the full system, in which the components in each slice exercise stimulus that matches the test template assigned to the slice.

SLAM overcomes many of the limitations of current practices for verifying large systems. It achieves better utilization of resources, since most of the system components are exercised by the various test cases. It stresses the system more intensively, since more stimuli are being simultaneously driven into the system. Moreover, the interactions among the test cases and the collisions on system resources can lead to interesting corner cases.

From a methodological perspective, we demonstrate that SLAM integrates well with the verification cycle, and in fact enhances it, while significantly reducing the manual effort involved in test case generation.

We successfully integrated SLAM into an IBM System-Level Test-Generator [9], which has been used to verify several generations of IBM System p servers [11]. We evaluated our method experimentally with real test templates on actual system models. Our results show that the SLAM method achieves better and faster coverage for large systems than other approaches, and that it hits interesting events otherwise not verified.

Our Contributions Are:

1. A novel method for verifying large systems, while boosting coverage and reducing manual effort.
2. Practical guidelines for implementing this method and integrating it into the verification cycle.
3. Experimental results from evaluating the method on an industrial high-end design.

The rest of the paper is organized as follows. We describe our method in Section 2 and how it fits into verification cycle in Section 3. Section 4 presents our experimental evaluation. Section 5 summarizes the related work, and Section 6 presents our conclusions.

2 Partitioning Method

The SLAM method is based on dividing the components in a system into several groups, called slices, and assigning a different scenario for each slice.

Figure 1 illustrates slicing of a multi-core, multi-threaded system. In the examples, the system was divided into two slices. The dark gray components belong to one slice and the light gray ones to the other. The white components are shared by the two slices.

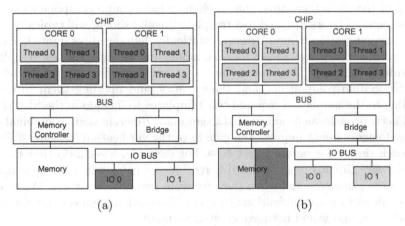

Fig. 1. Sample system and two possible slicing results

As shown in Figure 1, some components are divided between the slices while others are shared. Hardware threads and I/O components usually have their own instruction streams and therefore are more naturally divided. Buses, I/O bridges, and memory controllers are common resources needed by all the components in the system, and therefore cannot be divided.

The memory's address space can either be divided between the slices or shared between them. Shared address space can result in collisions between addresses used by the different test templates, which will create interactions between the scenarios. This enhances the simulation with events that would not have happened by running each of the test cases alone. On the other hand, dividing the address space will limit the interactions between scenarios, when such interactions are not desired.

In Figure 1a, the slicing was done on the basis of thread granularity, so threads from the same core belong to different slices. Each I/O component belongs to a different slice, and the memory is shared. This slicing results in more interactions (e.g., sharing internal core resources, cache lines, etc.) between the test cases of the different slices than the slicing in Figure 1b. In Figure 1b, the components are divided on the basis of core granularity, and the memory is divided between the slices. All I/O components belong to the light gray slice. This can be done if the test case assigned to the dark gray slice does not include any stimuli for I/O components. There is no preferred slicing method. The verification engineers should choose the degree of separation between the slices, based on the verification goals and the test templates used.

2.1 Slicing Techniques

We describe several approaches to the actual slicing of the system:

Pre-defined Slicing: The simplest way of slicing a system is to manually assign a subset of the components to each test case. This allows control over the *validity* of the slicing, ensuring that each slice has enough components of each type as required by its assigned test template. invalid slicing will typically result in test case generation failure. However, statically defining slices limits flexibility and requires defining new slicing for each model and for different test templates.

Random Slicing: The system can be sliced randomly, by taking all the dividable system components, and the memory, and dividing them to groups according to the number of required test templates to include in the SLAM test case. This approach can be automated to get many different slicing combinations. The randomness might improve the *quality* of the verification by using different slices each time we generate a test case. For example, a scenario that involves two hardware threads might reach different corner cases when the two threads are from the same core and when they are from two different cores. We can use this technique to get combinations that the verification engineer did not think of in advance, and would not have created manually.

Constrained-Random Slicing: Random slicing may result in choosing *invalid* subsets of the components. For example, there might be subsets that do not include enough components to run the scenario required by the test template. Constraint-random slicing overcomes this limitation by constraining the division process to a valid result. It can also be used to let the verification engineers control the division process by adding constraints of their own. This way, the simulation can be directed to more interesting scenarios or scenarios that were not reached so far.

2.2 Integration into Test Generators

In this section we demonstrate how SLAM can be integrated into an existing system level test generator.

High-end systems typically have numerous *configurations*, which may include different numbers of cores, chips, I/O bridges, and so on. Consequently, in many test generators there is a separation between the system description and the scenario description. This improves the efficiency of high end systems verification, since this way, the same test template can be used to generate test cases for different system configurations.

The separation between the system configuration and the test template is a key aspect that enables the implementation of the SLAM method. When the two are separated, it is the test generator's role to match between the components and the scenario described by the test template.

The test template consists of *statements*. Each statement represents a hardware transaction, (e.g., CPU accesses to memory or interrupt from an external I/O device to a CPU). The test generator parses the statements in the test template. For each statement it chooses system components that will participate in it, and generates a corresponding valid stimulus for these components. For example, stimulus may be an instruction stream for processors or a sequence of commands for I/O behavioral (which imitates the behavior of an external I/O device).

For SLAM, we extend the test generator to receive more than one test template as input. The components in the configuration are divided according to the number of input test templates and each group is assigned one test template. This is done either manually or automatically by the test generator, based on the techniques discussed in Section 2.1.

The generation of the test case is done by alternately parsing statements from each of the test templates. For each statement, participating components are chosen only from its assigned slice or from the shared components. During generation, the test generator maintains a *generation state* that contains the history of the generated statements, the current stimuli being generated, and the current state of the components in the system. This allows the generator to prevent contentions between the slices on important resources. For example, this can prevent a translation table used by CPU on one slice from being overwritten by another CPU from another slice. It also allows the test generator to create interactions between the slices. For example, this may include accesses to different addresses within the same cache line, which will enhance the resulting test case with interesting corner cases.

3   Adding SLAM to the Verification Cycle

SLAM offers two principle benefits to the verification process: reduced manual effort for test case creation and less time required for running regressions. In this section we suggest how to integrate SLAM into the verification methodology to exploit these benefits.

3.1   Reducing Manual Effort

In the first stage of verification, the verification team usually focuses on specific function in a system. A function might be a unit, such as a new I/O bridge, or a feature, such as cache coherency. The verification team starts testing basic usage of the function and bringing up the environment. They focuses on writing specific test templates, each exercising one aspect of the function under test. With SLAM, the same test templates will be reused in later stages in combination with other test templates to create more complex test cases, so planning ahead and preparing a set of high-quality test templates is important.

The next step involves performing more thorough testing of the individual functions. In this stage, the test scenarios are more sophisticated. The current practice in this stage involves writing complicated test templates that target specific scenarios. As we show in the experimental section, complex scenarios can be achieved by combining several simple test templates into a SLAM test case, without the need to write new test templates. This reuse reduces manual effort in covering complex scenarios. It also allows generating tests cases with many different combinations of directed scenarios without any additional effort.

In more advanced steps of the verification, once each function has been tested on how it operates individually and the system-level environment is stable, the verification is targeted at the various interactions between components and functionalities, and the stress on common system resources as a result of their simultaneous work. The current practice is to write test templates that combine several scenarios that have already been running. This is labor-intensive and only covers a subset of the possible combinations.

Using SLAM, the existing test templates from the previous stages can be combined without any additional effort to produce a rich variety of test cases that exercise the whole system in many different ways. As part of this stage, it is also useful to generate SLAM test cases from random test templates of the various units. This helps catch bugs by running unplanned and unexpected scenarios.

3.2   Saving Regression Time

As part of the verification process, the verification team collects a set of important scenarios, and runs all of them each time the design is changed, in addition to running them periodically. This technique is known as regression testing. With large systems, running regression takes a long time and occupies precious simulation resources.

SLAM dramatically speeds up this process by running several scenarios in parallel. As we show in the experimental results section, with large enough systems, running a scenario on a subset of a system would still fulfill its original intent. However, with SLAM test cases a trade-off exists between gaining speed and reaching new corner cases, since many contentions on resources cause delays in the execution of each scenario. For example, *false sharing*, which is sharing of addresses that are mapped to the same cache row, can cause data, brought to cache by CPU from one slice, to be evicted from the cache by CPU from another slice. This enhances the scenario with interesting new events. On the other hand, it also slows it down since the first CPU will have to fetch the data back from memory for the next time it is used.

4   Experimental Evaluation

We implemented SLAM in IBM System-level Test-Generator, which is used in the verification of IBM System p design. The method is already in extensive use in the verification of the next System p generation, but its effect on the verification was not empirically measured. We conducted a series of experiments to evaluate it.

The verification teams maintain a vast library of test templates that is updated for various hardware projects. From these test templates, the test generator creates numerous test cases that run on a hardware model. The library includes many test templates targeting different functions of a design. SLAM is being used as part of the verification of many different functions, including multi-core features and various I/O interfaces. In this experiment we focused on multi-core features. We used the following subset of test templates:

- CACHE—target various aspects of different cache levels across the system by moving cachelines from cache to cache, causing cacheline evictions, etc.
- RESERVATION—focused on the reservation mechanism, implemented in the POWER architecture[13] by *load-link/store-conditional* instructions.
- PREFETCH—exercise various automatic as well as software-triggered hardware prefetch mechanisms (e.g., "data cache block touch" instruction and its variants).
- NEW FEATURE—aimed at a **new feature** of POWER architecture, related to multi-core behavior.

We measured our results by counting coverage events that were collected as part of RTL simulation. We used the same coverage model used by the System p verification teams. This model has more than 400,000 events, divided into more than 8,000 *classes*. Examples of classes are: branch-related events, L2 state changes, fixed-point unit events, floating point, etc. It is important to note that while we used multi-core and multi-chip models, we counted each event only once, independent of the core or chip on which it was reached. On the other hand, we counted separately events that pertain to different threads, since in this case they are associated with different pieces of logic. We ignored the number of times each event was hit and simply counted whether it was hit or not. The coverage events were only collected from passing test cases.

Some simulations were done on a software simulator (usually each run is a few hundred thousand to one million cycles) and some on a hardware *accelerator platform*, a special purpose hardware that speeds up RTL simulation and allows simulations of up to several billion cycles. Our experiments ran on the same simulation resources used by the verification teams; therefore, the actual simulation time was affected by the changing workloads of the machines. To avoid this effect, we present the events as a function of simulation cycles.

The goal of the experiments was to verify the assumptions we based on when using SLAM: (1) exercising a stimulus on a subset of the model does not undermine its effectiveness, (2) SLAM achieves coverage faster than running individual test cases, and (3) using SLAM allows hitting events that are impossible to hit by each one of individual test cases.

4.1   Simulating a Subset of the System

SLAM relies on the assumption that exercising a stimulus on a subset of the model does not undermine its effectiveness. In the first part of the experiment we validate this assumption by comparing coverage obtained by running stimulus on a full system to running the same stimulus on a subset of the system - in this case, a subset of the hardware threads.

We used a large system model composed of several multi-core, multi-threaded chips, with a total of 64 hardware threads. We chose a CACHE test template in which all participating hardware threads perform various memory accesses and cache maintenance operations on a fixed set of cache lines. We generated several test cases from the same test template, with a varying number of participating threads. In each simulation, the threads that did not participate were idle. The participating threads were selected randomly from the entire model, not necessarily from the same core or chip.

We ran simulations of the generated test cases, and measured the coverage reached by the different test cases as a function of the number of participating threads. The results showed that the test template has a "saturation" point, at which adding more agents to participate in the scenario will not contribute to higher coverage.

The coverage is affected by many parameters such as test generator randomization and environment settings, which are random for each simulation run. To neutralize the great variance caused by that, we collected several simulation runs for each number of participating threads. We built the results graph by serially concatenating simulation results to each other. This gave us the accumulated coverage as a function of accumulated cycles

The order of concatenation was according to an *events per cycle* metric, which measures the efficiency of the simulation. The simulations were concatenated by order of events per cycle, from high to low, to create fair comparison of the graphs. The results are presented in Figure 2.

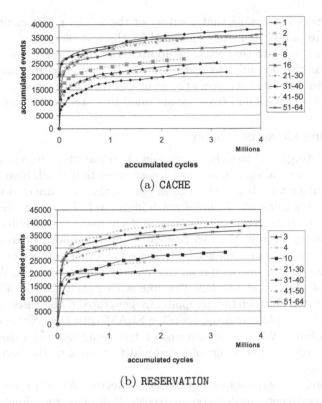

(a) CACHE

(b) RESERVATION

Fig. 2. Coverage of simulations with increasing number of participating threads for CACHE and RESERVATION test templates. Each line in the graphs represents the accumulated coverage achieved by a series of simulations with the specified number of participating threads.

We repeated the experiment with two test templates: CACHE and RESERVATION. The results show that as we increase the number of participating threads, we get higher coverage. But, there is a saturation point where the coverage stops growing, even as we add more and more threads until we add all 64. With the CACHE test template, the saturation point was at around 20 threads, while with the RESERVATION test template, it was at around 30 threads.

Beyond the saturation point, we sometimes even see that simulations with fewer threads achieve higher coverage. For example, in the RESERVATION graph we can see that both lines of 31-40 threads and of 41-50 threads are getting higher coverage than the 51-64 line. One possible explanation is that when most of the threads in each core are participating in the same scenario, we get similar behavior across the units of the system. But when in each core there is a different number of active threads, the asymmetry creates more events.

While the exact number of hardware threads at the saturation point might change with a different system model and different test template, the importance of these results is in showing that a subset of the model is sufficient to extract all the coverage points that can be reached by the test template.

These results indicate that SLAM's approach is based on a true assumption and indeed has the potential to increase coverage obtained by simulations. In the following subsections we present the results of comparisons between coverage obtained by SLAM tests and coverage obtained in a traditional way.

4.2   Reaching Coverage Faster

Because simulating large models is very slow, verification engineers always seek to optimize the simulation efficiency with test cases that reach high coverage in minimum simulation cycles. In the second part of the experiment, we show that running test cases using SLAM helps reach high level of coverage faster.

The idea is to take two test templates and compare the combined coverage we get by running each of the two templates several times, separately, on the full system, to the coverage we get by running the same number of simulations with SLAM test cases, generated from the same two test templates. We used two combination of test templates: NEW FEATURE with PREFETCH and NEW FEATURE with RESERVATION. For each test template, we generated 6 test cases. In addition, we generated 12 *SLAM test cases*, by using SLAM with the combination of the two test templates. We ran simulations of the resulting test cases. We then compared the combined coverage of individual test cases to the coverage of the SLAM test case.

Since running many simulations of a large model on a software simulator takes weeks, this experiment was done on an acceleration platform[1]. Each simulation was limited to one million cycles to get results typical for a software simulation platform. Because of the limited availability of the accelerators during the experiment period, we used a smaller multi-core, multi-threaded model, with a total of 32 hardware threads.

We built the results graph by serially concatenating simulation results to each other. This gave us the accumulated coverage as a function of accumulated cycles, similar to the way they were built in Section 4.1. However, here we wanted to compare how quickly the coverage increased, and this is affected by the order of the simulations. To overcome this, for each graph we took 10 random orders and built a graph based on their average.

Figure 3 shows only the NEW FEATURE related events. The dashed lines are the average results of running 6 simulations of each test template. The solid lines are the average results of running 12 simulations of SLAM test case of each of the combinations. We can see that although after 12 million cycles, the coverage reached by each setting is similar, the SLAM test cases graph grows much faster. For example, after around 3 million cycles it reaches the same coverage level reached by the individual simulations after 6 or 7 million cycles.

This shows that when limited to a small number of simulation cycles, SLAM achieves higher coverage than a combination of the individual test cases.

---

[1] An acceleration platform is a dedicated hardware, used for RTL simulation, which is much faster than traditional software simulation.

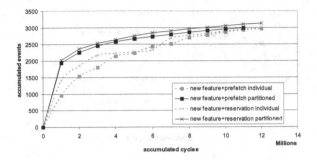

Fig. 3. NEW FEATURE related events covered by individual test cases vs. SLAM test cases

Figure 4 shows only the RESERVATION related events. We can see that even after 12 million cycles, the SLAM test case obtained more coverage than the original test cases running individually. This added coverage may indicate that the combination of the NEW FEATURE with RESERVATION triggers more events, which were not reached by the individual targeted reservation test. We expand on this topic in Section 4.3. Here also, we see that the individual test cases takes 6 million cycles to reach the same coverage attained by the SLAM test cases in only 2 million cycles.

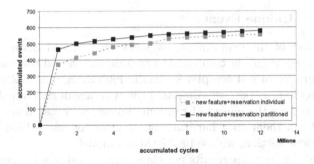

Fig. 4. RESERVATION related events covered by individual test cases vs. SLAM test cases

Figure 5 shows only the PREFETCH related events. There is a small number of events in this class. There is no visible difference between the PREFETCH related events obtained by SLAM test cases and individual test cases. We attribute this to the fact that the NEW FEATURE does not have much relevance to the PREFETCH mechanism. Recall that when we took the same combination of test cases and compared NEW FEATURE related events in Figure 3, we reached higher coverage more quickly. In this case, running the SLAM test case improved coverage of one related class and did not damage the coverage of the second class.

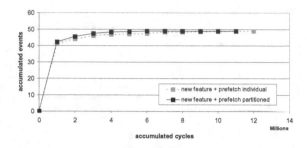

Fig. 5. PREFETCH related events covered by individual test cases vs. SLAM test cases

Interestingly, when we compare the total number of events of all classes that were hit by each setting, we can't see a difference between the number and the rate of event coverage for individual test cases compared to SLAM test cases. This can be explained by the fact that the number of events in the model is huge and our test cases cover less than 20% of them. Not all of the events are relevant to the test templates we selected, and many of them can happen regardless of the type of test case we are running. For example, the "instruction fetch" class of events can be hit by any test case. As we run more and more cycles we keep hitting more events, but they are not necessarily the ones we aim for in the test templates.

4.3   Covering Unique Events

In the third part of the experiment, we show that SLAM allows us to reach additional coverage events as compared to running individual test cases. We used the following groups of test templates: CACHE, PREFETCH, and NEW FEATURE.

As in the previous section, we compared the coverage of individual and SLAM test cases. To reduce the effects of random choices, we created several random test cases and ran them on a hardware accelerator for one billion cycles each. As in the previous section, we used a 32-thread model.

We analyzed the coverage results per class. Figure 6 shows the coverage levels of a small subset of the classes. We averaged the number of coverage events hit by different test cases (including CACHE with NEW FEATURE and PREFETCH with NEW FEATURE). For most of the classes, the accumulated number of events hit by individual test cases was similar to the number of events hit by SLAM test cases.

However, we identified a class of events that were *almost always* hit by SLAM test cases and *never* hit by individual test cases (marked by an oval in the figure). These events were associated with a specific piece of logic in the design that dealt with the TLBIE instruction when executed in conjunction with the NEW FEATURE. (The TLBIE instruction invalidates an entry in a translation look-aside buffer.) Apparently, the TLBIE instruction was never a part of the NEW FEATURE test templates, but because of its unique system-wide effect, (TLBIE has an effect

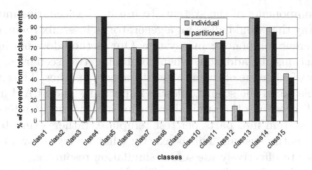

Fig. 6. Compared coverage of different classes

above the scope of the thread and the core that executed it) was included in
PREFETCH and CACHE test templates as part of the scenario.

Although the reader may argue that it was possible to create a test template
for the NEW FEATURE that would include TLBIE, this was not done; unless the
SLAM test cases caught it, this would result in a coverage hole. This result
demonstrates that with SLAM, simple test templates can be combined to create
new scenarios that would otherwise require writing new test templates. Moreover, SLAM will lead to events that the verification engineer did not think of in
advance, which may results in uncovering hidden bugs.

5   Related Work

Building a test case from several components is a known approach to verification. Modern verification languages and methodologies support this by allowing
a "top-level" scenario (coined *sequence* in some languages) to be composed of
several component sequences (e.g., [1,6,10,12]). This approach is commonly used
to build a complex scenario from several simpler steps or to execute several independent agents (e.g., PCIe, UART, Ethernet controller) in parallel on a test
bench. Alternatively, we provide both a method and a methodology for slicing
a large system for running several (possibly complex) scenarios in parallel. Furthermore, our technique can be used on top of these languages and methodologies
to address this challenge.

Another known technique of combining several scenarios involves using an
Operating System (OS). This is either a special-purpose OS built for verification purposes (e.g., Test Operating System [8]) or a real OS. The latter case is
described in many works on hardware/software co-verification (e.g., [4,5]). Our
approach does not require an OS, thus saving the overhead for both booting
and running time. In addition, the OS-based approach can only be used on a
fast (e.g., acceleration) platform, while our method can be used in a simulation
environment.

Interleaving [7] is another known method for combining several scenarios into
a single test case. Using this approach several scenarios can be intermixed to run

on the same components of the system. To use it, the scenarios must either be specified in a way that would allow for a generator to intermix them, or originally written for different components in a system. Our method does not impose either of these restrictions. In addition, when combining two scenarios, interleaving breaks the flow of each one of them to insert parts of another. Thus, this method is not applicable when the scenario flow is important. The SLAM approach, on the other hand, preserves the original scenarios intact. Lastly, interleaving does not divide the system into parts per test template, rather, every test template will occupy the entire system. This is exactly what we try to avoid with SLAM method in order to effectively use scarce simulation resources.

Another technique is *irritation* (e.g., [3]). Here, one or more components of a system under test are reserved to run (usually) a short code sequence in a loop in parallel to the other components executing the main scenario. The idea is to interfere ("irritate") with the main scenario to create interesting events. Irritation can be considered as a special case of SLAM. In our method, we allow any scenarios to run in parallel.

6   Conclusion

We presented *SLAM*, a method for test generation for large systems. With this method, a system is divided into several parts and each is assigned a different test template. Our approach achieves better utilization of simulation resources and allows reaching additional coverage events without defining new scenarios. Experimental results from a real-life verification project support our claims.

Our method was successfully integrated into the IBM System-level Test-Generator and is being used as part of the system level verification methodology for the IBM System p servers.

References

1. Accellera: UVM - Universal Verification Methodology, http://uvmworld.org/
2. Adir, A., Almog, E., Fournier, L., Marcus, E., Rimon, M., Vinov, M., Ziv, A.: Genesys-Pro: Innovations in test program generation for functional processor verification. IEEE Design and Test of Computers 21(2), 84–93 (2004)
3. Ludden, J.M., Rimon, M., Hickerson, B.G., Adir, A.: Advances in simultaneous multithreading testcase generation methods. In: Raz, O. (ed.) HVC 2010. LNCS, vol. 6504, pp. 146–160. Springer, Heidelberg (2010)
4. Altera: Hardware/Software co-verification using FPGA platforms, http://www.altera.com/literature
5. Andrews, J.: Co-verification of Hardware and Software for ARM SoC Design. Elsevier (2005)
6. Bergeron, J., Cerny, E., Hunter, A., Nightingale, A.: Verification Methodology Manual for SystemVerilog. Springer-Verlag New York, Inc., Secaucus (2005)
7. Copty, S., Jaeger, I., Katz, Y., Vinov, M.: Intelligent interleaving of scenarios: A novel approach to system level test generation. In: DAC, pp. 891–895 (2007)

8. Devins, R.: SOC verification software - test operating system. In: IEEE Electronic Design Processes Workshop (2001)
9. Emek, R., Jaeger, I., Naveh, Y., Bergman, G., Aloni, G., Katz, Y., Farkash, M., Dozoretz, I., Goldin, A.: X-Gen: A random test-case generator for systems and SoCs. In: IEEE International HLDVT Workshop, Cannes, France, pp. 145–150 (October 2002)
10. Glasser, M.: Open Verification Methodology Cookbook. Springer (2009), http://books.google.com/books?id=X49tFORdBtAC
11. IBM: System, http://www-03.ibm.com/systems/p/
12. Planitkar, S.: Design verification with e. Prentice-Hall (2003)
13. Power.org: PowerISA v2.06, http://www.power.org/resources/downloads

Improving Post-silicon Validation Efficiency by Using Pre-generated Data

Wisam Kadry, Anatoly Koyfman, Dmitry Krestyashyn,
Shimon Landa, Amir Nahir, and Vitali Sokhin

IBM Research – Haifa, Israel
{wisamk,anatoly,krest,shimonl,nahir,vitali}@il.ibm.com

Abstract. Post-silicon functional validation poses unique challenges that must be overcome by bring-up tools. One such major challenge is the requirement to reduce overhead associated with the testing procedures, thereby ensuring that the expensive silicon platform is utilized to its utmost extent. Another crucial requirement is to conduct high-quality validation that guarantees the design is bug-free prior to its shipment to customers. Our work addresses these issues in the realm of software-based self-tests.

We propose a novel solution that satisfies these two requirements. The solution calls for shifting the preparation of complex data from the run-time to the offline phase that takes place before the software test is compiled and loaded onto the silicon platform. This data is then variably used by the test-case to ensure high testing quality while retaining silicon utilization.

We demonstrate the applicability of our method in the context of bare-metal functional exercisers. An exerciser is a unique type of self-test that, once loaded onto the system, continuously generates test-cases, executes them, and checks their results. To ensure high silicon utilization, the exerciser's software must be kept lightweight and simple. This requirement contradicts the demand for high-quality validation, as the latter calls for complex test generation, which in turn implies extensive, complex computation. Our solution bridges these contradicting requirements.

We implemented our proposed solution scheme in IBM's Threadmill post-silicon exerciser, and we demonstrate the value of this scheme in two highly important domains: address translation path generation and memory access management.

1 Introduction

In today's state-of-the-art multi-processor and multi-threaded hardware systems, eliminating all functional bugs in the design before the first tapeout is virtually impossible. This is due to the intricacy of modern micro-architectures and the complexity of the system topology. Consequently, the development stage known as *post-silicon validation* [17,19,25], which is responsible for catching any remaining functional bugs before they escape to the field, is of growing importance.

V. Bertacco and A. Legay (Eds.): HVC 2013, LNCS 8244, pp. 166–181, 2013.
© Springer International Publishing Switzerland 2013

Post-silicon validation uses implementations of the system on silicon running at realtime speed. These platforms are relatively scarce and have high manufacturing costs. Moreover, when compared to simulation platforms, they offer realtime execution speed, but low dynamic *observability* into the system's state. A related limitation is the high overhead for loading and offloading memory and state information. These characteristics create challenges and impose trade-offs that shape the way post-silicon platforms are used for functional valida tion. While post-silicon platforms offer a huge number of execution cycles, their scarcity and high cost call for high machine utilization in terms of maximizing the time spent in executing test-cases and minimizing overhead. The overhead associated with loading a test-case image onto the platform and offloading its results may become a bottleneck. Under such circumstances, the silicon platform would be idle for a portion of the time.

A prominent technique of driving stimuli (as well as performing checking) in post-silicon validation is that of Software-Based Self-Tests [26], or SBSTs. SBSTs are actually simple programs that run on the silicon under test to verify its behavior. This approach is highly advocated as it requires no additional testing-specific instrumentation of the hardware.

A unique type of SBSTs is that of bare-metal exercisers [5, 29]. An exerciser is an SBST that, once loaded onto the system, continuously generates test-cases, executes them, and checks their results. (We omit the details involving the compilation of the exerciser into a loadable executable image.) The generated test-cases must be valid programs for the hardware threads to execute. They must also be sufficiently complex, such that they stress the design and trigger meaningful events in various areas.

We are, therefore, faced with two seemingly conflicting requirements when designing the stimuli generator of a post-silicon validation exerciser. On the one hand, achieving high machine utilization requires the exerciser's stimuli generation engine to be fast and light. On the other hand, achieving high validation quality requires that very same engine to be capable of generating complex test-cases. Moreover, if a single exerciser image is to be loaded and run for a long time on silicon at realtime speed, sufficient variability must exist among the generated test-cases. Consequently, these requirements constitute a considerable challenge to the design of a post-silicon exerciser.

Finally, an exerciser has to be simple. The low observability makes failures extremely difficult to debug, and therefore, simple software must be used to ease the effort. We also want to deploy the exerciser in the early stages of the post-silicon validation efforts when the OS cannot yet be run on the system and "complex" operations such as reading files from an I/O device are not supported.

Contributions. In this work, we address the problem of conducting high-quality design validation without harming the utilization of the expensive silicon platform under test in the realm of SBSTs. The novelty of our solution lies in preparing the input data off the platform and efficiently integrating it into the SBST. As the input data is prepared off platform, we can leverage sophisticated (and highly complex) techniques to ensure the data is of high quality. The data is formatted and structured in a way that enables the SBST to easily access it with minimal overhead.

We demonstrate the effectiveness of the proposed method in the context of bare-metal exercisers. Specifically, we implemented this approach in the IBM Threadmill post-silicon exerciser [5] to address two complex stimuli generation problems: the creation of address translation paths, and the selection of addresses for memory access management.

We achieve the high quality of the off-platform generated data by using well-established pre-silicon stimuli generation techniques. For this purpose, we employed the following pre-silicon tools: a) DeepTrans [4], a technology that specializes in generating sophisticated address translation paths for the functional verification of processors and b) Constraint satisfaction problem solver (CSP solver) [11], which takes the test-template and the system configuration as input to allocate memory regions and create address tables that are used by the exerciser during runtime. The solver outcome complies with memory requirements that are induced by the system configuration or specified by the user in the test-template. The CSP solver we used is a well-established technology and is used by IBM pre-silicon test-generators Genesys-Pro [2] and X-Gen [15]. We conducted several experiments that demonstrate the effectiveness of this method in the stimuli domains to which it was applied.

The rest of the paper is organized as follows: After discussing related work in the next section, we describe the general solution scheme for exercisers in Section 3. In Sections 4 and 5, we describe its implementation to address translation paths and memory access management (respectively) with the experiments we conducted and their results. Finally, we give our conclusions in Section 6.

2   Related Work

Post-silicon validation has been getting a lot of attention in recent years [22,23]. However, the majority of this attention has been directed towards constructing efficient mechanisms for collecting runtime data from the chip to enhance checking and debugging capabilities [1,12–14,21].

More recently, other aspects of post-silicon validation have been attracting research attention. In [3,27] an overall methodology for post-silicon is presented. Singerman et al. [28] and [8] address the issue of coverage in post-silicon.

The main topic of this paper is that of stimuli generation for post-silicon validation. Specifically, we focus on Software-Based Self-Tests, or SBSTs. In [26] authors provide a comprehensive survey on the subject. Additional recent publications on this matter can be found in [30,31]. In [10] the authors establish the effectiveness of SBSTs for the validation of the processor's memory model

The authors of [20] and [18] propose a variety of techniques to mutate failing SBSTs in order to shorten the time between bug occurrence and its detection.

In [29], the author presents the concept of post-silicon exercisers along with a simple generation technique.

Several papers describing Threadmill, its usage and internal mechanisms have also been published. A pre- to post-silicon verification methodology is described in [3], where Threadmill is presented as the tool enabling test-plan driven post-silicon validation. Industrial experience of applying the unified methodology to POWER7® processor chip is described in [6]. Some of the Threadmill generation techniques are presented in [5]. Specifically, a technique for floating-point instruction generation is presented, which is similar in essence to the concept presented in this paper, but is confined to floating-point. Adjusting stimuli generators to leverage the unique added value of different execution platforms is described in [24].

Finally, a different mechanism for memory management is described in [7], in which the selection of addresses is performed on-platform, in a more computationally expensive manner.

3   Solution Scheme

In this section we describe our high level approach to ensuring high quality of the post-silicon validation effort while guaranteeing high silicon utilization. While we focus on the implementation of the solution in the context of exercisers, we note that the same approach can be easily applied to the general case of SBSTs. One such example is described in Section 5.

The exerciser execution process consists of two consecutive parts: the off-platform exerciser image build and the actual online run on the platform. At the offline image build, the generator code as well as some data required for the next phase are integrated into one executable image. Notably, no generation of test-cases and instructions takes place during this offline phase. The second part takes place when the image is loaded onto the platform and it starts generating the test-cases, executing them, and checking their results.

To have high-quality test-cases, the exerciser needs to use interesting inputs while generating the instructions. For example, when generating loads or stores, the generator can pick random memory locations or, preferably, it might direct the accesses toward more interesting areas, such as cache lines' or pages' borders' affinities. One of our goals, along with high-quality tests, is to ensure high utilization of the machine by maximizing the time spent in executing test-cases. Therefore, the complex task of allocating these interesting memory areas should be avoided at runtime and shifted to the offline phase, saving more cycles for test-case executions.

Our method involves preparing interesting data whose preparation is a time-consuming task at the off-platform phase and then integrating it into the executable image. This data is needed when the exerciser generates the test-cases at runtime. Such data examples are the memory intervals to select addresses from and the translation paths. Having this data ready-to-use at runtime, enables faster generation of test-cases. Also, we use well-established pre-silicon tools to ensure that the off-platform generated data is of high quality.

In cases where pseudo-random techniques are used to generate the data, such as the cases described in this paper, it is essential to rely on pseudo-random methods, and to retain the list of seeds used to create the data. This is required

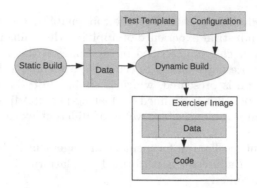

Fig. 1. Off-platform data preparation flow

so that if needed, during the debug process of a fail, the same test-case, including initial values and instruction stream, can be reproduced.

We distinguish between two different stages of the off-platform data preparation: *static-build* and *dynamic-build* (see Figure 1). In the static-build stage, we generate large amounts of data by using the relevant pre-silicon tools. This data is filtered in the subsequent dynamic-build stage and are then used by the exerciser. The static-build is an independent stage that does not require specific inputs, such as the test-template and the system configuration. For example, generating large amounts of possible translation paths for the entire physical memory is independent of the number of threads in the system and of the required scenario in the test-template. Furthermore, this independence allows us to employ sophisticated pre-silicon tools that have a long runtime.

On the other hand, the dynamic-build stage takes place every time we construct an exerciser image. This stage takes, in addition to the data created at the static build stage, the test-template and the system configuration as additional inputs. This stage must therefore be sufficiently efficient, enabling the user to construct a new exerciser image in a reasonable amount of time. For example, the verification engineer may have one test-template specifying multiple inter-thread collisions and another test-template targeting page-crossing events. Each of these cases calls for different allocation of memory intervals, and therefore, these intervals must be determined at the dynamic-stage in which the test-template is available.

Overall, the dynamic-build stage has four main roles: *a*) filtering the relevant data from the static-build stage; *b*) preparing new data based on new available inputs, such as the test-template and the system configuration; *c*) organizing the data created in both stages in structures that are optimized for efficient retrieval by the exerciser during the on-platform runtime; and *d*) integrating the code and the prepared data into one executable image.

Creating the efficient data structures depends on the data type and its usage. For example, in the memory management case, we hold all the offline prepared intervals in one primary table and sort it by certain translation properties, memory ownership, and size. A memory interval can cross a page or a cache line borders. In these cases, accesses to such intervals will cause interesting events. Our method enables the exerciser to do fast retrieval of these interesting intervals by using auxiliary look-up tables per each event. Each auxiliary table contains the indices of the entries from the primary table where the relevant interesting intervals reside.

Using this method, all the exerciser has to do during runtime is to retrieve and use the pre-made data structures for generating complex test-cases that trigger interesting, meaningful events throughout the design.

4 Address Translation

Address translation is an integral part of all modern computer architectures. In addition to supporting multiple virtual spaces, it commonly plays a part in memory protection and caching mechanisms by maintaining the related properties for basic translated memory units, e.g., pages or segments. The growing demand for performance complicates the address translation and memory management mechanisms, thereby increasing the risk of bugs.

To thoroughly validate all translation-related hardware mechanisms an SBST must support a large variety of events. These coverage requirements include the ability to produce a set of valid translation paths that cover a large physical memory region. This is required to ensure that the translation mechanisms are stressed, triggering events such as TLB cast-outs and invalidations. In addition, the randomization of the numerous translation path properties is desired. In PowerPC, for example, this includes the segment size, page size, protection bits and more. Finally, the SBST must generate translation paths that activate all possible inter-thread and inter-processor memory sharing scenarios, including translating different virtual pages into the same physical page, use of the same translation table entries by different threads, and others.

The task of generating a valid translation path is a complex one. In addition to ensuring the coverage of the different properties described above, a large set of rules must be obeyed. In the PowerPC architecture, two such examples are the rule requiring that each page starts at an address naturally aligned to its size, and the rule requiring the consistency of the cachability attribute across all translation paths. Every access to an address in physical memory can go through the cache (termed *a cachable access*) or bypass it (termed *a caching-inhibited access*). This caching property is an attribute of the page mapped to the given physical address. Therefore, for every accessible address in physical memory, the caching property must be consistent across all pages mapped to that address.

To address the problem of translation path generation at the pre-silicon verification stage a tool called DeepTrans [4] is used. DeepTrans contains rich built-in testing knowledge enabling the generation of interesting translation paths with or without specific user requests.

We propose to address the challenge of generating valid and interesting translation paths through a solution partitioned among the SBST run phases, namely,

Table 1. Distribution of page sizes and caching properties

	Small	Medium	Large	Huge
Cacheable	3230	3202	580	37
Caching-inhibited	386	380	62	36

the static-build stage, the dynamic-build stage, and the on-platform runtime stage.

At the static-build stage we leverage DeepTrans [4] to construct a large set of address translation paths for the entire physical memory. We iteratively activate DeepTrans to generate, at each iteration, a new translation path. Each of these translation paths is generated under different constraints. These constraints may request, for example, that the next translation path is generated to create a $4KB$ page access in a caching-inhibited way, leaving many other attributes for DeepTrans to randomize. By using these constraints we ensure that every location in physical memory is accessible in every possible mode, through more than one path. As DeepTrans has all PowerPC translation rules modeled in it, all generated paths are legal and consistent with each other.

To evaluate the quality of our approach we ran DeepTrans to generate $7,913$ translation paths covering a physical space of $8GB$. Overall, 20 hours were required to generate such a set of paths on a single Intel Xeon® Linux server running at $2.4GHz$ with $16GB$ of RAM.

Table 1 depicts the distribution of page sizes and the caching properties over the generated set of translation paths. We strongly bias DeepTrans towards generating pages that are accessed through the cache, as we wish to stress the entire memory hierarchy. In addition, we bias DeepTrans towards generating small or medium pages, as such pages provide us more freedom in triggering some interesting events. For example, a page crossing access, i.e., a memory access that spans more than one page, can only occur at the boundaries of pages. Partitioning memory to small pages provides a larger set of addresses where a page crossing event can be triggered.

A *translation collision* event occurs when same memory location is accessed using different translation paths (either from the same or different hardware threads). These accesses may vary in one (or more) of the different translation attributes. Recall that some attributes, such as the caching property, must be consistent across all paths accessing the same physical address.

We turn to evaluate the quality of the set of paths generated by DeepTrans with respect to the potential of triggering a translation collision event[1]. Specifically, we evaluate the potential of triggering a translation collision where the translation paths differ in page size. We divide the available page sizes in the PowerPC architecture into 4 categories: small ($4KB$ and $16KB$), medium ($1MB$),

---

[1] The set of translation paths only describes the potential to trigger a translation collision event; it is up to the memory management mechanism to create such events through an intelligent selection of addresses to access within a test-case.

Table 2. Different page size collisions

	Small	Medium	Large
Medium	203		
Large	97	603	
Huge	53	66	22

large ($8MB$), and huge ($8GB$). We measure the absolute number of cases when a physical page covered by a translation path with a larger page size contains a physical page covered by another translation path with a smaller page size. Results are shown in Table 2. The numbers inside the table cells show the absolute number of these cases; the corresponding row and column show the corresponding page sizes. As can be observed, we generated all possible collision combinations. The bias toward the collision with large pages represents the internal DeepTrans expert knowledge that these collisions are more valuable than the collisions with huge pages. For example, the number of collisions between large pages and medium size pages (603) is almost ten times higher than the number of collisions between huge pages and medium size pages (66).

At the dynamic-build stage the test-template and system configuration are accessible, in addition to the complete set of pre-generated translation paths. We use this data to pick and choose translations paths that best match the intent expressed in the test-template. For example, if the test-template targets page crossing accesses between caching-inhibited pages, we bias our path selection to ensure a variety of matching paths are incorporated in the exerciser image.

In addition to the selection of paths, we also arrange the data in a way that will facilitate an efficient access during runtime. For example, in our Threadmill implementation of this approach, translation paths are arranged in two tables. The first table is sorted by the test-case's runtime mode and the physical address – this is required to enable the memory management component (which selects physical addresses) to effectively map them to virtual addresses. The second table is sorted by the virtual address and is used by the translation exception handlers in order to facilitate an effective installation of the translation path.

At runtime, the memory management component and the translation exception handlers access the tables to extract the required data as explained above. Overall, about 9 seconds are needed for DeepTrans to generate a single translation path. Doing this on the silicon platform would sharply drop its utilization, and the majority of the run time would be spent building translation paths instead of actually executing test-cases. In addition, adding such complex algorithms to the exerciser would make it far more complex and difficult to debug.

Using this method, a diverse set of test-templates targeting different aspects of the translation mechanisms, coupled with several sets of pre-generated translation paths, enable us to address coverage holes and achieve an aggregated high coverage.

5   Memory Management

Modern high-end multi-threaded systems rely on *weak* consistency memory models [9, 16] that make it easier to implement performance boosting mechanisms such as caches, out-of-order, and speculative executions. Implementations of these weak consistency models are highly error-prone and hard to verify due to the vast test space and their distributed nature.

One desired attribute of SBSTs targeting the validation of the memory hierarchy is the ability to generate *collision events*. A collision event occurs when two (or more) hardware threads access the same memory location. Modern processors manage data transition in cache line granularity, that is, regardless of the size of the program access, the processor fetches data from memory in chunks of fixed size. Therefore, to stress the memory hierarchy, it is often enough to have the hardware threads access different locations within the cache line (termed *false sharing*) rather than the exact same location (termed *true sharing*).

The generation of memory access collisions must take into account the checking method. Threadmill employs a technique called *multi-pass consistency checking* [5]. In this technique, a test-case is run multiple times with the same resource initializations and verified to ensure that the same final values are produced each time. However, the final value in the collision location in memory after a write-write collision depends on the execution order of the write operations and may differ for different executions of the same multi-threaded test-case. Similarly, a write-read collision may result in different values in the target register of the read. For this reason, Threadmill checks neither the memory used for write-write collisions nor the registers used in write-read collisions. It still makes sense to generate these unchecked collision events because they stress the hardware and may cause failures that can be observed by other means (e.g., built-in hardware checkers).

Threadmill supports this by allocating, to each hardware thread, a number of *owned* intervals. Only the "owner" thread is allowed to write to these intervals. Additionally, all threads share *read-only* and *unowned* intervals. The unowned intervals can be written to and read by all threads but are left unchecked, while the read-only intervals are only read. This ownership scheme allows Threadmill to produce different types of true-sharing and false-sharing collision events while maintaining its checking method.

A user can explicitly direct certain memory accesses, for example, to target the same cache congruence class. This can be specified in the test-template by defining a *mask*, which is a bit-vector with don't-care (X) values for some of its bits. Each mask represents the set of addresses that can be obtained by determining don't-care bits. For example, the mask $8b11XXXX00$ represents all the 8-bit addresses that start with two 1s and end with two 0s.

Threadmill strives to place the intervals at interesting locations to increase the test-case quality. A memory location is considered *interesting* if accessing it stresses the design. Such locations include *a)* cache line or page/segment crossing; *b)* memory having certain attributes, for example, non-cacheable memory or memory obeying different consistency rules; and *c)* various memory affinity, such as memory located on a different chip.

We employ the CSP solver, feeding it with our requirements to produce the memory intervals that the exerciser will use during runtime. Some inputs to the solver, such as the test-template and the system configuration, are only available in the dynamic-build stage, thus making executing the solver in the static-build stage impossible. Our CSP technology proved to be time-efficient, taking less than 10 seconds for 48 threads, which is a typical bring-up configuration that satisfies the build time requirements of the dynamic-build stage. The resulting set of memory intervals includes: memory for the code and data areas of the exerciser application, memory for test-cases that will be generated during runtime, and the memory accessed by the generated load/store instructions. The intervals are embedded into the exerciser and organized such that they can be efficiently retrieved by it during runtime.

As in the case of the address translation paths, conducting such computations would drop silicon utilization dramatically. Our solution calls for moving this computation off to the dynamic-build stage. At runtime, the generator can randomly select one of the available entries from the table to find a memory location to access (details below).

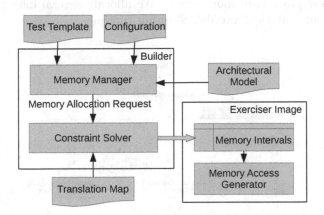

Fig. 2. Memory management architecture

The high-level architecture of Threadmill's memory management component is depicted in Figure 2. This component consists of two sub-components: a builder application and a memory access generator. The builder application runs during the dynamic-build stage and allocates all the memory intervals. The chosen intervals are incorporated into the exerciser image as tables organized for quick retrieval. The memory access generator component executes during runtime. It retrieves a matching interval address from the tables, based on the randomly generated memory access. Note that the tables are built to ensure sufficient variability in the address selection.

The builder retrieves the user requests from the test-template. It also retrieves the system topology, the number of threads, and the available memories from

the system configuration. The builder then accordingly creates memory allocation requests and feeds them to the CSP solver. The memory allocation requests
consist of instruction stream locations (test-cases), user-defined memory allocations, and allocations for random loads and stores (collision areas). The CSP
solver also accepts a memory map produced by the address translation component (see Section 4). The map describes page and segment boundaries as well as
page attributes, e.g., whether a page is cacheable or non-cacheable.

The CSP solver represents each memory allocation request as a pair of CSP
variables: interval start and interval length. There are two common mandatory
(also called *hard*) constraints: *a)* all intervals are disjoint and *b)* all intervals
reside in the available memory space. We also add specific hard constraints for
each memory allocation type. For example, for a user-defined memory allocation
request, the CSP solver must allocate an interval of the required size, starting at
an address that adheres to the specified mask. For random loads and stores, the
CSP solver must allocate the required number of intervals for each ownership
type (read-only, owned, and unowned). We also specify the size distribution of
the intervals, as well as the minimal number of cacheable and non-cacheable
intervals for random memory accesses, enabling Threadmill to find a matching
interval for any possible memory access. We allocate several intervals for each
request to ensure sufficient variability during runtime.

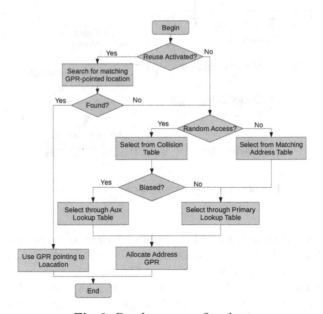

Fig. 3. Random access flowchart

In addition to hard constraints, the CSP solver is also passed a number of non-
mandatory (also called *soft*) constraints to enable the generation of high quality
test-cases. These soft constraints are satisfied on a "best effort" basis and used to

direct interval allocation to interesting areas such as multiple intervals residing within the same cache line. The builder creates data structures containing the allocated addresses and incorporates them into the exerciser. The instruction stream allocations and user-defined intervals are put into simple arrays. The collision area, however, requires some organization to facilitate quick retrieval during runtime. This is further explained below.

During runtime, the memory access generator first decides on the generated instruction and then decides on the memory access address (see Figure 3).

With an instruction at hand, we know whether the memory access is cacheable or non-cacheable, load or store. Cacheable and non-cacheable memory areas are mutually exclusive, thus we divide the collision area table into two parts. We also group all the memory intervals according to their ownership. Based on whether our memory access is load or store, checked or unchecked, we can choose the matching ownership regions and randomly select from them. We construct a primary look-up table for each thread. This table allows for fast and simple random choice (by just a single operation), while maintaining uniform distribution amongst entries. This look-up table contains indices into the main collision area table, grouped by access type (see Figure 4). Organizing the collision area tables in this way enables fast and efficient data retrieval, resulting in high machine utilization.

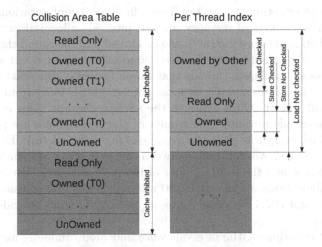

Fig. 4. Collision area tables

We also build auxiliary look-up tables per event. These table are used to support fast retrieval of addresses when the generation of a specific event is desired. These tables contain indices from the primary table that support the required event. Consider, for example, the case of a page-crossing access event. Only a subset of the chosen addresses may support this event, as it requires for the memory interval to start "near" the end of one page, and be long enough to cross into the next. All relevant memory intervals supporting this event are

Table 3. Average number of collisions

(a) Without collision bias

Threads	Rd-Rd	Wr-Wr	Rd-Wr	Total Intervals
2	17.2	0	0	40
4	74.6	0	0	60
8	508.6	0	0	100

(b) With collision bias

Threads	Rd-Rd	Wr-Wr	Rd-Wr	Total Intervals
2	35.6	33.6	53.8	40
4	147.6	80.8	156.2	60
8	714.2	207.4	420	100

identified at the dynamic-build stage, and their indices are places in the page-crossing look-up table. The auxiliary look-up tables are sorted by index number, and hence, by construction, maintain the same sorting attributes of the primary table.

To demonstrate the effectiveness of our scheme, we conducted two experiments. For both experiments, we ran Threadmill on 3 configurations: 2, 4, and 8 threads, all with $8GB$ of memory and 10 intervals allocated per ownership. We generated 50 load/store instructions per thread and measured the number of collision events generated for the checked accesses. A collision event is defined as a pair of accesses by different threads that target (possibly different) locations in the same cache line. For example, suppose thread 0 loads twice from some cache line and thread 1 stores three times to the same cache line. This is counted as six read-write collision events. The results of the experiments are presented in Table 3, in which every row gives the average of five different runs. Every column except the last one shows collisions between different types of memory accesses. The last column shows the total number of intervals allocated. For example, for 8 thread configurations we allocated 100 intervals and 714.2 collisions occurred between Read and 207.4 between Write accesses of different threads, as shown in Table 3b.

In the first experiment, the intervals were allocated randomly and uniformly distributed within the available memory. As the experiment results show, the probability of generating colliding memory accesses for randomly allocated intervals within a large memory space is negligible. Note that we still obtain Read-Read collisions since read-only intervals are shared among all threads.

In the second experiment, we used our CSP solver to bias interval allocation and increase the collision rate. We observe a considerable collision rate for all collision types, as shown in Table 3b.

While the above describes an implementation specific to Threadmill, a similar approach can be implemented to improve the quality of other tools. Consider, for example, the *Litmus* system described in [10]. The developers of the Litmus system acknowledge the need for multitude of address to efficiently utilize the hardware platform. To address this need, they opt to allocate arrays in memory (instead of a single address). However, compilers allocate arrays in contiguous memory, that is, all addresses reside consecutively in memory. Alternatively, applying our method and allocating multiple locations (and arranging their addresses in an array) would require a negligible addition to compilation time, and just one additional pointer traversal at runtime to reach the desired address.

6   Conclusions

We introduced a novel method that bridges two conflicting requirement, namely, to conduct high quality functional validation while ensuring high silicon utilization. Our method calls for shifting the preparation of complex data from the SBST's runtime to the offline phase that takes place before the software test is compiled and loaded onto the silicon platform.

We implemented this method in Threadmill and applied it to two domains: address translation path generation and memory access management. We used well-established pre-silicon technologies to ensure the quality of the generated data. Our results indicate that we are able to guarantee a high level of coverage, while keeping the on-platform complexity low. The addition of this method did not change any of Threadmill's attributes, specifically, its coverage (i.e., the type of test-cases that can be generated by Threadmill) and the ability to reproduce an exerciser image that re-generates the same test-cases.

While our results indicate a good balance between off-platform pre-computation and on-platform data usage, many additional research questions remain. One such question is the applicability of our proposed scheme when the target platform is an accelerator or emulator, as opposed to real silicon. Since accelerators/emulators are significantly slower than silicon, but significantly faster than software simulation, we believe the tradeoff might be different.

References

1. Abramovici, M., Bradley, P., Dwarakanath, K.N., Levin, P., Memmi, G., Miller, D.: A reconfigurable design-for-debug infrastructure for SoCs. In: DAC, pp. 7–12 (2006)
2. Adir, A., Almog, E., Fournier, L., Marcus, E., Rimon, M., Vinov, M., Ziv, A.: Genesys-pro: Innovations in test program generation for functional processor verification. IEEE Design & Test of Computers 21(2), 84–93 (2004)
3. Adir, A., Copty, S., Landa, S., Nahir, A., Shurek, G., Ziv, A., Meissner, C., Schumann, J.: A unified methodology for pre-silicon verification and post-silicon validation. In: DATE, pp. 1590–1595 (2011)
4. Adir, A., Emek, R., Katz, Y., Koyfman, A.: Deeptrans - a model-based approach to functional verification of address translation mechanisms. In: MTV, pp. 3–6 (2003)
5. Adir, A., Golubev, M., Landa, S., Nahir, A., Shurek, G., Sokhin, V., Ziv, A.: Threadmill: a post-silicon exerciser for multi-threaded processors. In: DAC, pp. 860–865 (2011)

6. Adir, A., Nahir, A., Shurek, G., Ziv, A., Meissner, C., Schumann, J.: Leveraging pre-silicon verification resources for the post-silicon validation of the IBM POWER7 processor. In: DAC, pp. 569–574 (2011)
7. Adir, A., Nahir, A., Ziv, A.: Concurrent generation of concurrent programs for post-silicon validation. IEEE Trans. on CAD of Integrated Circuits and Systems 31(8), 1297–1302 (2012)
8. Adir, A., Nahir, A., Ziv, A., Meissner, C., Schumann, J.: Reaching coverage closure in post-silicon validation. In: Raz, O. (ed.) HVC 2010. LNCS, vol. 6504, pp. 60–75. Springer, Heidelberg (2010)
9. Adve, S.V., Hill, M.D.: A unified formalization of four shared-memory models. IEEE Trans. Parallel Distrib. Syst. 4(6), 613–624 (1993)
10. Alglave, J., Maranget, L., Sarkar, S., Sewell, P.: litmus: Running tests against hardware. In: Abdulla, P.A., Leino, K.R.M. (eds.) TACAS 2011. LNCS, vol. 6605, pp. 41–44. Springer, Heidelberg (2011)
11. Bin, E., Emek, R., Shurek, G., Ziv, A.: Using a constraint satisfaction formulation and solution techniques for random test program generation. IBM Systems Jouranl 41(3), 386–402 (2002)
12. Chen, K., Malik, S., Patra, P.: Runtime validation of memory ordering using constraint graph checking. In: HPCA, pp. 415–426 (2008)
13. De Paula, F.M., Gort, M., Hu, A.J., Wilton, S.J.E., Yang, J.: Backspace: formal analysis for post-silicon debug. In: Proceedings of the 2008 International Conference on Formal Methods in Computer-Aided Design, pp. 1–10 (November 2008)
14. Deorio, A., Li, J., Bertacco, V.: Bridging pre- and post-silicon debugging with BiPeD. In: ICCAD (November 2012) (to appear)
15. Emek, R., Jaeger, I., Naveh, Y., Bergman, G., Aloni, G., Katz, Y., Farkash, M., Dozoretz, I., Goldin, A.: X-gen: a random test-case generator for systems and socs. In: HLDVT, pp. 145–150 (2002)
16. Gharachorloo, K., Lenoski, D., Laudon, J., Gibbons, P.B., Gupta, A., Hennessy, J.L.: Memory consistency and event ordering in scalable shared-memory multiprocessors. In: 25 Years ISCA: Retrospectives and Reprints, pp. 376–387 (1998)
17. Gray, R.: Post-silicon validation experience: History, trends, and challenges. In: GSRC Workshop on Post-Si Validation (June 2008)
18. Hong, T., Li, Y., Park, S.-B., Mui, D., Lin, D., Kaleq, Z.A., Hakim, N., Naeimi, H., Gardner, D.S., Mitra, S.: QED: Quick error detection tests for effective post-silicon validation. In: ITC, pp. 154–163 (2010)
19. Keshava, J., Hakim, N., Prudvi, C.: Post-silicon validation challenges: how EDA and academia can help. In: DAC 2010, pp. 3–7. ACM (2010)
20. Lin, D., Hong, T., Fallah, F., Hakim, N., Mitra, S.: Quick detection of difficult bugs for effective post-silicon validation. In: DAC, pp. 561–566 (2012)
21. Mitra, S., Lin, D., Hakim, N., Gardner, D.S.: Bug localization techniques for effective post-silicon validation. In: ASP-DAC, p. 291 (2012)
22. Mitra, S., Seshia, S.A., Nicolici, N.: Post-silicon validation opportunities, challenges and recent advances. In: DAC, pp. 12–17 (2010)
23. Nahir, A., Ziv, A., Galivanche, R., Hu, A.J., Abramovici, M., Camilleri, A., Bentley, B., Foster, H., Bertacco, V., Kapoor, S.: Bridging pre-silicon verification and post-silicon validation. In: DAC, pp. 94–95 (2010)
24. Nahir, A., Ziv, A., Panda, S.: Optimizing test-generation to the execution platform. In: ASP-DAC, pp. 304–309 (2012)
25. Patra, P.: On the cusp of a validation wall. IEEE Design and Test of Computers 24, 193–196 (2007)

26. Psarakis, M., Gizopoulos, D., Sánchez, E.E., Reorda, M.S.: Microprocessor software-based self-testing. IEEE Design & Test of Computers 27(3), 4–19 (2010)
27. Rotithor, H.G.: Postsilicon validation methodology for microprocessors. IEEE Design & Test of Computers 17(4), 77–88 (2000)
28. Singerman, E., Abarbanel, Y., Baartmans, S.: Transaction based pre-to-post silicon validation. In: DAC, pp. 564–568 (2011)
29. Storm, J.: Random test generators for microprocessor design validation (2006), http://www.oracle.com/technetwork/systems/opensparc/ 53-rand-test-gen-validation-1530392.pdf (accessed January 9, 2013)
30. Theodorou, G., Chatzopoulos, S., Kranitis, N., Paschalis, A.M., Gizopoulos, D.: A software-based self-test methodology for on-line testing of data tlbs. In: European Test Symposium (2012)
31. Theodorou, G., Kranitis, N., Paschalis, A.M., Gizopoulos, D.: Software-based self test methodology for on-line testing of l1 caches in multithreaded multicore architectures. IEEE Trans. VLSI Syst. 21(4), 786–790 (2013)

Development and Verification of Complex Hybrid Systems Using Synthesizable Monitors*

Andreas Abel[2], Allon Adir[1], Torsten Blochwitz[2], Lev Greenberg[1], and Tamer Salman[1]

[1] IBM Research - Haifa; Haifa, Israel
{adir,levg,tamers}@il.ibm.com
[2] ITI GmbH, Webergasse 1, 01067 Dresden

Abstract. Using simulation monitors that are formally defined and automatically synthesized is already part of the standard methodology of hardware design and verification. However, this is not yet the case in the domain of systems engineering for cyber-physical systems. The growing trend towards model-based systems engineering is making the use of simulation monitors more relevant and possible. Recent related work focuses almost exclusively on the aspects of requirements specification. In this work, we explain how monitors can play a much more pervasive role in systems engineering, going beyond merely checking requirements. We describe how monitors can be used along the entire product lifecycle, from early design alternative analysis to final field testing. This work also covers the special considerations that must be addressed when designing a monitor specification language, specifically in the context of systems engineering. Our focus is on the practical issues related to the use of monitors and describes a prototype monitor specification and synthesis platform applied to the hybrid simulation of an automotive subsystem.

Keywords: Simulation, Monitors, Cyber Physical Systems, Systems Engineering.

1 Introduction

A simulation monitor is a device that observes the progress of simulation and can detect and report specified behaviors of the simulated model. Its main purpose is to check for possible illegal behaviors, but it can also keep track of test coverage or collect data about a simulated system for later analysis. Simulation monitors have long been in use as part of the hardware development and verification methodology [1]. Industry-standard languages, such as Property-Specification-Language (PSL) [2] or SystemVerilog Assertions (SVA) [3], are used to formally specify the monitored behavior. Formal specifications in these languages can be synthesized [4,5] into monitor implementations in hardware-description languages and form an integral part of the simulated hardware. These specifications

* The research leading to these results has received funding from the European Union Seventh Framework Programme (FP7/2011-2014) under grant agreement n° 287716.

V. Bertacco and A. Legay (Eds.): HVC 2013, LNCS 8244, pp. 182–198, 2013.

can also be synthesized into software that uses the software simulator interfaces to keep track of the dynamic system state.

The development and common usage of such advanced monitoring technology was possible in the hardware domain dues to the ubiquitous use of formal models in the hardware development methodology. Today, the domain of systems engineering is undergoing a similar revolution as the use of formal models increases. This use is termed Model Based Systems Engineering (MBSE). The use of formally specified and automatically synthesizable monitors can now be added to the list of its many benefits.

To understand the need for simulation monitors, we must start by examining the field of systems engineering in general. According to the International Council on Systems Engineering (INCOSE), systems engineering is "an interdisciplinary approach and means to enable the realization of successful systems" [6]. The roles of the systems engineer correspond to the main stages in the product lifecycle. This lifecycle is commonly charted with a V-Model, such as the one shown in Figure 1. The process starts with the analysis and definition of the system requirements, which are then propagated and refined for the various subsystem and component design stages (occurring down the left side of the V). The components are then implemented, integrated, and tested (up the right side of the V-Model) so as to create a complete and verified system corresponding to the requirements.

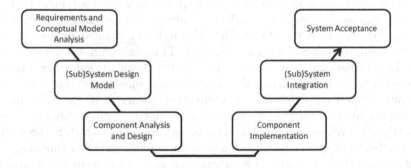

Fig. 1. The V-Model of a product development lifecycle

Many testing processes are carried out along the development lifecycle [7]. These include high-level early conceptual tests, testing the design, testing the implementation of components (by component suppliers or customers), system-integration-labs with hardware-in-the-loop simulators, and field testing environments for the final product. In all of these stages, monitors would be of great benefit as requirement checkers. Indeed, requirement engineering forms a crucial part of the systems engineer's role. Most existing works that mention simulation monitors in the context of systems focus on the requirement specification and checking aspects. For example, the Contract Specification Language (CSL) developed in the SPEEDS [8] project was designed to be used to formally define properties of systems or components as part of contracts [9] (i.e., assume-guarantee pairs of properties that serve in the compositional engineering of systems). Thus, the possible usage of CSL to specify monitors is only secondary, and indeed we explain below that a property specification language like CSL is limited when used to specify monitors. Maler and Nickovic also describe hybrid-system simulation monitors [10] only as requirement checkers.

Consequently, a generic monitor-specification language (and accompanying technology) is needed for the various uses of monitors. Furthermore, the needs and skills of systems engineers are different from those of, for example, hardware designers. Therefore, synthesizable specification languages like PSL cannot serve systems engineers without appropriate adaptations.

In this paper, we show how monitors can serve the systems engineering process in different stages of the development life cycle (Section 2). Section 3 provides observations and recommendations for the desired features of an industrial monitor specification language for systems engineers. Section 4 focuses on the considerations arising from hybrid simulation. Section 5 describes a prototype of a monitor specification and synthesis platform developed to demonstrate some of the ideas we presented here and Section 6 concludes the paper.

2   Performing Systems Engineering with Monitors

The definition and management of the requirements form a central part of the systems engineer's role. The high-level product requirements are reviewed and defined together with the stakeholders through well-defined processes, such as System-Requirement Specification (SysRS). This stakeholder-developer requirement based relationship is also repeated further down the sub-system hierarchy when each subsystem is further decomposed into constituent components. Complex multi-tiered supply chains are a universal feature in all the main industries of complex hybrid systems, such as the automotive, and aerospace & defense industries. Therefore, the formalization of requirements, which is the main feature needed to support a monitor-based systems engineering methodology, could greatly support the supply-chain structure of complex system development.

Different synthesis technologies could be used to create monitors corresponding to the same formal monitor definition but designed to be used in the various testing platforms. For example, a formal requirement could be used to synthesize a software monitor for an early executable high-level analysis model. Other monitors could be later synthesized to monitor the design simulations or integrated system simulation. Later in the product lifecycle, the same monitor definition could be used to synthesize another piece of software to analyze traces coming out of the system's diagnostic components during field testing of the actual system. All of these monitors would be synthesized from the same monitor specification and would use the same logic with different simulator interfaces.

2.1   Analysis of Test Coverage Requirements

Test requirements are an additional kind of requirements during the product's lifecycle. These are carefully planned in a test plan that serves the test team. The test plan can be authorized by the stakeholders of a particular lifecycle stage. As in the case of the system requirements, test requirements are also commonly defined in natural language and can be formal in the legal sense but are rarely formal in the mathematical sense.

The test plan that includes the test requirements mainly serves as the working document for the test team that actually conducts the testing. It also serves as an important tool for management to keep track of the progress of testing and decide when enough testing has been done. Monitors for test coverage are a crucial tool in enabling such progress analysis. Monitors are defined for the tasks in the test plan. These monitors would report that a testing task was covered during simulation or during field testing. Coverage reports could be created and used to evaluate the testing efficiency, progress, or to identify persistent coverage holes that need to be directly targeted [11].

2.2   Requirement Traceability

An important issue relating to requirement management is requirement traceability. Accepted safety standards, such as ISO 26262 [12] for automotive functional safety, or DO-178 [13] variants for software reliability in airborne systems, require explicit traceability between requirements and their hierarchic decomposition for subcomponents. Requirements must also be traceable to the components responsible for their implementation, and to the tests that are planned to verify them. Monitor specifications can serve as the formal definition of the system or test requirements. In such cases, the traceability information would relate formal objects and could serve automatic tools that would exploit this information for their analysis. For example, coverage monitors could be used to track the testing progress in the various components. The traceability information could then be used to produce coverage reports for the higher level subsystems, or to identify semantic coverage holes by considering the system's structure. For example, coverage hole analysis could detect that test objectives relating to performance under extreme conditions are consistently uncovered by tests traceable to the engine-control-unit. This could be due to defective testing or simulation of this subsystem, for example.

2.3   Data Harvesting and Dynamic Optimization

An additional usage of monitors is gathering information about the behavior of the model. The model can be an early analysis model or a later refined one. The gathered information can then be analyzed by other tools for various purposes. For example, monitors can gather overall system performance information, which can be used to create a formal statistical model of the performance aspects of the system. A typical example is the generation of a statistical model of an emergent behavior of a network system. This is carried out during the design space exploration phase of the system to evaluate different topologies or component selection. Other types of analysis could be carried out with the help of monitors, including power usage analysis, cost-performance optimization analysis, and usage patterns analysis. Such monitor measurements can be harvested from the high-level executable models that are used by the systems engineer for early analysis. This includes comparing alternative system functions, structures, or configurations against various measures-of-effectiveness (MOEs), such as price, performance, and time-to-market MOEs. The systems engineer optimizes the planned system with respect to these MOEs by either assessing several manually selected alternatives or by using automatic optimization tools. Dynamic optimization refers to the method of performing such optimization using simulation. Multiple simulations are performed for each of the various alternatives and the empirical results are compared.

Monitors could obviously serve such a process very well. According to our proposed monitor-based methodology, the monitors are formally defined and automatically synthesized to enable the collection of the required information from the simulator. Such automation supports the comparison of a greater number of alternatives. This is beneficial in cases in which static analysis tools are unavailable or are unable to cope with the system's complexity.

2.4   Use of Monitors in Hardware Development and Verification

Hardware design methods do not generally follow requirement engineering processes as rigorously as in systems engineering. However, in practice today, a part of the standard methodology for designers is to annotate their design code with assertions and with coverage monitors. This is done directly in the hardware description language or with dedicated languages like PSL [2] or SVA [3], which can be automatically synthesized into the hardware description language or to software monitors [4,5]. This results in a great number of monitors (thousands) in a typical hardware system, mostly on the low unit-level. Monitors for higher levels (i.e., for hardware features involving multiple units, such as memory coherence) are typically created separately by special verification experts.

A similar approach to monitor usage could also be taken by designers of components of complex hybrid systems. We expect, however, that the monitor definition languages would need to be adapted to the particular discipline of the design (electronic, aerodynamic, software, etc.). We can take a lot from the hardware monitoring domain and apply it to systems engineering, as was done in the prototype described in Section 5, especially in relation to property-specification languages and actual technologies used for automatic synthesis.

3   Language Considerations

Most languages in current use for hardware monitor specification were not primarily designed for such usage. These languages include software languages such as C, hardware description languages such as VHDL, and even formal property-specification-languages such as PSL. Properties defined in PSL could be formally verified with model-checking or dynamically checked with automatically synthesized checkers. However, as discussed in Section 2, the use of monitors as property checkers is only one of several possible uses—other uses include test coverage monitoring and data harvesting. Thus, a language designed for property specification is not necessarily the best one for monitors in general.

A monitor's specification should include (1) a specification of a behavioral property to monitor, (2) a mapping between formal attributes appearing in the monitored property and actual attributes of the system or model, and (3) the action to take when the monitor detects the specified behavior. The first part could use variants of existing property specification languages, like PSL or CSL. The second part relates attributes to actual model signals. For example, in the monitored behavior specified as "Every request must be followed by an acknowledgment after no more than 10 seconds", the formal attributes "request" and "acknowledgment" should be mapped to specific signals in the simulated system components. The mapping could be carried out with mapping tables or graphically using diagrams, e.g., with a UML profile that supports links between ports of the monitor block and the monitored component attributes. The third part of a monitor's specification is the action to be taken when the monitor detects the specified behavior. In the context of verification, the implied action is to declare a failure when the property is disproved (formally or empirically).

For other monitor uses, the action would be different. For example, when monitors are used for keeping track of test coverage, then the action would include updates to a coverage report. When monitors are used for data harvesting, the action may include updates to a statistics database or lead to an optimization analysis when used for dynamic optimization.

Such general actions can be directly specified in software code. The monitor specification platform could support a library of software utilities that can assist the coding of the action software. For example, accessors to coverage tables, or reporting utilities. However in specific systems engineering contexts, the possible monitor actions would be limited, only allowing the user to select and configure one of a short list of possible actions.

The monitor action specification should also indicate when the action is to be taken. For test coverage monitors this happens when the specified behavior occurs, while for checkers, when the behavioral property is violated. Omitting this part of the monitor specification is possible by always performing the action when the specified behavior occurs and to specify the negated behavior in the case of checkers. However, the resulting properties could become counter-intuitive. Properties for checkers are generally thought of as requirements and are often indeed expressed as assertions. In this case, the monitor looks for a violation of the specified behavior. Test coverage monitors are more intuitively expressed as test requirements. In this case the monitor should look for the occurrence of the specified behavior.

This difference between properties of which either the occurrence or the violation should be detected leads to a slightly different "flavor" in the way in which the property is specified. Properties whose occurrence is monitored are more conveniently specified as sequences of (possibly complex) events. PSL, for example includes a SERE style—Sequential-Extended-Regular-Expressions [2], in which regular expressions are used to specify the sequences. UML sequence-diagrams can also be used to define monitors with a sequence of occurrences—here the focus would be on the interactions between the system components. On the other hand, properties for which the violation is monitored are more conveniently expressed with some form of implication. This is because these properties originate from system requirements, which often take the form of "whenever some condition holds then some guarantee must also hold". For example, "Every request must be followed by an acknowledgment after no more than 10 seconds". With contract specifications [9], the assumptions and the guarantees are specified separately. The system or component requires that the assumptions hold and guarantees that guarantees hold.

The CSL language, for example, focuses on properties with explicit or implied implications. This is not surprising as it is designed to specify requirements. Thus, it is ill-suited as a monitor specification language, as it is difficult to use it to specify coverage monitors. On the other hand, languages that only focus on event sequences, such as UML sequence-diagrams, are also ill-suited to serve as monitor specification languages because of the difficulty of using them to define checkers. Live-Sequence-Charts diagrams [14] are much more suitable, because they include constructs of both "flavors".

The concept of vacuity [2] is relevant to the case of checker monitors keeping track of requirements with implications. A monitor would normally declare that a simulation run is consistent with the requirement even when the left side of the implication never occurs during the run. Such vacuous passes indicate insufficient testing and should be therefore be reported as such to the verification person.

3.1 Declarative vs. Operational Property Specification

The formal languages used to define properties for hardware verification (PSL or SVA) are declarative. I.e., the property itself is described rather than the operations that can be used to detect it. The description is formal and concise and can be automatically synthesized into hardware or software. However, these languages are geared to describe hardware properties. Moreover, writing properties in these languages requires some experience and a certain way of thinking not always present even in hardware designers. The result is that more checkers are still written directly in the hardware description language, rather than synthesized into the hardware description language from a declarative specification. Popular software programming languages such as C or C++ are also very commonly used for writing monitors. The simulator itself is a piece of software and can easily provide hooks for the attachment of monitor software that could observe the simulated behavior and detect violations or measure coverage. Figure 9 shows a declarative monitor specification and an operational specification of the same monitor. The operational specification is in C and uses the *SIG* function to access the dynamic value of the system attributes. Automatically synthesizing software (e.g., C code) from formally defined properties, such as in PSL, is actually possible, but in practice, as we noted above, designers typically prefer to write the monitor software directly.

We can expect to make the same considerations for using declarative property definition languages or operational languages in the systems engineering domain. In fact, in this domain, the problem would probably be more acute. Hardware designers are often expected to write pieces of operational software and even, sometimes though less frequently, might be willing to use formal property definition languages. Such tendencies could be only rarely assumed in the case of systems engineers. Systems engineers commonly come from one of the disciplines used in the respective system design and only incidentally from the software parts of the system. Moreover, the use of formal models is only recently being driven by the movement towards MBSE. The willingness to learn new sophisticated formal languages that can be used for requirement and monitors definition could only be expected in the long run. We expect that the adoption of formal languages for requirement and monitors definition depends on the success of MBSE as a part of the mainstream systems engineering discipline.

A compromise is possible, however, between a rich formal declarative language and an operational language. The idea is to come up with a short list of the most useful properties expressed in the formal declarative language and then to allow the user to configure or fill in the parameters of these "templates". The list should be short enough so as not to deter users but strong enough so as to be useful. This was the approach taken for the CSL language mentioned above. The language was designed for the definition of properties of systems or of components with contracts. The selection of the most useful templates was done together with the industrial partners of the SPEEDS [8] project.

We believe that a tool that would support a monitor-based systems engineering methodology and aspires to popular demand would need to include at least the option of selecting and configuring from such a list of most-commonly used monitor templates. The list would serve most users most of the times. However, as seen in Section 2, monitors can have very diverse usages by systems engineers. The skill sets and the levels of detail and sophistication needed at these various steps can be expected to differ. Some flexibility would need to thus be allowed in the monitor specification language and tool so as also to support richer specification constructs or even operational specification when an occasional need for greater detail is required. See Section 5 for an example.

4   Hybrid Simulation Monitors

In systems engineering, complex hybrid systems are modeled. In discrete systems modeling, time is represented by a discrete monotonic ascending process. Each signal representing a property of the model is assigned a value at each time step. In hybrid systems modeling, on the other hand, time is a continuous monotonic ascending process. Hybrid models can include both discrete and continuous signals. Discrete signals belong to behaviors that are discrete in nature, such as a signal representing a state of a switch that can be turned on and off. Continuous signals, on the other hand, represent properties that are continuous in nature, such as the temperature of a certain body.

The simulation of a hybrid system model involves sampling of the continuous signals at finite points in time. However, the simulator must still be able to capture interesting behaviors that might occur at any point in time. Various methods are applied in these simulators to enable the identification of these events and other interesting points in time, including the inspection of the signals' derivatives and their zero-crossings. Among the well-known simulation tools for hybrid models are MathWorks® Simulink® [15] and the Modelica® modeling language and tools [16]. These tools can simulate a hybrid model in two different modes—a fixed time-step mode and a variable time-step mode. In the first case, the simulation tool decides on a constant sampling rate, while in the second, the sampling rate varies to capture important events in the signals' behaviors.

The simulation-based verification process of hybrid models should take into account the monitors defined on the model. These monitors might seek events that are not necessarily captured in the simulation samples. This is due to the fact that interesting behaviors sought by the monitors might have not been considered interesting for the simulator. For example, the behavior of a continuous signal representing the temperature of a certain object is sampled by the simulation tool in accordance with the needs of the model and the simulation process. A monitor defined on the behavior of this signal might need a different sampling scheme and its results would be inaccurate with the existing samples. Figure 2(a) demonstrates a possible behavior of a signal representing a temperature over continuous time. The stars on the graph represent the sample points that were selected by the simulation tool according to its need to best describe the signal's behavior. Assume that the user wants to monitor the first point in time at which the temperature reaches 100°. Figure 2(b) shows the same signal in the vicinity of the required temperature (marked with a dashed ellipse in the left-side graph). It can be seen that the point in time at which the temperature equals 100° is not sampled, thus, inspection of the sample would not trigger the monitor. A valid hybrid monitor would therefore have to take measures that take into account the fact that the simulator works with samples. In the scope of this work, we have investigated three methods for implementing hybrid monitors. The first uses a restricted monitor language, the second manipulates monitors to adapt to hybrid systems, and the third uses a monitor-aware simulation. The three methods are presented in the following subsections.

4.1   Restricted Monitor Language

One method of dealing with hybrid monitors is the prohibition of writing monitors that might lead to false detection or non-detection of intended behaviors. An example of this would be to prohibit the use of the equality operator in hybrid monitor specifications. In general, monitoring continuous behavior could cause

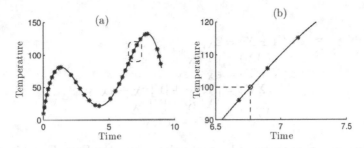

Fig. 2. (a) A sampling of a continuous signal representing a temperature. (b) A zoomed view of the signal. The point in time where the temperature reaches 100° is not sampled.

false reaction either with an equality or with a two-sided inequality using a small enough range. For example, consider a detection monitor "$a_1 \leq T \leq a_2$", where T is the continuous temperature signal of figure 2, ascending from beneath a_1 to above a_2. This monitor should be prohibited if the sampling of the temperature is sparse enough to allow for the satisfaction of the property to go undetected. A sufficient condition ensuring that this property is detected is given in Equation. 1, where $\frac{dT}{dt}$ is the derivative of the signal and S is the set of sampling-step sizes.

$$a_2 - a_1 \geq \max \left| \frac{dT}{dt} \right| \max S \tag{1}$$

This condition is conservative and can be used when the signal derivatives and sampling rates cannot be determined before the simulation. However, monitoring the actual derivatives and sample rates can relax this condition. The monitor manager could give a warning in time zones in which the condition does not hold during simulation, yet still allows the monitor to be used at other times.

4.2 Monitor Manipulation

A second method for dealing with hybrid monitors is the automatic manipulation of the monitored properties to accommodate the continuous nature of the signals. Each continuous signal X is assigned an inaccuracy parameter ε_X that represents the error in the signal due to sampling. These values can be gathered offline based on the derivative of the signal and the sample-step. Once the inaccuracy parameters are known, each monitored expression can be manipulated to adapt to the continuous system by error propagation techniques. The adaptation of the monitored expression is intended to catch sampled occurrences of the monitored expression as well as suspected occurrences. Let X and Y be two continuous signals in the system with inaccuracy parameters ε_X and ε_Y, respectively, and A be a discrete signal with no inaccuracy. The error propagation in arithmetic expressions can be computed as depicted in the following equations:

$$\varepsilon\,(A \pm X) = \varepsilon_X$$
$$\varepsilon\,(AX) = |A|\,\varepsilon_X$$
$$\varepsilon\,(X \pm Y) = \varepsilon_X + \varepsilon_Y$$
$$\varepsilon\,(XY) = |X|\,\varepsilon_Y + |Y|\,\varepsilon_X + \varepsilon_X\varepsilon_Y$$
$$\varepsilon\,(X/Y) = \frac{|X|\,\varepsilon_Y + |Y|\,\varepsilon_X}{Y^2 - |Y|\,\varepsilon_Y}$$

For each expression that can be manipulated into the form $E = 0$ in a monitor, the expression is modified to accommodate for the possible inaccuracy into $-\varepsilon\,(E) \le E \le \varepsilon\,(E)$. Similarly, expressions of the form $E < 0$ or $E > 0$ are modified into $E < \varepsilon\,(E)$ or $E > -\varepsilon\,(E)$, respectively. Such techniques may also allow the monitor to produce two kinds of detections; definitive and potential, where the latter is due to the manipulation of the monitored expression.

4.3 Monitor-Aware Simulation

Hybrid simulation tools use various techniques to determine the sample set during simulation. These techniques are meant to allow the simulator to capture all interesting events and behaviors in the system, according to the expressions and subexpressions containing signals of the system. A monitor management system could control the simulator's sampling policy, when such controls are available, so as to fit the needs of the monitors. Alternatively, the monitor logic could be integrated into the simulated model, and thus the simulator would automatically treat the monitor specification expressions as interesting to sample.

5 Monitor Specification and Synthesis Platform

In this section, we describe the prototype of a monitor specification and synthesis platform for systems engineers that we designed. We developed this platform to demonstrate the ideas and recommendations we presented in this paper. For our demonstration, we used an executable model of an automatic transmission gearbox (ATG). Figure 3 depicts the ATG model composed of a driver, engine, controller, gearbox and driveline components. The driver component models the driver acceleration-pedal input. The engine component transforms the acceleration-pedal input to mechanical torque. The controller component selects the required gear using five corresponding output ports, and the gearbox transforms mechanical torque from engine to driveline, according to the currently selected gear. Finally, the driveline component models the car dynamics. The resulting ATG model exhibits hybrid dynamics that includes both continuous (e.g., acceleration of the car between gear changes) and discrete (e.g., dynamics during gear switching) behaviors. Modeling of complex systems requires multiple engineering domains, each typically preferring its own modeling languages and tools. In the ATG example, the Modelica® language [16] in the

SimulationX® tool was used to model mechanical components (e.g., the gearbox) and a SysML [17] statechart in the IBM® Rational® Rhapsody® tool was used to model the controller component. The FMI standard [18] was used to integrate models from different tools. This standard provides a simple interface for the integration of models from different tools described by differential, discrete, and algebraic equations. In this work we used the SimulationX simulation engine to simulate and generate system signal traces.

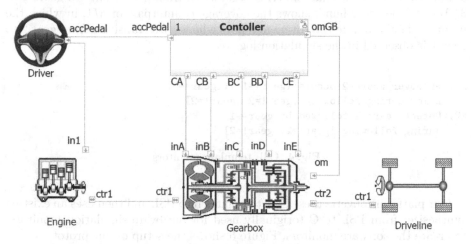

Fig. 3. A hybrid model of an automatic transmission gearbox

We would like to use monitors throughout the product lifecycle and thus several different simulation platforms would need to be monitored. We chose to have our monitors track the simulation through the simulation logs rather than directly from the simulator software interfaces. Every simulator can be expected to produce some log of its run and these logs of various formats could then be translated into traces of a standard form expected by the generic monitoring platform. The standard trace gives the values of the system attributes at any point in time, as reported by the simulator. Our prototype performed the monitoring offline after the simulation log was available, but the platform could easily be adapted to perform the monitoring online during simulation, by using a pipeline starting with the dynamically appended log file, translated into the standard trace, and "fed" into the monitors producing their reports.

A formally defined monitor specification language is outside the scope of this work, though we gave some recommendations in Section 3 for how such a language should be designed for systems engineers.

In our prototype, we supported a simple monitor specification language with a GUI for the specification and a back end for the automatic synthesis. This specification language addresses most of the issues we raised in Section 3. We would like our monitors to serve the different uses needed by systems engineers, as described in Section 2. Thus, the monitor-specification language would need to support both requirement checking and test coverage. As we mentioned above, CSL is based on a collection of useful templates but is focused on requirements. We therefore created a coverage counterpart of a couple of CSL templates.

For example, the CSL template "Whenever E occurs C holds during following [I1,I2]" specifies the requirement that whenever an even E occurs then the condition C holds during the next interval defined by the start and end events I1 and I2. Figure 4 depicts examples demonstrating use of the template. $M1$ specifies a monitor that checks that the ATG can switch from gear 2 only to gears 1 or 3. $M2$, on the other hand, shows the coverage counterpart of $M1$, in which the monitor should update the coverage report whenever a transition from gear 2 to gear 1 is observed in the simulation log.

```
M1: Whenever gear==2 occurs (gear==1 || gear==3)
    holds during following [gear!=2, gear!=2]
M2: Detect gear==2 followed by gear==1
    during following [gear!=2, gear!=2]
```

Fig. 4. CSL template monitors

Our platform converts these CSL templates into PSL and then uses an existing synthesizer from PSL to C (originally used for hardware simulation monitors) to create the software monitors. Figure 5 shows the setup of our prototype.

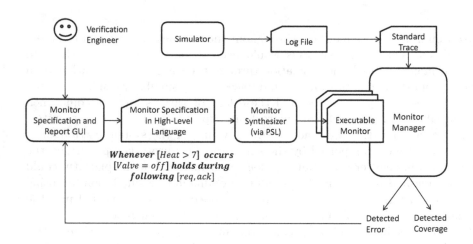

Fig. 5. Monitor specification, synthesis, and usage flow

In our prototype's monitor specification language, we can also specify monitors with logical expressions using the standard arithmetic and logical operators (from C with the added operator *implies* for logical implication). For such monitors, the user also indicates whether the monitor should report coverage when the expression holds true (a coverage monitor) or to report an error when the expression does not hold true (a requirement checker). Figure 6 shows examples of logical monitors. The checker monitor $M3$ reports an error whenever the speed rises above 200. The coverage monitor $M4$ updates the coverage report whenever the speed rises above 200. Figure 7 depicts additional CSL inspired temporal functions that enrich the language.

```
M3: speed <= 200
M4: speed > 200
```

Fig. 6. Logical monitors

```
[]
HeldDuring(expression e, integer t):  true whenever e is true for at least
                                      t seconds.
Timeout(expression e, integer t):     true t seconds after e is true.
Up(expression e):                     true when e becomes true.
Down(expression e):                   true when e stops being true.
```

Fig. 7. Additional temporal Templates

For example, in Figure 8, the monitor $M5$ checks the requirement that when the gas pedal (a floating number between 0 and 1) is fully pressed for 10 seconds, the car must reach at least 100 km/hr.

The monitors shown in Figure 7 are directly synthesized into C monitors, without using intermediate PSL descriptions.

```
M5: HeldDuring(gas=1, 10) implies speed >= 100
```

Fig. 8. Temporal monitor example

Finally, our platform supports monitor specification using operational C code. Figure 9 gives a specification of a checker monitor with equivalent behavior to monitor $M5$, but in this case the monitor is specified with operational C code. The monitor code is invoked on every simulation sampling as it is documented in the simulation log. The values of the system attributes (and the *time*) at the point of sampling can be accessed with the *SIG* function. This is a checker monitor, so the code must return true if and only if no violation of the requirement was detected in the sampled time. This situation is reversed for coverage monitors that must return true if and only if the desired specified event was

```
Declarative: HeldDuring(gas=1, 10) implies speed>=100
Operational:
static int lastSampleTime = 0;
static int lastFullGas = 0;
static int count = 0;

if (lastFullGas && (SIG(gas)==100)
  count += (SIG(time) - lastSampleTime);
else
  count = 0;
lastSampleTime = SIG(time);
lastFullGas=(SIG(gas)==1);

return (count<10 || SIG(speed)>=100);
```

Fig. 9. A monitor specification with declarative and operational code

detected in the sampled time. Monitors that are specified with operational code naturally require no synthesis, and they can be directly used by our monitoring platform.

The monitors were specified using a GUI in which the user could fill in the parameters of the CSL templates or specify monitors with logical expressions or code. The GUI also indicated the current status of the monitors. Checker monitors are either failed or are vacuously or non-vacuously passed. Coverage monitors are either detected or not. A more complete textual report could also be given with the number of failures/passes/detections.

During our work with the prototype, we adjusted and improved the monitor specification language so as to conveniently serve the various monitor specification types. We did not detect any actual violation of requirements with our monitors, but we were able to correct the specification of the requirement itself. This occurred through the use of the checker monitor $M1$ specified above. The monitor detected a violation, but when debugging the failing trace it was found that the ATG passes through a short intermediate neutral gear when shifting between any two gears. For the same reason, the coverage monitor $M2$ never reported coverage, even in simulation runs in which the car shifted from gear 2 to gear 1. Thus, we changed the requirement (and monitor) specification to take this fact into account. This demonstrates that monitors can also be used in the early requirement specification phase with high-level analysis models for the purpose of refining the requirements and making their phrasing more precise.

6   Conclusions

In this paper, we showed that a monitor-based development and verification methodology could benefit systems engineers in various different stages of the product development lifecycle. The benefits of model-based development with its use of formal languages have long been evident in the hardware development domain and have enabled the entire electronic design automation (EDA) technology and industry. The same benefits could also be expected in systems engineering, where monitors are a natural part of this expected revolution.

Our main claim is that monitor use could be pervasive along the entire product lifecycle and not be limited only to requirement checking. Various uses, such as requirement specification; early system alternative analysis; test coverage; data harvesting; and naturally, requirement checking; can be made throughout the development process. Many executable models, simulators, and testing platforms are already used during the development of complex cyber physical systems. These include high-level early analysis models, design and development models for the system and its components, integrated system models, hardware-in-the-loop models, and field testing environments.

Technology for automatic monitor synthesis is already available from the hardware domain. Several languages have also been proposed for formal specification of system requirements. We described how such languages should be extended and adjusted to serve the various recommended uses by systems engineers, and demonstrated our recommendations in a generally applicable monitor specification and execution platform. However, an actual formal definition of a monitor specification language was beyond the scope of this paper. The next step should be the design of such a language. We believe that this effort should take our recommendations into account and be carried out together with practicing systems engineers. The main challenge would be to come up with a language flexible enough to support the various uses and user skills that could still maintain a consistent interface and semantics.

Acknowledgments. The authors wish to thank Shinichi Hirose from IBM Research - Tokyo for the fruitful discussions and the valuable advice.

References

1. Wile, B., Goss, J.C., Roesner, W.: Comprehensive Functional Verification - The Complete Industry Cycle. Morgan Kaufmann (2005)
2. Eisner, C., Fisman, D.: A Practical Introduction to PSL. Springer US (2006)
3. Vijayaraghavan, S., Ramanathan, M.: A Practical Guide for SystemVerilog Assertions. Springer (2005)
4. Boulé, M., Zilic, Z.: Automata-Based Assertion-Checker Synthesis of PSL Properties. ACM Transactions on Design Automation of Electronic Systems (TODAES) 13(1), 4 (2008)
5. Abarbanel, Y., Beer, I., Gluhovsky, L., Keidar, S., Wolfsthal, Y.: FoCs - Automatic Generation of Simulation Checkers from Formal Specifications. In: Emerson, E.A., Sistla, A.P. (eds.) CAV 2000. LNCS, vol. 1855, pp. 538–542. Springer, Heidelberg (2000)
6. INCOSE: What is Systems Engineering?,
   http://www.incose.org/practice/whatissystemseng.aspx
7. Engel, A.: Verification, Validation, and Testing of engineered Systems. Wiley (2010)

8. SPEculative and Exploratory Design in Systems Engineering, http://www.speeds.eu.com
9. Benveniste, A., Raclet, J.B., Caillaud, B., Nickovic, D., Passerone, R., Sangiovanni-Vincentelli, A., Henzinger, T., Larsen, K.G.: Contracts for the Design of Embedded Systems, Part II: Theory (2011) (submitted for publication)
10. Maler, O., Nickovic, D.: Monitoring Properties of Analog and Mixed-Signal Circuits. International Journal on Software Tools for Technology Transfer, 1–22 (2013)
11. Lachish, O., Marcus, E., Ur, S., Ziv, A.: Hole analysis for functional coverage data. In: The 39th proceedings of Design Automation Conference. pp. 807–812. IEEE (2002)
12. ISO 26262-1:2011 Road vehicels - Functional safety (2011), http://www.iso.org/iso/catalogue_detail?csnumber=43464
13. StClair, B., King, T.: DO-178C brings modern technology to safety-critical software development. Military Embedded Systems (March 2012)
14. Werner, D., Harel, D.: LSCs: Breathing Life into Message Sequence Charts. Formal Methods in System Design 19(1), 45–80 (2001)
15. Mathworks: MATLAB/Simulink, a tool for modeling, simulating and analyzing multidomain dynamic systems, http://www.mathworks.com/products/simulink
16. Fritzson, P., Engelson, V.: Modelica - A Unified Object-Oriented Language for System Modeling and Simulation. In: Jul, E. (ed.) ECOOP 1998. LNCS, vol. 1445, pp. 67–90. Springer, Heidelberg (1998)
17. OMG Systems Modeling Language (2010), http://www.omgsysml.org
18. Functional Mock-up Interface, https://www.fmi-standard.org

Assertion Checking Using Dynamic Inference

Anand Yeolekar and Divyesh Unadkat

Tata Research Development and Design Centre, Pune
{anand.yeolekar,divyesh.unadkat}@tcs.com
www.tcs-trddc.com

Abstract. We present a technique for checking assertions in code that combines model checking and dynamic analysis. Our technique first constructs an abstraction by summarizing code fragments in the form of pre and post conditions. Spurious counterexamples are then analyzed by Daikon, a dynamic analysis engine, to infer invariants over the fragments. These invariants, representing a set of traces, are used to partition the summary with one partition consisting of the observed spurious behaviour. Partitioning summaries in this manner increases precision of the abstraction and accelerates the refinement loop. Our technique is sound and compositional, allowing us to scale model checking engines to larger code size, as seen from the experiments.

Keywords: Verification, Model Checking, Dynamic Inference, Scalability.

1 Introduction

Embedded software that is classified safety- or business-critical needs to be rigorously analyzed for bugs before deployment. Over the years, many dynamic and static approaches have been proposed to analyze software. Dynamic approaches scale to large-size code and may report test cases leading to bugs, but are of little help in proving their absence, as stated by Dijkstra, so crucial for safety-critical software. Static analysis techniques are sound and scale to large size code, but may report many false positives. Model checking techniques are precise and report traces violating assertions. These traces serve as valuable diagnostics for developers. Unfortunately, model checking algorithms run into the state space explosion problem analyzing even moderately-sized code. Even with SAT and SMT solvers scaling over the years [1] and abstraction techniques in place, model checking has not scaled to the level of static analysis tools [2]. This has led researchers to combine dynamic analysis and model checking in a variety of ways.

An approach to scale model checking using dynamically computed procedure summaries was proposed in [3]. This approach was limited to generating test cases due to the unsound approximation constructed using Daikon's [4] analysis. In this paper, we present a CEGAR-based [5,6] technique for checking assertions that overcomes this limitation by soundly constructing and refining procedure summaries, using possibly unsound dynamic inference.

V. Bertacco and A. Legay (Eds.): HVC 2013, LNCS 8244, pp. 199–213, 2013.

Figure 1 outlines our approach. We first decompose the code structurally into its procedures, called units, based on the location of the assertion to be checked. These units are summarized in the form of pre- and post-conditions. We choose an unconstrained pre and post to form the initial sound abstraction of the units. The given assertion is checked over the abstracted code. Following the abstraction-refinement paradigm, spurious counterexamples are used to refine the summary. We propose to refine the summary using dynamic analysis over the spurious traces to infer *likely* invariants, that can be used to partition the state space represented by the summary. The state space is partitioned into two parts such that, the spurious traces represented by the invariants form one part, with the remaining state space forming the second. Partitioning continues till the assertion is violated in the original code or reported safe in the abstraction. Iterative partitioning improves the precision of the summary and accelerates the refinement process.

Dynamic analysis may infer unsound invariants at program locations. We propose to overcome this limitation in the following way. The precondition invariants are cast as *assumes* and the post as *assertions* to be checked over the unit. This annotated unit is analyzed using a model checker. Violated invariants in the postconditions are dropped and counterexamples reported by the model checker are used to improve Daikon's inference over the unit. This is iterated till the model checker reports safety i.e. a sound pre-post pair is obtained. This pre-post pair is used to partition the summary, maintaining soundness of the resulting abstraction. Note that running a model checker at this level usually scales much better than at the application level.

We believe that our approach utilizing dynamic inference can discover stronger program properties with fewer refinements, in contrast to static approaches for abstraction refinement, such as predicate-refinement [5] and specification-refinement [7]. The approach is fully compositional and takes advantage of modularity in the program structure.

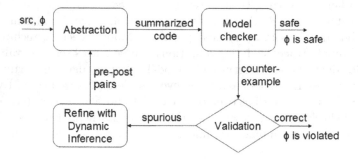

Fig. 1. Outline of our approach

The contributions of this work are as follows:

- A compositional approach to scale model checking using dynamic inference

- A fully automated tool that demonstrates the approach
- Case studies showing scalability of the method on benchmark code

The rest of the paper is organized as follows. In section 2, we define the summarization and refinement of code fragments, present an algorithm for assertion checking, and address theoretical issues. Section 3 explains the implementation of our algorithm in a tool called DIV. In section 4 we describe experiments conducted with DIV, SatAbs and CBMC. We discuss work related to our approach in section 5 and conclude in section 6.

2   Compositional Assertion Checking

In this section, we present the approach of computing and refining summaries of code fragments using dynamic inference. Our approach builds on the work of scaling test generation presented in [3] and overcomes the limitation of unsound summaries, making it suitable for verification.

2.1   Dynamic Inference Using Daikon

Daikon implements dynamic detection of *likely* invariants. Daikon analyzes data values from program traces to match a fixed template set of invariants. Invariant templates include constants $x = k$, non-zero $x \neq 0$, intervals $a \leq x \leq b$, linear relationships $y = ax + b$, ordering $x \leq y$, containment $x \in y$, sortedness, size of arrays $size[arr] \leq n$ and so on. Each invariant inferred is an (linear) expression instantiated on program variables, and can be translated to statements in C language. Invariants are reported at program points such as function entry and exit, expressing the function's preconditions and postconditions, respectively.

An invariant inferred by Daikon holds for traces *seen* so far. As trace data accumulates, new invariants can be reported as well as, some invariants can be dropped, due to the nature of the machine-learning algorithms of Daikon. With more trace data, crossing the *confidentiality threshold*[1] enables reporting of more invariants, and those violated are withdrawn. In addition, Daikon implements analysis to suppress redundant invariants, filter out non-useful ones and limit the number of instantiations from templates. As with any other dynamic analyses, Daikon's inference is unsound and incomplete. Invariants inferred from program traces, however, reveal useful information about the program behaviour, often complementing static approaches [8,9]. We next explain how to generate sound summaries of functions as abstraction units, with the inferred invariants as the starting point.

2.2   Summarizing Functions

Let S be a program containing assertion ϕ to be checked. Let f be a candidate function to be summarized, such that the location of ϕ is not reachable

---

[1] Minimum number of samples for an invariant to hold.

from entry location of f. Let $pre, post$ denote the set of pre and postcondition invariants inferred by Daikon over f. The summary of f is defined as a set $\hat{f} = \{\langle pre_0, post_0 \rangle, ..., \langle pre_k, post_k \rangle\}$, with the restrictions that (i) the preconditions are disjoint that is, $pre_i \wedge pre_j = \Phi$, (ii) each pre-post pair forms a Hoare triple $\{pre_i\}f\{post_i\}$, and (iii) the set of states represented by the union of preconditions over-approximates the set of states of S reachable at all call points of f in S. The pre-post pairs of the summary partition the function's input-output space. The summary permits a non-deterministic mapping of input points to output points within the state space defined by a pre-post pair.

```
int compare(int a,int b) {
1. if (sign(a)==sign(b))
2.    if (abs(a)>abs(b)) return a;
3.    else return b;
4. if (a>b) return a;
5. else return b;  }
int main() {
6. unsigned int x=nondet;
7. assert(compare(x,-x)==x);  }
        (a)
```

```
int compare'(int a,int b) {
1. int ret;
2. ret=nondet;
3. return ret;
   }
int main() {
4. unsigned int x=nondet;
5. assert(compare(x,-x)==x);
   }
           (b)
```

Fig. 2. Example code and the summarized version

Example 1. Consider the example code in figure 2(a), containing an assertion in main to be checked. compare returns the smaller of a,b when both are negative, otherwise the larger. Figure 2(b) illustrates a trivial summarization of compare obtained with $\{\langle true, true \rangle\}$ as the summary that is, unconstrained pre and postconditions. Newly introduced variable ret indicates the return value of the function.

Abstraction. A *trace* is a finite sequence $(..., \langle loc, s \rangle, ...)$ where s is the program state at location loc in the source code. Let $t = (\langle l_0, s_0 \rangle, \langle l_1, s_1 \rangle, ..., \langle l_k, s_k \rangle)$ and $\hat{t} = (\langle l_0, \hat{s}_0 \rangle, \langle l_k, \hat{s}_k \rangle)$ be traces of f and $\hat{f}$, respectively. For sequential code, the traces are equivalent $t \approx \hat{t}$ if $s_0 = \hat{s}_0$ and $s_k = \hat{s}_k$ i.e. the input-output mapping matches. Since the summary allows non-deterministic input-output behaviour, the set of traces of $\hat{f}$, denoted as $\|\hat{f}\|$, over-approximates the set of traces of f i.e., $\|\hat{f}\| \supseteq \|f\|$. Let $\hat{S}$ denote the program obtained by replacing f with $\hat{f}$ in S. Then it follows that $\|\hat{S}\| \supseteq \|S\|$ that is, $\hat{S}$ is an abstraction of S. In figure 2, compare' is an abstraction of compare.

2.3   Summary Refinement

The summary abstracts the function's computation but allows spurious behaviours. A model checker analysing code containing summarized functions may return spurious counterexamples, necessitating summary refinement. A summary $\hat{f}_2$ refines $\hat{f}_1$, denoted $\hat{f}_2 \prec \hat{f}_1$, if $\|\hat{f}_2\| \subseteq \|\hat{f}_1\|$. Correspondingly, $\hat{S}_2$ is a refinement of $\hat{S}_1$ and $\|\hat{S}_2\| \subseteq \|\hat{S}_1\|$.

We propose to refine summaries by using Daikon to infer new invariants from the spurious counterexamples that can strengthen the abstraction. The central idea of the refinement scheme is to partition the state space represented by the pre-post pairs into two parts such that, the spurious traces form the first part, with the remaining state space forming the second.

Let $\langle pre_i, post_i \rangle \in \hat{f}_1$ contain the spurious input-output mappings $(i_1, \hat{o}_1), ..., (i_n, \hat{o}_n)$, extracted from the counterexample obtained on $\hat{S}$ while checking ϕ. Let p_1, q_1 be the pre and postcondition invariants inferred by Daikon on executing f with inputs $I_1 = \{i_1, ..., i_n\}$. We use $\langle p_1, q_1 \rangle$ to partition $\langle pre_i, post_i \rangle$, with the first part as $\langle pre_i \wedge p_1, post_i \wedge q_1 \rangle$.

When refining summaries in this way using likely invariants, the problem is to soundly partition the pre-post pair. We solve this by using a model checker combined with Daikon to iteratively verify $\{pre_i \wedge p_1\} f \{post_i \wedge q_1\}$, with the pre and post translated appropriately as *assume* and *assert* statements respectively, in the language of the model checker. Counterexamples returned are added to I_1, improving the inference. Recall that Daikon's algorithms can report *more* invariants as traces accumulate, leading to simultaneous widening and strengthening. This terminates when the model checker verifies the pre-post pair over f. Note that the model checker is applied at unit level, where scalability does not pose a problem.

We obtain the pre-post pair of second part in the following manner. For the precondition, we complement the pre of the first, giving $p_2 = \neg p_1$. To obtain the corresponding postcondition q_2, constraints in $p_2 \wedge pre_i$ are used to synthesize inputs I_2 to execute f and infer invariants. Following the process above, we obtain the sound pre-post pair $\langle pre_i \wedge p_2, post_i \wedge q_2 \rangle$. These two pre-post pairs replace $\langle pre_i, post_i \rangle$ in $\hat{f}_1$ to give $\hat{f}_2$. Note that $\hat{f}_2$ meets all the requirements of a summary as defined above namely, preconditions being disjoint, soundness of all pre-post pairs and preconditions over-approximating state space at call points of f.

To show $\hat{f}_2 \prec \hat{f}_1$, consider a trace $(\langle l_0, i \rangle, \langle l_k, o \rangle)$ such that $i \triangleright pre_i \wedge p_1, o \triangleright post_i \wedge \neg q_1$, where $\triangleright$ denotes the point lies in the state space defined by the invariants. Such a trace, where the input lies in the first part and the output in the other, exists in $\hat{f}_1$ but is disallowed in $\hat{f}_2$. Further, every trace in $\hat{f}_2$ exists in $\hat{f}_1$ as $pre_i \wedge p_1 \Rightarrow pre_i, post_i \wedge q_1 \Rightarrow post_i$, etc. Clearly, $\|\hat{f}_2\| \subseteq \|\hat{f}_1\|$, establishing refinement. In algorithm 1, we explain how to refine summaries when inferred invariants are too weak to partition, and how to block the spurious mappings from reappearing in $\hat{f}_2$.

Example 2. Consider our running example compare' from figure 2(b). Assume that the model checker returned a counterexample (spurious) violating the assertion, with assignments a=4,b=-4 at entry of compare' and ret=7 at the exit. Figure 3(a) shows invariants, a>b,ret==a, inferred by Daikon after analyzing the

```
pre:            pre:
  a>b             a>b
post:           post:
  ret==a          ret==a or ret==b
   (a)              (b)
```

Fig. 3. Generating a sound pre-post pair

execution of `compare`. On verifying the pre-post invariants with a model checker, we obtain a counterexample violating `ret==a`. On running Daikon again with the newly added counterexample, we obtain invariants shown in figure 3(b). Subsequently, the model checker reports safety of this pre-post pair over `compare`. The second pre-post pair $\{\langle \neg(a > b)\rangle, \langle ret = a \vee ret = b\rangle\}$ is obtained as explained above. The parent summary $\{\langle true, true\rangle\}$ of figure 2(b) is partitioned as shown in figure 4(a), where `compare'` is refined to `compare''`.

```
int compare''(int a,int b) {          int compare'''(int a,int b) {
1. int pid=nondet,ret;                1. int pid=nondet,ret;
2. assume(pid>=0 && pid<2);           2. assume(pid>=0 && pid<3);
3  if (pid==0)                        3  if (pid==0) assume(a>b && a>0);
     assume(a>b);                     4. else if (pid==1)
4. else                                    assume(!(a>0) && (a>b));
     assume(!(a>b));                  5. else assume(!(a>b));
                                      6. ret=nondet;
5. ret=nondet;                        7. if (pid==0)
6. if (pid==0)                             assume(ret==a&&(ret==a||ret==b));
     assume(ret==a||ret==b);          8. else if (pid==1)
7. else                                    assume(ret==b&&(ret==a||ret==b));
     assume(ret==a||ret==b);          9. else assume(ret==a||ret==b);
8. return ret; }                      10. return ret; }
int main() {                          int main() {
9.  unsigned int x=nondet;            11. unsigned int x=nondet;
10. assert(compare(x,-x)==x); }       12. assert(compare(x,-x)==x); }
          (a)                                   (b)
```

Fig. 4. Refining a function summary

Example 3. Assume that model checking the code of figure 4(a) returned a spurious counterexample with `a=2,b=-2` at the entry and `ret=-2` at the exit of `compare''`. The final refinement is shown in figure 4(b), with $\langle a > b, ret = a \vee ret = b\rangle$ getting refined to $\{\langle a > 0 \wedge a > b, ret = a \wedge (ret = a \vee ret = b)\rangle, \langle \neg(a > 0) \wedge a > b, ret = b \wedge (ret = a \vee ret = b)\rangle\}$. The model checker reports safety of the assertion after analyzing `compare'''`.

Algorithm 1. Assertion checking

```
1: check(S, φ) =
2:   f̂ = {⟨true, true⟩}        // initial summary
3:   while true do
4:     ce = modelcheck(Ŝ, φ)
5:     if ce = null or ce = valid then
6:       terminate
7:     end if
8:     for all ⟨pre_k, post_k⟩ ∈ f̂ | k ∈ pid(ce, f̂) do      // partition the parent
9:       testdb = inputs(ce, f̂, k)
10:      repeat      // first child pre-post pair
11:        ⟨p_1, q_1⟩ = daikon(f, testdb)
12:        ⟨p_{k1}, q_{k1}⟩ = ⟨p_1 ∧ pre_k, q_1 ∧ post_k⟩
13:        ce' = modelcheck({p_{k1}}f{q_{k1}})
14:        testdb = testdb ∪ ce'
15:      until ce' is null
16:      p_{k2} = ¬p_{k1} ∧ pre_k
17:      testdb = synthinputs(f, p_{k2})
18:      repeat      // second child pre-post pair
19:        ⟨dummy, q_2⟩ = daikon(f, testdb)
20:        q_{k2} = q_2 ∧ post_k
21:        ce' = modelcheck({p_{k2}}f{q_{k2}})
22:        testdb = testdb ∪ ce'
23:      until ce' is null
24:      for all ⟨i, ô⟩ ∈ iopairs(ce, f̂, k) do      // process point pre-post pairs
25:        if ô ▷ q_{k1} then
26:          o = simulate(f, i)
27:          add(f̂, ⟨i, o⟩)
28:        end if
29:      end for
30:      remove(f̂, ⟨pre_k, post_k⟩)      // replace the parent with children
31:      add(f̂, (⟨p_{k1}, q_{k1}⟩, ⟨p_{k2}, q_{k2}⟩))
32:    end for
33:  end while
```

2.4 Algorithm for Assertion Checking

Algorithm 1 presents our approach for checking assertion ϕ using dynamically computed function summaries. For simplicity, we present the case with only one function f summarized in S.

The initial abstraction $\hat{f}$ for f is chosen as the unconstrained pre-post pair, $\{\langle true, true \rangle\}$ (line 2). By definition, the summary over-approximates the set of states reachable in S at all call sites of f. To compute this set is as hard as checking the assertion itself, so we choose $true$ as an over-approximation of this set.

The algorithm implements CEGAR [6] with dynamic inference in the loop, beginning line 3. We obtain $\hat{S}$ by replacing f with $\hat{f}$ in S. The summarized program is passed to the model checker, which may return a counterexample trace (line 4). The algorithm terminates if the model checker reports assertion safety or the counterexample violates ϕ in S (lines 5-7).

When the counterexample trace violating the assertion turns out to be spurious, we proceed to refining the summary (lines 8-33). We assume the availability of trace processing operators `pid, inputs, iopairs` that extract the values of $\hat{f}$'s pre-post identifiers, inputs and corresponding output variables respectively, from the trace when supplied with relevant arguments.

A trace is spurious due to incorrect input-output mapping within the pre-post pairs of the summary chosen by the model checker. Refinement proceeds by identifying such pre-post in $\hat{f}$ along the trace (line 8). The central idea is to increase precision of the abstraction by partitioning the pre-post pairs such that, the spurious traces form the first part, with the remaining state space forming the second. In the process, we also eliminate spurious mappings.

We collect inputs of f, extracted from the spurious trace, belonging to the pre-post pair (line 9). The algorithm executes f (at unit-level) with these inputs and invokes Daikon to infer invariants (line 11). These invariants are used to partition the state space represented by the pre-post pair (line 12). The model checker is invoked at unit level (line 13) to check whether the postcondition invariants hold over f, given the preconditions. Counterexamples reported, if any, are added to the set of executions (line 14) to repeat the process, improving Daikon's inference, yielding a sound pre-post pair.

The negated precondition of the first part is used to build the precondition of the second part (line 16), thus maintaining the correctness condition of the summary. `synthinputs` synthesizes values to input variables of f (line 17) from the precondition constraints, using an off-the-shelf constraint solver. Lines 18-23 repeat above steps to obtain the corresponding postcondition, completing the second part. The difference in loops on lines 10-15 and 18-23 is that in the former, Daikon is used to infer both pre and post, while in the latter, only post is inferred (pre being available by negating pre obtained earlier).

Due to the nature of Daikon's inferencing mechanism and loops 10-15 and 18-23 weakening the postconditions, we cannot guarantee that partitioning pre-post pairs will always eliminate the spurious input-output mapping in the ce. Lines 24-29 check this and create *point pre-post pairs* to eliminate spuriousness. For a spurious input-output pair $(i, \hat{o})$ retained in the newly created child pre-post pair (line 25), `simulate` executes f to discover the correct input-output mapping (i, o) (line 26) and appends to the summary (line 27), blocking a family of spurious mappings $(i, *)$ from reappearing in subsequent counterexamples. The newly created pre-post pairs replace the parent pre-post, refining the summary (lines 30-31).

2.5   Remarks

We discuss some properties of algorithm 1.

Soundness. $\hat{S}$ over-approximates the set of traces of S at any stage of refinement. Thus if ϕ is not violated in $\hat{S}$, then ϕ is safe in S, subject to the bound supplied to the model checker.

Progress. To guarantee progress, we need to ensure that spurious counterexamples are eliminated. As discussed earlier, spurious mappings from the *ce* retained within pre-post pairs are eliminated by inserting the corrected input-output mappings. This blocks the spurious system-level counterexample in subsequent model checking runs, ensuring progress.

To ensure faster convergence, refinement should significantly improve the precision of the abstraction. Summary refinement partitions the state space such that known spurious behaviours are separated out from the unknown ones. The partitioning crucially depends on Daikon (lines 11,19) to form new pre-post pairs. We depend on the conjunction $pre_k \wedge p_1$ to partition the parent. Precondition invariants inferred by Daikon with this *testdb* may turn out to be weaker than parent's pre that is, $pre_k \Rightarrow p_1$, which means the parent pre-post cannot be partitioned. This is still not a problem if Daikon is able to infer stronger postcondition invariants which are subsequently verified as sound by the modelchecker. In this case, the parent pre-post is refined through postcondition strengthening without getting partitioned.

The worst case occurs when both pre and postcondition invariants inferred are weaker than parent's pre-post, or the $repeat-until$ loop weakens the post. In this case, appending point pre-post pairs to the parent is the only refinement. In practice, this situation was observed only rarely, and did not impact scalability.

Termination. When algorithm 1 terminates, we have a (validated) counterexample or the assertion is proven safe. Every loop in the algorithm is terminating, as we use a bounded model checker and Daikon has a finite template set of invariants. In the worst case, the algorithm keeps on accumulating point partitions for each spurious counterexample.

Compositionality. Our choice of $\{true\}$ as the unconstrained initial precondition of summaries allows to decouple the units from the rest of the system. Summaries are computed and refined at unit-level, independent of others, making our approach fully compositional. Assertion ϕ is checked at system-level that is, when the summaries are composed to form $\hat{S}$.

An implication of our choice is that the summary can become too abstract and the model checker may be employed in checking behaviours that are infeasible in the context of S. Our experimental results indicate that this has not impacted the performance or scalability of our approach.

3   Implementation

Figure 5 depicts our technique for checking assertions in C code. We use Daikon[10] for invariant generation over C code and CBMC [11] for model checking. The *preprocessor* is built using our internally developed tool suite PRISM consisting of a front-end for parsing C code into an intermediate representation, program analysis framework and an unparser. It constructs the function call graph (fcg), identifies functions for abstraction, identifies input-output variables

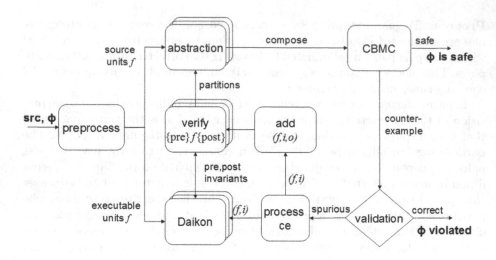

Fig. 5. Tool architecture

of these functions and generates a driver for execution. The functions chosen for abstraction are the roots of subtrees (in the fcg) of those functions *not* on the (statically computed) program call stack, when control reaches the location of the user-provided assertion on any path. The *abstraction* routine maintains a list of pre-post pairs for the abstracted functions. The *validation* routine replays counterexamples returned by CBMC on the original code to check for assertion violations. The *ce processing* routine extracts (abstracted) function partition ids, inputs and outputs from the XML trace. We use Kvasir, a tool from the Daikon toolsuite that instruments C code and generate traces for Daikon's consumption. Invariants inferred by Daikon are filtered and translated to CBMC *assume* and *assert* statements. The *verify* routine invokes CBMC to check $\{pre\}f\{post\}$; counterexamples if any, are fed back to Daikon to improve invariants. The *add* subroutine appends point pre-post pairs to the summary after executing the function. The routine *synthinputs* (not shown in the figure) synthesizes inputs for execution and inference, by using an off-the-shelf constraint solver over the negated preconditions generated by *verify*. The tool has been implemented in Java in about 3KLoC under Linux.

4   Experiments

This section furnishes details about the experimental setup, tool parameters, observations and results from the case-studies.

4.1   Setup and Tool Parameters

Table 1 lists the casestudies and results of experiments. For evaluating our strategy, we used benchmark programs (column 1) ranging from a simple program from [12] (row 1) to increasingly complex ones from Kratos [13] (rows 2-18). Columns 2 and 3 list the number of functions and lines of code, respectively. The code was seeded with assertions on line numbers given in column 4 (LoA - line of assert statement). These assertions were ones which could not be checked in [3] due to either timeouts or algorithm unsoundness. Due to runtime termination issues, Kratos sources were modified to exit the loops in functions *eval* and *start_simulation* after maximum 10 iterations. The preprocessing phase in our tool removed hard-coded variable initializations and assigned non-deterministic values to these global variables, converting them to program inputs. Some programs contained a non-deterministic initialization to local variables; this was replaced with initialization to a constant, removing the reactive behaviour.

A timeout of 1 hour was imposed on model checking. The unroll depth was set to the largest loop size in the application when running CBMC, to avoid loop-unwinding assertions. We synthesized 10 test inputs per partition (using preconditions) in addition to the inputs obtained via counterexamples, to improve Daikon's invariant detection. Uninteresting invariants were filtered out using Daikon's filtration options, such as disabling disequality comparisons. In addition, we implemented a filtering strategy that dropped invariants comparing unrelated variables, e.g. invariants comparing only the function's updated variables at the entry point (i.e. preconditions), and invariants relating only input variables at the exit (i.e. postconditions). The tool was fully automatic - no human intervention was required, and no user annotations were used for any of the case studies.

We also experimented with SatAbs[14] tool. We used SatAbs with default parameters and a timeout of 1 hour per assertion. All experiments were conducted on an Intel Xeon 4-core processor running at 2.4 GHz, with processes allowed to take 3GB of memory.

4.2 Results

Column 5 in table 1 presents the results of applying the SatAbs and DIV for checking assertions seeded in the code. `safe, unsafe, TO` indicates that the assertion was reported safe, the assertion was violated, or the model checker timed out, respectively. Column 6 reports the number of abstracted functions based on the call-graph approach. Column 7 reports the number of partitions generated across all abstracted functions (excluding point partitions). Column 8 reports average number of invariants generated per partition. Column 9 reports average number of iterations of the loops on lines 10-15 and 18-23 in algorithm 1. Finally, column 10 reports the number of refinements required by DIV to achieve the result.

4.3 Analysis and Observations

CBMC when applied alone on the assertions, without our summarization technique, either *timed out* or went *out of memory* for the chosen assertions, except

Table 1. Experimental Results

(1)	(2)	(3)	(4)	(5)		(6)	(7)	(8)	(9)	(10)
App	# Funcs	LoC	LoA	Result		#Abs Funcs	# Parts	Avg Invs	Avg Iters	#Refs
				SatAbs	DIV					
SimpleEx	3	24	17	safe	safe	1	1	6	2	1
bist_cell	18	449	299	safe	safe	8	14	26	25	2
			199	unsafe	unsafe	2	2	2	10	2
pc_sfifo3	19	555	358	safe	safe	8	13	9	7	1
			508	unsafe	unsafe	5	5	8	32	5
token_ring10	35	1567	1152	TO	safe	14	14	-	-	0
			451	TO	unsafe	23	23	-	-	0
			675	TO	unsafe	12	12	2	8	2
transmitter12	39	1777	1322	TO	safe	16	16	-	-	0
			519	TO	unsafe	27	27	2	9	1
			775	TO	TO	15	15	-	-	-
transmitter13	41	1899	1715	TO	safe	17	17	-	-	0
			560	TO	unsafe	29	29	2	4	2
			836	TO	TO	15	15	-	-	-
token_ring13	41	1936	1341	TO	safe	17	17	-	-	0
			127	TO	unsafe	29	29	1	2	1
			579	TO	unsafe	29	29	2	8	1
			875	TO	TO	15	15	-	-	-

row 1. SatAbs terminated successfully for rows 1-5 and timed out for the rest of the cases. DIV scaled better than both CBMC and SatAbs.

- **Scalability:** Our approach demonstrates that summarizing code fragments scales model checking. The novelty of our approach is to use relatively low-cost dynamic analysis to construct summaries and verify them at unit level, making the analysis sound, compositional and scalable.
- **Summary Refinement:** Our approach of forming a pre-post pair consisting of the observed spurious behaviour using inferred invariants yields highly precise summaries during refinement. This is confirmed by the low number of refinements required by DIV (column 10) to terminate with a result. Further, our approach shows that executing code fragments with *well chosen inputs* (derived from preconditions) enables Daikon to infer useful and stronger invariants.

As seen from columns 6 and 7, the number of pre-post pairs is comparable to the number of abstracted functions. This indicates that most of the pre-post pairs did not require partitioning and were refined by discovering stronger postconditions, sufficient to check the assertion. We confirmed this by observing the invariants.

- **Overhead of Dynamic Inference:** Columns 8-9 give an idea of the complexity of *repeat-until* loops of algorithm 1, used to form new pre-post pairs. Though several iterations were required to obtain sound pre-post pairs using Daikon per partition, the model checker was observed to quickly terminate within a minute. Our invariant filtration strategy combined with instantiating only selected invariants from Daikon's template resulted in low number of invariants representing pre-post, as seen from column 8.
- **Call Graph-Based Summarization:** The call-graph approach maximizes functions that can be summarized. Overall, we were able to summarize more than 50% functions, as seen from column 6. Even with this aggressive abstraction, for rows 11,14,18 CBMC timed out. In these cases, we observed that less than 40% functions could be summarized. When the call graph is unbalanced or the assertion is placed deep down in the graph, few functions can be abstracted, resulting in scalability issues.
- **Code Modularity:** Our abstraction technique is well suited to take advantage of modularity in code, where functions have low coupling. In particular, a summary is refined only when a counterexample trace passes through the function, optimising the refinement procedure. As seen in rows 6,7,9,12,15, the result was obtained with the initial abstraction $\hat{f} = \{\langle true, true \rangle\}$ in place, without any refinement. In all other cases, we observed that not all abstracted functions underwent refinement.

5   Related

Dynamic analysis to scale model checking has been used by various researchers [15,16,17,18,19,20]. Daikon has been used in conjunction with static analysis tools such as ESC/Java to infer properties and specifications for subsequent verification or user consumption [8], and to achieve both scale and automation of theorem proving [21].

Gulavani et.al. [22] propose a combination of DART-like dynamic and predicate-based static reasoning, called the Synergy algorithm. Test executions are used to refine an abstraction of the program, which in turn generates new test cases attempting to violate the given assertion. The abstraction and refinement strategies differ from our approach, which focuses on summarizing functions.

Kroening et.al. [23] proposed loop summarization using abstract transformers for checking assertions using CBMC. They abstract program loops with respect to a given abstract interpretation. Similar to our technique, they instantiate candidate invariants from a template and check which invariant holds over the loop, except that we use Daikon to guess invariants. Leaping counterexamples provide diagnostic information to user but can include spurious ones as they do not refine the abstraction. In contrast, our approach refines the abstraction to eliminate spurious counterexamples.

Taghdiri [7] proposed an approach to abstract procedures using statically computed specifications. The initial over-approximation is refined using spurious counterexamples returned by a SAT solver. Unsat cores reported by the solver while concretizing (spurious) traces are conjuncted with the existing specification, to iteratively strengthen the specification. Our approach differs in the way that, the abstraction is refined both by blocking (a family of) spurious counterexamples and increasing precision by adding new pre-post pairs, guided by dynamic inference.

6   Conclusion and Future Work

We have presented a CEGAR-based technique that combines model checking with dynamic analysis to check assertions. The central idea is to use dynamically inferred invariants to separate observed spurious behaviour, refining the abstraction. The technique is sound, compositional and scales better than some existing tools as seen from experiments.

As part of the future work, we envision the following:

 - Our technique can be generalized to include different reasoning techniques for the decomposed code fragments. In particular, we would like to use static analysis methods to obtain sound postconditions for dynamically inferred preconditions.
 - Daikon templates can be extended to infer suitable invariants over different domains. We would like to extend our approach to more challenging areas like heap analysis and concurrency.

Acknowledgements. The authors would like to thank their colleagues R. Venkatesh and Shrawan Kumar for their valuable inputs at various stages of this work. They would also like to thank the anonymous reviewers for their feedback.

References

1. Beyer, D.: Competition on software verification. In: Flanagan, C., König, B. (eds.) TACAS 2012. LNCS, vol. 7214, pp. 504–524. Springer, Heidelberg (2012)
2. D'Silva, V., Kroening, D., Weissenbacher, G.: A survey of automated techniques for formal software verification. IEEE Transactions on Computer-Aided Design of Integrated Circuits and Systems 27, 1165–1178 (2008)
3. Yeolekar, A., Unadkat, D., Agarwal, V., Kumar, S., Venkatesh, R.: Scaling model checking for test generation using dynamic inference. In: International Conference on Software Testing, Verification and Validation (ICST 2013). IEEE (2013)
4. Ernst, M.D., Perkins, J.H., Guo, P.J., McCamant, S., Pacheco, C., Tschantz, M.S., Xiao, C.: The daikon system for dynamic detection of likely invariants. Sci. Comput. Program. 69, 35–45 (2007)
5. Graf, S., Saïdi, H.: Construction of abstract state graphs with pvs. In: Grumberg, O. (ed.) CAV 1997. LNCS, vol. 1254, pp. 72–83. Springer, Heidelberg (1997)
6. Clarke, E.M., Grumberg, O., Jha, S., Lu, Y., Veith, H.: Counterexample-guided abstraction refinement. In: Emerson, E.A., Sistla, A.P. (eds.) CAV 2000. LNCS, vol. 1855, pp. 154–169. Springer, Heidelberg (2000)

7. Taghdiri, M.: Inferring specifications to detect errors in code. In: ASE, pp. 144–153 (2004)
8. Nimmer, J.W., Ernst, M.D.: Invariant inference for static checking. In: SIGSOFT FSE, pp. 11–20 (2002)
9. Polikarpova, N., Ciupa, I., Meyer, B.: A comparative study of programmer-written and automatically inferred contracts. In: ISSTA, pp. 93–104 (2009)
10. Ernst, M., et al.: The daikon invariant detector, http://pag.lcs.mit.edu/daikon
11. Clarke, E., Kroning, D., Lerda, F.: A tool for checking ANSI-C programs. In: Jensen, K., Podelski, A. (eds.) TACAS 2004. LNCS, vol. 2988, pp. 168–176. Springer, Heidelberg (2004)
12. Dillig, I., Dillig, T., Aiken, A.: Automated error diagnosis using abductive inference. In: Proceedings of the 33rd ACM SIGPLAN Conference on Programming Language Design and Implementation, PLDI 2012, pp. 181–192. ACM (2012)
13. Cimatti, A., Griggio, A., Micheli, A., Narasamdya, I., Roveri, M.: Kratos benchmarks, https://es.fbk.eu/tools/kratos/index.php?n=Main.Benchmarks
14. Clarke, E., Kroening, D., Sharygina, N., Yorav, K.: Predicate abstraction of ANSI–C programs using SAT. Formal Methods in System Design (FMSD) 25, 105–127 (2004)
15. Yuan, J., Shen, J., Abraham, J.A., Aziz, A.: On combining formal and informal verification. In: Grumberg, O. (ed.) CAV 1997. LNCS, vol. 1254, pp. 376–387. Springer, Heidelberg (1997)
16. Shacham, O., Sagiv, M., Schuster, A.: Scaling model checking of dataraces using dynamic information. J. Parallel Distrib. Comput. 67, 536–550 (2007)
17. Kroening, D., Groce, A., Clarke, E.: Counterexample guided abstraction refinement via program execution. In: Davies, J., Schulte, W., Barnett, M. (eds.) ICFEM 2004. LNCS, vol. 3308, pp. 224–238. Springer, Heidelberg (2004)
18. Gunter, E.L., Peled, D.: Model checking, testing and verification working together. Formal Aspects of Computing 17, 201–221 (2005)
19. Yorsh, G., Ball, T., Sagiv, M.: Testing, abstraction, theorem proving: better together! In: Proceedings of the 2006 International Symposium on Software Testing and Analysis, pp. 145–156. ACM (2006)
20. Păsăreanu, C.S., Pelánek, R., Visser, W.: Concrete model checking with abstract matching and refinement. In: Etessami, K., Rajamani, S.K. (eds.) CAV 2005. LNCS, vol. 3576, pp. 52–66. Springer, Heidelberg (2005)
21. Win, T., Ernst, M.: Verifying distributed algorithms via dynamic analysis and theorem proving (2002)
22. Gulavani, B.S., Henzinger, T.A., Kannan, Y., Nori, A.V., Rajamani, S.K.: Synergy: a new algorithm for property checking. In: Proceedings of the 14th ACM SIGSOFT International Symposium on Foundations of Software Engineering, SIGSOFT 2006/FSE-14, pp. 117–127. ACM, New York (2006)
23. Kroening, D., Sharygina, N., Tonetta, S., Tsitovich, A., Wintersteiger, C.M.: Loop summarization using abstract transformers. In: Cha, S(S.), Choi, J.-Y., Kim, M., Lee, I., Viswanathan, M. (eds.) ATVA 2008. LNCS, vol. 5311, pp. 111–125. Springer, Heidelberg (2008)

Formal Specification of an Erase Block Management Layer for Flash Memory

Jörg Pfähler, Gidon Ernst, Gerhard Schellhorn, Dominik Haneberg,
and Wolfgang Reif

Institute for Software & Systems Engineering
University of Augsburg, Germany
{joerg.pfaehler,ernst,schellhorn,haneberg,reif}
@informatik.uni-augsburg.de

Abstract. This work presents a formal specification and an implementation of an erase block management layer and a formal model of the flash driver interface. It is part of our effort to construct a verified file system for flash memory. The implementation supports wear-leveling, handling of bad blocks and asynchronous erasure of blocks. It uses additional data structures in RAM for efficiency and relies on a model of the flash driver, which is similar to the Memory Technology Device (MTD) layer of Linux. We specify the effects of unexpected power failure and subsequent recovery. All models are mechanized in the interactive theorem prover KIV.

Keywords: Flash File System, Specification, Refinement, Wear-Leveling, Power Failure, UBI, MTD, KIV.

1 Introduction

Flaws in the design and implementation of file systems already lead to serious problems in mission-critical systems. A prominent example is the Mars Exploration Rover Spirit [25] that got stuck in a reset cycle. This incident prompted a proposal to verify a file system for flash memory [18,12] as a small step towards Hoare's Grand Challenge [15]. In 2013, the Mars Rover Curiosity also had a bug in its file system implementation, that triggered an automatic switch to safe mode.

We are developing such a verified flash file system (FFS) as an implementation of the POSIX file system interface [29], using UBIFS [16]—a state-of-the-art FFS implemented in Linux—as a blueprint. In order to tackle the complexity of the verification of an entire file system implementation, we refine a top-level abstract POSIX specification in several steps down to an implementation.

File systems for flash memory differ from traditional ones because the hardware does not support overwriting data in-place (in contrast to magnetic disks). The memory is physically partitioned into *blocks*, each consisting of an array of *pages* that can be empty or programmed with data. There are three operations 1) Read a consecutive part of a block, possibly across page boundaries. Empty

V. Bertacco and A. Legay (Eds.): HVC 2013, LNCS 8244, pp. 214–229, 2013.

pages yield default values, typically bytes 0xFF. 2) Write/Program data to a whole page that was previously empty. Typically, there is an additional constraint that pages in a block must be written in order [11,8]. 3) Erase a whole block, i.e., empty all of its pages. The erase operation enables reuse of memory, though it comes at considerable costs: Erasing is slow and physically degrades the memory. The number of erase cycles until a block breaks down is thus limited – between 10^4 and 10^6 for typical hardware. Such broken blocks are called *bad*.

To deal with these characteristics, data is always written to new locations (out-of-place updates); and erasing is performed asynchronously and in parallel to read/write access to the flash device. The software component responsible for this is called the *Erase Block Management* (EBM) layer. It maintains the information which blocks are currently available. The interface offered to clients mirrors the hardware operations, but it is based on *logical* block numbers instead of physical ones. The primary task of the EBM is therefore to maintain a mapping from logical to physical block numbers.

Several significant benefits follow from such a mapping. The EBM layer can *transparently* migrate a logical block to a different physical one. This enables *wear-leveling*, a method to distribute erase cycles evenly between physical blocks to prolong the hardware's lifetime. Furthermore, the client may reuse a logical block number after issuing an erase request, even before the corresponding physical erase has been performed.

This work presents the formal models of our project that are related to erase block management. As the bottom layer (Sec. 2) we specify a thin abstraction of the driver for flash memory that supports the operations read, write and erase. It is modeled after the *Memory Technology Device* (MTD) interface of Linux. We also define a *simple* EBM specification (Sec. 3) to capture the behavior visible to the upper layers. The main design goal is to abstract from implementation details as far as possible to facilitate the verification of clients wrt. the specification.

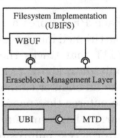

Fig. 1. Lower Layers

Note that this abstract model only needs to consider logical blocks. Finally, we give an implementation (Sec. 4) that supports wear-leveling, handling of bad blocks and asynchronous erasure of blocks using additional data structures in RAM for efficiency. Its design is inspired by the state-of-the-art *Unsorted Block Image* layer (UBI) [22,14]. Our implementation also provides strong guarantees in the event of an unexpected power failure. However, the effects are subtle and visible to the client (and thus occur in the abstract EBM as well). For the EBM specification and the MTD layer, we also contribute a proof of certain invariants.

Figure 1 visualizes some of the layers of our FFS. The part shaded in grey is subject of this paper, namely the abstract EBM, the implementation UBI and driver abstraction MTD. The dashed lines indicate functional equivalence, or more formally, *refinement* relations. The erase block management is utilized by the file system either directly or through a write-back cache (the write buffer "WBUF"). The interface symbol —c— denotes dependencies between the components. The refinement is already proved, but a description is out of scope for this paper. A correctness proof of the FFS then only has to consider the abstract specification of an EBM's behavior, which is much more suitable for the verification of clients – especially wrt. the effects of unexpected power failure.

We have previously published models of the top-level POSIX specification [10], of the Virtual Filesystem Switch (VFS) [9] and of an abstract version of UBIFS [28]; [10] also presents a correctness proof of VFS. These models constitute the upper layers of the refinement stack that are not shown in Fig. 1.

We use KIV to mechanize our models as ASMs [1] based on structured algebraic specifications [26] with freely and non-freely generated algebraic datatypes. For proofs about programs we use the wp-calculus. All our models and proofs are available online [24].

2   Hardware Model (MTD)

This section defines our assumptions about the hardware, captured by the behavior of an abstract interface representing the driver.

Flash memory is organized as an array of *physical erase blocks* (PEBs):

$$\textbf{state var } pebs : Array\langle Peb\rangle \qquad \textbf{where} \tag{1}$$

$$\textbf{data } Peb = \texttt{peb}(\texttt{data} : Array_{\texttt{PEB\_SIZE}}\langle Byte\rangle, \texttt{fill} : \mathbb{N}, \texttt{bad} : \mathbb{B})$$

Each PEB stores a byte-array **data** of fixed length **PEB_SIZE** that is implicitly partitioned into pages of length **PAGE_SIZE**. A PEB stores a page-aligned counter **fill** that tracks the part of the block that contains programmed pages, i.e., only data above **fill** is known to be EMPTY and can be written to. Note that the fill counter cannot be accessed by software. It is an auxiliary state only used to enforce that pages are written sequentially and never overwritten. PEBs also carry a hardware-supported marker **bad** that is set by the EBM or the file system after access failures to prevent future usage of the block.

Figure 2 shows the specification of the operations on this layer. Value parameters are separated from reference parameters by semicolon. The state variable is passed implicitly. The if-test at the beginning of operations reflects the *precondition*. With the exception of **mtd_isbad**, each operation requires that the respective physical erase blocks is not marked as bad. Furthermore, all offsets must be in bounds; offsets must additionally be page-aligned for **mtd_write**. We tacitly omit an additional precondition $n < \#pebs$ for all operations.

The operation **mtd_write** models the fact that pages are written sequentially by a loop. The function $\texttt{copy}(src, \mathit{off_0}, dst, \mathit{off_1}, n)$ returns the result of copying the value from index $\mathit{off_0} + i$ in src to index $\mathit{off_1} + i$ in dst, for all i with $0 \leq i < n$. We also specify the possibility of *hardware failures*: either the body of the loop executes normally, or writing of the current page fails nondeterministically and a corresponding error code EIO is returned. Similarly, all other operations may also fail nondeterministically. We omit the respective code in each operation for brevity.

This model makes the following assumptions about the hardware:

mtd_write($n, \mathit{off}, \mathit{len}, \mathit{buf}; \mathit{err}$)
  if $\mathit{pebs}[n].\mathtt{fill} \leq \mathit{off} \wedge \mathit{off} + \mathit{len} \leq$ PEB_SIZE $\wedge \neg\, \mathit{pebs}[n].\mathtt{bad}$
    $\wedge$ page-aligned(off) $\wedge$ page-aligned(len) then
  $\mathit{err} :=$ ESUCCESS, $m := 0$
  while $\mathit{err} =$ ESUCCESS $\wedge\, m \neq \mathit{len}$ do
      { $\mathit{pebs}[n].\mathtt{data} :=$ copy($\mathit{buf}, m, \mathit{pebs}[n].\mathtt{data}, \mathit{off} + m,$ PAGE_SIZE)
        $\mathit{pebs}[n].\mathtt{fill} := \mathit{off} + m +$ PAGE_SIZE
        $m := m +$ PAGE_SIZE }
    or $\mathit{err} :=$ EIO

mtd_read($n, \mathit{off}, \mathit{len}; \mathit{buf}, \mathit{err}$)
  if $\mathit{off} + \mathit{len} \leq$ PEB_SIZE $\wedge \neg\, \mathit{pebs}[n].\mathtt{bad}$ then
  $\mathit{buf} :=$ copy($\mathit{pebs}[n].\mathtt{data}, \mathit{off}, \mathit{buf}, 0, \mathit{len}$)

mtd_erase($n; \mathit{err}$)
  if $\neg\, \mathit{pebs}[n].\mathtt{bad}$ then
  $\mathit{pebs}[n] :=$ peb(EMPTY_PEB, 0, false)

mtd_isbad($n; \mathit{bad}$)
  $\mathit{bad} := \mathit{pebs}[n].\mathtt{bad}$

mtd_markbad($n; \mathit{err}$)
  if $\neg\, \mathit{pebs}[n].\mathtt{bad}$ then
  $\mathit{pebs}[n].\mathtt{bad} :=$ true

Fig. 2. MTD Operations

1. Page writes and block erasure can be viewed as atomic operations.
2. Success of an operation can be recognized, i.e., an error is not returned by mistake.
3. Conversely, hardware failure can also be detected reliably. In particular, reads that produce garbage can be recognized.
4. An unsuccessful page write/block erasure does not modify the state.
5. An unexpected power failure has no effect on the state of the flash device.

Assumption 4 is not realistic and we will relax it to a certain degree. For example, checksums can be used to recognize certain kinds of data corruption. However, on the level of MTD there is no possibility to express such application-specific concepts.

The model maintains the following invariant for all $\mathit{peb} = \mathit{pebs}[i]$ with $\neg \mathit{peb}.\mathtt{bad}$:

invariant   page-aligned($\mathit{peb}.\mathtt{fill}$) $\wedge\ \mathit{peb}.\mathtt{fill} \leq$ PEB_SIZE   (2)
        $\wedge\ \forall n.\ \mathit{peb}.\mathtt{fill} \leq n <$ PEB_SIZE $\rightarrow \mathit{peb}.\mathtt{data}[n] =$ EMPTY

It specifies that the fill count is a multiple of PAGE_SIZE and that all bytes above (inclusive) are empty. The invariance of this trivially follows from the preconditions of the operations.

3   Abstract EBM Layer Specification

The erase block management layer essentially provides the same functionality as the driver/MTD—namely read, write and erase—though it is based on *logical erase blocks* (LEBs). These are mapped on-demand to physical ones. This indirection enables a number of desirable features, namely asynchronous erase,

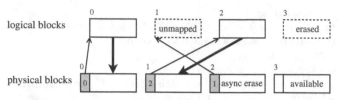

Fig. 3. Mapping of Logical Blocks to Physical Ones

hiding of bad blocks from the application, wear-leveling and trivial support for several *volumes* (i.e., partitions) on one device. However, the way this mapping is stored on flash leads to subtle differences between the behavior of the EBM and MTD in the presence of power failures. These effects can not be hidden completely by the implementation and are consequently present in the formal EBM specification as well. We therefore informally describe first how the implementation works, and then define an abstract EBM model.

Figure 3 shows the logical view of the device at the top with consecutive blocks numbered $0, 1, \ldots$, and the physical device at the bottom. Bold arrows denote which physical block is allocated for a logical one. For example, block 0 is mapped to 0, whereas the data of logical block 2 is stored in physical block 1. This forward mapping is kept in RAM.

An inverse mapping (displayed by thin arrows) is stored on flash in the grey headers of physical blocks. The in-memory representation of the forward mapping is initially built during system startup by reading the headers of each physical block, and it is lost during power-failure.

A logical block that has no associated physical one (such as the dashed blocks 1 and 3) is implicitly empty, i.e., it has previously been erased. As soon as a write to such a block occurs, a new physical block is allocated and the mapping is extended both in memory and on flash.

The mapping to a physical block is in general deallocated by requesting an *asynchronous* erase, also called *unmapping* the LEB. The logical block may be reused immediately after unmapping, however, the old physical block still contains the inverse mapping, as it is the case for LEB 1 in the example. When the system recovers from power failure in such a situation, the mapping for logical block 1 will *re-appear* with some old data. Since it would be rather difficult to prevent this effect without sacrificing the lazy allocation of physical erase blocks, the application/file system is expected to deal with it; or alternatively use a less efficient *synchronous* version of logical block erasure. Note that several PEBs with the same inverse mapping may exist simultaneously. These are distinguished by sequence numbers in PEB headers (see Sec. 4).

We will now formally specify the EBM layer in a way so that it only maintains logical blocks but encompasses the effect described above. The state of the model consists of a partial function *avols* mapping volume identifiers $\mathbb{V}$ to arrays of logical blocks: A mapped LEB stores an array **data** of bytes together with the counter **fill** similarly to MTD (1). However, a LEB has a smaller size than a PEB due to the inverse mapping stored at the beginning of each physical block by

ebm_write(v, l, off, len, buf)
  if $avols[v][l]$.ismapped $\wedge$ $avols[v][l]$.fill $\le off \wedge off + len <$ LEB_SIZE
    $\wedge$ page-aligned(off) $\wedge$ page-aligned(len) then
  choose n with $n \le len \wedge$ page-aligned(n) in
  $avols[v][l]$.data $:=$ copy(buf, 0, $avols[v][l]$.data, off, n)
  if $n \ne 0$ then $avols[v][l]$.fill $:= off + n$
  if $n = len$ then $err :=$ ESUCCESS else $err :=$ EIO

ebm_read($v, l, off, len; buf$)
  if $off + len \le$ LEB_SIZE then
    if $avols[v][l]$.ismapped then $buf :=$ copy($avols[v][l]$.data, off, buf, 0, len)
    else $buf :=$ fill-buffer(buf, len, EMPTY)

ebm_erase(v, l)
    { $avols[v][l] :=$ erased, $err :=$ ESUCCESS }
 or { $avols[v][l] :=$ unmapped, $err :=$ EIO }

ebm_map(v, l)   ebm_create_volume($n; v$)
  if $\neg$ $avols[v][l]$.ismapped then   choose v_0 with $\neg v_0 \in avols$ in $v := v_0$
    $avols[v][l] :=$ mapped(EMPTY_LEB, 0) $avols[v] :=$ mkarray$\langle Leb \rangle$(n)
                                  forall $l < n$ do
ebm_unmap(v, l) $avols[v][l] :=$ erased
  $avols[v][l] :=$ unmapped

Fig. 4. EBM Operations

the implementation. Mapped blocks *leb* are recognized by the test *leb*.ismapped. Otherwise, a logical block has been erased asynchronously (**unmapped**) or synchronously (**erased**). Note that the EBM implementation handles bad blocks transparently, i.e., there is no need to model them in the abstract interface and state.

    state var $avols : \mathbb{V} \nrightarrow Array\langle Leb \rangle$ where

    data $Leb =$ mapped(data : $Array_{\text{LEB\_SIZE}}\langle Byte \rangle$, fill : $\mathbb{N}$)
           | unmapped | erased

Figure 4 shows the operations on this layer. The preconditions—denoted by if-statements at the beginning of operations—are similar to the ones of MTD, namely the respective offsets must be in bounds and a multiple of PAGE_SIZE. Blocks are addressed by a volume identifier v and the logical block number l. We tacitly assume that v denotes a valid volume $v \in avols$, and that $l < \#avols[v]$. Additionally, the operation ebm_write requires the block l to be mapped.[1]

Writing to a block may fail nondeterministically. In contrast to Fig. 2 it is not realized by a loop but simply by writing a (non-strict) prefix of length n of the actual data. The operation succeeds if the whole data is written. The field fill is updated only if $n \ne 0$.

---

[1] The full model actually checks for this condition and maps the block on-demand. This is omitted for brevity here.

```
ebm_reset_recover(; err)
   choose avols', err' with (err' = ESUCCESS → inv(avols') ∧ avols ⊆ avols')
      avols := avols'
      err   := err'
```

Fig. 5. Effect of a Power-failure on the state of the EBM

A physical erase block for an LEB is allocated via the operation ebm_map. Operations ebm_erase and ebm_unmap request synchronous resp. asynchronous deallocation. Similar to our hardware model, nondeterministic failures may occur (partly omitted in Fig. 4), and we assume that failure as well as success can be detected reliably. In the case of such errors the state is not modified by any operation, with the exception of erase, which may set the respective logical erase block to **unmapped**. This means that erase may update the in-memory mapping although it failed to invalidate the remains of the inverse mapping stored on flash.

Unsurprisingly, an invariant inv analogous to formula (2) is maintained by all operations. We call a state of the EBM *consistent* if it satisfies this invariant.

Possible effects of a *power failure* and the subsequent recovery are specified by an extra operation ebm_reset_recover shown in Fig. 5. After a power failure, the EBM implementation reads the mapping stored in each physical erase block and tries to restore its state. This may fail due to read errors. For an unmapped logical erase block there may still be a physical erase block storing the inverse mapping, as for example PEB 2 in Fig. 3. Thus, the logical erase block 1 will be re-mapped with the contents found in PEB 2. In the model, this leads to a state $avols'$ that is "greater" than $avols$ before the crash, formally specified by the relation ⊆, which holds iff

1. $avols$ and $avols'$ contain the same volume identifiers and corresponding volumes have the same size
2. if $avols[v][l] \neq$ **unmapped** then $avols'[v][l] = avols[v][l]$.

Thus, both states are identical with the exception of previously unmapped logical erase blocks, which may be arbitrary after a reset.

4 EBM Implementation

This section describes the implementation of the functionality of Sec. 3 on top of the MTD hardware model of Sec. 2. The implementation has several subcomponents as visualized by Fig. 6. Grey boxes denote functional components. For example, the whole layer is represented by "interface operations" that provides the EBM interface to applications, as denoted by the knob at the top. It maintains the in-memory data structure that stores the forward mapping from logical to physical blocks, labeled "mapping table".

Allocation "get" and asynchronous erase "put" of physical blocks are managed by the wear-leveling subsystem; it maintains the erase queue and some information about the state of physical blocks in the "wear-leveling array". Asynchronous erasure and wear-leveling are background operations.

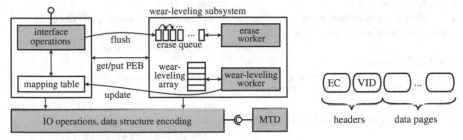

Fig. 6. Subsystems of the Implementation   **Fig. 7.** Layout of a PEB

The I/O layer provides operations not only to read and write parts of the flash memory, but also to convert on-disk data structures such as block headers and the volume table to and from a byte-representation.

This section is structured as follows: First the data structures needed for an implementation of the interface operations are discussed. Afterwards, the asynchronous erasure and wear-leveling subsystem are discussed. Finally, we outline how the in-memory state is recovered from flash.

4.1   Data Structures and Interface Operations

The forward mapping *vols* (bold arrows in Fig. 3) is stored in RAM. It maps ($\rightarrow$ indicates a finite map) each volume identifier $v \in vols$ to an array, which is indexed by logical block numbers. The value stored is either a physical block number if one has been allocated, or the constant **unmapped** otherwise.

state var $vols : \mathbb{V} \rightarrow Array\langle PebRef \rangle$ where

type $PebRef = \mathbb{N} + \mathbf{unmapped}$

Fig. 7 shows the layout of a PEB. The first two pages are used to store two headers. The remaining pages store application data. The first page contains an erase counter associated with the physical erase block (*erase counter-* or EC-header). The erase counter is used for wear-leveling.

The second page of allocated PEBs contains the inverse mapping (thin arrows in Fig. 3) as the *volume identifier header* (VID-header). It stores the corresponding volume identifier and logical block number. Sequence numbers **sqn** distinguish multiple PEBs with equal **vol**, **leb** pairs: During system startup/recovery, the highest sequence number denotes the newest block for a given inverse mapping. An (optional) size and checksum of the contents of the block are used for atomic block-writes during wear-leveling. Two headers are necessary, because every PEB must store its erase counter, but only once a PEB is allocated an inverse mapping is required. Formally, the headers are defined as:

data $EcHeader$ $= \mathtt{echdr}(\mathtt{ec} : \mathbb{N})$

data $VidHeader = \mathtt{vidhdr}(\mathtt{vol} : \mathbb{V}, \mathtt{leb} : \mathbb{N}, \mathtt{sqn} : \mathbb{N}, \mathtt{size} : \mathbb{N}, \mathtt{checksum} : \mathbb{N})$

write(v, l, off, len, buf)
    if $vols[v][l] \neq$ unmapped then
        io_write_data($vols[v][l], off, len, buf$)

read($v, l, off, len; buf$)
    if $vols[v][l] =$ unmapped then
        $buf :=$ fill-buffer($buf, len,$ EMPTY)
    else
        io_read_data($vols[v][l], off, len; buf$)

erase(v, l)
    unmap(v, l)
    wl_flush(v, l)

map(v, l)
    if $vols[v][l] =$ unmapped then
    wl_get_peb($; m$)
    io_write_vidhdr($m,$ vidhdr(v, l, max-$sqn, 0, 0$))
    max-$sqn := max$-$sqn + 1$
    if $err =$ ESUCCESS then $vols[v][l] := m$

unmap(v, l)
    if $vols[v][l] \neq$ unmapped then
        $vols[v][l] :=$ unmapped
        wl_put_peb($v, l, vols[v][l]$)

create_volume($n; v$)
    choose v_0
    with $v_0 \notin vols \land v_0 \neq$ VTBL_VOLID in
    $v := v_0$
    $vols[v] :=$ mkarray$\langle PebRef \rangle(n)$
    forall $l < n$ do
        $vols[v][l] :=$ unmapped
    io_write_vtbl($vols$)

Fig. 8. Implementation of the Operations (slightly simplified)

We specify I/O operations (prefixed by io_) for reading and writing EC/VID-headers and data pages. Their purpose is twofold: On the one hand encoding from and to byte-representations is performed. On the other hand the operations do the necessary offset computations. For example io_write_data(n, off, len, buf) simply calls mtd_write($n, 2 \cdot$ PAGE_SIZE $+ off, len, buf$). Furthermore, they add additional hardware failures on top of the hardware model of Sec. 2. Programming a VID-header for example may also fail by writing garbage, i.e., data that does not contain a valid VID-header, into the second page.

The main operations are shown in Fig. 8 in a slightly simplified version. In the actual implementation a hardware failure triggers several retries of an operation before giving up and returning an error.

Reading and writing of a logical block (v, l) evaluates the mapping $vols[v][l]$ to obtain the physical block number and calls the respective I/O-operation. The operation map requests a new physical block m from the wear-leveling subsystem by calling wl_get_peb and writes the VID-header using a new sequence number. If the write was successful, the mapping is updated. Conversely, unmap removes a logical block (v, l) from the mapping and releases the corresponding physical block with wl_put_peb which puts the PEB into the erase queue. Similarly, erase first removes the in-memory mapping. Additionally, all PEBs that still store an inverse mapping for the LEB are erased synchronously via wl_flush.

A new volume is created by selecting an unused volume identifier, setting the state of each logical block to unmapped and writing the new volume table to flash. The volume table encodes a partial function from user-accessible, existing volumes to their size. Apart from user-accessible volumes, there are also hidden

```
wl_put_peb(lebref, n)
  wla[n].status := erasing
  eraseq := enqueue(eq-entry(n, lebref), eraseq)

wl_get_peb(; n)
  let ecs = {wla[n].ec | wla[n].status = free ∧ n < #wla} in
  if ecs ≠ ∅ then
    choose m with wla[m].status = free ∧ φ(wla[m].ec, ecs) in
      n := m
      wla[n].status := used

atomic_change(v, l, m, len, buf, err)
  len := datasize(buf)
  io_write_vidhdr(m, vidhdr(v, l, max-sqn, len, checksum(buf, len)); err)
  max-sqn := max-sqn + 1
  if err = ESUCCESS ∧ len > 0 then
    io_write_data(m, 0, align↑(len, PAGE_SIZE), buf)
```

Fig. 9. The Wear-Leveling Subsystem

volumes. We currently only use the hidden volume VTBL_VOLID to store the volume table itself.

4.2 Asynchronous Erasure and Wear-Leveling

Whether a physical erase block is free, allocated, scheduled for erasure or is already unusable is stored alongside its erase counter in the wear-leveling array. It is used to find suitable free PEBs for the interface operations and appropriate free and used PEBs for wear-leveling.

> **state var** $wla : Array\langle WlEntry\rangle$ where
>
> **data** $WlEntry$ = wl-entry(ec : $\mathbb{N}$, status : $WlStatus$)
>
> **data** $WlStatus$ = free | used | erasing | erroneous

Every free and used PEB has a valid EC-header and its erase counter stored on flash and in memory match. The page for the VID-header and the data pages of a free physical erase block are not yet programmed. Erroneous PEBs are already marked as bad on flash.

The PEBs scheduled for erasure are additionally kept in a queue. It is used to assign work to the background operation for asynchronous erasure. For synchronous erasure of *one* LEB $(v, l) \in \mathbb{V} \times \mathbb{N}$ it is necessary to locate *all* PEBs that belonged to (v, l). To easily locate them without reading from flash, each entry of the queue caches the inverse mapping stored in the corresponding PEB.

> **state var** $eraseq : Seq\langle EraseqEntry\rangle$ where
>
> **data** $EraseqEntry$ = eq-entry(pnum : $\mathbb{N}$, lebref : $LebRef$)
>
> **data** $LebRef$ = none + $\mathbb{V} \times \mathbb{N}$

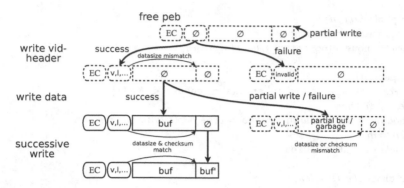

Fig. 10. States of the new PEB during and after `atomic_change`

Fig. 9 shows the implementation of allocation and deallocation of a physical erase block. Allocation choses a free PEB with certain restrictions φ on its erase counter—e.g. medium wear among the free PEBs—and marks it as used. Deallocation of a PEB n that was mapped at LEB *lebref* beforehand (or known to have an invalid VID-header if *lebref* is **none**) adds a corresponding entry to the erase queue.

The background operation for asynchronous erasure (not shown) dequeues an entry from the erase queue and then tries to erase the PEB synchronously by calling `mtd_erase` and to write a new EC-header with an increased erase counter multiple times. If this fails, the PEB is marked as bad via `mtd_markbad`. The operation `wl_flush` (not shown) iterates over the erase queue and similarly erases all PEBs that still belong to a specific LEB synchronously.

Wear-leveling is implemented as choosing a used and a free physical erase block of low resp. high wear. If the difference of the erase counters exceeds a certain threshold the VID-header and data region of the used PEB are read. The operation `atomic_change` as shown in Fig. 9 is the core of the wear-leveling algorithm. Conceptually, it must write a new inverse mapping for the logical erase block (v, l) and the buffer's contents into the free physical erase block m. However, there are two problems that need to be addressed. First, programming *all* pages of the data region of the new PEB could preclude successive write operations from the client that were allowed on the previous PEB. Therefore, only the contents up to the last non-`EMPTY` byte are written, calculated as `datasize`(buf). From the MTD invariant (2) it follows that successive writes by a client remain allowed. Second, additional measures are needed to ensure correct recovery from an unexpected power-loss during wear-leveling. Fig. 10 shows the different intermediate states of the target physical erase block during wear-leveling. At the top the contents of a free PEB are shown. The bold arrows denote state transitions due to a call of an I/O operation. An unsuccessful write to the VID-header is easily detectable during recovery, either the VID-header is empty or contains garbage. After a successful write of the VID-header, the recovery would read the PEB and discover that it stores the newest inverse mapping for the logical erase

ebm_change(v, l, n, buf)
  $avols[v][l] := \mathtt{mapped}(\mathtt{copy}(buf, 0, \mathtt{EMPTY\_LEB}, 0, n), n)$

Fig. 11. Atomically Exchange the Contents of an LEB

block (v, l). However, this is clearly wrong, since the actual data has not yet been copied to this PEB and successive read operations would just return bytes with the value EMPTY. Therefore, the data size of the contents of the original PEB is also stored in the VID-header. Rebuilding the mapping after a reset then only takes a PEB into consideration if the data size calculated over its data pages is at least as large as the value in the VID-header requires. This measure is also sufficient to detect a partial write of the data. We store a checksum in the VID-header and additionally allow failures during programming of the data pages that can be detected by either the data size or the checksum. If the copying was successful, the in-memory mapping is updated accordingly. Otherwise, the new physical erase block is scheduled for erasure and the old PEB is used.

Note that the checksum is only calculated up to the initial data size. Thus, a successive write to the LEB after wear-leveling maintains that the data size and checksum stored in the VID-header match the values calculated from the contents of the data region. In summary, these additional fields allow to distinguish *valid* (solid) from *invalid* (dotted) states of the target PEB.

The second problem is not specific to this implementation. Every model that either 1) updates the mapping before copying the actual data or 2) allows failures that write a valid mapping but invalid data simultaneously has to deal with this issue. In our model the inverse mapping must be updated first because it is stored in the second page and we enforce that pages are written sequentially.

If asynchronous erasure and wear-leveling are scheduled in between operations, do not fail and there are enough free PEBs to move to, the difference between erase counters of good PEBs is bounded by a constant. Thus, the device is worn out evenly.

With the operation atomic_change it is possible to implement an additional interface operation that atomically exchanges the contents of a logical erase block. On the abstract layer of Sec. 3 this is then specified as shown in Fig. 11. If the operation fails the LEB is unchanged. In contrast to ebm_write, ebm_change is more general and has a more favorable behavior wrt. failures. However, on the concrete layer this comes at the price of one additional erasure of a block. Thus, it is only desirable to use ebm_change if the additional guarantees are actually required. In UBIFS this functionality is for example used to write a new super block.

4.3   Power Failure and Recovery

The state of the EBM implementation is in RAM and only the MTD state is persistent. An unexpected power failure may invalidate the in-memory state, but is assumed to preserve everything stored on flash unaltered.

```
recover(; err)
  let recs = ∅ in
    scan_all(; recs, err)
    if (VTBL_VOLID, VTBL_LNUM) ∈ recs then let vtbl in
    io_read_vtbl(recs[VTBL_VOLID, VTBL_LNUM].pnum; vtbl, err)
    if err = ESUCCESS then
    init_volume_sizes(vtbl; )
    init_volume_mappings(recs; )
```

Fig. 12. Rebuilding of the in-memory State from Flash

Fig. 12 shows how the in-memory state is rebuilt from the data structures stored on flash. We assume that after a power failure this operation is first executed, before any client can issue a call. First, all physical erase blocks are scanned (`scan_all`), i.e., it is checked whether a PEB is marked as bad and has valid EC- and VID-headers. The PEB's entry in the wear-leveling array, the erase queue and maximum of the sequence numbers are updated accordingly. Instead of updating the in-memory mapping *vols* directly an intermediate data structure

$$recs \; : \mathbb{V} \times \mathbb{N} \nrightarrow RecoveryEntry \qquad \text{where}$$
$$RecoveryEntry = \texttt{recovery-entry}(\text{pnum} : \mathbb{N}, \text{sqn} : \mathbb{N})$$

is introduced. In contrast to *vols*, the data structure contains *all* encountered combinations (v, l) of volume identifiers and logical block numbers and the corresponding physical erase block. This includes hidden volumes and logical erase blocks beyond the—at this point unknown—size of the corresponding volume. The sequence number of the corresponding PEB is also cached. It is used to determine during the scanning which one of two PEBs belonging to the same LEB stores the most recent inverse mapping in case both are *valid*.

Afterwards, it is checked that a volume layout was found during scanning. Mounting fails if no layout is present. Otherwise, the volume table is read and for each non-hidden volume identifier a volume of the stored size initialized to **unmapped** is added to *vols* (`init_volume_sizes`). Finally, all mapping information from the intermediate data structure *recs* referring to an existing volume and within its bounds is transferred to *vols* (`init_volume_mappings`).

The recovery does not alter the MTD state. A power-loss during the operation therefore does not need any additional concepts.

It is crucial for the correctness of the recovery that the in-memory mapping corresponds to the *most recent* (inverse) mapping stored on-disk after each operation, among those PEBs that are *valid*.

To see that it is necessary to have the most recent mapping in RAM, assume the opposite: There are two PEBs A and B and both store a mapping for a LEB (v, l). In memory (v, l) is mapped to A, although B has the higher sequence number. If the contents of both data regions are identical, assume that a write operation is requested by the client on LEB (v, l) with non-empty data. Afterwards, A and B's contents definitely differ. In the event of a power failure, the subsequent recovery will restore a mapping from (v, l) to B. Reading the mapped LEB (v, l) before and after the power-loss will yield different results.

During wear-leveling there are intermediate states that do not yet have the correct data, but a newer version of the mapping—the dotted states in Fig. 10. Therefore, it is not sufficient to only consider the sequence number. The data size and checksum of the PEB also need to be taken into account, i.e., the mapped PEB must be valid.

5   Related Work

The models [4,3,2] in Z notation of an ONFI-compliant [11] device are conceptually below our model of a driver for flash memory. It would be possible to provide an implementation of our MTD model on top of their hardware model.

The block manager in the Alloy models [19,20] maps logical to physical pages and has a similar task as our EBM. However, storing and updating an on-disk mapping is not treated. Power failures are only considered during writing of a sequence of pages. Their specification of power failures and recovery is intertwined and uses auxiliary variables for the status of a pages. It is not immediately clear to us, how one would disentangle the specification in a real implementation.

Flash Translation Layers (FTLs) [5] and some FFSs [6,13] similarly store information about the state of a page or block in out-of-band (OOB) data, which allows programming of individual bits. This simplifies the recovery from power failures during wear-leveling, since it is possible to set a validity bit after copying the data. However, NOR flash devices do not have OOB data and some NAND devices use the whole area for error-correction codes [30]. Therefore, our EBM implementation is more generic. FTLs that support an operation similar to unmap (see "trim" command in Section 7.10 in [17], [21] clarifies the semantics) also have the problem that pages re-emerge after a power failure.

In the refinement-based approach [7] with Event-B, it is assumed that bookkeeping information is stored in every page, i.e., a page knows the version of the file it belongs to and the offset within the file. Updating the contents of one page is atomic. If two pages store the same inverse mapping after a power failure during wear-leveling, its contents are identical and chosing either suffices. However, this approach uses more memory for the mapping and requires reading every page of the flash device during startup in order to rebuild the mapping.

None of the formal models [4,19,7] considers the limitation to sequential writes within an erase block, although non-sequential writes are often not supported by newer ONFI-compliant devices [8,11].

6   Conclusion

We have presented a formal specification of an erase block management layer and an implementation based on an ONFI-compliant hardware model. Performance aspects such as asynchronous erasure and quality aspects such as wear-leveling are hidden from clients of the abstract model. Only power failure is visible, but its abstract specification is much more tractable for the verification of clients. As a consequence we can focus on the log-structure, indexing and write buffering of a FFS in the future.

The refinement proof between the abstract EBM model and the implementation is already completed and establishes that the implementation's behavior is captured by the abstract EBM specification. We also show that the recovery works as specified if a power failure occurs in between or *during* operations using the temporal logic of KIV [27]. Due to space limitations, we could not provide a description of these proofs in this paper. Quite some time was spent on understanding which concepts are relevant and what assumptions regarding failures are necessary to ensure that power loss during operations is handled correctly.

We are currently working on an automatic translation from our models to Scala [23] code, allowing us to run and test our implementation on top of a Memory Technology Device in Linux.

Several aspects remain for future work. In the implementation of UBI wear-leveling and erasure are performed in a background thread and concurrent write operations are permitted. The implementation uses locks on a per-LEB level to ensure that the background operations do not interfere with the interface operations. We did not yet verify this kind of concurrency. There is also an unresolved issue with *unstable bits* [31], resulting from a power cut during an erase operation. They are not covered by our hardware model.

References

1. Börger, E., Stärk, R.F.: Abstract State Machines—A Method for High-Level System Design and Analysis. Springer (2003)
2. Butterfield, A., Ó Catháin, A.: Concurrent models of flash memory device behaviour. In: Oliveira, M.V.M., Woodcock, J. (eds.) SBMF 2009. LNCS, vol. 5902, pp. 70–83. Springer, Heidelberg (2009)
3. Butterfield, A., Freitas, L., Woodcock, J.: Mechanising a formal model of flash memory. Sci. Comput. Program. 74(4), 219–237 (2009)
4. Butterfield, A., Woodcock, J.: Formalising flash memory: First steps. In: IEEE Int. Conf. on Engineering of Complex Computer Systems, pp. 251–260 (2007)
5. Chung, T.-S., Park, D.-J., Park, S., Lee, D.-H., Lee, S.-W., Song, H.-J.: A survey of flash translation layer. J. Syst. Archit. 55(5-6), 332–343 (2009)
6. Intel Corp. Intel Flash File System Core Reference Guide, version 1. Technical report, Intel Corporation (2004)
7. Damchoom, K., Butler, M.: Applying Event and Machine Decomposition to a Flash-Based Filestore in Event-B. In: Oliveira, M.V.M., Woodcock, J. (eds.) SBMF 2009. LNCS, vol. 5902, pp. 134–152. Springer, Heidelberg (2009)
8. Samsung Electronics. Page program addressing for MLC NAND application note (2009), http://www.samsung.com
9. Ernst, G., Schellhorn, G., Haneberg, D., Pfähler, J., Reif, W.: A Formal Model of a Virtual Filesystem Switch. In: Proc. of Software and Systems Modeling (SSV), pp. 33–45 (2012)

10. Ernst, G., Schellhorn, G., Haneberg, D., Pfähler, J., Reif, W.: Verification of a Virtual Filesystem Switch. In: Proc. of Verified Software, Theories Tools and Experiments (to appear, 2013)
11. Intel Corporation, et al.: Open NAND Flash Interface Specification (June 2013), http://www.onfi.org
12. Freitas, L., Woodcock, J., Butterfield, A.: POSIX and the Verification Grand Challenge: A Roadmap. In: ICECCS 2008: Proc. of the 13th IEEE Int. Conf. on Engineering of Complex Computer Systems (2008)
13. Gal, E., Toledo, S.: Algorithms and Data Structures for flash memory. ACM Computing Surveys, 138–163 (2005)
14. Gleixner, T., Haverkamp, F., Bityutskiy, A.: UBI - Unsorted Block Images (2006), http://www.linux-mtd.infradead.org/doc/ubidesign/ubidesign.pdf
15. Hoare, C.A.R.: The verifying compiler: A grand challenge for computing research. Journal of the ACM 50(1), 63–69 (2003)
16. Hunter, A.: A brief introduction to the design of UBIFS (2008), http://www.linux-mtd.infradead.org/doc/ubifs_whitepaper.pdf
17. INCITS. ATA/ATAPI Command Set - 2 (ACS-2), Revision 2 (August 3, 2009)
18. Joshi, R., Holzmann, G.J.: A mini challenge: build a verifiable filesystem. Formal Aspects of Computing 19(2) (June 2007)
19. Kang, E., Jackson, D.: Formal Modeling and Analysis of a Flash Filesystem in Alloy. In: Börger, E., Butler, M., Bowen, J.P., Boca, P. (eds.) ABZ 2008. LNCS, vol. 5238, pp. 294–308. Springer, Heidelberg (2008)
20. Kang, E., Jackson, D.: Designing and analyzing a flash file system with alloy. Int. J. Software and Informatics 3(2-3), 129–148 (2009)
21. Knight, F.: TRIM - DRAT/RZAT clarifications for ATA8-ACS2, Revision 2 (February 23, 2010)
22. Memory Technology Device (MTD) and Unsorted Block Images (UBI) Subsystem of Linux, http://www.linux-mtd.infradead.org/index.html
23. Odersky, M., Spoon, L., Venners, B.: Programming in Scala: A Comprehensive Step-by-step Guide, 1st edn. Artima Incorporation, USA (2008)
24. Pfähler, J., Ernst, G., Haneberg, D., Schellhorn, G., Reif, W.: KIV models and proofs of MTD, UBI and abstract UBI (2013), http://www.informatik.uni-augsburg.de/swt/projects/flash.html
25. Reeves, G., Neilson, T.: The Mars Rover Spirit FLASH anomaly. In: Aerospace Conference, pp. 4186–4199. IEEE Computer Society (2005)
26. Reif, W., Schellhorn, G., Stenzel, K., Balser, M.: Structured specifications and interactive proofs with KIV. In: Bibel, W., Schmitt, P. (eds.) Automated Deduction—A Basis for Applications, vol. II, pp. 13–39. Kluwer, Dordrecht (1998)
27. Schellhorn, G., Tofan, B., Ernst, G., Reif, W.: Interleaved programs and rely-guarantee reasoning with ITL. In: Proc. of TIME, pp. 99–106. IEEE Computer Society (2011)
28. Schierl, A., Schellhorn, G., Haneberg, D., Reif, W.: Abstract Specification of the UBIFS File System for Flash Memory. In: Cavalcanti, A., Dams, D.R. (eds.) FM 2009. LNCS, vol. 5850, pp. 190–206. Springer, Heidelberg (2009)
29. The Open Group. The Open Group Base Specifications Issue 7, IEEE Std 1003.1, 2008 edn. (2008), http://www.unix.org/version3/online.html (login required)
30. UBI - Out-of-Band Data Area, http://www.linux-mtd.infradead.org/faq/ubi.html
31. UBIFS - Unstable Bits Issue, http://www.linux-mtd.infradead.org/doc/ubifs.html

Attention-Based Coverage Metrics*

Shoham Ben-David[1],**, Hana Chockler[2], and Orna Kupferman[3]

[1] David Cheriton School of Computer Science, University of Waterloo, Canada
[2] Department of Informatics, King's College, London, UK
[3] School of Computer Science and Engineering, Hebrew University, Jerusalem, Israel

Abstract. Over the last decade, extensive research has been conducted
on coverage metrics for model checking. The most common coverage
metrics are based on mutations, where one examines the effect of small
modifications of the system on the satisfaction of the specification. While
it is commonly accepted that mutation-based coverage provides adequate
means for assessing the exhaustiveness of the model-checking procedure,
the incorporation of coverage checks in industrial model checking tools
is still very partial. One reason for this is the typically overwhelming
number of non-covered mutations, which requires the user to somehow
filter those that are most likely to point to real errors or overlooked
behaviors.

We address this problem and propose to filter mutations according
to the *attention* the designer has paid to the mutated components in
the model. We formalize the attention intuition using a multi-valued setting, where the truth values of the signals in the model describe their
level of importance. Non-covered mutations of signals of high importance
are then more alarming than non-covered mutations of signals with low
intention. Given that such "importance information" is usually not available in practice, we suggest two new coverage metrics that automatically
approximate it. The idea behind both metrics is the observation that designers tend to modify the value of signals only when there is a reason
to do so. We demonstrate the advantages of both metrics and describe
algorithms for calculating them.

1 Introduction

Today's rapid development of complex hardware designs requires reliable verification methods. A major challenge in these methods is to make the verification
process as exhaustive as possible. Exhaustiveness is crucial in simulation-based
verification [5]. There, coverage metrics have been traditionally used in order
to monitor progress of the verification process, estimate whether more input
sequences are needed, and direct simulation towards unexplored areas of the
design [12,22,24]. During the last decade, there has been an extensive research

---

* This work is partially supported by the EC FP7 programme, PINCETTE 257647,
  and by the ERC (FP7/2007-2013) grant agreement QUALITY 278410.
** Shoham Ben-David is grateful to the Azrieli Foundation for the award of an Azrieli
  Fellowship.

V. Bertacco and A. Legay (Eds.): HVC 2013, LNCS 8244, pp. 230–245, 2013.

on coverage metrics for model checking. Such metrics are used for assessing the exhaustiveness of the specification, and information obtained from them is used in order to reveal behaviors of the system that are not referred to in the specification [19,18,10,16,21,7].

The most common coverage metrics for model checking are based on mutations, where one examines the effect of small modifications of the system on the satisfaction of the specification. For example, *state-based* mutations flip the value of some (control or output) signal, and *logic-based* mutations fix the value of a signal to 0 or 1 [10,21]. While there is an agreement that mutation-based coverage provides adequate means for assessing the exhaustiveness of the model-checking procedure, the incorporation of coverage checks in industrial-strength model-checking tools is still very partial. One possible reason for this is the fact that coverage checking requires model checking many mutations. As it turns out though, the fact the mutations are only slightly different from the original system enables a reuse of much of the information gathered during model checking and leads to coverage algorithms that do not incur a significant computational overhead on top of the model-checking procedure [9,6,7]. Another reason for the slow integration of coverage checks in practice, is the overwhelming number of non-covered mutations that current metrics involve [3], a problem reported also in the context of test-case generation using model checking [15]. Typically, a user gets a long list of mutations that are non-covered, and is expected to analyze them and filter out the non-interesting ones. When a significant portion of the non-covered mutations are false alarms, it may cause the user to disregard coverage information altogether, potentially causing real problems to be ignored.

We address this problem and propose to filter mutations according to the *attention* the designer has paid to the mutated components in the original model. We first formalize the intuition of attention using a multi-valued setting. In this setting, the truth values of the signals in the model are real numbers taken from the range $[-1, 1]$. The higher the absolute value of a signal is, the "more intentional" this value is. In particular, 1 stand for "very intentional true", -1 for "very intentional false", and 0 corresponds to "don't care". We consider specifications described by means of formulas in linear temporal logic (LTL). The semantics of LTL can be adjusted to the multi-valued setting, lifting the intention interpretation from the output signals to the whole specification [1]. Recall that in the traditional approach to coverage, we check coverage by flipping the value of a signal in a state, and checking whether the specification is satisfied in the new model. In the multi-valued setting, mutations reduce the absolute value of the truth value of a signal, and we check the effect of this on the truth value of the specification. Non-covered mutations of signals with high intention are then more alarming than non-covered mutations of signals with low intention.

While the multi-valued setting offers a very precise ranking of mutations, it requires the user to manually provide the intention information, which is a serious drawback. Accordingly, we suggest two new coverage metrics that automatically approximate the intention information. The idea behind both metrics is the observation that designers tend to modify the value of signals only when there is a reason to do so. Thus, the value of a signal that has just been assigned is "more intentional" than the value of a signal that maintains its value. Before we turn to describe the new coverage metrics, let us point out that the above "lazy assignment" assumption, which is the key to our two metrics, is supported by power gating and clock gating considerations. Power consumption is an important consideration in modern chip design, from portable servers to large server farms. As the chips become more complex, the cost of powering a server farm can easily outweigh the cost of the servers themselves, thus design teams go to great lengths in order to reduce power consumption in their designs. Existing power saving techniques can be divided into electrical, such as using more efficient transistors, and logical, which attempt to introduce power-saving changes into designs without changing their logic. Logical power saving techniques attempt to reduce the number of changes in the values of signals, the main source of power consumption in chips. The most widely researched logical power saving techniques are *clock gating*, in which a clock is prevented from making a "tick" if it is redundant (c.f., [2]), and *power gating*, in which whole sections of the chip are powered off when not needed and then powered on again [20,13]. The goal of these techniques is to make sure that a change in the value of a signal happens only when there is a good reason for it, that is, leaving the value of a signal unchanged would result in a different logic than intended by the designer.

Our first coverage metric is *stuttering coverage*, where mutations flip the value of a signal along a sequence of states in which the signal is fixed (rather than flipping the value in a single state). Consider, for example, the property "every request is eventually granted" and a chip design where "grant" signals, once raised, only fall when the current transaction terminates. In this design, "grant" will stay up for several consecutive cycles. Applying the traditional mutation-based coverage metrics results in all these states being identified as non-covered with respect to the property and the "grant" signal. On the other hand, considering mutations that flip the value of a signal in the whole block at once will filter out these blocks, resulting in fewer and more meaningful coverage results.

Our second metric is applied to *netlist mutations*. Such mutations set a signal in the netlist to a constant value or make it "free" to change nondeterministically in every cycle. Here, the goal is to define as interesting mutations of signals whose values have received a lot of attention of the designer. We associate attention with the frequency in which signals flip their value. Thus, our metric filters mutations of signals that are not often flipped. We formalize "often" by means of windows of a fixed length along the computation.

We discuss the advantages of both metrics and describe algorithms for calculating them. Our algorithms output a "pass" result if all mutations are covered. If a non-covered block or signal (in the first and the second metrics, respectively) is found, it is presented as a counterexample. Note that, in contrast to existing algorithms for computing coverage, our algorithms do not output all non-covered mutations at once. There are two advantages to this strategy. First, it allows us to construct algorithms with the same complexity as model checking (essentially, we reduce coverage computation to model checking a property of almost the same size as the original one). Second, it mimics the real verification process, where bugs are found and corrected one by one. Since fixing a coverage hole results in a modification of either a property or a design, the rest of the coverage holes might become irrelevant, and the verification process should be re-executed.

2 Preliminaries

2.1 Linear Temporal Logic

We specify on-going behaviors of reactive systems using the linear temporal logic *LTL* [23]. Formulas of LTL are constructed from a set AP of atomic proposition using the usual Boolean operators and the temporal operators $\mathbf{X}$ ("next time"), $\mathbf{U}$ ("until"), $\mathbf{G}$ ("always"), and $\mathbf{F}$ ("eventually"). We define the semantics of LTL with respect to a *computation* $\pi = \sigma_0, \sigma_1, \sigma_2, \ldots$, where for every $j \geq 0$, we have that σ_j is a subset of AP, denoting the set of atomic propositions that hold in the j's position of π. We use $\pi \models \psi$ to indicate that an LTL formula ψ holds in the path π.

2.2 Circuits

We model reactive systems by *sequential circuits*. A sequential circuit (a *circuit*, for short) is a tuple $\mathcal{S} = \langle I, O, C, \theta, \rho, \delta \rangle$, where I is a set of input signals, O is a set of output signals, and C is a set of control signals that induce the state space 2^C. The sets I and C and the sets I and O are disjoint. Accordingly, $\theta \in 2^C$ is an initial state, $\rho : 2^C \times 2^I \to 2^C$ is a deterministic transition function, and $\delta : 2^C \to 2^O$ is an output function. Possibly $O \cap C \neq \emptyset$, in which case for all $x \in O \cap C$ and $t \in 2^C$, we have $x \in t$ iff $x \in \delta(t)$. Thus, $\delta(t)$ agrees with t on signals in C. We partition the signals in $O \cup C$ into three classes as follows. A signal $x \in O \setminus C$ is a *pure-output* signal. A signal $x \in C \setminus O$ is a *pure-control* signal. A signal $x \in C \cap O$ is a *visible-control* signal. While pure output signals have no control on the transitions of the system, a specification of the system can refer only to the values of the pure-output or the visible-control signals.

An input sequence $i_0 \cdot i_1 \cdot i_2 \cdots \in (2^I)^\omega$ induces a run $s_0, s_1, s_2, \ldots$ of states of $\mathcal{S}$, where $s_0 = \theta$ and $s_{j+1} = \rho(s_j, i_j)$ for all $j \geq 0$. Recall that only signals in $I \cup O$ are visible, thus LTL formulas that specify $\mathcal{S}$ are over the set $AP = I \cup O$ of atomic propositions, and a *computation* of $\mathcal{S}$ is a sequence $\sigma_0, \sigma_1, \sigma_2, \ldots \in (2^{I \cup O})^\omega$, such that there is an input sequence $i_0 \cdot i_1 \cdot i_2 \cdots \in (2^I)^\omega$, inducing the run $s_0, s_1, s_2, \ldots$, and $\sigma_j = i_j \cup \delta(s_j)$ for all $j \geq 0$.

2.3 Mutations in Circuits

Let $\mathcal{S}$ be a circuit that satisfies a specification φ. We consider two types of mutations – *state-based* and *logic-based* – reflecting the possible ways in which a small change (mutation) can be introduced into $\mathcal{S}$ (see also [10,21]).

State-Based Mutations. For a circuit $\mathcal{S} = \langle I, O, C, \theta, \rho, \delta \rangle$, a state $t \in 2^C$, and a signal $x \in C$, we define the x-*twin* of t, denoted $twin_x(t)$, as the state t' obtained from t by dualizing the value of x. Thus, $x \in t'$ iff $x \notin t$. A state-based mutation of x in t replaces t by $twin_x(t)$. The resulting mutant circuit is denoted by $\tilde{\mathcal{S}}_{t,x}$. The effect of this mutation for a pure-output signal x is changing the value of x in t. Mutations that dualize control signals introduce more aggresive changes. Indeed, dualizing a control signal x in a state s in $\mathcal{S}$ causes all transitions leading to t to be directed to its t-twin. In particular, the state t is no longer reachable in $\tilde{\mathcal{S}}_{t,x}$. Formally, given $\mathcal{S}$, s, and a signal $x \in O \cup C$, we define the *dual circuit* $\tilde{\mathcal{S}}_{s,x} = \langle I, O, C, \tilde{\theta}, \tilde{\rho}, \tilde{\delta} \rangle$ as follows.

- If x is a pure-output signal, then $\tilde{\theta} = \theta$, $\tilde{\rho} = \rho$, and $\tilde{\delta}$ is obtained from δ by dualizing the value of x in s, thus $x \in \tilde{\delta}(s)$ iff $x \notin \delta(s)$.
- If x is a pure-control signal, then $\tilde{\delta} = \delta$, and $\tilde{\theta}$ and $\tilde{\rho}$ are obtained by replacing all the occurrences of s in θ and in the range of ρ by $twin_x(s)$. Thus, if $\theta = s$, then $\tilde{\theta} = twin_x(s)$; otherwise, $\tilde{\theta} = \theta$. Also, for all $s' \in 2^C$ and $i \in 2^I$, if $\rho(s', i) = s$, then $\tilde{\rho}(s', i) = twin_x(s)$; otherwise, $\tilde{\rho}(s', i) = \rho(s', i)$.
- If x is a visible-control signal, then we do both changes. Thus, $\tilde{\delta}$ is obtained from δ by dualizing the value of x in s, and $\tilde{\theta}$ and $\tilde{\rho}$ are obtained by replacing all the occurrences of s in θ and in the range of ρ by $twin_x(s)$.

For a specification φ such that $\mathcal{S} \models \varphi$, a state t is x-*covered* by φ if $\tilde{\mathcal{S}}_{t,x}$ does not satisfy φ.

Note that it makes no sense to define coverage with respect to observable input signals. This is because an open system has no control on the values of the input signals, which just resolve the external nondeterminism of the system.

Logic-Based Mutations. These mutations describe changes resulting from freeing a control signal of $\mathcal{S}$ or fixing it to 0 or 1. Freeing a control signal is, from the design perspective, equivalent to turning this signal into an input signal. Fixing a signal to 0 or to 1 is known as "stuck-at-0" and "stuck-at-1" mutations, respectively, and these are the most commonly-used fault models in fault simulation and automatic test pattern generation (ATPG). For a circuit $\mathcal{S} = \langle I, O, C, \theta, \rho, \delta \rangle$ and a control signal $x \in C$, the mutant circuits are defined according to the type of the logic-based mutation applied to $\mathcal{S}$ as follows:

- The x-*freed* circuit $\mathcal{S}_x = \langle I', O, C', \theta', \rho', \delta' \rangle$ is obtained from $\mathcal{S}$ by moving x to the set of input signals (that is, $I' = I \cup \{x\}$, and $C' = C \setminus \{x\}$), and removing it from the definition of θ, from the range of ρ, and from the domain of δ.
- The x-*fixed-to-1* circuit $\mathcal{S}_{x,1} = \langle I, O, C, \theta', \rho', \delta \rangle$ is obtained from $\mathcal{S}$ by replacing all the occurrences of x in θ and in the range of ρ by 1; i.e., $\theta' = \theta \cup \{x\}$, and for all $s \in 2^C$ and $i \in 2^I$, we have $\rho'(s, i) = \rho(s, i) \cup \{x\}$.
- The x-*fixed-to-0* circuit $\mathcal{S}_{x,0}$ is defined by replacing all the occurrences of x in θ and in the range of ρ by 0.

A control signal x is *nondet-covered* if $\mathcal{S}_x$ does not satisfy φ, 1-*covered* if $\mathcal{S}_{x,1}$ does not satisfy φ, and 0-*covered* if $\mathcal{S}_{x,0}$ does not satisfy φ.

2.4   Mutations in Netlists

Hardware designs are frequently represented as *netlists*. A netlist is a collection of primitive combinational elements. *And-Inverter* graphs (AIGs) are often used to store the netlist; i.e., the netlist consists of input gates, AND-gates, inverters, and memory elements (registers). Formally, a netlist N is a directed graph $\langle V_N, E_N, \tau_N \rangle$, where V_N is a finite set of vertices, $E_N \subseteq V_N \times V_N$ is a set of directed edges, and $\tau_N : V_N \rightarrow \{AND, INV, REG, INPUT\}$ maps a node to its type. The in and out degree of the vertices respects the expected requirements from the corresponding type.

When a design is modeled as a netlist, the smallest possible mutation is changing the type of a single node. We use the definition from [7], where the mutation changes the type of a single node in V_N to an input. This new input can be kept open, in which case its value is non-deterministically set at each cycle, or it can be fixed to 0 or 1.

Netlists can be naturally represented as a special case of sequential circuits, where the registers are viewed as control signals, that is, a state of the netlist is defined by a combination of values of the registers. Changing the type of a single node in a netlist can, therefore, be viewed as a logic-based mutation in the corresponding circuit.

3   Attention-Based Coverage

Ranking of coverage results according to the level of alarm they should cause could have been a much easier task if the designer of the verified system had provided information regarding his understanding of the importance of the different components of the system. In this section we develop a multi-valued approach for ranking of coverage results in case such an information is provided. We are aware of the fact that current modeling formalisms do not require the user to provide such an information. We still find it interesting and useful, both as further motivation to future modeling standards (especially given the tendency today to move to multi-valued approaches), and as a starting point for methods that approximate the multi-valued settings without information from the user, like those we suggest in Sections 4 and 5.

3.1   Multi-valued Circuits

For our model of intention based coverage, we assume that the assignments to the pure-output variables are not Boolean. Rather, each output signal is assigned a real value in the range $[-1, 1]$, reflecting the level of importance that the designer gives to this assignment. Formally, in a multi-valued circuit $S = \langle I, O, C, \theta, \rho, \delta \rangle$, the output function is $\delta : 2^C \rightarrow [-1, 1]^O$, which is not Boolean. Note that $C \cap O$ need not be empty, in which case we require, for all states $s \in 2^C$ and visible-control signals $x \in C \cap O$, that either $x \in s$ and $\delta(s)(x) \geq 0$ or $x \notin s$ and $\delta(s)(x) \leq 0$. Note that the values of signals in I are still Boolean. For uniformity, we map them to $\{-1, 1\}$, in the expected way: a *computation* of the multi-valued circuit S is a sequence $\sigma_0, \sigma_1, \sigma_2, \ldots \in ([-1, 1]^{I \cup O})^\omega$, such that there is an input sequence $i_0 \cdot i_1 \cdot i_2 \cdots \in (2^I)^\omega$, inducing the run $s_0, s_1, s_2, \ldots$, and for all $j \geq 0$, the assignment σ_j describes the values of the input and output signals in the j-th position in the run. Thus, for an input signal $x \in I$ we have that $\sigma_j(x)$ is 1 if $x \in i_j$ and is -1 if $x \notin i_j$, and for an output signal $x \in O$, we have $\sigma_j(x) = \delta(s_j)$.

Intuitively, the higher the absolute value of a signal is, the "more intentional" this value is. In particular, 1 stand for "very intentional true", -1 for "very intentional false", and 0 corresponds to "don't care". The semantics of LTL can be adjusted to the multi valued setting, lifting the intention interpretation from the output signals to the whole specification. We use $val(\pi, \varphi)$ to denote the value (in $[-1, 1]$) of an LTL formula φ in a computation $\pi = \sigma_0, \sigma_1, \ldots ([-1, 1]^{I \cup O})^\omega$. The value $val(\pi, \varphi)$ is defined by induction on the structure of φ as follows (c.f., [1]).

- $val(\pi, p) = \sigma_0(p)$,
- $val(\pi, \neg\varphi_1) = -val(\pi, \varphi_1)$,
- $val(\pi, \varphi_1 \wedge \varphi_2) = \min\{val(\pi, \varphi_1), val(\pi, \varphi_2)\}$,
- $val(\pi, \mathbf{X}\varphi_1) = val(\pi^1, \varphi_1)$,
- $val(\pi, (\varphi_1 \mathbf{U} \varphi_2)) = \max\{val(\pi, \varphi_2), \min\{val(\pi, \varphi_1), val(\pi^1, (\varphi_1 \mathbf{U} \varphi_2))\}\}$.

Note that, by De-Morgan rules, we have that $val(\pi, \varphi_1 \vee \varphi_2) = \max\{val(\pi, \varphi_1), val(\pi, \varphi_2)\}$, which matches our intuition. When φ is propositional, we sometimes use $val(s, \varphi)$ (rather than $val(\pi, \varphi)$), for the first state s of π.

Example 1. Consider the computation π in Figure 1 and the property $\varphi = G(p \rightarrow Fq)$. The signal q is "strongly false" in states s_0, s_1, and s_2, and is "strongly true" in the state s_3. Afterwards, the value of q reduces to $\frac{1}{2}$, indicating a "weaker true", possibly because the value is kept on only in order to reduce power consumption or as a back-up for the case that the q that is true in state s_3 would fail.

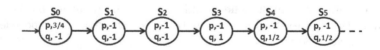

Fig. 1. A multi-valued computation

We compute the value of φ on π. By the multi-valued semantics, we have

$$val(\pi, \varphi) = \min_{0 \leq i \leq 5} \{val(\pi^i, \neg p \vee Fq)\}.$$

Opening $val(\pi^i, \neg p \vee Fq)$, we get

$$val(\pi, \varphi) = \min_{0 \leq i \leq 5} \{\max_{i \leq j \leq 5}\{val(s_j, \neg p), val(s_j, q), \ldots, val(s_5, q)\}\}.$$

In all indices i that correspond to states in which p is strongly false we get that the maximum is 1 (since p is negated in s_j, its -1 value contributes 1). When $i = 0$, we have that $val(s_0, p) = \frac{3}{4}$. But since $val(s_3, q) = 1$, the maximal value in $\max\{val(s_0, \neg p), val(s_1, q), val(s_2, q), val(s_3, q), val(s_4, q), val(s_5, q)\}$ is still 1. Hence, the value of φ on π is 1.

Theorem 1. *The model-checking problem for multi-valued LTL has the same complexity as the model-checking problem for regular (Boolean) LTL.*

Proof Sketch. Essentially, the states of the automata constructed from the LTL specifications are now extended to be associated with functions from formulas in the closure of the specification to values in $[-1, 1]$, rather than with subsets of the formulas in the closure [1]. □

3.2   Multi-valued Coverage

We now turn to the question of coverage in multi-valued circuits. Recall that in a regular (Boolean) model we check coverage by flipping the value of a signal in a state, and checking whether the specification is satisfied in the new model. In the multi-valued setting, mutations reduce the importance of a truth value of a signal, and check the effect of this on the truth value of the specification. Consider the example in Figure 1 again. If we reduce the truth value of q is state s_3 we expect to get a different coverage result from the case where the truth value of q is reduced in state s_4, since the value in s_3 is more important than that in s_4 to begin with.

We parameterize the coverage query by two values $v_1, v_2 \in (0, 1]$. The first value, v_1, describes the change in the truth value of the mutated signal. The second value describes the threshold for reporting non-coverage. That is, if after changing the truth value of the signal by v_1, the change in the truth value of the specification is less than v_2, then the signal is non-covered.

We now turn to formalize this intuition. For a state $s \in 2^C$ and an output signal $x \in O$ with $|\delta(s)(x)| \geq v_1$, we define the v_1-mutated value of x in s as the value obtained from $\delta(s)(x)$ by "bringing it closer to 0" by changing it by at most v_1. Note that since $|\delta(s)(x)| \geq v_1$, we do not have to worry about a signal switching its positivity in the definition below. Also note that the assumption about $|\delta(s)(x)|$ being at least v_1 matches the intuition behind multi-valued coverage, as it makes little sense to compute the effect of mutating signals that the designer does not care much about.

Formally,

$$val_{v_1}(s, x) = \begin{cases} \delta(s)(x) - v_1 & \text{if } \delta(s)(x) \geq 0. \\ \delta(s)(x) + v_1 & \text{if } \delta(s)(x) < 0. \end{cases}$$

For a circuit $\mathcal{S}$ we define $\tilde{\mathcal{S}}_{s,x,v_1}$ to be the circuit obtained from $\mathcal{S}$ by replacing $\delta(s)(x)$ with $val_{v_1}(s, x)$. It is not hard to prove that reducing the absolute value of a signal by v_1 can reduce the absolute value of the whole specification by at most v_1. Formally, for all circuit $\mathcal{S}$, states s, signals x, values v_1, and specifications φ, we have that $0 \leq val(\mathcal{S}, \varphi)$ iff $0 \leq val(\tilde{\mathcal{S}}_{s,x,v_1}, \varphi)$ and $|val(\mathcal{S}, \varphi) - val(\tilde{\mathcal{S}}_{s,x,v_1}, \varphi)| \leq v_1$. Hence, checking (v_1, v_2)-coverage, we take $v_2 \leq v_1$.

We say that x is (v_1, v_2)-covered in a state s by a formula φ in the model $\mathcal{S}$ if $|val(\mathcal{S}, \varphi) - val(\tilde{\mathcal{S}}_{s,x,v_1}, \varphi)| \geq v_2$.

Example 2. Consider again the computation π appearing in Figure 1. Suppose we want to evaluate the coverage of the signal q in state s_3 with respect to the specification $\varphi = G(p \to Fq)$ and the parameters $(\frac{1}{2}, \frac{1}{4})$. The value of q in s_3 is reduced to $\frac{1}{2}$ and we get that $\max\{val(s_0, \neg p), val(s_1, q), val(s_2, q), val(s_3, q), val(s_4, q), val(s_5, q)\}$ is now $\frac{1}{2}$, while the other values in the external minimum remain 1, so the value of φ in the mutated computation is $\min\{\frac{1}{2}, 1, 1, 1, 1\} = \frac{1}{2}$. Recall from Example 1 that $val(\pi, \varphi) = 1$. Thus $|val(\pi, \varphi) - val(\tilde{\pi}_{s_4,q,\frac{1}{2}}, \varphi)| = 1 - \frac{1}{2} \geq \frac{1}{4}$. Accordingly, we get that q is $(\frac{1}{2}, \frac{1}{4})$-covered in s_3 with respect to φ, we do not report a hole here, which matches our intuition.
Let us now check the $(\frac{1}{2}, \frac{1}{4})$-coverage of q in s_4. It is easy to see that $val(\tilde{\pi}_{s_4,q,\frac{1}{2}}, \varphi)$ is still 1. Thus, $|val(\pi, \varphi) - val(\tilde{\pi}_{s_4,q,\frac{1}{2}}, \varphi)| = 0 < \frac{1}{4}$. Accordingly, we report that q is $(\frac{1}{2}, \frac{1}{4})$-non-covered in s_4, which matches our intuition.

4   Stuttering Coverage

In a circuit, a mutation $\tilde{\mathcal{S}}_{s,q}$ switches the value of a visible control signal q in the state s of the circuit $\mathcal{S}$ (see Section 2.3). In many cases, such a mutation is too subtle, resulting in a spurious 'non-covered' result. To see this, consider the formula $\varphi = G(p \to Fq)$, and the execution path π shown in Fig. 2. Clearly, $\pi \models \varphi$. If we apply the standard mutation based coverage check, we shall flip the

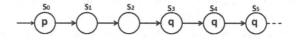

Fig. 2. An execution path in which existing metrics declare that q is not covered by $G(p \to Fq)$

value of q in each of the states s_3, s_4 or s_5, and find that none of them is covered. It could be the case however, that q was left active simply because there was no reason to deactivate it, and therefore the 'non-covered' result that we report is a false alarm.

In this section we introduce *stuttering coverage*, which regards a block of states that agree on the value of a propositional formula as one unit, and flips their value together. In the case of Figure 2, the value of q will be flipped in all the states s_3, s_4, and s_5 together, causing φ to fail on the mutated path, and thus we get that q is covered in all states. Consider now a slightly modified example, where q holds in states s_3 and s_5, but not in s_4. In this case, the stuttering coverage metric will indicate that both s_3 and s_5 are not covered, which seems a reasonable strategy, since the designer deliberately switched q off and on again.

Stuttering coverage is related to *statement coverage* metrics used in the context of code coverage [4,10]. There, a mutation modifies or skips an assignment statement in the code. The effect of this in the corresponding circuit is a change in the block of states that starts with the execution of the statement and ends when the next assignment takes place. Unlike stuttering coverage, all blocks as above are affected. In contrast, stuttering coverage flips the value of q in a single block. Also, the boundaries of the block are determined by a propositional formula that may depend not only in q. Below we present the formal definition of stuttering coverage and suggest an algorithm to easily detect it.

4.1   Finding Stuttering Coverage Holes

We examine mutations that flip the value of q in a sequence of states – a *block*. In the example, we define blocks as maximal sequences of states along which the mutated signal does not change its value. Here we generalize the setting to consider blocks defined by a predicate on the state space. For a Boolean assertion β over C, let $||\beta||$ denote the set of states that satisfy β. We are going to include in a block a sequence of states that are all satisfying β. That is, in stuttering coverage, we switch the value of q in β-blocks instead of in a single state. Note that typically there may be many β-blocks in a circuit, each suggesting a different mutation, and our metric considers them all.

Let $S = \langle I, O, C, \theta, \rho, \delta \rangle$ be the circuit, q the signal to be flipped and β the Boolean expression. We construct a mutant circuit $S' = \langle I', O', C', \theta', \rho', \delta \rangle$ that embodies all the mutations corresponding to a flip of q in a β-block. Essentially, as suggested in [8], we do so by nondeterministically guessing when a β-block starts. We now describe the details of the construction. We define $I' = I \cup \{x\}$ and $O' \cap C' = O \cap C \cup \{start, hold\}$. The new input signal x is used to nondeterministically select a starting point for a β-block. The visible control signals *start* and *hold* are used to find the borders of the β-block: The signal *start* is initiated to *false* and is set to *true* by the transition function if x is *true* and β is *false*. Once *start* is set to *true* it stays *true* forever. Thus *start* uses the input x to "guess" that β is going to become active in the next state of the computation. Since *start* may be wrong in its guess, we use the signal *hold* to verify the guess and to indicate when β is no longer valid. The signal *hold* is initiated to *true*, and stays active as long as *start* is *false*, or, if *start* is *true*, it stays active until β is *false*.

Formally, $\theta' = \theta \cup \{hold\}$ and $\rho'(s, i) = \rho(s \cap C, i \cap I) \cup \gamma$, where γ is defined as follows:

$$
\gamma = \begin{cases}
\{start, hold\} & \text{If } (start \notin s, x \in i, \text{ and } s \notin ||\beta||) \text{ or} \\
 & (start \in s, hold \in s, \text{ and } s \in ||\beta||). \\
\{start\} & \text{If } hold \notin s \text{ or } (hold \in s, start \in s \text{ and } s \notin ||\beta||). \\
\{hold\} & \text{If } start \notin s \text{ and } (x \notin i \text{ or } (x \in i \text{ and } s \in ||\beta||)). \\
\emptyset & \text{Otherwise.}
\end{cases}
$$

Note that a state s is in the selected β-block iff *start*, *hold* and β are all active together in s. We denote such states by the predicate $InBlock = start \wedge hold \wedge \beta$. This construction however, cannot select a β-block if it begins in the initial state. This is because *start* is initialized to *false* and thus can be active only starting in the second state. This can be easily fixed by introducing a new initial state $\tilde{\theta} = \{hold\}$, with a single outgoing transition leading to the original initial state, and adding a leading X (next) before the formula. This way the formula will be checked starting from the original initial state of the model, and a β-block can be selected from the original initial state as well.

Note that in $\mathcal{S}'$ there are execution paths on which *InBlock* is never active: this happens when the input signal x never holds, or when *start* becomes active in wrong place and "misses" the beginning of a β-block.

In order to flip q in the selected β-block, we introduce a new observable signal $q' = q \oplus InBlock$. Note that q' holds the flipped value of q exactly on the selected β-block, and is equal to q in all other states. We define $\varphi' = \varphi[q \leftarrow q']$, replacing every occurrence of q in φ with q'. Thus, φ' "reads" the flipped value of q exactly on the selected β-block.

In order to search for a non-covered case, we look for a computation path on which φ' holds, but also *InBlock* is active at some point. Thus we search for a computation path on which $\varphi' \wedge F(InBlock)$ holds. Such a computation path demonstrates a non-covered case of the original circuit $\mathcal{S}$.

The size of the $\mathcal{S}'$ is linear in the size of $\mathcal{S}$ and the Boolean expression β, size of the new property φ' is the same as the size of φ, and the algorithm performs model checking once, hence proving the following claim.

Claim. Finding a stuttering coverage hole is not harder than detecting a non-covered mutation as defined in Section 2.3, and is the same as model checking.

Remark 1. The logic LTL-X excludes the "next time" (**X**) operator from LTL and is used for the specification of stutter-invariant properties [14]. Formulas in LTL-X are particularly suitable for stuttering coverage. Indeed, while the next-time operator can impose requirements on particular states in a computation (say, some valuation of signals should occur immediately after some event happens), stutter-invariants properties impose requirements on blocks. Even in the presence of the next-time operator, stuttering coverage has the advantage of reducing the number of mutations that needs to be checked.

Remark 2. Since stuttering coverage introduces larger changes in the circuit than the standard mutation-based coverage metrics described in Section 2.3, it may seem that stuttering coverage is strictly stronger than the standard coverage (in other words, if a state is stutter-covered, then it is covered according to the standard mutation-based metric). This is true for most properties, and, in particular, for properties used in the verification of real hardware designs, making this metric especially attractive in practice. However, this implication does not hold in general. One example is the properties using the **X** operator, as Remark 1 points out. Another example are properties that require that a particular signal holds its value for a large block of cycles (or for the duration of the whole design), as in $p \rightarrow \mathbf{G}p$, which states that if a signal p holds in the initial state, then it should hold in the whole design.

5   Frequency-Based Coverage

We now consider logic-based mutations, typically modeling netlists [9]. Such a mutation takes a signal x and frees it or fixes it either to 0 or to 1. Here as well, coverage is reported when the specification holds on the mutated model.

In this metric we define as *important* signals that change a lot, assuming that a change in the signal's value is a result of an intentional action by the designer, whereas keeping the value constant whenever possible is the default behavior. We thus want to detect a signal that changes its value frequently, and yet, when mutated, does not influence the satisfaction of the specification.

We first have to formalize "frequently". There are different definitions that come to mind. We find the definition of *k-window*, specified below, to be most appropriate. It is possible to extend the idea here to other definitions. Let $\mathcal{S} = \langle I, O, C, \theta, \rho, \delta \rangle$ be the circuit modeling the netlist. For a control signal x, a computation π, and an integer $k \geq 1$, we say that x is *k-frequently flipped in* π if in each window of length k in π (that is, each subsequence of length k of assignments), the value of x is flipped at least once.

5.1   Finding Frequency-Based Coverage Holes

We are going to filter coverage results by frequency by defining a mutant circuit $\mathcal{S}'$ that keeps a log of flips of x in the last k transitions. , and enables the coverage check to restrict attention to computations in which x is flipped frequently. The circuit $\mathcal{S}'$ also applies the required mutation on x. The frequency check is, of course, with respect to the values of x before the mutation. Accordingly, $\mathcal{S}'$ keeps record of the original value of x in a new signal x'. In order to detect a change in the value of x', we also add a signal prev-x', recording the original value of x in the previous state.

We define the mutant circuit $\mathcal{S}' = \langle I, O', C', \theta', \rho', \delta \rangle$ as follows. First, we apply to x the desired mutation as specified in Section 2.3. We then add a set of control signals $V = \{x', \text{prev-}x', q_0, q_1, ..., q_k\}$. Thus, $C' = C \cup V$. The signals x' and prev-x' are described above. The signals $q_0, q_1, ..., q_k$ are used to count to k (note that as such, one could easily replace them by only $\lceil \log k \rceil$ signals. For simplicity, we describe the construction here with linearly many signals). Only q_k needs to be visible, thus $O' = O \cup \{q_k\}$.

The signal x' records the behavior of x in $\mathcal{S}$, namely, before the mutation was applied to it. The signal prev-x' records the value of x' in the previous state. Thus, we define $x' \in \theta'$ iff $x \in \theta$ and prev-$x' \in \theta'$ iff $x \notin \theta$. For all $s \in 2^{C'}$ and $i \in 2^I$, we set $\rho'(s, i) = \rho(s \cap C, i) \cup \{x'\}$ if $x \in \rho(s \cap C, i)$, and $\rho(s \cap C, i)$ otherwise. We set $\rho'(s, i) = \rho'(s, i) \cup \text{prev-}x'$ iff $x \in s$. A change in the value of x occurs in a state $s \in 2^{C'}$ if $s \models x' \oplus \text{prev-}x'$. That is, if $x' \in s$ and prev-$x' \notin s$ or $x' \notin s$ and prev-$x' \in s$.

In order to detect whether x is k-frequently flipped in the computations of $\mathcal{S}$, we record the behavior of x along k-windows. We do it using $q_0, ..., q_k$. For each state $s \in 2^{C'}$ we add exactly one of $q_0, ..., q_k$ as follows. We define $\theta' = \theta' \cup \{q_0\}$, and for all $s \in 2^{C'}$, $i \in 2^I$ and $0 \leq j < k$, we update ρ' as follows.

$$\rho'(s,i) = \begin{cases} \rho'(s,i) \cup \{q_k\} & \text{if } q_k \in s, \\ \rho'(s,i) \cup \{q_0\} & \text{if } s \models x' \oplus \text{prev-}x' \text{ and } q_k \notin s, \\ \rho'(s,i) \cup \{q_{j+1}\} & \text{if } s \not\models x' \oplus \text{prev-}x' \text{ and } q_j \in s. \end{cases}$$

It is easy to see that if x is k-frequently flipped in a computation, then q_0 would appear infinitely often on π. Otherwise, eventually a state with q_k would be reached, and from that point onwards q_k will appear in all states on π. Let ψ be the formula to be verified, and let $\mathcal{S}'$ be the mutated model as defined above. In order to check for coverage, we check for a computation satisfying $\psi' = \psi \wedge G \neg q_k$, asserting that ψ holds with the mutated behavior of x even though q_k is never reached. A path satisfying ψ' exhibit an interesting non-covered mutation.

6   A Case Study

We experimented with our ideas on a model of a PCI bus, taken from the NuSMV [11] example list. The model describes four master-slave units, communicating using the PCI bus protocol [17]. We briefly describe the protocol below, omitting details that are not essential for understanding our examples.

When a PCI master unit needs to start a transaction over the bus, it first asserts its request signal req, and keeps it asserted until permission is granted by the bus arbiter, indicated by the signal gnt being asserted. When permission is granted, the master can start a transaction by asserting its $frame$ signal. We omit the details of the actual transaction over the PCI bus. A transaction terminates when $frame$ is de-asserted, at which stage the bus is free for new transaction requests.

We note that in the formal PCI bus protocol, all signal are *active low*, meaning that they are considered active when their value is 0 and inactive when it is 1. In the PCI model we used, signals are *active high*, thus our example looks different than a typical PCI waveform.

The PCI model specifies more than 100 properties, which can roughly be divided into three categories. We examine each of the categories in light of the stuttering coverage method. The first are properties of the form

$$G((\neg req \wedge issue\_next) \rightarrow X req)$$

asserting that one event should be immediately followed by another event. As discussed in Remark 1, the advantage of stuttering coverage in formulas that impose requirements in specific states (in our example, those immediately after states with $\neg req$) is computational, and it does not change the coverage analysis.

The second type of properties have the form

$$G(req \rightarrow (req \ U \ grant)),$$

stating that once a signal becomes active, it should remain active until some other event occurs, similarly to the second type of properties discussed in Remark 2. Recall that coverage information is checked for specifications that hold in the system. Thus, checking the coverage of the signal req, we know that $G(req \rightarrow (req\ U\ grant))$ holds. When $\beta = req$, we flip the value of a full block of req. We distinguish between two cases: (1) We flip a block in which req is active. Then, the left hand side of the implication becomes false, and the formula continues to hold, thus req is not covered, which meets our intuition – we want the design to activate req only when required, thus the fact req is active high should be further challenged by other components of the specification. (2) We flip a block in which req is inactive. Here, the fact we flip the entire block puts the responsibility on the coverage on the signal $grant$, enabling the user to detect redundant activation of $grant$.

The third type of properties are eventual ones. For example,

$$\varphi = G((gnt \wedge \neg frame) \rightarrow F frame).$$

This specification states that if $frame$ is inactive and gnt is given, then a transaction must start eventually. We checked stuttering coverage of the signal $frame$ for the above specification with $\beta = frame$. That is, we switch $frame$ in blocks of consecutive states where $frame$ has value 1. As described in Section 4.1, this involves the introduction of the signal $block$, which is asserted during the selected β block, and the signal $frame'$, which agrees with $frame$ outside the selected block, and is the negation of $frame$ inside the block. We replaced the specification by

$$\varphi' = \neg(G((gnt \wedge \neg frame') \rightarrow F(frame')) \wedge F block).$$

The specification φ' failed, and Figure 3 presents the counterexample, which is an example of a non-covered block. In this example, three transactions take place. In cycles 5, $frame$ is asserted for a short transaction of 2 cycles. Then on cycle 9, $frame$ is asserted again for a longer transaction lasting until cycle 17. Finally, a last transaction starts on cycle 20. The block of consecutive $frames$ selected for coverage check is the middle transaction, from cycle 9 to 17, as indicated by signal 'block' being asserted. Note that the signal $frame$ is indeed

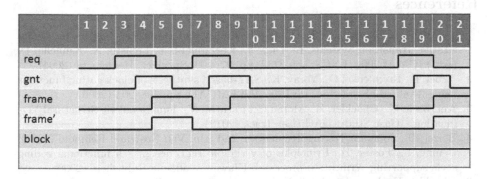

Fig. 3. A non-covered case for $G((gnt \wedge \neg frame) \rightarrow F(frame))$

not stutter-covered by φ. This is because many transactions take place on a typical execution path. Accordingly, a *gnt* is followed by many blocks of consecutive *frames*, and eliminating one such block is not sufficient for causing φ to change its value. In order to cover the behavior of *frame*, a more detailed property should be introduced. Note further, however, that by using stuttering coverage we dramatically reduce the number of non-covered cases: in traditional "single state" coverage, each of the *frames* in cycles 9 to 17 would be declared as non-covered.

7   Future Work

The algorithms we presented in this paper can be easily implemented on top of existing model checking tools – we need only to generate properties for detecting stuttering coverage and frequency-based coverage as described in Sections 4 and 5. As we already mentioned in the introduction, our algorithms generate one non-covered mutation at each run, hence mimicking the typical patterns of work of a verification engineer. Sometimes, however, we want to have a picture of how well our properties cover the design before we set up to fix coverage holes. In this context, a promising direction is to combine our definitions with the existing algorithms for efficient computation of coverage at once, for example those described in [7] and [6]. Based on our experience, the main obstacle in adoption of these algorithms as a part of the mainstream verification process is the sheer size of the output – the set of all non-covered mutations that need to be examined. We believe that using stuttering and frequency-based coverage will reduce the number of non-covered mutations by filtering the non-important mutations away, and we plan to perform these experiments as a future work. Finally, while the multi-value setting here comes mainly as a motivating framework to its approximation by stuttering and frequency-based coverage, we strongly believe that in the future we will see more and more quantitative specifications and systems, giving rise to quantitative verification methods, and making the multi-valued reasoning realistic in practice.

References

1. de Alfaro, L., Faella, M., Stoelinga, M.: Linear and Branching Metrics for Quantitative Transition Systems. In: Díaz, J., Karhumäki, J., Lepistö, A., Sannella, D. (eds.) ICALP 2004. LNCS, vol. 3142, pp. 97–109. Springer, Heidelberg (2004)
2. Arbel, E., Rokhlenko, O., Yorav, K.: SAT-based synthesis of clock gating functions using 3-valued abstraction. In: Proc. 9th FMCAD, pp. 198–204 (2009)
3. Auerbach, G., Chockler, H., Moran, S., Paruthi, V.: Functional vs. Structural Verification – Case Study. DAC User Track (2012)
4. Beizer, B.: Software Testing Techniques, 2nd edn. Van Nostrand Reinhold (1990)
5. Bening, L., Foster, H.: Principles of verifiable RTL design – a functional coding style supporting verification processes. Kluwer Academic Publishers (2000)
6. Chockler, H., Ivrii, A., Matsliah, A., Moran, S., Nevo, Z.: Incremental formal verification of hardware. In: Proc. 11th FMCAD, pp. 135–143 (2011)

7. Chockler, H., Kroening, D., Purandare, M.: Computing Mutation Coverage in Interpolation-Based Model Checking. IEEE Trans. on CAD of Integrated Circuits and Systems 31(5), 765–778 (2012)
8. Chockler, H., Kupferman, O., Kurshan, R.P., Vardi, M.Y.: A Practical Approach to Coverage in Model Checking. In: Berry, G., Comon, H., Finkel, A. (eds.) CAV 2001. LNCS, vol. 2102, pp. 66–78. Springer, Heidelberg (2001)
9. Chockler, H., Kupferman, O., Vardi, M.Y.: Coverage Metrics for Temporal Logic Model Checking. In: Margaria, T., Yi, W. (eds.) TACAS 2001. LNCS, vol. 2031, pp. 528–542. Springer, Heidelberg (2001)
10. Chockler, H., Kupferman, O., Vardi, M.Y.: Coverage Metrics for Formal Verification. STTT 8(4-5), 373–386 (2006)
11. Cimatti, A., Clarke, E., Giunchiglia, E., Giunchiglia, F., Pistore, M., Roveri, M., Sebastiani, R., Tacchella, A.: NuSMV 2: An OpenSource Tool for Symbolic Model Checking. In: Brinksma, E., Larsen, K.G. (eds.) CAV 2002. LNCS, vol. 2404, p. 359. Springer, Heidelberg (2002)
12. Dill, D.L.: What's between simulation and formal verification? In: Proc. 35st DAC, pp. 328–329. IEEE Computer Society (1998)
13. Eisner, C., Nahir, A., Yorav, K.: Functional verification of power gated designs by compositional reasoning. FMSD 35(1), 40–55 (2009)
14. Etessami, K.: Stutter-Invariant Languages, ω-Automata, and Temporal Logic. In: Halbwachs, N., Peled, D.A. (eds.) CAV 1999. LNCS, vol. 1633, pp. 236–248. Springer, Heidelberg (1999)
15. Fraser, G., Wotawa, F.: Mutant Minimization for Model-Checker Based Test-Case Generation. In: TAIC PART – MUTATION, pp. 161–168 (2007)
16. Große, D., Kühne, U., Drechsler, R.: Analyzing Functional Coverage in Bounded Model Checking. IEEE Trans. on CAD of Integrated Circuits and Systems 27(7), 1305–1314 (2008)
17. PCI Special Interest Group: PCI Local Bus Specification, 2.2 edn. (1998), http://www.ics.uci.edu/~harris/ics216/pci/PCI_22.pdf
18. Hoskote, Y., Kam, T., Ho, P.-H., Zhao, X.: Coverage estimation for symbolic model checking. In: Proc. 36st DAC, pp. 300–305 (1999)
19. Katz, S., Grumberg, O., Geist, D.: "Have I written enough properties?" - A method of comparison between specification and implementation. In: Pierre, L., Kropf, T. (eds.) CHARME 1999. LNCS, vol. 1703, pp. 280–297. Springer, Heidelberg (1999)
20. Keating, M., Flynn, D., Aitken, R., Gibbons, A., Shi, K.: Low Power Methodology Manual. Springer (2007)
21. Kupferman, O., Li, W., Seshia, S.A.: A Theory of Mutations with Applications to Vacuity, Coverage, and Fault Tolerance. In: Proc. 8th FMCAD, pp. 1–9 (2008)
22. Peled, D.: Software Reliability Methods. Springer (2001)
23. Pnueli, A.: The temporal logic of programs. In: Proc. 18th FOCS, pp. 46–57 (1977)
24. Tasiran, S., Keutzer, K.: Coverage Metrics for Functional Validation of Hardware Designs. IEEE Design and Test of Computers 18(4), 36–45 (2001)

Synthesizing, Correcting and Improving Code, Using Model Checking-Based Genetic Programming

Gal Katz and Doron Peled

Department of Computer Science, Bar Ilan University
Ramat Gan 52900, Israel

Abstract. The use of genetic programming, in combination of model checking and testing, provides a powerful way to synthesize programs. Whereas classical algorithmic synthesis provides alarming high complexity and undecidability results, the genetic approach provides a surprisingly successful heuristics. We describe several versions of a method for synthesizing sequential and concurrent systems. To cope with the constraints of model checking and of theorem proving, we combine such exhaustive verification methods with testing. We show several examples where we used our approach to synthesize, improve and correct code.

1 Introduction

Software development is a relatively simple activity: there is no need to solve complicated equations, to involve chemical materials or to use mechanical tools; a programmer can write tens of lines of code per hour, several hours a day. However, the number of possible combinations of machine states in even a very simple program can be enormous, producing frequently unexpected interactions between tasks and features. Quite early in the history of software development, it was identified that the rate in which errors are introduced into the development code is rather high. While some simple errors can be observed and corrected by the programmer, many design and programming errors survive shallow debugging attempts and find themselves in the deployed product, sometimes causing hazardous behavior of the system, injuries, time loss, confusion, bad service, or massive loss of money.

A collection of *formal methods* [20] were developed to assist the software developers, including testing, verification and model checking. While these methods were shown to be effective in the software development process, they also suffer from severe limitations. Testing is not exhaustive, and frequently, a certain percentage of the errors survive even thorough testing efforts. Formal verification, using logic proof rules, is comprehensive, but extremely tedious; it requires the careful work of logicians or mathematicians for a long time, even for a small piece of code. Model checking is an automatic method; it suffers from high complexity, where memory and time required to complete the task are sometimes prohibitively high.

V. Bertacco and A. Legay (Eds.): HVC 2013, LNCS 8244, pp. 246–261, 2013.
© Springer International Publishing Switzerland 2013

It is only natural that researchers are interested in methods to automatically convert the system specification into software; assuming that formal specification indeed represents the needed requirements fully and correctly (already, a difficult task to achieve), a reliable automatic process would create correct-by-design code. Not surprisingly, efficient and effective automatic synthesis methods are inherently difficult. Problems of complexity and decidability quickly appear. Unless the specification is already close in form to the required system (e.g., one is an automaton, and the other is an implementation of this automaton), this is hardly surprising. One can show examples where the required number of states of a reactive system that is described by a simple temporal specification (using Linear Temporal Logic) grows doubly exponential with the specification [16]. This still leaves open the question of whether there is always a more compact representation for such a specification, a problem that is shown [6] to be as hard as proving open problems about the equivalence of certain complexity classes.

Software synthesis is a relatively new research direction. The classical Hoare proof system for sequential programs [7] can be seen not only as a verification system, but also as an axiomatic semantics for programs, and also as a set of rules that can be used to preserve correctness while manually refining the requirement from a sequential system into correct code. The process is manual, requiring the human intuition of where to split the problem into several subparts, deciding on where a sequential, conditional or iterating construct needs to be used, and providing the intermediate assertions. Manna and Wolper [17] suggested the transformation of temporal logic into automata, and thence to concurrent code with a centralized control. A translation to an automaton (on infinite sequences) provides an operational description of these sequences. Then, the operations that belong, conceptually, to different processes, are projected out on these processes, while a centralized control enforces globally the communication to occur in an order that is consistent with the specification.

More recent research on synthesis is focused on the interaction between a system and its environment, or the decomposition of the specified task into different concurrent components, each having limited visibility and control on the behavior of the other components. The principle in translating the given temporal specification into such systems is based on the fact that the components need to guarantee that the overall behavior will comply with the specification while it can control only its own behavior. This calls for the use of some intermediate automata form. In this case, it is often automata on trees, which include the possible interactions with the environment. In addition, synthesis includes some game theoretical algorithms that refine the behaviors, i.e., the possible branches of the tree, so that the overall behavior satisfy the specification. The seminal work of Pnueli and Rosner [22] shows that the synthesis of an open (interactive) system that satisfies LTL properties can be performed using some game theoretical principles. On the other hand, Pnueli and Rosner show [23], that synthesis of concurrent systems that need to behave according to given distributed architecture (as opposed to centralized control) is undecidable.

The approach presented here is quite different. Instead of using a direct algorithmic translation, we perform a generate-and-check kind of synthesis. This brings back to the playground the use of verification methods, such as model checking or SAT solving, on given instances. An extreme approach would be to generate all possibilities (if they can be effectively enumerated) and check them, e.g., by using model checking, one by one. In the work of Bar-David and Taubenfeld [3], mutual exclusion algorithms arc synthesized by enumerating the possible solutions and checking them. We focus on a directed search that is based on *genetic programming*. In a nutshell, genetic programming allows us to generate multiple candidate solutions at random and to mutate them, again as a stochastic process. We employ enhanced model checking (model checking that does not only produce an affirmation to the checked properties or a counterexample, but distinguishes also some finer level of correctness) to provide the *fitness* level; this is used by genetic programming to increase or decrease the chance of candidate programs to survive. Our synthesis method can be seen as a heuristic search in the space of syntactically fitting programs.

2   Genetic Programming Based on Model Checking

We present a framework combining genetic programming and model checking, which allows to automatically synthesize software code for given problems. The framework we suggest is depicted at Figure 1, and is composed of the following parts:

- A *user* that provides a formal specification of the problem, as well as additional constraints on the structure of the desired solutions,
- an *enhanced GP engine* that can generate random programs and them evolves them, and
- a *verifier* that analyzes the generated programs, and provides useful information about their correctness.

The synthesis process generally goes through the following steps:

1. The user feeds the GP engine with a set of constraints regarding the programs that are allowed to be generated (thus, defining the space of candidate programs). This includes:
   (a) a set of functions, literals and instructions, used as building blocks for the generated programs,
   (b) the number of concurrent processes and the methods for process communication (in case of concurrent programs), and
   (c) limitations on the size and structure of the generated programs, and the maximal number of permitted iterations.
2. The user provides a formal specification for the problem. This can include, for instance, a set of temporal logic properties, as well as additional requirements on the program behavior.
3. The GP engine randomly generates an initial population of programs based on the fed building blocks and constraints.

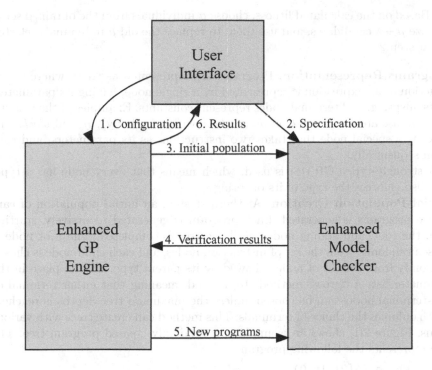

Fig. 1. The Suggested Framework

4. The verifier analyzes the behavior of the generated programs against the specification properties, and provides fitness measures based on the amount of satisfaction.

5. Based on the verification results, the GP engine then creates new programs by applying genetic operations such as mutation, which performs small changes to the code, and crossover, which cuts two candidate solutions and glues them together, to the existing programs population. Steps 4 and 5 are then repeated until either a perfect program is found (fully satisfying the specification), or until the maximal number of iterations is reached.

6. The results are sent back to the user. This includes a program that satisfies all the specification properties, if one exists, or the best partially correct programs that was found, along with its verification results.

For steps 4 and 5 above we use the following selection method, which is similar to the Evolutionary Strategies [24] $\mu + \lambda$ style:

- Randomly choose at set of μ candidate solutions.
- Create λ new candidates by applying mutation (and optionally crossover) operations (as explained below) to the above μ candidates.
- Calculate the fitness function for each of the new candidates based on "deep model checking".

– Based on the calculated fitness, choose μ individuals from the obtained set of size $\mu + \lambda$ candidates, and use them to replace the old μ individuals selected at step 2.

Programs Representation. Programs are represented as trees, where an instruction or an expression is represented by a single node, having its parameters as its offspring, and terminal nodes represent constants. Examples of the instructions we use are *assignment, while* (with or without a body), *if* and *block*. The latter is a special node that takes two instructions as its parameters, and runs them sequentially.

A strongly-typed GP [18] is used, which means that every node has a type, and also enforces the type of its offspring.

Initial Population Creation. At the first step, an initial population of candidate programs is generated. Each program is generated recursively, starting from the root, and adding nodes until the tree is completed. The root node is chosen randomly from the set of instruction nodes, and each child node is chosen randomly from the set of nodes allowed by its parent type, and its place in the parameter list. A "grow" method [15] is used, meaning that either terminal or non-terminal nodes can be chosen, unless the maximum tree depths is reached, which enforces the choice of terminals. This method can create trees with various forms. Figure 2(i) shows an example of a randomly created program tree. The tree represents the following program:

```
while (A[2] != 0)
    A[me] = 1
```

Nodes in bold belong to instructions, while the other nodes are the parameters of those instructions.

Mutation. Mutation is the main operation we use. It allows making small changes on existing program trees. The mutation includes the following steps:

1. Randomly choose a node (internal or leaf) from the program tree.
2. Apply one of the following operations to the tree with respect to the chosen node:
   (a) Replace the subtree rooted by the node with a new randomly generated subtree.
   (b) Add an immediate parent to the node. Randomly create other offspring to the new parent, if needed.
   (c) Replace the node by one of its offspring. Delete the remaining offspring of that node.
   (d) Delete the subtree rooted by the node. The node ancestors should be updated recursively (possible only for instruction nodes).

Mutation of type (a) can replace either a single terminal or an entire subtree. For example, the terminal "1" in the tree of Fig. 2(i), is replaced by the grayed subtree in 2(ii), changing the assignment instruction into A[me] = A[0]. Mutations of type (b) can extend programs in several ways, depending on the new parent node type. In case a "block" type is chosen, a new instruction(s) will be

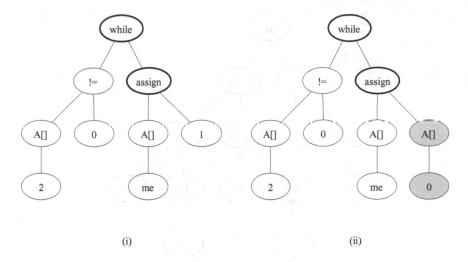

Fig. 2. (i) Randomly created program tree, (ii) the result of a replacement mutation

inserted before or after the mutation node. For instance, the grayed part of Fig. 3 represents a second assignment instruction inserted into the original program. Similarly, choosing a parent node of type "while" will have the effect of wrapping the mutation node with a while loop. Another situation occurs when the mutation node is a simple condition which can be extended into a complex one, extending, for example, the simple condition in Fig. 2 into the complex condition: A[2] != 0 and A[other] == me. Mutation type (c) has the opposite effect, and can convert the tree in Fig. 3 back into the original tree of Fig. 2(i). Mutation of type (d) allows the deletion of one or more instructions. It can recursively change the type, or even cause the deletion of ancestor nodes.

The type of mutation applied on candidate programs is randomly selected, but all mutations must obey strongly typing rules of nodes. This affects the possible mutation type for the chosen node, and the type of new generated nodes.

Crossover. The crossover operation creates new individuals by merging building blocks of two existing programs. The crossover steps are:

1. Randomly choose a node from the first program.
2. Randomly choose a node from the second program that has the same type as the first node.
3. Exchange between the subtrees rooted by the two nodes, and use the two new programs created by this method.

While traditional GP is heavily based on crossover, it is quite a controversial operation (see [2], for example), and may cause more damage than benefit in the evolutionary process, especially in the case of small and sensitive programs that we investigate. Thus, crossover is barely used in our work.

The Fitness Function. *Fitness* is used by GP in order to choose which programs have a higher probability to survive and participate in the genetic

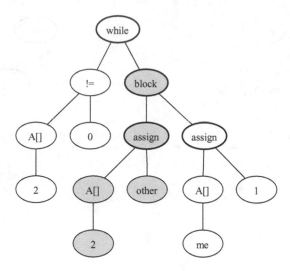

Fig. 3. Tree after insertion mutation

operations. In addition, the success termination criterion of the GP algorithm is based on the fitness value of the most fitted individual. Traditionally, the fitness function is calculated by running the program on some set of inputs (a training set) which suppose to represent all of the possible inputs. This can lead to programs that work only for the selected inputs (overfitting), or to programs that may fail for some inputs, which might be unacceptable in some domains. In contrast, our fitness function is not based on running the programs on sample data, but on an enhanced model checking procedure. While the classical model checking provides a yes/no answer to the satisfiability of the specification (thus yielding a two-valued fitness function), our *deep model checking* algorithm generated a smoother function by providing several levels of correctness. In fact, we have four levels of correctness, per each specification property, written in Linear Temporal Logic:

1. None of the executions of the program satisfy the property.
2. Some, but not all the executions of the program satisfy the property.
3. The only executions that do not satisfy the property must have infinitely many decisions that avoid a path that does satisfy the property.
4. All the executions satisfy the property.

We provided several methods for generating the various fitness levels:

- Using Streett Automata, and a strongly component analysis of the program graph [10].
- A general deep model checking logic and algorithm. [9,19].
- A technique inspired by probabilistic qualitative LTL model checking [13].

We use a fitness-proportional selection [8] that gives each program a probability of being chosen that is proportional to its fitness value. In traditional GP, after the μ programs are randomly chosen, the selection method is applied in order to decide which of them will participate in the genetic operations. The selected programs are then used in order to create a new set of μ programs that will replace the original ones.

3   Finding New Mutual Exclusion Algorithms

The first problem for which we wanted to synthesize solutions was the classical *mutual exclusion* problem [4]. The temporal specification (in Linear Temporal Logic) for the problem are given in Table 1.

Table 1. Mutual Exclusion Specification

No.	Type	Definition	Description
1	Safety	$\Box\neg(p_0$ in CS $\wedge\ p_1$ in CS)	Mutual Exclusion
2,3	Liveness	$\Box(p_{me}$ in Post $\rightarrow \Diamond(p_{me}$ in NonCS))	Progress
4,5		$\Box(p_{me}$ in Pre $\wedge\ \Box(p_{other}$ in NonCS)) $\rightarrow$ $\Diamond(p_{me}$ in CS))	No Contest
6		$\Box((p_0$ in Pre $\wedge\ p_1$ in Pre) $\rightarrow\ \Diamond(p_0$ in CS $\vee\ p_1$ in CS))	Deadlock Freedom
7,8		$\Box(p_{me}$ in Pre $\rightarrow \Diamond(p_{me}$ in CS))	Starvation Freedom
9	Safety	$\Box\neg($remote writing$)$	Single-Writer
10	Special	Bounded number of remote operations	Local-Spinning

Initially, we tried to rediscover three of the classical mutual exclusion algorithms - the *one bit* protocol (a deadlock-free algorithm for which we used properties $1-6$ from the above specification), and two starvation-free algorithms (satisfying also properties $7-8$) - *Dekker's* and *Peterson's* algorithms. Our framework (and tool) successfully discovered all of these algorithms [9], and even some interesting variants of them.

Inspired by algorithms developed by Tsay [25] and by Kessels [14], our next goal was to start from an existing algorithm, and by adding more constraints and building blocks, try to evolve into more advanced algorithms.

First, we allowed a minor asymmetry between the two processes. This is done by the operators *not0* and *not1*, which act only on one of the processes. Thus, for process 0, $not0(x) = \neg x$ while for process 1, $not0(x) = x$. This is reversed for $not1(x)$, which negates its bit operand x only in process 1, and do nothing on process 0.

As a result, the tool found two algorithms which may be considered simpler than Peterson's. The first one has only one condition in the *wait* statement, written here using the syntax of a *while* loop, although a more complicated atomic comparison, between two bits. Note that the variable turn is in fact A[2] and is renamed here turn to accord with classical presentation of the extra global bit that does not belong to a specific process.

```
Pre CS
A[me] = 1
turn = me
While (A[other] != not1(turn));
Critical Section
A[me] = 0
```

The second algorithm discovered the idea of setting the turn bit one more time after leaving the critical section. This allows the while condition to be even simpler. Tsay [25] used a similar refinement, but his algorithm needs an additional if statement, which is not used in our algorithm.

```
Pre CS
A[me] = 1
turn = not0(A[other])
While (A[2] != me);
Critical Section
A[me] = 0
turn = other
```

Next, we aimed at finding more advanced algorithms satisfying additional properties. The configuration was extended into four shared bits and two private bits (one for each process). The first requirement was that each process can change only its 2 local bits, but can read all of the 4 shared bits (the new constraint was specified as the safety property 9 in the table above). This yielded the following algorithm.

```
Pre CS
A[me] = 1
B[me] = not1(B[other])
While (A[other] == 1 and B[0] == not1(B[1]));
Critical Section
A[me] = 0
```

As can be seen, the algorithm has found the idea of using 2 bits as the "turn", were each process changes only its bit to set its turn, but compares both of them on the while loop. Finally, we added the requirement for busy waiting only on local bits (i.e. using local spins). The following algorithm (similar to Kessels') was generated, satisfying all properties from the table above.

```
Non Critical Section
A[other] = 1
B[other] = not1(B[0])
T[me] = not1(B[other])
While (A[me] == 1 and B[me] == T[me]);
Critical Section
A[other] = 0
```

4 Synthesizing Parametric Programs

Our experience with genetic program synthesis quickly hits a difficulty that stems from the limited power of model checking: there are few interesting fixed finite state programs that can also be completely specified using pure temporal logic. Most programming problems are, in fact, parametric. Model checking is undecidable even for parametric families of programs (say, with n processes, each with the same code, initialized with different parameters) even for a fixed property [1]. One may look at mutual exclusion for a parametric number of processes. Examples are, sorting, where the number of processes and the values to be sorted are the parameters, network algorithms, such as finding the leader in a set of processes (in order to reinitialize some mutual task), etc. In order to synthesize parametric concurrent programs, in particular those that have a parametric number of processes, and even a parametric architecture, we use a different genetic programming strategy.

First, we assume that a solution that is checked for a large number of instances/parameters is acceptable. This is not a guarantee of correctness, but under the prohibitive undecidability of model checking for parametric programs, at least we have a strong evidence that the solution may generalize to an arbitrary configuration. In fact, there are several works on particular cases where one can calculate the parameter size that guarantees that if all the smaller instances are correct, then any instance is correct [5]. Unfortunately, this is not a rule that can be applied to any arbitrary parametric problem. We apply a *co-evolution* based synthesis algorithm: we collect the cases that fail as counterexamples, and when suggesting a new solution, check it against the collected counterexamples. We can view this process as a genetic search for both correct programs and counterexamples. The fitness is different, of course, for both tasks: a program gets higher fitness by being close to satisfying the full set of properties, while a counterexample is obtaining a high fitness if it fails the program.

One way to observe this kind of co-evolution also as using model checking for instance of the parameters. For example, consider seeking a solution for the classical *leader election in a ring* problem, where processes initially have their own values that they can transfer around, with the goal of finding a process that has the highest value. Then, the parameters include the size of the ring, and the initial assignment of values to processes. While we can check solutions up to a certain size, and in addition, check all possible initial values, the time and state explosion is huge, for both size and permutation of initial values. We can then store each set of instances of the parameters that failed some solution, and, when checking a new candidate solution, check it against the failed instances.

In this sense, the model checking of a particular set of instances can be considered as a generalized *testing* for these values: each set of instances of the parameters provides a single finite state systems that is itself comprehensively tested using model checking. This idea can be used, independently, for model checking: for example, consider a sorting program with a parametric set of values and initial values to be sorted; for a particular size and set of values, the model checking provides automatic and exhaustive test, but the check is not exhaustive for all the array sizes or array values, but rather samples them.

5 Correcting Erroneous Program

Our method is not limited to finding new program that satisfy the given specification. In fact, we can start with the code of an existing program and try to improve or correct it. When our initial population consists of a given program, which is either non optimal, or faulty, we can start our genetic programming process with it, instead of with a completely random population. If our fitness measure includes some quantitative evaluation, the initial program may be found inferior to some new candidates that are generated. If the program is erroneous, then it would not get a very high fitness value by failing to satisfy some of the properties.

In [12] we approached the ambitious problem of correcting a known protocol for obtaining interprocess interaction called α-core [21]. The algorithm allows multiparty synchronization of several processes. It needs to function in a system that allows nondeterministic choices, which makes it challenging, as processes that may consider one possible interaction may also decide to be engaged in another interaction. The algorithm uses asynchronous message passing in order to enforce live selection of the interactions by the involved processes. This non-trivial algorithm, which is used in practice for distributed systems, contains an error. The challenges in correcting this algorithm are the following:

Size. The protocol is quite big, involving sending different messages between the controlled processes, and new processes, one per each possible multi-party interaction. These messages include announcing the willingness to be engaged in an interaction, committing an interaction, cancelling an interaction, request for commit from the interaction manager processes, as well as announcement that the interaction is now going on, or is cancelled due to the departure of at least one participant. In addition to the size of the code, the state space of such a protocol is obviously high.

Varying architecture. The protocol can run on any number of processes, each process with arbitrary number of choices to be involves in interactions, and each interaction includes any number of processes.

These difficulties make also the model checking itself undecidable [1] in general, and the model checking of a single instance, with fixed architecture, hard. In fact, we use our genetic programming approach first to find the error, and then to correct it. We use two important ideas:

1. Use the genetic engine not only to generate programs, but also to evolve different architectures on which programs can run.
2. Apply a co-evolution process, where candidate programs, and test cases (architectures) that may fail these programs, are evolved in parallel.

Specifically, the architecture for the candidate programs is also represented as code (or, equivalently, a syntactic tree) for spanning processes and their interactions, which can be subjected to genetic mutations. The fitness function directs the search into program that may falsify the specification for the current program. After finding a "bad" architecture for a program, one that causes the program to fail its specification, our next goal is to reverse the genetic programming direction, and try to automatically correct the program, where a "correct" program at this step, is one that has passed model checking against the architecture. Yet, correcting the program for the first found wrong architecture only, does not guarantee its correctness under different architectures. Therefore, we introduce a new algorithm (see Algorithm 1) which co-evolves both the candidate solution programs, and the architectures that might serve as counterexamples for those programs.

Algorithm 1: Model checking based co-evolution
MC-CoEvolution(initialProg, spec, maxArchs)

(1)	prog := initialProg
(2)	InstantList := ∅
(3)	while |archList| <maxArchs
(4)	arch := EvolveArch(prog, spec)
(5)	if arch = null
(6)	return true // prog stores a "good" program
(7)	else
(8)	add arch to archlist
(9)	prog := EvolveProg(archlist, spec)
(10)	if prog is null
(11)	return false // no "good" program was found
(12)	return false // can't add more architectures

The algorithm starts with an initial program *initProg*. This can be the existing program that needs to be corrected, or, in case that we want to synthesize some code, a randomly generated program. It is also given a specification *spec* which the program to be corrected or generated should satisfy. The algorithm then proceeds in two steps. First (lines $(4) - (8)$), the *EvolveArch* function is called. The goal of this function is to generate an architecture on which the specification *spec* will not hold. If no such architecture is found, the *EvolveArch* procedure returns *null*, and we assume (though we cannot guarantee) that the program is correct, and the algorithm terminates. Otherwise, the found architecture *arch* is added to the architecture list *archList*, and the algorithm proceeds to the second step (lines $(9) - (11)$).

In this step, the architecture list and the specification are sent to the *EvolveProg* function which tries to generate programs which satisfy the specification under *all* of the architectures on the list. If the function fails, then the algorithm terminates without success. Since the above function runs a Genetic Programming process which is probabilistic, instead of terminating the algorithm, it is possible to increase the number of iterations, or to re-run the function so a new search is initiated. If a correct program is found, the algorithm returns to the first step at line (4), on which the newly generated program is tested. At each iteration of the *while* loop, a new architecture is added to the list. This method serves two purposes. First, once a program was suggested, and refuted by a new architecture, it will not be suggested again. Second, architectures that were complex enough to fail programs at previous iterations, are good candidates to do so on future iterations as well. The allowed size of the list is limited in order to bound the running time of the algorithm.

Both *EvolveProg* and *EvolveArch* functions use genetic programming and model checking for the evolution of candidate solutions (each of them is equipped with relevant building blocks and syntactic rules), while the fitness function varies. For the evolution of programs, a combination of the methods proposed in [10,11] is used: for each LTL property, an initial fitness level is obtained by performing a deep model checking analysis. This is repeated for all the architectures in *archList*, which determines the final fitness value. For the evolution of the architectures, we reverse the goal of the fitness function, and give higher score for architectures that are having a better chances to falsify the program. At the end, the smallest architecture that manifested the failure included two processes, with two alternative communication between both of them.

6   A Tool for Genetic Programming Based on Model Checking

We constructed a tool, MCGP [13], that implements the our ideas about model checking based genetic programming. Depending on these setting, the tool can be used for several purposes:

- Setting all parts as *static* will cause the tool to just run the deep model checking algorithm on the user-defined program, and provide its detailed results.
- Setting the *init* process as *static*, and all or some of the other processes as *dynamic*, will order the tool to synthesize code according to the specified architecture. This can be used for synthesizing programs from scratch, synthesizing only some missing parts of a given partial program, or trying to correct or improve a complete given program.
- Setting the *init* process as *dynamic*, and all other processes as static, is used when trying to falsify a given parametric program by searching for a configuration that violates its specification (see [12]).
- Setting both the *init* and the program processes as *dynamic*, is used for synthesizing parametric programs, where the tool alternatively evolves various programs, and configurations under which the programs have to be satisfied.

7   Conclusions

We suggested the use of a methodology and a tool that perform a genetic programming search among versions of a program by code mutation, guided by

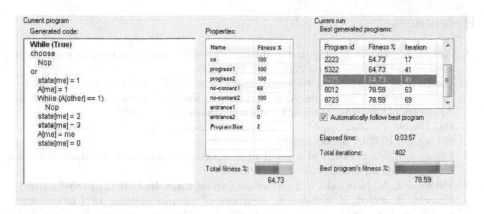

Fig. 4. User interface during synthesis of a mutual exclusion algorithm

model checking results. Code mutation is at the kernel of genetic programming (crossover is also extensively used, but we did not implement it). Our method can be used for

- synthesizing correct-by-design programs,
- finding an error in protocol with complicated architecture (where the architecture can also undergo genetic mutation),
- automatically correcting erroneous code with respect to a given specification, and
- improve code, e.g., to perform more efficiently.

We demonstrated our method on the classical mutual exclusion problem, and were able to find existing solutions, as well as new solutions.

In general, the verification of parametric systems is undecidable, and in the few methods that promise termination of the verification, quite severe restrictions are required. The same apply to code synthesis. Nevertheless, we provide a co-evolution method for synthesize parametric systems based on accumulating cases to be checked: architectures on which the synthesis failed before, or test cases based on previous counterexamples are accumulated to be checked later with new candidate solutions. As the model checking itself is undecidable, we finish if we obtain a strong enough evidence that the solution is correct on the accumulated cases.

Although our method does not guarantee termination, neither for finding the error, nor for finding a correct version of the algorithm, it is quite general and can be fine tuned through provided heuristics in a convenient human-assisted process of code correction.

An important strength of the work that is presented here is that it was implemented and applied on a complicated published protocol to find and correct an actual error.

References

1. Apt, K.R., Kozen, D.: Limits for automatic verification of finite-state concurrent systems. Inf. Process. Lett. 22(6), 307–309 (1986)
2. Banzhaf, W., Nordin, P., Keller, R.E., Francone, F.D.: Genetic Programming – An Introduction. In: On the Automatic Evolution of Computer Programs and its Applications, 3rd edn. Morgan Kaufmann, dpunkt.verlag (2001)
3. Bar-David, Y., Taubenfeld, G.: Automatic discovery of mutual exclusion algorithms. In: PODC, p. 305 (2003)
4. Dijkstra, E.W.: Solution of a problem in concurrent programming control. Commun. ACM 8(9), 569 (1965)
5. Emerson, E.A., Namjoshi, K.S.: Reasoning about rings. In: POPL, pp. 85–94 (1995)
6. Fearnley, J., Peled, D., Schewe, S.: Synthesis of succinct systems. In: Chakraborty, S., Mukund, M. (eds.) ATVA 2012. LNCS, vol. 7561, pp. 208–222. Springer, Heidelberg (2012)
7. Hoare, C.A.R.: An axiomatic basis for computer programming. Commun. ACM 12(10), 576–580 (1969)
8. Holland, J.H.: Adaptation in Natural and Artificial Systems: An Introductory Analysis with Applications to Biology, Control and Artificial Intelligence. MIT Press, Cambridge (1992)
9. Katz, G., Peled, D.: Genetic programming and model checking: Synthesizing new mutual exclusion algorithms. In: Cha, S(S.), Choi, J.-Y., Kim, M., Lee, I., Viswanathan, M. (eds.) ATVA 2008. Katz, G., Peled, D, vol. 5311, pp. 33–47. Springer, Heidelberg (2008)
10. Katz, G., Peled, D.: Model checking-based genetic programming with an application to mutual exclusion. In: Ramakrishnan, C.R., Rehof, J. (eds.) TACAS 2008. LNCS, vol. 4963, pp. 141–156. Springer, Heidelberg (2008)
11. Katz, G., Peled, D.: Synthesizing solutions to the leader election problem using model checking and genetic programming. In: Namjoshi, K., Zeller, A., Ziv, A. (eds.) HVC 2009. LNCS, vol. 6405, pp. 117–132. Springer, Heidelberg (2011)
12. Katz, G., Peled, D.: Code mutation in verification and automatic code correction. In: Esparza, J., Majumdar, R. (eds.) TACAS 2010. LNCS, vol. 6015, pp. 435–450. Springer, Heidelberg (2010)
13. Katz, G., Peled, D.: MCGP: A software synthesis tool based on model checking and genetic programming. In: Bouajjani, A., Chin, W.-N. (eds.) ATVA 2010. LNCS, vol. 6252, pp. 359–364. Springer, Heidelberg (2010)
14. Kessels, J.L.W.: Arbitration without common modifiable variables. Acta Inf. 17, 135–141 (1982)
15. Koza, J.R.: Genetic Programming: On the Programming of Computers by Means of Natural Selection. MIT Press, Cambridge (1992)
16. Kupferman, O., Vardi, M.Y.: Model checking of safety properties. Formal Methods in System Design 19(3), 291–314 (2001)
17. Manna, Z., Wolper, P.: Synthesis of communicating processes from temporal logic specifications. ACM Trans. Program. Lang. Syst. 6(1), 68–93 (1984)
18. Montana, D.J.: Strongly typed genetic programming. Evolutionary Computation 3(2), 199–230 (1995)
19. Niebert, P., Peled, D., Pnueli, A.: Discriminative model checking. In: Gupta, A., Malik, S. (eds.) CAV 2008. Niebert, P., Peled, D., Pnueli, A, vol. 5123, pp. 504–516. Springer, Heidelberg (2008)
20. Peled, D.: Software Reliability Methods. Springer (2001)

21. Perez, J.A., Corchuelo, R., Toro, M.: An order-based algorithm for implementing multiparty synchronization. Concurrency - Practice and Experience 16(12), 1173–1206 (2004)
22. Pnueli, A., Rosner, R.: On the synthesis of a reactive module. In: POPL, pp. 179–190 (1989)
23. Pnueli, A., Rosner, R.: Distributed reactive systems are hard to synthesize. In: FOCS, pp. 746–757 (1990)
24. Schwefel, H. P.P.: Evolution and Optimum Seeking: The Sixth Generation. John Wiley & Sons, Inc., New York (1993)
25. Tsay, Y.-K.: Deriving a scalable algorithm for mutual exclusion. In: Kutten, S. (ed.) DISC 1998. LNCS, vol. 1499, pp. 393–407. Springer, Heidelberg (1998)

Domain Types:
Abstract-Domain Selection Based on Variable Usage*

Sven Apel [1], Dirk Beyer [1], Karlheinz Friedberger [1],
Franco Raimondi [2], and Alexander von Rhein [1]

[1] University of Passau, Germany
[2] Middlesex University, London, UK

Abstract. The success of software model checking depends on finding an appropriate abstraction of the program to verify. The choice of the abstract domain and the analysis configuration is currently left to the user, who may not be familiar with the tradeoffs and performance details of the available abstract domains. We introduce the concept of *domain types*, which classify the program variables into types that are more fine-grained than standard declared types (e.g., 'int' and 'long') to guide the selection of an appropriate abstract domain for a model checker. Our implementation on top of an existing verification framework determines the domain type for each variable in a pre-analysis step, based on the usage of variables in the program, and then assigns each variable to an abstract domain. Based on a series of experiments on a comprehensive set of verification tasks from international verification competitions, we demonstrate that the choice of the abstract domain per variable (we consider one explicit and one symbolic domain) can substantially improve the verification in terms of performance and precision.

1 Introduction

One of the main challenges in software model checking is to automatically select, for each program variable, an abstract representation (also known as *abstract domain*) that allows to effectively prove the program correct or to identify an error path. Several abstract domains have been applied successfully to software-verification problems, with different strengths and weaknesses. Abstract domains can be based on explicit representations (e.g., hash tables for integers, memory graphs for the heap) and symbolic representations (predicates, binary decision diagrams (BDD)). For example, using an explicit-value domain [14] was efficient on many benchmarks from the recent competition on software verification [9], while using a BDD domain [15] was more efficient on event-condition-action (ECA) systems that involve only simple operations over integers in an ECA competition [30]. In the context of product-line verification, it has been shown that BDD-encodings of feature variables improve verification performance [5,24]. The key insight is that different abstract domains are successful on different programs, and for every abstract domain, we can find programs for which the abstract domain is not successful.

---

* A preliminary version was published as Technical Report MIP-1303 in May 2013 [3].

V. Bertacco and A. Legay (Eds.): HVC 2013, LNCS 8244, pp. 262–278, 2013.
© Springer International Publishing Switzerland 2013

So far, the choice of the abstract domain for a given verification problem (which often implies the choice of a certain verification tool as well) was left to the user. Our goal is to automate the choice of an effective abstract domain. We analyze the usage of program variables before the model checker starts the state-space exploration and assign each variable to a certain domain type. In addition to the declared type of a variable (e.g., int and char), the *domain type* represents information about the value range and the operations in which the variable is involved.

Our approach is based on the CPA verification framework, in which each abstract domain has a *precision* associated with it [11]. We use the domain types from the pre-analysis as guidance for assigning an abstract domain to each variable. In the experiments that we conducted to evaluate our approach, we use two abstract domains: an explicit-value domain and a BDD-based domain. For both domains, the precision is a set of variables that should be tracked in the domain. The precisions are initialized based on the variables' domain types. The domain assignment improves the overall verification performance, if each abstract domain tracks the kind of variables that it is suited for.

The analysis is implemented in the verification framework CPACHECKER [13], which implements configurable program analysis for C programs and provides abstract domains for an explicit-value analysis and a BDD-based analysis (we do not use the predicate analysis). We evaluate our approach on six sets of verification tasks from different application domains (a total of 2 435 files) that have been used by recent international competitions on software model checking (SV-COMP 2013 [9], RERS Challenge 2012 [30]).

Our evaluation reveals that the programs in the benchmark sets contain a significant number of variables that have a much narrower domain type than the declared type of the variable. We also demonstrate that the verification performance improves if these variables are tracked using a more suitable abstract domain, compared to using a single abstract domain for all variables. All results are available on the supplementary website [1].

Example. We illustrate our approach on the example program in Fig. 1. The program contains three variables that are declared by the programmer as int. The variables are used in different ways: the variable enabled is used as a boolean; the variables a and b are numeric and used in a greater-than comparison, b is also used in a multiplication. Neither the explicit-value analysis nor the BDD-based analysis is able to efficiently verify such a program: The explicit-value domain is perfectly suited to handle variable b, because b has a concrete value, and the multiplication

```
int enabled, a, b;
b = 20;
if (enabled) {
  if (a > 5) {
    if (a == 0) {
      b = 0;
    }
    assert (b * b > 200);
  }
}
```

Fig. 1. Example with int variables of different domain types

and the greater-than comparison can easily be computed; BDDs are known to be inefficient for multiplication [31]. The BDD domain can efficiently encode the variables enabled and a, whereas the explicit-value analysis is not good at encoding facts like a > 5.

---

[1] http://www.sosy-lab.org/projects/domaintypes/

Thus, without information about variable a, the explicit-value analysis does not know the value of variable b and cannot determine the result of the multiplication.

It has been proposed to use several abstract domains in parallel, with each domain handling all variables (e.g. [17]). If the domains are well communicating (reduced product), this could solve the verification task, but the load on each domain would be unnecessarily high, because every domain has to handle more variables than necessary.

Contributions. We make the following contributions:

– We introduced the concept of domain types and developed a pre-analysis that computes the domain types for all program variables.
– We extended an existing verification framework to use the two abstract domains 'explicit-value' and 'BDD' in parallel, while controlling the precision of each abstract domain (the variables to track) separately, based on domain types.
– We evaluate our approach on verification benchmarks from recent international software-verification competitions.

2   Background

We informally explain the concepts that we use, and provide references to the literature for details. As context, we assume to verify C programs with integer variables.

Abstract Domains and Program Analysis. Abstraction-based software model checkers automatically extract an abstract model of the subject program and explore this model using one or more abstract domains. An abstract domain represents certain aspects of the concrete program's states that the state exploration is supposed to track [1]. Different abstract domains can track different aspects of the program state space and complement each other. For example, a *shape domain* [12, 26, 34] stores, for each tracked pointer, the shape of the pointed-to data structures on the heap. Another example is the *explicit-value domain* that, for each tracked variable, tracks the explicit value of the variable [14, 28, 29]. These two examples illustrate that abstract domains can represent different information. However, it is also possible to use different abstract domains to represent the same information in different ways. Consider a program in which the value of variable x ranges from 3 to 9. This can be stored by an *interval domain* [17] using the abstract state $x \mapsto [3, 9]$, or by a *predicate domain* [7, 10, 27] using the abstract state $x \geq 3 \wedge x \leq 9$.

Every abstract domain consists of (1) a representation of sets of concrete states, defining the abstract states (lattice elements), (2) an operator to decide if one abstract state subsumes another abstract state (partial order), and (3) an operator that combines two abstract states into a new abstract state that represents both (join). Software verifiers use one or several abstract domains to represent the states of the program. The characteristics of the abstract domain have implications on the effectivity (low number of failures and false results) and efficiency (performance) of the program analysis.

Precision. Each abstract domain can operate at different levels of abstraction (i.e., it can be more fine-grained or more coarse-grained). The level of abstraction of an abstract domain is determined by the *abstraction precision*, which controls if the analysis is coarse or fine. For example, the precision of the shape domain could instruct the analysis which pointers to track and how large a shape can maximally grow; the precision of the

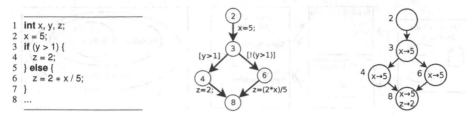

Fig. 2. Example program (left), control-flow automaton (CFA) that represents the program (middle), and abstract reachability graph (ARG, right) for the explicit-value domain. CFA edges model assume operations (e.g., [y > 1]) and assignment operations (e.g., z = 2;).

predicate domain is a set of predicates to track that can, for example, grow by adding predicates during refinement steps [23].

Next, we describe the two abstract domains that we consider in our experiments.

Explicit-Value Domain. The explicit-value domain stores explicit values for program variables. Each abstract state of this abstract domain is a map that assigns to each program variable that occurs in the precision, an integer value (or no value if an explicit value cannot be determined). For example, consider the code, the control-flow automaton (CFA), and the abstract reachability graph (ARG) in Fig. 2: the assignment of value 5 to variable x is stored in an abstract state for CFA node 3. Then, a conditional statement starts two possible execution paths, which the verifier has to explore. The explicit-value domain does not store a value for variable y, because there is no explicit value for y. After both branches of the CFA are explored, the ARG contains a 'frontier' abstract state that is the result of joining the abstract successors from both branches for CFA node 8. The explicit-value domain might suffer from a loss of information if no explicit values can be determined (e.g., for y > 1). On the one hand, this introduces imprecision and potentially false alarms. On the other hand, if values are present, all operations can be executed extremely fast. The precision controls which variables are tracked in the explicit-value domain. For the code fragment in Fig. 2, we could use a precision $\{x, z\}$ and omit y, if we knew beforehand that it is not necessary to represent variable y.

BDD Domain. The BDD domain stores information about program variables using binary decision diagrams (BDD). Each abstract state in the BDD domain is a BDD that represents a predicate over the variable values [18]. BDDs can be efficient in representing predicates and performing boolean operations. Because of this characteristic, BDDs have been used in model checking of systems with a large number of boolean variables, most prominently in hardware verification [20, 31]. Values of integer variables can be represented by BDDs using a binary encoding of the values (representing the integer values using, e.g., 32 boolean BDD variables). We can represent a variable with even fewer BDD variables if we can statically determine the set of values that the variable might hold at run time and that (non-) equality is the only arithmetical operation (nominal scale [37]). In our example, there is only one value for variable x (i.e., x = 5), and thus we need only one boolean variable for program variable x. The size of the BDD —and thus, the performance of the BDD operations— depends on the number of BDD variables; therefore, it is important to keep the number of BDD variables small.

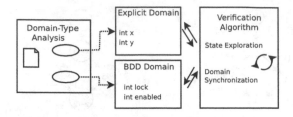

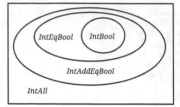

Fig. 3. A model-checking engine with two abstract domains and domain-type analysis

Fig. 4. Hierarchy of domain types

The abstraction precision of the BDD domain is (also) a set of program variables that an analysis should track using this abstract domain. Considering again our example of Fig. 2, if we knew beforehand that the explicit-value domain can efficiently represent variables x and z, we would not include them in the BDD precision, which would result in precision {y} for the BDD domain, and thus we would need only BDD variables for y. Because the performance of BDD operations decreases with a growing number of variables, the BDD domain should be used only for variables that the explicit-value analysis can not efficiently track. To achieve the goal of a better assignment of program variables to abstract domains, we introduce the concept of domain types in Section 3.

3 Domain Types

The domain-type-based verification process consists of three steps: (1) The subject program is type-checked to determine the domain type for each variable (pre-analysis). (2) Each variable is mapped to an abstract domain that the analysis will use to represent information about the variable. (3) The actual verification procedure with the initialized precisions per abstract domain is started. Fig. 3 illustrates the approach of a verification engine that is based on domain types. The state-exploration algorithm uses several abstract domains to represent the state space of the program.

3.1 Classification

In many statically-typed programming languages, variables are declared to be of a certain type. The type determines which values can be stored in the variable and which operators are allowed on the variable. For the assignment of abstract domains to variables in a program analysis, more specific information on the variables are valuable, in particular, which of the operators that the static type allows are actually applied to the variable. For example, consider boolean variables in the programming language C. The language C does not provide a type 'boolean'. In C, the boolean values true and false are represented by the integer values 1 and 0, respectively. When integer variables are read, the value 0 is interpreted as false and all other values

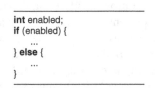

```
int enabled;
if (enabled) {
    ...
} else {
    ...
}
```

Fig. 5. Using an integer variable as boolean in C

SYNTAX DEFINITION

op	::=		*program operations:*
	|	[expr]	*assume*
	|	x = expr;	*assignment*
expr	::=		*expressions:*
	|	val	*value*
	|	! expr	*negation*
	|	expr == expr	*equality*
	|	expr != expr	*inequality*
	|	expr + expr	*addition*
	|	expr − expr	*subtraction*
	|	expr * expr	*multiplication*
	|	expr / expr	*division*
val	::=		*values:*
		0	*zero*
	|	c	*non-zero constant*
	|	x	*variable*

TYPE RULES FOR PROGRAM OPERATIONS

$$\frac{\text{expr} : \tau}{[\,\text{expr}\,] : \tau} \quad \text{(ASSUME)}$$

$$\frac{\text{expr} : \tau}{\text{x} = \text{expr}; \; : \tau} \quad \text{(ASSIGNMENT)}$$

$$\frac{uses(\text{op}_1, \text{x}) \quad \text{op}_1 : \tau_1 \quad uses(\text{op}_2, \text{x}) \quad \text{op}_2 : \tau_2}{\text{op}_1 : max(\{\tau_1, \tau_2\})} \quad \text{(CLOSURE)}$$

$$\frac{uses(\text{op}, \text{x}) \quad \text{op} : \tau}{\text{x} : \tau} \quad \text{(VARUSAGE)}$$

TYPE RULES FOR EXPRESSIONS

$$\frac{\text{expr} : \tau}{!\,\text{expr} : max(\{\tau, IntBool\})} \quad \text{(NEGBOOL)}$$

$$\frac{\text{val} : \tau}{\begin{array}{l}\text{val} == 0 : max(\{\tau, IntBool\})\\ \text{val} != 0 : max(\{\tau, IntBool\})\end{array}} \quad \text{(EQBOOL)}$$

$$\frac{\text{expr}_1 : \tau_1 \quad \text{expr}_2 : \tau_2}{\begin{array}{l}\text{expr}_1 == \text{expr}_2 : max(\{\tau_1, \tau_2, IntEqBool\})\\ \text{expr}_1 != \text{expr}_2 : max(\{\tau_1, \tau_2, IntEqBool\})\end{array}} \quad \text{(EQINT)}$$

$$\frac{\text{expr}_1 : \tau_1 \quad \text{expr}_2 : \tau_2}{\begin{array}{l}\text{expr}_1 + \text{expr}_2 : max(\{\tau_1, \tau_2, IntAddEqBool\})\\ \text{expr}_1 - \text{expr}_2 : max(\{\tau_1, \tau_2, IntAddEqBool\})\end{array}} \quad \text{(ADD)}$$

$$\frac{\text{expr}_1 : \tau_1 \quad \text{expr}_2 : \tau_2}{\begin{array}{l}\text{expr}_1 * \text{expr}_2 : max(\{\tau_1, \tau_2, IntAll\})\\ \text{expr}_1 / \text{expr}_2 : max(\{\tau_1, \tau_2, IntAll\})\end{array}} \quad \text{(MULT)}$$

DESCRIPTION

Predicate $uses(\text{op}, \text{x})$ states that a program operation op references a variable x; function $max(\{\tau_1, \ldots, \tau_n\})$ returns the maximal type for our defined set of types and the following (transitiv) type relation: $IntBool < IntEqBool < IntAddEqBool < IntAll$; a type constraint obj : τ states that the type of obj is equal or greater than τ, where obj can be either an expression, a program operation, or a variable; note that this first proposal for typing rules is very coarse and can be significantly refined, e.g., by eliminating the closure.

Fig. 6. Syntax definition and domain-type rules; a program is represented as control-flow automaton (CFA) [10], where nodes represent control-flow locations and edges represent program operations that are executed when control flows from one control-flow location to the next; CPACHECKER supports C, we use this largely abbreviated and adjusted grammar of program operations to simplify the presentation.

are interpreted as true. Let us consider the code in Fig. 5: The expression enabled in the if condition is internally expanded to the expression enabled != 0 [2]. As described in Sect. 2, such a variable should be represented in a BDD by one boolean variable, not by 32 boolean variables. Therefore, we introduce a domain type *IntBool* that represents this more precise type. To determine whether an integer variable has actually the domain type *IntBool*, our pre-analysis inspects all occurrences of the variable in the C expressions. If a variable is found to be of domain type *IntBool*, this fact can be considered during the assignment of the abstract domain, and thus the variable can be represented by data structures that efficiently store boolean values during the verification. Fig. 4 shows the four domain types that we consider in the static pre-analysis (more domain types are of course possible, but not yet evaluated). The pre-analysis assigns every program variable to one of these domain types, from which an appropriate abstract domain can be derived.

Other programming languages (e.g., JAVA) provide more restrictive types than C does, such as boolean and byte, but for the purpose of assigning the best abstract domain, even more precise information is beneficial. In dynamically-typed or even untyped languages, types of variables are unknown before program execution. A static analysis of domain types can lead to considerable improvements of the verification process, because it can infer more specific domain types, and thus, choose more efficient algorithms and data structures for representing abstract states.

3.2 Pre-analysis

In the first step, a static pre-analysis computes the domain type for each program variable, according to the type system in Fig. 6. For each program operation (either ASSUME or ASSIGNMENT), the analysis determines the maximal domain type that is needed according to the expression operators that occur in the program operation. Then, it constructs the type closure over all program operations that use some common variables, to determine the maximal domain type that the program operations for a program variable require. The type of a variable x is the (maximal) domain type of program operations that use variable x. For example, the program operations x == 0, x == x + 1, and y == x * (z + x) are of the domain types $IntBool$, $IntAddEqBool$, and $IntAll$, respectively. If all program operations occur in the program, the closure includes all of them (because all use variable x), and thus the domain type of x, y, and z is $IntAll$.

The domain type of an expression is $IntBool$ if all operators in the expression are negations (!) or comparisons with zero (== 0 and != 0). If an expression also contains equality tests with non-zero constant values or other variables (==, !=), then the domain type of the expression is $IntEqBool$. If an expression, in addition, contains linear arithmetic (+, −), arbitrary comparisons (==, !=, <, >, <=, >=), or bit operators (&, |, ^), then the domain type is $IntAddEqBool$ [2]. Expressions that contain any other operators (e.g., multiplication, division) are of the most general domain type $IntAll$.

The four domain types are in subtype relation, as illustrated in Fig. 4. Each variable that is of type $IntBool$ is also of the domain types $IntEqBool$, $IntAddEqBool$, and $IntAll$. The type system assigns the strongest (most restrictive, least) possible type that satisfies the type rules (i.e., the type system assigns domain type $IntBool$ instead of $IntAddEqBool$ if possible). To be able to refer to variables that are of a certain domain type and *not* of the corresponding weaker domain type (e.g., variables that are in $IntAddEqBool$ and not in $IntEqBool$), we introduce four new domain types, for brevity:

$$Bool = IntBool$$
$$Eq = IntEqBool \setminus IntBool$$
$$Add = IntAddEqBool \setminus IntEqBool$$
$$Other = IntAll \setminus IntAddEqBool$$

3.3 Domain Assignment

Once the domain type has been determined for each program variable, each domain type is assigned to a certain abstract domain that the analysis uses to track the variables

[2] The operators <, >, <=, >=, <<, >>, &, |, and ^ are omitted in the type rules in Fig. 6 for brevity.

of that domain type. Therefore, we define a *domain assignment* d to be a map that assigns an abstract domain to each domain type. To setup the program analysis, we add all variables of a domain type t to the abstraction precision of the abstract domain $d(t)$. In principle, every abstract domain can represent any variable, but each abstract domain has certain strengths and weaknesses. A perfect domain assignment would map each domain type to the abstract domain that is most appropriate for representing values of the variables.

It seems straightforward to assign the BDD domain to domain type *Bool*. The BDD domain can efficiently represent complex boolean combinations of variables, but is sensitive to the number of represented variables. We can also assign the BDD domain to the domain types Eq and *Add*. For domain type Eq, we know from the properties of the domain type that those variables only hold a limited and static set of values. Therefore, we can enumerate these values and represent them by $\log_2(n)$ BDD variables, where n is the number of values. The explicit-value domain can in principle be used for all domain types, but the more different combinations of variable assignments need to be distinguished in the analysis, the larger the state space grows, perhaps resulting in an out-of-memory exception. Moreover, the explicit-value domain is not appropriate for analyzing uninitialized variables.

In our experiments, we show that different domain assignments have significantly different performance characteristics for different sets of verification tasks. Automatically selecting an optimal domain assignment remains an open research problem. The goal of this paper is to show that the concept of domain types provides a promising technique to approach the problem.

4   Experimental Evaluation

To evaluate the domain-type-based analysis approach, we conduct a series of experiments with different configurations on a diverse set of verification tasks. The results provide evidence that the chosen domain assignment has a significant impact on effectiveness and efficiency. In particular, we address the following issues:

Domain Types. The subject systems contain a sufficient set of integer variables such that a domain-type analysis is able to classify them into more specific domain types.
Variable Partitioning. The verification performance significantly changes if variables are represented by different abstract domains, compared to representing all variables with the same abstract domain.
Advantage of Combinations. Using the BDD domain for some variables (e.g., all variables of the domain types *Bool* and Eq) and the explicit-value domain for other variables can improve the verification performance.

4.1   Implementation

For our experiments, we extended the open verification framework CPACHECKER [13], which provides various abstract domains and supports the concept of abstraction precisions in a modular way, such that it is easy to extend and configure. The tool is applicable to an extensive set of verification benchmarks, because it participated in the competition on software verification. This makes it possible to evaluate our approach on a large set of representative programs.

Explicit-Value Domain. We use the default explicit-value domain that is already implemented in CPACHECKER [14]. It uses a hash-map to associate variables with values. This implementation is efficient in handling variables with few different values that are used in complex operations.

BDD Domain. We extended CPACHECKER's BDD domain [15] to use —depending on the domain type— specialized encodings of variables in the BDD. For domain type *Bool*, we use exactly one BDD variable per program variable. For variables of domain type *Add*, we use 32 BDD variables to represent one program variable (we omit the details of bit-precise analysis). For variables of domain type *Eq*, we know from the pre-analysis how many different values the variable can hold. Therefore, we can re-map the values to a new set of values with the same cardinality (nominal scale [37]), which needs considerably fewer BDD variables (compared to 32 BDD variables). We use a simple bijective map from the original constants in the program to a (smaller, successive) set of integer values encoded with BDD variables. We also encode information about equality of uninitialized *Eq* variables (for example, in the expression x==y). To achieve this, we reserve a value in the encoding for each of the *Eq* variables. In total, we use $log_2(n+m)$ BDD variables per *Eq* program variable, where n is the number of program constants and m is the number of *Eq* variables.

4.2 Experimental Setup

We performed all experiments on a Ubuntu 12.04 (64-bit) system (LINUX 3.2 as kernel and OpenJDK 1.7 as JAVA VM) with a 3.4 GHz Quad Core processor (Intel Core i7-2600). Each verification run was limited to 2 cores, 15 GB of memory, and 15 min of CPU time. We used the version of CPACHECKER that is available as revision tag cpachecker-1.2.7-hvc13. Each verification task was verified using five different configurations:

Explicit: This configuration tracks all variables with the explicit-value domain.

BDD-IntBool: This configuration uses both abstract domains [3]; all variables of domain type *IntBool* are in the precision of the BDD domain and all other variables are in the precision of the explicit-value analysis.

BDD-IntEqBool: This configuration uses both abstract domains; all variables of domain type *IntEqBool* are in the precision of the BDD domain and all other variables are in the precision of the explicit-value domain.

BDD-IntAddEqBool: This configuration uses both abstract domains; all variables of domain type *IntAddEqBool* are in the precision of the BDD domain and all other variables are in the precision of the explicit-value domain.

BDD: This configuration tracks all variables with the BDD domain.

---

[3] We expected that the combined configurations (*BDD-IntBool*, *BDD-IntEqBool*, and *BDD-IntAddEqBool*) would suffer from the overhead of running two abstract domains. We measured this overhead in separate experiments (running one of the domains with empty precision) and found that the impact is negligible.

4.3   Verification Tasks

We evaluate our approach on six benchmark sets that, in total, consist of 2435 verification tasks. The benchmark sets are (number of verification tasks in parentheses):

CONTROL FLOW AND INTEGER VARIABLES (94)	LOOPS (79)
DEVICE DRIVERS LINUX 64-BIT (1 237)	SYSTEMC (62)
ECA (366)	PRODUCT LINES (597)

All verification tasks of the benchmark sets have been used in international competitions of software-verification tools [9, 30]; they are publicly available via the competition repository or the CPACHECKER repository [4]. The SV-COMP benchmark suite is the most comprehensive and diverse suite of this kind that currently exists. It covers various application domains, such as device drivers, software product lines, and event-condition-action-systems simulation.

The following description of the systems is partly taken from the report on the first competition on software verification [8]. Unless stated otherwise, the systems are taken from the 2013 edition of the competition. The set CONTROL FLOW AND INTEGER VARIABLES contains, among others, verification tasks that are based on device drivers from the WINDOWS NT kernel and verification tasks that represent the connection-handshake protocol between SSH server and clients with protocol-specific specifications. The set DEVICE DRIVERS LINUX 64-BIT contains verification tasks that are based on device drivers from the LINUX kernel. The verification tasks in the set SYS-TEMC are provided by the SYCMC project [21] and were taken (with some changes) from the SYSTEMC distribution. The benchmark set ECA contains event-condition-action (ECA) programs, a kind of systems that is often used in sensor-actor systems. The verification tasks in our benchmark set have been used in the RERS Grey-Box Challenge 2012 [30] on verifying ECA systems. The LOOPS benchmark set consists of verification tasks that require the analysis of loops with non-static loop bounds. The benchmark set PRODUCT LINES models three software product lines used in feature-interaction detection [5].

Domain Types. To evaluate whether we can assign a non-trivial set of variables to specific domain types, we measured how many variables could be classified as *Bool*, *Eq* or *Add* per benchmark set. We were able to classify as *Bool*, *Eq* or *Add*, on average, 60 % for CONTROL FLOW AND INTEGER VARIABLES, 26 % for DEVICE DRIVERS LINUX 64-BIT, 64 % for LOOPS, 52 % for PRODUCT LINES, 99 % for SYSTEMC, and 100 % for ECA of all program variables. This confirms that there is always a set of variables that have potential for improvement by alternative domain assignments. In most benchmark sets, the domain type with the largest number of variables is *Eq*. We expect that optimizations for the domain type *Eq* pay off, especially, in the benchmark sets ECA and SYSTEMC, because this domain type covers a large part of the variables in these sets. The benchmark set SYSTEMC also has a high number of *Add* variables in a significant number of verification tasks, so we expect a performance difference for the different domain assignments especially for this domain type.

---

[4] http://cpachecker.sosy-lab.org/

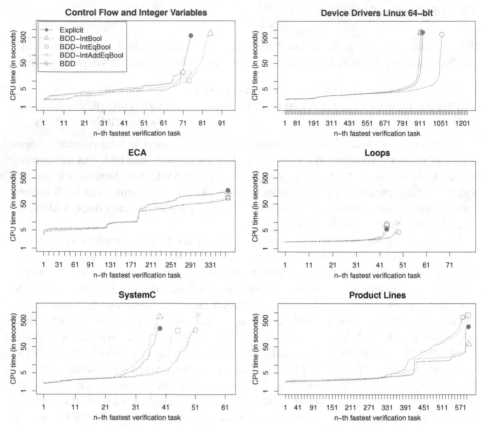

Fig. 7. The quantile plots show the performance of different configurations; each picture represents the data for one benchmark set; each data point (x, y) shows the x-th fastest verification run that needed y seconds of CPU time; the y-axes use logarithmic scales

4.4 Results

Due to the huge amount of verification results, we cannot provide the raw data of all verification runs. Instead, we discuss results aggregated by categories and configurations in Fig. 7. The diagrams show the performance of the configurations (*Explicit, BDD-IntBool, BDD-IntEqBool, BDD-IntAddEqBool*, and *BDD*) in quantile plots for each benchmark set. A point (x, y) in a quantile plot states that the x-th fastest verification run of the respective configuration took y seconds of CPU time. The right-most x value of a configuration indicates the total number of correctly solved verification tasks. The area below the graph is proportional to the accumulated verification time. We also provide a supplementary web page[5], where the detailed results of all verification runs (including the raw data and the log files) are available for download and as interactive plots.

---

[5] http://www.sosy-lab.org/projects/domaintypes/

Effectiveness. Figure 7 witnesses that many tasks are difficult to verify. For example, in the benchmark set LOOPS, most configurations solve only about half of the tasks correctly. Failures are caused by timeouts, out-of-memory exceptions, or limitations of the implemented abstract domains. The combined configurations often demonstrate good effectiveness results. In several benchmark sets, the configuration *BDD-IntBool* is among the configurations that can verify most files correctly (have one of the highest x values). However, there is no clear winner in terms of effectiveness, which suggests to further investigate verification based on domain types. The first plot (CONTROL FLOW AND INTEGER VARIABLES) demonstrates that using combinations of abstract domains allows solving verification tasks that are not solvable by one abstract domain alone.

Efficiency. The benchmark set CONTROL FLOW AND INTEGER VARIABLES covers a diverse set of verification tasks. Among others, it contains drivers of the WINDOWS NT kernel and SSH benchmarks. The plot (Fig. 7) shows that the configurations *BDD-IntEqBool* and *BDD-IntAddEqBool* are fast on many of the files, and that configuration *BDD-IntBool* can solve more tasks than any other configuration. This result can be explained by investigating the number of variables per domain type: the verification tasks in this category have many variables of domain types that can be efficiently handled in the BDD domain (*Bool*, *Eq*, *Add*). A certain set of verification tasks can only be solved using the configuration *BDD-IntBool*. These verification tasks illustrate a situation where two variables of types Eq and $Other$ interact in a special pattern. The variables must be handled by the same domain to verify the file. Only the configurations *Explicit* and *BDD-IntBool* track both variables in the explicit domain and compute a correct verification result. Configuration *Explicit* fails on other tasks in this set, such that its effect on these tasks cannot be seen easily in the plot.

On the benchmark set DEVICE DRIVERS LINUX 64-BIT, all configurations, except the *BDD* configuration, show identical performance. Configuration *BDD* performs so well because some of the $Other$ variables, which are ignored in configuration *BDD*, do not have an effect on the verification result. It would be interesting to combine our approach with CEGAR [23] (where such variables would be ignored in all configurations). The combination configurations perform similarly because only 26 % of all variables have been classified as $IntAddEqBool$, and therefore these tasks do not have much potential for the domain-type optimization.

For the benchmark set ECA, the configurations that encode Eq variables in BDDs are most efficient. All variables in the ECA verification tasks are of domain type Eq, and therefore the configurations that represent Eq variables with the BDD domain are performing best (*BDD-IntEqBool*, *BDD-IntAddEqBool*, and *BDD*). This indicates that tracking Eq variables with BDDs can be beneficial. The configurations *Explicit* and *BDD-IntBool* perform worse, because they represent the variables of domain type Eq using the explicit-value domain. The performance result is in line with the results of a recent paper on BDD-based software model checking [15].

In the benchmark set LOOPS, the *BDD-IntAddEqBool* and *BDD* configurations can solve a specific group of tasks that the other configurations can not solve. These tasks model a token-ring architecture with a varying number of nodes. The verification tasks each contain pairs of Add variables that are difficult to track with the explicit-value domain, because they are not initialized at program start. One of the variables is assigned to the other, then both are incremented (which makes them *Add*), and then the values are compared again. This unique usage profile requires to represent these variables in the BDD domain, which explains the results.

The benchmark set SYSTEMC shows that the configurations *BDD-IntAddEqBool* and *BDD-IntEqBool* can verify a considerable number of tasks more than the other combination configuration and configuration *Explicit*. This is easy to understand: the tasks contain many $IntEqBool$ (avg. 93 %) and $IntAddEqBool$ (avg. 99 %) variables. This result shows that it can be extremely efficient to track such variables with BDDs. The good performance of configuration *BDD* shows that the non-$IntAddEqBool$ variables can be ignored during verification.

The configuration *BDD-IntBool* performs well on the verification tasks in benchmark set PRODUCT LINES. The benchmark set has been used for research projects on product-line verification [4, 5], from which we know that these files contain many variables of type $Bool$ and Eq. Some of the files that are most difficult to verify contain $Bool$ variables that guide the control flow and are critical for the verification process. Therefore, it is no surprise that the *BDD-IntBool* configuration performs best on these tasks.

4.5 Discussion

Our experimental study has shown that the performance of the combined configurations (*BDD-IntBool*, *BDD-IntEqBool*, and *BDD-IntAddEqBool*) depends heavily on the domain types of the variables in the program. If the verification tasks contain variables of domain type $IntAddEqBool$, then representing these variables with the BDD domain can significantly improve the performance.

The experiments have also shown that configuration *BDD* exhibits a good performance on many verification tasks, even though it cannot track variables of domain type $Other$. This means that variables of domain type $Other$ are ignored during verification, and still the verification result is correct. But, in the interest of soundness and reliable results, we are more interested in configurations without obvious 'blind spots'.

Let us briefly re-visit —based on the experimental results— the issues that we listed at the beginning of the section. The first issue concerning the domain types has already been discussed (Sect. 4.3). Concerning the variable–domain mapping, our experiments confirm that analyzing variables of different domain types with different abstract domains can make a huge difference, in terms of effectiveness and efficiency. Combined configurations sometimes outperform the single-domain configurations (only explicit-value domain or only BDD domain) on several benchmark sets. The configuration *BDD* performs well on most benchmark sets, in particular on the DEVICE DRIVERS LINUX 64-BIT tasks. However, it is apparent that including the support of the explicit analysis for $Other$ variables is critical to obtain reliable verification results. Overall, it might be beneficial to use the BDD domain for variables of domain type $IntAddEqBool$, and the explicit-value domain for the $Others$. This is confirmed by the performance of configurations *BDD-IntEqBool* and *BDD-IntAddEqBool*.

5 Related Work

We infer domain types for program variables according to their usage in program operations. This principle is also used by the type- and memory-safety analysis of C programs with *liquid types* [33]. There, a static program analysis is used to determine, for each variable, a predicate that restricts the possible values of the variable (the *liquid type*). In a second step, each usage of the variable is checked for type safety, or if it could lead to an unsafe memory access. In contrast to domain types, *liquid types* use a predicate for each variable. *Liquid types* are fine-grained, domain types are coarse-grained in comparison, but the granularity is flexible in both approaches. Our type checker for domain types does not depend on an SMT solver, which is an advantage in terms of computational complexity.

Roles of variables are used to analyze programs submitted by students [16]. Program slicing and data-flow analysis is applied to determine the role of each variable (e.g., *constant* or *loop index*). The role is then compared to the role that the students have assigned to the variables. Variable roles are also used to understand COBOL programs [38, 39], to understand novice-level programs [35], and to classify programs into categories [25]. These works on variable roles fall into the area of automated program comprehension. The rather strong behavioral variable types might be interesting to extend our work.

JAVA PATHFINDER [40] has an extension that combines the standard explicit analysis with a BDD-based analysis for boolean variables [5, 32]. In that approach, the variables that are to be tracked by BDDs were manually selected, based on domain knowledge. Our new approach handles a broader set of domain types and categorizes them automatically.

BEBOP [6], a model checker for boolean programs, encodes all program variables (only booleans, in this case) in BDDs, and uses explicit-state exploration for the program counter. Our domain-type analysis would correctly classify all variables as *Bool* and encode them with BDDs; thus, we subsume this approach. A similar strategy was followed by others [22].

A hybrid approach combining explicit and BDD-based representations analyzes the program variables with BDDs and the states of the property automaton explicitly [36]. In our setting, this translates to encoding all program variables in BDDs, because the property automaton runs separately and explicitly in parallel in CPACHECKER. This case can be represented in our general framework as configuration *BDD*.

The two symbolic domains BDDs and Presburger formulas have been previously used as representation for boolean and integer variables [19]. The approach was evaluated on two systems, a control software for a nuclear reactor's cooling system and a simplified transport-protocol specification. In contrast to our work, this work is not based on a separate analysis to determine domain types of variables, but includes the type analysis in the actual model-checking process. By performing the domain-type analysis in advance, we avoid overhead during the model-checking process.

6 Conclusion

We introduced the concept of *domain types*, which makes it possible to assign variables to certain abstract domains based on their usage in program operations. We define a static pre-analysis that maps each variable of type 'integer' to one of four more specific domain types, which reflect the usage of variables in the program.

We performed many experiments with two abstract domains, to demonstrate that the domain assignment based on domain types has a significant impact on the effectiveness and efficiency of the verification process. We considered five domain assignments: one for each considered abstract domain that tracks all program variables in one single abstract domain, without considering the different domain types, and three with different assignments of the variables to the two abstract domains according to the domain type.

A key insight is that the concept of domain types is a simple yet powerful technique to create verification tools that implement a better choice for the domain assignment. State-of-the-art is to use either one single abstract domain, or a fixed combination of abstract domains that adjust precisions via CEGAR or otherwise dynamically, during the verification run. Our benchmark set contains a significant number of variables for which we can determine different, narrower domain types. The domain type $IntEqBool$ (and even more its subtype $IntBool$) dramatically decreases the size of the internal BDD representation of the variable assignments, and thus can lead to a significant improvement in verification efficiency. Overall, our experiments show that performance can be improved substantially if the variables are tracked in an abstract domain that is suitable for the domain type of the variable. Not only the performance is improved: combinations of abstract domains make it possible to solve verification problems that are not solvable using one abstract domain alone.

Acknowledgements. S. Apel and A. von Rhein have been supported by the DFG grants AP 206/2, AP 206/4, and AP 206/5.

References

1. Aho, A.V., Sethi, R., Ullman, J.D.: Compilers: Principles, Techniques, and Tools. Addison-Wesley (1986)
2. American National Standards Institute. ANSI/ISO/ IEC 9899-1999: Programming Languages — C. American National Standards Institute, 1430 Broadway, New York, USA (1999)
3. Apel, S., Beyer, D., Friedberger, K., Raimondi, F., von Rhein, A.: Domain types: Selecting abstractions based on variable usage. Technical Report MIP-1303, University of Passau (2013), http://arxiv.org/abs/1305.6640
4. Apel, S., Speidel, H., Wendler, P., von Rhein, A., Beyer, D.: Detection of feature interactions using feature-aware verification. In: Proc. ASE, pp. 372–375. IEEE (2011)
5. Apel, S., von Rhein, A., Wendler, P., Größlinger, A.: Strategies for product-line verification: Case studies and experiments. In: Proc. ICSE, pp. 482–491. IEEE (2013)
6. Ball, T., Rajamani, S.: Bebop: A symbolic model checker for boolean programs. In: Proc. SPIN, pp. 113–130 (2000)
7. Ball, T., Rajamani, S.K.: The SLAM project: Debugging system software via static analysis. In: Proc. POPL, pp. 1–3. ACM (2002)
8. Beyer, D.: Competition on software verification (SV-COMP). In: Flanagan, C., König, B. (eds.) TACAS 2012. LNCS, vol. 7214, pp. 504–524. Springer, Heidelberg (2012)
9. Beyer, D.: Second competition on software verification. In: Piterman, N., Smolka, S.A. (eds.) TACAS 2013 (ETAPS 2013). LNCS, vol. 7795, pp. 594–609. Springer, Heidelberg (2013)

10. Beyer, D., Henzinger, T.A., Jhala, R., Majumdar, R.: The software model checker BLAST. Int. J. Softw. Tools Technol. Transfer 9(5-6), 505–525 (2007)
11. Beyer, D., Henzinger, T.A., Théoduloz, G.: Program analysis with dynamic precision adjustment. In: Proc. ASE, pp. 29–38. IEEE (2008)
12. Beyer, D., Henzinger, T.A., Théoduloz, G., Zufferey, D.: Shape refinement through explicit heap analysis. In: Rosenblum, D.S., Taentzer, G. (eds.) FASE 2010. LNCS, vol. 6013, pp. 263–277. Springer, Heidelberg (2010)
13. Beyer, D., Keremoglu, M.E.: CPACHECKER: A tool for configurable software verification. In: Gopalakrishnan, G., Qadeer, S. (eds.) CAV 2011. LNCS, vol. 6806, pp. 184–190. Springer, Heidelberg (2011)
14. Beyer, D., Löwe, S.: Explicit-state software model checking based on CEGAR and interpolation. In: Cortellessa, V., Varró, D. (eds.) FASE 2013 (ETAPS 2013). LNCS, vol. 7793, pp. 146–162. Springer, Heidelberg (2013)
15. Beyer, D., Stahlbauer, A.: BDD-Based Software Model Checking with CPACHECKER. In: Kučera, A., Henzinger, T.A., Nešetřil, J., Vojnar, T., Antoš, D. (eds.) MEMICS 2012. LNCS, vol. 7721, pp. 1–11. Springer, Heidelberg (2013)
16. Bishop, C., Johnson, C.G.: Assessing roles of variables by program analysis. In: Proc. CSEIT, pp. 131–136. TUCS (2005)
17. Blanchet, B., Cousot, P., Cousot, R., Feret, J., Mauborgne, L., Miné, A., Monniaux, D., Rival, X.: A static analyzer for large safety-critical software. In: Proc. PLDI, pp. 196–207. ACM (2003)
18. Bryant, R.: Symbolic boolean manipulation with ordered binary-decision diagrams. ACM Computing Surveys 24(3), 293–318 (1992)
19. Bultan, T., Gerber, R., League, C.: Composite model-checking: Verification with type-specific symbolic representations. ACM TOSEM 9(1), 3–50 (2000)
20. Burch, J.R., Clarke, E.M., McMillan, K.L., Dill, D.L., Hwang, L.J.: Symbolic model checking: 10^{20} states and beyond. In: Proc. LICS, pp. 428–439. IEEE (1990)
21. Cimatti, A., Micheli, A., Narasamdya, I., Roveri, M.: Verifying SystemC: A software model checking approach. In: Proc. FMCAD, pp. 51–59. IEEE (2010)
22. Cimatti, A., Roveri, M., Bertoli, P.G.: Searching powerset automata by combining explicit-state and symbolic model checking. In: Margaria, T., Yi, W. (eds.) TACAS 2001. LNCS, vol. 2031, pp. 313–327. Springer, Heidelberg (2001)
23. Clarke, E.M., Grumberg, O., Jha, S., Lu, Y., Veith, H.: Counterexample-guided abstraction refinement for symbolic model checking. J. ACM 50(5), 752–794 (2003)
24. Classen, A., Heymans, P., Schobbens, P.-Y., Legay, A.: Symbolic model checking of software product lines. In: Proc. ICSE, pp. 321–330. ACM (2011)
25. Demyanova, Y., Veith, H., Zuleger, F.: On the concept of variable roles and its use in software analysis. Technical Report abs/1305.6745, ArXiv (2013)
26. Dudka, K., Müller, P., Peringer, P., Vojnar, T.: Predator: A verification tool for programs with dynamic linked data structures. In: Flanagan, C., König, B. (eds.) TACAS 2012. LNCS, vol. 7214, pp. 545–548. Springer, Heidelberg (2012)
27. Graf, S., Saïdi, H.: Construction of abstract state graphs with PVS. In: Grumberg, O. (ed.) CAV 1997. LNCS, vol. 1254, pp. 72–83. Springer, Heidelberg (1997)
28. Havelund, K., Pressburger, T.: Model checking Java programs using Java PATHFINDER. Int. J. Softw. Tools Technol. Transfer 2(4), 366–381 (2000)
29. Holzmann, G.J.: The SPIN model checker. IEEE Trans. Softw. Eng. 23(5), 279–295 (1997)
30. Howar, F., Isberner, M., Merten, M., Steffen, B., Beyer, D.: The RERS grey-box challenge 2012: Analysis of event-condition-action systems. In: Margaria, T., Steffen, B. (eds.) ISoLA 2012, Part I. LNCS, vol. 7609, pp. 608–614. Springer, Heidelberg (2012)
31. McMillan, K.L.: The SMV system. Technical Report CMU-CS-92-131, CMU (1992)

32. von Rhein, A., Apel, S., Raimondi, F.: Introducing binary decision diagrams in the explicit-state verification of Java code. In: JavaPathfinder Workshop (2011),
    http://www.infosun.fim.uni-passau.de/cl/publications/
    docs/JPF2011.pdf
33. Rondon, P., Bakst, A., Kawaguchi, M., Jhala, R.: CSolve: Verifying C with liquid types. In: Madhusudan, P., Seshia, S.A. (eds.) CAV 2012. LNCS, vol. 7358, pp. 744–750. Springer, Heidelberg (2012)
34. Sagiv, M., Reps, T.W., Wilhelm, R.: Parametric shape analysis via 3-valued logic. ACM TOPLAS 24(3), 217–298 (2002)
35. Sajaniemi, J.: An empirical analysis of roles of variables in novice-level procedural programs. In: Proc. HCC, pp. 37–39. IEEE (2002)
36. Sebastiani, R., Tonetta, S., Vardi, M.Y.: Symbolic systems, explicit properties: On hybrid approaches for LTL symbolic model checking. In: Etessami, K., Rajamani, S.K. (eds.) CAV 2005. LNCS, vol. 3576, pp. 350–363. Springer, Heidelberg (2005)
37. Stevens, S.S.: On the theory of scales of measurement. Science 103(2684), 677–680 (1946)
38. van Deursen, A., Moonen, L.: Type inference for COBOL systems. In: Proc. WCRE, pp. 220–230. IEEE (1998)
39. van Deursen, A., Moonen, L.: Understanding COBOL systems using inferred types. In: Proc. IWPC, pp. 74–81. IEEE (1999)
40. Visser, W., Havelund, K., Brat, G., Park, S., Lerda, F.: Model checking programs. J. ASE 10(2), 203–232 (2003)

Efficient Analysis of Reliability Architectures via Predicate Abstraction

Marco Bozzano, Alessandro Cimatti, and Cristian Mattarei

Fondazione Bruno Kessler, Trento, Italy
{bozzano,cimatti,mattarei}@fbk.eu

Abstract. The overall safety of critical systems is often based on the use of redundant architectural patterns, such as Triple Modular Redundancy. Certification procedures in various application domains require an explicit evaluation of the reliability, and the production of various artifacts. Particularly interesting are Fault Trees (FT), that represent in a compact form all the combinations of (basic) faults that are required to cause a (system-level) failure. Yet, such activities are essentially based on manual analysis, and are thus time consuming and error prone.

A recently proposed approach opens the way to the automated analysis of reliability architectures. The approach is based on the use of Satisfiability Modulo Theories (SMT), using the theory of Equality and Uninterpreted Functions ($\mathcal{EUF}$) to represent block diagrams. Within this framework, the construction of FTs is based on the existential quantification of an $\mathcal{EUF}$ formula. Unfortunately, the off-the-shelf application of available techniques, based on the translation into an AllSMT problem, suffers from severe scalability issues.

In this paper, we propose a compositional method to solve this problem, based on the use of predicate abstraction. We prove that our method is sound and complete for a wide class of system architectures. The presented approach greatly improves the overall scalability with respect to the monolithic case, obtaining speed-ups of various orders of magnitude. In practice, this approach allows for the verification of architectures of realistic systems.

Keywords: Formal Verification, Reliability Architectures, Fault Tree Analysis, Satisfiability Modulo Theory, Redundant Systems.

1 Introduction

Redundancy is a well known solution used in the design of critical system. In order to increase the dependability of a system, components carrying out important functions are replicated, and their effects combined by means of dedicated modules such as voters. A typical schema is Triple Module Redundancy (TMR) where three components are connected by a voter. This solution can be instantiated multiple times within the same system, in cascading stages organized in different structures [3,37,28].

V. Bertacco and A. Legay (Eds.): HVC 2013, LNCS 8244, pp. 279–294, 2013.

The reliability analysis for such architectures is based on the construction of so-called Fault Trees [45]. A Fault Tree (FT) identifies all the configurations of faults that can lead to an undesired event (e.g., loss of a system function). The construction of FT's from a model are in general not carried out automatically, and are thus costly, tedious and error prone. A recent exception is the work in [13], where the problem of analyzing reliability architectures is cast in the framework of Satisfiability Modulo Theories (SMT) [6]. Functional blocks are represented in the theory of Equality and Uninterpreted Functions ($\mathcal{EUF}$) as uninterpreted functions. Redundancy is modeled by the repetition of the same function block, combined with blocks representing the voting mechanisms. The possible occurrence of faults is modeled by the introduction of Boolean fault variables. Within this framework, FTs are directly generated by the collection of values to the fault variables that make an $\mathcal{EUF}$ formula satisfiable. In fact, the construction of such FTs is a variation of the AllSMT problem [35] where the assignments to the fault variables are required to be minimal with respect to set inclusion. Unfortunately, the techniques based on [35] can be seen as a monolithic enumeration of the disjucts of the DNF of the resulting formula, are are often subject to a blow up. This prevents the construction of FT (and ultimately the reliability analysis) for systems of realistic size.

In this paper, we propose a new method for the compositional computation of FTs for the analysis of redundancy architectures. The key technical insight is the use of predicate abstraction to partition the construction of FT. More specifically, the computation of the FT for a DAG of concrete components proceeds in two steps: first, we combine the abstraction of the individual components under a suitable set of predicates, carrying out an SMT-based quantification, thus obtaining a pure Boolean model; then, we compute the FT for such model using BDD-based projection techniques [14]. We prove that the approach is sound, i.e. the FTs computed on the abstract system are the same as the ones computed directly on the original, concrete system.

The approach was implemented within the NuSMV3 system, on top of the MathSAT5 [21] SMT solver, and we carried also out an experimental evaluation to test the scalability. On small-sized examples, where the monolithic approach requires already a significant computation time, the new method performs orders of magnitude better. Even more important, the new method scales dramatically better, and is able to generate fault trees with hundreds of blocks in less than one minute. The increased capacity allowed us to analyze some classical architectures (e.g. [3,46,37,28]) that are out of reach for the previous technique [13].

The paper is structured as follows. In Section 2 we discuss some relevant related work. In Section 3 we present some logical background. In Section 4 we define the problem, and discuss the limitations of the previous solutions. In Section 5 we present our approach. In Section 6 we formally define the approach and prove its soundness. In Section 7 we describe the experimental evaluation. In Section 8 we draw some conclusions, and discuss future work.

2   Related Work

In recent years, there has been a growing interest in techniques for model-based safety assessment [33]. The perspective of model-based safety assessment is to represent the system by means of a formal model and perform safety analysis (both for preliminary architecture and at system-level) using formal verification techniques. The integration of model-based techniques allows safety analysis to be more tractable in terms of time consumption and costs. Such techniques must be able to verify functional correctness and assess system behavior in presence of faults [17,4,11,16].

A key difference with respect to our approach is that these techniques focus on the analysis of the *behavior* of dynamical systems, whereas our approach aims at evaluating characteristics of redundancy architectures, independently of components' behavior. Our approach builds upon the work in [13], which is based on the calculus of Equality and Uninterpreted Functions ($\mathcal{EUF}$), and makes use of Satisfiability Modulo Theory (SMT) techniques for verification [7,27].

The techniques based on Markov Decision Process and Probabilistic Petri Nets [34,29,44,19,40] are widely used in industry for the quantitative evaluation and reliability analysis. However, such approaches are not able to provide a uniform and completely automated process, and in fact, the link between the reliability evaluation and the qualitative safety assessment analysis is performed manually. Thus, this is a key difference between the approach proposed in [13] and the current techniques for the analysis of reliability architectures.

In this work we rely on *NuSMV3*, that is a complete verification and validation framework for model based analysis. *NuSMV3* is based on an open source verification engine [20], that supports BDD-based and SAT-based finite state model checking. At its core, *NuSMV3* uses the SMT solver MathSAT [10,21], that supports several theories like linear arithmetic over reals and integers, difference logic, bit vectors, uninterpreted functions, and equality. In addition to verification, *NuSMV3* also provides complex capabilities to perform safety assessment, in particular, FTA [14] and reliability evaluation.

3   Background

Traditionally, dynamical systems are modeled as finite state systems: their state can be represented by means of assignments to a specified set of variables [30]. In symbolic model checking, they are represented by means of Boolean logic, where (Boolean) variables are combined together via Boolean connectives (e.g. conjunction, disjunction, negation). In this approach, sets of states are represented by the Boolean formula corresponding to the characteristic function of the set. The symbolic analyses of dynamic systems, most notably symbolic model checking techniques (e.g. [39,8,38]) rely on efficient ways to represent and manipulate Boolean formulae, in particular Binary Decision Diagrams [18], and, more recently, Boolean satisfiability (SAT) solvers [41].

Boolean logic, however, is a rather limited representation, and fails to represent many important classes of systems. This limitation has been lifted with the advent of Satisfiability Modulo Theory (SMT) [6], where the formula is not pure Boolean, but it is expressed in some background theory such as Real and Integer Arithmetic $(\mathcal{LA}(\mathbb{Q})/\mathcal{LA}(\mathbb{Z}))$, Difference Logic $(\mathcal{DL})$, and Bit Vectors $(\mathcal{BV})$. On top of SMT solver there are many different verification algorithms that can be used [25,43,22,23]. In this paper we will focus primarily on the theory of Equality and Uninterpreted Functions $(\mathcal{EUF})$, where variables range over an unspecified domain, and function symbols can be declared, but have no specific property, except for the fact that they are functions, i.e. $(x = y) \rightarrow (f(x) = f(y))$. Moreover, we use predicate abstraction in order to approximate a concrete system using a set of formulas (predicates). Our approach makes use of an AllSMT procedure [35] that efficiently implements predicate abstraction by enumerating all the satisfying assignments over the set of predicates using an SMT solver.

The target of our approach is to improve the analysis of reliability architectures, and in particular the techniques for Model-Based Safety Assessment such as the construction of Fault Trees and Failure Mode and Effects Analysis (FMEA) tables, which can be performed automatically by reduction to symbolic model checking [16,11,15,14,12].

4   The Problem: Analysis of Reliability Architectures

The evaluation of architectural patterns is an essential ingredient for the development of safety critical system, due to the fact that such systems have to guarantee an high reliability. When a specific component is essential to guarantee correct and safe operation of the system, a standard practice in safety engineering is to encapsulate it in a redundant architectural pattern. This practice aims at increasing the reliability of the redunded component.

One of the most well-known architectural pattern is the Triple Modular Redundancy (TMR) architecture [3,5,26,42,31]. It consists in triplicating the module that is critical for the reliability of the system, and feeding one voter with their outputs. Specifically, considering each redundant module as a functional component, receiving an input and providing an output, the voter returns the value computed by the majority of the redunded modules. This approach allows us to varying, and hopefully increase, the reliability of the system, which depends on the reliability of each voter and each component, in addition to the displacement and connections between them. The analysis of reliability architectures, in general, is performed manually, due to the lack of specific techniques addressing both modeling and verification. The manual approach is supported by several specific algorithms [28,36] that can aid the verification and analysis of reliability of TMR chains. However, such approaches cannot be generalized in order to cover a full set of architectural patterns.

Recent studies on the verification of architectural patterns [13] aim at automating the analysis of reliability architectures. The idea proposed in [13] consists in defining the behavior of components using uninterpreted functions. Such formalism has the capability to describe the functional behavior of the components without giving any details of their implementation. Uninterpreted functions have no specific properties, except that they have to provide the same

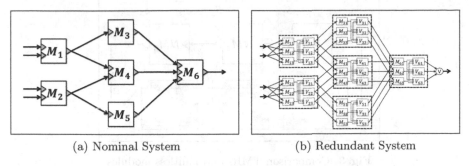

(a) Nominal System   (b) Redundant System

Fig. 1. Network of combinatorial components [3]

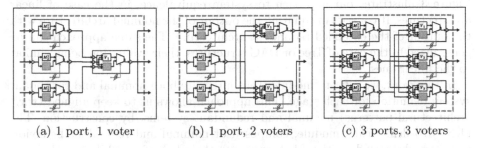

(a) 1 port, 1 voter   (b) 1 port, 2 voters   (c) 3 ports, 3 voters

Fig. 2. Modular redundancy examples

outputs when given the same inputs. Moreover, faulty behavior can be modeled simply by leaving the output of a faulty component unconstrained.

5   The Approach

In this work we concentrate on the equivalence checking between nominal and faulty systems with redundant modules. The idea is to provide the same inputs to both structures and evaluate under which conditions the outputs are different. This evaluation relies on Model-Based Fault Tree Analysis [14], which consists of generating all the faults configurations such that it is possible to reach an undesirable behavior (a.k.a. Top Level Event). A faults configuration, also called cut-set, is minimal if it is not possible to reach the TLE by removing a fault from this set, and in this work we concentrate on the minimal cut-sets generation.

Figure 1 shows a graphical representation of the nominal (1a) and redundant (1b) configurations of the network example introduced in [3]. Each redundant module, as shown in Figure 2, is then extended to take into account faults, namely by placing the nominal (the M and V modules) and faulty behaviors (the light red modules) in parallel. Figure 2 illustrates some examples of this extension, for different architectures. The selection between nominal and faulty behaviors is realized by a multiplexer that receives a fault event as input. Finally,

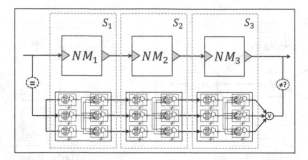

Fig. 3. Comparison TMRs and faultless modules

Figure 3 illustrates our approach to system equivalence, in the case of linear architectures. It consists in equating the output of the nominal architecture with the output of the extended redundant architecture. The same approach can be generalized to the case of Tree or DAG structures, their evaluation being similar to the linear ones.

In this work, we refer to modules that integrate both nominal and redundant system definition for each stage. This approach allows us to keep aligned (w.r.t architectural patterns) nominal and redundant systems, by construction. The idea is to define each module, composed of nominal and redundant behavior, using an abstract definition that preserves their behavior, while permitting a significant improvement of the performances of the routines that analyze them.

The predicate abstraction is defined for each individual redundant component, and formalized in Equation 1. Specifically, given a component defined as an SMT formula $\Gamma_{\mathbb{B}\cup\mathbb{D}}(I, O, F)$ over input and output ports, and faults events, we want to define a Boolean formula $\Psi_{\mathbb{B}}(A_I, A_O, F)$ over input and output predicates (defined as ϕ_I and ϕ_O, then bound to A_I and A_O) by performing a quantifier elimination over concrete input and output ports (the sets I and O), and fault events. The relation between these predicates and concrete ports is defined by

$$\Psi_{\mathbb{B}}(A_I, A_O, F) = \exists I, O.(\Gamma_{\mathbb{B}\cup\mathbb{D}}(I, O, F) \wedge$$
$$A_I \iff \phi_I(I) \wedge A_O \iff \phi_O(O)) \tag{1}$$

From the Boolean formula representing an abstract component, it is possible to generate an SMV module that encodes it. On top of this, we can encode a network composed of individual abstract components. In Section 6 we show that this network is equivalent to the abstraction of a network composed of concrete components, and use this result for FTA.

Given that abstract formulas are Boolean, we can analyze them using a BDD-based engine. Moreover, the network definition that we introduced in this paper allows for the generation of an optimal variable ordering that guarantees high verification performances. Equation 2 describes a system as the composition of different modules; in particular, it represents the configuration shown in Figure 1. This notation, similar to the relational language introduced in [32], consists of defining two operators: sequential composition ($\triangleright$) and parallel composition ($|$). The former relates components that are connected in a sequential fashion, linking outputs of the first component with inputs of the second one. Parallel composition, on the other hand, juxtaposes the set of ports from different components, which run in parallel.

$$(M_1|M_2) \triangleright (D|D) \triangleright (M_3|M_4|M_5) \triangleright M_6 \qquad (2)$$

The framework described in this paper enables the definition of any tree- or DAG-shaped structure. Three special combinatorial components can be used to connect inputs and outputs of different components, in order to implement: duplication of values (module D), simple propagation of input values (I module, a.k.a. identity) and arbitrary reconfiguration of signals (R module). For instance, in Equation 2 we use D modules in order to duplicate outputs of the M_1 and M_2 components.

6 Abstraction

In this section we formally define our approach, based on predicate abstraction, and we show that it allows for an efficiently generation of FTs. We concentrate on networks of combinatorial components used to define TMR architectures. A combinatorial component, according to Definition 1, is a system with input and output ports, a set of faults signals and a formula. Intuitively, such components do not have time evolution (i.e., they are combinatorial) and the values of the output ports are computed only over current inputs and faults.

Definition 1 (Combinatorial component). *A combinatorial component is a tuple $S = \langle P, F, \pi \rangle$, where:*

- *$P = P_O \| P_I$ are the terms representing vector ports, sequentially split into input and output (i.e. the symbol $\|$ defines vectors concatenation). Each port can have Boolean ($\mathbb{B}$) or Data ($\mathbb{D}$) type, while faults are only Boolean;*
- *F is the set of faults events;*
- *$\pi(P_I, P_O, F)$ is an SMT formula over ports and faults, where each term belongs to $\mathbb{B}$ or $\mathbb{D}$.*

We also define two special combinatorial components whose purpose is to formalize the abstraction. Specifically, the *abstractor component* (compare Definition 2) is used to translate a set of concrete values into their abstract counterpart, whereas the *concretizer component* (Definition 3) generates instances of concrete values satisfying the input predicates.

Definition 2 (Abstractor combinatorial component). *A combinatorial component $A = \langle P, F, \alpha \rangle$ is called abstractor if:*

- *$F = \emptyset$;*
- *$P = P_I \| P_O$;*
- *P_I is the vector of input ports belonging to $\mathbb{D}$;*

- $\boldsymbol{P_O}$ is the vector of output ports belonging to $\mathbb{B}$;
- $\alpha(\boldsymbol{P_I}, \boldsymbol{P_O}, \emptyset)$ is an SMT formula over input and output ports.

Definition 3 (Concretizer combinatorial component). *A combinatorial component $C = \langle P, F, \gamma \rangle$ is called concretizer if:*

- $F = \emptyset$;
- $\boldsymbol{P} = \boldsymbol{P_I} \| \boldsymbol{P_O}$;
- $\boldsymbol{P_I}$ is the vector of input ports belonging to $\mathbb{B}$;
- $\boldsymbol{P_O}$ is the vector of output ports belonging to $\mathbb{D}$;
- $\gamma(\boldsymbol{P_I}, \boldsymbol{P_O}, \emptyset)$ is an SMT formula over input and output ports.

Definition 4 formalizes the sequential composition of two components S' and S''. The idea is to connect the output ports of S' to the input ports of S''. The resulting component S has the same input ports as S', the same output ports of S'' and the union of the faults of S' and S''. Concretizer and abstractor components allow us to express the abstraction of module S as the sequential composition $C \triangleright S \triangleright A$.

Definition 4 (Sequential composition). *Given two combinatorial components $S' = \langle \boldsymbol{P'}, F', \pi' \rangle$ and $S'' = \langle \boldsymbol{P''}, F'', \pi'' \rangle$, such that $|\boldsymbol{P'_O}| = |\boldsymbol{P''_I}|$, the sequential composition $S = \langle \boldsymbol{P}, F, \pi \rangle$, denoted $S = S' \triangleright S''$ is defined by:*

- $\boldsymbol{P_I} = \boldsymbol{P'_I}$;
- $\boldsymbol{P_O} = \boldsymbol{P''_O}$;
- $F = F' \cup F''$;
- $\pi(\boldsymbol{P_I}, \boldsymbol{P_O}, F) = \exists \boldsymbol{P'_O}, \boldsymbol{P''_I}.\pi'(\boldsymbol{P'_I}, \boldsymbol{P'_O}, F') \wedge$
  $\pi''(\boldsymbol{P''_I}, \boldsymbol{P''_O}, F'') \wedge \boldsymbol{P'_O} = \boldsymbol{P''_I}$.

Similarly, parallel composition of two components is defined as follows.

Definition 5 (Parallel composition). *Given two combinatorial components $S' = \langle \boldsymbol{P'}, F', \pi' \rangle$ and $S'' = \langle \boldsymbol{P''}, F'', \pi'' \rangle$, such that $F' \cap F'' = \emptyset$, the parallel composition $S = \langle \boldsymbol{P}, F, \pi \rangle$, denoted $S = S' | S''$, is defined by:*

- $\boldsymbol{P_I} = \boldsymbol{P'_I} \| \boldsymbol{P''_I}$;
- $\boldsymbol{P_O} = \boldsymbol{P'_O} \| \boldsymbol{P''_O}$;
- $F = F' \cup F''$;
- $\pi(\boldsymbol{P_I}, \boldsymbol{P_O}, F) = \pi'(\boldsymbol{P'_I}, \boldsymbol{P'_O}, F') \wedge \pi''(\boldsymbol{P''_I}, \boldsymbol{P''_O}, F'')$.

Definition 6 expresses the equivalence between combinatorial components. Intuitively, two combinatorial components are equivalent if their relational formulas have the same value for each assignment to input and output ports, and faults.

Definition 6 (System equivalence). *Given two combinatorial components $S' = \langle \boldsymbol{P'}, F', \pi' \rangle$ and $S'' = \langle \boldsymbol{P''}, F'', \pi'' \rangle$, such that $F' = F''$ and $\boldsymbol{P'} = \boldsymbol{P''}$, they are called system equivalent, denoted $S' \equiv S''$, if and only if*
  $\forall M = \langle p_{I1}, ..., p_{In}, p_{O1}, ..., p_{Om}, f_1, ..., f_{Ik} \rangle : \pi'(M) \iff \pi''(M).$

In this work we concentrate on Fault Tree Analysis [45], and specifically on the generation of the Minimal Cut-Sets (MCSs) as formally defined in 8. This analysis provides a subset of the cut-sets (see Definition 7), which represents all fault configurations such that there exists an assignment to input and output ports making a specific event, called top level event (TLE), true. In this case, we consider to have two different systems, nominal and redundant, and the TLE is the predicate representing the difference between the outputs, by providing to them the same input.

Definition 7 (Cut-Sets). *Given a combinatorial component* $S = \langle P, F, \pi \rangle$ *and a predicate* $\mathcal{T}(P_O)$, *called Top Level Event; the set of cut-sets, denoted* CS, *is defined as follows:*

$$CS(S, \mathcal{T}) = \{f \in 2^F | \exists p_I \in 2^{P_I}, p_O \in 2^{P_O}.\pi(p_I, p_O, f) \wedge \mathcal{T}(p_O) = \top\}$$

A minimal cut-set is defined as follows, by keeping only cut-sets that are minimal fault configurations.

Definition 8 (Minimal Cut-Sets). *Given a combinatorial component* $S = \langle P, F, \pi \rangle$ *and a predicate* $\mathcal{T}(P_O)$, *the set of minimal cut-sets, denoted* MCS, *is defined as follows:*

$$MCS(S, \mathcal{T}) = \{cs \in CS(S, \mathcal{T}) | \forall cs' \in CS(S, \mathcal{T}), cs' \subseteq cs \implies cs' = cs\}$$

6.1 Modular Abstraction Equivalence

In this work we evaluate redundant networks by using modular predicate abstraction. In order to show the soundness of our approach, we prove that, given a system composed of concrete modules, it is possible to substitute each individual module with its abstract counterpart. This result is stated in Theorem 1. We organize the proof using the following lemmas. Lemma 1 states that the if two combinatorial components are equivalent, it is possible to sequentially combine them with a third component and preserve the equivalence. Lemma 2 states a similar result for parallel composition.

Lemma 1 (Reduction equivalence). *Given the combinatorial components* S, S', *and* S'', *if* $S' \equiv S''$ *then* $S \triangleright S' \equiv S \triangleright S''$ *and* $S' \triangleright S \equiv S'' \triangleright S$.

Lemma 2 (Parallel equivalence). *Given the combinatorial components* S_1', S_1'', S_2', S_2'', *if* $S_1' \equiv S_1'' \wedge S_2' \equiv S_2''$ *then* $S_1'|S_2' \equiv S_1''|S_2''$.

Theorem 1 allows us to generate an equivalent network of combinatorial components by using only abstract modules. Namely, it enables substitution of a concrete module with its abstract counterpart, provided that the application of abstraction and concretization on inputs preserves the behavior of the outputs in the abstract domain, as formally defined by the hypothesis.

Theorem 1 (Modular abstraction equivalence). *Given a combinatorial component* $S = S_1 \triangleright \ldots \triangleright S_n$, *a set of abstractors* $A_1, A_2, \ldots, A_n$ *and a set of* concretizers $C_1, C_2, ..., C_n$, where $\mathcal{C}(S) = C_1 \triangleright S_1 \triangleright S_2 \triangleright ... \triangleright S_{n-1} \triangleright S_n \triangleright A_n$ and $\mathcal{A}(S) = C_1 \triangleright S_1 \triangleright A_1 \triangleright ... \triangleright C_n \triangleright S_n \triangleright A_n$, such that $\forall i \in \{1, ..., n\}$. $|\boldsymbol{P}_O^{C_i}| = |\boldsymbol{P}_I^{S_i}| \wedge |\boldsymbol{P}_O^{S_i}| = |\boldsymbol{P}_I^{A_i}|$

$\quad$ if $\qquad\qquad \forall i \in \{2, ..., n\}. A_{i-1} \triangleright C_i \triangleright S_i \triangleright A_i \equiv S_i \triangleright A_i$

$\quad$ then $\qquad\qquad\qquad\qquad\qquad \mathcal{C}(S) \equiv \mathcal{A}(S)$

Proof. by hypothesis $\qquad S_n \triangleright A_n \equiv A_{n-1} \triangleright C_n \triangleright S_n \triangleright A_n$

$\quad$ then (by Lemma 1) $\quad \mathcal{C}(S) \equiv (C_1 \triangleright S_1 \triangleright S_2 \triangleright ... \triangleright S_{n-1}) \triangleright (S_n \triangleright A_n) \equiv$
$$(C_1 \triangleright S_1 \triangleright S_2 \triangleright ... \triangleright S_{n-1}) \triangleright (A_{n-1} \triangleright C_n \triangleright S_n \triangleright A_n)$$

$\quad$ then (by hypothesis) $\quad S_{n-1} \triangleright A_{n-1} \equiv A_{n-2} \triangleright C_{n-1} \triangleright S_{n-1} \triangleright A_{n-1}$

$\quad$ then (by Lemma 1) $\quad ... \triangleright S_{n-2}) \triangleright (S_{n-1} \triangleright A_{n-1}) \triangleright (C_n \triangleright S_n \triangleright A_n) \equiv$
$$... \triangleright S_{n-2}) \triangleright (A_{n-2} \triangleright C_{n-1} \triangleright S_{n-1} \triangleright A_{n-1}) \triangleright (C_n \triangleright S_n \triangleright A_n)$$

$\quad$ then, keep applying hypothesis and Lemma 1 it is possible to conclude that
$$(C_1 \triangleright S_1) \triangleright (S_2 \triangleright A_2) \triangleright (C_3 \triangleright ... \equiv$$
$$(C_1 \triangleright S_1) \triangleright (A_1 \triangleright C_2 \triangleright S_2 \triangleright A_2) \triangleright (C_3 \triangleright ... \equiv \mathcal{A}(S)$$

The results stated in Theorem 1 is very general; it can be applied to different abstractions, provided that the hypothesis of the theorem holds. In the case of stages that are a parallel composition of modules, the hypothesis can be proved with Lemma 2, and this is an important aspect when dealing with Tree and DAG systems. As a corollary, we obtain that it is possible to compute the MCSs for the concrete system on the abstract system.

Corollary 1 (Computation of Minimal Cut-Sets). *If a combinatorial component $S = S_1 \triangleright ... \triangleright S_n$, the abstractors $A_1, ..., A_n$, and the concretizers $C_1, ..., C_n$ satisfy the hypothesis of Theorem 1, then $MCS(\mathcal{C}(S), \mathcal{T}) = MCS(\mathcal{A}(S), \mathcal{T})$.*

7 Experiments

7.1 Implementation

We implemented our approach on top of the NuSMV3 system, a verification tool built on top of NuSMV2 [20] and MathSAT [21]. NuSMV3 provides various SMT-based verification algorithms, and various engines for predicate abstraction [1,2]. The functionalities that are relevant for this paper are the ability to deal with $\mathcal{EUF}$ theory, predicate abstraction via AllSMT [35], and the capability to generate Fault Trees with probabilistic evaluations as described in [13].

Our implementation takes a description of a nominal model, its counterpart expressed with redundancy schemas, and can generate either the monolithic problem or the compositional problem, where the various components are modeled with fault variables and predicates describing discrepancies between the nominal and redundant flow.

We instantiated the framework described in Section 5 using the following abstraction, which expresses, given a set of input and output ports, the equivalence between nominal values and their extended version. More precisely, considering a stage with a nominal component having i_n, o_n as input and output ports, and a redundant module duplicating the signals with i_1, i_2, o_1, o_2 as ports, our abstraction generates the predicates $\{(i_n = i_1), (i_n = i_2)\}$ as input, and $\{(o_n = o_1), (o_n = o_2)\}$ as output.

In order to use the results of Section 6, we have to prove that the hypothesis of Theorem 1 holds for our predicates. For this purpose, we carried out an equivalence checking using the MathSAT SMT solver. Specifically, we proved that the formula $\nexists M : \neg(\pi_\alpha(M) \iff \pi_\gamma(M))$ is unsatisfiable for each SMV module implementation, where π_α and π_γ represent, respectively, abstract and concrete formula modulo predicates, as expressed in Theorem 1. Thus, each sequence $C_i \triangleright S_i \triangleright A_i$ explicitly represents an abstract component, and it is used as a single module that is computed using AllSMT-based predicate abstraction techniques.

The generation of Fault Trees, in the form of Binary Decision Diagrams [18], provided the best performance by disabling dynamic reordering, and using a statically computed ordering, based on the topology of the analyzed system. In detail, considering the example in Expression 2, the ordering starts with faults and output predicates for the module M_1, followed by the variables of M_2, then the ones from M_3 (D modules do not have variables), and so on.

The setting for the experimental evaluation comprises the generation of the abstract modules, for each of the possible pair of nominal and redundant components represented in Figure 2, and then caching their machine representation. The time needed to perform such process is not taken into account in the scalability evaluation, however this operation takes on average 5 seconds with a maximum time of 10 seconds. The target of our evaluation consists in Fault Tree Analysis (generation of MCSs), with a top level event stating that the output of the nominal network differs from the redundant one. The library of abstract components consists of 12 different redundancy configurations with 1, 2 and 3 voters per stage. The system configuration for the standard methodology of [13], without predicate abstraction, is similar to the setting with modular abstraction with the difference that each module is a concrete representation with real variables and $\mathcal{EUF}$ functions. The algorithms used in both cases are based on Fault Tree generation as proposed in [14]; given the difference between concrete and abstract, in the first case we use SMT-based techniques, whereas for the latter we use the BDD-based ones.

7.2   Experimental Evaluation

We compared the performance of the monolithic and compositional approaches on a wide set of benchmarks, including randomly generated and real-world architectures. Whenever both techniques terminated, we checked the correctness by comparing the Fault Trees. We ran the experiments on an Intel Xeon E3-1270 at 3.40GHz, with a timeout of 1000 seconds, and a memory limit of 1 GB.

Linear Structures. We first analyzed the scalability of the approach on linear TMR structures. The TMR chains experiments consider networks of length n with 1, 2 and 3 voters, with different combinations of structures. The results of this comparison are presented in Figure 4: the x axis represents the length of the chain, while on the y axis there is the time needed to compute the minimal cut-sets. The concrete generation reaches the timeout starting from a TMR chain with 1 and 2 voters of length 20, while with 3 voters, it is not able to evaluate more than 10 stages within the timeout. The modular abstraction approach is able to perform FTA in less than 110 seconds for a TMR chain of length 140, both with 1, 2 and 3 voters.

The two and three voters schemas are much harder to deal with (as witnessed by the relative degrade in performance of both techniques). In fact, the presence of additional voters increases the number of fault variables, and the overall number of cut-sets. In the case of compositional, partitioning helps to limit the impact on performance. However, the compositional approach is vastly superior to the monolithic one which shows a significant degrade in performance.

Scalability on Tree and DAG Structures. We then analyzed tree and DAG diagrams, first considering the design description presented in [3], that describes a DAG redundant structure as shown in Figure 1. In this case, the modular abstraction technique is able to perform FTA in 0.025 seconds, while the concrete case takes 4.5 seconds. Both methods construct the set of 102 minimal cut-sets.

The analysis of a real-word system architecture concerned the verification of the redundancy management of the Boeing 777 Primary Flight Computation, as described in [46]. The model considers a system with 36 redundant modules and 123 possible faults. In this case, the technique based on predicate abstraction takes 1.07 seconds to generate the Fault Tree composed of 195 minimal cut-sets. Differently, the monolithic approach takes 4680 seconds (1 hour and 18 minutes).

In order to evaluate the performance of modular abstraction, we built a random generator of Tree and DAG structures. The problems are generated by picking a module type from the set of possible ones, adding it to the network with inputs selected from inputs of the system or outputs of previously introduced modules, until the target system size is reached. In order to be able to relate numbers of modules and verification complexity, we imposed that the increase of system diameter between two consecutive layers is at most two modules. This means that a random tree structure with length 140 has a maximum diameter of 22 modules (i.e. max diameter with n modules is $2 * \sqrt{n} - 1$).

The set of possible components is defined with modules with 1, 2, and 3 inputs and a single output, in addition to the special components D, which replicates the input to two equal set of outputs, and an identity module I.

The random generation of Tree and DAG networks allows us to compare the performances of two approaches. Figure 5 shows a scatter plot of the results for networks of size until 25, with red and blue points representing respectively Tree and DAG architectures. The results of this test clearly illustrate the improvement due to the abstraction, which is able to perform the analysis in less than 1.5

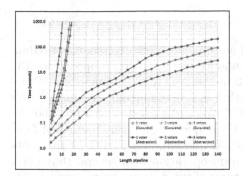

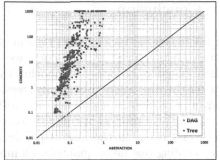

Fig. 4. Scalability evaluation on linear structures

Fig. 5. Tree (Red) and DAG (Blue) comparison

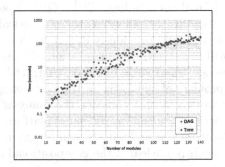

Fig. 6. Tree and DAG scalability: abstraction

seconds for each instance, with an average gain in performance that is in the order of 10^2 (i.e. Gain (Min, Avg, Max) = $(2, 6 * 10^2, 7 * 10^3)$).

The scalability evaluation of the modular approach in the case of Tree and DAG structure is shown in Figure 6. In this chart, the x axis represents the number of modules composing the network, while the y axis shown the total time to compute the full set of minimal cut-sets. The module count in the case of DAG does not consider the components of type D or I, due to the fact that they essentially express links between stages. The results shows that the performance in the case of Linear, Tree or DAG structure are almost comparable, in fact almost all the time is spent on the BDD quantification of predicates.

In the monolithic case, the bottleneck is clearly the AllSMT procedure (with optimizations described in [14]), due to the excessive number of cut-sets. In the compositional case, the time for initializing the library accounts in total for less than 1 minute. This cost is payed only once, and the necessary abstractions can be cached. Once the library is initialized, the main source of inefficiency is the generation of the BDD. This cost appears hard to limit, but we remark that we are obtaining an expensive quantification by partitioning and inlining.

8   Conclusion

In this paper we tackled the problem of automated safety assessment of redundancy architectures. In this work, we enhance the approach proposed in [13], where functional blocks are modeled within the SMT($\mathcal{EUF}$) framework. We focus on the construction of Fault Trees, that is a fundamental step in [13]: this step was tackled as a problem of AllSMT [35] and turned out to be a bottleneck. Here we propose a compositional technique for the construction of fault trees that relies on the idea of predicate abstraction, and partitions the problem, trading one large quantifier-elimination operation with several (but much simpler) operations. We prove the correctness of the decomposition, and provide an implementation realized on top the MathSAT5 solver. An experimental evaluation demonstrates dramatic improvements in terms of scalability with respect to the monolithic quantification. This makes it possible to construct Fault Trees with more than 400 minimal cut-sets from 2^{6*140} (10^{250}) possible fault configurations. The availability of this tool allows us to automatically obtain results for realistic configurations that were previously out of reach.

In the future, we will investigate the integration of these techniques into an architecture decomposition framework, based on contract-based design [24]. We will also analyze the problem of synthesizing the best configuration for a given cost function. Future work will also consider the analysis of various forms of deployment, where functions are run on the same platform. This form of analysis, also known as Common Cause Analysis, can be expressed in the modeling framework, but it is currently unclear if the compositional analysis is retained.

References

1. Proc. of Formal Methods in Computer-Aided Design, FMCAD 2007, Austin, Texas, USA, November 11-14. IEEE Computer Society (2007)
2. Proc. of 9th International Conference on Formal Methods in Computer-Aided Design, FMCAD 2009, Austin, Texas, USA, November 15-18. IEEE (2009)
3. Abraham, J.A., Siewiorek, D.P.: An algorithm for the accurate reliability evaluation of triple modular redundancy networks. IEEE Trans. on Comp. 100(7), 682–692 (1974)
4. Akerlund, O., Bieber, P., Boede, E., Bozzano, M., Bretschneider, M., Castel, C., Cavallo, A., Cifaldi, M., Gauthier, J., Griffault, A., et al.: ISAAC, A framework for integrated safety analysis of functional, geometrical and human aspects. In: Proc. ERTS (2006)
5. Anderson, T., Lee, P.A.: Fault tolerance, principles and practice. Prentice/Hall International (1981)
6. Barrett, C.W., Sebastiani, R., Seshia, S.A., Tinelli, C.: Satisfiability modulo theories. In: Biere, et al. (eds.) [9], pp. 825–885
7. Bensalem, S., Ganesh, V., Lakhnech, Y., Munoz, C., Owre, S., Rueß, H., Rushby, J., Rusu, V., Saïdi, H., Shankar, N., et al.: An overview of sal. In: Proc. of the 5th NASA Langley Formal Methods Workshop (2000)
8. Biere, A., Cimatti, A., Clarke, E.M., Strichman, O., Zhu, Y.: Bounded model checking. Advances in Computers 58, 117–148 (2003)

9. Biere, A., Heule, M., van Maaren, H., Walsh, T. (eds.): Handbook of Satisfiability. FAIA, vol. 185. IOS Press (2009)
10. Bozzano, M., Bruttomesso, R., Cimatti, A., Junttila, T., van Rossum, P., Schulz, S., Sebastiani, R.: MathSAT: Tight Integration of SAT and Mathematical Decision Procedures. Journal of Automated Reasoning 35, 265–293 (2005)
11. Bozzano, M., Cimatti, A., Katoen, J.P., Nguyen, V.Y., Noll, T., Roveri, M.: Safety, dependability, and performance analysis of extended AADL models. The Computer Journal (March 2010), doi:10.1093/com
12. Bozzano, M., Cimatti, A., Lisagor, O., Mattarei, C., Mover, S., Roveri, M., Tonetta, S.: Symbolic model checking and safety assessment of altarica models. ECE-ASST 46 (2012)
13. Bozzano, M., Cimatti, A., Mattarei, C.: Automated analysis of reliability architectures. In: ICECCS, pp. 198–207. IEEE Computer Society (2013)
14. Bozzano, M., Cimatti, A., Tapparo, F.: Symbolic Fault Tree Analysis for Reactive Systems. In: Namjoshi, K.S., Yoneda, T., Higashino, T., Okamura, Y. (eds.) ATVA 2007. LNCS, vol. 4762, pp. 162–176. Springer, Heidelberg (2007)
15. Bozzano, M., Villafiorita, A.: The FSAP/NuSMV-SA Safety Analysis Platform. International Journal on Software Tools for Technology Transfer 9(1), 5–24 (2007)
16. Bozzano, M., Villafiorita, A.: Design and Safety Assessment of Critical Systems. CRC Press (Taylor and Francis), An Auerbach Book (2010)
17. Bozzano, M., Villafiorita, A., Åkerlund, O., Bieber, P., Bougnol, C., Böde, E., Bretschneider, M., Cavallo, A., et al.: ESACS: An integrated methodology for design and safety analysis of complex systems. In: Proc. ESREL 2003, pp. 237–245 (2003)
18. Bryant, R.E.: Graph-based algorithms for boolean function manipulation. IEEE Trans. Computers 35(8), 677–691 (1986)
19. Ciardo, G., Muppala, J., Trivedi, K.: SPNP: stochastic Petri net package. In: Proc. of the Third International Workshop on Petri Nets and Performance Models, PNPM 1989, pp. 142–151. IEEE (1989)
20. Cimatti, A., Clarke, E., Giunchiglia, F., Roveri, M.: NuSMV: A new symbolic model checker. International Journal on Software Tools for Technology Transfer (STTT) 2(4), 410–425 (2000)
21. Cimatti, A., Griggio, A., Schaafsma, B.J., Sebastiani, R.: The MathSAT5 SMT Solver. In: Piterman, N., Smolka, S.A. (eds.) TACAS 2013. LNCS, vol. 7795, pp. 93–107. Springer, Heidelberg (2013)
22. Cimatti, A., Mover, S., Tonetta, S.: SMT-Based Verification of Hybrid Systems. In: Hoffmann, J., Selman, B. (eds.) AAAI (2012)
23. Cimatti, A., Mover, S., Tonetta, S.: SMT-based scenario verification for hybrid systems. Formal Methods in System Design 42(1), 46–66 (2013)
24. Cimatti, A., Tonetta, S.: A property-based proof system for contract-based design. In: 2012 38th EUROMICRO Conference on Software Engineering and Advanced Applications (SEAA), pp. 21–28. IEEE (2012)
25. de Moura, L., Owre, S., Rueß, H., Rushby, J., Shankar, N., Sorea, M., Tiwari, A.: SAL 2. In: Alur, R., Peled, D.A. (eds.) CAV 2004. LNCS, vol. 3114, pp. 496–500. Springer, Heidelberg (2004)
26. Favalli, M., Metra, C.: TMR voting in the presence of crosstalk faults at the voter inputs. IEEE Transactions on Reliability 53(3), 342–348 (2004)
27. Fränzle, M., Herde, C., Teige, T., Ratschan, S., Schubert, T.: Efficient solving of large non-linear arithmetic constraint systems with complex boolean structure. J. on Satisfiability, Boolean Modeling and Computation 1(3-4), 209–236 (2007)

28. Hamamatsu, M., Tsuchiya, T., Kikuno, T.: On the reliability of cascaded TMR systems. In: 2010 IEEE 16th Pacific Rim International Symposium on Dependable Computing (PRDC), pp. 184–190. IEEE (2010)

29. Hinton, A., Kwiatkowska, M., Norman, G., Parker, D.: PRISM: A tool for automatic verification of probabilistic systems. In: Hermanns, H., Palsberg, J. (eds.) TACAS 2006. LNCS, vol. 3920, pp. 441–444. Springer, Heidelberg (2006)

30. Holzmann, G.J.: The model checker spin. IEEE Transactions on Software Engineering 23(5), 279–295 (1997)

31. Johnson, J.M., Wirthlin, M.J.: Voter insertion algorithms for fpga designs using triple modular redundancy. In: Proc. of the 18th Annual ACM/SIGDA International Symposium on Field Programmable Gate Arrays, pp. 249–258. ACM (2010)

32. Jones, G., Sheeran, M.: Relations and refinement in circuit design. In: 3rd Refinement Workshop, vol. 90, pp. 133–152. Citeseer (1990)

33. Joshi, A., Whalen, M., Heimdahl, M.P.E.: Modelbased safety analysis: Final report. Technical report (2005)

34. Katoen, J.-P., Khattri, M., Zapreevt, I.S.: A markov reward model checker. In: Second International Conference on the Quantitative Evaluation of Systems, pp. 243–244. IEEE (2005)

35. Lahiri, S.K., Nieuwenhuis, R., Oliveras, A.: SMT Techniques for Fast Predicate Abstraction. In: Ball, T., Jones, R.B. (eds.) CAV 2006. LNCS, vol. 4144, pp. 424–437. Springer, Heidelberg (2006)

36. Tan, L., Tan, Q., Li, J.: Specification and verification of the triple-modular redundancy fault tolerant system using csp. In: The Fourth International Conference on Dependability, DEPEND 2011, pp. 14–17 (2011)

37. Lee, S., Jung, J.I., Lee, I.: Voting structures for cascaded triple modular redundant modules. IEICE Electronic Express 4(21), 657–664 (2007)

38. McMillan, K.L.: Interpolation and SAT-based model checking. In: Hunt Jr., W.A., Somenzi, F. (eds.) CAV 2003. LNCS, vol. 2725, pp. 1–13. Springer, Heidelberg (2003)

39. McMillan, K.L.: Symbolic Model Checking. Kluwer Academic Publishers (1993)

40. Sanders, W.H., Obal II, D., Qureshi, M.A., Widjanarko, F.: The ultrasan modeling environment. Perf. Evaluation 24(1), 89–115 (1995)

41. Silva, J.P.M., Lynce, I., Malik, S.: Conflict-driven clause learning sat solvers. In: Biere, et al. (eds.) [9], pp. 131–153

42. Thaker, D.D., Amirtharajah, R., Impens, F., Chuang, I.L., Chong, F.T.: Recursive TMR: Scaling fault tolerance in the nanoscale era. IEEE Design & Test of Computers 22(4), 298–305 (2005)

43. Tonetta, S.: Abstract model checking without computing the abstraction. In: Cavalcanti, A., Dams, D.R. (eds.) FM 2009. LNCS, vol. 5850, pp. 89–105. Springer, Heidelberg (2009)

44. Trivedi, K.S.: Sharpe 2002: Symbolic hierarchical automated reliability and performance evaluator. In: Proc. International Conference on Dependable Systems and Networks, DSN 2002, p. 544. IEEE (2002)

45. Vesely, W.E., Stamatelatos, M., Dugan, J., Fragola, J., Minarick III, J., Railsback, J.: Fault Tree Handbook with Aerospace Applications (2002)

46. Yeh, Y.C.: Triple-triple redundant 777 primary flight computer. In: Proc. of the IEEE Aerospace Applications Conference, vol. 1, pp. 293–307. IEEE (1996)

Lazy Symbolic Execution through Abstraction and Sub-space Search

Guodong Li and Indradeep Ghosh

Fujitsu Labs of America, CA
{gli,ighosh}@fla.fujitsu.com

Abstract. We present an approach to address a main performance bottleneck in symbolic execution. Despite a powerful method to produce test cases with high coverage, symbolic execution often suffers from the problem of exploring a huge number of paths without (1) significantly increasing the coverage, and (2) going deep enough to hit hot spots. The situation becomes worse for modern programming languages such as C/C++ which extensively use library calls and shared code. In this paper we use a novel "lazy" execution approach to evaluate functions, library calls, and other entities commonly used in a high level language. Specifically, the symbolic executor uses high level abstractions and sub-space search to control and guide symbolic execution so that only necessary paths are visited to produce valid test cases. This method is able to avoid exploring many useless or duplicate paths. Experimental results show that it can help solve path constraints and produce test cases in much less time. For many programs, it can improve the performance by several orders of magnitude while maintaining the same source code coverage.

1 Introduction

Traditionally, software quality has been assured through manual testing which is tedious, difficult, and often gives poor coverage of the source code especially when availing of random testing approaches. This has led to much recent work in the formal validation arena. One such formal technique is symbolic execution [5,15,16,19] which can be used to automatically generate test inputs with high structural coverage for the program under testing.

Some widely used symbolic execution engines such as [6,5] handle high level languages such as C and Java. We have extended KLEE [5] to a tool KLOVER [15] for the automatic validation and test generation for C++, the language of choice for most low-level scientific and performance critical applications in academia and industry. To avoid dealing with the complex syntax of a high level language, these tools [5,19,15] handle the bytecode (*e.g.* LLVM bytecode [12] in [5,15,16]) generated by a compiler. So does the approach proposed in this paper; however it is a general method independent of the input language or the intermediate bytecode, although an OO language like C++ containing large libraries can benefit more from the approach.

V. Bertacco and A. Legay (Eds.): HVC 2013, LNCS 8244, pp. 295–310, 2013.

Typically, a symbolic executor forks two new states (or paths) when the condition of a branch is evaluated to be **unknown** (*i.e.* both this condition and its negation are satisfiable). If n unknown branches are called in a sequence, then $O(2^n)$ states are produced. It is possible that a small program (*e.g.* with embedded loops containing unknown branches) leads to hundreds of thousands of states; and the executor gets stuck in exploring too many paths. On the other hand, we usually do not need all these states to test the program, *e.g.* $O(n)$ states are sufficient to cover all the branches of this sequence. Hence a question is: which $O(n)$ states are needed, and how to produce these states automatically?

Many modern symbolic executors [6,5,19] have applied some techniques to mitigate the state explosion problem. For example, the EXE tool [6] has incorporated a RWSet analysis [4] to merge the states which are equivalent modulo live variables. At an execution point, two states can be merged if their stacks, heaps, and path conditions are the same after non-live variables are eliminated. For another example, KLEE [5] provides an experimental feature which allow a user to specify where to merge the states. Ite (if-then-else) expressions are used to combine expressions from different states. Recently, a more advanced merging approach [11] is proposed which merges states according to the impact that each symbolic variable has on solver queries that follow a potential merge point. This can be guided by search strategies that are more likely to reach the bugs or missed branches. This paper proposes a different approach.

State explosion becomes more severe for a language like C/C++ which comes with a large standard library containing the implementation of commonly-used APIs. Unfortunately, the library is highly optimized only for concrete execution. A simple API function call may contain a vast number of unknown branches. For example, consider the code "if (f(x) > g(x)) ...; else ...;", we need only two paths (states) to cover the two branches, while the symbolic execution of $f(x)$ or $g(x)$ may lead to path explosion. State merging may help in this case, however there is another approach — the focus of this paper — which needs no state merging at all! After all, state merging is costly and it is very hard to find out appropriate merging points and strategies. One of our key ideas is that *we do not spawn states unless they are indeed needed*. That is, the states are spawned *lazily* such that (1) useless or duplicate paths are avoided whenever possible; and (2) the execution can terminate early without coverage penalty.

Now we summarize our techniques and contributions:

- We use function abstraction and lazy function evaluation to avoid path explosion. Specifically, we first use abstractions to divide the state space into sub-spaces, then search each sub-space efficiently for one valid solution. Once a solution is found in a sub-space, we safely skip the rest of this sub-space. This divide-and-conquer technique enables us to explore only a small portion of the entire space without scarifying source coverage.

- We use a generic declarative language to describe the abstractions and control the execution. We show how to abstract some commonly-used data structures and APIs. Our method allows us to define operations, recursive

abstractions, quantified expressions, and so on, in a slight extension of the source language; hence is very general and extensible. (Section 3.1)
- We present how to search sub-spaces through early termination (Section 3.2). We give some analysis and preliminary experimental results to demonstrate the effectiveness of our method.

As far as we know, the presented work is the first effort to apply lazy symbolic execution through functional abstraction and optimized sub-space search to mitigate path explosion, especially for C/C++ programs. With this technique, our symbolic executor is able to improve the performance by orders of magnitude, yet produce valid test cases without source coverage penalty. Although there are some prior works on using summaries to help symbolic execution [1,9], or using lazy methods to initialize data structures [10] or generate path constraints [17], our method contains new features such as two-level execution, sub-space based early termination, and so on. In this paper we describe how to (1) introduce the abstraction phase and the search phase; and (2) handle general data structures and apply search and solving mechanisms.

We organize the paper by first giving motivating examples and an overview, then describing the lazy execution method in details, and then presenting experimental results. Finally we discuss and conclude.

2   Backgroup and Motivation

Our executor is built on top of a symbolic execution engine KLEE [5] to handle C++ programs. The C++ standard includes a library for all commonly used data structures and algorithms. Instead of using the standard library provided with GCC, we choose and optimize the simpler uClibc++ library [20] to improve the performance of symbolic execution. This paper uses this library to illustrate how lazy execution is performed. Note that the method is general, *e.g.* it is applicable to other libraries in other languages.

Motivating Example 1 (Strings). We start with the simple String library in C++. The following is a part of the C++ version of the main benchmark program in [2], where input *str* is a symbolic string. The full version is presented in the Appendix.

```
int i = str.find_last_of('/');
if (i == string::npos) return false; // exit 1
...
if (t == "live.com") return true;   // exit 5
```

In order to reach exits 1 and 5, we need to solve the following two paths constraints. Suppose we use the default uClibc++ implementation. If *str* is given a fixed length n, then the executor explores $O(n)$ paths for exit 1. However we need only visit 1 path to cover this exit, *e.g.* when *str* is an empty string. Other valid paths are simply duplications. Exit 5 is much more challenging.

The minimum length of *str* is 29; unfortunately the executor fails to find out a solution within the 2-hour time-out limit after exploring $> 10,000$ paths. The case where *str*'s length is not fixed becomes worse since more paths need to be visited.

> Exit 1: str.find_last_of('/') $\neq$ *npos*
> Exit 5: i = str.find_last_of('/') $\wedge$ i != npos $\wedge$ rest = str.substr(i+1) $\wedge$
>   rest.find("EasyChair") $\neq -1$ $\wedge$ str.compare(0, 7, "http://") = 0 $\wedge$
>   t = str.substr(7, i-7) $\wedge$ t.compare(0,4,"www.") = 0 $\wedge$
>   t' = t.substr(4) $\wedge$ t' = "live.com"

One main problem of using the default library implementation is that many new states will be spawned in the very beginning, while these states may lead to only invalid paths in subsequent execution. For example, for exit 5, all the trials on lengths less than 29 are fruitless. In fact, for these lengths, the executor should not execute the bodies of the involved string APIs at all!

Motivating Example 2 (C++ Containers). C++ containers are data structures parametrized for generic types. Take map for example, it supports insertion, deletion, search, and so on. The keys and elements can be integers, strings, or even user-defined objects. Similar to the string case, using the default library implementation will inevitably lead to path explosion even for small programs. To see this, consider inserting n elements with symbolic keys into a set. A naive implementation may lead to $O(n^n)$ paths, and an optimized one (*e.g.* the elements are sorted) may result in $O((log(n))^n)$ paths. This poses a big challenge to executing realistic programs which usually use containers extensively.

Two issues further complicate the problem: (1) C++ containers use iterators to traverse the elements, where an iterator is a pointer referring the elements objects in the heap; and (2) the key can be of object (*e.g.* string) type such that each comparison of two keys may produce a large number of paths.

Motivating Example 3 (User-defined Class). A user may define a class converting a long number (*e.g.* read from a hardware register) to a date of customized format. For example, the following code converts an input to a date and then sees whether the date is the first date of 2012. The `fromNum` function usually involves many division operations and branches over the results. This may overload the SMT solver. In contrast, lazy execution can quickly find out a valid solution for exit 1, *e.g.* $n = 2012 \times 366 + 0 \times 31 + 0$. Basically it first identifies a candidate dt = "2012-01-01" in the abstraction phase, then converts it back to a valid number in the search phase. The conversion is fast since the target number has been given in this case.

```
long n;  // symbolic value
Date dt = Date::fromNum(n);   // delayed execution
if (dt.isValid() && dt == "2012-01-01")
   ...; // exit 1
```

2.1 Overview

Our lazy execution approach delays state spawning to the point where the new states are indeed needed. For a library function call, we first regard it as an "atomic" operation by refraining its execution from spawning paths. Specifically, we do not execute this function's body at this moment; instead we use an abstraction to model this function's semantics and mark its atomic space. In addition, an invocation to the declarative implementation of this function is added into the path condition. Take `find_last_of` for example. A valid abstraction requires that the return value is either *npos* (indicating character c is not found) or an unsigned integer less than the string length. The abstraction marks the relation between the return value i and the string length; while the DI maintains the relation of i and the string value.

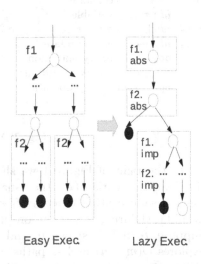

Easy Exec   Lazy Exec

Fig. 1. Lazy execution with abstraction and subspace search: the main flow

Abstraction : $i = str.find\_last\_of$ (c) $\land$ ($i = npos \lor 0 \leq i < str.len$)
DI Invocation : $find\_last\_of\_imp(i, str, c)$

As shown on the left of Figure 1, in an abstraction phase, only the abstractions are used to determine the satisfiability of a branch. When the end of a path is reached, the executor enters the "search" phase, where the DIs are expanded in their original call order. Consider exit 1 with path condition $str.find\_last\_of$ (c) = *npos*. To cover this exit we take the requirement as an assumption, then execute the function body to search a solution within the "sub-space" associated with this exit. Once a solution is found, *e.g.* str = "", the executor can stop exploring other paths since they won't increase coverage. This *early termination* technique avoids exploring useless or duplicate paths in a sub-space. A key point here is that the abstractions are used as assumptions, *e.g.* the return value must be *npos*, then the DIs are executed with respect to this fact. This avoids exploring other values which lead to invalid solutions.

The case of exit 5 is similar. The abstractions imply that str's minimum length is 29, and $i = 19$. This immediately specifies str's length and the values of all intermediate symbolic integer variables. Then, the executor can explore only one path to find out a valid solution, *e.g.* str = "http://www.live.com/EasyChair".

Hence we use the abstractions to (1) mark atomic operations; (2) divide the state space into coverage sub-spaces; (3) constrain the values of variables in the DIs; and (4) guide the search. For each sub-space, we only need to find one solution (*i.e.* explore only one path).

$$
\begin{array}{llll}
\tau := \texttt{i1}, \texttt{i2}, \ldots & \text{bitvector type} & \tau' := \tau \mid \tau \times \ldots & \text{primitive, vector type} \\
e := c : \tau & \text{constant} & \tau_f := \tau' \to \tau' & \text{function type} \\
\quad\mid \; id : \tau & \text{variable} & \tau_p := \tau' \to \texttt{bool} & \text{predicate type} \\
\quad\mid \; id[e] & \text{array read} & e := \lambda v.\, e(v) & \text{lambda expression} \\
\quad\mid \; id[e \mapsto e] & \text{array update} & \quad\mid \; \forall v \in [e,e] : (e : \tau_p)\, v & \text{forall expression} \\
\quad\mid \; \texttt{op}_\texttt{u}\, e & \text{unary operation} & \quad\mid \; \exists v \in [e,e] : (e : \tau_p)\, v & \text{exists expression} \\
\quad\mid \; e\; \texttt{op}_\texttt{b}\, e & \text{binary operation} & \quad\mid \; (id : \tau_f)(e,\ldots,e) & \text{function application} \\
\quad\mid \; \texttt{op}_\texttt{t}(e,e,e) & \text{trinary operation} & \quad\mid \; (id : \tau_p)(e,\ldots,e) & \text{predicate} \\
& & \quad\mid \; \texttt{f}_\texttt{abs}(e,\tau') & \text{unintrp. abstraction}
\end{array}
$$

Fig. 2. Main syntax of IL

On the right of Figure 1 we show pictorially why lazy execution is better than eager execution (*i.e.* the usual one without abstractions and DIs). In the eager case, executing function f_1 spawns many paths, most of which may be invalidated during f_2's execution (marked by black filled nodes in the diagram). Suppose f_1 and f_2 spawn m and n states respectively, then eager execution explores $O(m \times n)$ useless paths. In contrast, lazy execution first collects the abstractions without path spawning, then use them to rule out most of f_1's invalid paths. In one sense, it utilizes the subsequent control- and data- flow information to avoid visiting useless paths. In many cases this can reduce the number of paths to $O(n)$, and further to $O(1)$ through early termination.

Important questions include: (1) how to find out and define the abstractions? (2) how to combine the abstractions and DIs at run-time? and (3) how to efficiently search the sub-space? We address these questions in the next section.

3   Lazy Symbolic Execution

We use an immediate language to help define function abstractions and control the execution. The Intermediate Language (IL) extends KLEE's expression language by adding advanced expressions such as quantified expressions, function applications, *etc.*, plus mechansims to evaluate these advanced expressions in the execution engine. In Figure 2, we show the syntax of the primitive expressions inherited from KLEE (left) and some advanced expressions introduced by IL (right). Note that new abstract functions or operations are introduced.

3.1   Function Abstraction and Declarative Implementation

An abstraction records the abstract information about a function, while encapsulating other details in a *declarative implementation (DI)*. For example, function find_last_of is abstracted as below, where i marks c's position in the string, and input *pos* specifies the first position to consider. Here i is either npos or an unsigned integer less than the string's length. When the executor encounters this function, it adds into the current path condition the abstraction and an invocation to the DI. The DI constrain the values of i and *str* in a declarative style, *i.e.* it captures the exact semantics: if $i = npos$, then $c \notin str$; otherwise, $str[i] = \text{'c'} \land \forall k > i : str[i] \neq \text{'c'}$. Here primitive _assume adds the constraint into the current path condition, and _test is similar but terminates the path if the constraint is false. Note that find_last_of_imp is marked _LAZY so that the symbolic executor will execute it later (*e.g.* at the end of a path).

```
size_t string::find_last_of(char c, size_t pos = npos) {    // abstraction
  size_t len = str.length(); pos = pos > len ? len : pos;
  size_t i = _create_symbolic_variable(sizeof(size_t), "i");
  _assume(i == npos || i < len);
  _assume(find_last_of_imp(i, *this, c, pos));
  return i;
}
// the following is the DI (declarative implemenation)
_LAZY void find_last_of_imp(size_t i, string& str, char c, size_t pos) {
  for (size_t k = pos; k > 0; --k)
    if (str[k-1] == c) { _test(i == k - 1); return; }
  _test(i == npos);
}
```

We show below two other DI versions: the first one uses IL's syntax parser to introduce a built-in forall expression (_assume_IL accepts various argument formats similar to printf); the second one specifies the DI as a recursion, whose unrolling can be customized at run-time (see Section 3.2). Note that both the abstractions and the DIs are directly specified in the source code.

```
_LAZY void find_last_of_imp_1(size_t i, string& str, char c, size_t pos) {
  if (i == npos) _assume_IL("@x [0,%0] : %1[x] <> %2", pos-1, str, c);
  else
  { _assume_IL("@x [%0,%1] : %2[x] <> %3", i+1, pos-1, str, c);
    _test(str[i] == c); }
}
_LAZY void find_last_of_imp_2(size_t i, string& str, char c, size_t pos) {
  if (pos == -1) { _test(i == npos); return; }
  if (str[pos-1] == c) { _test(i == pos - 1); return; }
  _assume(find_last_of_imp_2(i, str, c, pos - 1));
}
```

We show below the abstractions for exit 5. Figure 3 shows some other string operations. Some length constraints are also used in [2]. For example, operator $A(s)$ introduces an integer variable for s to reason about the relation between strings, *e.g.* $s_1 > s_2 \land s_1 < s_2$ is unsat since $A(s_1) > A(s_2) \land A(s_1) < A(s_2)$ is unsat for uninterpreted function A.

Abs.(Length constraints)

$0 \leq i < str.len \land$
$i + 1 + rest.len \leq str.len \land 9 \leq rest.len \land$
$7 \leq str.len \land$
$t.len = i - 7 \land 4 \leq t.len \land$
$t'.len + 4 \leq t.len \land t'.len = 8$

DI (Lazy function calls)

find_last_of_imp(i, str, '/') $\land$
find_imp(0, rest, "EasyChair") $\land$
compare_imp(0, str, 0, 7, "http://") $\land$
compare_imp(0, t, 0, 4, "www.") $\land$
eq_imp(t', "live.com")

Figures 3 and 4 show some example abstractions. For C++ set, elements are associated with pointers (positions) as chars in a string; hence the abstraction is somehow similar to the string case. To model the mutations better, we introduce an "add" operator to model element insertion, and specify some DIs in recursive form. An interesting point is that the abstraction of operation **erase** can use function call **find** to facilitate subsequent query on the element. We give below an example where the executor explores only one path to cover the target branch.

```
code:    set<int> s; set<int>::iterator it;
         s.insert(b); s.insert(c); s.insert(a); s.insert(a+1); cout << "s: " << s << endl;
         it = myset.find(a+2);
         if (*it > 100 && s.size() > 3)   // the target branch
             cout << "found: a + 2 = " << _get_solution(*it) << endl;
```

output: the set: $a + 1 \oplus a \oplus c \oplus b \oplus \{\}$
          found: $a + 2 = 101$

3.2   Sub-space Search with Early Termination

Let us consider exit 5 in the string example. With a valid assignment to the numeric variables, e.g. $str.len = 29 \wedge t'.len = 8 \wedge t.len = 12 \wedge rest.len = 9 \wedge i = 19$, the executor can expand the DIs to obtain a valid string. It should be noted that such assignment calculation is done implicitly, and the executor will not enumerate concrete values. The executor will give a solution once all the abstractions together with the explored parts of the DIs are found satisfiable.

Hence, the length constraints are the "initial" assumption of the search phase. The DIs are symbolically executed one by one, each of which may result in multiple paths. Once a path terminates normally (i.e. without violating any _test), the executor terminates this sub-space and returns a valid test case. For instance, **find_last_of_imp** is expanded to produce value constraints: $str[19] = '/' \wedge str[20] \neq '/' \wedge str[17] \neq '/' \wedge \cdots \wedge str[28] \neq '/'$. Finally we obtain a solution str = "http://www.live.com/EasyChair".

It is not uncommon that the search phase needs to explore more than one path to find out a valid solution. For example, consider constraints t = "live.com" and !t.compare(0,4, "www."), the length constraints imply that t's minimum length is 8; however it should be 12 when considering the string value. the executor will find out this fact in the search phase, and try larger lengths. Here lazy execution starts from length 8 rather than 0 (a substantial improvement already).

3.3   Sub-space Search with Abstractions

Eager execution spawn paths immediately, while in lazy execution, extra assumptions (e.g. abstractions) are used to rule out a portion of the invalid paths. Figure 5 gives two branching trees starting from a node with path condition pc. This node spawns n paths with constraints $C_1^1, \ldots, C_n^1$ respectively. On the left, each

Operation	Abstraction	Decl. Imple.
$s[i]$	$0 \le i < |s|$	return (s[i])
$s_2 = s.\text{concat}(s_1)$	$|s_2| = |s| + |s_1|$	$\forall k \in [0, |s_2|) : s_2[k] = \texttt{ite}(k < |s|, s[k], s_1[k])$
$i = s.\text{lastIndexOf}(c)$	$i = -1 \vee$ $(0 \le i < |s| \wedge$ $s[i] = c)$	$(i = -1 \wedge \forall k \in [0, |s|) : s[k] \ne c) \vee$ $(0 \le i < |s| \wedge \forall k \in [i+1, |s|) : s[k] \ne c)$
$i = s.\text{find}(s')$	$i = -1 \vee 0 \le i \wedge$ $0 \le i \le |s| - |s'|$	$(i = -1 \wedge \forall k \in [0, |s| - |s'|) : s[k, k + |s'|) \ne s')$ $\vee (0 \le i \le |s| - |s'| \wedge s[i, i + |s'|) = s' \wedge$ $\forall k \in [0, i) : s[k, k + |s'|) \ne s')$
$s.\text{substr}(i_1, i_2)$	$0 \le i_1 + i_2 \le |s|$	return $(s[i_1, \ i_1 + i_2))$
$s = s_1$	$|s| = |s_1| \wedge$ $A(s) = A(s_1)$	$\forall k \in [0, |s|) : s[k] = s_1[k]$
$s > s_1$	$A(s) > A(s_1)$	$(|s| > 0 \wedge |s_1| = 0) \vee s[0] > s_1[0] \vee$ $s[1, |s|) > s_1[1, |s|)$

Fig. 3. An example abstraction for string operations (excerpt). Operator $||$ gives the length of a string, $s[i, j]$ gives a substring of s starting from position i and ending at j; and $s[i, j) = s[i, j - 1]$. Operator $A(s)$ introduces an integer variable for s. **return** returns an expression as the result.

Operation	Abstraction	Decl. Imple.
$S.\text{insert}(v)$: return $(v \oplus S, p)$	$*p = v \wedge 0 \le p < |S|$	insert_imp$(e \oplus S, v, p, k = 0) =$ if $e = v$ then $p = k$ else insert_imp$(S, v, p, k + 1)$
$p = S.\text{find}(v)$	$p = -1 \vee$ $0 \le p < |S| \wedge *p = v$	find_imp$(e \oplus S, v, p, k = 0) =$ if $e = v$ then $p = k$ else find_imp$(S, v, p, k + 1) \wedge$ find_imp$(\{\}, v, -1, k)$
$S_1 = S.\text{erase}(v)$	$S_1.\text{find}(v) = -1$	$(\forall p \in [0, |S|) : *p \ne v \Rightarrow *p \in S_1)$

Fig. 4. An example of abstracting C++ unsorted set (excerpt). We use p, S, k and v to denote iterator (pointer), set, key, and value respectively. We use $\oplus$ for adding an element in the front, $*$ for dereferencing an iterator, and $\{\}$ for an empty set. A set is a sequence of pointers indexing from 0; each pointer refers to an element. $v \in S$ is implemented by iterating over S's elements.

node continues spawning and generates a large sub-tree of height k. The nodes in each bottom sub-tree at the last level have constraints $C_1^k, \ldots, C_m^k$. There are $O(n \times \cdots \times m)$ paths, which is exponential to the height k. Suppose all the leaf nodes except the rightmost one are invalid (marked by $\bullet$), e.g. $C_1^k, \ldots, C_{m-1}^k$ conflict with pc, then only the rightmost path is valid (marked by $\circ$). In this case exploring the others is fruitless. This can be avoided through the lazy method shown on the right: the abstraction moves $C_1^k, \ldots, C_{m-1}^k$ to be closer to pc. Then the first $m - 1$ paths are found to be invalid quickly at level 2, and all related sub-trees are cut immediately. The number of visited paths is reduced by $m - 1$ times, e.g. if level k corresponds to a function with $m = 1,000$ internal paths, then we obtain a speed-up of 999x. Furthermore, the remaining sub-tree itself is also subject to lazy execution, hence we may need to explore only a couple of paths. This can bring improvement of several orders of magnitude.

Here we introduce some notations to facilitate subsequent discussions. Expression $(c_1 + \neg c_1) \cdot c_2$ describes a tree that first branches over condition c_1 and then encounters c_2. Here operators $\cdot$ and $+$ denote "fork" and "concat" respectively. Obviously this expression equals to $c_1 \cdot c_2 + \neg c_1 \cdot c_2$. Notation $\Lambda \vdash \Gamma$ denotes the tree Γ with abstraction Λ, $i.e.$ the tree simplified under assumption Λ. For example, $c_1 \vdash (c_1 + \neg c_1) \cdot c_2$ is $c_1 \vdash c_1 \cdot c_2$ or simply $c_1 \vdash c_2$. The number of visited paths (including unsat paths) in a tree Γ is $|\Gamma|$, $e.g.$ $|(c_1 + \neg c_1) \cdot c_2| = 2$ and $|c_1 \vdash c_2| = 1$. The basic theorem about lazy execution is: $\forall \Lambda, \Gamma : |\Lambda| \times |\Lambda \vdash \Gamma| \leq |\Gamma|$, hence adding extra non-forking abstractions ($i.e.$ $|\Lambda| = 1$) will not increase the number of paths. This indicates that, with non-forking abstractions, the lazy approach always performs better than the eager one w.r.t. path number.

As illustrated in Section 3.1, our abstractions are mostly non-forking logical formulas. Even for forking ones, the conclusion is virtually the same since abstraction Λ's paths usually exist in the original implementation Σ as well. That is, $(|\Lambda| \leq |\Gamma_1|) \Rightarrow (|\Lambda \vdash \Gamma \cdot \Gamma_1| \leq |\Gamma \cdot \Gamma_1|)$. The main overhead brought by abstractions is on the solver. Fortunately this overhead is marginal because (1) Λ are light-weight constraints; and (2) KLEE uses many powerful optimizations such as cache solving and independence solving that handle extra constraints well.

Does the quality of the abstractions matter? Let us consider two extreme cases. First, if the abstractions contain no useful information ($e.g.$ tautologies), then the lazy method is the same as the eager one: $|\vdash \Gamma_1| = |\Gamma_1|$. Second, if the abstractions are precise, then there is no need to use the DIs to find out a valid solution: $|\Gamma_1 \vdash \Gamma_1| = |\Gamma_1|$. In general, the more precise the abstractions are, the faster a lazy executor can find the answer.

We give below some properties about lazy execution, where $\Gamma_1 \preceq \Gamma_2$ denotes that (1) $\Gamma_1 = \Gamma_2$ ($i.e.$ they have the set of end paths), and (2) $|\Gamma_1| \leq |\Gamma_2|$. This indicates that Γ_1 is a sound reduction of Γ_2. These self-explanatory properties specify how to introduce, lift and merge abstractions.

$$
\begin{aligned}
\text{Abs. Intro.:} \quad & (\Gamma \Rightarrow \Lambda) \implies \Lambda \vdash \Gamma_1 \cdot \Gamma \cdot \Gamma_2 \preceq \Gamma_1 \cdot \Gamma \cdot \Gamma_2 \\
\text{Abs. Absort:} \quad & \Lambda_1 \vdash (\Lambda_2 \vdash \Gamma) \equiv \Lambda_1 \wedge \Lambda_2 \vdash \Gamma \\
\text{Abs. Union:} \quad & \Lambda \vdash \Gamma_1 + \Gamma_2 \preceq (\Lambda \vdash \Gamma_1) + (\Lambda \vdash \Gamma_2) \\
\text{Abs. Concat:} \quad & \Lambda_1 \wedge \Lambda_2 \vdash \Gamma_1 \cdot \Gamma_2 \preceq (\Lambda_1 \vdash \Gamma_1) \cdot (\Lambda_2 \vdash \Gamma_2)
\end{aligned}
$$

An important property about DIs is that their declarative style allows us to exchange DIs and form DI groups based on dependency information, $e.g.$ give higher execution priorities to DI groups that will be more likely to incur path reduction. The executor can use simple heuristics for DI scheduling which include: (1) grouping dependency DIs with respect to data dependency; (2) unrolling recursive DIs partially based on look-up information, and grouping the rest; and (3) searching the sub-space in favor of sub-trees with less dependency. Due to space constraint we do not elaborate this optimization.

Example. Consider an example where a map is searched to find an element with key $s_1 + s_2$ (here + adopts its C++ semantics to denote the concatenation of

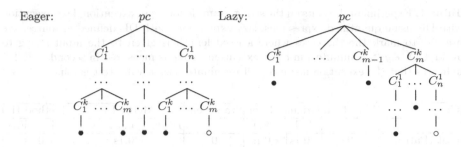

Fig. 5. Comparing lazy and eager execution

strings and characters). For brevity we ignore C++ iterators and the abstractions over the map operations, and model the map as a sequence of (key,value) pairs: $(k_1, v_1) \oplus (k_2, v_2) \oplus \dots$. The `find` operator can be specified in a functional style: find(empty_m, k') = null $\land$ find((k,v)$\oplus$m, k') = (if k = k' then v else find(m,k')). Suppose we want to find an element with key $s_1 + s_2$ in the following map under path condition $s_3.find(s_2) = 1 \land s_1[0] > 'a'$. An abstraction of this condition is $s_2.len + 1 \leq s_3.len \land s_1.len > 0 \land s_1[0] > 'a'$.

Key:	$s_1 + s_2 + s_3$	"A" $+ s_1 + s_2$	$s_1 + s_2[0] + $ "A"	...
Value:	...	...	...	...

We can unroll the `find` function three times to match $s_1 + s_2$ over the first three symbolic keys. Since the first key uses variable s_1, s_2 and s_3, while the other two use only s_1 and s_2, the search might be in favor of keys 2 and 3. For key 2, the derived abstraction is $1 + s_1.len + s_2.len = s_1.len + s_2.len$, which immediately invalidates this case. The abstraction for key 3 is $s_1.len + 1 + 1 = s_1.len + s_2.len$; hence constraint $s_2.len = 2$ is added into the path condition. Now $s_3.find(s_2) = 1$ can be unrolled to get $s_3[0, 1] \neq s_2 \land s_3[1, 2] = s_2$. For this constraint together with $s_2[0] + $ "A" $= s_2$, the executor can quickly find a valid solution, $e.g.$ $s_2 = $ "0A" and $s_3 = $ "00A". Another DI "$s_1[0] > 'a'$" is executed next, where a valid assignment to s_1, $e.g.$ $s_1 = $ "b", can be found by exploring only one path.

4   Evaluation Results

We run KLOVER on benchmark programs on a laptop with a 2.40GHz Intel Core(TM)2 Duo processor and 4GB memory. We compare lazy execution with eager execution, in terms of the number of visited paths and the execution time.

Results I: String Solving through Lazy Execution. We first test the main benchmark program in [2]: example 1 described in Section 2. Table 1 compares the results when using the default uClibc++ implementation, IL quantified expressions, or IL predicates. Both the value and the length of the string are symbolic. Lazy execution can achieve much higher performance. The eager approach can also use "early termination" to make the execution reasonably fast

Table 1. Experimental results on the string example for eager execution, lazy execution with DIs using quantified expressions, lazy expressions with DIs defined in source. We use "*" to mark the the cases where a fixed length is given to the input string to avoid T.O (*e.g.* > 5 minutes) in eager execution. Time is measured in seconds. "E.T." indicates that the execution instance will terminate once a valid test is found.

Case	Min. Len.	Original Impl.		Start Len.	Method I	Method II
		- E.T.	+ E.T.		DI w. Quant. Expr.	DI in Source
Exit (Path) 1	0	<0.1s	<0.1s	0	<0.1s	<0.1s
Exit (Path) 2	1	<0.1s	<0.1s	1	<0.1s	<0.1s
Exit (Path) 3	10	0.1s	<0.1s	10	<0.1s	<0.1s
Imme. Path 1	17	5.2s*	1.8	17	0.1s	0.2s
Imme. Path 2	21	T.O*	T.O	21	0.7s	1s
Exit 4, Path I	17	T.O*	T.O	17	0.2s	0.3s
Exist 5, Path I	29	T.O*	T.O	29	2.1s	2.5s
All 9 paths	32	T.O*	T.O	–	4.4s	5.7s

when a path condition is short; but it rapidly blows up when the path conditions are complicated. This indicates that early termination is not the key reason why lazy execution is much faster.

When the DIs are modeled using quantified expressions (*e.g.* find_last_of_imp_1), the execution is a little faster than the case where DIs are modeled as predicates in source code (*e.g.* find_last_of_imp). This is because KLOVER is able to solve quantified expressions directly in the solver rather than search the DI state space. Executing DIs may spawn many paths, hence KLEE's various search heuristics can be applied here (we use DFS only). In addition, KLEE's cache solver is essential to speed-up the solving since these paths have similar path conditions. Note that KLOVER always finds the *minimum* lengths.

We also test KLOVER on string sequences generated randomly. The operations in each sequence are related by data dependency such that the result or the side-effect of an operation may be used by subsequent operations. We are able to obtain 10–500x speed-ups by adopting the lazy execution method. Moreover, the longer a sequence is, the better lazy execution work. In general, using quantified expressions in DIs works better for larger strings and longer sequences; but defining DIs in the source code is more general and requires less support from the executor and its solver. Note that the eager approach often times out, in which case the lazy approach achieves higher speed-ups.

To summarize, with lazy execution we can define a built-in string solver that can rival with external solvers [2,7,14,8]. In particular, the solver in [8] uses a lazy solving technique to avoid fruitless iterations between the numeric domain and the string domain. Our approach is general and flexible, *e.g.* easy to support new operations or different operation semantics.

Results II: Road Test. Table 2 shows the results for 63 programs for unit testing the STL library (*e.g.* from http://www.cplusplus.com/reference) and

Table 2. Road test results on programs for unit testing. "#path" gives the number of valid paths.

Library	#programs	Original Method		Lazy Execution		Time Impr.
		time	#path	time	#path	
bitset,set	10	141s	2,559	1.1s	23	128x
bitset2,container	15	>20m	>35,200	9.4s	31	>127x
string	20	>20m	>21,330	7.2s	35	>166x
regexp	8	>20m	>37,100	47.5s	12	>25x
date,math	10	>20m	>1,540	8.4s	39	>142x

user-defined data structures. We compare the original *eager* method and our lazy method in terms of the completed paths leading to valid test cases. The original method is given a 20-minute timeout. As shown in the table, the lazy method can reduce the total execution time from around minutes to a few seconds without losing source line coverage. In fact for those time-out cases, with lazy execution we are able to not only finish the execution of all programs in reasonable time, but also achieve higher coverage (10-30%) since more paths are visited using the lazy method. In these unit-testing programs, typically 1-2 inputs are symbolic.

Results III: Lazy Execution for Small Programs. We test KLOVER on programs using various data structures and multiple input variables. The data structures include bitset, container, string, regular expression, date and user-defined ones. We manually define their abstractions and DIs. Table 4 shows the results for 5 programs (of small-medium size) developed by us. More complicated programs often result in time-out even with the lazy execution method, hence they are not the subject of the performance evaluation. The evaluation results show that: lazy execution can reduce the number of paths and execution times by 1-3 orders of magnitude for non-trivial programs. For example, when prog 1 has less symbolic inputs or elements, the eager method explores 16,384 valid paths (and many more invalid paths) while the lazy method explores only 931 paths, among which 145 paths lead to valid test cases. These 145 tests constitute a coverage-preserving subset of the 16,384 ones. The improvement is more significant when more conflicts exist in the program such that many tentative paths turn out to be unsat in the end.

Cost of Defing DIs. We observe that the more accurate and restrictive the DIs, the faster our lazy method can find out the solutions and terminate the execution. Defining abstractions and DIs in the IL is quite straight-forward, however identifying the right abstractions requires efforts. Typically, it takes a couple of hours to identify and specify non-trivial abstractions and DIs for a library; and it takes a few hours to write test cases to verify and check their correctness and efficiency. Fortunately, it is possible to use symbolic execution or other symbolic techniques to (1) calculate program invariants [9], and (2) check the correctness of likely invariants. It is also possible to derive predicates

Table 3. Experimental results on programs using multiple libraries. T.O denotes a 10-minute time-out. Eager "#path" gives the number of valid paths by the eager method; lazy "#path" is of format valid path number / tried path number for the lazy method. "Impr." indicates the time improvement by the lazy method over the eager one.

Program	Less Sym. Input/Element					More Sym. Input/Element				
	Eager		Lazy		Impr.	Eager		Lazy		Impr.
	time	#path	time	#path		time	#path	time	#path	
prog. 1	398s	16384	17.1s	145/931	23.2x	T.O	>22100	40.3s	203/1651	>14.8x
prog. 2	T.O	>34450	0.8s	9/88	≥750x	T.O	>34460	2.1s	9/144	>285x
prog. 3	T.O	>45780	29s	9/227	>26.7x	T.O	>38700	41.9s	14/344	>14.3x
prog. 4	324s	2940	4.3s	9/1851	75.3x	T.O	>2087	15.4s	9/6851	>77.9x
prog. 5	69s	625	4.9s	13/72	14.1x	195s	545	14.5s	53/155	13.4x

from the assembly or bytecode of a function and formally verify their correctness automatically [13]. We plan to explore these directions to automatically derive, refine and verify the abstractions and DIs.

5   Discussion and Conclusion

Lazy execution enables us to infer information about subsequent executions and use it to prune useless and duplicate paths. A typical way to gather such information is to apply static analysis on the source program [3]. In this paper we show how to provide a general framework to use this information in symbolic execution. For example, KLOVER supports defining the information in an abstraction-search architecture, and iteratively applies the declarative implementations to search for a solution. KLOVER extends the engine's kernel to introduce IL for controlling lazy execution. This method is not only general but also efficient. For example, KLOVER can reuse all facilities built in a high-performance executor such as KLEE, *e.g.* use optimizations such as expression rewriting, value concretization, constraint independence, *etc.*, to process and solve IL expressions.

A main advantage of lazy execution is to avoid exploring many useless or duplicate paths, and define sophisticated built-in solvers in the source code. State merging techniques [4,11] have a similar purpose. However our method is more systematic and may work better since it utilizes the information in the very beginning and in a declarative way. There also exist some works on using summaries in symbolic execution. For example, Anand *et al.* [1] found feasible interprocedural program paths by composing symbolic executions of feasible intraprocedural paths. They summarize procedures at various levels of detail and of composing those using logic formulas in a demand-driven way. Godefroid *et al.* [9] computed both may and must information compositionally and store them as summaries, and use them to check specific properties and help directed testing. In addition, Khurshid *el al.* [10] performed symbolic execution of commonly used library classes at the abstract level only. Our abstraction-DI-search flow is orthogonal to these methods.

The most related work is [17] and [18]. The main goal of [17] is to handle constraints involving data structures that cannot be handled by the solver, such as pointers, non-linear constraints, hidden external functions. The basic idea is to obtain concrete values in one run, then use these values to resolve complex elements (*e.g.* non-linear functions) in subsequent runs. It contains no concepts of abstraction, sub-space search, etc.

The lazy method in [18] first explores an abstraction of a function by replacing each called function with an unconstrained input, then expands a (possibly spurious) trace to a concretely realizable one by recursively expanding the called functions and finding concrete executions. It two-phase execution scheme is similar to ours, but it uses no predicate abstractions and DIs during the execution.

Our future work includes (1) identifying high-quality abstractions automatically; (2) improving DI specification and sub-space search; and (3) testing larger C/C++ programs.

References

1. Anand, S., Godefroid, P., Tillmann, N.: Demand-driven compositional symbolic execution. In: Ramakrishnan, C.R., Rehof, J. (eds.) TACAS 2008. LNCS, vol. 4963, pp. 367–381. Springer, Heidelberg (2008)
2. Bjørner, N., Tillmann, N., Voronkov, A.: Path feasibility analysis for string-manipulating programs. In: Kowalewski, S., Philippou, A. (eds.) TACAS 2009. LNCS, vol. 5505, pp. 307–321. Springer, Heidelberg (2009)
3. Blanc, N., Groce, A., Kroening, D.: Verifying C++ with STL containers via predicate abstraction. In: Automated Software Engineering, ASE (2007)
4. Boonstoppel, P., Cadar, C., Engler, D.: RWset: Attacking path explosion in constraint-based test generation. In: Ramakrishnan, C.R., Rehof, J. (eds.) TACAS 2008. LNCS, vol. 4963, pp. 351–366. Springer, Heidelberg (2008)
5. Cadar, C., Dunbar, D., Engler, D.R.: KLEE: Unassisted and automatic generation of high-coverage tests for complex systems programs. In: Operating Systems Design and Implementation (OSDI) (2008)
6. Cadar, C., Ganesh, V., Pawlowski, P.M., Dill, D.L., Engler, D.R.: EXE: automatically generating inputs of death. In: Conference on Computer and Communications Security, CCS (2006)
7. Ganesh, V., Kieżun, A., Artzi, S., Guo, P.J., Hooimeijer, P., Ernst, M.: HAMPI: A string solver for testing, analysis and vulnerability detection. In: Gopalakrishnan, G., Qadeer, S. (eds.) CAV 2011. LNCS, vol. 6806, pp. 1–19. Springer, Heidelberg (2011)
8. Ghosh, I., Shafiei, N., Li, G., Chiang, W.-F.: JST: An automatic test generation tool for industrial java applications with strings. In: International Conference on Software Engineering, ICSE (2013)
9. Godefroid, P., Nori, A.V., Rajamani, S.K., Tetali, S.: Compositional may-must program analysis: unleashing the power of alternation. In: Symposium on Principles of Programming Languages, POPL (2010)
10. Khurshid, S., Păsăreanu, C.S., Visser, W.: Generalized symbolic execution for model checking and testing. In: Garavel, H., Hatcliff, J. (eds.) TACAS 2003. LNCS, vol. 2619, pp. 553–568. Springer, Heidelberg (2003)
11. Kuznetsov, V., Kinder, J., Bucur, S., Candea, G.: Efficient state merging in symbolic execution. In: Programming Language Design and Implementation (PLDI) (2012)

12. Lattner, C., Adve, V.S.: LLVM: A compilation framework for lifelong program analysis & transformation. In: Symposium on Code Generation and Optimization (CGO) (2004)
13. Li, G.: Validated compilation through logic. In: Butler, M., Schulte, W. (eds.) FM 2011. LNCS, vol. 6664, pp. 169–183. Springer, Heidelberg (2011)
14. Li, G., Ghosh, I.: PASS: String solving with parameterized array and interval automaton. In: Bertacco, V., Legay, A. (eds.) HVC 2013. LNCS, vol. 8244, pp. 15–31. Springer, Heidelberg (2013)
15. Li, G., Ghosh, I., Rajan, S.P.: KLOVER: A symbolic execution and automatic test generation tool for C++ programs. In: Gopalakrishnan, G., Qadeer, S. (eds.) CAV 2011. LNCS, vol. 6806, pp. 609–615. Springer, Heidelberg (2011)
16. Li, G., Li, P., Sawaga, G., Gopalakrishnan, G., Ghosh, I., Rajan, S.P.: GKLEE: Concolic verification and test generation for GPUs. In: Symposium on Principles and Practice of Parallel Programming (PPoPP) (2012)
17. Lin, M., Li Chen, Y., Yu, K., Shi Wu, G.: Lazy symbolic execution for test data generation. IET Software 5(2), 132–141 (2011)
18. Majumdar, R., Sen, K.: LATEST: Lazy dynamic test input generation. Tech. Rep. UCB/EECS-2007, EECS Department, University of California, Berkeley (2007)
19. Tillmann, N., de Halleux, J.: Pex–white box test generation for .NET. In: Beckert, B., Hähnle, R. (eds.) TAP 2008. LNCS, vol. 4966, pp. 134–153. Springer, Heidelberg (2008)
20. uClibc++: An embedded C++ library, http://cxx.uclibc.org

Appendix

```
bool IsEasyChairQuery(string str) {
1:  // (1) check that str contains "/" followed by anything
2:  // not containing "/" and containing "EasyChair"
3:  int lastSlash = str.find_last_of('/');
4:  if (lastSlash == string::npos)
5:  { printf("exit (path) 1 \n"); return false; }
6:
7:  string rest = str.substr(lastSlash + 1);
8:  if (rest.find("EasyChair") == -1)
9:  { printf("exit (path) 2 \n"); return false; }
10:
11: // (2) Check that str starts with "http://"
12: if (str.compare(0, 7, "http://"))
13: {  printf("exit (path) 3 \n"); return false; }
14:
15: // (3) Take the string between "http://" and the last "/".
16: // if it starts with "www." strip the "www." off
17: string t = str.substr(7, lastSlash-7);
18: if (!t.compare(0,4,"www.")) { t = t.substr(4); // imme. path 2}
19: // imme. path 1
20: // (4) Check that after stripping we have either "live.com" or "google.com"
21: if (!(t == "live.com") && !(t == "google.com"))
22: { printf("****** exit (path) 4 ****** \n"); return false; }
23:
24: printf("****** exit (path) 5 ****** \n");
25: return true;
}
```

Fig. 6. The full motivating example I: a C++ version of the example program in [2]

SPIN as a Linearizability Checker under Weak Memory Models*

Oleg Travkin, Annika Mütze, and Heike Wehrheim

Institut für Informatik
Universität Paderborn, Germany
{oleg82,amuetze,wehrheim}@upb.de

Abstract. Linearizability is the key correctness criterion for concurrent data structures like stacks, queues or sets. Consequently, much effort has been spent on developing techniques for showing linearizability. However, most of these approaches assume a sequentially consistent memory model whereas today's multicore processors provide relaxed out-of-order execution semantics.

In this paper, we present a new approach for checking linearizability of concurrent algorithms under weak memory models, in particular the TSO memory model. Our technique first compiles the algorithm into intermediate low-level code. For achieving the out-of-order execution, we (abstractly) model the processor's architecture with shared memory and local buffers. Low-level code as well as architecture model are given as input to the model checker SPIN which checks whether the out-of-order execution of the particular algorithm is linearizable. We report on experiments with different algorithms.

1 Introduction

With the increased usage of multicore processors concurrent data structures implementing stacks, queues or sets find their way into standard programming libraries (e.g., `java.util.concurrent`). To allow for a high degree of concurrency these often restrict locking to small parts of the data structure or even completely dispose with locking. However, the performance gain achieved by such lock-free algorithms often comes at the price of an increased complexity in verification: The intricate interplay between concurrent processes makes such algorithms particularly hard to prove correct.

The standard correctness criterion for concurrent data structures is *linearizability* [11]. A fine-grained implementation of a data structure (e.g., an implementation of a stack by a linked list) is linearizable if its operations (e.g., pop and push) appear to be atomic. As Herlihy and Wing put it, "they seem to take effect instantaneously at some point in time" [11]. This is an important characterization as most proof techniques rely on fixing this point in time, also called

---

* This work has been partially funded by the German Research Foundation (DFG LINA, WE 2290/8-1).

V. Bertacco and A. Legay (Eds.): HVC 2013, LNCS 8244, pp. 311–326, 2013.

the *linearization point* (LP). In addition, linearizability definitions assume to have an abstract model of the data structure at hand (for comparison) in which all operations are executed atomically.

Today, a vast amount of techniques is available for showing linearizability, ranging from manual proofs (usually done by the algorithm designers), to model checking [20] and theorem proving [16,19]. These techniques mostly assume a sequentially consistent (SC) memory model [14]: statements in a sequential program are executed in program order; an execution of a concurrent program is an interleaving of the sequential program orders. However, multicore processors like x86, SPARC, POWER provide relaxed out-of-order executions [1]. These arise because – besides main memory – the cores possess local store buffers, and thus reads and writes to shared variables become visible to processes in different orders. In recent years, a large amount of work has been done on formalising the semantics of such weak memory models [17,2], on checking robustness of algorithms against reordering [3] and on model checking under relaxations [5]. To the best of our knowledge, there is only a single approach for checking linearizability under relaxed memory models [4]. The approach, which has also been applied in an SC setting [6], proceeds by having a model checker generate all concurrent and sequential histories (roughly, sequences of invokes and returns), and afterwards employing a particular check procedure for comparing them with respect to linearizability. To this end, the model checker needs to have a state variable for storing histories. A similar approach to checking linearizability based on recording histories (for SC executions) has been proposed in [20].

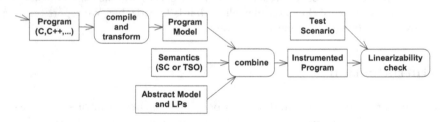

Fig. 1. Approach overview

In this paper, we present a new approach to checking linearizability under weak memory models which avoids the overhead of recording histories. In contrast to [4,20], we use the model checker to generate the state space *as well as* to carry out the linearizability check. Alike them, we use finite[1] test scenarios specifying particular usages of the concurrent data structure to limit state space exploration. To faithfully model out-of-order executions, we compose the scenario and the data structure with a model of the processor's architecture. This model includes local store buffers and the main memory, and provides operations for local reads and writes as well as memory fences (operations carrying out buffer flushes). To allow for a precise interaction with this model, we need exact information about the read and write operations in our algorithms. To

---

[1] The scenario has to be finite in terms of observable states.

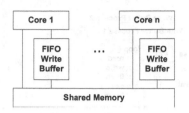

Fig. 2. TSO architecture as it is common for x86-based multicore processors

$$Initially : x = 0 \land y = 0$$

Process 1	Process 2
$write(x, 1);$	$write(y, 1);$
$read(y, r1);$	$read(x, r2);$

$$r1 = 0 \land r2 = 0$$

Fig. 3. Test program for detection of $Write \to Read$ reordering, also known as litmus test

this end, the algorithms (written in high-level languages like C or C++) are compiled into intermediate code by the LLVM compiler framework. Then the intermediate code (LLVM IR) is transformed into input for the model checker (which in our case is SPIN [12]). The model checker runs this code, and checks whether the operation conforms to its abstract model at all linearization points. Thus, our approach relies on a priori fixing linearization points. This is the price we pay for dispensing with history recordings. Although the idea of performing checks against an abstract model is not new, we are the first to combine such checks in a model checking framework with weak memory model semantics. The whole approach is summarized in Figure 1.

We have experimented with a number of algorithms, both ones being linearizable in SC as well as ones known to exhibit incorrect behaviour under weak memory models. Besides providing a linearizability checker, one contribution is also a Promela model of weak memory which is ready to be used for arbitrary property verification of concurrent algorithms.

2   Modelling Memory Model Behavior in SPIN

In our approach, a memory model is part of the input to the model checker SPIN. Currently, we offer two memory models: Sequential Consistency (SC) and Total Store Order (TSO). SPIN supports SC execution semantics, i.e., program order of each process is preserved during execution and concurrency is achieved by interleaving of all processes. Hence, support of SC as a memory model is straightforward. However, one of our design goals was to allow to switch between several memory models. In the following, we explain the relaxations introduced by TSO and our implementation of it.

TSO Architecture and Its Behavior. TSO allows two relaxations compared to SC. First of all, program order is not guaranteed. In particular, writes may appear as if they were executed after a later read, i.e., the order $Write \to Read$ is relaxed. However, instructions can only be reordered if they are independent, i.e., if a write and its following reads access different addresses. Figure 2 illustrates the architecture of a modern multicore processor providing a TSO memory model.

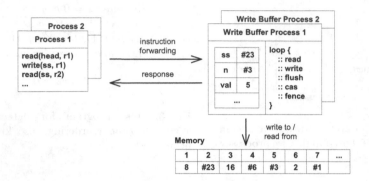

Fig. 4. Simulating TSO behavior by use of write buffer processes

Each processor has a write buffer to store its writes before they are flushed to the shared memory, i.e., the writes are pending, and subsequent read access may be granted before write access. Hence, reads can be executed while an earlier written value is still pending and the instructions appear to be reordered w.r.t. program order. Figure 3 shows a test program for detection of this behavior. Initially both shared variables x and y hold the value 0. The test detects reordering if both registers have values $r1 = 0 \land r2 = 0$ at the end of its execution and hence at least one process must have had its instructions reordered. Simple interleaving, as in an SC setting, does not allow this outcome.

A second relaxation allows processes to read their own writes early. If a write buffer contains a pending write to an address requested by a read, the value from the buffer is read. This behavior is called *early-read* [1] or also *Intra-Process-Forwarding* [13], because a reading processor is allowed to see its own writes before they are committed to the memory and hence before other processes can see them.

TSO as a Promela Model. In order to allow for flexibly switching between different memory models, we separate program specification from the underlying memory model and define an interface between both. Hence, a single program specification can be reused for checks against different memory models. As an interface we use a basic set of memory instructions as supported by most common processors. Each memory model specification implements *inline* statements for each type of instruction to define its semantics. To make sure that the memory model semantics is used, a program has to be specified in terms of the inline statements for the instructions. Thus, a program has no direct access to the memory, but only accesses it through the inlined instructions. Inlines are automatically replaced by the respective definitions from the memory model specification before runtime. The main memory is implemented by an array of statically fixed but adjustable length.

Write buffers introduce non-deterministic behavior by delaying writes. We model this non-determinism by assigning a dedicated write buffer process to each

```
inline read(addr, register) {
  atomic {
    ch ! R, addr, NULL, NULL;
    ch ? R, addr, register, _;
  }
}
```

```
do
:: ch? R, addr, value, _ → execRead;
:: ch? W, addr, value, _ → execWrite;
:: ch? CAS, add, old, new → execCAS;
:: ch? F, _, _, _ → execFence;
:: buffer ≠ ∅ → execFlush;
od
```

Fig. 5. Inline statement for read instruction; executed by program process

Fig. 6. Selection of next action; executed by write buffer process

program process. Figure 4 shows the basic components of a verification model. A program is defined within a process using the instruction set as defined by the memory model specification. Control flow and process local operations can be modelled in terms of regular Promela[2] statements because they are not visible to other processes. Memory instructions, such as read or write, are forwarded to the write buffer process via a synchronous channel that is dedicated to both processes only. The write buffer process stores pending writes as an address-value pair in an array-based FIFO queue and implements the actual execution of program instructions. Our model produces an error for full buffers in order to avoid loss of observable behavior. Larger buffers allow for more instructions to be reordered and hence may reveal behavior that is not observable in combination with small buffers. The execution of program instructions is performed in a loop, in which the write buffer process reacts to incoming messages. Messages encode the type of instruction that is to be executed as well as parameters that are necessary for its execution.

Instruction Forwarding and Execution. In our TSO model, inlines of the program process basically forward the actual execution of an instruction to the write buffer process. The actual execution is defined in the write buffer process. Figure 5 shows the inline statement for a read instruction. The part shown in the figure is executed in the program process. A read request (encoded by message type R) for a particular address $addr$ is send to the write buffer process. Variable $register$ is used to store the received value in a process local variable. A loop in the write buffer process (see Fig. 6) implements a non-deterministic choice between several actions. An incoming message triggers the execution of the instruction by the write buffer process. Note, that the communication for the read instruction is a two-way communication and it is performed atomically. Atomic steps in SPIN are allowed to pass control flow to other processes, e.g., via synchronous communication. When a process reaches the end of its control flow, the control flow is returned to the initiating process. No other non-involved processes can execute during this step and hence atomicity is preserved although several processes are involved in an atomic step.

Our memory model offers a basic set of memory instructions, which is also the interface to program specifications:

1. **read(**$addr$, reg**)**: read from memory address $addr$ into register reg

---

[2] Promela is the input specification language for the model checker SPIN.

2. **write**(*addr*, *reg*): write value *reg* to memory address *addr*
3. **mfence**(): causes a buffer to flush its content to memory[3]
4. **CAS**(*addr*, *oldReg*, *newReg*, *resReg*): compares memory value at address *addr* with value *oldReg*. Swaps memory value at *addr* with value *newReg* if compared values are equal. Fail or success is returned to *resReg*.

An overview of the communication structure (including the involved steps) between program and write buffer processes is given in Figure 7, where 1) shows the execution of a read instruction. The instruction is performed atomically, i.e., request, fetching the value from the buffer or memory, and response are performed in one single step. 2) shows the execution of write. A write message

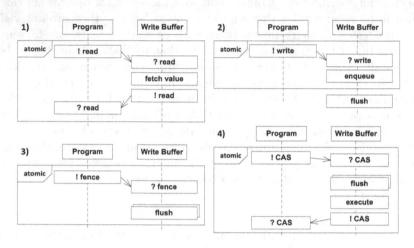

Fig. 7. Structure of communication between program and write buffer

is send to the write buffer process, which enqueues the address-value pair in its queue immediately. To model the delay of writes by a write buffer, the address-value pair is allowed to stay in the buffer for an unlimited amount of time until it is flushed. A flush commits a pending write from the buffer to the memory. Since the buffer implements a FIFO queue, the flushed write is always the oldest pending write. However, a flush can only be performed on a non-empty buffer. If the buffer is flushed immediately after enqueueing a write, the observable behavior is equivalent to a direct write to the memory.

3) shows the execution of a fence instruction. Fences are used to avoid reordering of program instructions. To achieve that, the write buffer is emptied by a sequence of flush steps, all of which are executed within one single atomic step. Note, the buffer process may flush non-deterministically during program execution. Hence, no behavior is lost by executing the fence atomically.

4) shows the execution of an atomic CAS. After receiving a CAS request the write buffer is emptied in order to avoid reordering with pending writes and

---

[3] Real processors have further kinds of fences. However, we use mfence only, because it captures the semantics of the other more specific fences.

hence to avoid violation of atomicity of CAS. When the buffer is empty, the actual CAS instruction is executed, which may or may not modify the memory. In the same step a response of success or failure is send to the program process, which stores the result in program local register variable.

So far, we have defined the semantics of a TSO architecture and a basic low-level interface similar to instructions as they are offered by common processors. In the following, we will use the interface to compose program specifications.

3   Program Encoding

One objective of our approach is to enable verification of programs written in several languages. Since memory models are defined for low-level instructions [1,17] similar to assembly languages, a program needs to be compiled before verification. In our approach, we use the LLVM[4] compiler framework, which transforms a program into an intermediate representation (LLVM IR) before a final transformation towards an executable. The intermediate representation is used for static program analysis and for optimization of the program. We reuse the intermediate representation for verification of the program. Using LLVM has two advantages over other compilers: 1. LLVM supports compilation of many languages and hence ensures a broad applicability of our verification approach. 2. The intermediate representation is easier to understand than assembly code, because it preserves variable and function naming in the code. We extract the Promela model from the LLVM IR code of a program. Currently this task is manual, but we plan to automate it in future extensions. The LLVM IR code is already low-level code and hence consists of instructions syntactically close to our memory interface (see Section 2). We use a C++ implementation of a stack to present the program transformation steps.

```
class Node {                         class Stack {
public:                              public:
    Node():val (0) {};                   Node* head;
    int val;                             void push(int);
    Node *next;                          Node* pop();
};                                   };

void Stack::push(int v) {            Node* Stack::pop() {
    Node *n, *ss;                        Node *ss, *ssn;
    n = new Node;                        do {
    n->val = v;                              ss = head;
    do {                                     if(ss == NULL)
        ss = head;                               return NULL;
        n->next = ss;                        ssn = ss->next;
    }while (0 == CAS(&head, ss, n));      }while (0 == CAS(&head, ss, ssn));
}                                        return ss;
                                     }
```

Fig. 8. C++ implementation of the Treiber stack [18]

The code in Figure 8 implements a Treiber stack [18], which is known to be linearizable [9] for SC. It is a list-based implementation and relies on the fine-grained synchronisation primitive compare-and-swap (CAS). A Node stores an

---
[4] www.llvm.org

```
define %Node* @_ZN5Stack3popEv(%Stack* %this) {
entry:
  %retval = alloca %Node*
  %this.addr = alloca %Stack*
  %ss = alloca %Node*
  %ssn = alloca %Node*
  store %Stack* %this, %Stack** %this.addr
  %this1 = load %Stack** %this.addr
  br label %do.body
do.body:
  %head = getelementptr %Stack* %this1, i32 0, i32 0
  %0 = load %Node** %head
  store %Node* %0, %Node** %ss
  %1 = load %Node** %ss
  %cmp = icmp eq %Node* %1, null
  br i1 %cmp, label %if.then, label %if.end
if.then:
  store %Node* null, %Node** %retval
  br label %return
if.end:
  %2 = load %Node** %ss
  %next = getelementptr %Node* %2, i32 0, i32 1
  %3 = load %Node** %next
  store %Node* %3, %Node** %ssn
  br label %do.cond
do.cond:
  %head2 = getelementptr %Stack* %this1, i32 0, i32 0
  %4 = bitcast %Node** %head2 to i32*
  %5 = load %Node** %ss
  %6 = ptrtoint %Node* %5 to i32
  %7 = load %Node** %ssn
  %8 = ptrtoint %Node* %7 to i32
  %9 = cmpxchg i32* %4, i32 %6, i32 %8 seq_cst
  %10 = icmp eq i32 %9, %6
  %conv = zext i1 %10 to i32
  %cmp3 = icmp eq i32 0, %conv
  br i1 %cmp3, label %do.body, label %do.end
do.end:
  %11 = load %Node** %ss
  store %Node* %11, %Node** %retval
  br label %return
return:
  %12 = load %Node** %retval
  ret %Node* %12
}
```

```
inline pop(returnvalue)
{
  short retval, head, head2, thisAddr,
  ss, ssn, this1, v, v0, v1, v2, v3, v4,
  v5, v7, v9, v11, next;

entry:
atomic {
  alloca(Ptr, retval);
  alloca(Ptr, thisAddr);
  alloca(Ptr, ss);
  alloca(Ptr, ssn); }
  write(thisAddr, this);
  read(thisAddr, this1);
doBody:
  getelementptr (Stack, this1, 0, head);
  readPopFail (head, v0);
  write (ss, v0);
  read(ss, v1);
  if
  :: ss == NULL -> write(retval, NULL);
                        goto retLabel;
  :: else -> skip;
  fi
  ->
ifend:
  read (ss,v2);
  getelementptr (Node, v2, 1, next);
  read (next, v3);
  write (ssn, v3);
doCond:
  getelementptr(Stack, this1, 0, head2);
  read (ss, v5);
  read (ssn, v7);
  casPop(head2, v5, v7, v9);
  if
  :: v9 == false -> goto doBody;
  :: else skip;
  fi
  ->
retLabel:
  read(ss,v11);
  write(retval, v11);
  returnvalue = v11;
}
```

Fig. 9. LLVM-IR code for pop operation from Figure 8; slightly simplified for brevity

Fig. 10. Promela model for the code in Fig. 9

integer value and a next-pointer to the next element in the list. The head-pointer of Stack points to the top element of a stack. Note that the loop in the method push (pop) tries to replace the head-pointer with a new value (the value of next). The CAS is successful, if no other process replaces head in the time between the first read of head and the CAS attempt. Each new loop iteration retries to perform the CAS until it is successful or, in case of pop, the stack is empty.

Promela Model of the Program. In order to verify program correctness under a particular memory model, we need a low-level representation of the program. For this, the program has to be compiled. An excerpt, the pop operation, of the compiled stack implementation from Figure 8 is shown in Figure 9. We slightly reduced the representation by removing additional instruction parameters for brevity (e.g., *alignment*). A manually transformed Promela model for the pop operation is shown in Figure 10.

The LLVM IR code is structured by operations and labeled blocks. An operation may contain several blocks. We tried to preserve this structure during transformation by defining inlines for operations and creating similarly labeled blocks. The instructions load, store and cmpxchg correspond to read, write and CAS instructions in our memory model (see Section 2). Depending on its parameters a branching instruction br represents a conditional or unconditional goto. Instruction alloca allocates memory and getelementptr is used for pointer computation, e.g., to determine the memory address of a particular attribute of an object. Variables in LLVM IR are prefixed by % for register variables and by @ for static variables. Note that memory addresses are stored within registers (as well as their values) and hence instruction parameters are always register variables or primitive values. For readability and understandability, we preserve variable naming during transformation.[5] Pointer casts are ignored during transformation, e.g., ptrtoint, because the memory address does not change for pointers of different types. Hence, the Promela model has fewer variables than the LLVM IR code. However, the word size of a read may vary with the pointer type (32bit, 64bit or more) and can lead to non-atomic reads for larger word sizes. Our model assumes atomicity of a read and hence is only valid if all reads of a program can be performed atomically, which is the case for the Treiber stack.

Memory Layout and Type Information. Low-level programs have to allocate memory. In order to simulate memory allocation in our model, there are two options: 1. Manually reserve portions of memory for each variable, which must be adapted whenever a test scenario is changed, e.g., number of operation calls. 2. We define some allocation mechanism, which performs allocation automatically. In order to allow simple application of our approach, we chose the latter. Type information is encoded as an integer indicating the length of an object in the memory array. A pointer Ptr has length one to store the pointer value. Similarly, a Stack instance has length 1, because it has exactly one head pointer to the top element. A Node instance has length 2. To store a Node instance, two array slots are necessary, one to store the element value and another one to store a pointer reference to the next node.

Memory allocation is implemented by a counter pointing to the next free memory slot. An alloca instruction increments the counter by the amount of slots to reserve after assigning the counter value to its second parameter, which becomes a pointer pointing to a free memory slot. Allocated memory is never freed in order to avoid the complexity inherent to a garbage collection mechanism. Hence, our model excludes the ABA problem as it is closely related to

---

[5] We prefixed nameless register variables (e.g., %1, %2,...) with "v" in our program specification in order to fit to Promela syntax.

the memory reclamation of a garbage collector. To access a particular attribute of an object, e.g., next pointer of a Node, the memory location containing the attribute must be computed. This computation is a simple offset computation which is local and is performed by getelementptr. Since different programs use different types, the instructions alloca and getelementptr must be adapted for each program and hence are part of the program model, although they can be seen as a part of the interface introduced in Section 2.

With this encoding of type information, we can model dynamic allocation of memory and avoid the effort of manually allocating memory for each test scenario. However, dynamic memory allocation results in different possible memory distributions due to interleaving and increases the number of observable states. More important, it usually does not affect correctness of the program. To reduce possible memory distributions in our Promela model, we allocate memory in atomic blocks. A fully static memory allocation would be optimal, but it would require us to allocate memory manually. The effort for creation and adaption of test scenarios would increase by far.

```
#include "tso.pml"                    init{ atomic{
proctype process1(chan ch){              alloca(Stack, this)
   short returnvalue;                     run process1(channelT1);
   push(this, 42);                        run bufferProcess(channelT1);
   pop(returnvalue);                      run process1(channelT2);
}                                         run bufferProcess(channelT2);
                                       }}
```

Fig. 11. Test scenario: two processes performing push and pop operations under TSO

Towards Verification. So far, we have defined an interface between memory models and program models. The program model is defined in terms of the interface provided by memory models and hence executes with the semantics as defined by a memory model. In order to start verification of correctness properties, we have to compose test scenarios, i.e., define which instructions a process should execute and under which memory model. The test scenario composition is straightforward in the sense that processes have to be defined as well as their initialisation. The underlying memory model is specified by an include instruction. Figure 11 shows a process definition on the left, which performs a push operation followed by a pop operation. The initialisation on the right simply allocates memory for a stack that is used throughout the test and starts pairs of program processes (process1) and write buffer processes (bufferProcess).

4   Checking Linearizability

Earlier sections have presented the construction of a program model and its combination with TSO execution semantics. In the following, we enrich the resulting model with correctness checks in order to identify violations of linearizability.

Linearizability is expressed in terms of histories of events, where the events are invocations and returns of operations. Roughly speaking, if all concurrent histories produced by an implementation have a matching sequential history of the abstract sequential specification, then the implementation is linearizable. In the original setting [11], "matching" is defined by (a) the sequential history having exactly the same invocations and returns as the concurrent history, and (b) the ordering between non-overlapping operations to be kept. Two operations do not overlap if the return of the first precedes the invocation of the second. A consequence of this definition is that the implementation looks as though the operation takes effect instantaneously at some point in time, this point being called the *linearization point* (LP). For weak memory models it is now condition (b) which becomes less clear: what do we mean by non-overlapping? In sequentially consistent memory, an operation has definitely finished when it has returned; in weak memory, an operation has only definitely finished when its results have been flushed, which might actually happen after the return (delayed writes).

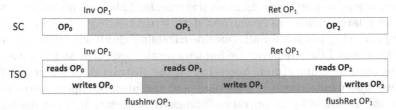

Fig. 12. Comparison of operation execution by one process for SC and TSO

Therefore, recently, two new definitions of linearizability for TSO were proposed [4,10], none of which we are however going to use. The first one [4] (TSO-to-TSO linearizability) considers the delay of writes by enriching the histories with two new events. The events mark the beginning (*flushInv* OP_1) and the end (*flushRet* OP_1) of an execution interval, in which writes of an operation are flushed, see Figure 12. The core of the definition in [4] is to preserve the order of *Ret* or *flushRet* events and their following *Inv* or *flushInv* events in the history produced by the abstract sequential specification. In order to produce such a history, the abstract sequential specification is executed on a TSO memory model as well and hence can be subject to errors due to TSO-behavior itself. A second definition [10] (TSO-to-SC linearizability) rather sticks to the original definition [11] and considers the order of *Ret* and *Inv* events only. Hence, the implementation has to have its LP within the interval between *Inv* and *Ret*, which is equivalent to allowing behavior that is observable on SC only. To make implementations in which the effect of an operation can take place between *Ret* and *flushRet* linearizable under this criterion, the authors propose to weaken the abstract sequential specification by allowing operations to fail for no reason.

We do not use the first definition because it does not keep the essential idea behind proving linearizability, namely that once linearizability has been proven the programmer can think of such operations as behaving like atomic operations. We do not use the second definition because we always want to start with the established sequential specification of the data structure (a push is a push, and not sometimes a push and sometimes an empty operation), and our linearizability check should detect whether the implementation running on TSO deviates from this specification. Nevertheless, our notion of linearizability is close to the definition by Gotsman et al., and hence also to the original one, it only differs in the sense that we consider the full execution interval of an operation running on TSO. Regarding Figure 12, the full execution interval of OP_1 is the interval between $InvOP_1$ and $flushRetOP_1$. Two operations being non-overlapping thus means that the return or flushReturn (whatever is later) of the first operation needs to preceed the invocation of the second. This is the ordering which has to be kept when finding a matching sequential history.

In order to check for our notion of linearizability with SPIN, we use a Promela model of the sequential abstract specification of the data structure in which all operations are atomic. By executing operations of this sequential data structure, we therefore get sequential histories. We assume that the implementations of the data structures have linearization points (LPs) which have a fixed position in the code, i.e., belong to particular program statements. This is an assumption which is true for a large number of concurrent data structures, e.g., Treiber Stack [18] or MS Queue [15], but not for all. Our linearizability check now makes use of the knowledge about LPs: whenever the implementation executes an LP, we also execute the corresponding atomic operation on the abstract data structure. When these two statements (the LP statement and the abstract operation) disagree in the result returned by an operation, the current execution is not linearizable with this LP. If they always agree, the sequence of abstract operations gives us the sequential history we look for.

In case of our stack, agreement or disagreement can be checked by comparing the values returned by pop operations: if the pop LP in the implementation extracts a value from the list which is not equal to the return value of the abstract pop on a stack, the implementation is not linearizable. Thus it is the pop operation which acts as an observer for the correctness of previous push operations. For the push, the LP in the implementation and the atomic push on the stack are just executed together; no check is necessary here since the push operation is not returning a value. In order to carry out this check of agreement between implementation and abstract data structure, the low-level operations have to be instrumented such that the corresponding abstract operation is executed at the LPs. Next, we first describe how we model the abstract data structure in Promela, then the instrumentation of the implementation and finally give some results of an experimental evaluation.

Abstract Model. For the linearizability check, we use an abstract atomic model of the data structure which is shared by all processes. For each LP of the implementation, we create an abstract atomic operation. If an operation has more than one LP, e.g., one LP for failure and one for success, we encode separate abstract operations w.r.t. the behavior at the LP. Abstract model and implementation model are wired during the instrumentation, which is explained in Section 4.

For the stack example, we use the abstract model in Figure 13. An array is used to store stack content with up to SSIZE elements. The variable asTop always has the index value of the first free slot in the stack array. For each LP

```
#define SSIZE 4                              inline asPopFail() {
short asStack[SSIZE];                            assert (asTop == 0)
short asTop = 0;                             }

inline asPopSucc(asValue) {                  inline asPush(asValue) {
  atomic {                                     atomic {
    asTop--;                                     assert (asTop < SSIZE)
    assert (asStack[asTop] == asValue);          asStack[asTop] = asValue;
    asStack[asTop] = 0;                          asTop++;
  }                                            }
}                                            }
```

Fig. 13. Abstract stack model; allows to stack up to SSIZE elements

of the Treiber stack we define an inline. The Treiber stack has three LPs [8], one for push and two for pop. Both push and pop have their LPs at the CAS instruction, if the CAS execution is successful. A pop operation can fail if the stack is empty. In this case, the LP is the first read of variable head. Assertions to ensure consistency of implementation and abstract model are included in the inline definitions. Variable asValue is used to forward the input value (in case of push) from the implementation to the abstract stack or the result value (in case of pop). Finally, we need to instrument the implementation in order to execute the abstract model at the LPs.

Instrumentation for Linearizability Checking. So far, we have provided a stack implementation model that is executed w.r.t. TSO memory model semantics and an abstract model of the stack. For a linearizability check, both models must pass the LP synchronously. Hence, both models have to execute a low-level instruction for the LP together with the corresponding abstract operation atomically. However, we cannot always put an atomic block around a low-level instruction in the program model followed by an abstract operation to achieve this. Instructions can be delayed by write buffers, which would be prevented by an atomic block.

```
inline readPopFail(addr, target)            inline casPop(addr, old, new, return)
{                                           {
  atomic{                                     atomic{
    ch ! R, addr, NULL, NULL;                   ch ! CAS, addr, old, new;
    ch ? R, addr, target, NULL;                 ch ? CAS, addr, return, _;
    if                                          if
      :: target == NULL -> asPopFail();           :: return -> asPopSucc(memory[old]);
      :: else -> skip;                            :: else -> skip;
    fi                                          fi
  }                                           }
}                                           }
```

Fig. 14. Instrumentation of LPs for the pop operation

Hence, instead of wiring both models at the program level, we extend the semantics model. The idea is not to change the execution semantics of the memory model, but to find the right step to perform the abstract operation. In other words, we define copies of existing instruction definitions and customize them for each LP. Afterwards, we replace the standard instructions by the customized instructions at LPs in the program model. In Figure 14 two customized instruction definitions for the LPs of the pop operation are shown. Both replace the standard instructions (read and cas) in the model in Figure 10, readPopFail in the doBody block and casPop in the doCond block. Since both instructions are atomic, we can add the instrumentation code to the atomic block of the corresponding instruction. Depending on the instruction result the LP is reached and hence, the abstract operation is triggered. In case of the read instruction the LP is reached, if the read value is NULL. In case of the CAS, the LP of the pop operation is a successful execution of CAS.

Writes have to be instrumented differently from reads and CAS instructions. Because a write becomes visible to other processes during its flush into memory, the actual LP is the flush. Hence, the abstract operation has to be performed during the flush of the write. For correct instrumentation of LPs corresponding to writes, the flush semantics need to be extended, s.t. flushing a write corresponding to an LP also triggers the execution of the corresponding abstract operation. In our instrumentation of writes, we send a third value besides the address-value-pair to the buffer process. This value represents a particular abstract operation to trigger or none if the write is a non-LP write. During the execution of a flush a simple case distinction encodes whether and, if so, which abstract operation is triggered. Examples for instrumented writes can be obtained from our SVN repository. In particular, we instrumented writes in our models of Seqlock, Spinlock and Burns Mutex.

The instrumentation is the final step of the model composition for checking linearizability. Executions leading to inconsistent results of the abstract model and implementation model are reported as errors and indicate non-linearizability of the implementation or a wrong instrumentation of LPs. In the following section, we discuss our experience with the proposed approach.

Experimental Results. As a proof of concept, we tested our approach on a few well-known concurrent data structure implementations. We implemented each of the data structures in C/C++ and applied our approach to it as presented throughout this paper. All implementations, the corresponding Promela models including test scenarios and our memory models are available for download at our SVN repository[6]. We performed an exhaustive search for each of the program models and test scenarios. The results are presented in Figure 15 for SC and TSO separately. The column buffer# (memory#) denotes the minimum write buffer (memory resp.) size that is required for the test scenarios.

We were able to identify known bugs in the Burns Mutual Exclusion algorithm, which can be easily avoided by introducing fence instructions. The other implementations did not show non-linearizable behavior, neither with SC nor with TSO semantics. Our results confirm existing verification results [3,4], which were not able to find bugs due to TSO memory model relaxations. However, the stack and queue implementations are known to show incorrect behavior, when run on weaker memory models [5].

---

[6] http://code.google.com/p/lina-rmm-verification/

		SC		TSO			
test scenario		states	time [s]	states	time [s]	buffer#	memory#
Treiber stack [18]	U‖O	627	0	14292	0.07	6	13
	UO‖UO	16772	0.04	262742	1.38	6	23
	UOU‖OUO	135708	0.29	4145402	29.4	10	33
	UUUU‖OOOO	896528	2.55	33589805	294	16	43
	U‖O‖U	47214	0.1	5893891	52.4	6	19
	UO‖UO‖UO	37269425	157	oom	769	6	33
	U ≙ push, O ≙ pop, oom ≙ out of memory						
M&S Queue[15]	E‖D	2203	0.01	94354	0.52	7	20
	ED‖ED	88933	0.24	1113224	28.2	9	34
	EDE‖DED	1401240	4.53	oom	873	19	48
	E ≙ enqueue, D ≙ dequeue, oom ≙ out of memory						
Seqlock [10]	W‖R	676	0	11099	0.05	6	10
	WW‖RR	10570	0.02	1050382	6.9	12	13
	WWW‖RRR	103873	0.16	63211488	538	18	16
	W‖R‖R	71571	0.12	4467945	31.2	6	14
	W ≙ write pair, R ≙ read pair						
Spinlock [4]	p‖p	193	0	1004	0	1	2
	p‖p‖p‖p	48995	0.11	3741610	26.8	1	2
	p is infinite loop, selecting non-det. operations: acquire, release, tryacquire						
Burns unfenced [7]	p1‖p2	43	0	4	0	2	3
Burns (fenced)	p1‖p2	54	0	474	0	2	3
	p1 and p2 enter and leave critical section in an infinite loop						

Fig. 15. All tests were performed on a virtual machine, Ubuntu Linux, Intel Core i5, 2.53GHz and 3GB dedicated to SPIN 6.2.3

5   Conclusion

In this paper, we have presented an approach for linearizability checking under consideration of different architectures and hence different memory models. Our approach can be viewed as a step-by-step guide that leads developers from the implementation of a concurrent program to the verification of its correctness. Since we carry out checks based on given test scenarios, our approach is – like others – a testing and not a verification technique. Thus, we see our linearizability checker as a first step of getting confidence in the correctness of an algorithm before starting a formal proof, for instance in a theorem prover supported approach. Moreover, we provide a Promela model of TSO memory model that is ready to use for arbitrary correctness properties.

The relation between our and other notions of linearizability on TSO [4,10] has already been discussed. In the future, we also intend to study what kind of compositionality our notion of linearizability guarantees. On the practical side, we plan to automate the transformation from LLVM IR code to our Promela model, which would reduce a developer's effort in applying our approach. We also plan to offer weaker memory models, e.g., Partial Store Order (PSO), for verification and to extend the provided instruction set in order to be applicable to a greater variety of programs. However, it is yet unclear how linearizability could be defined for the even weaker memory model PSO.

References

1. Adve, S.V., Gharachorloo, K.: Shared Memory Consistency Models: A Tutorial. IEEE Computer 29(12), 66–76 (1996)

2. Alglave, J., Fox, A., Ishtiaq, S., Myreen, M.O., Sarkar, S., Sewell, P., Nardelli, F.Z.: The Semantics of Power and ARM Multiprocessor Machine Code. In: Proceedings of the 4th Workshop on Declarative Aspects of Multicore Programming, DAMP 2009, pp. 13–24. ACM, New York (2008)
3. Bouajjani, A., Derevenetc, E., Meyer, R.: Checking and Enforcing Robustness against TSO. In: Felleisen, M., Gardner, P. (eds.) ESOP 2013. LNCS, vol. 7792, pp. 533–553. Springer, Heidelberg (2013)
4. Burckhardt, S., Gotsman, A., Musuvathi, M., Yang, H.: Concurrent Library Correctness on the TSO Memory Model. In: Seidl, H. (ed.) ESOP 2012. LNCS, vol. 7211, pp. 87–107. Springer, Heidelberg (2012)
5. Burckhardt, S., Alur, R., Martin, M.M.K.: CheckFence: checking consistency of concurrent data types on relaxed memory models. In: PLDI, pp. 12–21 (2007)
6. Burckhardt, S., Dern, C., Musuvathi, M., Tan, R.: Line-up: A complete and automatic linearizability checker. In: PLDI, pp. 330–340 (2010)
7. Burns, J., Lynch, N.A.: Mutual Exclusion Using Indivisible Reads and Writes. In: Proceedings of the 18th Annual Allerton Conference on Communication, Control, and Computing, pp. 833–842 (1980)
8. Derrick, J., Schellhorn, G., Wehrheim, H.: Proving Linearizability Via Non-atomic Refinement. In: Davies, J., Gibbons, J. (eds.) IFM 2007. LNCS, vol. 4591, pp. 195–214. Springer, Heidelberg (2007)
9. Derrick, J., Schellhorn, G., Wehrheim, H.: Mechanically verified proof obligations for linearizability. ACM Trans. Program. Lang. Syst. 33(1), 4 (2011)
10. Gotsman, A., Musuvathi, M., Yang, H.: Show no weakness: Sequentially consistent specifications of TSO libraries. In: Aguilera, M.K. (ed.) DISC 2012. LNCS, vol. 7611, pp. 31–45. Springer, Heidelberg (2012)
11. Herlihy, M.P., Wing, J.M.: Linearizability: a correctness condition for concurrent objects. ACM Trans. Program. Lang. Syst. 12(3), 463–492 (1990)
12. Holzmann, G.: The Spin model checker: Primer and Reference Manual, 1st edn. Addison-Wesley Professional (2003)
13. Intel, Santa Clara, CA, USA. Intel 64 and IA-32 Architectures Software Developer's Manual Volume 3A: System Programming Guide, Part 1 (May 2012)
14. Lamport, L.: How to Make a Multiprocessor Computer That Correctly Executes Multiprocess Programs. IEEE Trans. Computers 28(9), 690–691 (1979)
15. Michael, M.M., Scott, M.L.: Simple, Fast, and Practical Non-Blocking and Blocking Concurrent Queue Algorithms. In: The 15th Annual ACM Symposium on Principles of Distributed Computing, pp. 267–275 (May 1996)
16. Schellhorn, G., Wehrheim, H., Derrick, J.: How to Prove Algorithms Linearisable. In: Madhusudan, P., Seshia, S.A. (eds.) CAV 2012. LNCS, vol. 7358, pp. 243–259. Springer, Heidelberg (2012)
17. Sewell, P., Sarkar, S., Owens, S., Nardelli, F.Z., Myreen, M.O.: x86-TSO: A rigorous and usable programmer's model for x86 multiprocessors. Commun. ACM 53(7), 89–97 (2010)
18. Treiber, R.K.: Systems programming: Coping with parallelism. Technical Report RJ 5118, IBM Almaden Res. Ctr. (1986)
19. Vafeiadis, V., Herlihy, M., Hoare, T., Shapiro, M.: Proving correctness of highly-concurrent linearisable objects. In: Torrellas, J., Chatterjee, S. (eds.) PPOPP, pp. 129–136 (2006)
20. Vechev, M., Yahav, E., Yorsh, G.: Experience with Model Checking Linearizability. In: Păsăreanu, C.S. (ed.) Model Checking Software. LNCS, vol. 5578, pp. 261–278. Springer, Heidelberg (2009)

Arithmetic Bit-Level Verification
Using Network Flow Model

Maciej Ciesielski[1], Walter Brown[1], and André Rossi[2]

[1] University of Massachusetts
ECE Department
Amherst, MA 01003, USA
ciesiel@ecs.umas.edu, webrown@umass.edu
[2] Université de Bretagne-Sud
Lab-STICC UMR 6285
56321 Lorient Cedex France
andre.rossi@univ-ubs.fr

Abstract. The paper presents a new approach to functional, bit-level verification of arithmetic circuits. The circuit is modeled as a network of adders and basic Boolean gates, and the computation performed by the circuit is viewed as a flow of binary data through such a network. The verification problem is cast as a Network Flow problem and solved using symbolic term rewriting and simple algebraic techniques. Functional correctness is proved by showing that the symbolic flow computed at the primary inputs is equal to the flow computed at the primary outputs. Experimental results show a potential application of the method to certain classes of arithmetic circuits.

Keywords: Formal verification, Functional verification, Arithmetic verification, Bit-level arithmetic.

1 Introduction

One of the most challenging problems encountered in hardware design is functional verification of arithmetic circuits and datapaths. Boolean logic techniques, based on BDDs, so successfully used in logic synthesis, cannot solve large arithmetic problems as they require "bit-blasting", i.e., flattening of the design into bit-level netlists. Similarly, Boolean satisfiability (SAT) and Satisfiability Modulo Theories (SMT) solvers cannot handle complex arithmetic designs and require solving computationally expensive decision problems. On the other hand, theorem provers, popular in industry, require a significant human interaction and intimate knowledge of the design to guide the proof process. Typical approach in industry is to use a host of methods, including simulation-based and formal methods, which requires large teams of experts with high degree of expertise. While datapath verification has reached certain level of maturity [1,2], certain areas of arithmetic verification remain open for more research. According to Slobodova [3] "Multiplication function is beyond the capacity of BDDs and

V. Bertacco and A. Legay (Eds.): HVC 2013, LNCS 8244, pp. 327–343, 2013.
© Springer International Publishing Switzerland 2013

SAT solvers"; it requires decomposition into smaller entities, while there is "No automatic way of finding properties on the decomposition boundary".

The work described in this paper addresses some of those issues. It focuses on *functional verification*, i.e., proving correctness of arithmetic design w.r.t. its intended function, rather than targeting a specific property or checking equivalence between the implementation and specification. In this sense, functional verification can be viewed as a more general problem, as it has to overcome the issue of generating a complete set of properties that describe the intended functionality. Our approach is based on modeling an arithmetic circuit as a network of half adders and basic Boolean connectors and viewing the computation performed by the circuit as a flow of binary data through the network. The verification problem is cast as a special case of a Network Flow problem and solved using symbolic term rewriting and linear algebraic techniques.

1.1 Related Work

Several approaches have been proposed to check an arithmetic circuit against its functional specification. Different variants of canonical, graph-based representations have been proposed, including Binary Decision Diagrams (BDDs), Binary Moment Diagrams (BMDs), Taylor Expansion Diagrams (TED), and others [4]. Application of BDDs to verification of arithmetic circuits is somewhat limited due to prohibitively high memory requirement for complex arithmetic circuits, such as multipliers. BDDs are being used, along with many other methods, for local reasoning, but not as monolithic data structure [3,1,2]. BMDs and TEDs offer a linear space complexity but require word-level information of the design, which is often not available or is hard to extract from bit-level netlists. A number of SAT solvers have been developed to solve generic Boolean decision problems. The one potentially relevant to our work is CryptoMiniSAT, which targets XOR-rich bio-informatics circuits by replacing traditional CNF formula with XORs [5]. However, it is still based on a computationally expensive DPLL decision process and does not scale with the design size. Several techniques combine linear arithmetic constraints with Boolean SAT in a unified algebraic domain [6] or use ILP to model the modulo semantics of the arithmetic operators [7] [8]. In general, ILP models are computationally expensive and are not scalable. Some techniques combine a word-level version of automatic test pattern generation (ATPG) and modular arithmetic constraint-solving techniques for the purpose of test generation and assertion checking [9]. SMT solvers integrate different theories (Boolean logic, linear integer arithmetic, etc.) into a DPLL-style SAT decision procedure [10]. However, in their current format, the SMT tools are not efficient at solving decision problems that appear in arithmetic circuits.

A number of Computer Algebra methods have been introduced to model arithmetic components as polynomials [11,12]. Automated techniques for extracting arithmetic bit level (ABL) information from gate level netlists have been proposed in the context of property and equivalence checking [13]. ABL components are modeled by polynomials over unique ring, and the normal forms are computed w.r.t. Grobner basis over rings $Z/2^n$ using modern computer algebra algorithms. In our view this model is unnecessarily complicated and not scalable to practical designs. A simplified version of this technique replaces the expensive Grobner base computation with a direct generation of polynomials representing circuit components [15]. However, no practical method for deriving such large polynomials and no systematic comparison against the specification have been proposed. Our work addresses this issue using a more efficient network flow model.

Industry also uses Theorem Provers, deductive systems for proving that an implementation satisfies a specification, using mathematical reasoning. The proof system is based on a large (and problem-specific) database of axioms and inference rules, such as simplification, rewriting, induction, etc. Some of the known theorem proving systems are: HOL, PVS, and Boyer-Moore/ACL2. The success of verification depends on the set of available axioms, rewrite rules, and on the *order* in which they are applied during the proof process, with no guarantee for a conclusive answer. Similarly, term rewriting techniques, such as [14], are incomplete, as they rely on simple rewriting rules (distributivity, commutativity, and associativity) and use non-canonical representations.

An entirely different approach to functional arithmetic verification has been proposed in [16]. In this approach the arithmetic circuit, composed of adders and connecting logic gates, is described by a system of linear equations. The resulting set of linear equations is then reduced to a single algebraic expression (the "signature" of the circuit) using Gaussian elimination and linear algebra techniques. If the resulting signature matches the input and output expressions (specified by input bit positions and binary output encoding) and does not contain any internal signals, then the circuit is considered functionally correct. The difficulty of this method lies in proving the case when not all signals can be eliminated and the signature contains a "residual expression"(RE), in those variables. In this case, for the circuit to be functionally correct, the residual expression must evaluate to zero. Proving this requires solving a separate and difficult Boolean problem. Furthermore, such an expression is not unique and the method does not offer means for choosing RE that would be easiest to solve.

1.2 Novelty and Contribution

In this work we follow the algebraic approach similar to [16], but solve the problem by modeling it as a computationally simpler *network flow* problem. Specifically, the computation performed by the circuit is modeled as a flow of binary data, represented as an algebraic, pseudo-Boolean expression. This representation provides important information about the circuit functionality and location of possible bugs. The verification proof reduces to showing the equivalence between the input and output expressions. Any possible discrepancy between the two expressions is captured in an algebraic expression, which, in contrast to "residual expression" in [16], is unique and related to fanouts and other signals that can be identified a priori. This feature greatly simplifies the final proof which can be solved using purely algebraic methods.

In contrast to theorem provers and traditional term rewriting techniques, the proposed method is complete. It is based on a complete set of algebraic expressions describing internal circuit modules, used as the rewriting rules. The result does not depend on the order in which the rules are applied; the order is fixed and unique. The method does not require expertise in formal verification, can be fully automated, and always terminates with a conclusive answer. Furthermore, no assumption is made about any structural similarity between the implementation and the specification, required by commercial verification tools.

2 Technical Approach

In this work we are concerned with a class of arithmetic circuits, i.e., combinational circuits with binary inputs that compute a (signed or unsigned) integer function; the result computed by the circuit is encoded in a finite number of binary outputs. The internal operators (circuit modules) are assumed to be binary adders (single-bit half adders and full adders) and basic Boolean logic gates. Such circuits are often referred to as Arithmetic Boolean Level (ABL) circuits [13]. Techniques exist that can convert a gate-level arithmetic circuit into such an ABL network, although a highly bit-optimized arithmetic circuits may contain a sizable number of logic gates that cannot be mapped onto (half) adders. Those gates will be modeled using arithmetic operators, such as half adders, and described as linear equations, as described in Section 3.1.

2.1 Basic Terminology

The arithmetic function computed by the circuit is expressed as a polynomial in terms of the primary inputs. We refer to such a polynomial as *input signature*, denoted by $Sig_{in}(N)$, for some circuit N. Such a polynomial is unique, as it uniquely describes an arithmetic function computed by the circuit; it can be linear or nonlinear. For example, the input signature of a 7-3 counter N_C, shown in Fig. 2 is simply $Sig_{in}(N_C) = x_1 + x_2 + x_3 + x_4 + x_5 + x_6 + x_7$. For a n-bit binary adder N_A with inputs $\{a_0, \cdots, a_{n-1}, b_0, \cdots, b_{n-1}\}$, the input signature is $Sig_{in}(N_A) = \sum_{i=0}^{n-1} 2^i a_i + \sum_{i=0}^{n-1} 2^i b_i$, etc. The integer coefficients, called *weights*, w_i), associated with the corresponding signals, are uniquely determined by the circuit structure and its specification. For the 7-3 counter the input weights are $w_i = 1$ for each signal x_i, while for an adder, $w(a_i) = w(b_i) = 2^i$ for inputs a_i, b_i at bit position i.

Input signature for non-linear networks can be similarly obtained. For example, input signature of a 2-bit signed multiplier can be directly obtained from its high-level specification: $F = (-2a_1 + a_0)(-2b_1 + b_0) = 4a_1b_1 - 2a_0b_1 - 2a_1b_0 + a_0b_0$. By substituting product terms by new variables, $x_3 = a_1b_1, x_2 = a_1b_0, x_1 = a_0b_1, x_0 = a_0b_0$, we obtain a linear input signature of the multiplier network in terms of these fresh variables: $Sig_{in}(M) = 4x_3 - 2x_2 - 2x_1 + x_0$. Again, the signal weights are uniquely defined by the specification.

The result computed by an arithmetic circuit can also be expressed as a polynomial in the *output* variables. This polynomial is always linear as it represents a unique binary encoding of an integer number computed by the circuit. We refer to such a polynomial as *output signature*. For example, the output signature of a 2-bit signed multiplier M with outputs Z_3, Z_2, Z_1, Z_0 is $Sig_{out}(M) = -8Z_3 + 4Z_2 + 2Z_1 + Z_0$. In general, output signature of any arithmetic circuit with n output bits S_i is represented as $Sig_{out}(N) = \sum_{i=0}^{n-1} 2^i S_i$. The output signal weights are also uniquely defined, in this case by the output bit position.

We also introduce the notion of a *cut* in the circuit, defined as a set of signals separating primary inputs from primary outputs. Each cut has its own algebraic signature, defined similarly to the input and output signatures. Specifically, a cut signature is a linear polynomial in the cut signals with coefficients specified by the integer signal weights. The computation of those weights is one of the basic steps of our verification procedure, to be described in detail in Section 3.4.

For nonlinear circuits, such as multipliers, the nonlinear part (contained between the primary inputs and the linear variables) is typically very shallow. This is the case not only for simple array multipliers mentioned above, but also for all signed and Booth-encoded multipliers and other circuits containing adder network structures (typical of all arithmetic circuits). Such a nonlinear block can be independently and easily verified using Boolean methods or word-level diagrams (BMD or TED). In this work we assume that the boundary between the linear and nonlinear blocks is known (as in the multiplier example above).

2.2   Overview of the Method

Since the input and output signatures describe the same circuit, albeit in different sets of variables, in a functionally correct circuit the two signatures must be equivalent, in the sense that they must evaluate to the same integer value for any integer input vector. The proof goal of functional verification is then to show that one signature can be transformed into the other using expressions of the internal operators: adders and logic gates. This can be done by symbolically rewriting the input signature, using the properly linearized internal logic and arithmetic operators, and checking if the polynomial obtained by such transformation matches the output signature. This check can be easily done using canonical word level diagrams, such as BMD or TED. The transformation can also be done in the opposite direction, from outputs to inputs, and the resulting expression compared to the input signature. If the input signature is not known, it can be computed directly from the output signature by such a backward transformation.

The presumed equivalence between the input and output signatures suggests that the functional verification problem in an arithmetic circuit can be viewed as a *Network Flow Problem*: the data is injected into input bits and flows through the network to be collected at the output bits. The network modules act like nodes in a transportation network, distributing data according to the edge capacities, here represented as signal weights. In the functionally correct circuit, the total flow into the inputs, described by the input signature, must be equal to the flow at the output of the circuit, described by the output signature.

   While conceptually the equivalence between the input and output signatures can be determined by symbolic rewriting, it is actually accomplished by *computing the signal weights*. The concept of rewriting is presented here only to prove the correctness of our method. In an actual implementation, the proof will be accomplished by i) computing weights of the intermediate polynomials involved in the transformation; ii) checking if such computed weights are compatible with the input/output signatures; and iii) if the weights satisfy additional equivalence relations required for functional correctness. The details of this procedure are provided in Sections 3.4 and 3.5.

3   Arithmetic Network Model

For the presented network model to work, we have to make sure that each network node (represented by circuit module) satisfies *Flow Conservation Law (FCL)*. As we will see in the next section, this is automatically guaranteed by basic arithmetic operators, such as adders. Logic gates and fanouts are modeled in a similar fashion, to make sure that each satisfies FCL.

3.1   Algebraic Models

This section describes algebraic models of the circuit modules used in our method. They include: half-adders (HA), full-adders (FA), inverters (INV), buffers (BUF), and basic logic gates (AND, XOR, OR). Each of them is modeled with a single linear equation which satisfies FCL.

• A half-adder (HA) with binary inputs a, b, and a full adder (FA) with binary inputs a, b, c_0 and outputs S (sum) and C (carry out) are represented by the following equations:

$$HA: a + b = 2C + S; \quad FA: a + b + c_0 = 2C + S \tag{1}$$

• Logic gates, AND and XOR, can be obtained directly from the HA using a linear HA model: the XOR(a, b) is derived from the sum output S, and the AND(a, b) from the carry-out output C of HA(a, b), as shown in Fig. 1(a). If only one gate (say an AND) is used/needed, the other output (in this case corresponding to an XOR) is left unconnected. We refer to such an unused signal as a *floating signal*. The role of the floating signals in our model is to pick up the "slack" in the flow, so that the used output always assumes the correct binary values and the module satisfies the FCL.

• The OR gate, $R =$ OR(a, b), can be similarly derived from the HA using deMorgan's law, resulting in $\{a + b = 2C + S; \; C + S = R\}$. By combining the two equations we obtain a general OR model: $a + b = 2R - S$, see Fig. 1(b). Here, S represents an unused, floating signal. The set of equations for OR can often be simplified if $C = a \cdot b = 0$, i.e., when inputs a, b to the HA are never both 1. This happens often in arithmetic circuits whenever a, b come as reconvergent fanouts from the C and S outputs of another HA, where they cannot be both 1. In this case the equation for the OR gate, denoted as OR*, simplifies to $a + b = R$, see Fig. 1(c). In summary, the OR gate is modeled as follows:

$$OR : a + b = 2R - S; \quad OR^* : a + b = R \tag{2}$$

• An inverter gate $y =$ INV(x) is modeled by the equation: $x = 1 - y$. Similarly, a buffer with input x and output y can be modeled by the simple equation $x = y$.
• Special attention must be given to fanouts, which can be viewed as trivial modules. Such modules do not compute any arithmetic or logic function and simply replicate the signal as needed. In its original form a fanout node may not satisfy algebraic flow conservation law. For example, if signal x_1 fans out into two signals, x_2, x_3 then the equation $x_1 = x_2 + x_3$, with a constraint $x_1 = x_2 = x_3$, does not satisfy the algebraic flow conservation law. To fix this problem, we create a dummy fanout module, called $FBox$, with inputs x_0, x_s and outputs $x_1, \ldots x_k$ for a fanout with factor k, as shown in Fig. 1(d). Here x_s is a slack variable added to compensate for the difference between $x_1 + \ldots x_k$ and x_0. We refer to such a variable as *fanout slack*. The equation satisfying FCL for the FBox is: $w_0 x_0 + w_s x_s = w_1 x_1 + \ldots + w_k x_k$, where w_i is the weight associated with signal x_i.

Fig. 1 shows algebraic models for the basic modules, and the truth table to verify the logical correctness of the models. It is easy to verify that each such module satisfies the FCL.

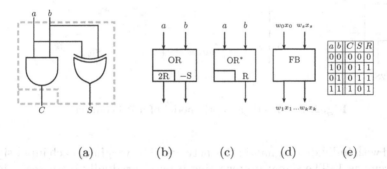

(a)   (b)   (c)   (d)   (e)

Fig. 1. Modeling logic gates: (a) $C =$ AND(a, b), $S =$ XOR(a, b), derived from half-adder: $a + b = 2C + S$; (b) generic model for OR: $a + b = 2R - S$; (c) simplified XOR* model: $a + b = R$; (d) model of fanout box; (e) truth table for C, S, R.

3.2 Signature Rewriting

Before formalizing our verification model, we illustrate the verification approach with an example of a 7-3 counter, shown in Fig. 2. The circuit counts the number of 1s on the seven input bits and encodes the result in a 3-bit output word. Its structure is described by the following set of linear equations.

$$\begin{cases} FA_1 : x_1 + x_2 + x_3 = 2x_{11} + x_{12} \\ FA_2 : x_4 + x_5 + x_6 = 2x_{13} + x_{14} \\ FA_3 : x_{12} + x_{14} + x_7 = 2x_{15} + x_{10} \\ FA_4 : x_{11} + x_{13} + x_{15} = 2x_8 + x_9 \end{cases} \qquad (3)$$

The input signature, $Sig_{in} = cut_0 = x_1+x_2+x_3+x_4+x_5+x_6+x_7$ is rewritten into an expression (cut signature) $cut_1 = (2x_{11} + x_{12}) + (2x_{13} + x_{14})$ using equations for FA$_1$: $(x_1+x_2+x_3 = 2x_{11}+x_{12})$ and FA$_2$: $(x_4+x_5+x_6 = 2x_{13}+x_{14})$. Similarly, expression for cut_1 is rewritten into cut_2 using equation for FA$_3$, and then into expression cut_3 using FA$_4$. The resulting expression $cut_3 = 4x_8 + 2x_9 + x_{10}$ matches exactly the output signature, $Sig_{out} = 4S_2 + 2S_1 + S_0$, which indicates that the circuit is correct (i.e., performs its intended function). Notice the weights

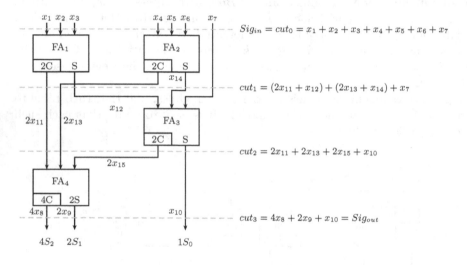

Fig. 2. Arithmetic network model of a 7-3 counter

associated with individual signals in this network. The weight of each input signal in this circuit is 1. The signature rewriting process gradually increases weights of some of the signals, eventually producing higher weights at the output bits. For example, one unit of x_1, x_2, x_3 each, when applied to FA$_1$, will produce one unit of x_{12} generated at output S of the adder, and two units of x_{11} (denoted in the figure as $2x_{11}$), generated at output C. This is a direct consequence of equation (1) of the adder. Then, signals x_{11}, x_{13}, x_{15}, each with weight 2, will produce outputs x_8 and x_9 with weights 4 and 2, respectively. This is simply the result of replacing the subexpression $2x_{11} + 2x_{13} + 2x_{15} = 2(x_{11} + x_{13} + x_{15})$ in cut_2 by $2(2x8 + x9)$, or, equivalently, of multiplying the equation (3) for FA$_4$ by constant 2.

In summary, the weights, which represent the amount of flow carried by the signals play an important role in computing the flow in the network. The next two sections describe the process of computing the weights by propagating them from the primary outputs to primary inputs, without actually performing signature rewriting.

3.3 Weight Compatibility Constraints

As discussed in the preceding section, linear models of the arithmetic modules used in the network naturally impose constraints on signal weights. We refer to those rules as *Weight Compatibility* constraints. The weights which satisfy the compatibility condition are *unique*, and are determined solely by the output encoding and the network structure. These rules are simply a consequence of linear equations modeling the internal modules (adders, gates, inverters, and fanout boxes). Let w_x denote the weight of signal x. Then, the FA equation $a + b + c_0 = 2C + S$ imposes the following condition:

$$w_a = w_b = w_{c0} = w_S; \quad \text{and} \quad w_C = 2w_S$$

For the HA, the first constraint simply reduces to $w_a = w_b = w_S$. Note that for the AND and XOR gates, which use the FA/HA model, these rules will determine weights of the *floating signals*, i.e., the S signal for the AND gate and the C signal for the XOR gate.

Similar relation can be derived for the generic OR gate, modeled by $a + b = 2R - S$, namely:

$$w_a = w_b = -w_S, \quad \text{and} \quad w_R = -2w_S$$

The simplified OR* gate, governed by the equation $a + b = R$, has only one constraint, namely $w_a = w_b = w_R$.

The first constraint in each group simply means that the input weights must be the same. Changing any of the weights in a manner inconsistent with this constraint, would correspond to multiplying individual signals by different constants, which would invalidate the algebraic model (equations 1 and 2). The same is true for the buffer: one must not multiply each side of the equation by a different constant as this will change the relation between the two signals. On the other hand, multiplying the entire equation for any given module by a constant, will not change the relationship between the signals and will only increase the flow carried by those signals. This happens during the process of weight propagation, as shown in the 7-3 counter circuit.

Similarly, the compatibility constraints for an $FBox$ are derived directly from the $FBox$ equation: $w_0x_0 + w_sx_s = w_1x_1 + \ldots + w_kx_k$.
For a known set of signal weights $w_0, w_1, \ldots, w_k$ this will automatically determine weight of the *slack signal* x_s. The weight propagation procedure, described in the next section, guarantees that such weights can always be computed and have unique value.

In addition to the weight compatibility constraints, a *connectivity* rule needs to be imposed on the connections between the modules to correctly propagate the weights along the network wires. Such a rule is intuitively obvious: the weights of the signals on the two ends of a wire (buffer) must be equal. This, too, can be justified by the mathematical model of the buffer, described by the equation $x_i = x_j$. This trivially imposes the constraint that $w_i = w_j$.

3.4   Weight Propagation

Computation of signal weights is an important first step in our verification procedure. The weights are computed by traversing the network from primary outputs (where they are determined by the binary encoding) to primary inputs, starting with the least significant bit, S_0. The assignment of weights must satisfy the compatibility conditions derived earlier. The weight assignment process is illustrated with an example of a parallel prefix adder, with input signature $Sig_{in} = 8(a_3 + b_3) + 4(a_2 + b_2) + 2(a_1 + b_1) + a_0 + b_0 + c_0$ and output signature $\{16C_{out} + 8S_3 + 4S_2 + 2S_1 + 1S_0\}$ imposed by the output encoding.

Fig. 3 shows the original gate-level design and Fig. 4(a) shows the network flow model of the circuit, obtained from gate level netlist using ABL extraction technique. In this design, each OR is represented by a simple OR* model $(R = a + b)$, because it satisfies the simplifying conditions discussed earlier. The signals S_6, S_7, C_{10}, S_{11}, shown at the bottom of the circuit, are the *floating signals* coming from the output of HAs, which do not propagate any further. The signals d_9, d_8, d_7, d_{16}, shown at the top of the circuit, are the *fanout slack variables*, added as inputs to the FBoxes. In contrast to the input and output signatures, the weights of the floating and fanout slack signals are not known a priori and are computed during the weight propagation procedure.

The procedure starts with the least significant bit of the output, S_0. The weight 1 of signal S_0, connected to the S output of FA$_0$, matches the weight of that signal generated by FA$_0$. At the same time weight 2 is imposed on signal d_1 at the C output of that adder (to be denoted by $2d_1$). This assignment of weights at FA$_0$ is compatible with the weight (1) of its inputs. If the input weights were not known, this would also impose weights $=1$ on the inputs a_0, b_0, c_0. Propagation of $2S_1$ upwards similarly satisfies the weight compatibility at FA$_1$ (whose all inputs have weight 2) and imposes weight 4 on signal d_{16}. Propagation of $4S_2$ through HA$_7$ generates weights $(4d_7, 4d_{16})$ at the input to HA$_7$ and weight $8d_{18}$ at the C output of HA$_7$, see Fig. 4(a), etc. The procedure continues as long as the weights satisfy the weight compatibility conditions.

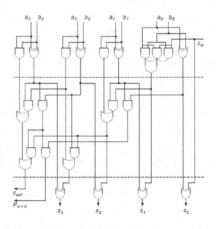

Fig. 3. Gate-level parallel prefix adder

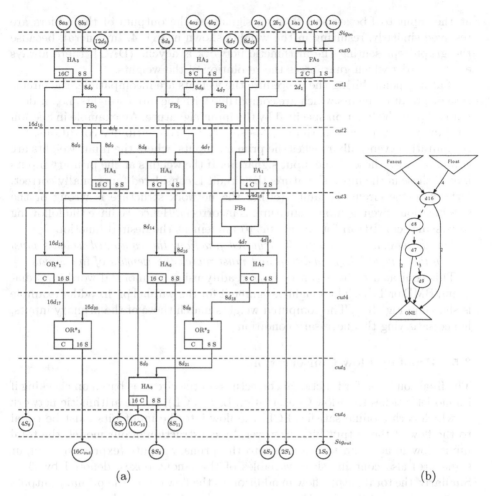

Fig. 4. (a) Network flow for parallel prefix adder; (b) TED showing equivalence between fanouts and floating signals

The floating and slack signals must be computed from the weights of already computed signals. Consider, for example, $Fbox_3$ associated with signal d_{16}. The weight of the right output signal, $4d_{16}$ has been already determined by back-propagating $4S_2$, but the other output from this Fbox will not be known until both inputs to HA_6 have been determined. This is made possible by the computation of weights originating at $16C_{out}$, resulting in the following sequence of weights:

$$16C_{out} \rightarrow 16d_{20} \rightarrow \{8d_{14}|8d_{16}\}$$

which fixes the left output of $Fbox_3$ to $8d_{16}$. The slack variable for this fanout box is then computed as the difference between the outgoing and incoming flow associated with this signal, i.e., $8d_{16} + 4d_{16} - 4d_{16} = 8d_{16}$. Other slack variables at the input to Fboxes and floating signals at the outputs of the adders are resolved similarly, resulting in the weights shown in Fig. 4. In general, because the graph representing the arithmetic network is acyclic (DAG), there always exist an order which guarantees the resolution of the weights.

If at any point during the procedure the weights are incompatible, the circuit cannot produce weights which are compatible with the input weights, i.e., it does not compute the function specified by the input signature. An example in Section 3.6 illustrates this case. If the weights satisfy the compatibility conditions, the computation eventually reaches the primary inputs, where the input weights are compared with those in the input signature. If the weights at the primary inputs match those in the input signature, the circuit is considered functionally correct. Otherwise the circuit is faulty (either the network structure is wrong or the specification, given as input signature, is incorrect). Hence we have the following **necessary condition** for the circuit to implement the desired function:

For the circuit to compute the required function, the computed weights must satisfy the compatibility condition and must match the weights of the inputs.

This equivalence check can be done readily using a canonical word-level diagram, BMD or TED. The weight assignment for the parallel prefix adder example is shown in Fig. 4(a). The computed weights match those of the primary inputs, hence satisfying this necessary condition.

3.5   Proof by Flow Conservation

The final condition for functional correctness of the circuit is based on checking if its model satisfies the Flow Conservation Law (FCL). In the arithmetic network in which each module satisfies FCL, the flow into the input bits must be equal to the flow at the output bits. However, by construction of our model, the total input flow in addition to the flow into the primary inputs (expressed as input signature) also contains slack variables of the fanout boxes, denoted by Δ_{fn}. Similarly, the total output flow in addition to the flow out of the primary outputs (expressed as output signature) also contains floating signals associated with the unused variables, denoted Σ_{fl}. That is, in an arithmetic circuit which, by construction, satisfies flow conservation law, we have:

$$Sig_{in} + \Delta_{fn} = Sig_{out} + \Sigma_{fl} \qquad (4)$$

where Δ_{fn} and Σ_{fl} are the weighted sums of the slack fanouts and the floating signals introduced in the network, respectively. In our example, $\Delta_{fn} = 8d_{16} + 12d_9 + 8d_8 + 4d_7$; and $\Sigma_{fl} = 16C_{10} + 8S_{11} + 8S_7 + 4S_6$. Intuitively, for the input signature to be equal to the output signature, the flow added by the fanouts must be compensated by the flow removed by the floating signals. As a result, if the input and output signatures match, the proof of functional correctness of the network reduces to proving that

$$\Delta_{fn} - \Sigma_{fl} = 0 \qquad (5)$$

In summary: *The circuit is functionally correct if and only if: (i) there exists a compatible assignment of weights consistent with the input signature Sig_{in};*

and (ii) the amount of the flow introduced by fanouts Δ_{fn} is equal to the flow consumed by floating signals Σ_{fl}.

The first condition guarantees that the input signature can be rewritten into an output cut whose weights match those of the output signature, while the second condition satisfies the flow conservation law in this pseudo-Boolean network.

A naive way to solve this problem would be to express each of those terms as a function of primary inputs and prove that the resulting expression is zero. However, we only need to express Σ_{fl} in terms of the fanout variables. We then need to prove that $\Sigma_{fl} = \Delta_{fn}$ in terms of the fanout signals only. We perform this verification using TED. Figure 4(b) shows the TED for Δ_{fn} and Σ_{fl}, both expressed in terms of fanout variables only, clearly indicating that they are identical.

3.6 Debugging Faulty Circuits

The described method for functional verification can also help identify and localize bugs in a faulty circuit. Consider again the circuit in Fig. 2 but with wires x_{12} and x_{13} swapped. The question is whether this circuit will still work as a 7-3 counter; and if not, what causes the malfunction and how can the bug be identified. In this faulty configuration the equations for the affected adders, FA_3 and FA_4, are:

$$\begin{cases} FA_3 : x_{13} + x_{14} + x_7 = 2x_{15} + x_{10} \\ FA_4 : x_{11} + x_{12} + x_{15} = 2x_8 + x_9 \end{cases} \tag{6}$$

With this, the following cuts are generated during the rewriting process, starting with cut_0:

$$\begin{cases} cut_1 : (2x_{11} + x_{12}) + (2x_{13} + x_{14}) + x_7 \quad \text{(same as before)} \\ cut_2 : (2x_{11} + x_{12}) + x_{13} + (2x_{15} + x_{10}) \quad \text{(different)} \\ cut_3 : x_{13} - x_{12} + 4x_8 + 2x_9 + x_{10} \quad \text{(different)} \end{cases} \tag{7}$$

In this arrangement, the weight of x_{12} does not match the weights of other signals, $2x_{11}, 2x_{15}$, at the input to FA_4. Similarly, the weight of signal $2x_{13}$ does not match the weights of x_{14} and x_7, at the input to FA_3. This violates the weight compatibility discussed earlier. While the resulting expression of cut_3 contains the output signature $4x_8 + 2x_9 + x_{10}$, it also contains a "residual expression" $(x_{13} - x_{12})$. This indicates that the circuit computes a function that differs from the intended one by $(x_{13} - x_{12})$, hence it is incorrect. (It can be easily shown that $x_{13} - x_{12} \neq 0$). The identification of such a residual expression is useful in determining the source of the bug: it must be related to signals x_{13}, x_{12}.

4   Results

We tested our verification method on a number of signed multipliers up to 62 $\times$ 62 bits. First, a structural verilog code was generated for each multiplier using a generic multiplier generator software (courtesy of the University of Kaiserslautern). The verilog code was parsed to transform the multiplier circuit into a network of HA, FA and basic logic gates from which a set of equations was generated in the required format. The structure of those designs made it possible to easily extract input signature required in our method. In general, however, transformation of an arbitrary gate-level circuit into an ABL network is a known difficult problem that can be computationally expensive; it may also result in different configurations since such a mapping is not unique. This, however, does not affect our approach; the different structures will only affect the effectiveness of the method but not the result. Each mapping will have its own, unique set of transformations and any of those will lead to the same conclusive answer regarding the circuit functionality.

The results of our experiments are shown in Fig. 5. The CPU time includes all phases of the process: preprocessing (which takes a negligible fraction of the entire process, taking only 3 sec for the 62-bit multiplier); computing signal weights; checking weight compatibility with input signature; creating symbolic equation for $\Delta_{fn} - \Sigma_{fl}$; generating script for TED; and using TED to check the equivalence condition (5). The experiments were run on a PC with an Intel i7 CPU @ 2.30GHz and 7.7 GB memory. Since most of the research in this

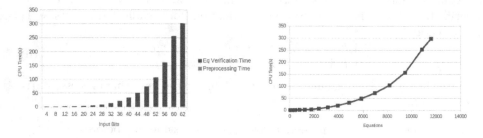

Fig. 5. CPU time for multipliers (a) in the number of bits (b) in number of equations

field has been done in the context of property checking rather than functional verification, we could not find suitable data for comparison. the CPU runtimes [1,2]. The runtime complexity of the procedure to compute algebraic signature of the network is quadratic in the number of equations (or, equivalently in the number of gates), c.f. Figure 5.

Comparison with SMT Solvers: In principle, the network can be described by a system of linear equations $Ax = b$ derived directly from the equations describing the network modules. The test for functional correctness can be obtained by checking if the network $Ax = b$ is compatible with the expected input and output signatures. This can be modeled as satisfiability (SAT) problem as follows. Let $Sig_{in}(N)$ and $Sig_{out}(N)$ be the primary input and output signature as defined in Section 3.1. Then, we need to show that: $(Ax = b) \wedge (Sig_{in}(N) \neq Sig_{out}(N)$ is unsatisfiable (unSAT). We performed this test on a number of multipliers using three SMT solvers that support Linear Integer Arithmetic: MathSAT, Yices, and Z3. The results, reported in Table 1 show that the SMT solvers were not able to solve the problem for multipliers larger than 8 bits, while our method can verify the functional correctness of multipliers up to 62 bits in several minutes. Z3 ran out of memory (3 GB), while Yices was unable to complete the computation in 30 minutes. In some cases, MathSAT was "unable to perform computation" and is not reported here. We also attempted to solve the problem using BDDs, but (as expected) we were unable to build BDD for multipliers larger than 14 bits, due to the memory explosion.

Table 1. Comparison with SMT solvers (MO=memory out with 3 GB, TO=timeout after 1800 sec)

Design	Z3 (sec)	Yices (sec)	Our method (sec)
$mult\ 3 \times 3$	0.23	0.02	0.21
$mult\ 4 \times 4$	466.36	0.05	0.28
$mult\ 8 \times 8$	MO	TO	0.57
$mult\ 16 \times 16$	MO	TO	1.52
$mult\ 24 \times 24$	MO	TO	3.63
$mult\ 32 \times 32$	MO	TO	12.22
$mult\ 40 \times 40$	MO	TO	31.57
$mult\ 48 \times 48$	MO	TO	71.93
$mult\ 56 \times 56$	MO	TO	157.24
$mult\ 62 \times 62$	MO	TO	297.59
$PrefixAdder(4b)$	160.31	0.05	0.25

5   Conclusions

The goal of this paper was to present a novel idea of modeling the functional verification of arithmetic circuits without resorting to expensive Boolean or bit-blasting methods. As such, this approach has a potential application in formal verification and could be used in conjunction with existing methods for functional verification. Currently the method is applicable to designs with well defined input signature, expressed as a multivariate (possibly nonlinear) polynomial in the input variables. Typically such a signature is given as part of the specification; otherwise it can be extracted from the design by transforming the known output signature (binary encoding) backwards towards the inputs. In this sense, the method is directly applicable to extract circuit functionality from its hybrid arithmetic/gate-level structure.

An important application where this method can be particularly useful is the identification and localization of bugs in the design. This can be accomplished by analyzing areas containing incompatible weights, as illustrated in Section 3.6. Typically this will happen due to miss-wiring, crossing, or missing wires, which will result in incompatible weights. It seems that the module which violates the weight assignment and the bit position that imposes a violating assignment should provide important information about the bug location. We are not aware of any other approach that can so efficiently address this debugging issue.

The major limitation of this method is in generating ABL networks from an arbitrary gate-level arithmetic circuit, which in general is a difficult problem. Nevertheless, the method can be useful in verifying new arithmetic circuit architectures based on novel computer architecture algorithms, were the design is already specified in terms of adders and some connecting gates. The method can be readily extended to sequential circuits by converting them to bounded models, which is a part of the ongoing research effort. The extension to floating point arithmetic will need to be investigated.

Acknowledgment. This work has been supported by a grant from the National Science Foundation under award No. CCF-1319496.

References

1. Kaivola, R., Ghughal, R., Narasimhan, N., Telfer, A., Whittemore, J., Pandav, S., Slobodová, A., Taylor, C., Frolov, V., Reeber, E., Naik, A.: Replacing Testing with Formal Verification in Intel® Core™ i7 Processor Execution Engine Validation. In: Bouajjani, A., Maler, O. (eds.) CAV 2009. LNCS, vol. 5643, pp. 414–429. Springer, Heidelberg (2009)
2. Seger, C.-J.H., Jones, R.B., OLeary, J.W., Melham, T., Aagaard, M.D., Barrett, C., Syme, D.: An Industrially Effective Environment for Formal Hardware Verification. IEEE Transactions on Computer-Aided Design of Integrated Circuits and Systems 24(9), 1381–1405 (2005)
3. Slobodova, A.: A Flexible Formal Verification Framework. In: MEMCODE 2011 (2011)
4. Pradhan, D.K., Harris, I.G. (eds.): Practical Design Verification. Cambridge University Press (2009)
5. Soos, M.: Enhanced Gaussian Elimination in DPLL-based SAT Solvers. In: Pragmatics of SAT (2010)
6. Fallah, F., Devadas, S., Keutzer, K.: Functional Vector Generation for HDL Models using Linear Programming and 3-Satisfiability. In: Proc. Design Automation Conference, pp. 528–533 (1998)
7. Brinkmann, R., Drechsler, R.: RTL-Datapath Verification using Integer Linear Programming. In: Proc. ASPDAC, pp. 741–746 (2002)
8. Zeng, Z., Talupuru, K., Ciesielski, M.: Functional Test Generation based on Word-level SAT. J. Systems Architecture 5, 488–511 (2005)
9. Huang, C.-Y., Cheng, K.-T.: Using Word-level ATPG and Modular Arithmetic Constraint-Solving Techniques for Assertion Property Checking. IEEE Trans. on CAD 20(3), 381–391 (2001)
10. Biere, A., Heule, M., Maaren, H.V., Walsch, T.: Satisfiability Modulo Theories in Handbook of Satisfiability, ch. 12. IOS Press (2008)
11. Raudvere, T., Singh, A.K., Sander, I., Jantsch, A.: System Level Verification of Digital Signal Processing application based on the Polynomial Abstraction Technique. In: Proc. ICCAD, pp. 285–290 (2005)
12. Shekhar, N., Kalla, P., Enescu, F.: Equivalence Verification of Polynomial Data-Paths Using Ideal Membership Testing. IEEE Trans. on Computer-Aided Design 26, 1320–1330 (2007)

13. Wienand, O., Wedler, M., Stoffel, D., Kunz, W., Greuel, G.: An Algebraic Approach for Proving Data Correctness in Arithmetic Data Paths. In: Proc. ICCAD, pp. 473–486 (July 2008)
14. Vasudevan, S., Viswanath, V., Sumners, R.W., Abraham, J.A.: Automatic Verification of Arithmetic Circuits in RTL using Stepwise Refinement of Term Rewriting Systems. IEEE Trans. on Computers 56, 1401–1414 (2007)
15. Pavlenko, E., Wedler, M., Stoffel, D., Kunz, W.: STABLE: A new QF-BV SMT Solver for hard Verification Problems combining Boolean Reasoning with Computer Algebra. In: Proc. Design Automation and Test in Europe, pp. 155–160 (2011)
16. Basith, M.A., Ahmad, T., Rossi, A., Ciesielski, M.: Algebraic approach to arithmetic design verification. In: Formal Methods in CAD, pp. 67–71 (2011)

Performance Evaluation of Process Partitioning Using Probabilistic Model Checking

Saddek Bensalem[1], Borzoo Bonakdarpour[2], Marius Bozga[1], Doron Peled[3], and Jean Quilbeuf[1]

[1] UJF-Grenoble 1 / CNRS VERIMAG UMR 5104, France
{saddek.bensalem,marius.bozga,jean.quilbeuf}@imag.fr
[2] School of Computer Science, University of Waterloo, Canada
borzoo@cs.uwaterloo.ca
[3] Department of Computer Science, Bar Ilan University, Israel
doron.peled@gmail.com

Abstract. Consider the problem of *partitioning* a number of concurrent interacting processes into a smaller number of physical processors. The performance and efficiency of such a system critically depends on the tasks that the processes perform and the partitioning scheme. Although empirical measurements have been extensively used a posteriori to assess the success of partitioning, the results only focus on a subset of possible executions and cannot be generalized. In this paper, we propose a probabilistic state exploration method to evaluate a priori the efficiency of a set of partitions in terms of the speedup they achieve for a given model. Our experiments show that our method is quite effective in identifying partitions that result in better levels of parallelism.

Keywords: Concurrent programming, Scheduling, Speedup, Efficiency, Parallel programming, Formal methods.

1 Introduction

In concurrent programming, a program consists of multiple interacting *processes* that may run in parallel. Processes can potentially reside on different physical *processors* in order to speedup execution. Typically, there are far more processes than actual available physical processors. *Partitioning* is the problem of assigning processes to processors, so that the best level of parallelism and, ideally, maximum *speedup* is achieved. This problem is known to be notoriously challenging in the context of concurrent systems, as an intelligent scheduler must be able to make predictions about the state and temporal execution of interactions among processes. The research activities that deal with this problem range over a wide spectrum: from theoretical parallel and distributed algorithms and analytical performance analysis methods to empirical and experimental approaches. In all these activities, one measures the executions of different processes and utilization of processors of the system over time. Rules of thumb that involve static analysis of the system can be useful but of limited effect, since it is the dynamic

V. Bertacco and A. Legay (Eds.): HVC 2013, LNCS 8244, pp. 344–358, 2013.

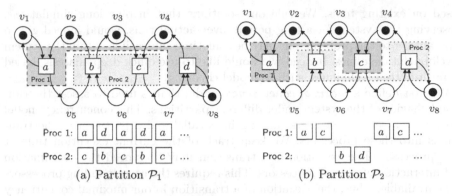

Fig. 1. An example of the effect of partitioning on concurrent scheduling

behavior that actually affects the efficiency. Empirical approaches provide us with an insight about specific dynamic behavior of the system under analysis, but typically they only focus on a very small subset of possible executions and cannot be generalized.

The focus of this paper is on evaluating and comparing partitions for concurrent programs by using state exploration techniques. Consider the abstract model of a concurrent program in Figure 1(a) running on two processors Proc 1 and Proc 2. The model has Boolean variables $v_1 \cdots v_8$, where the values of $v_1 \cdots v_4$ and v_8 are initially true and the rest are false. The transitions of this program are labeled by a, b, c, and d. For example, transition a updates the value of variables as follows: $v_2 = false$, $v_5 = true$, and the value of v_1 does not change. We assume that transitions that share variables cannot execute simultaneously (e.g., a and b). A *partition* maps transitions to processors. Let $\mathcal{P}_1$ be the partition, such that processor Proc 1 executes transitions a and d, and processor Proc 2 executes transitions b and c. Since transitions a and c are enabled in the initial state, Proc 1 and Proc 2 can execute them concurrently. After this execution, the values of variables are updated as follows: $v_2 = v_3 = v_4 = false$, $v_5 = v_6 = v_7 = true$. In this state, transitions b and d are enabled and, hence, Proc 1 and Proc 2 can concurrently execute d and b. Thus, both processors are always busy executing.

Now, consider a different scenario, where transitions are mapped to processors according to partition $\mathcal{P}_2$ (see Figure 1(b)). In the initial state, a and c are enabled, but Proc 1 can only execute one of them. If Proc 1 executes transition a, the system reaches a state from where only transition c is enabled. Since this is the only choice of execution, Proc 1 executes c and the system reaches a state where b and d are enabled. Since these transitions are both handled by Proc 2, they are executed sequentially. Thus, during that execution, partition $\mathcal{P}_2$ allows utilizing only half of the resources, that is one processor over two.

We propose an effective and relatively inexpensive test for assessing a priori the efficiency of concurrent execution of a system deployed according to a given partition. The task needs to be based on a simple but affordable analysis, and based on existing tools. We rule out solutions that involve long simulations. Observing the system for a long period, over actual runs, would indeed give a good answer to the problem, but may be sometimes unfeasible within the system development deadlines. Instead, we would like to use quick deep analysis, based on push-button techniques, such as model checking.

We first define a *maximal concurrency* model that is used to assess the run-time behavior of the system under different partitions. This concurrency model consists of a set of processors running in parallel and a partition of the transitions into these processors. We keep track of the current execution time at each processor. The execution of a transition may thus need the coordination and interaction of several processors. This requires the corresponding processors to be available. Thus, the execution of a transition in our maximal concurrency model involves first waiting for a time where all involved processors are available, and then consuming the time required to execute the transition in each one of them. Obviously, the different mapping of transitions into processors makes a big impact on execution time.

Our method analyzes the value of variables that keep track of execution time for each processor. We provide a probabilistic analysis, assuming that different nondeterministic and concurrent choices are selected randomly. The analysis relies on comparing execution time and the probability of speedup for finite prefixes of execution sequences according to a partition. We aim at keeping the complexity of conducting the analysis as low as possible. This is in particular challenging, as any analysis that takes into account the performance needs to, in some sense, sum up behavior parameters (e.g., some measurement of the duration of the execution) over time. This can potentially explode the size of the state space very quickly. Our solution is to provide an analysis for a limited execution sequence, say, of length k. As starting this analysis from only the initial state would be biased (perhaps the system always performs first the same constant initialization sequence), our method analyzes execution prefixes from the entire reachable state space of the system. This means that we take into account the probability of reaching some state, and, from there, the probability of speedup of executing a sequence of length k.

By experimenting with various values of k, we can tune between precision and additional complexity. More formally, one needs to identify the answer to the following question: with what probability can random executions according to one partition be faster by a factor of f. We, in particular, use the probabilistic model checker PRISM [10] to solve this problem. Our experiments clearly show the benefit of using our technique to assess the efficiency of different partitions.

Organization. In Section 2, we present our computation and concurrency model. Section 3 is dedicated to our method for comparing the performance of two given partitions. We present our case study in Section 4. Related work is discussed in Section 5. Finally, in Section 6, we make the concluding remarks and discuss future work.

2 Computation Model

2.1 Transition Systems

Definition 1. *A transition system $\mathcal{T}$ is a tuple $\langle V, S, T, \iota \rangle$, where*

- *V is a finite set of finite-domain variables.*
- *S is the set of states that are valuations of the variables V,*
- *T is a set of transitions. With each transition $\tau \in T$, we have:*
  - *An enabling condition $en_\tau : S \to \{ true, false \}$ over the variables V that must be true for the transition τ to execute.*
  - *A transformation $f_\tau : S \to S$ that modifies the current state on execution of τ.*
- *$\iota \in S$ is the initial state, that is the initial valuation of the variables.* □

For example, the model in Figure 1 has Boolean variables $v_1 \cdots v_8$ and four transitions a, b, c, and d. The initial state is where $v_1 = v_2 = v_3 = v_4 = v_8 = true$ and $v_5 = v_6 = v_7 = false$. Moreover, en_a is $v_1 = v_2 = true$. In Section 1, we described how the transitions update the state of the program.

Definition 2. *An execution σ is a maximal sequence of states $\sigma = s_0 s_1 s_2 \ldots$, such that*

- *$s_0 = \iota$.*
- *For each $0 \leq i < |\sigma|$, there exists some $\tau \in T$, such that $en_\tau(s_i)$ holds and $s_{i+1} = f_\tau(s_i)$.* □

We choose to use simple transition systems, as they can already illustrate our approach without the need to use complicated details. In particular, we abstract away processes; concurrency between transitions is allowed when they use disjoint set of variables. In fact, when the system is divided logically into processes, there is no need to use a more complicated model: the program counter of each process is an additional variable that makes all the transitions of a single process interdependent.

2.2 Maximal Concurrency Model

Given a transition system $\mathcal{T} = \langle V, S, T, \iota \rangle$, in order to reason about concurrency and speedup, we need to take the execution of transitions and their duration into account. Let P be a fixed finite set of *processors*. The mapping of the system $\mathcal{T}$ on the processors P is specified through a partition $\mathcal{P}$ of the set $V \cup T$. Each class in $\mathcal{P}$ corresponds to a set of variables and/or transitions handled by a given processor in P. Thus, for a variable $v \in V$ (respectively, transition $\tau \in T$), $\mathcal{P}(v)$ (respectively, $\mathcal{P}(\tau)$) returns a processor in P. Specifying the mapping of the variables explicitly allows us to determine which processor is used when accessing the variables.

Since computing en_τ and f_τ, where $\tau \in T$, involves dealing with a set of variables, execution of τ will engage a *set* of processors. Formally, given a partition $\mathcal{P}$, if transition τ is associated with variables V_τ, then the set of processors engaged in executing τ is

$$P_\tau^\mathcal{P} = \{p \in P \mid p = \mathcal{P}(\tau) \vee \exists v \in V_\tau : p = \mathcal{P}(v)\}$$

We assume that executing a transition τ engages each processor in $P_\tau^\mathcal{P}$ for some (not necessarily equal) constant time. Given a processor $p \in P_\tau^\mathcal{P}$, we call this time the *duration* of transition τ on processor p, and denote it by $p_\tau^\mathcal{P}$. Furthermore, in order to analyze and keep track of the duration for which a processor is still engaged in a transition, we introduce a *history (time) variable* $t_p^\mathcal{P}$ for each processor $p \in P$.

In order to measure execution time of processors for $\mathcal{T}$, we augment executions of $\mathcal{T}$ with history variables.

Definition 3. *Let ρ be a finite segment (suffix of a prefix) of an execution sequence σ and $\mathcal{P}$ be a partition. The augmented execution of ρ according to partition $\mathcal{P}$ includes updates to the variables $t_p^\mathcal{P}$ for each processor $p \in P$ as follows:*

- *In initial state ι, $t_p^\mathcal{P} = 0$, for all $p \in P$.*
- *Executing τ involves the following updates:*
  - *We let $c = \max\{t_p^\mathcal{P} \mid p \in P_\tau^\mathcal{P}\}$; i.e., the maximum value among the value of history variables of processes associated with τ.*
  - *We let $t_p^\mathcal{P} = c + p_\tau^\mathcal{P}$, for each process $p \in P_\tau^\mathcal{P}$; i.e., after synchronization, the history variable $t_p^\mathcal{P}$ is updated, as $p_\tau^\mathcal{P}$ time units elapsed in the local time of process p.*   □

Figure 2 shows the effect of executing a transition that involves processors p_1, p_3, and p_4 on the value of history variable for each processor. Notice that first, the value of all variables are updated with the maximum time value, and then, the time durations of each processor are added, respectively. The augmented execution of any two transitions involving a common processor is sequentialized through the history variable of the common processor. In particular, two transitions involving a common variable v are never executed concurrently, since they both involve processor $\mathcal{P}(v)$.

3   Evaluating the Effect of Partitions on Speedup

3.1   The Notion and Metrics for Execution Speedup

Our main goal is to compare the execution time of each processor through analyzing history variables under different partitions. The comparison relies on the following definitions of respectively execution time, sequential execution time, and speedup, for a finite prefix of execution sequences according to a partition.

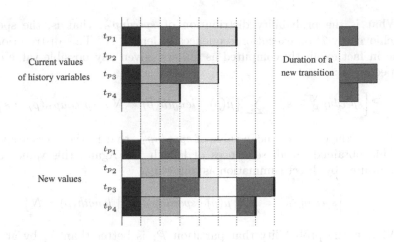

Fig. 2. The effect of a new transition involving processors $\{p_1, p_3, p_4\}$ on history variables

Definition 4. *Given a set P of processors, a partition $\mathcal{P}$, and a finite execution prefix ρ,*

- *the execution time of ρ is $exec_{\mathcal{P}}(\rho) = \max\{t_p^{\mathcal{P}} \mid p \in P\}$, where $t_p^{\mathcal{P}}$ are obtained from augmented execution of ρ according to the partition $\mathcal{P}$,*
- *the sequential execution time is*

$$seqexec_{\mathcal{P}}(\rho) = \sum_{\tau \in T} \#(\rho, \tau) \cdot \max\{p_\tau^{\mathcal{P}} \mid p \in P_\tau^{\mathcal{P}}\}$$

where $\#(\rho, \tau)$ denotes the number of times τ is executed in ρ,
- *the speedup achieved by partition $\mathcal{P}$ when executing ρ is the ratio*

$$speedup_{\mathcal{P}}(\rho) = \frac{seqexec_{\mathcal{P}}(\rho)}{exec_{\mathcal{P}}(\rho)}$$

□

In order to provide a detailed analysis, one needs information about the timing duration of transitions. This information is based on the processor partition and the actual protocol used to provide the correct interactions between all the elements (in particular the participating processors) involved in its execution. Moreover, to combine all results obtained on different execution sequences, we need a probability distribution on the occurrences of such sequences. In particular, this can be obtained from a probability distribution of execution of different transitions of the system, whenever several of them are simultaneously enabled. In case a probability distribution of simultaneously enabled transitions is not given, then one can assume identical probability of execution for all of them. If the probability distribution μ on finite prefixes of execution ρ is given, then we can answer the following questions:

(i) What is the probability distribution of $speedup_{\mathcal{P}}^N$, that is, the speedup achieved by $\mathcal{P}$ on execution sequences of length N? This distribution can be in fact explicitly computed as follows, given any possible value of the speedup s :

$$\mathbb{P}\left[speedup_{\mathcal{P}}^N \geq s\right] = \sum \left\{\mu(\rho) \mid length(\rho) = N \wedge speedup_{\mathcal{P}}(\rho) \geq s\right\}$$

(ii) What is the expected mean value of $speedup_{\mathcal{P}}^N$, that is, the average speedup value obtained on all sequences of length N? Again, this value can be computed by direct summation as follows:

$$\mathbb{E}\left[speedup_{\mathcal{P}}^N\right] = \sum \left\{\mu(\rho) \cdot speedup_{\mathcal{P}}(\rho) \mid length(\rho) = N\right\}$$

(iii) What is the probability that partition $\mathcal{P}_1$ is better than $\mathcal{P}_2$ by at least, for instance, 20% on sequences of length N? The answer can be directly computed as:

$$\mathbb{P}\left[\frac{speedup_{\mathcal{P}_1}^N}{speedup_{\mathcal{P}_2}^N} \geq 1.2\right] = \sum \left\{\mu(\rho) \mid length(\rho) = N \wedge \frac{speedup_{\mathcal{P}_1}(\rho)}{speedup_{\mathcal{P}_2}(\rho)} \geq 1.2\right\}$$

We note the following about our analysis method:

1. Probabilities on executing transitions can be given as input. Otherwise, the method assumes that all transitions enabled at some state are executed with equal probability.
2. Execution duration of transitions can also be given as input in terms of time units. Otherwise, we assume that the duration of a transition is 1 time unit for each participating processor. Thus, the sequential execution time $seqexec_{\mathcal{P}}(\rho)$ of any finite prefix ρ is equal to the length of the prefix $length(\rho)$ and, hence, independent of the partition $\mathcal{P}$. In this case, we can use the speedup as a performance indicator. That is, a greater speedup means equivalently smaller (faster) execution time for a partition.
3. Complete analysis is expensive. Timing analysis explodes the state space and makes even a finite state system, potentially, an infinite one. We will, thus, analyze limited segments of executions. To avoid biasing the measurement, we will not always start the analysis from the initial state, but from any reachable state. Furthermore, we will weigh these measurements according to the probability to reach and execute such finite fragments.

3.2 Our Assessment Solution

Because of the high complexity of timing analysis for arbitrarily long sequences, we choose to check only executions of limited size k, with $k \ll N$ and depending on the amount of time and memory available, e.g., running $k = 10$ execution steps. However, a naive implementation of this idea would be quite biased. For example, an ATM system may start with verifying the PIN code, not revealing within the first few transitions executed a whole lot about the nature of the rest of the execution.

For this reason, we check the behavior of sequences of k transitions from *all* reachable states, based on the calculated probability (under the stated assumptions in Subsection 3.1) of reaching that state. We start building augmented execution prefixes from that point. Let zero be the proposition that states that the value of all history variables are zero. For an arbitrary expression η encoding the property of interest, we compute the probability of temporal properties of the form

$$\phi(k, \eta) \equiv \Diamond(\text{zero} \wedge \bigcirc^k \eta)$$

where $\bigcirc^k$ is the application of the next-time operator $\bigcirc$ in temporal logic k times.

Using specific η properties, we can compute approximate answers to questions (i)-(iii) mentioned in Subsection 3.1. For example, to answer questions (i) and (ii) for a fixed partition $\mathcal{P}$, we consider $\eta \equiv exec_{\mathcal{P}} \leq \frac{k}{s}$ (where s is a given possible value of the speedup) and approximate

$$\mathbb{P}\left[speedup_{\mathcal{P}}^N \geq s \right] \approx \mathbb{P}\left[\phi(k, exec_{\mathcal{P}} \leq \tfrac{k}{s}) \right]$$

$$\mathbb{E}\left[speedup_{\mathcal{P}}^N \right] \approx \sum_{j=1}^k \tfrac{k}{j} \cdot \mathbb{P}\left[\phi(k, exec_{\mathcal{P}} = j) \right]$$

Likewise, the average speedup value is approximated as the weighted average of all potential speedups $\{\frac{k}{j} \mid 1 \leq j \leq k\}$ that can be achieved on sequences of length k. To answer question (iii), we must consider execution of two partitions $\mathcal{P}_1$ and $\mathcal{P}_2$ simultaneously. Accordingly, the two partitions will have different durations for transitions. In order to make a comparison between partitions, we allow using multiple history variables and constants per a transition system. Thus, we may use two sets of processors P_1 and P_2, two sets of history variables and two sets of duration constants per partition. In this case, we consider

$$\eta \equiv \frac{exec_{\mathcal{P}_2}}{exec_{\mathcal{P}_1}} \geq 1.2$$

and approximate:

$$\mathbb{P}\left[\frac{speedup_{\mathcal{P}_1}^N}{speedup_{\mathcal{P}_2}^N} \geq 1.2 \right] \approx \mathbb{P}\left[\phi\left(k, \frac{exec_{\mathcal{P}_2}}{exec_{\mathcal{P}_1}} \geq 1.2\right) \right]$$

In order to efficiently construct augmented prefixes for k steps at each state, we provide *two copies* of the transitions: one copy that does not count (i.e., no augmented executions), before zero becomes true. Then, a transition that causes zero to hold, exactly once, occurs, it sets up a flag and the second copy of the transitions starts to apply augmented executions. This replication of the transitions guarantees that the analyzed property does not count the time in doing a reachability analysis, but rather constrain the counting to the k last steps. The transition that guarantees zero has its own probability, and on the

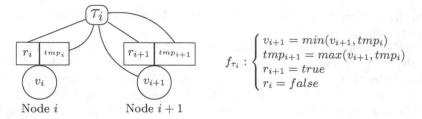

$$f_{\tau_i} : \begin{cases} v_{i+1} = min(v_{i+1}, tmp_i) \\ tmp_{i+1} = max(v_{i+1}, tmp_i) \\ r_{i+1} = true \\ r_i = false \end{cases}$$

Fig. 3. Detail of a propagation transition

face of it, one needs to normalize the probability of $\phi(k, \eta)$ with the probability to execute this transition. However, the probability of skipping this transition forever is zero. Hence no actual normalization is needed.

4   Case Study : Sorting Chain

Our case study to evaluate our technique is a chain of nodes that sorts values through a propagation mechanism. Values to sort enter the chain through the leftmost node. Each node compares the incoming value on its left with its current value, keeps the smaller one and propagates the greater one to its right. This propagation scheme sorts the values in ascending order from left to right.

We model the node i as a set of variables (v_i, tmp_i, r_i), where v_i is the current value stored in the node, tmp_i is the value to be propagated to the right, and r_i is a Boolean variable that is true whenever the node has to propagate a value to the right. Propagation of a value from node i to node $i + 1$ is modeled through the transition τ_i, as shown in Figure 3. The enabling condition is that the node i has a value to propagate and $i + 1$ has not. Formally, $en_{\tau_i} = r_i \wedge \neg r_{i+1}$. The effect of the propagation can be described as follows. The propagation transitions compare the current value of $i + 1$ with the value propagated by i. The smaller one becomes the new value of $i + 1$ while the greater one is propagated by $i + 1$. The variables r_{i+1} and r_i are updated to indicate that i has propagated its value and $i + 1$ has now a value to propagate. Note that transitions τ_i and τ_{i+1} cannot execute simultaneously since both access variables of node $i + 1$.

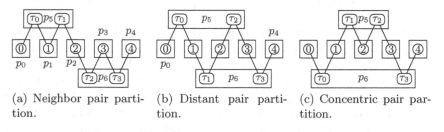

(a) Neighbor pair partition.   (b) Distant pair partition.   (c) Concentric pair partition.

Fig. 4. Different partitions for sorting chain of 5 nodes

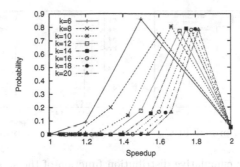

Fig. 5. Approximations of speedup distribution, for the model with 5 nodes using the neighbor pair partition

We assume that each node i is maintained by its own private processor p_i. Then, we consider additional support processors for executing transitions. Execution of a transition implies its support processor and the two processors hosting the corresponding nodes. For simplicity, we assume that the number of transitions is even (and, hence, the number of variables is odd). We consider the following partitions:

- Neighbor pairs ($\mathcal{P}_1$): we add one processor for each pair (τ_{2i}, τ_{2i+1}), where $i \in \{0, \ldots, \frac{n}{2}\}$. With 5 variables, we have p_5 for executing τ_0 and τ_1, p_6 for executing τ_2 and τ_3, as depicted in Figure 4(a).
- Distant pairs ($\mathcal{P}_2$): we add one processor for each pair of transitions $(\tau_i, \tau_{i+\frac{n}{2}})$, where $i \in \{0, \ldots, \frac{n}{2}\}$. With 5 variables, transitions τ_0, τ_2 are executed by p_5 and transitions τ_1, τ_3 are executed by p_6, as depicted in Figure 4(b).
- Concentric pairs ($\mathcal{P}_3$): we add one processor for each pair of transitions $(\tau_i, \tau_{n-(i+1)})$, where $i \in \{0, \ldots, \frac{n}{2} - 1\}$. With 5 variables, transitions τ_0, τ_3 are executed by p_5 and transitions τ_1, τ_2 are executed by p_6, as depicted in Figure 4(c).

4.1   Approximating Speedup

Our first experiment shows how the approximation behaves when increasing the length k of the considered execution sequences. We compute an approximation of the distribution of $speedup_{\mathcal{P}_1}$ for different values of k. This is obtained by checking with PRISM [10] the probability of $\phi(k, speedup_{\mathcal{P}_1} = s)$, where $s \in \{\frac{k}{j} \mid 1 \leq j \leq k\}$.

Figure 5 shows the speedup distribution for different values of k for the neighbor pairs partition $\mathcal{P}_1$. The lines are added for readability, the actual results are the points that correspond to the possible values of speedup. When k increases, there are only three speedup values with a strictly positive probability. Namely,

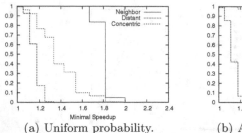
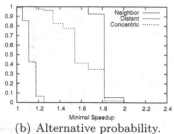

(a) Uniform probability.   (b) Alternative probability.

Fig. 6. Complementary cumulative distribution function of the speedup for the three proposed partitions, for the chain of 5 nodes

these are 2, $\frac{k}{\frac{k}{2}+1}$ and $\frac{k}{\frac{k}{2}+2}$. To obtain a speedup of 2, each support processor is used at every time slot. A speedup of $\frac{k}{\frac{k}{2}+1}$ is obtained when one of the processors is unused during one time slot. Similarly, a speedup of $\frac{k}{\frac{k}{2}+2}$ is obtained when there are two time slots where one processor is unused. Thus, in that example $speedup_{\mathcal{P}_1}^{N}$ converges toward 2 as N goes to ∞, which is visible in the successive distributions obtained.

By checking the probability of $\phi(k, speedup_{\mathcal{P}} \leq s)$, we obtain an approximation of the complementary cumulative distribution function for the speedup, given a partition $\mathcal{P}$. Since, the probabilities on executing transition can be given as input, we compare here the uniform probability and an alternative probability. In the latter, the probability of executing a given transition is higher, if it was enabled and not executed for a greater number of steps. To compute the probability of $\phi(k, speedup_{\mathcal{P}} \leq s)$, we take $k = 20$ for the chain of 5 nodes. The time for PRISM to build the model and compute the probabilities is about 20 minutes on a 3GHz dual-core machine running Debian Linux. For the chain of 7 nodes, we take $k = 12$. The time for computing the probabilities is then about 9 hours.

The obtained functions are shown in Figure 6, for the chain of 5 nodes and Figure 7 for the chain of 7 nodes. Consider the chain of 5 with uniform probability (Figure 6(a)). The probability of "the speedup is 1.4 or greater" is 0 for the partition $\mathcal{P}_2$ (distant pair partition), roughly 0.4 for the partition $\mathcal{P}_3$ (concentric pair partition), and 1 for the partition $\mathcal{P}_1$ (neighbor pair partition). For the chain of 5 nodes, the speedup is at most 2, since there are only 2 support processors for transitions. For the chain of 7 nodes, it ranges between 1 and 3.

The alternative probability yields a higher average speedup than uniform probability. Indeed, if two transitions can be executed in parallel, executing one of them increases the probability of executing the other one immediately after, thus enforcing parallelism. Table 1 summarizes the results by giving the average speedup for each configuration. This gives us the first method for assessing the efficiency of partitions. Note that the probabilities or the average can be computed independently for each partition.

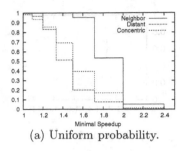
(a) Uniform probability.

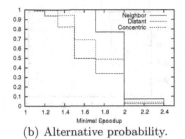
(b) Alternative probability.

Fig. 7. Complementary cumulative distribution function of the speedup for the three proposed partitions, for the chain of 7 nodes

4.2   Comparing Partitions

In order to compare more precisely two partitions $\mathcal{P}_1$ and $\mathcal{P}_2$, we compare their speedup by considering $\frac{speedup_{\mathcal{P}_1}}{speedup_{\mathcal{P}_2}}$. By checking the probability of the property

$$\phi\left(k, \frac{speedup_{\mathcal{P}_1}}{speedup_{\mathcal{P}_2}} \geq \alpha\right)$$

for the possible speedup ratios α, we obtain again a complementary cumulative distribution function. Figure 8(a) and Figure 8(b) compare partitions $\mathcal{P}_1$ and $\mathcal{P}_2$ for the chains of 5 and 7 nodes. Note that equation

$$\mathbb{P}\left[\frac{speedup_{\mathcal{P}_1}}{speedup_{\mathcal{P}_2}} \geq 1\right] = 1$$

means that partition $\mathcal{P}_1$ cannot exhibit a smaller speedup than the partition $\mathcal{P}_2$. Furthermore, with probability 0.6, the speedup of partition $\mathcal{P}_1$ is 20% better than the speedup of partition $\mathcal{P}_2$, and with probability 0.2 it is 40% better. These results come from the fact that $\mathcal{P}_1$ preserves the intrinsic parallelism of the model, whereas $\mathcal{P}_2$ prevents some interactions to execute in parallel. Here, partition $\mathcal{P}_1$ is clearly better than partition $\mathcal{P}_2$.

Figures 9(a) and 9(b) compare $\mathcal{P}_2$ and $\mathcal{P}_3$, for the models of 5 and 7 nodes. In this case, both partitions are restricting the intrinsic parallelism of the model, but none of them is always better than the other. For the chain of 5 nodes,

Number of nodes	Uniform Probability			Alternative Probability		
	Partition $\mathcal{P}_1$	Partition $\mathcal{P}_2$	Partition $\mathcal{P}_3$	Partition $\mathcal{P}_1$	Partition $\mathcal{P}_2$	Partition $\mathcal{P}_3$
5	1.80	1.16	1.38	1.82	1.13	1.60
7	1.88	1.46	1.56	1.96	1.67	1.79

Table 1. Average speedup

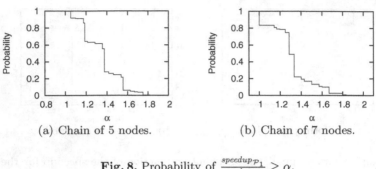

(a) Chain of 5 nodes.   (b) Chain of 7 nodes.

Fig. 8. Probability of $\frac{speedup_{\mathcal{P}_1}}{speedup_{\mathcal{P}_2}} \geq \alpha$.

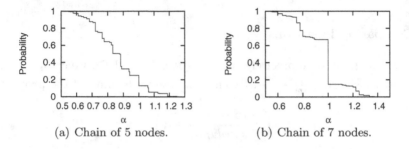

(a) Chain of 5 nodes.   (b) Chain of 7 nodes.

Fig. 9. Probability of $\frac{speedup_{\mathcal{P}_2}}{speedup_{\mathcal{P}_3}} \geq \alpha$

$$\mathbb{P}\left[\frac{speedup_{\mathcal{P}_1}}{speedup_{\mathcal{P}_2}} \geq 0.5\right] = 1$$

since both speedups are between 1 and 2. Likewise,

$$\mathbb{P}\left[\frac{speedup_{\mathcal{P}_1}}{speedup_{\mathcal{P}_2}} \geq 2\right] = 0$$

However, the probability that $\mathcal{P}_2$ strictly outperforms $\mathcal{P}_3$ ($\alpha > 1$) is less that 0.2, meaning that the probability that $\mathcal{P}_3$ outperforms or performs as well as $\mathcal{P}_2$ is more than 0.8. Hence, $\mathcal{P}_3$ seems apriori better than $\mathcal{P}_2$.

5   Related Work

The $(\max, +)$ discrete event systems theory [7] provides conditions about the existence of asymptotic values for throughput, growth rates, cycle time, etc, as well as analytic methods for their computation. Nonetheless, these results are usually restricted to particular classes of systems. As an example tightly related to our work, one can mention the study of the asymptotic growth rate for heaps of pieces in Tetris games, as presented in [9]. Using our computational model, this problem is equivalent to the computation of the limit/asymptotic speedup for transition systems where transitions are continuously enabled and fire according to a uniform probability. For this particular problem, the (max, +) systems theory guarantees the existence of the limit speedup. However, the computation of this limit, known as the Lyapunov exponent, is to the best of our knowledge still an open problem actively studied within the (max, +) community.

Schedulability analysis using verification has been addressed in different contexts. For example, in [1], the authors model jobshop and precedence task scheduling using timed automata. The schedulability problem is then reduced to reachability problem in timed automata. On the contrary, the focus of our work is not on schedulability analysis, but rather on evaluating and comparing two existing partitions using quantitative analysis. Likewise, the work in [8,11] discusses partitioning and execution of concurrent Petri nets, but fall short in evaluation of partitions.

The work in [4,3,5] proposes transformations for automated implementation of concurrent (e.g., multi-threaded, multi-process, or distributed) systems from a component-based abstract model. One input to the transformation algorithms is a partition scheme that maps concurrent components and schedulers to processors and/or machines. Although the focus of the work in [4,3,5] is on automating the implementation of a concurrent system, it falls short on evaluating different partition schemes to choose the one that results in the best speedup for the concurrent implementation. The evaluation technique presented in this paper can assist in choosing a better input partition to automatically implement concurrent programs.

Finally, most approaches based on classic performance evaluation (e.g., in [6,2]) are limited to specific network topologies. On the contrary, our technique is independent of topology and it benefits from the push-button model checking technology. This makes the tedious task of performance evaluation for different topologies much easier.

6   Conclusion

In this paper, we studied the problem of evaluating and comparing two given *partitions*, where each transition and variable of a transition system is mapped to a processor and the system allows some concurrency among its transitions. We defined a notion of *maximal concurrency* that is used to assess the runtime behavior of the system under different partitions. Our notion of maximal concurrency model consists of a set of processors, a partition, a variable per processor that keeps track of the current execution time at the processor, and a constant, which describes the duration of transition.

We developed an effective and relatively inexpensive test for assessing and comparing a priori the efficiency of two partitions. Our method on observing the system for a long period, over actual runs, or empirical studies. It analyzes the value of variables that keep track of execution time for each processor. The analysis relies on comparing execution time, sequential execution time, and the probability of speedup, for finite prefixes of execution sequences of some constant size k according to a partition. We utilized a probabilistic model checker to answer the abstract question: with what probability can random executions according to one partition be faster by a factor of f. Our experiments on popular distributed algorithms clearly showed the effectiveness of our technique to assess the efficiency of different partitions.

For future work, we are planning to design methods that automatically generate partitions that are likely to perform well. Another interesting research direction is to incorporate other parameters, such as power consumption (e.g., in sensor networks), network load, etc in assessing the efficiency of partitions.

Acknowledgments. This research was supported in part by Canada NSERC Discovery Grant 418396-2012 and NSERC Strategic Grant 430575-2012.

References

1. Abdeddaïm, Y., Asarin, E., Maler, O.: Scheduling with timed automata. Theoretical Computer Science 354(2), 272–300 (2006)
2. Bianchi, G.: Performance analysis of the IEEE 802.11 distributed coordination function. IEEE Journal on Selected Areas in Communications 18, 535–547 (2000)
3. Bonakdarpour, B., Bozga, M., Jaber, M., Quilbeuf, J., Sifakis, J.: Automated conflict-free distributed implementation of component-based models. In: IEEE Symposium on Industrial Embedded Systems (SIES), pp. 108–117 (2010)
4. Bonakdarpour, B., Bozga, M., Jaber, M., Quilbeuf, J., Sifakis, J.: A framework for automated distributed implementation of component-based models. Journal on Distributed Computing (DC) 25(1), 383–409 (2012)
5. Bonakdarpour, B., Bozga, M., Quilbeuf, J.: Automated distributed implementation of component-based models with priorities. In: ACM International Conference on Embedded Software (EMSOFT), pp. 59–68 (2011)
6. Cao, M., Ma, W., Zhang, Q., Wang, X., Zhu, W.: Modelling and performance analysis of the distributed scheduler in IEEE 802.16 mesh mode. In: ACM International Symposium on Mobile Ad Hoc Networking and Computing (MobiHoc), pp. 78–89 (2005)
7. Olsder, G.J., Bacelli, F., Cohen, G., Quadrat, J.P.: Synchronization and Linearity. Wiley (1992)
8. Ferscha, A.: Concurrent execution of timed Petri nets. In: Winter Simulation Conference, pp. 229–236 (1994)
9. Gaubert, S.: Methods and applications of (max,+) linear algebra. Technical Report 3088, INRIA (January 1997)
10. Kwiatkowska, M., Norman, G., Parker, D.: PRISM 4.0: Verification of probabilistic real-time systems. In: Gopalakrishnan, G., Qadeer, S. (eds.) CAV 2011. LNCS, vol. 6806, pp. 585–591. Springer, Heidelberg (2011)
11. Cortadella, J., Kondratyev, A., Lavagno, L., Passerone, C., Watanabe, Y.: Quasi-static scheduling of independent tasksfor reactive systems. In: Esparza, J., Lakos, C.A. (eds.) ICATPN 2002. LNCS, vol. 2360, pp. 208–227. Springer, Heidelberg (2002)

Improving Representative Computation in ExpliSAT*

Hana Chockler[1,**], Dmitry Pidan[2], and Sitvanit Ruah[2]

[1] King's College, London, UK
[2] IBM Haifa Research Lab, Haifa University Campus, Haifa 31905, Israel

Abstract. This paper proposes a new algorithm for computing path representatives in the concolic software verification tool ExpliSAT. A path representative is a useful technique for reducing the number of calls to a decision procedure by maintaining an explicit instantiation of symbolic variables that matches the current control flow path. In the current implementation in ExpliSAT, the whole representative is guessed at the beginning of an execution and then recomputed if it does not match the currently traversed control flow path. In this paper we suggest a new algorithm for computation of a representative, where the instantiation is done "on demand", that is, only when a specific value is required in order to determine feasibility. Experimental results show that using representatives improves performance.

1 Introduction

The notion of *concolic* verification is typically used in the context of static analysis and testing and refers to a hybrid software verification technique that combines concrete values of control variables with symbolic representation of data. This technique is now used in many *symbolic execution* tools, such as DART [1], CUTE [2], Klee [3] and others. ExpliSAT [4] is based on a similar algorithm, but instead of executing the program on each of the control paths, it, essentially, builds a model of each explicit control flow path with symbolic data variables and invokes a decision procedure (usually SAT or SMT) to determine whether there exists an instantiation of this path that violates correctness assertions. One common problem of the concolic approach is how to determine whether the current control flow path is feasible. Tools that perform formal analysis of the program apply some decision procedure on the path in order to determine its feasibility; however, it is useful to know whether the current path is feasible on-the-fly, to avoid lengthy executions of infeasible paths.

In contrast to tools that use concrete evaluations of symbolic variables for guiding the execution, ExpliSAT uses the concept of *path representatives*, which

---

* This work is partially supported by the European Community under the call FP7-ICT-2009-5 – project PINCETTE 257647.
** This work was done while this author was an employee of IBM Research Lab in Haifa.

V. Bertacco and A. Legay (Eds.): HVC 2013, LNCS 8244, pp. 359–364, 2013.
© Springer International Publishing Switzerland 2013

are computed on the fly and hold a feasible instantiation of the symbolic values. Representatives are used to reduce the number of calls to the decision procedure (SAT) as follows: in a branching point, if a branch fits the current representative, then it is feasible, and no call to SAT is necessary. In case both branches are feasible, they both are explored according to the search algorithms and heuristics. In the current implementation, initial instantiation of all symbolic values in the representative is *guessed* at the beginning of the execution. If a guess is unsuccessful, the representative is recomputed from scratch, thus invalidating most of its benefits.

In this paper, we suggest a new algorithm for computing and maintaining the path representative, in which the symbolic values are instantiated "on demand" – only when needed to determine feasibility. The key point of our algorithm is that unassigned symbolic variables are not assigned random values, but are *left unevaluated* in the formula. The experimental results show that, while our approach always results in more calls to the decision procedure than in the previous implementation, these calls are small and do not incure a significant computational overhead. We compared our new implementation with the current implementation with the complete representative and with an implementation that does not use represenatives at all, on several case studies of different types of programs written in C. In all case studies, the new algorithm with instantiation of the representative "on demand" outperforms both the implementation with the full representative and the implementation without path representatives.

2   Preliminaries

Let V be a set of **variables** of the program under verification and Φ be a set of **expressions** over V, C operators, and constants.

Definition 1 (CFG). *A control flow graph (CFG) G is a tuple $\langle N, E, n_0 \rangle$, where N is a set of nodes, $E \subseteq N \times N$ is a set of directed edges, and $n_0 \in N$ is the initial node. Every node $n \in N$ has a type corresponding to a particular program construct as follows: (1) a terminal node: has no outgoing edges, represents an error or a final state of the program; (2) an* assignment $v := \varphi$, *where $v \in V$ and $\varphi \in \Phi$; these nodes have a single outgoing edge $(n, n') \in E$; (3) an* if *statement θ ? n' : n'', where $\theta \in \Phi$, $n', n'' \in N$ and $(n, n'), (n, n'') \in E$. the node n' corresponds to the next program statement if θ evaluates to* **true**, *and n'' corresponds to the next program statement if θ evaluates to* **false**.

Definition 2 (Guard). *For a path π in the CFG, let $n_1, \ldots, n_k$ be the nodes of π corresponding to if statements. Let θ_i ? n'_i : n''_i be the statement of n_i. A guard $\varphi_\pi \in \Phi$ for π is a boolean expression that satisfies $n_{i+1} = n'_i \leftrightarrow (\varphi_\pi \to \theta_i)$ for all $1 \leq i \leq k$.*

We say that a variable v has a *symbolic value* $v_s \in$ SV, where SV stands for the set of *symbolic values*, if v can be assigned any value in SV. We denote by Φ_{SV} the set of expressions over symbolic values, constants and C operators.

Definition 3 (Symbolic valuation). *Given a symbolic mapping $S : V \rightarrow \Phi_{SV}$ of V, symbolic valuation φ_S of expression $\varphi \in \Phi$, substitutes every variable v in φ with $S(v)$.*

ExpliSAT[4] traverses the CFG of a program under verification path by path. A path π is denoted by the pair $\langle n, \varphi_\pi \rangle$, where n is the last node of π and φ_π is its guard. On every assignment statement, ExpliSAT calculates a symbolic valuation of the assignment operation and assigns it to a variable on the left. On an if statement, ExpliSAT checks which branch is feasible and continues its traversal to the feasible branches. Algorithm 1 describes the main ExpliSAT procedure.

---

input : CFG $G = \langle N, E, n_0 \rangle$, program variables V, set of symbolic values SV
Queue of active paths $P \leftarrow \{\langle n_0, true \rangle\}$;
Symbolic mapping $S : V \rightarrow \Phi_{SV}, \forall v \in V, S(v) = v_s \in$ SV;
while $P \neq \emptyset$ **do**
    $\langle$node n, guard $\varphi \rangle \leftarrow$ pop P;
    if n *is terminal* **then** stop;
    else if n *is an assignment* $v := \varphi$ **then**
        $S(v) \leftarrow \varphi_S$;
        push P, $\langle n', \varphi \rangle$;
    end
    else if v *is if statement* θ ? n' : n'' **then**
        if $isFeasible(\varphi \wedge \theta_S)$ **then** push P, $\langle n', \varphi \wedge \theta_S \rangle$;
        if $isFeasible(\varphi \wedge \neg \theta_S)$ **then** push P, $\langle n'', \varphi \wedge \neg \theta_S \rangle$;
    end
end

Algorithm 1. *ExpliSAT algorithm*

The simplest way to check feasibility of the path in the *isFeasible* function in Algorithm 1 is to perform a call to a SAT solver to find a satisfying assignment. If a satisfying assignment exists, the path is feasible and can be traversed. While this approach is clearly sound and complete, it requires many computationally heavy SAT calls. In order to reduce the number of these calls, ExpliSAT maintains a *representative* of each path. A representative is a single *concrete* assignment that satisfies a path guard up to the current execution point. Within the *isFeasible* function, ExpliSAT first checks whether the current representative satisfies a new guard, and if yes, the path is clearly feasible and no SAT call is needed.

Definition 4 (Instantiation). *Let Dom(SV) be a domain of the set of symbolic variables SV, and let $I :$ SV $\rightarrow$ Dom(SV) be a concrete mapping that assigns every symbolic value with a concrete value from its domain. Given a mapping I, $\varphi \in \Phi_{SV}$ the instantiation $I^*(\varphi) \in$ Dom(SV) is the result of evaluating φ, after substituting every $v_s \in$ SV in φ by $I(v_s)$.*

Definition 5 (Representative). *Given guard φ and symbolic mapping $S : V \rightarrow \Phi_{SV}$, a representative is a concrete mapping I such that $I^*(\varphi_S) = true$.*

3   Our Algorithm and Experimental Results

Partial representative In the current representative computation algorithm, every symbolic variable $v_s \in \text{SV}$ is initialized to a randomly guessed value, and the symbolic mapping I (the representative) is updated in every SAT call. When the initial value satisfies the guard, no SAT call is needed.

Let $\text{SV}_p \subseteq \text{SV}$ be a subset of symbolic values. A *partial concrete mapping* $I|_{\text{SV}_p} : \text{SV}_p \to \text{Dom}(\text{SV}_p)$, is a projection of $I : \text{SV} \to \text{Dom}(\text{SV})$ to SV_p. We define *partial instantiation* $I^*|_{\text{SV}_p}$ and *partial representative* using Definitions 4, 5 with SV and I replaced by SV_p and $I|_{\text{SV}_p}$, respectively. The new *isFeasible* function using partial representative is presented in Algorithm 2.

> **input** : partial concrete mapping $I^*|_{\text{SV}_p} : \text{SV}_p \to \text{Dom}(\text{SV}_p)$
> **function** isFeasible(*symbolic expression* φ_S)
> **begin**
>   **if** $I^*|_{\text{SV}_p}(\varphi_S) = true$ **then** return true;
>   **else if** $\exists A : \text{SV} \to \text{Dom}(\text{SV})$ *s.t.* $A^*(I^*|_{\text{SV}_p}(\varphi_S)) = true$ **then**
> $\forall v_s \in symval(\varphi_S) \setminus \text{SV}_p, \quad I(v_s) \leftarrow A(v_s);$
> $\text{SV}_p \leftarrow \text{SV}_p \bigcup symval(\varphi_S);$
>   return true;
>   **end**
>   **else if** $\exists A : \text{SV} \to \text{Dom}(\text{SV})$ *s.t.* $A^*(\varphi_S) = true$ **then**
> $\forall v_s \in symval(\varphi_S), \quad I(v_s) \leftarrow A(v_s);$
> $\text{SV}_p \leftarrow symval(\varphi_S);$
>   return true;
>   **end**
>   **else** return false;
> **end**

Algorithm 2. *isFeasible* with partial representative

The execution starts with $\text{SV}_p = \emptyset$. Then, each call to *isFeasible* updates the SV_p with $symval(\varphi_S)$ - symbolic values appearing in the guard φ_S, and the *partial* concrete mapping $I|_{\text{SV}_p}$ (the representative) with the values of those variables from the satisfying assignment. Note that, contrary to the previous algorithm, unassigned symbolic variables are not getting random values, but are *left unevaluated in the formula*. When the previously assigned values do not satisfy the current guard, the whole representative is re-computed as previously. While this approach generates more SAT calls than the previous one (since there are no guesses of the concrete values), each of these calls is *incremental* and is very light-weight in practice. Since the symbolic values are assigned concrete values based on the output of the SAT solver, there are fewer cases when the heavy SAT call is required to re-compute the representative.

Experimental Results. We implemented all the algorithms within a prototype tool that performs symbolic execution of the program, built on top of the Cprover framework [5]. An IBM SAT solver [6] is used for checking the path feasibility.

Table 1. Comparison of path feasibility checking algorithms

	Total CPU time	Imp.	Algorithm CPU time	Calls	Solver CPU time	Avg.
TCAS						
Solver only	0:0:5.14		0:0:4.576	74	0:0:4.445	0.06
Full representative	0:0:4.772	7.16%	0:0:4.321	55	0:0:3.920	0.071
Partial representative	**0:0:4.412**	**14.16%**	0:0:3.963	56	0:0:3.606	0.064
Driver testcase						
Solver only	77:25:42.814		31:21:30.152	56885	30:56:10.846	1.958
Full representative	74:41:44.834	3.53%	29:45:25.496	46777	27:15:31.462	2.098
Partial representative	**66:46:38.931**	**13.76%**	22:45:15.305	54428	20:21:46.061	**1.347**
Credit card validation testcase						
Solver only	3:23:44.884		3:16:3.524	11429	3:13:40.263	1.017
Full representative	2:0:55.146	40.65%	1:52:50.230	7231	1:46:20.714	0.882
Partial representative	**1:34:27.025**	**53.64%**	1:26:50.890	7245	1:20:35.568	**0.667**
Control application testcase						
Solver only	3:35:06.587		3:31:13.139	4101	3:27:19.262	3.033
Full representative	3:29:40.822	2.52%	3:25:44.211	3621	3:18:59.129	3.297
Partial representative	**2:34:48:432**	**28.03%**	2:30:54.631	3851	2:25:24.401	**2.265**

Table 2. Characteristics of test cases

	Feasible paths ratio	Full representative hit ratio	Partial representative hit ratio Before SAT	After SAT	Total
TCAS	50%	36.54%	34.62%	19.23%	**53.85%**
Driver	4.18%	29.91%	7.27%	37.05%	**44.32%**
Credit card validation	55.89%	54.76%	54.65%	10.78%	**65.32%**
Control application	55.44%	15.01%	11.23%	76.82%	**88.05%**

We compared three algorithms: an algorithm without representative (SAT is called for every path), current ExpliSAT algorithm with full representative, and our new algorithm with partial representative (Algorithm 2). The comparison was performed on the open source aircraft collision avoidance system TCAS [7], and on three proprietary input programs representing different domains of software engineering. The first program is a unit from a hardware driver. The second program is a procedure simulating the process of a credit card number validation. The third program is a control application that performs navigation of the Cassette Multifunctional Mover (CMM) robot in the ITER project (see http://www.iter.org/). The experimental results are shown in Table 1. The time in all columns is given in hh:mm:ss format, except for _Avg_(sec.). The column "Algorithm CPU time" gives the total time for the verification algorithm, including simplifications and the computation of the representative; in particular, in includes the CPU time of SAT solving.

Each program under test has its own special characteristics. The driver unit contains long linear blocks of code, making the portion of branching instructions less significant, while in the credit card number validation program and in the control application, branching instructions comprise a much larger portion of the code. This difference can be seen by comparing columns 1 and 3 in Table 1. In the driver testcase, the portion of time spent by all three algorithms on path feasibility checking (column 3) is less than 40%, contrary to others, where this portion is near or above 90%. Intuitively, this means that both representative-based algorithms are more likely to make a larger impact on the latter testcases. The column *Imp.* in Table 1 shows the improvement in overall running time achieved by each of the representative-using algorithms, compared to the algorithm that uses no representative. It is easy to see that both algorithms improve the performance in all three cases, with the partial representative being the best one. The significance of improvement varies depending on the following ratios : the ratio of feasible paths (see column 1 in Table 2), and the ratio of representative hits (the ratio of times the representative succeeded to prove the feasibility of the path, see columns $2 - 5$ in Table 2). The larger those ratios are, the more significant the impact of the representative algorithm is.

We also note that our intuition that many small SAT calls are better than fewer large calls is reaffirmed by the results in columns $4 - 6$ in Table 1. Average time spent on a call to the SAT solver in the partial representative algorithm is smaller than in the full representative algorithm, and thus even though the number of calls is higher, the overall CPU time spent in the SAT solver is much lower for partial representative algorithm.

References

1. Godefroid, P., Klarlund, N., Sen, K.: Dart: directed automated random testing. In: PLDI, pp. 213–223 (2005)
2. Sen, K., Agha, G.: CUTE and jCUTE: Concolic unit testing and explicit path model-checking tools. In: Ball, T., Jones, R.B. (eds.) CAV 2006. LNCS, vol. 4144, pp. 419–423. Springer, Heidelberg (2006)
3. Cadar, C., Dunbar, D., Engler, D.R.: Klee: Unassisted and automatic generation of high-coverage tests for complex systems programs. In: OSDI, pp. 209–224 (2008)
4. Barner, S., Eisner, C., Glazberg, Z., Kroening, D., Rabinovitz, I.: ExpliSAT: Guiding SAT-based software verification with explicit states. In: Bin, E., Ziv, A., Ur, S. (eds.) HVC 2006. LNCS, vol. 4383, pp. 138–154. Springer, Heidelberg (2007)
5. The CBMC Homepage, http://www.cprover.org/cbmc
6. RuleBase PE Homepage,
   http://www.haifa.il.ibm.com/projects/verification/RB_Homepage
7. Software-artifact Infrastructure Repository,
   http://sir.unl.edu/portal/index.php

Author Index